# Handbook of Research on Technology Tools for Real-World Skill Development

Yigal Rosen
*Harvard University, USA*

Steve Ferrara
*Pearson, USA*

Maryam Mosharraf
*Pearson, USA*

## Volume II

A volume in the Advances in Higher Education
and Professional Development (AHEPD) Book
Series

Information Science
**REFERENCE**
An Imprint of IGI Global

Published in the United States of America by
Information Science Reference (an imprint of IGI Global)
701 E. Chocolate Avenue
Hershey PA, USA 17033
Tel: 717-533-8845
Fax: 717-533-8661
E-mail: cust@igi-global.com
Web site: http://www.igi-global.com

Library of Congress Cataloging-in-Publication Data

Handbook of research on technology tools for real-world skill development / Yigal Rosen, Steve Ferrara, and Maryam Mosharraf, editors.
    pages cm
Includes bibliographical references and index.
ISBN 978-1-4666-9441-5 (hardcover) -- ISBN 978-1-4666-9442-2 (ebook) 1. Educational technology--Study and teaching--Handbooks, manuals, etc. 2. Computer literacy--Study and teaching--Handbooks, manuals, etc. 3. Problem solving--Study and teaching. I. Rosen, Yigal, 1978- editor of compilation.
LB1028.3.H36 2016
371.33--dc23
                    2015028792

This book is published in the IGI Global book series Advances in Higher Education and Professional Development (AHEPD) (ISSN: 2327-6983; eISSN: 2327-6991)

British Cataloguing in Publication Data
A Cataloguing in Publication record for this book is available from the British Library.

For electronic access to this publication, please contact: eresources@igi-global.com.

# Advances in Higher Education and Professional Development (AHEPD) Book Series

Jared Keengwe
*University of North Dakota, USA*

ISSN: 2327-6983
EISSN: 2327-6991

## MISSION

As world economies continue to shift and change in response to global financial situations, job markets have begun to demand a more highly-skilled workforce. In many industries a college degree is the minimum requirement and further educational development is expected to advance. With these current trends in mind, the **Advances in Higher Education & Professional Development (AHEPD) Book Series** provides an outlet for researchers and academics to publish their research in these areas and to distribute these works to practitioners and other researchers.

**AHEPD** encompasses all research dealing with higher education pedagogy, development, and curriculum design, as well as all areas of professional development, regardless of focus.

## COVERAGE

- Adult Education
- Assessment in Higher Education
- Career Training
- Coaching and Mentoring
- Continuing Professional Development
- Governance in Higher Education
- Higher Education Policy
- Pedagogy of Teaching Higher Education
- Vocational Education

IGI Global is currently accepting manuscripts for publication within this series. To submit a proposal for a volume in this series, please contact our Acquisition Editors at Acquisitions@igi-global.com or visit: http://www.igi-global.com/publish/.

# Titles in this Series

*For a list of additional titles in this series, please visit: www.igi-global.com*

*Furthering Higher Education Possibilities through Massive Open Online Courses*
Anabela Mesquita (CICE – ISCAP / Polytechnic of Porto, Portugal & Algoritmi RC, Minho University, Portugal)
and Paula Peres (CICE – ISCAP / Polytechnic of Porto, Portugal)
Information Science Reference • copyright 2015 • 312pp • H/C (ISBN: 9781466682795) • US $175.00 (our price)

*Handbook of Research on Teacher Education in the Digital Age*
Margaret L. Niess (Oregon State University, USA) and Henry Gillow-Wiles (Oregon State University, USA)
Information Science Reference • copyright 2015 • 722pp • H/C (ISBN: 9781466684034) • US $415.00 (our price)

*Handbook of Research on Enhancing Teacher Education with Advanced Instructional Technologies*
Nwachukwu Prince Ololube (Ignatius Ajuru University of Education, Nigeria) Peter James Kpolovie (University
of Port Harcourt, Nigeria) and Lazarus Ndiku Makewa (University of Eastern Africa, Kenya)
Information Science Reference • copyright 2015 • 485pp • H/C (ISBN: 9781466681620) • US $315.00 (our price)

*Handbook of Research on Advancing Critical Thinking in Higher Education*
Sherrie Wisdom (Lindenwood University, USA) and Lynda Leavitt (Lindenwood University, USA)
Information Science Reference • copyright 2015 • 568pp • H/C (ISBN: 9781466684119) • US $325.00 (our price)

*Measuring and Analyzing Informal Learning in the Digital Age*
Olutoyin Mejiuni (Obafemi Awolowo University, Nigeria) Patricia Cranton (University of New Brunswick, Canada)
and Olúfẹ́mi Táíwò (Cornell University, USA)
Information Science Reference • copyright 2015 • 336pp • H/C (ISBN: 9781466682658) • US $185.00 (our price)

*Transformative Curriculum Design in Health Sciences Education*
Colleen Halupa (A.T. Still University, USA & LeTourneau University, USA)
Medical Information Science Reference • copyright 2015 • 388pp • H/C (ISBN: 9781466685710) • US $215.00
(our price)

*Handbook of Research on Innovative Technology Integration in Higher Education*
Fredrick Muyia Nafukho (Texas A&M University, USA) and Beverly J. Irby (Texas A&M University, USA)
Information Science Reference • copyright 2015 • 478pp • H/C (ISBN: 9781466681705) • US $310.00 (our price)

*New Voices in Higher Education Research and Scholarship*
Filipa M. Ribeiro (University of Porto, Portugal) Yurgos Politis (University College Dublin, Ireland) and Bojana
Culum (University of Rijeka, Croatia)
Information Science Reference • copyright 2015 • 316pp • H/C (ISBN: 9781466672444) • US $185.00 (our price)

DISSEMINATOR of KNOWLEDGE

www.igi-global.com

701 E. Chocolate Ave., Hershey, PA 17033
Order online at www.igi-global.com or call 717-533-8845 x100
To place a standing order for titles released in this series, contact: cust@igi-global.com
Mon-Fri 8:00 am - 5:00 pm (est) or fax 24 hours a day 717-533-8661

# Editorial Advisory Board

# List of Contributors

# Table of Contents

## Volume I

### Section 1
### Defining Real-World Skills in Technology-Rich Environments

*Lars Vavik, Stord/Haugesund University College, Norway*
*Gavriel Salomon, Hiafa University, Israel*

*Edith Avni, Toward Digital Ethics Initiative, Israel*
*Abraham Rotem, Toward Digital Ethics Initiative, Israel*

*Susan Malone Back, Texas Tech University, USA*
*Heather Greenhalgh-Spencer, Texas Tech University, USA*
*Kellilynn M. Frias, Texas Tech University, USA*

# Volume II

# Detailed Table of Contents

## Volume I

### Section 1
### Defining Real-World Skills in Technology-Rich Environments

*This section includes chapters on curricula and frameworks for teaching real-world skills.*

**Chapter 1**
    *Lars Vavik, Stord/Haugesund University College, Norway*
    *Gavriel Salomon, Hiafa University, Israel*

This paper addresses the tension between a discipline-based and a skill and competences-based approach to today's curriculum. The competences-based approach emphasizes the cultivation of market-oriented skills and competencies that people acquire in the knowledge society; it is the driving force behind many educational reforms. The other, more traditional approach emphasizes the acquisition of well organized disciplinary knowledge such as history and chemistry. The differences between learning guided by pre-determined educational goals, designed to acquire disciplined knowledge, and the acquisition of daily, net-related interest-driven partly out-of-school skills learning is too large to be ignored. Each of the two approaches has its advantages and drawbacks but jointly they can constitute fruitful curricula. On the one hand, such curricula address the three main purposes of school – qualification, socialization and subjectification – while on the other they address the needs of cultivating 21st Century skills and competences. The latter comes to serve the attainment of the former.

    *Edith Avni, Toward Digital Ethics Initiative, Israel*

    *Abraham Rotem, Toward Digital Ethics Initiative, Israel*

This chapter presents a proposal for a conceptual framework of digital competence, which is a civil right and need and is vital for appropriate, intelligent study and functioning in the real world, through means that technology and the internet offer the citizen. Digital competence in the 2010s is a multifaceted complex of a net of literacies that have been updated, reformulated and transformed under the influence of technology. The framework of the digital competency includes eight fields of digital literacies. At the top of the net is digital ethics literacy, outlines the moral core for proper use of technology; at the base are technological literacy and digital reading and writing literacy, comprising the foundation and interface for all the digital literacies, and in between are the digital literacies in these fields: information literacy, digital visual literacy, new media literacy, communication and collaboration literacy and social media literacy. These interconnected literacies compose a synergetic complex of the digital competence framework.

    *Susan Malone Back, Texas Tech University, USA*

    *Heather Greenhalgh-Spencer, Texas Tech University, USA*

    *Kellilynn M. Frias, Texas Tech University, USA*

The authors describe the application of transdisciplinary theory and practice to Science, Technology, Engineering and Mathematics (STEM) education at the undergraduate level. The modular approach which makes use of student collaboration within and across disciplines and input from outside experts holds promise for preparing students to address society's "wicked" problems – those with interconnected causes and for which a solution often causes additional problems. Transdisciplinary theory and practice are described and their application to STEM education is proposed along with a model of measuring transdisciplinary skills. Recommendations are proposed for future research on cross-cultural/cross disciplinary models, pedagogy, measuring student collaboration, determining effective partnership models and institutional supports, and the potential role of the social sciences in contributing to research on transdisciplinary practice and education.

    *Carolyn Harper Knox, University of Oregon, USA*

    *Lynne Anderson-Inman, University of Oregon, USA*

    *Fatima Terrazas-Arellanes, University of Oregon, USA*

    *Emily Deanne Walden, University of Oregon, USA*

    *Bridget Hildreth, University of Oregon, USA*

Students often struggle when conducting research online, an essential skill for meeting the Common Core State Standards and for success in the real world. To meet this instructional challenge, researchers at the University of Oregon's Center for Advanced Technology in Education (CATE) developed, tested, and refined nine SOAR Strategies for Online Academic Research. These strategies are aligned with well-established, research-based principles for teaching all students, with particular attention to the instructional needs of students with learning disabilities. To support effective instruction of the SOAR Strategies, researchers at CATE developed a multimedia website of instructional modules called the SOAR Toolkit. This chapter highlights the real world importance of teaching middle school students to conduct effective online research. In addition, it describes the theoretical and historical foundations of the SOAR Strategies, instructional features of the SOAR Toolkit, and research results from classroom implementations at the middle school level.

## Chapter 5

Sammy Elzarka, University of La Verne, USA
Valerie Beltran, University of La Verne, USA
Jessica Decker, University of La Verne, USA
Mark Matzaganian, University of La Verne, USA
Nancy T. Walker, University of La Verne, USA

The purposes of this chapter are threefold: to explore the research on and relationships among metacognition, reflection, and self-regulated learning; to analyze students' experiences with metacognition, reflection, and self-regulated learning activities in computer-based learning (CBL) courses; and to provide strategies that can be used in a CBL environment to promote students' metacognition, reflection, and self-regulation. A review of underlying frameworks for and prior study findings in metacognition and reflection are presented. Case study findings are also described and form the basis for the suggested strategies. The value and implications of using such strategies are also offered. Finally, future research should address the teaching of metacognition and reflection in CBL environments with an emphasis on real world application.

## Chapter 6

J. Christine Harmes, Assessment Consultant, USA
James L. Welsh, University of South Florida, USA
Roy J. Winkelman, University of South Florida, USA

The Technology Integration Matrix (TIM) was created to provide a resource for evaluating technology integration in K-12 instructional settings, and as a tool for helping to target teacher-related professional development. The TIM is comprised of 5 characteristics of meaningful learning (Active, Constructive, Authentic, Collaborative, and Goal-Directed) and 5 levels (Entry, Adoption, Adaptation, Infusion, and Transformation), resulting in 25 cells. Within each cell, descriptions are provided, along with video sample lessons from actual math, science, social studies, and language arts classrooms that illustrate a characteristic at the indicated level. Throughout development, focus groups and interviews were conducted with in-service teachers and technology specialists to validate the progression of characteristics and descriptive components.

*Patricia Eckardt, Stony Brook University, USA*

*Brenda Janotha, Stony Brook University, USA*

*Marie Ann Marino, Stony Brook University, USA*

*David P. Erlanger, Stony Brook University, USA*

*Dolores Cannella, Stony Brook University, USA*

Nursing professionals need to assume responsibility and take initiative in ongoing personal and professional development. Qualities required of nursing graduates must include the ability to, "translate, integrate, and apply knowledge that leads to improvements in patient outcomes," in an environment in which "[k]nowledge is increasingly complex and evolving rapidly" (American Association of Colleges of Nursing, 2008, p. 33). The ability to identify personal learning needs, set goals, apply learning strategies, pursue resources, and evaluate outcomes are essential. Nursing professionals must be self-directed learners to meet these expectations. Team-based learning (TBL) is a multiphase pedagogical approach requiring active student participation and collaboration. Team-based learning entails three stages: (1) individual preparation, (2) learning assurance assessment, and (3) team application activity.

## Section 2
## Technology Tools for Learning and Assessing Real-World Skills

*Chapters in this section deal with core topic of technology tools and the wide range of applications aimed for learning and assessing of real-world skills.*

# Chapter 8

*Edys S. Quellmalz, WestEd, USA*

*Matt D. Silberglitt, WestEd, USA*

*Barbara C. Buckley, WestEd, USA*

*Mark T. Loveland, WestEd, USA*

*Daniel G. Brenner, WestEd, USA*

Simulations have become core supports for learning in the digital age. For example, economists, mathematicians, and scientists employ simulations to model complex phenomena. Learners, too, are increasingly able to take advantage of simulations to understand complex systems. Simulations can display phenomena that are too large or small, fast or slow, or dangerous for direct classroom investigations. The affordances of simulations extend students' opportunities to engage in deep, extended problem solving. National and international studies are providing evidence that technologies are enriching curricula, tailoring learning environments, embedding assessment, and providing tools to connect students, teachers, and experts locally and globally. This chapter describes a portfolio of research and development that has examined and documented the roles that simulations can play in assessing and promoting learning, and has developed and validated sets of simulation-based assessments and instructional supplements designed for formative and summative assessment and customized instruction.

# Chapter 9

Issues in higher education, such as the rising cost of education, career readiness, and increases in the achievement gap have led to a movement toward accountability in higher education. This chapter addresses the issues related to career readiness by highlighting an assessment tool, the Collegiate Learning Assessment (CLA), through two case studies. The first examines the college-to-career space by comparing different alternatives for predicting college success as measured by college GPA. The second addresses an identified market failure of highly qualified college graduates being overlooked for employment due to a matching problem. The chapter concludes with a proposal for a solution to this problem, namely a matching system.

# Chapter 10

High fidelity measures have proven to be powerful tools for measuring a broad range of competencies and their validity is well documented. However, their high-touch nature is often a deterrent to their use due to the cost and time required to develop and implement them. In addition, given the increased reliance on technology to screen and evaluate job candidates, organizations are continuing to search for more efficient ways to gather the information they need about one's capabilities. This chapter describes how innovative, interactive rich-media simulations that incorporate branching technology have been used in several real-world applications. The main focus is on describing the nature of these assessments and highlighting potential solutions to the unique measurement challenges associated with these types of assessments.

# Chapter 11

Fulfilling the promise of educational technology as one mechanism to promote college and career readiness compels educators, researchers, and technologists to pursue innovative lines of collaborative investigations. These lines of mutual inquiry benefit from adopting and adapting principles rooted in design-based implementation research (DBIR) approaches. The purposes of this chapter are to: (a) provide the research foundation on which a personalized learning platform was developed, (b) present the evolution of EdSphere, a personalized learning platform that resulted from a deep and long-term collaboration among classroom teachers, school and district administrators, educational researchers, and technologists, and (c) describe a need for development of innovative technologies that promote college and career readiness among our earliest readers.

# Chapter 12

Often in our daily lives we learn and work in groups. In recognition of the importance of collaborative and problem solving skills, educators are realizing the need for effective and scalable learning and assessment solutions to promote the skillset in educational systems. In the settings of a comprehensive collaborative problem solving assessment, each student should be matched with various types of group members and must apply the skills in varied contexts and tasks. One solution to these assessment demands is to use computer-based (virtual) agents to serve as the collaborators in the interactions with students. The chapter presents the premises and challenges in the use of computer agents in the assessment of collaborative problem solving. Directions for future research are discussed in terms of their implications to large-scale assessment programs.

# Chapter 13

The purpose of our project is to explore the measurement of cognitive skills in the domain of science through collaborative problem solving tasks, measure the collaborative skills, and gauge the potential feasibility of using game-like environments with avatar representation for the purposes of assessing the relevant skills. We are comparing students' performance in two conditions. In one condition, students work individually with two virtual agents in a game-like task. In the second condition, dyads of students work collaboratively with two virtual agents in the similar game-like task through a chat box. Our research is motivated by the distributed nature of cognition, extant research on computer-supported collaborative learning (CSCL) which has shown great value of collaborative activities for learning, and the framework for the Programme for International Student Assessment (PISA) framework. This chapter focuses on the development and implementation of a conceptual model to measure individuals' cognitive and social skills through collaborative activities.

# Chapter 14

The study described in this chapter is based on a joint World ORT, Israeli Ministry of Education and Pearson initiative to provide an opportunity for international student collaboration on a series of complex science problems. Students from four schools in Israel, three in the United States and one in Mexico, participated in collaborative complex problem-solving on science topics selected by teachers at the participating schools. The intent was to expose students to the realities of collaborating with people under unfamiliar conditions (such as different cultures, languages, and time zones) in order to reach a shared goal, and to foster the value of this practice. The chapter presents the rationale for the project, describes the Animalia mini-course in detail, presents major findings and discusses implications for future curriculum development and further research.

## Chapter 15

*Belinda Brunner, Pearson, UK*
*Kirk A. Becker, Pearson, USA*
*Noel Tagoe, Chartered Institute of Management Accountants, UK*

Innovative item formats are attractive to the sponsors of professional certification or qualification examinations because they provide greater fidelity to the real world than traditional item formats. Using the design of the Chartered Institute of Management Accountant's professional qualification examinations as a case study, this chapter presents an in-depth exploration of the issues surrounding the use of innovative items to assess higher-order thinking skills required for professional competency, beginning with a discussion of approaches taken by various academic disciplines to define and characterize higher order thinking. The use of innovative, authentic assessments is examined in the context of validity arguments. A framework for principled thinking about the construct map of the assessment is introduced, and a systematic process for designing innovative items to address the desired constructs is provided.

# Volume II

## Chapter 16

*Mahmoud Emira, City & Guilds of London Institute, UK*
*Patrick Craven, City & Guilds of London Institute, UK*
*Sharon Frazer, City & Guilds of London Institute, UK*
*Zeeshan Rahman, City & Guilds of London Institute, UK*

This chapter aims to address assessment in the modern age in terms of its importance, challenges and solutions by examining the views of 1,423 users at UK test centres following their recent experience of using two systems which employ computer-based assessment (CBA) and computer-assisted assessment (CAA). Generally speaking, based on the research, which informs the findings presented in this chapter, both systems face similar challenges but there are challenges which are specific to the CAA system. Similarly, both systems may require common solutions to improve user's future experience, but there are solutions which are more relevant to the CAA system. The chapter concludes with a discussion around the UK apprenticeship and a case study of a pilot apprenticeship programme in which CBA and CAA are also integrated.

*Diane M. Browder, University of North Carolina at Charlotte, USA*
*Alicia Saunders, University of North Carolina at Charlotte, USA*
*Jenny Root, University of North Carolina at Charlotte, USA*

For students with moderate and severe developmental disabilities, including autism spectrum disorders and intellectual disability, technology can provide critical support for learning and life functioning. A growing body of research demonstrates the benefits of technology for these students to acquire academic skills, improve social functioning, and perform tasks of daily living. This chapter provides a description of this population and their learning needs. The research on technology applications for students with developmental disabilities is reviewed and synthesized. The review includes literature on technology to assist instruction and to provide options for student responding. Examples are provided of how technology can be applied to both instruction and assessment.

*Raffaela Wolf, CAE, USA*
*Doris Zahner, CAE, USA*

The assessment of higher-order skills in higher education has gained popularity internationally. In order to accurately measure the skills required for working in the 21st century, a shift in assessment strategies is required. More specifically, assessments that only require the recall of factual knowledge have been on the decline, whereas assessments that evoke higher-order cognitive skills are on the rise. The purpose of this chapter is to discuss and offer strategies for mitigating bias for a computer-administered performance-based assessment of higher-order skills. Strategies to abate the effects of bias are discussed within the test design and test implementation stages. A case study of a successful adaptation and translation of CAE's Collegiate Learning Assessment (CLA+) is presented to guide the discussion throughout the chapter.

*Yigal Rosen, Harvard University, USA*
*Maryam Mosharraf, Pearson, USA*

A concept map is a graphical tool for representing knowledge structure in the form of a graph whose nodes represent concepts, while arcs between nodes correspond to interrelations between them. Using a concept map engages students in a variety of critical and complex thinking, such as evaluating, analyzing, and decision making. Although the potential use of concept maps to assess students' knowledge has been recognized, concept maps are traditionally used as instructional tools. The chapter introduces a technology-enabled three-phase Evidence-Centered Concept Map (ECCM) designed to make students' thinking visible in critical thinking assessment tasks that require students to analyze claims and supporting evidence on a topic and to draw conclusions. Directions for future research are discussed in terms of their implications to technology tools in large-scale assessment programs that target higher-order thinking skills.

The current chapter deals with the use of Facebook as a social network for learning. Collaborative learning, metacognition and reflectivity are theoretically discussed and assessed in the current Facebook learning environment, as essential skills of the 21st century. The case study presented examines the relationship between attitudes and achievements of high school students learning an English play in the Facebook closed-group environment. Its findings reveal a significant improvement in students' attitudes at the end of the sessions. However, these were not found to correlate with students' final achievements. In addition, low achieving students preferred to study collaboratively, as they did in the Facebook closed group, more than higher achieving students. These findings may indicate the contribution of other factors to achievement in addition to positive attitudes and satisfaction in the Facebook learning environment. A metacognitive analysis of the students' written responses supports and expands the findings of this study.

The goal of this chapter is to present a theoretical and practical frame for PD of teachers at the digital age. The main question we ask is how to develop life competencies and skills of teachers in order to change their learning and teaching in a way that enables school graduates to acquire relevant skills for life. The chapter inquires this issue by a qualitative methodology case study . The case is an online course for teachers' professional development. The chapter presents evidence from reflective diaries, interviews and scripts of students' and teachers' discussions, focusing on identification of the effects of the course's learning environments on the development of the teachers' self determination learning and skills. The findings indicate the useful effects of the combination between LMS environments and social media, such as Web 2.0 tools. The conclusions suggest new directions for teachers' professional development that encourage the design of a flexible fractal net which enable fostering teachers' leadership and innovation.

## Section 3
## Automated Item Generation and Automated Scoring Techniques for Assessment and Feedback

*The five chapters in this section address a wide range of technologies for automated scoring, automated item generation and feedback.*

    *Mark Gierl, University of Alberta, Canada*
    *Syed F. Latifi, University of Alberta, Canada*
    *Hollis Lai, University of Alberta, Canada*
    *Donna Matovinovic, CTB/McGraw-Hill, USA*
    *Keith A. Boughton, CTB/McGraw-Hill, USA*

The purpose of this chapter is to describe and illustrate a template-based method for automatically generating test items. This method can be used to produce a large numbers of high-quality items both quickly and efficiency. To highlight the practicality and feasibility of automatic item generation, we demonstrate the application of this method in the content area of junior high school science. We also describe the results from a study designed to evaluate the quality of the generated science items. Our chapter is divided into four sections. In section one, we describe the methodology. In the section two, we illustrate the method using items generated for a junior high school physics curriculum. In section three, we present the results from a study designed to evaluate the quality of the generated science items. In section four, we conclude the chapter and identify one important area for future research.

    *Michael B. Bunch, Measurement Incorporated, USA*
    *David Vaughn, Measurement Incorporated, USA*
    *Shayne Miel, LightSide Labs, USA*

Automated scoring of essays is founded upon the pioneer work of Dr. Ellis B. Page. His creation of Project Essay Grade (PEG) sparked the growth of a field that now includes universities and major corporations whose computer programs are capable of analyzing not only essays but short-answer responses to content-based questions. This chapter provides a brief history of automated scoring, describes in general terms how the programs work, outlines some of the current uses as well as challenges, and offers a glimpse of the future of automated scoring.

    *William Lorié, Questar Assessment, Inc., USA*

Assessment of real-world skills increasingly requires efficient scoring of non-routine test items. This chapter addresses the scoring and psychometric treatment of a broad class of automatically-scorable complex assessment tasks allowing a definite set of responses orderable by quality. These multicomponent tasks are described and proposals are advanced on how to score them so that they support capturing gradations of performance quality. The resulting response evaluation functions are assessed empirically against alternatives using data from a pilot of technology-enhanced items (TEIs) administered to a sample of high school students in one U.S. state. Results support scoring frameworks leveraging the full potential of multicomponent tasks for providing evidence of partial knowledge, understanding, or skill.

## Chapter 25

*Peter W. Foltz, Pearson, USA & University of Colorado – Boulder, USA*

The ability to convey information through writing is a central component of real-world skills. However, assessing writing can be time consuming, limiting the timeliness of feedback. Automated scoring of writing has been shown to be effective across a number of applications. This chapter focuses on how automated scoring of writing has been extended to assessing and training of real-world skills in a range of content domains. It illustrates examples of how the technology is used and considerations for its implementation. The examples include 1) Formative feedback on writing quality, 2) scoring of content in student writing. 3) improving reading comprehension through summary writing, and 4) assessment of writing integrated in higher-level performance tasks in professional domains.

## Chapter 26

*Joshua Wilson, University of Delaware, USA*
*Gilbert N. Andrada, Connecticut State Department of Education, USA*

Writing skills are essential for success in K-12 and post-secondary settings. Yet, more than two-thirds of students in the United States fail to achieve grade-level proficiency in writing. The current chapter discusses the use of automated essay evaluation (AEE) software, specifically automated feedback systems, for scaffolding improvements in writing skills. The authors first present a discussion of the use of AEE systems, prevailing criticisms, and findings from the research literature. Then, results of a novel study of the effects of automated feedback are reported. The chapter concludes with a discussion of implications for stakeholders and directions for future research.

## Section 4
## Analysis, Interpretation, and Use of Learning and Assessment Data from Technology Rich Environments

*This section introduces tools for analysis, interpretation and use of learning and assessment data in technology environments.*

## Chapter 27

*Jean-Francois Rouet, University of Poitiers, France*
*Zsofia Vörös, University of Poitiers, France*
*Matthias von Davier, Educational Testing Service, USA*

The spread of digital information system has promoted new ways of performing activities, whereby laypersons make use of computer applications in order to achieve their goal through the use of problem solving strategies. These new forms of problem solving rely on a range of skills whose accurate assessment is key to the development of postindustrial economies. In this chapter, we outline a definition of problem solving in technology-rich environment drawn from the OECD PIAAC survey of adult skills. Then we review research studies aimed at defining and using online indicators of PS-TRE proficiency. Finally, we present a case study of one item that was part of the PIAAC PS-TRE assessment.

# Chapter 28

A key task emerging in item analysis is identification of what constitutes valid and reliable measurement information, and what data support proposed score interpretations. Measurement information takes on many forms with computerized tests. An enormous amount of data is gathered from technology-based items, tracing every click and movement of the mouse and time stamping actions taken, and the data recorded falls into two general categories: process and outcomes. Outcomes are traditional scored answers that students provides in response to prompts, but technology-based item types also provide information regarding the process that students used to answer items. The first consideration to the practical use of such data is the nature of the data generated when learners complete complex assessment tasks. The chapter we propose serves to discuss some possible methodological strategies that could be used to analyze data from such technology-rich testing tasks.

# Chapter 29

This chapter draws on process data recorded in a computer-based large-scale program, the Programme for International Assessment of Adult Competencies (PIAAC), to address how sequences of actions recorded in problem-solving tasks are related to task performance. The purpose of this study is twofold: first, to extract and detect robust sequential action patterns that are associated with success or failure on a problem-solving item, and second, to compare the extracted sequence patterns among selected countries. Motivated by the methodologies of natural language processing and text mining, we utilized feature selection models in analyzing the process data at a variety of aggregate levels and evaluated the different methodologies in terms of predictive power of the evidence extracted from process data. It was found that action sequence patterns significantly differed by performance groups and were consistent across countries. This study also demonstrated that the process data were useful in detecting missing data and potential mistakes in item development.

**Chapter 30**

Task persistence is defined as the continuation of activity in the face of difficulty, obstacles, and/or failure. It has been linked to educational achievement, educational attainment, and occupation outcomes. A number of different psychological approaches attempt to explain individual and situational differences in persistence and there is mounting evidence that interventions can be implemented to increase persistence. New technological capabilities offer the opportunity to seamlessly gather evidence about persistence from individuals' interactions in digital environments. Two examples of assessment of persistence in digital games are presented. Both demonstrate the ability to gather information without interruption of activity and the use of in-game actions as evidence. They also both require consideration of the student/player model, task model, and evidence models. A design pattern outlining each of these elements is presented for use by those considering assessment of persistence in digital environments.

**Chapter 31**

The assessment of real-world skills will often require complex and innovative types of computer-based test items to provide more authentic assessment. Having information about how students remain engaged with the various innovative elements during an assessment is useful in both assessing the utility of different types of innovative test items and assessing the validity of the inferences made about the test scores of individual students. This chapter introduces the Item Engagement Index (IEI) and the Student Engagement Index (SEI) and demonstrates their use with a variety of innovative items that were pilot tested for a nursing licensure exam. The IEI provided useful information about the amount of student effort each innovative item received, while the SEI was found useful in identifying disengaged test takers.

# Foreword

We need to think harder about how we prepare young people for tomorrow's world. In the past, education was about teaching students something. Now, it's about making sure that students develop a reliable compass and the navigation skills to find their own way through an uncertain, volatile, and ambiguous world. Now, schools need to prepare students for a world in which most people will need to collaborate with people of diverse cultural origins and appreciate different ideas, perspectives and values; a world in which people need to decide how to trust and collaborate across such differences; and a world in which their lives will be affected by issues that transcend national boundaries. Technology has become the key to bridge space and time in all of this.

These days, we no longer know exactly how things will unfold. We are often surprised and need to learn from the extraordinary, and sometimes we make mistakes along the way. And it will often be the mistakes and failures, when properly understood, that create the context for learning and growth. A generation ago, teachers could expect that what they taught would last their students a lifetime. Today, schools need to prepare students for more rapid economic and social change than ever before, for jobs that have not yet been created, to use technologies that have not yet been invented, and to solve social problems that we don't yet know will arise.

How do we foster motivated, engaged learners who are prepared to conquer the unforeseen challenges of tomorrow, not to mention those of today? The dilemma for educators is that routine cognitive skills—the skills that are easiest to teach and easiest to test—are also the skills that are easiest to digitize, automate, and outsource. There is no question that state-of-the-art knowledge and skills in a discipline will always remain important. Innovative or creative people generally have specialized skills in a field of knowledge or a practice. And as much as 'learning to learn' skills are important, we always learn by learning something. However, educational success is no longer about reproducing content knowledge, but about extrapolating from what we know and applying that knowledge in novel situations. Put simply, the world no longer rewards people for what they know—Google knows everything—but for what they can do with what they know. Because that is the main differentiator today, education today needs to be much more about ways of thinking, involving creativity, critical thinking, problem-solving, and decision-making; about ways of working, including communication and collaboration; about tools for working, including the capacity to recognize and exploit the potential of new technologies; and, last but not least, about the social and emotional skills that help us live and work together.

Conventionally, our approach to problems was to break them down into manageable bits and pieces and then to teach students the techniques to solve them. But today we create value by synthesizing the disparate bits. This is about curiosity, open-mindedness, and making connections between ideas that previously seemed unrelated, which requires being familiar with and receptive to knowledge in other fields than our own. If we spend our whole life in a silo of a single discipline, we will not gain the imaginative skills to connect the dots where the next invention will come from.

Equally important, the more content knowledge we can search and access, the more important becomes the capacity to make sense of this content—the capacity of individuals to question or seek to improve the accepted knowledge and practices of their time. In the past, you could tell students to look into an encyclopedia when they needed some information, and you could tell them that they could generally rely on what they found to be true. Today, literacy is about managing non-linear information structures, building your own mental representation of information as you find your own way through hypertext on the Internet, and dealing with ambiguity—interpreting and resolving conflicting pieces of information that we find somewhere on the Web.

Perhaps most importantly, in today's schools, students typically learn individually and at the end of the school year, we certify their individual achievements. But the more interdependent the world becomes, the more we need great collaborators and orchestrators. Innovation today is rarely the product of individuals working in isolation but an outcome of how we mobilize, share, and link knowledge. In the flat world, everything that is our proprietary knowledge today will be a commodity available to everyone else tomorrow. Expressed differently, schools need to drive a shift from a world where knowledge is stacked up somewhere, depreciating rapidly in value, towards a world in which the enriching power of communication and collaborative flows is increasing. And they will need to help the next generation to better reconcile resilience (managing in an imbalanced world) with greater sustainability (putting the world back into balance).

This is a tough agenda. What is certain is that it will never materialise unless we are able to clearly conceptualise and measure those 21st century knowledge areas and skills. Without rigorous conceptualisation, we will not be able to build meaningful curricula and pedagogies around these knowledge areas and skills. And, at the end of the day, what is assessed is what gets taught. This volume makes a major step in advancing this frontier. It examines a range of skills that are important; it looks at innovative measurement methods to make these skills amenable to quantitative assessment in ways that they become activators of students' own learning, and it looks at how we can learn to drink from the firehose of increasing data streams that arise from new assessment modes.

*Andreas Schleicher*
*Organisation for Economic Co-Operation and Development (OECD), France*

# Foreword

In its landmark report *Education for Life and Work in the 21st Century*, the National Research Council (2012) described "deeper learning" as an instructional approach important in preparing students with sophisticated cognitive, intrapersonal, and interpersonal skills. The approaches recommended by advocates of deeper learning are not new, and historically these instructional strategies have been described under a variety of terms. Until now, however, they have been rarely practiced within the schools (Dede, 2014), resulting in the sad situation that students who excel in school may struggle in the real world. And students who struggle in school are likely to sink in the real world. Various "deeper learning" approaches are described below.

- Case-based learning helps students master abstract principles and skills through the analysis of real-world situations;
- Multiple, varied representations of concepts provide different ways of explaining complicated things, showing how those depictions are alternative forms of the same underlying ideas;
- Collaborative learning enables a team to combine its knowledge and skills in making sense of a complex phenomenon;
- Apprenticeships involve working with a mentor who has a specific real-world role and, over time, enables mastery of their knowledge and skills;
- Self-directed, life-wide, open-ended learning is based on students' passions and is connected to students' identities in ways that foster academic engagement, self-efficacy, and tenacity;
- Learning for transfer emphasizes that the measure of mastery is application in life rather than simply in the classroom;
- Interdisciplinary studies help students see how differing fields can complement each other, offering a richer perspective on the world than any single discipline can provide;
- Personalized learning ensures that students receive instruction and supports that are tailored to their needs and responsive to their interests (U.S. Department of Education, 2010; Wolf, 2010; Rose & Gravel, 2010);
- Connected learning encourages students to confront challenges and pursue opportunities that exist outside of their classrooms and campuses (Ito et al., 2013); and
- Diagnostic assessments are embedded into learning and are formative for further learning and instruction (Dede, 2012).

These entail very different teaching strategies than the familiar, lecture-based forms of instruction characteristic of industrial-era schooling, with its one-size-fits-all processing of students. Rather than requiring rote memorization and individual mastery of prescribed material, they involve in-depth, differentiated content; authentic diagnostic assessment embedded in instruction; active forms of learning, often collaborative; and learning about academic subjects linked to personal passions and infused throughout life.

The chapters in this book demonstrate that new tools and media can be very helpful to many teachers who would otherwise struggle to provide these kinds of instruction for deeper learning (Dede, 2014). By analogy, imagine that you wish to visit a friend 20 miles away. You could walk (and some people would prefer to do so), but it would be much easier to use a bicycle, and it would be far easier still to use a car. In short, teachers who wish to prepare their students for the real world, as well as for further academics, don't have to use educational technology; they may prefer to walk. Realistically, however, many, if not most, teachers will be hard-pressed to get from industrial-style instruction to deeper learning without the vehicles of digital tools, media, and experiences.

In an extensive review of the literature on technology and teaching for the forthcoming American Educational Research Association (AERA) Handbook of Research on Teaching (5th Edition), Barry Fishman and I (in press) note the important distinction between using technology to do conventional things better and using technology to do better things (Roschelle et al., 2000). While there may be value in doing some types of conventional instruction better (i.e., more efficiently and effectively), the real value in technology for teaching lies in rethinking the enterprise of schooling in ways that unlock powerful learning opportunities and make better use of the resources present in the 21st-century world.

In our review, we consider how and under what conditions technology can be productively employed by teachers to more effectively prepare students for the challenges presented by a rapidly evolving world. We argue that technology as a catalyst is effective only when used to enable learning with richer content, more powerful pedagogy, more valid assessments, and links between in- and out-of-classroom learning. The examined the following technologies in depth:

- Collaboration tools, including Web 2.0 technologies and tools that support knowledge building;
- Online and hybrid educational environments, which are increasingly being used to broaden access to education but also have the potential to shift the way we conceive of teaching and learning;
- Tools that support learners as makers and creators, which have their deep roots in helping students learn to become programmers of computers (and not just users of them);
- Immersive media that create virtual worlds to situate learning or augment the real world with an overlay of computational information; and
- Games and simulations that are designed to enhance student motivation and learning.

This book provides examples of these and other powerful technologies to aid this type of instruction. If used in concert, these deeper-learning technologies can help prepare students for life and work in the 21st century, mirroring in the classroom some powerful methods of knowing and doing that pervade the rest of society. Further, they can be used to create a practical, cost-effective division of labor, one that empowers teachers to perform complex instructional tasks. In addition, these media can address the learning strengths and preferences of students growing up in this digital age, including bridging formal instruction and informal learning. And, finally, these technologies can provide powerful mechanisms for teacher learning; by which educators deepen their professional knowledge and skills in ways that mirror the types of learning environments through which they will guide their students.

At a time in history when civilization faces crises that we need the full capacity of people across the world to resolve, this volume provides an exemplary suite of practical ways to move forward with curricula, instruction, and assessments that are truly oriented to 21st-century life and work.

*Chris Dede*
*Harvard University, USA*

## REFERENCES

Dede, C. (2012). *Interweaving assessments into immersive authentic simulations: Design strategies for diagnostic and instructional insights* (Commissioned White Paper for the ETS Invitational Research Symposium on Technology Enhanced Assessments). Princeton, NJ: Educational Testing Service.

Dede, C. (2014). *The role of technology in deeper learning*. New York, NY: Jobs for the Future.

Fishman, B., & Dede, C. (in press). Teaching and technology: New tools for new times. In D. Gitomer & C. Bell (Eds.), *Handbook of research on teaching* (5th ed.). New York, NY: Springer.

Ito, M., Gutiérrez, K., Livingstone, S., Penuel, B., Rhodes, J., & Salen, K. … Watkins, S. C. (2013). Connected learning: An agenda for research and design. Irvine, CA: Digital Media and Learning Research Hub.

National Research Council. (2012). *Education for life and work: Developing transferable knowledge and skills in the 21st century*. Washington, DC: The National Academies Press. Retrieved from http://www.nap.edu/catalog.php?record_id=13398

Roschelle, J. M., Pea, R. D., Hoadley, C. M., Gordin, D. N., & Means, B. M. (2000). Changing how and what children learn in school with computer-based technologies. *The Future of Children: Children and Computer Technology, 10*(2), 76–101. doi:10.2307/1602690 PMID:11255710

Rose, D. H., & Gravel, J. W. (2010). Universal design for learning. In E. Baker, P. Peterson, & B. McGaw (Eds.), *International Encyclopedia of Education* (3rd ed.). Oxford, UK: Elsevier. doi:10.1016/B978-0-08-044894-7.00719-3

U.S. Department of Education. (2010). *Transforming American education: Learning powered by technology (National Educational Technology Plan 2010)*. Washington, DC: Office of Educational Technology, U.S. Department of Education.

Wolf, M. A. (2010, November). *Innovate to educate: System [re]design for personalized learning*. Washington, DC: Software and Information Industry Association.

# Preface

Changes in the world economy, specifically toward information industries, have changed the skillset demand of many jobs (Organization for Economic Development [OECD], 2012a). Information is created, acquired, transmitted, and used—rather than simply learned—by individuals, enterprises, organizations, and communities to promote economic and social development. Major employers and policy makers are increasingly asking teachers and educators to help students develop so-called real-world skills (Gallup, 2013). While learning basic numeracy and literacy skills still is crucial to success in the job market, developing real-world skills also is essential to success in the job market and worldwide economic development.

Real-world skills, or "21st century skills," include critical thinking, collaborative problem solving, creativity, and global competency. These skills that facilitate mastery and application of science, mathematics, language arts, and other school subjects will grow in importance over the coming decade (National Research Council, 2012; OECD, 2012a, 2012b). A wide range of initiatives and programs in education promote learning and assessment of real-world skills. These include, for example, the Common Core State Standards (National Governors Association Center for Best Practices and Council of Chief State School Officers, 2010a, 2010b), Next Generation Science Standards (National Research Council, 2013), Common European Framework of Reference (Council of Europe, 2011), Partnership for 21st Century Skills (Partnership for 21st Century Skills, 2009), Education for Life and Work (National Research Council, 2012), and assessment frameworks in the Programme for International Student Assessment (PISA) (OECD, 2013).

Because of the importance of promoting these skills, we have embarked on a journey to create a *Handbook of Research on Technology Tools for Real-World Skill Development*. Because conceptions and educational applications of real-world skills are evolving rapidly, we have welcomed a wide range of skills in the *Handbook*. The following four strands of skills are represented in the chapters: *Thinking skills* refer to higher-order cognition and dispositions such as critical thinking, complex problem solving, metacognition, and learning to learn. *Social skills* refer to attitudes and behaviors that enable successful communication and collaboration. *Global skills* refer to attitudes and behaviors that emphasize the individual's role in, and awareness of, the local as well as the global and multicultural environment. *Digital skills* emphasize information and digital literacies needed in the technology-rich world in which we live. Similarly, the chapters in this *Handbook* describe a range of technology tools to support teaching, learning, assessment for learning (e.g., Stiggins, 2005; Wiliam, 2011), feedback for learning (e.g., Hattie, & Timperley, 2007; Shute, 2008), and scoring of student responses. For example, section 1 includes chapters on curricula and frameworks for teaching real-world skills; the chapters in section 2 describe specific technology tools for teaching, learning, and assessing real-world skills; the chapters in section 3 describe automated scoring tools for assessment and learning; and section 4 contains chapters on techniques for analyzing data from technology-based performance assessments. Helping students learn real-world skills—that is, to internalize them and use them flexibly across a range of challenges and contexts in their everyday and work lives—is a significant educational challenge. Real-world skills cannot be taught in a single course or in a single year of schooling. And assessing real-world skills to provide feedback to guide development of those skills cannot be accomplished using conventional, large-scale assessment and score reporting methods alone. The technology tools described here represent the range of current and developing capabilities of technology tools to support teaching, learning, assessment, and feedback for learning.

As technology-rich environments for teaching, learning, assessment, and feedback are being integrated into educational processes, there is much to be learned about how to leverage advances in technology, learning sciences, and assessment to develop real-world skills for the 21st century. Research findings on what works best are just emerging, possibly due to the strong multi-disciplinary approaches required to extract the greatest value. This *Handbook* is intended to serve as a first body of research in the expanding area of technology tools for teaching, learning, assessment, and feedback on real-world skills that educators can turn to in the coming years as a reference. Our aim is to bring together top researchers to summarize concepts and findings. The *Handbook* contains contributions of leading researchers in learning science, educational psychology, psychometrics, and educational technology. Assuming that many readers will have little grounding in those topics, each chapter outlines theory and basic concepts and connects them to technology tools for real-world skill development. We see this as one of the most crucial contributions of the *Handbook*, seeking to establish strong theoretical principles that can inform educational research and practice and future research and development. The *Handbook* also provides brief overviews in each topic section for more knowledgeable readers. The *Handbook* is organized into four sections.

## SECTION 1: DEFINING REAL-WORLD SKILLS IN TECHNOLOGY-RICH ENVIRONMENTS

The seven chapters in Section 1 explore conceptualization of real-world skills and the role of technology. The section includes chapters on curricula and frameworks for teaching real-world skills. To aid readers in selecting specific chapters to study, we list the technology tools described in these chapters.

**Chapter 1:** A principled approach for developing digital competency.
**Chapter 2:** A model for teaching digital competency.
**Chapter 3:** A model for measuring problem solving skills in science, technology, engineering, and mathematics (STEM).
**Chapter 4:** A model for teaching Internet research skills.
**Chapter 5:** Another model for teaching Internet research skills.
**Chapter 6:** A matrix for evaluating technology integration in K-12 instructional settings, and teacher-related professional development.
**Chapter 7:** An online team-based learning model in nursing education.

# SECTION 2: TECHNOLOGY TOOLS FOR LEARNING AND ASSESSING REAL-WORLD SKILLS

Chapters 8 through 21 deal with the core topic of technology tools and a wide range of applications aimed at learning and assessing of real-world skills. The technology tools described in these chapters include the following.

**Chapter 8:** Technology-rich simulations for learning and assessing science skills.

**Chapter 9:** The Collegiate Learning Assessment, a test to evaluate the critical thinking and written communication skills of college students.

**Chapter 10:** Guidance, based on lessons learned from developing rich-media simulations, for assessment for organization staff promotion and development.

**Chapter 11:** A personalized learning platform for developing early reading.

**Chapter 12:** Computer agent technology for assessing collaborative problem solving skills.

**Chapter 13:** A model for assessing cognitive and social skills through online collaboration.

**Chapter 14:** An approach for technology-rich learning and formative assessment of collaborative problem solving skills.

**Chapter 15:** A framework for principled thinking about a construct map assessment of a higher-order thinking skills.

**Chapter 16:** Computer-based and computer-assisted approaches for assessment of knowledge and skills.

**Chapter 17:** Technology tools for learning for students with moderate and severe development and intellectual disabilities.

**Chapter 18:** Strategies for mitigating bias for a computer-administered performance-based assessment of higher-order skills.

**Chapter 19:** An evidence-centered concept map for a critical thinking assessment.

**Chapter 20:** Facebook as a social network for learning.

**Chapter 21:** A framework for teachers' professional development in the digital age.

# SECTION 3: AUTOMATED ITEM GENERATION AND AUTOMATED SCORING TECHNIQUES FOR ASSESSMENT AND FEEDBACK

The five chapters in Section 3 address a range of technologies for automated scoring, automated item generation, and learner feedback. The technology tools described in these chapters include the following.

**Chapter 22:** Procedures for automated generation of science items.

**Chapter 23:** Automated scoring approaches for development of writing proficiency.

**Chapter 24:** A principled framework for designing automated scoring of multicomponent assessment tasks.

**Chapter 25:** Automated scoring as the basis for feedback to support improvement of writing skills.

**Chapter 26:** Automated feedback to improve writing quality.

## SECTION 4: ANALYSES OF PROCESS DATA IN TECHNOLOGY-RICH PERFORMANCE TASKS

Chapters 27 through 31 deal with analysis, interpretation, and use of learning and assessment data in technology environments. The technology tools described in these chapters include the following.

**Chapter 27:** Analysis of solution paths in a technology-rich problem solving assessment.
**Chapter 28:** Analysis of solution paths in technology-rich critical thinking assessment.
**Chapter 29:** Use of a chi-square features selection algorithm (i.e., sequential pattern mining) and N-grams representation model to analyze process data in technology-rich problem solving tasks.
**Chapter 30:** Analytic methods to induce a persistence measure from game play click stream data and a design pattern to guide future development of persistence measures in digital environments.
**Chapter 31:** An Item Engagement Index (IEI) and Student Engagement Index (SEI) for assessing engagement during the online assessment of real-world skills.

Our goal in collecting and organizing these excellent chapters is to begin a process of crystalizing what our field has accomplished to date and what it knows, collectively, about technology tools and how those tools can be used to support and enhance teaching and learning of real-world skills. Knowing what we know should help us identify what we need to know. And it should guide further development of practical applications and empirical research on the efficacy of using technology tools for teaching, learning, assessing, and providing feedback as learners work to develop the skills they need for today's high-tech, higher-order knowledge and skills world. We hope this *Handbook* will serve as a tool to encourage collaborations among researchers, educators, policy makers, employers, and the general public to promote learning, assessment, and personalized feedback technologies. By compiling the rich research and knowledge in this *Handbook*, we hope to spark innovation in education.

The *Handbook* is a recommended reading source to the following audiences:

*Educators*: This book will share essential insights for policy makers, principals, curriculum experts, and teachers who are interested in better understanding the practical challenges and opportunities in introducing new technology-rich programs aimed to promote learning, assessment, and feedback on real-world skills.

*Researchers*: This book will provide a valuable springboard to researchers in psychology, education, assessment, and computer science to engage with the concept of technology-rich assessment and learning of higher-order thinking skills and work on new research directions. This will be aided by the emphasis of key gaps in existing research and providing details on what areas need more careful research and empirical validation.

*General audiences* with interest in upcoming trends in learning, assessment, and feedback: This book will cover a range of topics related to real-world skills and value of real-world skills in next-generation education.

# REFERENCES

Council of Europe. (2011). *Common European framework of references for languages: Learning, teaching, assessment*. Strasburg: Author.

Gallup. (2013). *21st century skills and the workplace: A 2013 Microsoft-Pearson Foundation study on 21st century skills and the workplace*. Washington, DC: Author.

Hattie, J., & Timperley, H. (2007). The power of feedback. *Review of Educational Research, 77*(1), 81–112. doi:10.3102/003465430298487

National Governors Association Center for Best Practices and Council for Chief State School Officers. (2010a). *Common core state standards for mathematics*. Washington, DC: Author.

National Governors Association Center for Best Practices and Council for Chief State School Officers. (2010b). *Common core state standards for English language arts and literacy in history/social, science, and technical subjects*. Washington, DC: Author.

National Research Council. (2012). *Education for life and work: Developing transferable knowledge and skills in the 21st century*. Washington, DC: The National Academies Press.

National Research Council. (2013). *Next generation science standards: For states, by states*. Washington, DC: The National Academies Press.

Organization for Economic Development (OECD). (2012a). *Better skills, better jobs, better lives: A strategic approach to skills policies*. OECD Publishing.

Organization for Economic Development (OECD). (2012b). *Education at a glance 2012: OECD indicators*. OECD Publishing.

Organization for Economic Development (OECD). (2013). *PISA 2015 collaborative problem solving framework*. OECD Publishing.

Partnership for 21st Century Skills. (2009). *P21 framework definitions*. Washington, DC: Author.

Shute, V. J. (2008). Focus on formative feedback. *Review of Educational Research, 78*(1), 153–189. doi:10.3102/0034654307313795

Stiggins, R. J. (2005). From formative assessment to assessment FOR learning: A path to success in standards-based schools. *Phi Delta Kappan, 87*(4), 324–328. doi:10.1177/003172170508700414

Wiliam, D. (2011). *Embedded formative assessment*. Bloomington, IN: Solution Tree Press.

# Acknowledgment

In the writing and editing this book we have to thank the conceptual visionaries who pushed our thinking and contributed greatly to the formation of the ideas presented here. At Pearson, Dr. Kimberly O'Malley, a thoughtful leader who provided executive support during all the stages of our work on the *Handbook*. Our colleagues, Dr. Peter Foltz and Dr. Katie McClarty who have been key in developing these ideas as part of 21st Century Skills project. Prof. Andreas Schleicher, OECD and Prof. Chris Dede, Harvard University shared their invaluable insights and directions for further research in Foreword section of the *Handbook*. And then there is the outstanding group of authors from a wide range of organizations and geographies who contributed their chapters to this volume. Along the way, the authors graciously served as each other's reviewers as we passed drafts around, nurturing each other's chapters and adding new perspectives. We thank you all for making our own work on the *Handbook* a great pleasure.

# Chapter 16
# Assessment in the Modern Age:
## Challenges and Solutions

**Mahmoud Emira**
*City & Guilds of London Institute, UK*

**Sharon Frazer**
*City & Guilds of London Institute, UK*

**Patrick Craven**
*City & Guilds of London Institute, UK*

**Zeeshan Rahman**
*City & Guilds of London Institute, UK*

## ABSTRACT

*This chapter aims to address assessment in the modern age in terms of its importance, challenges and solutions by examining the views of 1,423 users at UK test centres following their recent experience of using two systems which employ computer-based assessment (CBA) and computer-assisted assessment (CAA). Generally speaking, based on the research, which informs the findings presented in this chapter, both systems face similar challenges but there are challenges which are specific to the CAA system. Similarly, both systems may require common solutions to improve user's future experience, but there are solutions which are more relevant to the CAA system. The chapter concludes with a discussion around the UK apprenticeship and a case study of a pilot apprenticeship programme in which CBA and CAA are also integrated.*

## INTRODUCTION

Assessment is a major facet of education and one of the key activities in candidate learning (Apampa, Wills & Argles, 2010) because of its transformative impact on the learning process, regardless of the mode of delivery, i.e. traditional or online assessment. The first part of this chapter examines, through a literature review, assessment in the modern age in terms of its importance, challenges and potential solutions to address these challenges. It starts with a brief comparison between traditional and e-assessment. In the second part of the chapter the research findings are presented, discussed and linked to the literature. The findings, which are split in two online surveys, are based on the views of 1,423 users at UK test centres on e-assessment. The surveys focused on two systems, which employ computer-based assessment (CBA) and computer-assisted assessment (CAA). The chapter concludes with a discussion around the UK apprenticeship and

DOI: 10.4018/978-1-4666-9441-5.ch016

a case study of a pilot apprenticeship programme in which CBA and CAA are also integrated to explore the topics examined in part 1.

## PART 1: BACKGROUND AND LITERATURE REVIEW

This part, which is *mainly* a literature review, begins with a brief comparison between traditional and e-assessment. It then discusses e-assessment in much more detail in relation to its definition, importance, types, challenges and solutions to overcome these solutions.

### Traditional and E-Assessment Comparison[1]

Both assessment types have common characteristics when it comes to the principles of quality assessment (ANTA 2001 cited in Booth et al., 2003; DTWT, 2012), i.e. both should be:

- **Valid:** E.g. the assessment has measured what it is supposed to measure and evidence will prove that the individual has the required skills and/or knowledge.
- **Reliable:** E.g. same results would be obtained overtime.
- **Flexible:** E.g. assessments can be either on/off-the job, and at a convenient time and place.
- **Fair:** E.g. objective (Livingston Institute of Vocational Training, 2010) and adjusted to meet particular needs of candidates in terms of disabilities/cultural differences. No unnecessary higher levels of English or literacy than what is required to meet the standards in the competencies being assessed.

Traditional assessment are commonly considered as manual face to face tests taken with paper and pencil that are usually true/false, matching,

or multiple choice. These assessments are easy to grade, but only test isolated application, facts, or memorised data at lower-level thinking skills (Learn NC, 2014). However, this is not to suggest that traditional assessment does not use other forms of tests or assess higher level thinking skills. E-assessment, on the other hand, uses computers to create, deliver or mark candidates' work (Marriott & Teoh, 2012). A brief comparison could be made between the operation and delivery of both assessments. *Operationally,* in the short to medium term, traditional assessment methods may be less expensive (Nekoueizadeh & Bahrani, 2013). However, once developed, e-assessment methods become less costly in the long run (see also challenges of e-assessment below). E-assessment may reduce the time assessors spend in marking (with the exception of human marking on screen), but this is merely a reflection of the shift in their focus of effort to before, rather than after, the examination period (Kumar, 2012). In relation to the *delivery* of both assessment types, e-assessment is believed to be fairer to candidates in the sense that it is less "susceptible" to subjectivity, only when used in CBA mode (Nekoueizadeh & Bahrani, 2013, p. 95). E-assessment can support personalisation and the facility to be taken anytime and anywhere unlike traditional assessment. It might also have the upper hand when it comes to the improvement of candidates' (including those with cognitive and some physical disabilities) experiences of being more engaged in their learning (Kumar, 2012). Despite opponents to this view, it is argued that e-assessment is more likely than traditional assessment to enhance "candidates' critical thinking, effective decision-making, collaborative skills, or the ability to solve practical problems" (ibid, p.16) and this largely depends on the topic of assessment and form chosen (see types of e-assessment).

Regardless of these differences, there are key points to develop valid, reliable, flexible and fair assessment (Booth et al., 2003) such as a) making assessment a coherent part of the e-learning process b) using a range of methods to collect evidence of competence c) managing the expectations of candidates in relation to the timeliness and level of feedback right from the beginning d) knowing the suitability of the available e-assessment technology and offering alternatives where appropriate, especially if e-assessment creates access issues, and considering the opportunities of 'blended' approach. Despite technology's role in assessment, a blended delivery (online and face-to-face assessment) is "generally favoured by experienced designers and deliverers" (ibid, p.24).

## Definition of E-Assessment[2]

'E-assessment' refers to any type of assessment that has an electronic (digital) component and incorporates one or more of e-testing, e-portfolios and e-marking (see below types of e-assessment). Forms of e-assessment may be used to evaluate candidate[3]'s progress at different stages of learning with varied objectives (JISC, 2007a):

- *Diagnostic* assessment is normally used prior to/at the beginning of a programme of learning to 'diagnose' candidate's current knowledge and/or skills.
- *Formative* assessment may be used at a later stage during the course. Its priority is to evaluate current level of candidate's understanding with the aim of providing constructive feedback to 'form'/enhance their knowledge/skills and the most effective next stage of learning. It is also described as 'assessment *for* learning'. It does not determine whether the candidate should get the final award/qualification, but it can provide him/her with an opportunity to reflect on their learning and act accordingly. Therefore, the security of e-assessment might not be a top priority for low-stakes assessment (Phelps, 2006).
- *Summative* is the final assessment of a candidate's learning during a programme of study and its priority is to define their

achievement, hence referred to as 'assessment *of* learning'. The awarding of a formal qualification or certification of a skill relies on this form of assessment. Hence, high stakes assessment places much more emphasis on issues like the security of assessment (ibid, 2006) because of the significance of its objective. In this research, which informs the book chapter, the focus is *mostly* on the use of e-assessments at this summative stage. However, both systems could be used for formative purposes (see types of e-assessment).

## The Importance of E-Assessment

The importance of e-assessment is multifaceted and relevant to a wide range of stakeholders including candidates and assessors. E-assessment suits the way *candidates* now work and engage with information. Today's candidates are often referred to as digital natives where they are used to communicating and typing homework and coursework on screen (Ofqual, 2010) compared to their instructors who can be described as digital immigrants, i.e., not skilled enough with technology or less exposed to digital solutions (Prensky, 2001). E-assessment can widen participation by increasing accessibility for disabled candidates (e.g. with physical/visual impairment) and the breadth of what can be evidenced (JISC, 2007a).

For the *assessor*, e-assessment can be "more objective", provides "consistent marking" and "marks [are] available instantly" which makes it "easy to analyse candidate performance overall and gauge the complexity of individual questions" (Marriott & Teoh, 2012, p.6). In relation to higher stakes external assessment or the practice of awarding bodies, use of online tests, such as City & Guilds testing services (the UK leading vocational awarding body) has increased sharply since 2002 (JISC, 2007a). In 2008 EAL (EMTA Awarding Limited) enhanced their online exams system to increase its capability and improve customer satisfaction. The flexibility of e-assessment services allows centres, for example, to schedule exams at short notice or well in advance, and thus reduce administration time (Ofqual, 2010). Furthermore, e-assessment facilitates the process of tracking and analysing candidates' behaviour, performance and results (Al-Smadi & Gütl, 2008). It performs sophisticated e-assessment tasks (Boyle & Hutchinson, 2009), which include video, sound, simulations and animations. All of these features can be a tremendous benefit to the candidate and educational institution providing greater flexibility and precision in the learning and assessment services offered.

E- assessment could offer (JISC, 2010a):

1. Varied and authentic design forms;
2. Improved candidate engagement (e.g. interaction);
3. Choice in timing and locations (including various designs to ensure fairness to all candidates);
4. Potential to assess wider skills/attributes (e.g. through simulations, e-portfolio);
5. Efficient marking and storage of data;
6. Data consistency and accuracy;
7. Instant feedback;
8. More opportunities for candidates to act on feedback (e.g. by reflection in e-portfolios);
9. Creative and innovative approaches (e.g. to "interact with the question resources and present their response, or to rich media – providing a variety of realistic and stimulating content to allow more authentic assessment activity" such as use of audio, text editing and adaptive assessment (Winkley, 2010, p.5). The use of audio "can broaden the extent to which the assessment covers the curriculum quite broadly" (ibid, p.6); and
10. Accurate, timely and accessible evidence on the effectiveness of curriculum design and delivery (e.g. outcomes of assessments can feed into curriculum review processes) (JISC, 2010a, pp.8, 9). The efficiency of e-

assessment (e.g. saving time) could be used to "improve the design of the curriculum" (JISC, 2010b, p.3). The results of summative e-assessment are used as a "basis for addressing misconceptions and providing supplementary teaching", which is another way of tying to curriculum design (Sharples et al., 2012, pp. 3-4). E-assessment can provide automatic scoring (Winkley, 2010) and "real time, programme-level feedback loop" in ways that traditional assessment "simply cannot" (Prineas & Cini, 2011, p.10).

## Types of E-Assessment

Broadly speaking, there are two main categories of e-assessment: computer-based assessment (CBA) and computer-assisted assessment (CAA) which includes e-portfolio.

## CBA

CBA is a term that refers to the use of computers to "deliver, mark and analyse assignments or examinations" (Bull & McKenna, 2004, p.1). For the purpose of this chapter CBA, refers to assessments which: 1) are distributed, completed, marked automatically and administered electronically using local "intranets/networks and individual workstations" 2) are distributed, completed, marked automatically and administered electronically using the "internet" and 3) comprise a combination of "automatic marking and manual marking" that are delivered in either of the two ways described in points 1 and 2 (QCA, 2007, p.6). Examples of CBA (Figure 1), which are most commonly used, are: multiple-choice tests and true/false tests (Dikli, 2003).

Multiple-choice tests are widely used because they are 1) quick and easy to mark by a computer 2) more likely to be objective and fairer compared to other forms of assessment. In true/false tests guessing might increase the probability of success by 50%. In general, this CBA is high stakes

*Figure 1. Examples of multiple choice and true/false tests*

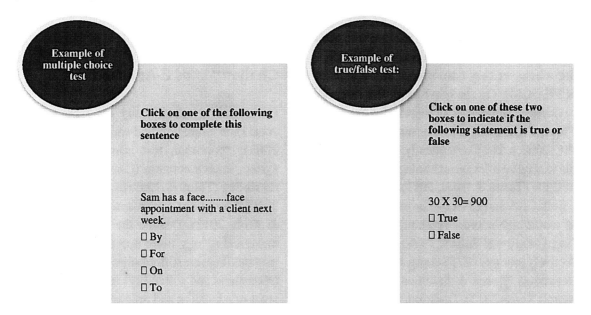

summative assessment where candidates take an end test. Its objective is to mark candidates' final assessment for the unit/qualification they were doing and ensure they have met their learning outcomes. However, the CBA in question comprises a small proportion of mid-high stakes assessments, which could be used as practice tests/ for formative purposes.

## CAA

In addition to CBA, there is computer-assisted assessment (CAA), which is called authentic assessment (Mueller, 2014a). This is also known as alternative assessment, performance/performance-based assessment and direct assessment in which candidates are asked to find solutions/ strategies to real world scenarios (see end of this section) that demonstrate how they can apply the knowledge and skills they acquired (ibid, 2014). Examples[4] of CAA include, but not restricted to, e-portfolio[5] and some types of projects[6]. This research focusses on the use of an e-portfolio, which is a directed collection of candidate's work in which s/he demonstrates their skills, progress

and achievement (Dikli, 2003). It is used to store and manage candidates' evidence electronically, which may include a range of multimedia formats for submitting assessment (QCA, 2007). E-portfolio has been in use for almost a decade and half so it is not something new[7] (JISC, 2008). E-portfolio may include diagnostic, formative and summative assessments (FD Learning, 2004) as part of the learning process but is most often used when presenting a claim of final achievement to an awarding body. Once candidates upload evidence of their learning, this can be accessed remotely by their tutor, assessor, manager and internal quality assurance staff (or any combination of these) (NCFE, 2014). In this research, the CAA's main objective is to support summative assessment and this is what the service license is for. Yet, test centres could use it for formative assessment if they wish.

E-portfolio has its own pros and cons. On the one hand, it offers efficient but gradual marking and verification (JISC, 2008) internally and externally. This efficiency could be described in terms of reduction in travel and contact costs (NCFE, 2014). E-portfolios facilitates more creative (e.g.

multimedia format) and efficient approaches to assessment reducing stationery costs (SQA, 2014a). It allows candidates to interact with their own qualification and have more control over their work whenever they have access to a computer (NCFE, 2014). On the other hand, the diversity of evidence included in an e-portfolio can make it "harder and more time consuming to assess" (JISC, 2008, p. 16). Consequently, centre staff may need to acquire relevant technological knowledge and skills (Tosun & Baris, 2011).

Both CBA and CAA can be used in assessing real world/higher order thinking skills (HOTS) (King, Goodson & Rohani, 1998). CBA can more effectively promote HOTS compared to traditional assessments (Rosen & Salomon, 2007 cited in Rosen & Tager, 2013). Traditional assessment often fails (Lin & Dwyer, 2006) and finds it difficult (Christensen & Knezek, 2014) to assess HOTS. However, when using CBA to assess HOTS, "it may be necessary to use more sophisticated assessment tools" (QAA, 2005, p.24), which are more likely to be found in CAA. For example, e-portfolios "develops reflective skills" (Ferrell & Gray, 2014, para 28) and "promote self-awareness, knowledge, esteem and confidence" (JISC infoNet, 2014, para 15). However, designing test questions to assess these skills can be "time consuming and requires skill and creativity" (Anohina & Grundspenkis, 2007, p. 265). There is no one type of assessment that is likely to be capable of covering "all levels of twenty-first century skills" (Christensen & Knezek, 2014, p. 836).

## Challenges of E-Assessment

E-assessment raises many challenges for the vocational education and training (Booth et al., 2003): economic, test administration/design system implementation (Craven, 2009) and accessibility (Thurlow, Lazarus, Albus & Hodgson, 2010). The cost of e-assessment is high (Marriott & Teoh, 2012). Despite the constant efforts to make technology more accessible and easier to manage, there are still questions about its reliability (robustness and suitability) for application in all areas of education and training as well as scale of delivery at both national and international levels. Reliability of power supply and internet availability can be additional challenges (Marriott & Teoh, 2012). Another major aspect of the practical challenges of online assessment is security (Al-Smadi & Gütl, 2008). Marais, Argles & von Solms (2006) distinguish between two types of the security of e-assessment: a) web security, i.e., the servers where the web application is running and b) e-assessment security, i.e., the authenticity of users and supervision of assessment location to minimise impersonation threats. It is equally important to protect candidates' privacy and

*Figure 2. Types of assessment*

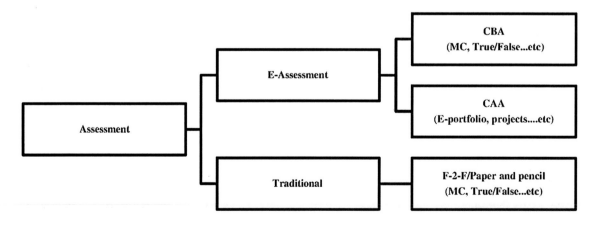

ensure their data are inaccessible by other users (Al-Smadi & Gütl, 2008). While flexibility is highlighted as an important aspect of e-assessment (Ofqual, 2010), Callan and Clayton (2010) argue that flexibility actually reduces quality[8], e.g. in relation to standardisation. E-assessment can also pose challenges for candidates and assessors alike (Marriott & Teoh, 2012). For candidates, who are not digital native, they may not be comfortable using computers. Assessors may also need to spend time to master necessary ICT skills (Marriott & Teoh, 2012), although this may vary depending on their age and whether they are digital natives or digital migrant.

Moreover, quality of assessment/e-assessment could be undermined by malpractice. Indeed, malpractice is not restricted to a certain type of assessment, but it could be avoided by the authentication process, which aims to "ensure fairness, consistency and validity of assessment and of the outcome of assessment" (FETAC, 2007, p. 28). It involves internal verification and external verification.

## Solutions to Overcome Challenges in E-Assessment

The main points to consider when using technology in assessment are about the a) rationale b) process and c) quality. The requirements of the assessment drive the technology; the technology should not drive the assessment (Ofqual, 2010). The choice and design of e-assessment methods are influenced by the candidates' needs, access to technology and the available resources.

To be more specific, the solutions to overcome challenges in e-assessment could be discussed at two levels: micro and macro. At micro level, awarding bodies must ensure that technology does not create new challenges for candidates/ test centres. Although candidates today are digital natives, awarding bodies must provide a user-friendly interface for centres and candidates so

that e-assessment systems can be easy to navigate (QCA, 2007). Technology should allow users, where appropriate, to engage in e-assessment activities from a variety of locations (not bound to a specific place) to avoid challenges to flexibility. Awarding bodies must provide opportunities for all users to familiarise themselves with the mode of delivery, for example through a) the provision of professional development opportunities to train staff where necessary and b) preparatory activities for candidates, e.g. to practise on-screen test questions. To overcome challenges related to the security of e-assessment, the following points need to be considered (Marais et al., 2006):

1. Authenticity of the candidate (e.g. use of passwords and biometrics).
2. Integrity to deter electronic corruption (e.g. multiple logging).
3. Privacy and confidentiality (e.g. marks and information should be confidential).
4. Secure client and server software (e.g. use of firewall).

At a macro level, more efforts are needed to further enhance reliability of technology. Organisations should have a clear rationale for opting for e-assessment; not just a hope that it may solve all problems of traditional assessment approaches. Awarding bodies must thoroughly understand the process of e-assessment. Organisations should also be realistic and not overambitious. This will be guided by finding out their service users' preferences to e-assessment; some such as schools may be reluctant whereas others (for instance, employers) might consider e-assessment as an "essential tool to help them to implement education and training" (Boyle, May & Sceeny, 2011, p.14).

## Conceptual Framework

Based on the above literature review, assessment in the modern age should:

- Reinforce its *importance* by ensuring it a) is convenient (Kumar, 2012), consistent, accurate (Marriott & Teoh, 2012), more objective (Nekoueizadeh & Bahrani, 2013) b) leads to efficient instant timely marking/feedback creating opportunities for reflection on feedback (JISC, 2010a) c) increases participation/accessibility for disabled candidates (JISC, 2007a) d) facilitates a wider range of what can be assessed e.g. media-rich (SQA, 2014a) using creative approaches (JISC, 2010a) e) improves monitoring of candidates' performance (Al-Smadi & Gütl, 2008) and reduces costs (SQA, 2014a), administration time (Ofqual, 2010) and loss of work (NCFE, 2014).

- **Be Prepared to Face a Number of E-Assessment Challenges:** Economic (Marriott & Teoh, 2012), test administration/design, system implantation (Craven, 2009), accessibility (Thurlow et al., 2010), reliability of power supply and internet availability (Marriott & Teoh, 2012), security (Al-Smadi & Gütl, 2008). Some types of e-assessment can be harder and more time consuming (JISC, 2008) and therefore assessors may need to spend time to master necessary ICT skills (Marriott & Teoh, 2012).

- **Offer Solutions to Overcome Likely Challenges:** At micro level e-assessment should be easy to navigate, accessible from a variety of locations (QCA, 2007) and secure (Marais et al., 2006). Users should be familiar with the delivery mode, e.g. training and practice tests (QCA, 2007) and given ongoing support/communication. At a macro level, it should be suitable for the target user (Boyle et al., 2011). The software should have good functionality, be efficient, easy to use, reliable (Milbradt,

2008) and match the users' skills (Anctil & Adams, 2002) while managing their expectations (Booth et al., 2003).

## Survey Background

A mixed method approach (Tashakkori & Teddlie, 1998) generating both quantitative and qualitative data was adopted in this research. Two surveys comprising five-point Likert scale from 'strongly disagree' to 'strongly agree') and open-ended questions were administered online. Both surveys were designed specifically for this research and focused on three topics: importance of e-assessment (CBA and CAA), challenges of using e-assessment and solutions to overcome these challenges. The reliability (internal consistency) of the survey items was high (0.8). The closer the value to 1, the greater the reliability would be (Pallant, 2007). Data analysis was carried out using descriptive statistics and interpretive reading of the data to explore any emerging themes. The data was triangulated using the validating quantitative data model where qualitative findings validate the quantitative findings (Creswell & Plano Clark, 2007). The respondents were assured of respecting their autonomy (right of withdrawal) and protecting their privacy (confidentiality of the data) (Hammersley & Trainianou, 2012).

This research focused on the views of staff at UK test centres with regard to specific examples of CBA and CAA. The CBA system in question was an innovative e-assessment platform, allowing candidates to take assessments when they want, giving instant feedback and exam results. The CAA system is used to deliver vocational qualifications by hundreds of colleges, training providers, councils and other organisations. The research sample consists of a range of users of both systems, e.g. assessors, internal verifiers (IVs), examiners and administrators. Examining the views of candidates is beyond the scope of this research. Assessors are responsible for assessing candidates' work against an agreed assessment criteria. The main role of IVs is to monitor the work of all assessors involved with the qualification to ensure that they are applying the assessment criteria throughout all assessment activities. IVs liaise with assessors, candidates and external verifiers to quality assure the assessment process and support assessors (SQA, 2014b). The total number of respondents for each survey is as follows: CBA (n=526) and CAA (n=897). Yet, they did not answer all the questions hence the variation in the total number of responses (Table 1).

## PART 2: RESEARCH FINDINGS[9]

In part 2, the research findings are presented, discussed and linked to the literature, which was reviewed in part 1. The findings were collected using two online surveys and focussed on two systems: CBA and CAA. The structure of these surveys is similar; they included questions, which relate to the importance of each system, challenges each system might face and solutions to overcome these challenges.

*Table 1. Research sample*

| CBA Survey | Percent | N= |
|---|---|---|
| Centre Manager | 12.99% | 56 |
| Centre Administrator | 18.33% | 79 |
| Exam Officer | 25.29% | 109 |
| Invigilator | 29.70% | 128 |
| Other | 13.69% | 59 |
| **Total** | 100.00% | 431 |
| CAA Survey | Percent | N= |
| Assessor/Examiner | 74.78% | 430 |
| Internal verifier | 14.61% | 84 |
| Administrator | 5.04% | 29 |
| Registrar | 3.83% | 22 |
| Other | 1.74% | 10 |
| **Total** | 100.00% | 575 |

## Findings: CBA Survey

### Importance of Using the CBA

The respondents (n=526[10]) were given the following eight statements on a Likert scale. These were designed to assess their views on the importance of CBA. The statements were related to topics like security, navigation, convenience, accessibility, efficiency, punctuality, online support and marking time, which to a large extent confirm the advantages of e-assessment discussed above:

- 74.7% strongly agreed/agreed that CBA provides a secure system to work with, which may suggest the issue of security of e-assessment (Marais et al., 2006) is taken very seriously as it is a high stakes assessment (Phelps, 2006).
- Similarly, 68.9% strongly agreed/agreed that navigation within the system is easy (QCA, 2007) and 66.1% were happy with the convenience of the system which enables them to access it anytime from anywhere (Kumar, 2012), which is one of the advantages highlighted above.
- Yet, nearly half of them (48.7%) strongly agreed/agreed that the CBA system in question facilitates accessibility and cater for the special needs of certain users (JISC, 2007a), which may imply that more work needs to be done in this respect.
- For them, CBA is efficient (JISC, 2010a) because it saves times and reduces admin and paperwork (57.4%) (Ofqual, 2010).
- Just over half of the respondents strongly agreed/agreed with the punctuality of the system in terms of the timely (52.2%) and useful communication and the availability of information of the CBA system (50.4%).
- 22.3% of the respondents strongly agreed/agreed that examiner marked tests are processed quickly. This is different to automatic marked tests which provide instant feedback (JISC, 2010a).

While there is clearly a scope for improvement in the current CBA system, nearly half of the respondents (47.7%) were extremely satisfied (or slightly less), i.e. those who rated the system between 8 and 10[11] following their most experience of using this system.

Their open-ended responses (n=223) to the question about the importance and challenges of using the CBA are shown in Table 2. Some of the respondents suggested more than one point hence the difference in the total number of responses. These points confirm and add to the advantages of e-assessment discussed above.

The respondents thought the CBA system is *efficient* (JISC, 2010a) because it 'works well both online and offline', has 'no issues' and is 'very reliable', which makes it 'an excellent system in comparison to other exam boards'. Efficiency takes a "closer look at the relationship between the level of performance of the software and the amount of resources that are used under stated conditions" (Milbradt, 2008, p.53). Others found the 'invigilation screen and the candidates screen efficient to use'. One administrator noted that 'downloading the exam is quick' and this is why it was considered to be a 'really convenient labour examination system'. Candidates too 'prefer online assessment' because they are digital natives (Ofqual, 2010), according to one of the respondents.

The second importance is that the CBA system is *easy to use* as it requires 'minimal effort', is 'simple to follow' and 'straightforward'. The system usability is "concerned with the effort needed for use as well as the individual judgment of such use by a stated or implied set of users" (Milbradt, 2008, p. 53). From candidate, invigilator and administrator perspectives, the CBA system makes it 'easy to book tests and for candidates to navigate, easy to use for exam invigilation and result checking' (Ofqual, 2010). The system is 'very easy to use and navigate as an administrator'. One respondent compared its ease of use to other CBA systems used by other awarding bodies: 'In the last three weeks I have had to learn all the awarding body systems this CBA system is the most user friendly and is fantastic because I can set up and remove users with different statuses. It is the only system with these functions'. These are supported by a 'software [which] seems easy to use and install'.

The third is about the *support* they received when using the CBA system, including access to 'available information either online or by phoning customer service' which is 'very easy to get through'. This support is provided by a 'great team', who is 'very helpful' giving 'quick response that solves issues with one call'. Others commented on the quality of training (QCA, 2007) they received before starting to use the CBA system: 'I received training and have only needed to ask advice since then on one occasion. I am extremely happy with this service'.

*Table 2. Respondents' views of the importance and challenges of using CBA*

| Importance | N= | Challenges | N= |
|---|---|---|---|
| Efficiency of the CBA system | 55 | Technical issues | 69 |
| Easy to use CBA system | 41 | Timescale of marking | 57 |
| Available support to use the system | 11 | Poor support | 16 |
| | | Poor content | 12 |
| | | Poor admin | 4 |
| Total | 107 | Total | 158 |

## Challenges of Using CBA

A number of challenges were identified such as inter-related *technical* issues:

1. *Internet and intranet related issues* (Marriott & Teoh, 2012): 'the only issues are internet related electronic hiccups'. It 'seems to require a high speed internet connection for example with 1MB by 1MB it can support at most 5 candidates during exams'. Others highlighted the difficulty to use the CBA with an 'authenticating proxy'. In some cases, the respondents had to bring their 'server computer back to base, upload the assessments and then access the results'.

2. *Software issues*: Although software is a "means to an end in the assessment process, it is a necessary condition for a CBA to work" (Milbradt, 2008, p. 53). Software can be problematic if it is 'outdated', has 'little connection to the real software candidates use' or 'does not accurately assess candidates' IT ability'. Sometimes the software 'does not let [users] expand the page, flip in and out' or increase font size, which can be 'difficult to read'. From an administrative perspective, they cannot 'use filter system' (limited search facility and reporting) or 'track first time pass rates' over a period of time, the latter should be an important feature of e-assessment (Al-Smadi & Gütl, 2008).

3. *Printing issues*: these include the respondents' inability to print a selection of the invigilation pack. Printing the 'whole pack' means a large 'amount of paper that needs generating for candidate keycodes/results sheets', which is not environment friendly and defies the objective of reducing stationery costs (SQA, 2014a). Also, the CBA system will let users 'print one test at a time and will not let them print out all the keycodes at once', which can be 'frustrating'.

4. *Inconsistent reliability issue* (Craven, 2009): some users described the CBA system as 'unreliable' and 'unpredictable'. Reliability refers to the "question if the software is capable to maintain its level of performance under stated conditions for a stated period of time" (Milbradt, 2008, p.53). Sometimes the tests 'do not work/crash', which may require multiple log in. This might raise questions about the security of the system (Marais et al., 2006). Others referred to the mismatched results generated by the CBA system and those on the online administration website (OAW)'. The latter is a free online administration service provided by the awarding body that enables approved centres to carry out a range of day-to-day functions quickly and efficiently via the internet including the submission of results to certificate candidates.

5. *Not user-friendly system*: some respondents found the user 'interface poor' and the CBA system 'confusing to use', 'difficult to navigate', which counteracts one of the objectives of e-assessment of being user-friendly (QCA, 2007). In addition, the time it takes for the tests to load individually can be infuriating for the candidates too. User interface is "often neglected" in software although it is one of the key elements of Usability (Milbradt, 2008, p.57).

Although most of the respondents who answered this question seem to be satisfied with the current *timescale of marking*, for some this was the 2nd biggest challenge: 'there does not seem to be any rhyme nor reason for the delay'. Part of the problem, which confirms the findings presented in Figure 3, is that 'there is no consistency with the time frame of marking'. This is 'quite distressing for candidates' who are 'eager to know how well they have done'. This challenge might imply the CBA system gives priority to the security of this high stakes e-assessment over other aspects.

There might be a need to better communicate this (i.e., CBA objectives and priorities) with *these* system users.

Some respondents experienced *poor support* when using the system: 'We get little or no help'. Others did not get the advice they expected: 'The technical advice was to turn my laptop off and on again'. This was confirmed by other respondents who believed 'sometimes support team do not have the required knowledge' or 'understand the problem'. This might highlight the need to provide staff with professional development opportunities (QCA, 2007), where necessary. One respondent complained about the channel through which the query was directed: 'I prefer going straight to the technical support team not the main number; sometimes it can be time consuming'.

*Poor content:* questions are 'sometimes completely incorrect' or 'do not reflect the candidates' experiences with ICT in the workplace', which might raise questions about the assessment validity (DTWT, 2012), let alone the feasibility of assessing wider skills using CBA. For example, one respondent indicated the 'formula section, which includes average formula, was inaccurate'. Exams are 'stressful enough for the candidates

without the added errors with the online testing'. There were other examples which related to poor design: 'In one of the exams creating graphs is poorly designed and the candidate is unfairly penalised for the amount of time this can take'. The main point that was highlighted as an example of *poor admin* is the notification required or 'speed of booking tests, which e-assessment should support (Ofqual, 2010): 'I have to now give seven day notice to book tests. This doesn't work with some professions'.

## SOLUTIONS AND RECOMMENDATIONS TO IMPROVE THE CBA SYSTEM

At the end of the 1st survey, the respondents (n=526[12]) were given an open-ended question to suggest ways for improving the CBA system. Their responses, which correlate with the findings in Table 2, were analysed and grouped in the order shown in Figure 4.

36.5% believed there is a need for an *improved technical provision*, which can be achieved in a number of ways:

*Figure 3. Responses to statements about the importance of CBA*

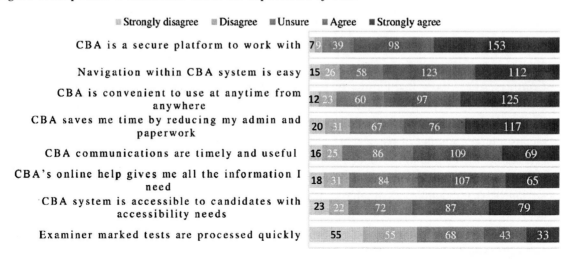

*Figure 4. Solutions and recommendations to improve the CBA system*

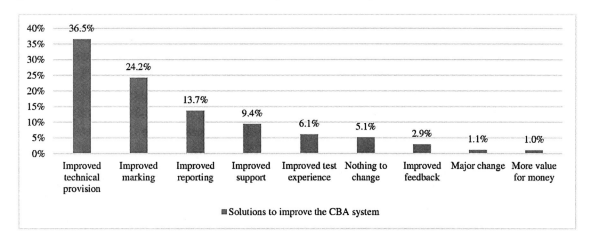

1. Make the CBA system more *user-friendly* (QCA, 2007): through a 'redesign of the test interface', 'word count for some writing assessment', 'bigger font and icons' and allowing candidates to 'see all of the information and input their answers without having to scroll up and down' between 'separate windows'. If they need to navigate to see the test questions, then they should have 'more online practice'; as it is a high stakes assessment. Making the system more user-friendly is also required for users other than candidates: 'make the invigilator screen editable and allow the invigilator to save the personalised layout'.

2. Adopt effective *up to date software*: at present this can 'confuse' some candidates. The software should be updated and 'compatible with Windows' and perhaps 'look like the Microsoft package'. Indeed, assessors "need to consistently monitor the knowledge and skill requirements of software on the network against their current competencies and only use software that is congruent with their capabilities" (Anctil & Adams, 2002, p. 12). Using up-to-date software is likely to 'improve the simulation software in some of the online tests' and increase the overall effectiveness of the platform.

3. Improve the *printing facility*: by allowing admin staff to 'print off a copy of all keycodes rather than one test at a time' or even print off individual invigilation packs by time (am/pm) and not the whole day together' to make the desired saving in stationery (SQA, 2014a). It might be easier if users can print off 'larger and score reports without being on the internet' and are given the option to amend 'positioning of printed A4 reports; some information tends to 'bleed' off the page'.

4. Make *scheduling and re-scheduling of exams easier* (Ofqual, 2010): for some users this process was 'long winded'. They would like to be able to book/schedule exams using 'one system' only and 'amend date and time for exam without re-booking'. Others indicated the need to speed up the 'enrolment' process and 'get rid of the system where you have to give so much notice for tests to be booked', which confirm the findings in Table 2.

5. Simplify *access rights* on the CBA system: to enable users to 'add access arrangement from the CBA system for a candidate when the exam has been booked' or have this 'automatically uploaded'. To speed up the process of candidates' login, two respondents suggested to 'get rid of pin numbers' or 'use

one log in' at all times. This very small number might suggest *most* of the respondents were aware of the implication of doing so in high stakes assessments, i.e., undermine its security (Marais et al., 2006).

Consistent with the above challenges of using the CBA system, nearly a quarter of the respondents wanted an *improved marking* (consistency and quicker results) (JISC, 2010a). The turnaround for results may vary depending on the exam. Sometimes candidates can get the results instantly/ within a day, but they could wait for up to 3-4 weeks. Users seem to be happy if the results are released within 48 hours up to a week. Managing the expectations of users is likely to contribute to the improvement of their future experiences.

The third solution the respondents proposed, which might be related to these mid-high stakes e-assessment, was to bring about an *improved reporting* and add more information, i.e., 'putting percentages on candidate score reports and candidate summary lists'. The inclusion of the words 'pass/fail' or 'achieve/did not achieve' may not be sufficient. This call for an improved reporting might imply a) a small number of respondents use these mid-high stakes CBA as practice tests/for formative purposes or b) most of the respondents are satisfied with the current reporting feature. Although for some test centres, 'the most important is the percentage %', this may not be very informative just like the words 'pass/fail'. They spend 'a lot of time printing off the reports and then writing the percentage'. They want to filter/ sort results (Al-Smadi & Gütl, 2008) by 'subject/ candidate name or candidate number', search for those results older 'than a year', which are 'ordered alphabetically'.

Almost a tenth of the respondents called for *improved support*, i.e. 'better knowledge from the support team and better attitude too'. Improved support is also about faster ongoing consistent communication: 'Faster admin loading/response times during periods of high demand', 'If it is going to take a little while to get exams back when previously it has taken less than a week, communicate this with your users', 'make the instructions given by your support team universal so that…I do not get contradicting advice'. It might be useful to offer the users of the CBA system 'training' (QCA, 2007) or 'a refresher course', if needed.

Others suggested *improvement in the test experience* in terms of a) question wording: 'correction of questions that come up as incorrect' to 'ensure the exams are worded better' and avoid questions using obsolete terminology: 'Mercer gauge instead of DTI (Dial Test Indicator)' b) the provision of more sample tests to prepare for this high stakes assessment: 'place more differentiated practice tests on the site to help candidates' (QCA, 2007) and c) the validity of the questions (DTWT, 2012): 'some candidates have complained about the Maths test being more like an ICT test. They have experienced difficulty when creating graphs so it would be good to improve this'.

Yet, there are respondents who were satisfied with the CBA system and believed there was *nothing to change*: 'all seems good to be honest', 'it does not need any improvements as long as the user knows how to navigate the system, 'I cannot think of anything at the moment. Overall very good service and very helpful people', 'keep it as it is' and 'my experience of the CBA system has been excellent'. On the other hand, there was a very small number who called for *major change:* 'a complete overhaul', 're-design the whole system'.

The last two solutions they made to improve the CBA system were *about improved feedback* (JISC, 2010a) and having *more value for money.* The former might refer to the mid-high stakes CBA, which tests centres might use as practice tests/for formative purposes: 'more detailed feedback on which answers are wrong', 'more in depth information about areas identified for development for candidates', 'on the multiple choice exams, instead of giving the candidates feedback on objective topics they got wrong, actually inform them of the question they got wrong'. However, it is important to manage the expectations of candidates in relation to the level of detail (and reporting) they should get (Booth et al., 2003), which should be aligned with the test objective. In terms of value for money, two respondents pointed out that CBA should get more value for money (Nekoueizadeh & Bahrani, 2013): 'charge less for the tests', 'void and refund when tests don't work correctly. It would help to have reusable practice tests'. Candidates normally have a free 'navigation test' to familiarise themselves with the CBA environment. Depending on the subject they study (e.g. Functional Skills), candidates will have free mock exams. The point about 'value for money' is likely to refer to the respondents' (n=2) preference to have more materials/support as part of the unit/ qualification rather than denote a criticism of the CBA system. This seems to confirm the above point about having more 'sample tests'.

## Findings: CAA Survey

## Importance of CAA

Similar to the CBA survey, the respondents (n=897) were given the following six statements (Figure 6) on a five point Likert scale and were related to candidate progress, value for money, quality assurance processes, training delivery, participation and engagement and planning of activities, which confirm the above advantages of e-assessment:

- 77.5% strongly agreed/agreed that CAA gives them better visibility of candidate's progress, which confirms the literature (Al-Smadi & Gütl, 2008), but they have to pay for this. Only 36% of them pointed out that CAA delivers good value for money. This might imply the need to make CAA less expensive (Nekoueizadeh & Bahrani, 2013).

*Figure 5. Summary of CBA challenges and solutions*

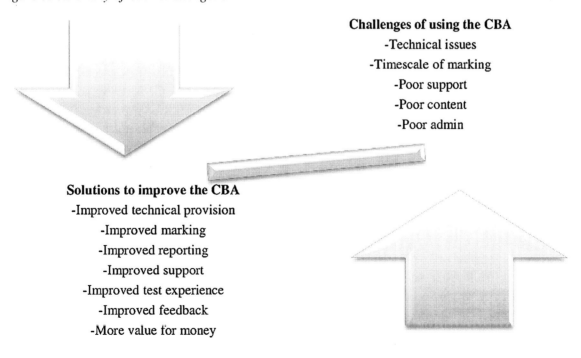

**Challenges of using the CBA**
-Technical issues
-Timescale of marking
-Poor support
-Poor content
-Poor admin

**Solutions to improve the CBA**
-Improved technical provision
-Improved marking
-Improved reporting
-Improved support
-Improved test experience
-Improved feedback
-More value for money

*Figure 6. The importance of CAA*

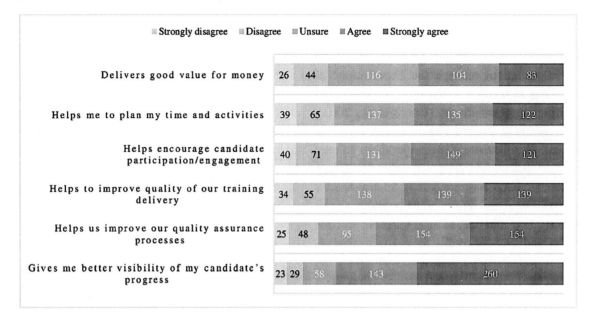

- The findings also show that CAA helped the respondents (59.2%) improve their quality assurance processes, i.e., data consistency and accuracy (JISC, 2010a).
- The majority of the respondents strongly agreed/agreed that CAA helped to improve the quality of their training delivery (53.4%) and encourage candidate participation and engagement (52%) (JISC, 2007a).
- Nearly half of the respondents (49.5%) thought CAA was useful in planning their time and activities. Being able to track candidate's progress, CAA results can drive curriculum design and delivery accordingly.

Nearly half of the respondents were extremely satisfied (or slightly less). They were asked to describe their overall satisfaction by choosing a number between 1 (extremely dissatisfied) and 10 (extremely satisfied). 47.9% rated the system between 8 and 10 following their most experience of using this system. This is almost identical to the percentage of those who rated their experience with the CBA system.

Their open-ended responses (n=367) to the question about the importance and challenges of using the CAA, which confirm and add to the advantages of e-assessment discussed above, are shown in Table 3[13].

They thought the CAA system was *easy to use* and navigate (QCA, 2007): 'As an assessor I find it quite easy to use', 'It evolved over the years and improved in functionality. The system is easy to use as an Assessor/Verifier'. In fact, this feature exceeded the expectations of some respondents: 'The CAA design and format are quite straightforward. I was expecting something more technical and could not believe that this was it'. The easiness of the system is consistent 'no matter what role I am using it for', i.e. assessor/ verifier role.

Consistent with their responses to the statement about 'visibility of candidate's progress' (Figure 6), to some extent, 41 respondents were happy with the system because it enabled them to *monitor candidates' progress* (Al-Smadi & Gütl, 2008): 'A very useful tool to plan, maintain and encourage candidate development'. It was very useful especially 'when I have candidates across a large region' and 'assess work remotely', which shows how e-assessment can offer choice in timing and locations (JISC, 2010a). Despite this remote assessment, the CAA 'allowed the candidates to have regular contact with assessor by remote access'. The CAA is useful because they could find all the information they require in 'one place… which is great for tracking purposes'. Eventually this 'makes assessing less time consuming' (ibid, 2010a). It is so convenient that some respondents 'could not imagine going back to paper-based portfolios after using the CAA system'. In relation to candidates, they too 'can see at a quick glance where they are and how they are doing, which helps with motivating them to continue their training'.

The CAA is *efficient,* e.g. assessors 'rarely have problems with the system', 'everything is working properly' and enables them to 'have their job done and completed quickly'. In fact, it is not only useful for assessors but also the candidates; it 'meets their needs' (Ofqual, 2010). Others described it as 'slick', 'very reliable' and 'one of the best e-portfolios systems available on the market at present'. It is a 'robust system' because it 'ensures that candidates' work [evidence] is safe, can't be lost' (JISC, 2010a) and thus minimises the likelihood of crashing: 'It has never crashed. I have used this system since late 2012'.

This robustness/reliability was backed up by the *available support to use the system* (QCA, 2007): 'Any queries/questions are always handled promptly and if not possible referred to someone else'; 'The helpline members of staff have been exceptionally helpful'; 'very professional, knowledgeable staff who has quickly understood my issue'; 'the way they talk though issues and explain in language I understand (not overly technical)'.

## Challenges of Using CAA

A number of challenges of the CAA system were highlighted such as *not being user friendly*, which contradicts the requirement for awarding bodies (QCA, 2007): 'I do not find the system easy to use'. Some assessors thought their candidates had similar views: 'candidates do find it difficult and require additional support from me'. For some it was not user friendly because the 'software is unsuitable', difficulty to 'choose the font size'/'some of the colouring' and 'terminology'. It is interesting that they were unaware some of these points had been addressed in recent updates: 'since the update, you have made the font size larger'. This might reflect why just over half of the respondents (52.19%) strongly agreed/ agreed about the timeliness of communicating the system upgrades (Figure 3). However, some recent changes/updates are to blame for making the CAA system less user friendly: 'some of the new changes are confusing and unnecessary'; 'it was easier before the Wizard was changed'. Making changes "always bears the risk of building in new errors which might not show up in software tests or if they do show up cannot easily be traced back to their cause" (Milbradt, 2008, p.55). This might explain the need to rectify these issues in further changes.

Working with a 'non-user friendly' system is likely to be *time-consuming* (JISC, 2008) in terms of a) the process of assessment: 'slow to upload and access candidates' portfolios' and b) its overall speed: 'it takes time going between each page'. Therefore, a few preferred to switch to the traditional paper-based assessment: 'I am at the point of going back to paper-based portfolios or suggesting we use a different e-portfolio'. However, this does not mean that it should be abandoned altogether: 'it is a fabulous tool but it can be time consuming', 'it saves time in some areas and takes more time in others'. The slow speed is likely to be the result of 1) means of connection, i.e., 'when being used offsite in a remote situation/using a laptop', 'unless you have high speed broadband you just sit for hours looking at a blank screen while it buffers between pages' and 2) recent changes/updates, which confirm the above findings: 'since it has been updated…. it is slow and seems to take long to upload work'.

*Reliability issues* with the system (rather than its assessment) include examples of 1) losing the data (NCFE, 2014): 'I did have a problem today with a unit which had disappeared and made life difficult' 2) crashing: 'it is constantly crashing' and 3) inaccuracy, which contradicts the literature (JISC, 2010a): 'useful but not accurate', 'It is unreliable and does not always work'. Again, some of these issues could be the result of 1) means of connection: 'It doesn't work very effectively on some types of tablets', 'the app for android just keeps crashing', 'iPhone app keeps freezing and loses or cuts short recorded discussions' or 2) recent updates/changes: 'despite an excellent start, the CAA has gone downhill over the last 3 months'. However, these issues 'seem to be intermittent' and respondents 'keep on trying throughout the day but it is frustrating'. For others these had been resolved: 'I have had so many problems but finally things are starting to work'.

Some of the *limited functionality* of the CAA system might make it slow or time consuming. Functionality is one of the major quality criteria of software (Milbradt, 2008). For some, the CAA system was 'restrictive in some of its processes and facilities'. For example, 'I have just spent twenty minutes referencing a discussion to find that the 'save' button is missing'. In fact, it was 'so limited in its functionality that a decent excel spreadsheet can outdo it', added another respondent. Part of this limited functionality was the

limited 1) feedback: 'It is very difficult to provide feedback', 'it doesn't show feedback of all the standards/outcomes/units that their evidence covered', 'you can't link the candidate's paper-based PDP (Personal Development Plan) to the e-portfolio as evidence' 2) reporting: 'reporting is very basic' and 3) interaction: 'there is no interaction between the candidate and CAA functions/features'. These examples might contradict the literature that e-assessment approaches should be creative and innovative and facilitate candidate engagement (JISC, 2010a).

The reliability issues seem to be related to another challenge, which is *poor support/communication*, which confirms the findings in Table 3: 'Changes had been made overnight and I was delivering a training session to new candidates without knowing of the changes'. Changes were not likely to be communicated effectively because the CAA is 'consistently on the change, which does not give users time to adapt before they have yet another change'. This might be complicated by the 'little support' and 'training' test centres receive from awarding bodies: 'I think it'd be beneficial if there was some form of active training when you first use this system', 'videos don't tell me what I need to do'. The implication is that awarding bodies might need to do more to fulfil their obligation towards their users and ensure they are familiar with the e-assessment being implemented (QCA, 2007).

*Table 3. Respondents' views on the importance and challenges of CAA*

| Importance | N= | Challenges | N= |
|---|---|---|---|
| Easy to use CAA system | 73 | Not user friendly | 95 |
| Monitor candidate progress | 41 | Time consuming | 92 |
| Efficiency of the CAA system | 35 | Reliability issues | 53 |
| Available support to use the system | 16 | Limited functionality | 39 |
| | | Poor support/communication | 22 |
| | | Security and access | 11 |
| | | Poor monitoring of candidates' progress | 7 |
| Total | 165 | Total | 319 |

*Security and access* can be another challenge (Al-Smadi & Gütl, 2008), which was highlighted by 11 respondents: 'a report was made by an assessor that a candidate was able to view private verification feedback'. In terms of access, 'sometimes the username and password work and sometimes they don't', 'I can't upload work for a candidate as the system is not allowing me to save it'. However, this seemed to vary depending on the respondent's role: 'only administrators seem to be able to add tasks'. As mentioned above, this might be the result of 1) means of connection: 'there are times when it is not accessible, but this is due to the internet server' or 2) new changes: 'the CAA has changed very recently, I cannot access candidate's work directly from assessor's tasks page'.

Although three quarters of the respondents (77.5%) strongly agreed/agreed the CAA system enabled them to track candidates' development (NCFE, 2014) (Figure 6), very few respondents criticised the *poor monitoring of candidates' progress*: 'not clear in regards to candidate's progress', 'it does not support their progression or awareness', 'there is no direct link to a plan for the next visit to actually carrying out the assess-ment'. This lack of clarity might be because the 'percent achievement display is unrealistic....... candidates get discouraged because they think they are behind'.

## SOLUTIONS AND RECOMMENDATIONS TO IMPROVE THE CAA SYSTEM

The respondents (n=897) were given an open-ended question to suggest ways for improving the CAA system. Their responses (n=384) were ana-lysed and grouped in the order shown in Figure 7.

Again, several respondents listed more than one suggestion hence the variation between the grand totals. They made specific suggestions to improve the *navigation and display* (QCA, 2007) of the CAA: 'make it easier to move around'; 'add a tool for changing the background colour and text in order to support candidates with dyslexia/other learning difficulties'. However, other suggestions they made are in response to the recent changes/updates: 'put evidence wizard back the way it was', 'put the hovering feature back in'. It is likely that these new changes were in response to the

*Figure 7. Solutions and recommendations to improve the CAA system*

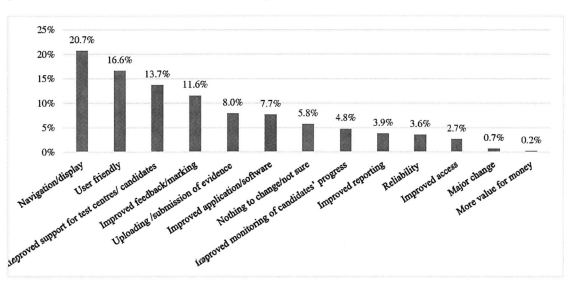

feedback submitted previously from other users, which shows that users had different preferences and it would not be an easy task for awarding bodies to meet their needs.

Consistent with the responses (Table 3), the second important solution was to make the *CAA more user friendly* in general, which is something awarding bodies strive to achieve (QCA, 2007): 'make it more user friendly, simple; at the moment we feel we are working in a sort of maze'. Others want to make it more user friendly in terms of a) search facility: 'As an assessor I mark work in date order so would like to search my list of candidates by submission date' and b) speed: 'Speed it up it is really slow to use'.

Fifty seven respondents called for *improved support for test centres and candidates*, including training (QCA, 2007), which also confirm the CBA findings: 'More support accessing training options', 'have some expansion to the support team accessibility'. This support might be improved if made available from the beginning and visible to users: 'once a centre has agreed to take on the CAA system, have someone assigned to ensure they are doing ok'. To reduce this pressure on awarding bodies to provide support, one respondent suggested a 'forum for assessors to give each other support'. Yet, there are respondents who were completely satisfied with the current level of support: 'whenever I ring the help desk for support the two members of staff that we speak to have been great'.

Nearly a tenth of the respondents suggested changes that would *improve their feedback and marking* (JISC, 2007b; 2010a): 'an online chat facility would be good for instant communication with candidates' to improve their engagement (ibid, 2010a). The other suggestions they made would a) speed up the assessment process e.g. 'being able to mark/work online without downloading and uploading', 'ability to multi assess several candidates at any one time' b) minimise plagiarism: using a software to 'assist in the authentication of assessment material' and c) cater for other

types of assessment: 'having a system that allows holistic assessment'. The last point might suggest very few users seemed unaware the CAA system facilitates the assessment of real world skills and compilation of student-structured evidence, which are the essence of holistic/authentic assessment. Occasionally, however, respondents had opposing views about giving feedback: 'to be able to give feedback on the assignment rather than the outcome' and 'being able to give feedback on more than one learning outcome at a time'.

Closely associated with this process is to make changes to the *uploading and submission of evidence* in terms of it's a) quantity: 'allow multiple uploading of items of evidence' b) type (Boyle & Hutchinson, 2009): 'ensure audio and video files are uploaded in a universal format' and c) size: 'allow larger file uploads for video'. These changes are likely to 'streamline the whole process and simplify it'. Despite these calls for improvement, these examples show how e-assessment can incorporate innovative approaches, e.g. use of multimedia format (Winkley, 2010).

The introduction of an *improved application/ software* is likely to facilitate the proposed solutions and address the limited functionality identified in Table 3, 'allow the apps on tablets and phones to do as much as the pc'. It is important to have the "ability to apply general software interface principles to independently explore new software" (Beetham & Sharpe, 2013, p.295). Again, it seems that some respondents were/were not aware of the entire features such as the availability of the application on portable devices (Apple and Android tablets and phones): 'I'd like to see an online app for android/ iPhone'; 'make the app on IOS and Android more detailed'.

Yet, there are respondents who were completely satisfied with the system as it is and believed there was *nothing to change/unsure* if they required any changes: 'nothing keep it as it is please', 'not sure as yet'. While there are constant support available to test centres to make necessary changes to the system where appropriate: 'I have put forward recommendations in the past to which most have been met or explained why would not be possible, so no new recommendations', there was one respondent who couldn't see the rationale for doing so: 'why you constantly feel the need to add/change things; it is simple and effective to use as it is'. Additional changes based on user's "experiences and further developments made it necessary to include new features in the software" (Milbradt, 2008, p. 55).

Very few respondents believed *major change* was required. This view might not necessarily reflect major issues with the system but rather a a) preference to a certain type of assessment (Marriott & Teoh, 2012): 'not my preferred method' b) *reliability of the system* (Milbradt, 2008): 'fix the slowness and crashing!', 'ensure that the system is working properly'.

Nearly 5% highlighted the need to *improve the monitoring of candidates' progress* (Al-Smadi & Gütl, 2008), which confirms the findings in Figure 6: 'an easier way to observe gap analysis would be helpful', 'improve the percentage bar'. Again, some respondents had contradicting views about how candidates' progress should be monitored: 'I would like the gap analysis to just show the gaps and not all of completed parts', 'for assessors and candidates to be able to see what they have covered and what they still need to do'. Others called for an *improved reporting* (3.9%): 'improve the reporting systems' to 'identify trends' and 'track candidate's progress'. These two suggestions might imply a) very small number of respondents use CAA for formative purposes or b) most of the respondents are satisfied with the current reporting feature. For others, it might be necessary to develop some of the reporting functions and have an *improved access*: 'give me one login for everything', 'allow the registrar to have access to the evidence folder'. However, others were against the idea of giving more permission to certain users, which can be a threat to the security of e-assessment (Al-Smadi & Gütl, 2008): 'only an assessor should have the permission to ensure candidates do not alter

previously assessed work'. Similar to the findings in Table 4 only one respondent called for *more value for money*: 'cut the price'. Although the CAA is almost comparable with that of other providers, this call for a reduction in the license cost (Scheuermann & Guimarães Pereira, 2008) suggests that most users weren't concerned about it, which may contradict the literature (Nekoueizadeh & Bahrani, 2013).

## PART 3: USING CBA AND CAA ON AN APPRENTICESHIP PROGRAMME- CASE STUDY

### Introduction

Apprenticeship has a number of key features (European Commission, 2013). Apprenticeship is a part of a formal education and training programme. The provision should include work-based training and theoretical education to help candidates acquire knowledge, practical skills and competences required for a specific occupation. Aspects of apprenticeships are often explicitly defined in the apprenticeship contract between the apprentice and the employer directly or indirectly via the educational institution. Apprentices typically have an equal status to that of an employee, and when compared to graduates, research shows that three out of four small to medium sized enterprises (SMEs) would prefer to hire apprentices because they have more practical skills than their university counterparts (Tovey, 2014). So, how can the apprenticeship be assessed given the emphasis on practical skills?

### Apprenticeship: Assessment and Challenges

Internationally, there is a need to progress in the apprenticeship system to compete effectively on a global scale and improve the UK "inconsistent assessment standards", compared to the equivalent

*Figure 8. Summary of CAA challenges and solutions*

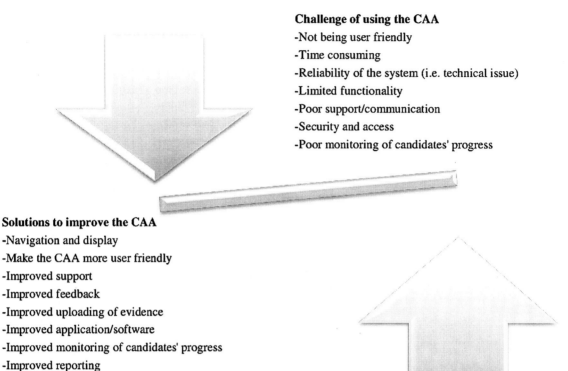

**Challenge of using the CAA**

-Not being user friendly

-Time consuming

-Reliability of the system (i.e. technical issue)

-Limited functionality

-Poor support/communication

-Security and access

-Poor monitoring of candidates' progress

**Solutions to improve the CAA**

-Navigation and display

-Make the CAA more user friendly

-Improved support

-Improved feedback

-Improved uploading of evidence

-Improved application/software

-Improved monitoring of candidates' progress

-Improved reporting

-Improved reliability

-Improved access

-More value for money

apprenticeship standards in Germany (Campbell, Thompson & Pautz, 2011, p. 375). Therefore, a relatively new approach is being implemented by a range of Awarding Bodies, centres and employers in a bid to reform the UK apprenticeship system. This approach is mainly established on pulling together existing methodology and resources to create the 'overall package'. It is crucial to ensure employers have confidence and value apprenticeships and therefore "there must be no incentive to pass individuals" who are deemed as not yet competent (BIS, 2013, p.15).

The UK Government Proposal for the New Apprenticeship (Trailblazers) calls employers to be radical (i.e., innovative and technology based) in their thinking about the needs of their industry and business when developing assessment activities for the new apprenticeships, therefore

employers should not feel constrained by existing qualifications or assessment approaches. Among the multiple assessment methods required for the new apprenticeship is "virtual assessment, such as online tests or video evidence as appropriate to the content" (DBIS, 2014, p. 11). Although apprentices are likely to be digital natives, these e-assessment methods might be challenging. E-assessment poses a number of challenges, which may also apply to the assessment of apprenticeship programmes. The nature of apprenticeship programmes, which often aim to develop apprentices' practical skills, may add another layer of complexity to the inclusion of technology when assessing such skills.

Another key reform of the assessment of apprenticeship is that assessment should occur at the end. It is worth noting here that the principles of quality assessment still stand whether applied to apprenticeship or any other programme of learning. These principles are: independence (fair), consistency (reliable and valid) and flexibility (BIS, 2013). Many stakeholders in the Richard Review (Richard, 2012, p.47) indicated that apprenticeship should be flexible in response to the constant changes in technology and certainly the inclusion of "new techniques or procedures". The following case study addresses the inclusion of technology in an apprenticeship programme, yet there is a need for more research and development leading to the development of technologies specifically designed to facilitate an integrated assessment approach to support formative and summative assessment of knowledge and practical skills for apprenticeships.

## Apprenticeship: Case Study

Forty apprentices joined a pilot UK-based apprenticeship programme run by a global multi-billion ICT business to develop their ICT skills between October 2013 and February 2014. This apprenticeship programme delivered mainly online learning and assessed using CBA (e.g. a software with multiple features including collaborative work, desktop sharing and electronic voting) and CAA (e.g. e-portfolio). To evaluate their views of the programme, the apprentices were asked to complete an online questionnaire, which mainly comprised closed questions with an option to add their own views, where appropriate. Of the 40 apprentices, 28 responded to the survey. The response received from them about this pilot programme has been positive. Most of them indicated that the programme met/exceeded their expectations (n=23): 'I feel I am learning fast and growing in competence'.

## The Current Level of Support

Most of the apprentices (n=25) were satisfied with the level of induction at the beginning of the programme, which helped them understand the process. Nineteen apprentices considered the e-learning materials they used on their own to be 'good/fair'. One of the factors which facilitated this process is probably the convenience of using technology (Kumar, 2012): 'The simple way of submitting work to my tutor has meant that I can get on with my workplace work as well as other coursework'. This confirms the advantages of e-assessment (i.e. flexibility of offering choice in locations). Indeed, they (n=20) found it 'very/fairly easy' to use technology to upload and submit evidence for assessment on the programme. Similarly, they (n=17) found the process of mapping evidence for the assessment of their apprenticeship 'very/fairly easy'. The support they received from their assessors had also been identified as an important factor: 'my assessor is very helpful and provides me with all the information I need'. The vast majority were satisfied with the current frequency of meeting their assessors and the length of time they spent with them. In terms of the overall support received during the main part of the apprenticeship programme, including its assessment, the majority (n=19) described it as 'about right'. The majority of support was offered remotely, i.e., using email, telephone and online forums, but the most valuable form of support (n=14) was the traditional face-to-face contact. Most of them (n=24) found the process of getting used to the technology used for teaching, assessment and communication on the programme 'very/fairly easy'. However, this does not mean they had no challenges.

## Challenges

The programme challenged the apprentices and thus enabled them to enhance their skills and change their mindset about the use of CBA and CAA in such programmes: 'Doing remote training sessions is a hard way to learn. However this has helped me in a way that most people wouldn't understand....it has helped me be more confident in my work'. Although the apprentices 'thoroughly enjoyed the apprenticeship programme' and that the online 'remote learning worked well', some of them had different expectations such as 'more regular [face-to-face] visits' from their assessor. One apprentice called for the inclusion of traditional delivery and assessment (face-to-face): 'I do believe there should *also* be face to face lessons'. While this might be the result of the difficulties encountered in using specific technology on the programme, it could also reflect a preference/familiarity with this type of assessment. Technology has not been used previously in the assessment of apprenticeship programmes and this could be another challenge especially with the UK government shift towards e-assessment in the new apprenticeships. Other apprentices highlighted a few technical challenges (e.g. reliability, access and difficulty to upload multiple files) of using technology in assessment, which resonates with the findings in Figure 6: 'the e-portfolio is not very reliable and I feel it is overly complicated for what it is. I have had password reset problems, site going down', 'provide an easier environment in which apprentices can connect to the software, i.e., (without the need to create an account)', 'it is not necessarily difficult, but it can be time-consuming. For instance, when I have about 6-7 files to upload I have to upload them individually rather than all at the same time'.

## Solutions

This might imply the need to improve the CAA software being used and resolve these issues. When asked about the additional support (in general and in relation to the use of technology in assessment), which the apprentices might require, their responses were generally positive: 'currently I am happy with how the process is run and cannot add further support suggestions', 'the current level of support is fine', 'I am happy with the use of Apprenticeship technology'.

Although the apprentices identified a number of challenges and proposed some solutions (e.g. improved reliability, improved access, improved submission/uploading of evidence) based on their experiences of using CBA and CAA systems in the apprenticeship programme, these are less comprehensive than those discussed in Part 2, e.g. security of e-assessment. This could be due to a number of factors. First, these findings from the apprenticeship programme are based on such a small sample compared to the number of respondents who completed the two surveys, which means that the inclusion of more apprentices might have coloured the overall findings. Research on a large scale in this area is required to further examine challenges of using e-assessment on apprenticeship programmes other than those in ICT and how these could be overcome. Second, the respondents to the two surveys (Part 2) comprised a wide range of users, excluding candidates, therefore they were more likely to have a broader perspective (than apprentices) of using technology in assessment. Finally, due to the familiarity of the apprentices with ICT and the nature of the apprenticeship programme (i.e., being run by a global IT business) it would make sense to assume a) they are likely to face less challenges when using technology in assessment and b) they may be in a better position to deal with technical issues as they arise and thus minimise the need for huge amount of support. This might suggest that a sufficient level of support should be factored in when using e-assessment in non-ICT apprenticeship programmes. It is interesting that this apprentice would like a 'blended' model rather than a case of either or. This confirms the importance of exploring the possibilities of blended delivery and assessment methods (Booth et al., 2003).

## FUTURE RESEARCH DIRECTIONS

Future researchers might wish to investigate CBA and CAA from candidate's perspective, which was beyond the scope of this chapter. They might also want to compare challenges and solutions required to overcome these challenges when these systems are used for diagnostic, formative and summative assessments or even across different awarding bodies. Using CBA and CAA on the pilot apprenticeship programme examined has been well-received. Due to its nature and emphasis on practical skills, skills had been assessed using traditional assessment methods until recent UK government proposals. The integration of technology in this process is a novelty thing and it might not be surprising the apprentices experienced a number of challenges with e-assessment such as preference/familiarity with traditional types of assessment. Other challenges were more technical and related to the reliability of e-assessment, access and difficulty to upload multiple files, which resonates with the survey findings. Similar solutions to those discussed in the main surveys were proposed. However, the findings of this case study may not be generalised to other apprenticeship programmes because of the small sample size and the apprentices' background in ICT, hence the need for further research.

## CONCLUSION

This chapter discussed assessment in the modern age in terms of its importance, challenges and solutions. The respondents' views are based on their recent experience of using two systems which employ CBA and CAA (*mostly* at summative stage, although both could be used for formative purposes). Generally speaking, both systems face similar challenges such as technical issues and poor support, but there are challenges which are specific to the CAA system, i.e., poor monitoring

of candidates' progress. Similarly, both systems may require some common solutions to improve user's future experience to ensure they are more user friendly and bring about improvement in the software. Again, some solutions are more relevant to the CAA system like the call for improvement in the uploading of candidates' evidence and monitoring of their progress.

To be more specific, the CBA survey findings, which confirm to a large extent the literature on the advantages of e-assessment in part 1, show that security of e-assessment is a top priority; it is high stakes assessment. Nearly half of the respondents are extremely satisfied/satisfied with their experience of using the system, despite a number of challenges. The biggest challenges they face relate to technical issues and timescale of marking. Accordingly, their proposed solutions call for an improved technical provision.

The CAA survey findings, which are also consistent with the literature, including that on the advantages of e-assessment, indicate that 'visibility' of candidates' progress is highly significant since the system facilitates gradual marking. The respondents' level of satisfaction with the CAA system is almost identical to that of the users of CBA system. They too highlight a number of challenges, which confirm the literature apart from the poor monitoring of candidates' progress. The top challenges are technical too (e.g. not user friendly, reliability issues and limited functionality), which echo the CBA findings. Sometimes the respondents are unaware these challenges (e.g. not being user friendly) have been addressed in recent updates of the system, which might suggest there is need to improve communication. The second possible cause of these challenges could be related to the means of connection (i.e. internet, application). Better navigation and display (improved technical provision) are the top two solutions.

They listed other solutions, which add to the literature (e.g. forum for assessors to give each other support and an online chat facility with candidates). This is likely to ease the pressure on awarding bodies to offer constant instant support, which should suit the needs of all users. Users might have expectations when using e-assessment systems for different purposes. However, these should be managed to suit the test objectives and the latter should be better communicated with the system users. Occasionally, they have opposing needs, e.g. giving feedback and monitoring of candidates' progress, and eventually opposing solutions. Unless e-assessment can be personalised for every user (where possible) or their expectations of what e-assessment can/cannot offer are managed, it will be a rather difficult task to meet their needs.

# REFERENCES

Al-Smadi, M., & Gütl, C. (2008). *Past, present and future of e-assessment: Towards a flexible e-assessment system.* Paper presented at the International Conference on Interactive Computer Aided Learning, Villach. Retrieved from http://bit.ly/1qDK7JY

Anctil, T. M., & Adams, N. J. (2002). Computer-based testing in vocational assessment and evaluation: A primer for rehabilitation professionals. *Vocational Evaluation and Work Adjustment Journal, 34,* 5-15. Retrieved from http://bit.ly/1jRKfZ5

Anohina, A., & Grundspenkis, J. (2007). A concept map based intelligent system for adaptive knowledge assessment. In O. Vasilecas, J. Eder & A. Caplinskas (Eds.), *Databases and information systems IV: selected papers from the Seventh International Baltic Conference DB&IS* (pp. 263-276). Amsterdam: IOS Press.

Apampa, K. M., Wills, G., & Argles, D. (2010). User security issues in summative e-assessment security. *International Journal of Digital Society, 1*(2), 135–147. Retrieved from http://bit.ly/1erjJ6e

Beetham, H., & Sharpe, R. (Eds.). (2013). Re-thinking pedagogy for a digital age (2nd ed.). London: Routledge.

Booth, R., Clayton, B., Hartcher, R., Hungar, S., Hyde, P., & Wilson, P. (2003, May 13). *The development of quality online assessment in vocational education and training.* National Centre for Vocational Education Research. Retrieved from http://bit.ly/1gNYKK5

Boyle, A., & Hutchinson, D. (2009). Sophisticated tasks in e assessment: What are they and what are their benefits? *Assessment & Evaluation in Higher Education, 34*(3), 305–319. doi:10.1080/02602930801956034

Boyle, A., May, T., & Sceeny, P. (2011). *From the festival hall to functional skills: A history of three e-assessment initiatives.* Paper presented at the AEA-Europe conference, Belfast.

Bull, J., & McKenna, C. (2004). *Blueprint for computer-assisted assessment.* London: Routledge Falmer. doi:10.4324/9780203464687

Callan, V. J., & Clayton, B. (2010). *Bridging the divide: the challenges and solutions around e-assessment as voiced by practitioners and auditors.* Paper presented at Australian Vocational Education and Training Research Association Conference, Queensland. Retrieved from http://bit.ly/RhC77j

Campbell, J., Thompson, E., & Pautz, H. (2011). Apprenticeship training in England: Closing the gap? *Journal of Contemporary European Studies, 19*(3), 365–378. doi:10.1080/14782804.2011.610606

Christensen, R., & Knezek, G. A. (2014). Measuring technology readiness and skills. In J. M. Spector, M. D. Merrill, J. Elen, & M. J. Bishop (Eds.), *Handbook of research on educational communications and technology* (4th ed.; pp. 829–840). New York, NY: Springer. doi:10.1007/978-1-4614-3185-5_67

City and Guilds. (2013). *Managing cases of suspected malpractice in examinations and assessments: guidance notes.* Retrieved from http://bit.ly/1lncKIp

Craven, P. (2009). History and challenges of e-assessment. *Cambridge Assessment.* Retrieved from http://bit.ly/1iU33mY

Creswell, J., & Plano Clark, V. (2007). *Designing and conducting mixed methods research.* London: Sage.

Department for Business. Innovation and Skills. (2013). *The future of apprenticeships in England: Next steps from the Richard Review.* Retrieved from http://bit.ly/1jK7rYe

Department for Business. Innovation and Skills. (2014). *The future of apprenticeships in England: Guidance for Trailblazers.* Retrieved from http://bit.ly/1fduGlq

Department of Training and Workforce Development. (2012). *Guidelines for assessing competence in VET.* Retrieved from http://bit.ly/SvMnJW

Dikli, S. (2003), Assessment at a distance: Traditional vs. alternative assessments. *The Turkish Online Journal of Educational Technology, 2*(3), 13-19. Retrieved from http://bit.ly/SJBvaD

European Commission. (2013). *Apprenticeship and traineeship schemes in EU27: Key success factors.* Retrieved from http://bit.ly/1sqazb8

Ferrell, G., & Gray, L. (2014). *Enhancing student employability through technology-supported assessment and feedback: how the curriculum can help develop the skills and competencies needed in the world of work.* Retrieved from http://bit.ly/1hYHPSA

Further Education and Training Awards Council. (2007). *Quality assuring assessment: Guidelines for providers.* Retrieved from http://bit.ly/1h7kAoq

Hammersley, M., & Traianou, A. (2012, May). *Ethics and educational research. British Educational Research Association on-line resource.* Retrieved from http://bit.ly/1x113gJ

Joint Council for Qualifications. (2013). *General and vocational qualifications suspected malpractice in examinations and assessments: Policies and procedures.* Retrieved from http://bit.ly/1qKJuOE

Joint Information Systems Committee. (2007a). *Effective practice with e-Assessment: An overview of technologies, policies and practice in further and higher education.* Retrieved from http://bit.ly/1igM2SK

Joint Information Systems Committee. (2008). *Effective practice with e-portfolios: supporting 21st century learning.* Retrieved from http://bit.ly/1hLnYeG

Joint Information Systems Committee. (2010a). *Effective assessment in a digital age: a guide to technology-enhanced assessment and feedback.* Retrieved from http://bit.ly/1hJwt7V

Joint Information Systems Committee. (2010b). *Making the most of a computer-assisted assessment system, University of Manchester.* Retrieved from http://bit.ly/1HDjK2j

Joint Information Systems Committee. (2007b). *E-portfolios: an overview of JISC activities.* Retrieved from http://bit.ly/SJKrwI

Joint Information Systems Committee infoNet. (2014). *Learners' perspectives.* Retrieved from http://bit.ly/1EQG1FA

King, F. J., Goodson, L., & Rohani, F. (1998). *Higher order thinking skills: definition, teaching strategies and assessment.* Retrieved from http://fla.st/1xek82v

Kumar, R. (2012). Effective practice with e-assessment: challenges and barriers. *RADIX International Journal of Research in Social Science, 1*(6). Retrieved from http://bit.ly/1qi9N0u

Learn, N. C. (2014). *Performance assessments versus traditional assessments, University of North Carolina.* Retrieved from http://bit.ly/1od3v50

Learning, F. D. (2004). *E-portfolios: their use and benefits.* Retrieved from http://bit.ly/1xCGdHB

Lin, H., & Dwyer, F. (2006). The fingertip effects of computer-based assessment in education. *TechTrends, 50*(6), 27–31. http://bit.ly/1upkbWT doi:10.1007/s11528-006-7615-9

Livingston Institute of Vocational Training. (2010). *TAE40110 Certificate IV training and assessment: Candidate manual assessment.* Retrieved from http://bit.ly/1qJHx7d

Marais, E., Argles, D., & von Solms, B. (2006). *Security issues specific to e-assessments.* Paper presented at the 8th Annual Conference on WWW Applications, Bloemfontein. Retrieved from http://eprints.soton.ac.uk/261433/

Marriott, P., & Teoh, L. (2012). *Computer-based assessment and feedback: Best practice guidelines. Higher Education Academy.* Retrieved from http://bit.ly/1jkdRZ2

Milbradt, A. (2008). Quality criteria in open source software for computer-based assessment. In F. Scheuermann & A. Guimarães Pereira (Eds.), Towards a research agenda on computer-based assessment: Challenges and needs for European educational measurement (pp. 53–57). Luxembourg: European Commission. Retrieved from http://bit.ly/1myPtUd

Mueller, J. (2014a). *Authentic assessment toolbox.* Retrieved from http://bit.ly/1hudUS8

Mueller, J. (2014b). *Portfolios.* Retrieved from http://bit.ly/1oUpEos

Nekoueizadeh, M., & Bahrani, T. (2013). Considering challenges in educational system for implementation of e-assessment. *International Journal of Language Learning and Applied Linguistics World, 4*(2), 89–99. Retrieved from http://www.ijllalw.org/finalversion429.pdf

Northern Advisory Council for Further Education. (2014). *E-portfolio systems.* Retrieved from http://bit.ly/1hLQ75s

Office of Qualifications and Examinations Regulations. (2010). *E-assessment.* Retrieved from http://bit.ly/1nTsRo9

Pallant, J. (2007). *SPSS survival manual: A step by step guide to data analysis using SPSS for Windows* (3rd ed.). Maidenhead, UK: Open University Press.

Phelps, R. P. (2006). Characteristics of an effective student testing system. *Educational Horizons, 85*(1), 19–29. Retrieved from http://bit.ly/1tK9MCR

Prensky, M. (2001, October). Digital natives, digital immigrants. *On the Horizon, 9*(5), 1–6. doi:10.1108/10748120110424816

Prineas, M., & Cini, M. (2011). *Assessing learning in online education: The role of technology in improving student outcomes.* National Institute for Learning Outcomes Assessment. Retrieved from http://bit.ly/1vsSyOF

Qualifications and Curriculum Authority. (2007). *Regulatory principles for e-assessment.* Retrieved from http://bit.ly/1dGAkNy

Quality Assurance Agency. (2005). *Reflections on assessment: Volume II.* Retrieved from http://bit.ly/1AZPTMP

Richard, D. (2012, November). *The Richard review of apprenticeships*. School for Startups. Retrieved from http://bit.ly/QFz6gX

Rosen, Y., & Tager, M. (2013). *Computer-based performance assessment of creativity skills: A pilot study*. Pearson. Retrieved from http://bit.ly/1yMHkU2

Scheuermann, F., & Guimarães Pereira, A. (Eds.). (2008). Towards a research agenda on computer-based assessment: Challenges and needs for European educational measurement. Luxembourg: European Commission. Retrieved from http://bit.ly/1myPtUd

Scottish Qualifications Authority. (2014a). *E-portfolios*. Retrieved from http://www.sqa.org.uk/sqa/42718.html

Scottish Qualifications Authority. (2014b). *CPD toolkit for assessors and internal verifiers of SVQ*. Retrieved from http://bit.ly/1qGbq8f

Sharples, M., McAndrew, P., Weller, M., Ferguson, R., FitzGerald, E., Hirst, T., . . . Whitelock, D. (2012). *Innovating Pedagogy 2012: Exploring new forms of teaching, learning and assessment to guide educators and policy makers*. Open University Innovation Report 1. Retrieved from http://bit.ly/1uwYH78

Tashakkori, A., & Teddlie, C. (1998). *Mixed methodology: Combining qualitative and quantitative approaches*. London: Sage.

Thurlow, M., Lazarus, S., Albus, D., & Hodgson, J. (2010, September). *Computer-based testing: Practices and considerations*. Retrieved from http://bit.ly/1q3azPj

Tosun, N., & Baris, M. (2011). E-portfolio applications in education. *The Online Journal of New Horizons in Education, 1*(4), 42-52. Retrieved from http://bit.ly/SuGFqE

Tovey, A. (2014, July 17). Degree losing attraction for smaller employers. *The Telegraph*. Retrieved from http://bit.ly/1jAxm5m

Trading Standards Institute. (2014). *Internal verifier*. Retrieved from http://bit.ly/1lotOBT

Winkley, J. (2010). *E-assessment and innovation*. AlphaPlus. Retrieved from http://bit.ly/1HD3IFD

## ADDITIONAL READING

Chapman, G. (2005). Drivers and barriers to the adoption of computer assisted assessment for UK awarding bodies. Proceedings of the 9th CAA Conference. Loughborough: Loughborough University; Retrieved from http://bit.ly/1FJfrhY

Conole, G., & Warburton, B. (2005). A review of computer-assisted assessment. *ALT-J. Research in Learning Technology, 13*(1), 17–31. http://1.usa.gov/1zL6ItF doi:10.1080/0968776042000339772

Scheuermann, F., & Björnsson, J. (2009). *The transition to computer-based assessment: New approaches to skills assessment and implications for large-scale testing*. Ispra: European. Commission. Retrieved from http://bit.ly/1w0lRdm

Scottish Qualifications Authority. (2003). *SQA guidelines on online assessment for further education*. Retrieved from http://bit.ly/1qJ1Cus

Scottish Qualifications Authority. (2007). *E-assessment: Guide to effective practice*. Retrieved from http://bit.ly/12kx0sv

## KEY TERMS AND DEFINITIONS

**Apprenticeship:** Commonly perceived to be a long-term training offered in collaboration between employers and educational institutions.

**External Verification:** Process by which providers can get an external independent confirmation that their assessment is valid, reliable and meet standards which they must adhere to.

**High-Stakes Assessment:** Outcomes are of high importance to both centre and candidates, affecting progression to subsequent roles and activities.

**Internal Verification:** Process by which providers (e.g. test centres) monitor and verify the assessment process and procedures internally.

**Low-Stakes Assessment:** Usually formative, with results recorded locally.

**Malpractice:** In assessment, this could be any act or practice which breaches the regulations and may undermine the process of assessment and its validity.

**Medium-Stakes Assessment:** Results may be recorded locally and nationally, but is not life changing.

**Test Centres:** Issue certificates of competence to learners and liaise with a number of stakeholders, e.g. they forward learners' results to awarding bodies and coordinate with them on quality assurance.

**Trailblazers:** Major UK reforms to apprenticeships which involves eight groups of employers working together to design new standards for occupations in their industries.

## ENDNOTES

[1]    It is beyond the scope of this chapter to cover all types of e-assessment, e.g. observations.

[2]    E-assessment and 'online'/'electronic' /'remote' assessment are used interchangeably. For the sake of simplicity, 'e-assessment' will be used throughout the chapter.

[3]    The word 'candidate' is used to refer to 'learner' or 'student.'

[4]    Other examples include short answer tests and essays (Dikli, 2003). In short answer tests candidates are required to fill a space with a short answer. Essays, which are more difficult and time consuming to assess, allow a) assessors to assess the higher order learning skills of candidates such as critical thinking and problem solving and b) candidates to respond freely.

[5]    It is argued that portfolios are not really assessments at all; they are compilation of evidence of candidates' learning (Mueller, 2014b).

[6]    In projects, candidates often apply their problem solving skills to provide a solution to a situation in a given task (Dikli, 2003).

[7]    In fact, portfolio has "long been part of the traditional assessment process" (SQA, 2014a, p. 36).

[8]    This is also in terms of perceptions and attitude of practitioners around some forms of e-assessment.

[9]    References cited throughout the findings indicate that the findings confirm and support the literature.

[10]    Although more responses might have changed the overall findings, the response rate to this question was almost 64%.

[11]    Where 1= extremely dissatisfied and 10= extremely satisfied.

[12]    The data collection resulted in 227 statements which were grouped under nine themes.

[13]    Some of the respondents suggested more than one point hence the difference in the total number of responses.

# Chapter 17
# Technology–Assisted Learning for Students with Moderate and Severe Developmental Disabilities

**Diane M. Browder**
*University of North Carolina at Charlotte, USA*

**Alicia Saunders**
*University of North Carolina at Charlotte, USA*

**Jenny Root**
*University of North Carolina at Charlotte, USA*

## ABSTRACT

*For students with moderate and severe developmental disabilities, including autism spectrum disorders and intellectual disability, technology can provide critical support for learning and life functioning. A growing body of research demonstrates the benefits of technology for these students to acquire academic skills, improve social functioning, and perform tasks of daily living. This chapter provides a description of this population and their learning needs. The research on technology applications for students with developmental disabilities is reviewed and synthesized. The review includes literature on technology to assist instruction and to provide options for student responding. Examples are provided of how technology can be applied to both instruction and assessment.*

## INTRODUCTION

Technology has transformed everyday life for many people in the 21st century, but for individuals with moderate and severe developmental disabilities it has especially opened doors of opportunity not previously available. Multiple studies have demonstrated that students with moderate and severe developmental disabilities can benefit from technology in learning academic skills (Knight, McKissick, & Saunders, 2013; Pennington, 2010), managing social skills (Ramdoss, et al., 2011), or

DOI: 10.4018/978-1-4666-9441-5.ch017

performing daily living skills (Mechling, Gast, & Seid, 2010). Technology can also promote job-related learning (Morgan & Horrocks, 2011).

Ironically, students with developmental disabilities may not access these opportunities to the extent students who are nondisabled do. While the use of technology in schools may be as high as 98% of students overall (National Center for Education Statistics, 2008), school access for students with intellectual disability may be much lower (Edyburn, 2013; Wehmeyer, Smith, Palmer, & Davies, 2004). Educators need more information on how technology can be used to assist instruction and promote new opportunities for learning.

Technology also can offer a means for students with developmental disabilities to show what they know. All states are required to provide alternate assessments for students who cannot participate in the state's general assessment with or without accommodations. Students with moderate and severe disabilities often are candidates for these alternate assessments. In contrast, Towles-Reeves, Kearns, Kleinert, and Kleinert (2009) found from 17-26% of these students only had emerging symbolic communication and another 8-11% were presymbolic. As Kleinert, Kearns, and Kleinert (2010) note communication is critical to learning and demonstrating achievement in state assessments. Technology can be crucial to promoting communicative competence for students who lack speech.

Given the proliferation of technology in today's world and its potential to promote learning and quality of life for individuals with moderate and severe developmental disabilities, the need exists to identify the research on how to use technology effectively with these students. This chapter includes a brief overview of the population, research on technology for this group of students, and examples of how the technology can be applied in interventions. The implications for practice, including assessment, will also be reviewed. The objectives of this chapter are:

1. To provide a brief overview of students with moderate and severe developmental disabilities and their learning characteristics that may be relevant to technology use.
2. To synthesize the research on the use of technology with this population focusing on academic, social/ communicative, and daily living skills.
3. To offer examples of how this research can be used to plan instruction and assessment.

## BACKGROUND

Before identifying effective technology applications, it is important to clarify the population of focus and the learning characteristics that are relevant to planning for technology use. This chapter focuses on the subgroup of students with disabilities who participate in alternate assessments. Students in these alternate assessments work towards alternate achievement of their states' academic content standards. To define this alternate achievement, educators target content from the students' grade level, then prioritize specific standards and translate these into learning targets with a lower level of complexity. For example, if the 4th grade expectation is for students to identify the author's point of view after reading a chapter book, the learning target for alternate achievement may be to identify the author's point of view by using a simplified summary of the book that is read aloud. The student may also respond by selecting from an array of answers rather than generating a response. Students who take alternate assessments are sometimes referred to as the "1%" in the United States because schools can report scores based on alternate achievement standards for up to 1% of their school population (U.S. Department of Education, 2003). One way to think about students with disabilities broadly is to consider whether they are working towards grade level or alternate academic achievement in schools. The focus of this chapter will be on those working towards alternate academic achievement.

## Who Are the Students?

The term "developmental disabilities" is inclusive of individuals with intellectual disabilities and autism spectrum disorders (ASD). The cognitive level of individuals with developmental disabilities can vary widely, but the focus of this chapter will be those who have a moderate level of intellectual disability and may also have an ASD. Students with moderate and severe developmental disabilities have a large overlap with those considered to have "significant cognitive disabilities" and who take the alternate assessment based on alternate achievement standards for their state. In the United States the term "significant cognitive disabilities" was introduced with the 1997 Amendments of the Individuals with Disabilities Education Act and then retained in No Child Left Behind and the reauthorization of IDEA to refer to this alternate assessment group. In contrast, it is not a specific disability category in IDEA. As Kleinert et al. (2010) note, every disability group is represented in students who take alternate assessments. The term "significant cognitive disabilities" includes primarily students with moderate and severe developmental disabilities, but also some others who take alternate assessments (e.g., a student who has both an intellectual disability and sensory impairment). The term "intellectual disability" now replaces "mental retardation" (Schalock et al., 2010). Handleman (1986) proposed the term "severe developmental disabilities" as an umbrella term to refer to individuals with autism, severe intellectual disability, and multiple disabilities. A developmental disability is one that: (1) is manifested before the age of 22, (2) is chronic and severe, (3) can be attributed to a mental or physical impairment or both, (4) results in substantial functional limitations in major life activities, and (5) requires lifelong need for special services that are individually planned and coordinated

(Handleman, 1986). Sometimes the term "low functioning" is used to refer to students with ASD who also have an intellectual disability, but this term, like "mental retardation," often is considered pejorative. In summary, given that multiple terms have been used to describe this population, the umbrella term "developmental disability" provides a way to denote students who have either ASD or intellectual disability (or both). The population is further delineated as those working towards alternate achievement of their schools' academic standards contrasted with those with mild developmental disabilities who pursue grade level achievement.

## How Do the Students Learn?

In planning for technology applications, it will be important to understand some of the characteristics of this population. One common feature is the slower rate of learning often demonstrated with poorer generalization and maintenance of newly learned skills. Students with moderate and severe developmental disabilities also typically have deficits in self-help and daily living skills compared to their same-age peers. Most have deficits in communication skills and some must rely on alternatives to speech to communicate. These students also may engage in stereotypic and challenging behavior. Some may have physical challenges that make it difficult to perform motor tasks like writing and typing. Students with ASD may also have impaired social interactions, rigidity about changes in routine, be overly or under sensitive to stimuli, and may perseverate on topics of interest to them. Many of these challenges can be overcome with environmental supports and evidence-based interventions.

### Evidence-Based Interventions

A common finding of many reviews of research for students with moderate and severe developmental disabilities is that they respond well to highly specific, systematic instruction (Ault, Wolery, Doyle, & Gast, 1989; Spooner, Knight, Browder, & Smith, 2012). Systematic instruction is based on principles of applied behavior analysis. Using systematic prompting and feedback, the teacher works to transfer stimulus control from some target prompting stimulus (e.g., a color cue or teacher model) to the target discriminative stimulus (e.g., target word to be read; math equation to be solved). Ault et al. (1989) found time delay, least intrusive prompts, and graduated guidance to be effective prompting systems when teaching students with moderate to severe disabilities. Time delay has been used effectively to teach literacy to students with severe disabilities (Browder, Ahlgrim-Delzell, Spooner, Mims, Baker, 2009) and mathematics (Polychronis, McDonnell, Johnson, Riesen, & Jameson, 2004). In time delay, the teacher provides an immediate prompt along with the target stimulus. For example, the teacher might provide an array of four sight words and say, "Point to 'men'" while pointing to the correct answer. The student imitates the response to be correct without error. Then over trials, the teacher gradually inserts a small amount of time (e.g., 4 seconds) between the target stimulus and providing the prompt. When the student begins to anticipate the correct response, transfer of stimulus control has occurred. In the system of least prompts, the teacher only provides as much assistance as needed, for example, moving from a verbal direction to a model and then some physical guidance. This prompting system has been used in skills like mathematics (Jimenez, Browder, & Courtade, 2008), reading (Mims, Hudson, & Browder, 2012), and daily living skills (Mechling, Gast, & Fields, 2008). In graduated guidance, the teacher provides increasing amounts of physical assistance as needed until the student makes the motoric response required. For example, when teaching a student to eat with a spoon, a teacher would provide the initial cue, "eat your food," and then would follow with a specific verbal cue, "pick up your spoon" paired with physical assistance

(placing hand over students hand and picking up spoon) if the student does not respond. The pairing of specific verbal prompts and physical prompts continues until the student did does not resist the prompt and demonstrates readiness to move to a less intrusive physical prompt paired with a specific verbal prompt, such as a hand on the elbow. The decreasing assistance continues until the teacher is only shadowing the motor responses, providing physical assistance as needed to ensure correct responses. This prompting system has been used to teach skills like eating, rolling a ball (Denny et al., 2000), and dressing (Resse & Snell, 1991).

## How Might Technology Promote Learning

There are numerous benefits to instructional technology, which make it ideal for this population, including that it can (a) promote correct implementation of instructional strategies; (b) be delivered in one setting and generalized to another; (c) reduce the amount of time needed for organization and presentation of materials because everything is stored in a database; (d) reduce the number of staff needed to implement instructional strategies; (e) allow teachers to randomize the order and position of content presentation; (f) increase the number of instructional opportunities for students; and (g) be implemented by personnel other than teachers, such as paraprofessionals (Kodak, Fisher, Clements, & Bouxsein, 2011). Although computer-assisted instruction is not intended to replace teacher-delivered instruction entirely, these benefits make it ideal for learners who need explicit, consistent instruction with repeated opportunities for practice.

Besides these benefits to instructional delivery, technology may help students compensate for learning that is slow and challenged by additional deficits in communication or problem behavior. For example, Langone, Shade, Clees, and Day (1999) found multimedia technology helped students with moderate and severe intellectual disability improve their matching skills. Students may find instructional technology more motivating than face-to-face instruction due to the appealing visual and auditory design capabilities (Hitchcock & Noonan, 2000; Moore & Calvert, 2000; Shane & Albert, 2008; Whalen, Liden, Ingersoll, Dallaire, & Liden, 2006). Technology may provide students with a means for expressing responses. For example, in one study students who were nonverbal were able to demonstrate phonetic segmenting with a voice output device (Ahlgrim-Delzell, Browder, & Wood, 2014). While students may use technological applications both for motivation and enhanced responding, simply providing technology for this population will not be enough. Students will likely need explicit and systematic instruction to learn to use the technology to achieve target goals.

## RESEARCH-BASED STRATEGIES FOR TECHNOLOGY USE

### Issues, Controversies, and Problems

The primary problem in technology use for individuals with moderate and severe developmental disabilities is availability. As noted earlier, access to technology has not kept pace for these students compared with the general school population. One reason for this may be low expectations for students with severe disabilities and the lack of information about what benefits can be derived from access to computers and other technology. Browder et al. (2004) noted how curricular expectations have evolved for students with moderate and severe disabilities over the last four decades towards increasingly higher goals. These expectations went from assuming students could only do preschool tasks (1970s), to providing functional life skills instruction with no academic counterpart (1980s), to promoting inclusion in general education primarily for social benefits (1990s), then to

consideration of how students might participate in large stakes assessments (2000s). This focus on assessment fueled the current focus on how students can achieve academic content standards. With the focus on academic content learning, educators need new options for teaching these more challenging constructs and for students to express learning.

Similarly, there has been an evolution in thinking about the extent to which students with moderate and severe developmental disabilities can direct their own lives and learning. Prior to the 1980s, many individuals with developmental disabilities spent their lives in segregated institutions and schools. As advocates pushed for more inclusive opportunities, interest arose in how students could learn to have more self-determination. Wehmeyer (2014) has described this important link between inclusive practices and promoting the opportunity for students with disabilities to make things happen in their own lives or that is, to be the causal agent. For educators to invest in technology, they will need to identify how this tool can help students with moderate and severe disabilities have more influence over their lives and learning.

Besides the challenges of access to technology, students with moderate and severe developmental disabilities have additional barriers to overcome once technology, like computer-assisted instruction. Computer-assisted instruction (CAI) incorporates different formats of multimedia (e.g., text, graphics, animations, voice, music, and slides) in a single system that is delivered via a computer program on a variety of devices (e.g., computer, tablet, smartphone, interactive whiteboard). There are two main barriers for students with moderate and severe developmental disabilities using and benefiting from CAI, including limitations in cognitive ability domains and the lack of universal design features accounting for the cognitive accessibility of these learners (Wehmeyer et al., 2004). Carefully designed programs can address these limitations. Today's CAI incorporates many of the same principles of B. F. Skinner's Programmed Instruction (1954), including presenting materials in small and sequenced steps, providing immediate feedback, using conditioned reinforcers, autonomy of instruction, and minimizing the rate of error in responses (Lockee, Larson, Burton, & Moore, 2008; McDonald, Yanchar, & Osguthorpe, 2005). In addition to these necessary design features, many improvements have been made over the past decade that addresses some of the limitations of the earlier forms of Programmed Instruction and CAI.

There are several key strategies in using CAI with students with moderate and severe developmental disabilities. First and foremost, CAI should be integrated with other empirically-based teaching strategies within the overall design of the technology in order for learning to occur (Babbitt & Miller, 1996; Seo & Bryant, 2009). Simply adding technology, which delivers the instruction, is not sufficient for learning to take place. Second, CAI may need to be adapted for the individual learning needs of these students. For example, authoring software or programs which serve as templates that teachers or researchers can adapt and design are especially important for responding to diverse needs (Higgins & Boone, 1996; McDonald et al., 2005). Third, principles of self-determination must be embedded within the instructional design itself, such as active student participation, decision making, and appropriate feedback to provide support (Lockee et al., 2008; Seo & Bryant, 2009). Rather than controlling student responses, the student needs to be the causal agent in executing the program to improve motivation and maintain student interest. Finally, ongoing evaluation of the program and student's progress should take place throughout implementation (Lockee et al., 2008). In a busy classroom, the temptation may exist to use computer time simply for independent engagement while working with other students. In contrast, to reap the full benefits of CAI, data are needed to determine if the student is mastering goals for learning. Finally, programs should be designed with principles of universal design

of learning to make them easily accessible for independent student use, such as multimodality features (e.g., text to speech and visual cues), visual examples, multiple methods for users to locate and use controls (e.g., touch screens), and sufficient wait times and allotment for errors (Wehmeyer et al., 2004). The instructional and program design features are pivotal to the success of CAI program for students with moderate and severe developmental disabilities.

## Practices from Research for Students with Moderate and Severe Disabilities

Evidence-based practices, like systematic methods of prompting, are typically identified for students with moderate and severe developmental disabilities through the synthesis of single case research (e.g., Browder, et al., 2009). Because this is a low incidence population, researchers often use experimental interventions designed for small sample sizes, such as a multiple baseline design across participants design (Gast, 2010). Threats to internal validity are controlled through replications between or across participants. The What Works Clearinghouse of the U.S. Department of Education has recognized single case designs as a type of experimental research that can be used to build support for the effects of a practice (What Works Clearinghouse, 2014). In contrast, because of the low sample size, researchers have advocated that multiple single case studies are needed to identify a practice as evidence-based (Horner et al., 2005). While practices like time delay now have numerous studies to support the practice (Browder et al., 2009), applications of technology for this population are newer and the evidence base is newly emerging. Also, not all of these studies adhered to the Horner et al. (2005) criteria for rigor in single case design. In contrast, we have only chosen to review studies that provided at least three demonstrations of effects as recommended by the What Works Clearinghouse so all had this minimal level of rigor for making inferences about the effects of treatment. The following sections will describe potential ways to use technology effectively with students with moderate and severe disabilities. Given the limited number of studies, small sample sizes, and variance in rigor of applications of design methodology, educators should view each of these as promising practices that need further research validation.

## Using Technology to Promote Academic Learning

Academic skills are important for increasing the quality of life for individuals with developmental disabilities and providing better post-school outcomes. In contrast, students whose disabilities are moderate or severe may have difficulty in accessing this content because of physical or cognitive limitations or a lack of prerequisite skills. Computer-based technologies may enhance access to the general curriculum by removing barriers that students with disabilities face when interacting with traditional materials (Ketterlin-Geller & Tindal, 2007). Portable devices also can be less stigmatizing and more socially inclusive than traditional augmentative and assistive communication devices. Computer-assisted instruction (CAI) has been shown to be an effective method to teach a variety of academic skills (Blischak & Schlosser, 2003; Mechling & Hunnicutt, 2011; Pennington, 2010; Ramdoss et al., 2011). Reviews of the literature have shown advantages of CAI for both students with ASD (Knight et al., 2013; Pennington, 2010) and for students with an intellectual disability (Wehmeyer et al., 2004).

Wehmeyer et al. (2004) identified over 20 studies in which technology was used to teach skills to students with intellectual disability in an educational setting. The academic skills included handwriting, telling time, word recognition, addition, and subtraction. Similarly, Pennington (2010) found 15 articles conducted with students with ASD. All studies targeted literacy skills, with eight

targeting reading instruction (e.g., identifying nouns, letters, numbers, and food words; acquisition of target vocabulary; decoding skills), and seven targeting written expression (e.g., sentence construction; Japanese character construction; and essay writing skills). Only two of the 15 studies involved using CAI to teach more complex skills, such as decoding skills and essay writing skills. Knight et al. (2013) updated Pennington's work and found 14 additional studies, most of which focused on literacy skills.

Many of the studies using CAI have focused on teaching discrete skills, such as picture, object, and symbol identification (Bosseler & Massaro, 2003; Chen & Bernard-Opitz, 1993; Clark & Green, 2004; Hetzroni, Rubin, & Konkol, 2002; Hetzroni & Shalem, 2005; Kelly, Green, & Sidman, 1998; Reagon, Higbee, & Endicott, 2007; Simpson & Keen, 2010; Sugasawara & Yamamoto, 2007; Whalen et al., 2010). In these studies, the computer presented targeted skills via some form of interactive multimedia. For example, Simpson and Keen (2010) successfully taught three preschool-aged students with ASD, using Microsoft PowerPoint®, which incorporated Boardmaker® symbols projected on an interactive whiteboard, to identify graphic symbols in order to communicate during interactive songs. Although these studies suggest positive effects of CAI programs for most students with ASD, a small number of studies have shown CAI can be used to teach students with ASD and intellectual disability more complex academic skills.

For example, Spooner, Ahlgrim-Delzell, Kemp-Inman, and Wood (2014) paired an iPad2® with systematic instruction, specifically constant time delay and a modified system of least prompts, to teach grade-appropriate literature in a shared story format to four elementary-aged students with autism and moderate intellectual disability. All students had limited verbal ability. Students learned to perform the steps of a task analysis to access the text (e.g., finding the title, turning the page). All response options for listening comprehension questions were presented in a four choice array with pictures, words, and auditory cueing. Although students needed longer to learn to answer comprehension questions than simply accessing the text, they did develop the strategy of using text prompts to answer comprehension questions.

Burton, Anderson, Prader, & Dyches et al. (2013) demonstrated how CAI also can be used to teach mathematics. In this study, four middle school students with ASD and intellectual disabilities learned to solve everyday problems using video self modeling. Students were given a seven-step task analysis to follow for solving. Students received a worksheet with five problems, which consisted of five items with five price tags, as well as a cash register with simulated money. Students were able to view videos of themselves solving the problems using the seven-step task analysis on an iPad as many times as needed. Students were asked to estimate the amount needed to purchase the item using the smallest number of bills, hand the money to the teacher, then estimate, calculate, and provide exact change. The technology allowed students to independently prompt themselves while problem solving, thus increasing independence and decreasing teacher dependency, an important self-determination skill.

Saunders (2014) used CAI to teach mathematical word problem solving across two problem types to three elementary-aged students with ASD and moderate intellectual disability. Word problems, videos, a student self-instruction checklist, and template were presented in a researcher-created program using SMART Notebook software. Students viewed videos of how to complete each step of a 12-step task analysis, and then were given an opportunity to try each step. Students monitored their progress using a self-instruction checklist with the embedded task analysis steps supported by picture supports and text-to-speech capability. Problems and numbers varied with each trial to provide multiple exemplars and build generalization. Students acquired mathematical word problem solving skills and were able to differentiate between the two problem types. Like Burton et al. (2013), the technology allowed students greater independence and promoted self-monitoring of their behavior.

One pivotal study evaluated the effects of CAI on the acquisition of science content in a general education classroom with older students. Smith, Spooner, and Wood (2012) evaluated the effects of embedded, computer-assisted explicit instruction on teaching science terms and application of those terms to general education science activities with three middle school students with autism and intellectual disabilities in an inclusive, general education science classroom. Science terms, pictures, and definitions were presented in 12 instructional slides on an iPad2®, which provided instruction on a set of three science terms per unit, using a model-test explicit instruction format. Students viewed the slideshow three times per class. All students were able to reach the mastery criterion of 14 out of 18 terms and applications correct in few sessions (range 6-8). Embedded instruction was successful, used high quality instructional practices, and was non-invasive to the overall flow of the general education classroom.

In Knight, Wood, Spooner, Browder, and O'Brien (2014) students with ASD and intellectual disabilities used supported e-text to learn science content. In e-text, material is presented to the student in an electronic format rather than a hard copy book or paper. In Knight et al., (2014) e-books were developed using CAST (2009) free software, *Book Builder* and had hyperlinks to an online glossary, and embedded coaches/avatars. The researchers found these universal design features were not sufficient to promote learning, and so they added embedded coaches/avatars to provide explicit instruction. Even with the new explicit instruction design feature, the authors noted the need for students to receive systematic feedback and praise that the program design could not deliver. In summary, research to date suggests that CAI can provide high quality, consistent academic instruction while limiting barriers for students with developmental disabilities. More studies are needed to demonstrate the generalizability of these findings across more participants especially in some academic content areas. A plethora of research exists on teaching discrete academic skills, especially for literacy; however, research is emerging on teaching more complex academic skills to students with developmental disabilities and in the areas of mathematics and science (e.g., Burton et al., 2013; Smith et al., 2012). There is a need to expand this research using students with moderate and severe intellectual disability without ASD, as well as older students at the secondary level. It is important to note, that across all CAI academic studies, the key culprit to developing effective programs is using sound, evidence- and research-based instructional strategies, such as systematic instruction with prompting and feedback, as well as other principles of applied behavior analysis.

## Technology to Enhance Daily Living Skills

Students with moderate and severe developmental disabilities often lag behind their same-age peers in management of skills of daily living like personal grooming, household chores, and use of community resources. Technology can provide a resource for either acquiring needed life skills or managing activities in daily living.

One way that technology can promote learning and performance of these skills is through offering visual supports to compensate for challenges in memory or executive planning thereby reducing dependence on caregivers. The National Professional Development Center defines a visual support as "any visual display that supports the learner engaging in a desired behavior or skills independent of prompts" (Wong et al., 2014, p. 22). Forms of technology-based visual supports commonly used to teach individuals with moderate to severe intellectual disability include pictures and videos. Picture supports display each step

of the task to be completed (e.g., on a handheld tablet or phone). Video supports either present the total task to be performed or break each step of the targeted skill into separate videos.

Van Laarhoven et al. (2010) compared the effectiveness of picture prompting and video prompting strategies on the daily living skills (folding laundry and meal preparation) of two adolescents with autism and moderate intellectual disability. In the picture prompts condition, a laptop was used to display a PowerPoint presentation with pictures depicting each step of the skill. In the video prompts condition, a laptop displayed a PowerPoint presentation of videos with audio narration for each step of the task analysis. While both picture prompts and video prompts were effective in increasing the number of correct responses and decreasing the amount of external prompts and prompts to use technology, video prompting resulted in a quicker acquisition of skills and was more efficient.

Interventions that combine video and picture prompts also have been found to be effective to teach the daily living skill of meal preparation. Mechling et al. (2010) taught three high school students with moderate intellectual disability to independently use a personal digital assistant (PDA) to self-prompt as they completed simple cooking tasks across three types of food preparation (e.g., stove top, microwave, and toaster oven). The PDA provided an embedded system of least prompts using (a) still pictures, (b) audio prompts, and (c) video models with audio prompts. The students were able to self-manage the amount of prompting they needed to complete the steps in the task analysis, or complete the steps independently without using the PDA at all. Students were able to determine the amount of prompting they needed, generally using more intrusive prompts (videos with audio prompting) as they acquired skills and then self-faded as needed.

Computer based video instruction (CBVI) also is used in classrooms to teach functional daily living skills as a means to conserve resources.

Systematic instruction is delivered through or in conjunction with video and computer-based instruction. For example, Ayers and Cihak (2010) taught three middle school students with moderate intellectual disability to make a sandwich, use a microwave to heat up soup, and set a table using CBVI. The "I Can! Daily Living and Community Skills" software program provided video models and opportunities for simulated practice with an embedded system of least prompts. One benefit of using CBVI was its cost-effectiveness. It decreased the need for consumable products for daily living tasks such as food preparation.

By using CBVI to teach transportation skills, practitioners also can save both instructional time as well as monetary resources required of community-based instruction alone. For example, Mechling and O'Brien (2010) taught three young adults, one with ASD and two with moderate intellectual disabilities to use public bus transportation through CBVI. CBVI sessions occurred in the individual's classroom and community based sessions took place on a city bus. A laptop with a touch screen was used to display a PowerPoint program. The researcher created a simulated instructional program by traveling the city bus route the individuals would be taking. The CBVI program consisted of video models and video prompts. The video model contained still photographs of the target destination, a video model of the bus ride from a person first perspective, and verbal cues related to the landmarks and instructions for when to stop the bus at the target destination. The video prompts were recorded to align with each step of the task analysis for riding the city bus to the target destination to be used during constant time delay instruction. Students were taught to identify landmarks along the route to the target destination and request to stop the bus. Similarly, Kelly, Test, and Cooke (2013) taught four young adults with intellectual disability to navigate a college campus. Photographs of landmarks for navigating around the college campus were displayed on a video iPod in the sequence necessary to arrive at a targeted location. If a participant was stuck, the researcher used a system of least prompts. Participants were able to navigate to untrained routes using the iPod alone without the presence of the researcher.

Perhaps one of the most important ways to use technology for daily living skills is to promote safety through simulations of emergencies. Mechling, Gast, and Gustafson (2009) used video modeling to teach three young adults with moderate intellectual disabilities how to extinguish cooking related fires and measured generalization through exposure to actual cooking-related fires with novel stimuli. Individuals were taught three methods of extinguishing cooking related fires through a model-test procedure. Students first watched the video model of extinguishing the fire on a portable DVD player and then were taken to the natural setting (kitchen or barbeque area) and exposed to a cooking fire to test their ability to follow the extinguishing steps presented in the video model. Individuals were able to quickly acquire fire-extinguishing skills and generalize them to novel examples, with maintenance of performance demonstrated following the removal of video modeling. Mechling et al. (2009) emphasized value of video modeling to prime individuals for events that may happen in the future to increase predictability and the individual's performance. Video models also can be used to teach safety skills that cannot or should not be taught in real world circumstances due to ethical and safety concerns.

In addition, recent research is showing technology can be used as a support for individuals with disabilities while they are in the community to manage their money. For example, Ayers, Langone, Boon, and Norman (2006) taught four middle school students with moderate intellectual disability to use the dollar plus strategy (rounding up) to pay for purchases in the community. Students were taught this strategy using Project Shop (Langone, Clees, Rieber, & Matzko, 2003), a software program that showed a video of a cashier stating a price, with the price shown on the screen, and required students to indicate the number of dollars they needed to pay and click "finished" when they had the correct amount. The students also were taken into community grocery stores for natural opportunities to practice purchasing skills. Similarly, Scott, Collins, Knight, and Kleinert (2013) taught three college students with moderate intellectual disability to operate iPods with pre-loaded podcasts with video models to withdraw money from an ATM.

Videos also have been an effective visual support for teaching job skills to individuals with developmental disabilities. Video self-modeling involves watching oneself perform the desired behavior. Goh and Bambara (2013) evaluated the effectiveness of video self-modeling alone or in combination with other instructional strategies (instructor feedback and practice) with three adults with intellectual disability and autism. Individuals watched videos of themselves carrying out the chained vocational tasks such as shoe storing, using the photocopier, and cleaning shoes in their natural employment settings (thrift store, department store, office) and were then asked to carry out the task in vivo. Additional interventions were put into place if the participants' performance plateaued, which involved video self-modeling plus instructor feedback, and feedback and practice of discrete skills within the chained task that needed improvement. Participants were able to reach mastery of chained job tasks, but the number of video self-modeling conditions required to achieve performance criteria varied by participant as well as job task. Goh and Bambara hypothesized the variability in effectiveness of the video self-modeling conditions may be explained by the participants' learning history with the tasks. Perhaps video self-modeling alone can be effective when individuals have experience with the task or setting as other studies have found (Lasater & Brady, 1995; McGraw-Hunter, Faw, & Davis, 2006); however, if it is a novel task, additional strategies such as feedback and practice may be needed.

Another method of video modeling is called subjective point of view modeling. This method displays a video from the point of view of the individual if they were completing the task. Mechling and Ortega-Hurndon (2007) used subjective point of view modeling in their investigation of CBVI to teach competitive job skills in a simulated environment that were complex and multiple step. Three young adults with moderate intellectual disability accessed a CBVI program on PowerPoint using a touch screen. The young adults were taught the steps of the task analysis for each job skill (e.g., watering a plant, delivering mail, and changing paper towels) using constant time delay. When the young adults selected the target photo of the correct step of the task analysis, a corresponding video was automatically played. All three young adults were able to correctly identify the sequence of steps in the task analysis using CBVI and generalize their respective skills to a natural office setting.

Allen et al. (2012) showed that a combination of technologies, settings, and strategies for teaching job skills can be effective. Researchers used a combination of video modeling and audio cueing ("bug in ear") to teach targeted job skills. Three young adults with ASD and moderate intellectual disability gained competitive employment as WalkaRound ® characters for retail promotions. WalkaRounds are good jobs for individuals with disabilities because an attendant is always recommended to accompany them, the bug in ear cannot be seen due to the costume, and the pay is competitive ($15-$20 an hour). First, a standard training video provided by the employer was used which demonstrated required actions in scripted and natural settings. Next, audio cueing using a Radio Shack TRC-508 s FM transceiver with a microphone and earphones training took place in a warehouse. Finally, job probes took place at a local discount retail store for retail product promotion. Here, the attendant gave audio cues for the targeted job skills – head actions such as nodding, arm/hand actions such as waving, and leg/torso actions such as jumping. The standard training video alone did not produce multiple skill use; however, when audio cueing was introduced, rates of multiple skill use increased for all participants. The efficacy of audio cueing was related to the frequency the prompts were delivered.

In summary, this research provides examples of how technology can be used in the area of daily living skill instruction for individuals with ASD and/or moderate intellectual disability as a means to provide visual supports both during simulated instruction and in vivo instruction. With the majority of daily living skills consisting of chained tasks, technology has been used to display or teach steps of a task analysis for the activity. Simulated instruction has used technology to provide picture or video supports in the form of custom or commercial programs followed by in vivo practice, either of carrying out the task in the classroom environment (Ayers & Cihak, 2010) or in the community (Mechling & O'Brien, 2010). In vivo instruction has used visual supports as a prompting system, such as to navigate a college campus (Kelly et al., 2010) or withdraw money from an ATM (Scott et al., 2013). Both commercial products, custom products, and a combination have been found to be effective. Although there are more studies using technology for daily living skills than for academics, additional research is still needed to demonstrate the generalizability of these findings across more participants. Also, it is important to note that most of these studies included some measure of the students' generalization of the simulated instruction to real life contexts. In both future research and practice, it is critical to measure that generalization occurs from technology to real life applications.

## Technology to Enhance Social and Communication Skills

Students with moderate and severe disabilities often have underdeveloped social and communication skills and also may exhibit challenging behavior related to these deficits. For example, a student who has no means to communicate the need for a change in an activity may use yelling or hitting to create an escape. Students with underdeveloped communication repertoires may lack age appropriate ways to interact with peers, request assistance, or convey information.

Technology can provide a platform for students to acquire and practice these critical skills. Hetzroni and Tanous (2004) enhanced the communication functions of five children with ASD in a natural classroom setting using the software program "I Can Word It Too" (available in English, Arabic, and Hebrew). In the software, three settings with various scenarios were presented to the child (play, food, and hygiene) with opportunities for question asking and answering. For example, in the play condition a voice would ask, "What would you like to play?" and the child could select an activity, such as ball with dad or rocking on a horse, which would activate an animation of the activity. Within the activity, the child could initiate requests as well as answer questions. All children decreased sentences with delayed echolalia, increased relevant speech, and generalized the new skills to their general education classroom setting.

Whalen et al. (2006) evaluated the effectiveness of TeachTown Basics, an applied behavior analysis based program for preschoolers with developmental delays that teaches receptive language, social understanding, self-help, attention, memory, auditory processing, and early academic skills. Four children with autism and four with developmental delays used TeachTown Basics for 15 min three days per week in their home for eight weeks. The children acquired receptive language, social, and cognitive skills. They also increased their spontaneous commenting, looking at the parent, and positive affect, while on the computer and decreased rates of inappropriate behavior.

Software programs can be used to teach higher-level social skills as well. Beaumont and Sofronoff (2008) implemented a seven-week program called the Junior Detective Training Program to teach skills in emotion recognition, regulation, and social interaction. Small group therapy was used to generalize the computer game content. Twenty-six participants with autism in the Junior Detective program demonstrated greater improvements in social skills according to parent and teacher reports and were able to suggest more appropriate emotion management strategies for story characters than the participants with autism in the control group ($n = 23$). Their treatment gains were maintained at five months post intervention and generalized to the home environment. Although intensive in the staff contact hours and time spent in the computer program required, the short duration needed for participants to show benefits provided overall cost effectiveness.

In addition to software programs, video models have been used to teach appropriate social and communication skills. Avcioglu (2013) used video modeling to teach four, 10 to 11 year old children in Greece with intellectual disability to greet familiar persons appropriately. Components of the target skill included becoming aware of a familiar person nearby, approaching the familiar person, looking at the person's face, and saying words like "Good Morning/Hello/Hi", and waiting for an answer from the familiar person. Both the teachers and mothers of the participants rated the social validity of the intervention highly, commenting that the children immediately practiced this skill at home, school, and in the community.

Social stories are another intervention often used with individuals with disabilities to present social information to increase the appropriateness and effectiveness of their responses. The social story describes how an individual engages in a skill the student needs to acquire in a narrative format. Social stories have been successfully used to teach social skills related to both positive and negative social behaviors (Walton & Ingersoll, 2013). Social stories presented using technology have been shown not only to be effective, but a preferred method by children with autism. For example, Mancil, Haydon, and Whitby (2009)

evaluated the differential effects of the presentation of paper or technology-based social stories on the inappropriate behaviors of three children with autism who pushed other students during transitions to lunch and during recess. A social story consisting of seven sentences was developed and put in both paper format and PowerPoint, with both formats having the same text and pictures. However, the computer-assisted social skills training (CASST) was made interactive by the pushing of the space bar causing the text to change colors. The students read the story each day before the transition to lunch. There was a reduction in frequency of pushing for all students with both formats, but the CASST format led to slightly better results. The students were able to generalize the skill learned for one environment (transition to lunch) to a non-taught environment (recess). Teacher reports indicated that the PowerPoint format was feasible for their classroom. Additionally, all students reported they preferred the CASST format to paper.

Social stories also have been used to improve the communication and social skills of individuals with severe disabilities in order to influence their self-determined behavior. For example, Richter and Test (2011) used multimedia social stories to increase the knowledge of adult outcomes and opportunities of three transition-age students with moderate intellectual disability. Researchers created six multimedia social stories about adult outcomes, residential opportunities, educational opportunities, and recreational opportunities. Writing with Symbols was used to place picture symbols above the text in the stories, which were presented using PowerPoint. All students increased their knowledge of adult outcomes and opportunities. In addition, individuals showed generalization of knowledge in a preference assessment where they indicated which adult outcome area they would like to explore with a supporting reason. Generalization was further demonstrated by participation at the individuals' transition planning meetings.

The increase in use of the Internet in society for communication and socializing through platforms such as Facebook ™ and Twitter ™ has also increased opportunities for individuals with developmental disabilities to expand social networks and opportunities for instruction. Avatars can enhance social interaction through the creation of three-dimensional physical representations of an online persona or character that can be personalized in any way to depict fantasy or reality. Avatars interact in virtual worlds like Second Life ® through socializing in settings such as virtual bars or cafes, speaking on specific topics in classes or workshops, or conducting business in virtual stores or market places (Stendal, Balandin, & Molka-Danielson, 2011). The ability to customize the appearance and persona of an Avatar also allows individuals to take on roles or abilities not available to them in real life. For individuals with disabilities, they have the option to adopt an Avatar with the same disability, or not (Stendal et al., 2011). Virtual worlds such as Second Life ® also provide opportunities for individuals with disabilities to socialize with others who share their disability. Stendal et al. (2011) reported an island on Second Life ® that was only for individuals with ASD and a nightclub called "Wheelies" for individuals who use wheelchairs. Research is needed to demonstrate how students with developmental disabilities respond to these websites.

Virtual worlds also may offer the opportunity to provide social skills training in a simulated environment. Parsons, Leonard, and Mitchell (2006) conducted social skills training with two adolescent boys with ASD within two specifically designed virtual environments. A café environment had four levels of difficulty that went from a quiet scene with empty tables to choose from to a busy café with a long line and the requirement to ask someone if they could sit down with them. The target behaviors were to get in line, find a place to sit, and ask appropriate questions. The bus environment had five levels of difficulty – from no line for the bus with empty scenes, to a long

line with a busy noisy bus that had no empty seats, requiring them to ask someone to move bags or stand in the aisle. Although there continued to be signs of repetitive behaviors and literal interpretations of the scenes, the participants found the exercise to be meaningful and enjoyed discussing appropriate social responses with a facilitator who was sitting with them. They reported enjoying using the virtual environment and were able to give specific examples of how this could be helpful to them in the real world. One participant shared how he had generalized skills learned in the virtual environment (asking someone to move their bags and asking if a seat was available) to a train and subway over his summer break.

In summary, technology presents unique advantages for promoting communication and social skills. Research indicates promise for technology to teach social and communication skills without inhibiting spontaneous language or social interaction (Whalen et al., 2006). In addition, individuals with disabilities are able to generalize skills to natural settings, such as transition meetings (Richter & Test, 2011), their homes and communities (Avcioglu, 2013), and classrooms (Hetzroni & Tannous, 2004). More research is needed demonstrating that students can both acquire and generalize these critical social skills.

Technology allows for instructors to customize programs to the needs and interests of individuals with disabilities. This can increase the motivation of individuals with disabilities to engage in the task, increasing the rate of learning, and also target specific skill deficits of the individual. This tailoring of instructional targets and delivery methods is especially crucial in social and communication skills where levels of functioning and understanding can vary wildly. Simulated instruction presented through CBVI or virtual instruction also reduces risks sometimes involved in social skills instruction. The risk of embarrassment or uncontrollable contingencies is removed in a virtual environment and the instructor has control over the level of difficulty, allowing the individual with a disability to master skills of increasing difficulty with the opportunity to ask questions and receive redirection.

## RECOMMENDATIONS FOR USING TECHNOLOGY WITH STUDENTS WITH MODERATE AND SEVERE DEVELOPMENTAL DISABILITIES

From the examples provided in the research review, several recommendations can be offered for using technology for students with moderate and severe developmental disabilities. First and foremost, the use of technology must incorporate effective instructional techniques for this population. Nearly all of the studies used applied principles of systematic instruction, including prompting in the use of the technology with feedback until the student mastered its use. Second, if the technology is to be used in real life settings, the intervention must include training for this generalization. Ramdoss et al. (2011) recommended stimuli and consequences within instruction resemble those of natural settings, such as the reactions of strangers to inappropriate behaviors (Parsons et al., 2006). These may also include models using peers typical of the students' setting, simulations of activities or problems (e.g., emergencies), and videos of real contexts (e.g., community). Instruction also should teach multiple appropriate responses to give students a wide repertoire of skills, such as several greeting phrases (Avcioglu, 2013). Third, technology may need to be adapted to the individual learner's needs. For example, the student may need pictorial instructions in the form of screen shots of the steps to access a website. Or the student may need adapted switches or keyboards that simplify motor response demands. Most importantly, students need access to technology to gain the benefits described. In the following sections, specific recommendations are provided for how students can use four specific technology

applications: (a) computer-based video instruction, (b) internet access, (d) electronic text, and (d) portable devices.

## Use Computer-Based Video Instruction

CAI interventions that embed actual videos within the intervention are referred to as computer-based video instruction (CBVI). CBVI uses the evidence-based practice of video modeling (VM) within the computer program to explicitly demonstrate and teach targeted skills (Bellini & Akullian, 2007). VM has been shown to be an effective medium for making positive behavior changes in individuals with ASD, and it has been shown to result in rapid skill acquisition, maintenance of skills over time, and generalization of skills (Bellini & Akullian, 2007). Many researchers believe that CBVI and VM are effective because they pair learning a new targeted skill or behavior with the highly preferred activity of watching videos (Bellini & Akullian, 2007; Delano, 2007; McCoy & Hermansen, 2007; Shukla-Mehta, Miller, & Callahan, 2010). CBVI and VM also provide learners with the opportunity to acquire skills through social models, but without the face-to-face interaction which may cause increased anxiety in some individuals with ASD (Sherer et al., 2001). Finally, CBVI and VM have the ability to reduce attention to irrelevant stimuli, to focus on the most pertinent aspects of the behavior being modeled, and to reduce the amount of verbal language to essential language only (Bellini & Akullian, 2007; Delano, 2007; McCoy & Hermansen, 2007; Sherer et al., 2001; Shukla-Mehta et al., 2010).

The first step is to determine the skills for which the CBVI will be used and to make the videos that create the context for learning and practicing the skill. The video should include the common physical stimuli and/or social context. For example, if a social skill for a young teen, some contexts may be the bus, a ballgame, and the lunch room with other teens present. It will be important to have multiple videos to help students sample the range of contexts in which the skill may be needed. The video also should demonstrate the natural consequences for engaging or not engaging in the behavior using a model that will gain the student's attention. Then a software platform is selected for displaying the videos and additional instructions. For example, Mechling, Gast, & Langone (2002) used a multimedia program, with digital photographs and videotapes imported into Hyperstudio 3.1 (Roger Wagner Publishing, Inc.), to teach vocabulary acquisition of words found on grocery store aisle signs to four students with moderate intellectual disability, one of whom had autism. All students generalized the learned skills to three different grocery stores to find the location of grocery items. In contrast, Kinney et al. (2003) used Microsoft PowerPoint® with embedded video models and video rewards to teach generative spelling to one student with autism. Not only was this student able to learn to spell 55 new words, but she was also able to generalize to novel words with similar beginning consonants and word endings that had been used in the matrix training.

## Teach Students to Access the Internet

One of the most important skills in the 21st century is to be able to access the internet to gain or share information, perform job tasks, and socialize. Zisimopoulos, Sigafoos, and Koutromanos (2011) demonstrated how three elementary age students with moderate intellectual disability could learn to access the internet to download pictures related to a class History project. The researchers developed a task analysis of 29 steps for accessing the Internet and downloading photos. Videos were created for each step of the task analysis using point of view modeling. The interventionist then used systematic prompting, specifically time delay and a video model, to prompt students to perform each step of the task analysis. During the 0s delay round

of intervention, students watched the video clip and then imitated the model to perform the step of the task analysis. During the 5s delay round, students had the opportunity to perform the step independently but then used the video model if needed. All three students learned to independently access the Internet and download pictures, as well as generalize to a novel instructor, task direction, and setting.

In teaching internet use, the first step is to select the type of sites to be accessed. For example, internet sites that have specific utility to the student for doing school work, leisure pursuits, community access, or job functioning might be targeted. Once the website is specified, each exact step needed to access the site is recorded as a task analysis. The task analysis is then converted to some type of visual support. This might be screenshots of what appears on the computer during each step with the tab or key to be indicated (e.g., circled, highlighted). In contrast to online support that often provides this type of technical assistance, these screen shots may need to use greatly enhanced highlighting, or as demonstrated by Zisimoupolis et al. (2011), the student may actual need to see a video model of a person performing the step (e.g., moving the mouse to select the tab). Also as indicated in this study, this video should be taken from the point of view of the user (e.g., looking down at the hand on the mouse). Although one demonstration may be needed for how the technology-based intervention works, the student should then be able to access the website using the provided video or screen shot models.

## Use Electronic Text to Improve Comprehension

Advances in technology have increased the accessibility of text. While some individuals may just prefer to listen to books through Audible ™ out of convenience, or use the text-to-speech (TTS) feature on documents to assist with comprehension, removing the requirement of decoding makes those texts accessible for everyone. The advent of e-text is another technology that has expanded opportunities for interaction with text for individuals with disabilities who are not able to read independently. For school age students with disabilities, the availability of e-text also provides access to the general curriculum. While the use of listening comprehension through e-text should not entirely replace instruction in other aspects of reading, assistive technology will give greater access to the wide range of texts of same age peers (Edyburn, 2007). For example, Coyne, Pisha, Dalton, Zeph, and Smith (2012) used e-books for eight students with severe disabilities that included a digitized human voice with highlighting to read the text, hyperlinked glossary for vocabulary, videos and photo essays to build background knowledge, and story illustration enhancements. Knight et al. (2014) used a similar format to present science content with four middle schools students with ASD and intellectual disability.

Although e-text is a valued form of assistive technology, a series of studies reported by Douglas, Langone, Bell, and Meade (2009) found that individuals with moderate intellectual disabilities required more than just audio support (TTS) or audio support with visuals (text highlighting) to increase comprehension of texts. Increased visual supports such as videos, photographs, and pictures above key vocabulary words are other components that are needed to increase accessibility and comprehension. In addition, individuals with disabilities must be taught how to use these tools just like any other new strategy or support that is incorporated into instruction.

To create an e-text intervention, the first step is to select the literature or informational text. This text should be appropriate to the student's chronological age and assigned grade such as a novel or chapter from a textbook. Consideration then needs to be given to whether the complexity of the original text is appropriate to the student's level of understanding. If not, the text can be summarized using simplified language. For example, a novel might be summarized in short summaries for each chapter. Additional supports for understanding the material may be selected. These might include video clips to build background knowledge, which often can be gleaned from online resources related to the topic or novel. The text then can be presented using a variety of software formats that have a text-to-speech function. It should be noted that some internet sites like Discovery Learning already have electronic text available. If the text does not have to be adapted, many resources (e.g., textbooks) are already available in electronic text formats. To benefit from e-texts students with moderate and severe developmental disabilities will likely need some form of systematic instruction to learn to comprehend text. For example, if the student cannot answer a comprehension question, the teacher may highlight the key text with the answer to show the student how to locate or derive the answer.

## Promote Independence with Portable Electronic Devices (e.g., IPad)

The use of portable electronic devices to assist with daily tasks is a common practice. For example, keeping reminders on a smart phone, using a tablet to refer to a grocery list, or keeping track of daily tasks and schedules using a PDA are socially acceptable. The increasing accessibility of portable devices has benefited individuals with disabilities by providing assistive technology that is not stigmatizing and can be easily customized to their needs.

Personal digital assistants (PDAs) are useful devices for individuals with disabilities due to their capacity for customization, portability, and capacity for large amounts of data. Wireless connectivity and 3G mobile technologies add to the benefits of PDAs (Mechling, 2011). In a synthesis of the literature from 2000-2010 on the use of portable electronic devices by individuals with moderate intellectual disability and ASD, Mechling found PDAs were categorized as having (a) text, sound,

461

and light; (b) picture cueing with and without voice recording; and (c) video recordings. The purposes of the devices were identified as (a) reminders and tools for time management, (b) transition aids, and (c) prompts and models for completing multistep functional skills.

Expanded reviews of the literature have found portable devices to be effective across a variety of domains. Kagohara et al. (2013) conducted a systematic review of the literature on the use of iPods, iPads, and other devices, specifically investigating the skills that have been taught using these devices, the software applications used, and the overall effectiveness of their use. A total of 15 studies were published between 2008 and 2012. The majority of studies taught communication skills ($n=8$), with seven out of eight targeting requesting skills and one teaching participants to name items. The other studies focused on academics ($n=1$), employment ($n=2$), leisure ($n=3$), and transition skills ($n=1$). Overall the studies had positive results, indicating these devices are effective in delivering instruction or serving as assistive technology for individuals with disabilities.

Research has found that individuals with disabilities continue to have difficulty using some portable devices and require additional modifications and instruction. For example, Taber, Alberto, Seltzer, and Hughes (2003) taught six students with disabilities to use speed dial when they had trouble dialing numbers. When students with moderate intellectual disability continued to have difficulty using cell phones, Stock, Davies, Wehmeyer, and Palmer (2008) taught them to use a program on a PDA to make calls that provided a picture phone book. Mechling (2011) suggested with the advances in cell phone technology and prevalence of smart phones with video technology, these could be of use for individuals with disabilities, but at the time of her review there were no investigations into the application of this technology for this population.

In teaching students with moderate and severe developmental disabilities to use portable devices, it is important to select technology that matches the students' abilities. For example, voice command software has limited utility for individuals with articulation problems or who have limited speech. Once selected, there will be the need to provide systematic instruction in use of the device. In their review of PDA use with individuals with developmental disabilities, Limbrick and Stephenson (2013) found that the more successful and rigorous studies included behavioral instructional strategies along with the device. The video modeling described earlier provides one potential way to teach the student to use the device. For example, the video clips might demonstrate each step to make a phone call or upload a picture to a social media site.

## Technology-Enhanced Assessment

One of the important implications of the research on technology for students with moderate and severe developmental disabilities is that it can be used to assess what students know and can do. First, technology may make the content of the assessment item more accessible to the student. Projection of an assessment item on an interactive white board may make it more salient or visible. The use of a brief video application may anchor the question in a familiar context (e.g., activity of daily living like shopping) that would then make it possible for the student to generalize what he or she has learned to the assessment context. An electronic display can make it possible for the student to use text-to-speech functions if the student is not able to read the material presented.

Technology also can increase the students' options for responding in an assessment. A student may be able to indicate understanding by selecting a response on a tablet or computer touch screen through either a motoric response or adapted switch. Projecting response options on an interactive whiteboard can make it possible for other students to be able to indicate answers through gross motor responses (e.g., swiping an item down on the board using an arm movement) or indicate responses through holding an eye gaze on one section of the board. Technology also can make it possible to record responses so that teachers can be fully engaged in the instructional strategies and later access the data needed to make decisions about progress.

In addition, technology provides a unique way to assess preferences of students with moderate and severe developmental disabilities for future life options. For example, Morgan and Horrocks (2011) presented three young adults with web-based examples of jobs and then found a correspondence between the jobs selected during this assessment and their actual work performance. The high school students selected from an array of four icons that presented a 2-4 minute video clip of an employee performing the job. Each student was asked to touch the picture of the job he or she liked better. Mechling and Bishop (2011) illustrated how to assess students' preference for different types of technology in three students who had profound and multiple disabilities. Students showed a preference for technology-based formats when compared to nontechnology-based materials. Two showed some preference for projection of images on a large interactive whiteboard over a traditional computer screen. Similar comparisons might be used to discover the type of technology most amenable to students expressing learning in an academic context.

## FUTURE RESEARCH DIRECTIONS

There are several directions needed for future research in technology for students with moderate and severe developmental disabilities. One of the most important is to improve the overall quality of the research designs to strengthen their internal validity. The Knight et al. (2013) literature review illustrates this need for stronger designs. Knight et al. used the Horner et al. (2005) for determining evidence-based practices in single-case research and Gersten et al. (2005) criteria for group experimental/quasi-experimental designs. Only four of the 17 single case studies met acceptable quality according to Horner et al.'s (2005) criteria (i.e., Hetzroni, Rubin, & Konkol, 2002; Hetzroni & Shalem, 2005; Mechling et al. 2002; Pennington, Stenoff, Gibson, & Ballou, 2012) and no group design studies were of acceptable or high quality. Future studies need to give careful consideration to these criteria, for example, by using comparison groups and random assignment in group designs. In single case design, experimental control is demonstrated through having three or more demonstrations of effects across participants or skills. In both cases, interventions need to be powerful enough to show strong effect sizes (group) or clear data patterns (single case). Data also need to be collected on the dosage and fidelity of the intervention.

Besides improving the quality of the experimental designs used in technology research, this research needs to be updated to include the most current and popular technology applications. In their review of PDAs, Stephenson and Limbrick (2013) focused on what devices were used for what purposes, the success of the device, how people were taught to use the device, and the level of evidence produced by the studies. More studies were conducted using the iPod Touch than other devices, although iPad publications were seeing an increasing trend. No research used any gaming software applications which are popular among children and teenagers. Mechling (2011) also noted the need for updated research in cell phone technology given the prevalence of smart phones with video technology.

A third recommendation for future research is to include a precise description of the methodology used to teach the use of the technology. Stephenson and Limbrick (2013) found the most successful interventions included precise behavioral strategies for implementation of the technology use in their review of PDAs. Systematic instruction, which incorporates behavioral strategies, has a strong evidence-base for use in teaching new skills to students with moderate and severe disabilities (Spooner et al., 2013).

A fourth recommendation is for all research that incorporates technology to report information for a cost-benefit analysis. Some interventions described in the literature required hundreds of hours for the researchers to create or adapt the needed software. If it is not commercially available for future use, the feasibility of replication is minimal. Some interventions rely on technology that may require an initial investment but produce gains that suggest the ongoing benefits justify the initial costs.

Finally, future research is needed that evaluates how technology transforms the overall school achievement for this population of students. Currently, there is inconsistency among schools in the extent to which technology is incorporated in instruction. In some classrooms for students with moderate and severe developmental disabilities, teachers are working with interactive whiteboards, portable tablets, and computers throughout their lessons. In others, a computer might only be used for keeping students occupied during free time. Research is needed to compare how the amount of access influences students' academic, daily living, and social/communicative performance.

## CONCLUSION

For enhanced quality of life in the 21st century and to be able to fully access the curriculum on today's schools, students with moderate and severe developmental disabilities need to gain technology competence. Gaining this competence will require access, adaptations, and systematic instruction.

For access, schools need to consider what technology students will need both for academic learning in school and for future functioning as an adult. This technology will likely continue to evolve rapidly requiring updating for all students, including those with disabilities. The numerous studies and reviews included in this chapter provide a strong foundation of support for the benefits of providing this access. Once procured, teachers may need some professional development in both how to use the technology and incorporate it into instruction.

In considering adaptations, students with moderate and severe developmental disabilities present unique and divergent needs. Some students might be able to access any text in an electronic format for their age level. Others will need to have this text simplified for understanding. Some students might be able to learn to access a website with one or two demonstrations. Others will need an ongoing visual referent like a series of screen shots. Some also may need video modeling of each step. Likewise, some students will be able to generalize daily living or social skills from a few exposures to realistic video models. Others will need extensive practice making the responses shown in the videos before they can apply them in real life. Teachers will need to consider how students acquire other skills and apply similar levels of adaptations to instruction in the use of technology.

For instruction, most students with moderate and severe developmental disabilities will need systematic prompting and feedback to acquire a new skill like using a new cell phone or locating information on a website. In some cases, the technology itself may be able to provide this systematic instruction. For example, video models embedded in PowerPoint may show the student how to locate an application on a cell phone. In contrast, other situations may require teacher-delivered prompting and feedback like a teacher instructing the student how to comprehend an electronic text passage or perform the steps in a math software program.

In summary, technology has the potential to be a powerful form of support for students with moderate and severe developmental disabilities to learn and self-direct their lives. To achieve this benefit begins with having high expectations for this population of students and providing equitable access to technology resources. With this supportive context, teachers can then use research-based strategies to optimize students' skill in technology use.

# REFERENCES

Ahlgrim-Delzell, L., Browder, D. M., & Wood, L. (2014). Effects of systematic instruction and an augmentative communication device on phonics skills acquisition for students with moderate intellectual disability who are nonverbal. *Education and Training in Autism and Developmental Disabilities*, *49*, 517–532.

Allen, K. D., Burke, R. V., Howard, M. R., Wallace, D. P., & Bowen, S. L. (2012). Use of audio cuing to expand employment opportunities for adolescents with autism spectrum disorders and intellectual disabilities. *Journal of Autism and Developmental Disorders*, *42*(11), 2410–2419. doi:10.1007/s10803-012-1519-7 PMID:22456818

Ault, M. J., Wolery, M., Doyle, P. M., & Gast, D. L. (1989). Review of comparative studies in the instruction of students with moderate and severe handicaps. *Exceptional Children*, *55*, 346–356. PMID:2521602

Avcioglu, H. (2013). Effectiveness of video modeling in training students with intellectual disabilities to greet people when they meet. *Educational Sciences: Theory and Practice*, *13*, 466–477.

Ayres, K., & Cihak, D. (2010). Computer- and video-based instruction of food-preparation skills: Acquisition, generalization, and maintenance. *Intellectual and Developmental Disabilities*, *48*(3), 195–208. doi:10.1352/1944-7558-48.3.195 PMID:20597730

Ayres, K. M., Langone, J., Boon, R. T., & Norman, A. (2006). Computer-based instruction for purchasing skills. *Education and Training in Developmental Disabilities*, *41*, 253–263.

Babbitt, B. C., & Miller, S. P. (1996). Using hypermedia to improve the mathematics problem-solving skills of students with learning disabilities. *Journal of Learning Disabilities*, *29*(4), 391–401. doi:10.1177/002221949602900407 PMID:8763554

Beaumont, R., & Sofronoff, K. (2008). A multicomponent social skills intervention for children with Asperger syndrome: The Junior Detective Training Program. *Journal of Child Psychology and Psychiatry, and Allied Disciplines*, *49*(7), 743–753. doi:10.1111/j.1469-7610.2008.01920.x PMID:18503531

Bellini, S., & Akullian, J. (2007). A meta-analysis of video modeling and video self-modeling interventions for children and adolescents with autism spectrum disorders. *Exceptional Children*, *73*(3), 264–287. doi:10.1177/001440290707300301

Blischak, D. M., & Schlosser, R. W. (2003). Use of technology to support independent spelling by students with autism. *Topics in Language Disorders*, *23*(4), 293–304. doi:10.1097/00011363-200310000-00005

Browder, D., Ahlgrim-Delzell, L., Spooner, F., Mims, P. J., & Baker, J. N. (2009). Using time delay to teach literacy to students with severe developmental disabilities. *Exceptional Children*, *75*, 343–364.

Browder, D., Flowers, C., Ahlgrim-Delzell, L., Karvonen, M., Spooner, F., & Algozzine, R. (2004). The alignment of alternate assessment content with academic and functional curricula. *The Journal of Special Education*, *37*(4), 211–223. doi:10.1177/00224669040370040101

Coleman-Martin, M. B., Heller, K. W., Cihak, D. F., & Irvine, K. L. (2005). Using computer-assisted instruction and the nonverbal reading approach to teach word identification. *Focus on Autism and Other Developmental Disabilities, 20*(2), 80–90. doi:10.1177/10883576050200020401

Coyne, P., Pisha, B., Dalton, B., Zeph, L. A., & Smith, N. C. (2012). Literacy by design: A universal design for learning approach for students with significant intellectual disabilities. *Remedial and Special Education, 33*(3), 162–172. doi:10.1177/0741932510381651

Delano, M. E. (2007). Improving written language performance of adolescents with Asperger syndrome. *Journal of Applied Behavior Analysis, 40*(2), 345–351. doi:10.1901/jaba.2007.50-06 PMID:17624076

Denny, M., Marchand-Martella, N., Martella, R. C., Reilly, J. R., Reilly, J. F., & Cleanthous, C. C. (2000). Using parent-delivered graduated guidance to teach functional living skills to a child with Cri du Chat Syndrome. *Education & Treatment of Children, 23*, 441–454.

Douglas, K. H., Ayres, K. M., Langone, J., Bell, V., & Meade, C. (2009). Expanding literacy for learners with intellectual disabilities: The role of supported eText. *Journal of Special Education Technology, 24*, 35–44.

Edyburn, D. L. (2007). Technology-enhanced reading performance: Defining a reading agenda. *Reading Research Quarterly, 42*(1), 136–141. doi:10.1598/RRQ.42.1.7

Edyburn, D. L. (2013). Critical issues in advancing the special education technology evidence base. *Exceptional Children, 80*, 7–24.

Gast, D. L. (2010). *Single subject research methodology in behavioral sciences*. New York, NY: Routledge Publishing Co.

Gersten, R., Fuchs, L. S., Compton, D., Coyne, M., Greenwood, C., & Innocenti, M. S. (2005). Quality indicators for group experimental and quasi-experimental research in special education. *Exceptional Children, 71*(2), 149–164. doi:10.1177/001440290507100202

Goh, A. E., & Bambara, L. M. (2013). Video self-modeling: A job skills intervention with individuals with intellectual disability in employment settings. *Education and Training in Autism and Developmental Disabilities, 48*, 103–119.

Handleman, J. S. (1986). Severe developmental disabilities: Defining the term. *Education & Treatment of Children, 9*, 153–167.

Hetzroni, O., Rubin, C., & Konkol, O. (2002). The use of assistive technology for symbol identification by children with Rett syndrome. *Journal of Intellectual & Developmental Disability, 27*(1), 57–71. doi:10.1080/13668250120119626-1

Hetzroni, O. E., & Shalem, U. (2005). From logos to orthographic symbols: A multilevel fading computer program for teaching nonverbal children with autism. *Focus on Autism and Other Developmental Disabilities, 20*(4), 201–212. doi:10.1177/10883576050200040201

Hetzroni, O. E., & Tannous, J. (2004). Effects of a computer-based intervention program on the communicative functions of children with autism. *Journal of Autism and Developmental Disorders, 34*(2), 95–113. doi:10.1023/B:JADD.0000022602.40506.bf PMID:15162930

Hitchcock, C. H., & Noonan, M. J. (2000). Computer-assisted instruction of early academic skills. *Topics in Early Childhood Special Education, 20*(3), 145–158. doi:10.1177/027112140002000303

Horner, R. H., Carr, E. G., Halle, J., McGee, G., Odom, S., & Wolery, M. (2005). The use of single-subject research to identify evidence-based practice in special education. *Exceptional Children, 71*(2), 165–179. doi:10.1177/001440290507100203

Jimenez, B. A., Browder, D. M., & Courtade, G. R. (2008). Teaching an algebraic equation to high school students with moderate developmental disabilities. *Education and Training in Developmental Disabilities, 43,* 266–274.

Kagohara, D. M., van der Meer, L., Ramdoss, S., O'Reilly, M. F., Lancioni, G. E., Davis, T. N., ... Sigafoos, J. (2013). Using iPods and iPads in teaching programs for individuals with developmental disabilities: A systematic review. *Research in Developmental Disabilities: A Multidisciplinary Journal, 34,* 147-156

Kelley, K. R., Test, D. W., & Cooke, N. L. (2013). Effects of picture prompts delivered by a video iPod on pedestrian navigation. *Exceptional Children, 79,* 459–474.

Ketterlin-Geller, L. R., & Tindal, G. (2007). Embedded technology: Current and future practices for increasing accessibility for all students. *Journal of Special Education Technology, 22,* 1–15.

Kleinert, J. O., Kearns, J. F., & Kleinert, H. L. (2010). *Students in the AA-AAS and the importance of communicative competence. Alternate assessment for students with significant cognitive disabilities: An educator's guide.* Baltimore, MD: Brookes.

Knight, V., McKissick, B. R., & Saunders, A. (2013). A review of technology-based interventions to teach academic skills to students with autism spectrum disorder. *Journal of Autism and Developmental Disorders, 43*(11), 2628–2648. doi:10.1007/s10803-013-1814-y PMID:23543292

Knight, V., Wood, C., Spooner, F., Browder, D., & O'Brien, C. (2014). An Exploratory Study Using Science eTexts with Students with Autism Spectrum Disorder. *Focus on Autism and Other Developmental Disabilities.* doi:10.1177/1088357614559214

Kodak, T., Fisher, W. W., Clements, A., & Bouxsein, K. J. (2011). Effects of computer-assisted instruction on correct responding and procedural integrity during early intensive behavioral intervention. *Research in Autism Spectrum Disorders, 5*(1), 640–647. doi:10.1016/j.rasd.2010.07.011

Langone, J., Clees, T. J., Rieber, L., & Matzko, M. (2003). The future of computer-based interactive technology for teaching individuals with moderate to severe disabilities: Issues relating to research and practice. *Journal of Special Education Technology, 18,* 5–16.

Langone, J., Shade, J., Clees, T. J., & Day, T. (1999). Effects of multimedia instruction on teaching functional discrimination skills to students with moderate/severe intellectual disabilities. *International Journal of Disability Development and Education, 46*(4), 493–513. doi:10.1080/103491299100470

Lasater, M. W., & Brady, M. P. (1995). Effects of video self-modeling and feedback on task fluency: A home-based intervention. *Education & Treatment of Children, 18,* 389–407.

Mancil, G. R., Haydon, T., & Whitby, P. (2009). Differentiated effects of paper and computer-assisted social stories™ on inappropriate behavior in children with autism. *Focus on Autism and Other Developmental Disabilities, 24*(4), 205–215. doi:10.1177/1088357609347324

McCoy, K., & Hermansen, E. (2007). Video modeling for individuals with autism: A review of model types and effects. *Education & Treatment of Children, 30*(4), 183–213. doi:10.1353/etc.2007.0029

McGraw-Hunter, M., Faw, G. D., & Davis, P. K. (2006). The use of video self-modelling and feedback to teach cooking skills to individuals with traumatic brain injury: A pilot study. *Brain Injury: [BI], 20*(10), 1061–1068. doi:10.1080/02699050600912163 PMID:17060139

Mechling, L., & O'Brien, E. (2010). Computer-based video instruction to teach students with intellectual disabilities to use public bus transportation. *Education and Training in Autism and Developmental Disabilities, 45*, 230–241.

Mechling, L. C. (2011). Review of twenty-first century portable electronic devices for persons with moderate intellectual disabilities and autism spectrum disorders. *Education and Training in Autism and Developmental Disabilities, 46*, 479–498.

Mechling, L. C., & Bishop, V. A. (2011). Assessment of computer-based preferences of students with profound multiple disabilities. *The Journal of Special Education, 45*(1), 15–27. doi:10.1177/0022466909348661

Mechling, L. C., Gast, D. L., & Fields, E. A. (2008). Evaluation of a portable DVD player and system of least prompts to self-prompt cooking task completion by young adults with moderate intellectual disabilities. *The Journal of Special Education, 42*(3), 179–190. doi:10.1177/0022466907313348

Mechling, L. C., Gast, D. L., & Gustafson, M. R. (2009). Use of video modeling to teach extinguishing of cooking related fires to individuals with moderate intellectual disabilities. *Education and Training in Developmental Disabilities, 44*, 67–79.

Mechling, L. C., Gast, D. L., & Langone, J. (2002). Computer-based video instruction to teach persons with moderate intellectual disabilities to read grocery aisle signs and locate items. *The Journal of Special Education, 35*(4), 224–240. doi:10.1177/002246690203500404

Mechling, L. C., Gast, D. L., & Seid, N. H. (2010). Evaluation of a personal digital assistant as a self-prompting device for increasing multi-step task completion by students with moderate intellectual disabilities. *Education and Training in Autism and Developmental Disabilities, 45*, 422–439.

Mechling, L. C., & Hunnicutt, J. R. (2011). Computer-based video self-modeling to teach receptive understanding of prepositions by students with intellectual disabilities. *Education and Training in Autism and Developmental Disabilities, 46*, 369–385.

Mechling, L. C., & Ortega-Hurndon, F. (2007). Computer-based video instruction to teach young adults with moderate intellectual disabilities to perform multiple step, job tasks in a generalized setting. *Education and Training in Mental Retardation and Developmental Disabilities, 42*, 24–37.

Mims, P. J., Hudson, M. E., & Browder, D. M. (2012). Using read-alouds of grade-level biographies and systematic prompting to promote comprehension for students with moderate and severe developmental disabilities. *Focus on Autism and Other Developmental Disabilities, 27*(2), 67–80. doi:10.1177/1088357612446859

Moore, M., & Calvert, S. (2000). Brief report: Vocabulary acquisition for children with autism: Teacher or computer instruction. *Journal of Autism and Developmental Disorders, 30*(4), 359–362. doi:10.1023/A:1005535602064 PMID:11039862

Morgan, R. L., & Horrocks, E. L. (2011). Correspondence between video-based preference assessment and subsequent community job performance. *Education and Training in Autism and Developmental Disabilities, 46*, 52–61.

National Center on Educational Statistics. (2008). *Computer and internet use by children and adolescents in 2008*. Washington, DC: U.S. Department of Education.

Odom, S. L., Collet-Klingenberg, L., Rogers, S. J., & Hatton, D. D. (2010). Evidence-based practices in interventions for children and youth with Autism Spectrum Disorders. *Preventing School Failure, 54*(4), 275–282. doi:10.1080/10459881003785506

Parsons, S., Leonard, A., & Mitchell, P. (2006). Virtual environments for social skills training: Comments from two adolescents with autistic spectrum disorder. *Computers & Education, 47*(2), 186–206. doi:10.1016/j.compedu.2004.10.003

Pennington, R. C. (2010). Computer-assisted instruction for teaching academic skills to students with autism spectrum disorders: A review of literature. *Focus on Autism and Other Developmental Disabilities, 25*(4), 239–248. doi:10.1177/1088357610378291

Pennington, R. C., Stenhoff, D. M., Gibson, J., & Ballou, K. (2012). Using simultaneous prompting to teach computer-based story writing to a student with autism. *Education & Treatment of Children, 35*(3), 389–406. doi:10.1353/etc.2012.0022

Polychronis, S. C., McDonnell, J., Johnson, J. W., Riesen, T., & Jameson, M. (2004). A comparison of two trial distribution schedules in embedded instruction. *Focus on Autism and Other Developmental Disabilities, 19*(3), 140–151. doi:10.1177/10883576040190030201

Ramdoss, S., Lang, R., Mulloy, A., Franco, J., O'Reilly, M., Didden, R., & Lancioni, G. (2011). Use of computer-based interventions to teach communication skills to children with autism spectrum disorders: A systematic review. *Journal of Behavioral Education, 20*(1), 55–76. doi:10.1007/s10864-010-9112-7

Reese, G. M., & Snell, M. E. (1991). Putting on and removing coats and jackets: The acquisition and maintenance of skills by children with severe multiple disabilities. *Education and Training in Mental Retardation, 26*, 398–410.

Richter, S., & Test, D. (2011). Effects of multimedia social stories on knowledge of adult outcomes and opportunities among transition-aged youth with significant cognitive disabilities. *Education and Training In Autism and Developmental Disabilities, 46*, 410–424.

Schalock, R. L., Borthwick-Duffy, S. A., Bradley, V. J., Buntinx, W. E., Coulter, D. L., Craig, E. M., & Yeager, M. H. et al. (2010). *Intellectual disability: definition, classification, and systems of supports* (11th ed.). Washington, DC: American Association On Intellectual And Developmental Disabilities.

Scott, R., Collins, B., Knight, V., & Kleinert, H. (2013). Teaching adults with moderate intellectual disability ATM use via the iPod. *Education and Training in Autism and Developmental Disabilities, 48*, 190–199.

Seo, Y. J., & Bryant, D. P. (2009). Analysis of studies of the effects of computer-assisted instruction on the mathematics performance of students with learning disabilities. *Computers & Education, 53*(3), 913–928. doi:10.1016/j.compedu.2009.05.002

Shane, H. C., & Albert, P. D. (2008). Electronic screen media for persons with autism spectrum disorders: Results of a survey. *Journal of Autism and Developmental Disorders, 38*(8), 1499–1508. doi:10.1007/s10803-007-0527-5 PMID:18293074

Shukla-Mehta, S., Miller, T., & Callahan, K. J. (2010). Evaluating the effectiveness of video instruction on social and communication skills training for children with autism spectrum disorders: A review of the literature. *Focus on Autism and Other Developmental Disabilities, 25*(1), 23–36. doi:10.1177/1088357609352901

Skinner, B. F. (1954). The science of learning and the art of teaching. *Harvard Educational Review, 24*, 86–97.

Smith, B. R., Spooner, F., & Wood, C. L. (2013). Using embedded computer-assisted explicit instruction to teach science to students with autism spectrum disorder. *Research in Autism Spectrum Disorders, 7*(3), 433–443. doi:10.1016/j.rasd.2012.10.010

Spooner, F., Knight, V. F., Browder, D. M., & Smith, B. R. (2012). Evidence-based practices for teaching academics to students with severe developmental disabilities. *Remedial and Special Education, 33*(6), 374–387. doi:10.1177/0741932511421634

Standen, P. J., & Brown, D. J. (2005). Virtual reality in the rehabilitation of people with intellectual disabilities [Review]. *Cyberpsychology & Behavior, 8*(3), 272–282. doi:10.1089/cpb.2005.8.272 PMID:15971976

Stendal, K., Balandin, S., & Molka-Danielsen, J. (2011). Virtual worlds: A new opportunity for people with lifelong disability? *Journal of Intellectual & Developmental Disability, 36*(1), 80–83. doi:10.3109/13668250.2011.526597 PMID:21070118

Stephenson, J., & Limbrick, L. (2013). A review of the use of touch-screen mobile devices by people with developmental disabilities. *Journal of Autism and Developmental Disorders*, 1–15. PMID:23888356

Stock, S. E., Davies, D. K., & Wehmeyer, M. L. (2004). Internet-based multimedia tests and surveys for individuals with intellectual disabilities. *Journal of Special Education Technology, 19*, 43–48.

Stock, S. E., Davies, D. K., Wehmeyer, M. L., & Palmer, S. B. (2008). Evaluation of cognitively accessible software to increase independent access to cellphone technology for people with intellectual disability. *Journal of Intellectual Disability Research, 52*(12), 1155–1164. doi:10.1111/j.1365-2788.2008.01099.x PMID:18647214

Taber, T. A., Alberto, P. A., Seltzer, A., & Hughes, M. (2003). Obtaining assistance when lost in the community using cell phones. *Research and Practice for Persons with Severe Disabilities, 28*(3), 105–116. doi:10.2511/rpsd.28.3.105

Towles-Reeves, E., Kearns, J., Kleinert, H., & Kleinert, J. (2009). An analysis of the learning characteristics of students taking alternate assessments based on alternate achievement standards. *The Journal of Special Education, 42*(4), 241–254. doi:10.1177/0022466907313451

U.S. Department of Education. (2003, December 9). *Improving the academic achievement of the disadvantaged: Final rule*, 68 Fed. Reg. 236.

Van Laarhoven, T., Johnson, J. W., Van Laarhoven-Myers, T., Grider, K. L., & Grider, K. M. (2009). The effectiveness of using a video iPod as a prompting device in employment settings. *Journal of Behavioral Education, 18*(2), 119–141. doi:10.1007/s10864-009-9077-6

Walton, K. M., & Ingersoll, B. R. (2013). Improving social skills in adolescents and adults with autism and severe to profound intellectual disability: A review of the literature. *Journal of Autism and Developmental Disorders, 43*(3), 594–615. doi:10.1007/s10803-012-1601-1 PMID:22790427

Wehmeyer, M. L. (2014). Framing for the future: Self-determination. *Remedial and Special Education.* doi:10.1177/0741932514551281

Wehmeyer, M. L., Smith, S. J., Palmer, S. B., & Davies, D. K. (2004). Technology use by students with intellectual disabilities: An overview. *Journal of Special Education Technology, 19*, 7–21.

Whalen, C., Liden, L., Ingersoll, B., Dallaire, E., & Liden, S. (2006). Behavioral improvements associated with computer-assisted instruction for children with developmental disabilities. *The Journal of Speech and Language Pathology-Applied Behavior Analysis, 1*(1), 11–26. doi:10.1037/h0100182

What Works Clearinghouse. (2014). *Procedures and standards handbook. Version 3.0.* Retrieved December 4, 2014. http://ies.ed.gov/ncee/wwc/pdf/reference_resources/wwc_procedures_v3_0_standards_handbook.pdf

Wong, C., Odom, S. L., Hume, K., Cox, A. W., Fettig, A., Kucharczyk, S., ... Schultz, T. R. (2014). Evidence-based practices for children, youth, and young adults with Autism Spectrum Disorder. Chapel Hill, NC: The University of North Carolina, Frank Porter Graham Child Development Institute, Autism Evidence-Based Practice Review Group.

Zisimopoulos, D., Sigafoos, J., & Koutromanos, G. (2011). Using video prompting and constant time delay to teach an internet search basic skill to students with intellectual disabilities. *Education and Training in Autism and Developmental Disabilities, 46,* 238–250.

## KEY TERMS AND DEFINITIONS

**Academic Learning:** The acquisition of skills that form the core of the general curriculum in schools including mathematics, language arts, social studies, and science.

**Alternate Assessment:** A system used by the state for students who cannot take the general assessment with our without accommodations. The alternate assessment is based on the state's grade level content standards, but sets alternate achievement standards that reduce the complexity and scope of the content.

**Computer-Assisted Instruction:** CAI is an evidence-based practice for students with ASD and includes the use of computers for teaching students academic skills and promoting communication and language development (Odom et al., 2010).

**Daily Living Skills:** Ability in activities that relate to everyday functioning in life including personal care and grooming, food preparation, household chores, use of community resources, community mobility, and leisure skills.

**Moderate and Severe Developmental Disabilities:** Disabilities that (1) are manifested before the age of 22, (2) are chronic and severe, (3) can be attributed to a mental or physical impairment or both, (4) result in substantial functional limitations in major life activities, and (5) require lifelong need for special services that are individually planned and coordinated (Handleman, 1986).

**Portable Device Applications:** Personal digital assistants (PDAs) are portable, palmtop computers used for personal organization and have features such as customizability and capacity for large amounts of data.

**Social and Communication Skills:** Ability in being able to convey information to another person, comprehend messages received, understand the social demands of a context and respond appropriately.

**Visual Supports:** "Any visual display that supports the learner engaging in a desired behavior or skills independent of prompts" (Wong et al., 2014, p. 22).

# Chapter 18

# Mitigation of Test Bias in International, Cross–National Assessments of Higher–Order Thinking Skills

**Raffaela Wolf**
*CAE, USA*

**Doris Zahner**
*CAE, USA*

## ABSTRACT

*The assessment of higher-order skills in higher education has gained popularity internationally. In order to accurately measure the skills required for working in the 21st century, a shift in assessment strategies is required. More specifically, assessments that only require the recall of factual knowledge have been on the decline, whereas assessments that evoke higher-order cognitive skills are on the rise. The purpose of this chapter is to discuss and offer strategies for mitigating bias for a computer-administered performance-based assessment of higher-order skills. Strategies to abate the effects of bias are discussed within the test design and test implementation stages. A case study of a successful adaptation and translation of CAE's Collegiate Learning Assessment (CLA+) is presented to guide the discussion throughout the chapter.*

## INTRODUCTION

International academic institutions of higher education are under pressure to enhance the quality of instruction in order to equip the next generation's workforce with the skills necessary to meet the demands of careers evolving in the 21st century. Research suggests that employers seek individuals who are able to think critically and communicate effectively (Hart Research Associates, 2006). In order to meet the demands of today's world, a shift in assessment strategies is necessary to measure the skills now prized in a complex global environment. More specifically, assessments that only foster the recall of factual knowledge have been on the decline, whereas assessments that evoke

DOI: 10.4018/978-1-4666-9441-5.ch018

higher-order cognitive skills, such as analytic and quantitative reasoning, problem solving, and written communication are on the rise. CAE's Collegiate Learning Assessment (CLA+) is a computer-administered instrument that purports to measure these higher-order skills within the United States and internationally. In general, instruments that allow for cross-national comparisons of higher-order competencies in higher education are scarce, mainly due to an array of methodological challenges, such as differences in educational systems, socio-economic factors, and perceptions as to which constructs should be assessed (Blömeke, Zlatkin-Troitschanskaia, Kuhn, & Fege, 2013). From a more specific psychometric perspective, measuring competencies within an international framework poses challenges that pertain to test development, scoring, and the validity of score interpretations (R. K. Hambleton & Murphy, 1992). Different forms of bias are considered the main sources of in-equivalence in cross-national research (F. J. Van de Vijver, 1998; F. J. Van de Vijver & K. Leung, 1997). Van de Vijver and Leung (1997) identified three common forms of bias within an international context; which include construct bias, method bias, and item bias.

The purpose of this chapter is to discuss and offer strategies to minimize different sources of bias, such as construct bias, method bias, and item bias for a computer-administered performance based assessment of higher-order skills. Rather than viewing and/or treating each source of bias in isolation, a holistic approach that combines a mixture of qualitative and quantitate methodologies was employed with the hope of collecting evidence for valid cross-national score interpretations. The proposed strategies to abate the effects of bias are discussed within the test design (i.e., construct definition, item and rubric development) and test implementation (i.e., translation process, training of scorers, administration (delivery platform)) stages. A case study of a successful test adaptation and translation of CAE's CLA+ will be presented to guide the discussion throughout the chapter.

## BACKGROUND

Increased globalization, among other factors, has created an increased interest in making cross-national comparisons on underlying constructs that the research instrument purports to measure. Occasionally, this necessitates translation of the instrument into a different language.

Due to differences in culture and language, among other differences in the population, it is evident that an examination of the degree to which the instrument measures the same construct across these cultural and language groups is a precursor to drawing valid score interpretations. In order to draw valid score inferences, it is assumed that individuals who earn the same observed score on these instruments have the same standing on the constructs underlying the measurement instrument. The evaluation of several criteria could aid in meeting the aforementioned assumption:

1.  The construct measured exists across nations.
2.  The construct is measured in the same manner across nations.
3.  Items that are believed to be equivalent across nations are linguistically and statistically equivalent.
4.  Similar scores across different adapted versions of the assessment reflect similar degrees of proficiency.

In order to address the points above and in an attempt to mitigate bias in the test translation and adaptation phase, quantitative methods should co-exist with both qualitative and cognitive methodologies to ensure quality control throughout the test adaptation process.

## Bias in Cross-National Comparisons

Bias occurs when observed differences on the constructs of interest are not due to the underlying trait. Consequently, score inferences drawn on biased results may lead to erroneous results and invalid score interpretations. Since the causes of bias may be multifaceted, it is helpful to classify bias into three broad categories for the purpose of evaluation: construct bias, method bias, and item bias (F. J. Van de Vijver & K. Leung, 1997; F. J. Van de Vijver & Poortinga, 1997). It should be noted that bias is not a property of the measurement instrument itself but a characteristic of a cross-national evaluation resulting from the application of a measurement instrument. In other words, the properties of a measurement instrument, person characteristics, and the way the test is administered may induce bias.

The question as to whether individuals from different cultures ascribe the same meaning to the construct definition of higher-order skills is of great importance in any assessment system. Construct comparability rests upon the assumption that test scores are contingent upon the same definition of higher-order skills across the countries. If the constructs are comparable, then test-score differences across countries may reflect a true representation of the discrepancies in student performance. However, within the context of such comparisons, differences in scores may be influenced by confounding variables, such as test translation and adaptation, familiarity with item-response formats, and other socio-cultural factors. Therefore, a holistic approach that examines all possible sources of bias may enhance the validity of score interpretations across cultures.

Method bias can be attributed to several factors, such as characteristics of the sample, the instrument, and administration procedures. Heterogeneity of samples on aspects that are not related to the outcome variable could confound real population differences on the outcome variable. For example, differences in motivation between the groups could cause method bias as introduced by the heterogeneity of the samples. Characteristics of the instrument itself also could pose another aspect of method bias. For example, the familiarity with different item formats, such as selected-response versus constructed-response items, could be a source of method bias. Administration problems also may be considered as an additional source of bias. The use of similar testing platforms and scoring procedures is imperative to ensure similar administration conditions across cultures.

Bias at the item-level, also referred to as differential item functioning (DIF; (Holland & Wainer, 1993), occurs when individuals from different demographics but have the same latent ability (i.e., total test score) do not have the same expected score on the item. Items are expected to be equally difficult cross-culturally for individuals who earn the same score on the construct of interest. Items that exhibit DIF would need to be examined further empirically, through a content analysis, to determine if item bias is present. Examples of sources that could cause item bias include the following: poor item translation, ambiguous item stems and response options, appropriateness of item content within cultural contexts, and awkward item wording.

## Qualitative Approaches to Alleviating Bias

A thorough discussion of qualitative strategies to mitigate bias is beyond the scope of the present chapter. For a detailed review on qualitative strategies for identifying and dealing with different forms of bias, see F. Van de Vijver and Tanzer (2004). In the current chapter the presentation of methodological approaches is restricted to the most prominent techniques for addressing different types of construct bias, method bias, and item bias.

One method to control for construct bias is through the simultaneous development of the same instrument in several countries, which affords the opportunity for cultural decentering (Werner &

Campbell, 1970). By using this approach, words and/or concepts that are favored predominantly in one country can be eliminated during the test development phase. Another approach to minimizing construct bias includes the development of an instrument within each country, which is followed by subsequent cross-national administration of all instruments (Campbell, 1986). Further approaches that may be used to mitigate construct and method bias may include the collaboration of experts who are familiar with the culture of different countries. Collaborative efforts between measurement scientists, cognitive scientists, and experts within the tertiary education system from different countries may aid in the development of instruments that are within appropriate cultural contexts. Different translation procedures (i.e., forward and back translations) also may be used to ensure adequate translations (Werner & Campbell, 1970). The translated instrument may be pilot tested with bilingual students to assess the appropriateness of the adapted version (Hocevar, El-Zahhar, & Gombos, 1989) However, findings may need to be interpreted with caution since the bilingual students may not be representative of the target population. Another pilot study could include non-standard instrument administrations where respondents to the instrument are asked to apply think-aloud techniques, which may be used as a tool to identify whether respondents attach the same meaning to the underlying construct (Johnstone, Bottsford-Miller, & Thompson, 2006; Zucker, Sassman, & Case, 2004).

In an attempt to minimize method bias, extensive training of individuals involved in the assessment process could ensure that test administration and test scoring procedures are applied in a similar manner across countries. The development of a detailed protocol for test administration, test scoring, and score interpretation is necessary to ensure similar procedures across nations. If different item formats (i.e., multiple choice versus constructed response) are part of the assessment, it may be worthwhile to provide practice items

so that students from different nations can become accustomed to different item formats (R. Hambleton, 2005; R. K. Hambleton, 1996; R. K. Hambleton & Patsula, 1999; F. Van de Vijver & K. Leung, 1997).

Although numerous quantitative procedures exist for detecting DIF, a few additional qualitative approaches could be utilized to ensure that items are behaving as intended. Individual items should be reviewed in terms of poor translation, complex wording, and whether the items invoke unintended additional traits. These procedures are judgmental methods that include linguistic and psychological analysis of each item. Experts typically are asked to examine and judge whether items elicit the construct of interest. This approach is conducted to establish evidence for construct validity (F. Van de Vijver & Tanzer, 2004).

The degree to which these approaches may reduce bias is contingent on the appropriateness of judgmental decisions. For this reason, it may be useful to collect multiple sources of evidence such as feedback from content item reviews and cognitive laboratories to ensure appropriateness of the subjective conclusions. Furthermore, these qualitative approaches should be used in combination with quantitative evidence obtained through psychometric analyses of the data.

## Psychometric Procedures for Mitigating Bias

A measure is considered to be invariant when members from different cultural and/or language groups have the same standing on the underlying construct, by attaining the same observed score on the assessment. The evaluation of the degree to which instruments are invariant across different groups has been facilitated by the development of several analytical techniques that are grounded on item response theory (IRT), and structural equation modeling (SEM). IRT employs mathematical models to relate a person's latent construct and item characteristics (e.g., slope, location, and/or guessing parameters) to the likelihood of a correct response on a particular item. For example, if dichotomous IRT models (e.g., multiple-choice items) are utilized, then one-, two-, and three-parameter logistic (i.e., 1PL, 2PL and 3PL) or normal ogive models can be applied. The difference between the logistic and normal ogive mathematical functions in terms of probabilities and parameter estimates is diminutive. However, in practice, logistic models are applied more frequently due to their simplicity in computation (Embretson & Reise, 2000).

Equation 1 models the probability of a successful performance on item *j* for the 3PL model

$$P(X_{ij} = 1 \mid \theta_j, a_i, b_i, c_i) = c_i + \frac{1 - c_i}{1 + \exp^{-Da_i(\theta_j - b_i)}}$$

(1)

This model defines the probability of a successful performance on an item $(X_{ij})$ as a function of one latent trait or person parameter $(\theta_j)$ and three item parameters ($a_i$ (item discrimination), $b_i$ (item difficulty), and $c_i$ (pseudo-guessing). $D$ is a scaling constant (1.7). The 3PL model reduces to the 2PL model if the pseudo-guessing parameter is zero. In addition, if it is assumed that all items have the same slope, then only the difficulty parameters are utilized to describe the response data; thus, a 1PL or Rasch model can be applied.

Several polytomous IRT models exist for situations in which a person may obtain one of several different scores, such as on a constructed-response (CR) item, which could be scored on a scale of 0 to 4. Popular models in the psychometric literature include the graded partial credit (GPC) model (Muraki, 1998), the graded response (GR) model (Samejima, 1997), and the nominal response model (D. R. Bock, 1972). Detailed theoretical discussions on these types of models are well documented in the literature (Baker & Kim, 2004;

De Ayala, 2009; Embretson & Reise, 2000). Reckase (2009) provides a detailed discussion of commonly used Multidimensional IRT (MIRT) models and the important methods needed for their practical application.

Successful implementation of IRT rests upon some stringent assumptions, such as monotonicity, local independence, and dimensionality. Monotonicity asserts that the likelihood of successful performance is a non-decreasing function of a person's proficiency. Local independence implies that item performance is provisionally independent given a person's trait level, whereas the dimensionality of an assessment refers to the quantity of latent aptitudes required to capture the construct of interest (Embretson & Reise, 2000). SEM is a multivariate analysis technique that includes specialized versions of a number of analysis methods as special cases (i.e., path analysis, confirmatory factor analysis, second order factor analysis, regression analysis, covariance structure analysis, correlation structure analysis). A key characteristic of SEM is the capability of linking observed indicators to latent variables. Latent variables are hypothetical variables that are free from random or systematic measurement errors and are observed indirectly through their effects on observed or manifest variables (Bollen, 1989). For example, the confirmatory factor analysis (CFA) model is one of the simplest SEM models. The model can be conceptualized as follows

$$x = \Lambda_x \xi + \delta \,,$$

(2)

where $\Lambda_x$ is a matrix of factor loadings, $\xi (xi)$ is a matrix of latent variables with a covariance matrix ($\phi$-phi), and $\delta$ (delta) is a matrix of residual errors, one for each observed variable $x_i$ with a covariance matrix, $\Theta_\delta$. An illustrative example of a six variable two-factor model (Equation 3) is as follows

$$\begin{pmatrix} x_1 \\ x_2 \\ x_3 \\ x_4 \\ x_5 \\ x_6 \end{pmatrix} = \begin{pmatrix} \lambda_{11} & 0 \\ \lambda_{21} & 0 \\ \lambda_{31} & 0 \\ 0 & \lambda_{42} \\ 0 & \lambda_{52} \\ 0 & \lambda_{62} \end{pmatrix} \begin{pmatrix} \xi_1 \\ \xi_2 \end{pmatrix} + \begin{pmatrix} x_1 \\ x_2 \\ x_3 \\ x_4 \\ x_5 \\ x_6 \end{pmatrix} \qquad (3)$$

In this example, $x_1$, $x_2$, and $x_3$ load on the first factor, $\xi_1$, and the remaining variables $x_4$, $x_5$, and $x_6$ load on the second factor, $\xi_2$. The factors are allowed to freely correlate (i.e., relate to each other) and the variances of the factors are fixed to 1.0 for model identification purposes.

Measurement equivalence, also known as factorial invariance, can be tested at the scale level through examining construct comparability and at the item level through DIF. In scale-level analyses, the set of items comprising a test typically are examined together using multi-group confirmatory factor analyses (MG-CFA; Byrne, 1998; Jöreskog, 1971), which involves testing several measurement invariance hypotheses. In the item-level analyses, the focus is on the invariant characteristics of each item, one item at a time, which can be examined through various DIF detection methods (Dorans & Kulick, 1986; Edelen, Thissen, Teresi, Kleinman, & Ocepek-Welikson, 2006; Holland & Thayer, 1988; Morales, Flowers, Gutierrez, Kleinman, & Teresi, 2006; Muthén & Lehman, 1985; Shealy & Stout, 1993; Swaminathan & Rogers, 1990; Thissen, 1991; Thissen, Steinberg, & Wainer, 1993). While IRT and SEM methods for testing measurement equivalence are conceptually similar, each method may yield unique information regarding the equivalence of the samples under investigation (Tremblay, Lalancette, & Roseveare, 2012).

Both frameworks examine the relationship between a theoretical construct and a set of observed variables (i.e., item scores). Furthermore, both approaches assess the degree to which item/subscale-level true scores are equivalent for individuals with the same ability score in the different populations under investigation. When measurement nonequivalence does not hold, both approaches can be used to identify the extent and the source of the problem. Within the IRT framework, individual items are assessed for DIF, whereas, within the CFA context, the proposed model is tested for its goodness of fit to the data for each group separately before examining the sources of measurement invariance. Additionally, IRT models may provide some advantages over CFA. Advantages include increased model flexibility and modeling of more item parameters. CFA assumes that item responses are continuous and linear, while IRT can model item responses that are either nominal or ordinal. Numerous IRT models exist that can accommodate different types of relationships between item responses and the underlying latent trait. When items are scored dichotomously (0 or 1), CFA methods can produce expected item scores that are out of bounds, such as less than zero or greater than one, with some estimates of ability. IRT rests upon a non-linear function that connects the item characteristics (e.g., slope, location, and/or guessing parameters) and the underlying latent proficiency responsible for the item response and, thus, expected observed responses cannot exceed the boundaries of 0 to 1 (R. D. Bock, 1997). In the case of polytomous data, CFA produces a single item intercept per item, whereas IRT typically yields multiple parameters akin to item intercepts per item because IRT models polytomous data as categorical. The CFA methodology is well versed to handle multiple latent constructs and multiple populations simultaneously. IRT-based measurement equivalence methodology is confined to scales that are unidimensional. Multidimensional approaches (Oshima, Raju, & Flowers, 1997) have been proposed in the psychometric literature, but the application thus far has been scarce.

Despite the differences in the two methodologies yielding unique information, the CFA and IRT approaches may produce corroborating results, particularly when there are mean differences across groups resulting in higher item parameters in one group relative to another (Stark, Chernyshenko, & Drasgow, 2006)a more thorough discussion on the similarities and differences between the two methodologies can be found in Raju, Laffitte, and Byrne (2002).) The current chapter focuses on SEM methodology.

## Scale-Level Analysis: Measurement (Factor) Equivalence

Measurement equivalence takes on numerous different forms that create a nested hierarchy predominantly characterized by increasing levels of cross-group equality constraints imposed on factor loading, item intercept or thresholds, and residual variance parameters (Vandenberg & Lance, 2000). The different forms of factorial invariance can be classified into dimensional invariance, configural invariance, metric invariance (weak factorial invariance), strong (scalar) factorial invariance, and strict factorial invariance (Horn & McArdle, 1992; Meredith, 1993; Selig, Card, & Little, 2008). Each form attempts to address a different question:

1. **Dimensional Invariance:** Is the number of common factors present in the data equivalent in each group?
2. **Configural Invariance:** Do the same items load on common factors across groups?
3. **Metric Invariance:** Do the common factors have the same meanings across groups?
4. **Strong Factorial Invariance:** Do comparisons of group means represent meaningful comparisons?
5. **Strict Factorial Invariance:** Can group-mean and observed-variance comparisons be justified?

Dimensional invariance is the least restrictive form of measurement invariance because it requires an instrument to represent the same number of common factors across groups. Exploratory factor analysis (EFA) can be utilized to assess whether the number of common factors are equivalent across groups when no hypothesis exists regarding the number of common factors. If the instrument has been validated previously, a hypothesis regarding the number of common factors can be tested within the confirmatory factor analysis (CFA) context. It is evident that this form of invariance should be met in order to justify any quantitative cross-national comparisons.

Assuming that dimensional invariance has been met, configural invariance requires that each common factor is associated with identical item clusters across groups. The configural model does not impose any constraints on the model parameters, and it serves as a baseline model against which all subsequent tests for equivalence are compared. Configural invariance is said to hold when a hypothesized statistical model that specifies which items measure each construct fits the data across cultures. Configural invariance can be assessed within the CFA framework, which entails the specification of item clusters and a formal test of the configural invariance hypothesis. Configural invariance is an improvement over dimensional invariance, but it is not sufficient to defend direct quantitative cross-national score comparisons.

Assuming configural invariance has been attained, metric invariance can be tested by placing constraints on the factor loadings. Metric invariance is expected to hold when the factor loadings are equal across groups. This form of invariance implies that common factors appear to have the same meaning across groups. More specifically, the relationships between the common factors and the responses to a common set of relevant items are identical across groups. The use of a multi-group CFA model allows for concurrent estimation of factor loadings across groups. Furthermore, a statistical test of the equal-loadings hypothesis can be conducted. An alternative is to compare the fit of two nested models (configural vs. metric); if model fit becomes distorted then the equal factor loadings hypothesis may not hold.

If the hypothesis does not hold, then one or more of the common factors, or a cluster of items, may have different meanings across cultures. This condition is considered to be a prerequisite in order for subsequent tests of measurement equivalence to be meaningful.

Assuming metric invariance, strong factorial invariance, or scalar invariance, require that regressions of items onto their associated common factors yield a vector of intercept terms that is invariant across groups. In order to test for strong factorial invariance, equality constraints are imposed on factor loadings and item intercepts to sample data from each group concurrently. Good model fit indicates that the model constraints are consistent with the data. Alternatively, strong factorial invariance also can be tested through the comparison of nested models (metric vs. strong factorial) where a significant worsening of fit would suggest that the equal item intercepts hypothesis is not supported by the data. Within the CFA framework, item intercepts reflect systematic additive influences on item responses that are constant in each group and are unrelated to the common factors. If strong factorial invariance holds, then group differences in factor means are expected to be unbiased. Moreover, group differences in observed means are then directly related to group differences in factor means.

Another form of invariance—strict factorial invariance—takes into account the residual variances. If the goal is to compare observed variance estimates across cultural groups, then the comparison should reflect the differences in the common factor variation rather than differences in residual variances. Assuming metric (weak factorial) invariance, residual invariance requires that corresponding item residual variances are invariant across groups. The strict factorial invariance model imposes cross-group equality constraints on corresponding factor loadings, item intercepts, and item residual variances. In other words, the strong factorial invariance model is restricted further so that corresponding item residual variances are invariant across groups. Some researchers have contended that this type of equivalence is too stringent and irrelevant in most applications (Bentler & Wu, 2005; Little, Card, Slegers, & Ledford, 2007).

When it is not feasible to establish invariance at one of the aforementioned levels, researchers may proceed with the test of a model that includes separate estimates of a subset of the subgroup parameters, such as some factor loadings and item intercepts. These types of models and the test of fit of these types of models are referred to as tests of partial invariance. It should be noted that the procedures, as described above, pertain to measurement scales that are composed of continuous variables. The steps for measurement invariance testing may need to be modified for measurement scales that consist of categorical data. The following resources provide detailed discussions on the topic: Bengt, Muthen, & Asparouhov (2002) and Bengt, Muthen, & Christoffersson (1981). Complete reference is available in *Additional Readings*.

## Structural Equivalence

Structural equivalence tests for equivalence on the latent variables, whereas measurement equivalence focuses on the observed indicator variables. These types of tests provide evidence of the psychometric properties of the scale, in particular within the context of construct validity. The examination of structural equivalence affords researchers the opportunity to examine whether the dimensionality of the hypothetical construct is the same across cultures (Byrne & Shavelson, 1987; Byrne & Watkins, 2003). At the structural level, invariance can be assessed in terms of group differences in latent factor means, variances, and covariances. More specifically, testing for structural equivalence attempts to answer the following questions:

1. Are the factor variances the same across groups?

2.  Is the factor covariance the same across groups?
3.  Are the factor means the same across groups?

Given that structural equivalence refers to examining relationships among theoretical constructs it is evident that these types of tests are useful only when measurement equivalence has been established (Meredith, 1993). Testing for structural equivalence can be an important component when establishing construct validity if interest lies in testing whether the dimensionality of the construct, as delineated through theoretical beliefs, holds true.

## Item-Level Analysis: Differential Item Functioning (DIF)

Persons with the same underlying trait who belong to the same group membership are expected to attain the same test or item scores. In order to ensure test fairness and valid score interpretations, it is imperative to demonstrate that items do not differentiate among persons based on gender, race, or ethnic background. There are at least two groups, i.e., focal and reference groups, in any DIF study. The focal group is the potentially disadvantaged group, whereas the group that may be potentially advantaged by the test is called the reference group. Furthermore, there are two types of DIF, namely uniform and non-uniform DIF. Uniform DIF transpires when a group outperforms another group across the range of ability levels. More specifically, almost all members of a group outperform almost all members of the other group who are at the same ability levels. In the case of non-uniform DIF, members of one group are favored up to a particular point on the ability scale and, from that point on, the relationship is reversed. In other words, there is an interaction between the grouping variable and ability level.

There are two main approaches to DIF detection. The first is the use of IRT models (Thissen & Steinberg, 1988; Thissen, Steinberg, & Gerrard, 1986; Thissen et al., 1993), while the second relies on observed-score analyses (Mantel-Haenszel [MH]; (Holland & Thayer, 1988), logistic regression (LR; (Swaminathan & Rogers, 1990), standardization (Dorans & Kulick, 1986), or simultaneous item bias test (SIBTEST; (Shealy & Stout, 1993). These observed-score methodologies also have been extended for use with polytomous data. These methods include: generalized Mantel-Haenszel (GMH; (Zwick, Donoghue, & Grima, 1993), standardized mean difference (SMD) procedure (Dorans & Schmitt, 1993), polytomous logistic regression (French & Miller, 1996), logistic discriminant function analysis (Miller & Spray, 1993), ordinal logistic regression (B. D. Zumbo, 1999), and Poly-SIBTEST (Chang, Mazzeo, & Roussos, 1996).

It is evident that several factors may influence the choice of a DIF method, including a preference for one of the above mentioned methodological approaches (IRT vs. non-IRT), the type of DIF effect (uniform, non-uniform, or both), model assumptions (parametric vs. nonparametric), the number of groups being compared, and the characteristics of the available data (e.g., dichotomous, polytomous, and missing data).

While IRT methods provide useful information when the IRT model fits the data and when the sample size is sufficiently large enough to obtain accurate IRT parameter estimates, observed-score methods are often employed in practice with smaller sample sizes and ease of interpretation. Within an IRT framework, DIF can be studied in a number of different ways provided that the IRT model fits the data. Three IRT methodologies to study DIF are the following: (a) parameter comparison, (b) area comparison, and (c) likelihood comparison.

In parameter comparisons, the difference in item response functions (IRFs) is examined through a comparison of item parameters between the reference and focal groups. For example, under the 1PL model, a test for uniform DIF can be performed by testing the following null hypothesis, $H_0 : b = 0$, with a normal approximation test statistic

$$Z = \frac{\hat{b}_F - \hat{b}_R}{s(\hat{b})} \cdot Z = \frac{\hat{b}_F - \hat{b}_R}{s(\hat{b})} \, Z = \frac{\hat{b}_F - \hat{b}_R}{s(\hat{b})},$$

(4)

where $\hat{b}_F$ and $\hat{b}_R$ are the item difficulty parameters of the focal and reference groups and $s(\hat{b})$ reflects the standard error of the difference. A multivariate test of item parameter differences may be more appropriate when the 2PL or 3PL models are implemented (Camilli & Shepard, 1994).

In area comparisons, the difference between the IRFs may be indicative of DIF through observing either signed or unsigned differences (Raju, 1988). The smaller the area between the IRFs, the lower the magnitude of DIF, which is examined through effect sizes. (See Raju (1990) for a thorough discussion on how to obtain statistical significance tests.) The signed area test focuses on uniform DIF, whereas the unsigned area test aims to assess non-uniform DIF. Parameter and area comparisons of IRFs can provide useful information for dichotomous response data. However, applications of the above mentioned procedures to polytomous data are scarce in the literature. The likelihood comparison approach can be easily applied to both dichotomous and polytomous response data. The procedure is discussed in more detail below.

The IRT likelihood ratio test procedure (Thissen, Steinberg, & Wainer, 1988) is a parametric, model-based procedure for detecting both uniform and non-uniform DIF. The IRT likelihood-ratio approach for DIF detection tests the hypothesis that item parameters (i.e., item discrimination, item difficulty) do not differ between the reference and focal groups. The difference in the item difficulty parameters between groups tests for uniform DIF, whereas the difference in the item discrimination parameters tests for non-uniform DIF. When testing the null hypothesis of no DIF, a compact model (constrained model) is compared to an augmented model (unconstrained model). In the compact model, the item parameters for the common-item(s) are constrained to be equal across reference and focal groups. In the augmented model, the item parameters for the item under investigation are unconstrained and the remaining items are constrained to be equal across the two groups.

The likelihood ratio test statistic can then be computed as follows

$$G^2 = -2LL_C - (-2LL_A),$$

(5)

where $LL_C$ is the log likelihood for the compact model given the maximum likelihood estimates of the parameters of the compact model, and $LL_A$ is the log likelihood for the augmented model given the maximum likelihood estimates of the parameters of the augmented model. The value of $G^2$ is distributed as the chi-square statistic with degrees of freedom being equal to the difference in the number of parameters in the compact and augmented model. If the result of the difference testing is found to be significant, then the studied item is flagged for DIF. The focus of this chapter is on traditional methodologies, such as logistic and ordinal regression.

Logistic regression models the probability of endorsing an item correctly by group membership (i.e., reference and focal groups, such as males versus females) and a criterion variable, such as scale or subscale total score.

The logistic regression equation is

$$P(Y_j = 1 \mid X_j, G_j) = \frac{e^{f_j}}{1 + e^{f_j}},$$

(6)

where $Y_j$ is the item response for person $j$, $X_j$ reflects the matching variable (i.e., total score), $G_j$ corresponds to group membership (dummy coded as 1 = reference, 2 = focal) for person $j$, and $f_j$ is the logit for person $j$.

The logit for person $j$ can be expressed as

$$f_j = \ln\left[\frac{p_j}{(1-p_j)}\right] = \\ \beta_0 + \beta_1 X_j + \beta_2 G_j + \beta_3 (XG)_j \qquad (7)$$

The logistic regression approach uses item responses coded as 0 or 1 for binary responses as the dependent variable, whereas total score for each subject $(X_j)$, the grouping variable $(G_j)$ (dummy coded as 1 = reference, 2 = focal), and a total score by group interaction term $(XG)_j$ are used as independent variables. Bruno (1999) extended the logistic regression approach for use with polytomous test items, where the logit for person $j$ to score scoring category $k$ or below is conceptualized as

$$\text{logit}\left[P(Y_j \le k \mid X_j, G_j) = \log\left[\frac{P(Y_j \le k)}{P(Y_j > k)}\right]\right]. \\ = \beta_0 + \beta_1 X_j + \beta_2 G_j + \beta_3 (XG)_j \qquad (8)$$

Coefficients of the logistic regression model are reflected through $\beta_0, \beta_1, \beta_2,$ and $\beta_3$, where $\beta_0$ is the intercept and $\beta_1, \beta_2, \beta_3$ reflect the slopes of the model. An item under investigation is said to exhibit uniform DIF when $\beta_2$ is non-zero and $\beta_3$ is zero, whereas non-uniform DIF is present if $\beta_3$ is nonzero.

The statistical significance of DIF can be examined through hypothesis testing that is akin to testing whether the group $(G_j)$ and interaction variables $(XG)_j$ are statistically significant in addition to the criterion (i.e., total score) variable. These two null hypotheses can be tested with a likelihood ratio test statistic that has a chi-square distribution with the degrees of freedom equal to the difference in the number of parameters:

$H_0$: The effect of group membership $(G_j)$ on the log odds of probability of correct endorsement for item $i$ is equal to zero.

$H_0$: There is no interaction $(XG)_j$ between group membership and ability.

For example, a simultaneous test of uniform and non-uniform DIF can be administered by subtracting the chi-square test statistic from a model that includes the interaction between the grouping variable and total score from the model that includes only the criterion variable (i.e., total score). The difference in the chi-squared values can then be compared to its distribution function with two degrees of freedom.

Measuring the magnitude of DIF follows the same concept as statistical hypotheses testing, except that R-squared values are compared at each step. B. Zumbo and Thomas (1997) recommend an examination of both the difference in chi-square value of the likelihood-ratio test along with a measure of effect size in order to identify DIF. The effect size provides an outlet for identifying practical significance, in particular when large sample sizes may statistically identify negligible effects. Recommended guidelines are followed to set cut off values for DIF identification. More specifically, an item exhibits DIF when $p \le .01$ for the chi-square difference tests, and when R-square values are at least .035 (Zumbo, 1999).

The DIF detection methods as outlined above are suitable for studies that focus on two group comparisons, such as the current study comparing university students from the United States and Italy. However, typically, different methodological approaches are employed in international large-scale assessment systems, such as the Programme for International Student Assessment (PISA), the Trends in International Mathematics and Science Study (TIMSS), and the Assessment of Higher Education Learning Outcomes (AHELO), since a number of different countries are being compared. The utilization of simultaneous procedures for multi-group comparisons has several advantages over traditional two-group methods: (a) simultaneous testing may increase power for detecting DIF compared to individual pairwise tests, (b) inflation of Type I error when DIF is tested in numerous individual pairwise tests can be mitigated by a simultaneous analysis, and (c) more efficiency when testing for DIF simultaneously compared to running multiple tests (i.e., time and computing resources).

As an example, some of the methods as outlined above, such as generalized logistic regression (Magis, Raîche, Béland, & Gérard, 2011), generalized Lord's test (Kim, Cohen, & Park, 1995), and generalized Mantel-Haenszel (Fidalgo & Madeira, 2008; Penfield, 2001), have been generalized for use when comparing more than two groups. Since these methods have been developed recently, the literature on the performance of these methods within the context of large-scale international comparative studies, such as PISA or TIMSS, is scarce (Svetina & Rutkowski, 2014). PISA and TIMSS both borrow statistical models from the IRT framework to scale and score student responses. However, measurement equivalence at the item level for PISA has been examined through an analysis of variance-like approach, which tests for item-by-country interactions (OECD, 2012).

## Practical Implementation

An array of methodological procedures are available to test for measurement equivalence at the scale and item levels. Consequently, a number of computational tools are available to conduct the aforementioned statistical analyses. A detailed treatment of each of those packages is beyond

the scope of this chapter; therefore, this section highlights some of the prominent software packages that can be utilized as computational tools to conduct these types of analyses.

Two widely available commercial software packages that can handle factor models for dichotomous and polytomous measures in multiple populations are: LISREL (Jöreskog & Sörbom, 2014) and Mplus (B. Muthén & L. Muthén, 2010). These packages allow for a vast variety of statistical analysis methods, including regression and path analysis, exploratory factor analysis (EFA), CFA, SEM, and mixture modeling. Multigroup and multilevel data also are supported. Several user-friendly IRT software packages have been developed recently to allow for item-level analysis. Two well-known packages, flexMIRT (L. Cai, 2013) and IRTPRO (L Cai, Thissen, & du Toit, 2011), support a variety of unidimensional and multidimensional IRT models that embrace multiple groups and multiple response categories. Furthermore, both packages are capable of handling multi-level structures. Non-IRT based item-level analyses can be implemented with any suitable software that performs logistic regression modelling such as SAS (SAS, 2011) or SPSS (IBM, 2013) see B. D. Zumbo (1999) for an application of non-IRT based item level analyses in SPSS, including syntax for analysis.)

Non-commercial or open source software that facilitates the analysis of scale- and item-level measurement equivalence within the *R* (R, 2014) environment is also available. For example, the package *lavaan* (Rosseel, 2012) can be used to test for measurement equivalence within a SEM framework. See Hirschfeld and von Brachel (2014) for a tutorial on how to test measurement invariance with the package *lavaan*. The package *difR* (Magis, Béland, Tuerlinckx, & De Boeck, 2010) is a useful package for item-level analysis. The package includes several DIF detection procedures for dichotomous data, which includes comparisons for two or more groups.

## EMPIRICAL ILLUSTRATION

This case study aims to provide empirical support for the recommendation found in the *International Test Commission Guidelines for Adapting Educational and Psychological Tests* (R. K. Hambleton, 1996), which urges researchers to carry out empirical studies to demonstrate measurement (factor) equivalence of their instrument across language groups and to identify any item-level DIF that may be present (R. K. Hambleton & Patsula, 1999; F. Van de Vijver & Hambleton, 1996).

In the current example, CAE's CLA+ was translated and adapted for use in Italy.

### Instrumentation

### CLA+

CLA+ is a performance-based assessment that measures higher-order competencies, such as critical-thinking and written-communication skills, by using a combination of both performance tasks (PTs) and selected-response questions (SRQs). The adapted version of CLA+ was used in this study and consisted of one PT and 20 SRQs. Higher-order skills are elicited by presenting students with an authentic task set within a real-world context. Students must them demonstrate their level of mastery of these skills (analysis and problem solving, critical reading and evaluation, scientific and quantitative reasoning, critiquing an argument, writing effectiveness, and writing mechanics). The PTs are designed so that students must analyze the information presented in a document library that contains information in the form of, as examples, newspaper articles, research abstracts, maps, graphs, or charts and write a recommended course of action or solution to the given problem. The PT is composed of three subscales: analysis and problem solving (identifying, interpreting, evaluating, and synthesizing pertinent information and proposing a solution in terms of how to proceed in case of uncertainty), writing effectiveness (producing an organized and cohesive essay with supporting arguments), and writing mechanics (demonstrating command of standard written English). An example PT scenario and task can be found in the Appendix. Similar to the PT, the SRQs also are developed with the intent to elicit higher-order cognitive skills rather than the recall of factual knowledge. Students are presented with a set of questions that pertain to documents from a range of information sources. The SRQ subscales were identified as critical reading and evaluation (eight items), scientific and quantitative reasoning (seven items), and critique an argument (five items). See the following chapter (Using the Collegiate Learning Assessment to Address the College-to-Career Space) for an example SRQ. Students were given 60 minutes to construct a response to the PT and 30 minutes to respond to the 20 SRQs.

### Task Selection, Translation, and Adaption of CLA+

Italian representatives of Agenzia Nazionale di Valutazione del Sistema Universitario e della Ricerca (ANVUR) were presented with an assortment of PT and SRQ sets and a committee of bilingual educators and administrators chose items that they felt were culturally appropriate and adaptable for use in the Italian context. The selected PT and SRQs were then translated and adapted by a third-party translation group and verified by ANVUR and CAE. ANVUR was provided with a translation and adaptation guide to help facilitate the process. Following the translation and adaptation of the PT and SRQs, ANVUR conducted cognitive labs and a pilot study with Italian university students to verify that the translated and adapted version of CLA+ was clear and elicited the appropriate types of student responses.

## Participants

ANVUR recruited 12 universities to participate in this feasibility study, four from each of three geographical regions (i.e., north, central, and south). The student participants from the 12 universities (n = 5853) comprised graduating students in their third and fourth year at their respective institutions. These students took the Italian CLA+ during the spring semester of 2013. A sample of American students (n = 3697) were selected for comparative purposes. The American student participants were university seniors who took CLA+ in the spring semester of 2014. The sampled institutions (public and private) consisted of small liberal arts colleges and large research institutions from the various regions of the United States.

The American sample was comprised of a slightly higher proportion of females (60.3%) than males (39.7%). This representation was similar for the Italian sample (females [59.4%], males [40.6%]).

## Test Administration

The Italian CLA+ was administered on ANVUR's testing platform. Students had a total of 90 minutes to complete the assessment: 60 minutes for the PT and 30 minutes for the 20 SRQs. The American students had a similar administration of CLA+ except through a different test delivery platform. The test administration of the Italian CLA+ was vetted and approved by CAE, prior to administration, to assess comparability of the testing platforms. A customized testing platform was created for the Italian students so that testing conditions were uniform between the two countries.

## Scoring

The PT of the adapted version of CLA+ was scored in Italy by a team of trained scorers. CAE measurement scientists led a series of trainings both virtually and on-site in Rome. The ANVUR scorers prepared a translated version of the CLA+ scoring rubric. This team of Italian lead scorers then trained a set of Italian scorers to complete the scoring of the student PT responses.

The CLA+ scoring rubric for the PTs consists of three subscales: Analysis and Problem Solving (APS), Writing Effectiveness (WE), and Writing Mechanics (WM). Each of these subscales is scored from a range of 1–6, where 1 is the lowest level of performance and 6 is the highest, with each score pertaining to specific response attributes. For all task types, blank or entirely off-topic responses are flagged for removal from results. Scorers receive prompt-specific guidance, in the form of a scoring handbook, in addition to the scoring rubrics as part of the scorer training. Additionally, the reported subscores are not adjusted for difficulty like the overall CLA+ scale scores, and, therefore, are not directly comparable to each other. These PT subscores are intended to facilitate criterion-referenced interpretations as defined by the rubric.

The selected-response section of the adapted CLA+ consists of 20 items distributed across three subscales: scientific and quantitative reasoning (seven items), critical reading and evaluation (eight items), and critique an argument (five items). Subscores in these sections are determined according to the number of questions correctly answered, with scores adjusted for the difficulty of the particular question set received.

## Data Analysis

### Descriptive Statistics

Table 1 provides descriptive statistics for the adapted CLA+. Both countries showed similar results for the PT (Italy: $M = 9.17$, $SD = 2.95$; US: $M = 9.06$, $SD = 2.54$) and SRQs (Italy: $M = 12.31$, $SD = 2.85$; US: $M = 12.65$, $SD = 3.71$).

*Table 1. Descriptive statistics for CLA+ for Italian vs. American students*

|  | Italy | | US | |
|---|---|---|---|---|
|  | **SRQ** | **PT** | **SRQ** | **PT** |
| **Items (N)** | 20 | 1 | 20 | 1 |
| **Students (N)** | 5853 | 5853 | 3697 | 3697 |
| **Min Score** | 0 | 3 | 0 | 3 |
| **Max Score** | 19 | 18 | 20 | 18 |
| **Mean** | 12.31 | 9.17 | 12.65 | 9.77 |
| **SD** | 2.85 | 2.95 | 3.71 | 2.28 |

Table 2 reports the descriptive statistics for each subscale of CLA+. Students in the US scored slightly higher on the subscales compared to students from Italy. The discrepancy appeared largest on the scientific and quantitative reasoning section of the SRQ scale (Italy: $M = 4.29$, $SD = 1.69$; US: $M = 5.02$, $SD = 1.70$) and the analysis and problem solving section of the PT scale (Italy: $M = 3.01$, $SD = .87$; US: $M = 3.24$, $SD = .91$). One possible explanation for the score difference on the SRQs could be related to differences in the familiarity with item format. For example, selected-response items are widely used in the United States, whereas many European countries make use of performance or constructed-response tasks (R. M. Wolf, 1998). The lack of familiarity with a particular item type could create a source of construct irrelevant variance and, thus, limit the validity of score interpretations.

## Reliability

The performance tasks were scored through a combination of automated and human scoring. Inter-rater reliability for the CLA+ assessment ranged from .77 - .88. Coefficient alpha for the selected-response tasks had values of .76 for the combined scale whereas values ranged from .51-.58 on the subscales of the selected response items.

## Factor Analyses Results

In an attempt to examine whether students accredit the same meaning to the underlying construct, MG-CFA was conducted (Byrne, Shavelson, & Muthén, 1989) at the scale level to test whether a hypothesized model fit in both populations. CFA models were estimated first without restrictions and then with constraints added progressively. Configural invariance was tested by imposing the same factor structure on both countries. The factor structure was tested separately in each country first before conducting MG-CFA. MG-CFA, as recommended by Cole, Bergin, and Whittaker (2008), were applied to categorical data where the item factor loadings and thresholds were varied in tandem (Table 3). Strong invariance was tested by constraining factor loadings and item thresholds to be equal in both countries and the residual variances were fixed at 1 in one group and freely estimated in the other. Strong invariance was tested by imposing equal factor loadings and

*Table 2. Descriptive statistics for CLA+ subscale scores for Italian vs. American students*

| | | US | | Italy | |
|---|---|---|---|---|---|
| **Scale** | | **Mean** | **SD** | **Mean** | **SD** |
| **SRQ** | **Scientific and Quantitative Reasoning** | 5.02 | 1.70 | 4.29 | 1.69 |
| **SRQ** | **Critical Reading and Evaluation** | 4.57 | 1.60 | 3.93 | 1.66 |
| **SRQ** | **Critique an Argument** | 3.06 | 1.41 | 2.60 | 1.42 |
| **PT** | **Analysis and Problem Solving** | 3.24 | .91 | 3.01 | .87 |
| **PT** | **Writing Effectiveness** | 3.40 | .87 | 3.04 | .89 |
| **PT** | **Writing Mechanics** | 3.69 | .77 | 3.41 | .78 |

*Table 3. Testing for measurement invariance with categorical data*

| Model | Factor Loadings | Thresholds | Residual Variances | Factor Means | Factor Variances |
|---|---|---|---|---|---|
| **Configural invariance** | * | * | Fixed at 1 | Fixed at 0 | Fixed at 1 |
| **Strong invariance** | Fixed | Fixed | Fixed at 1 | Fixed at 0/* | Fixed at 1 |
| **Strict invariance** | Fixed | Fixed | Fixed at 1 | Fixed at 0/* | Fixed at 1/* |

Note. The * indicates that the parameter is freely estimated. Fixed at 0/*= the factor means are fixed at 0 in one group and freely estimated in the other group. Fixed at 1/* = the factor variance is fixed at 1 in one group and freely estimated in the other group.

equal thresholds on both countries. Subsequently, strict invariance was tested by constraining all measurement parameters to be equal across groups. The various models were fit using an adjusted weighted least squares method (WLSM) using the Mplus software (BO Muthén & L Muthén, 2010). All models in this analysis were evaluated in terms of goodness of fit criteria. Exact fit was evaluated using the model $\chi^2$, whereas close fit was evaluated using the comparative fit index (CFI), the Tucker-Lewis non-normed fit index (TLI), and root mean squared error of approximation (RMSEA). In this study, values of less than .05 were used for the RMSEA and values greater than .95 were used for the TLI (Hu & Bentler, 1999). All fit indices were used in conjunction to determine model fit.

The first step was to test whether the proposed factor model fits the empirical data for the American and Italian samples. Results indicated that the hypothesized one-factor model was supported in both groups (Italian: $\chi^2 = 1926.80$; $df = 227$; $RMSEA = .041$; $CFI = .988$; $TLI = .986$;

American: $\chi^2 = 1267.05$; $df = 227$; $RMSEA = .035$; $CFI = .985$; $TLI = .983$). The second step was to move from a single-group CFA to a MG-CFA in order to cross-validate the one-factor model across the two groups (configural invariance). Table 4 indicates that Model 1 provided a good fit ($\chi^2 = 3185.68$; $df = 457$; $RMSEA = .038$; $CFI = .987$; $TLI = .985$) to the data, indicating that the factorial structure of the construct is equal across the two groups. In other words, persons ascribe the same meaning to the definition of higher-order skills between countries. Given that configural invariance was confirmed, the factor loadings and thresholds were then constrained to be equal to test for strong invariance. Table 5 provides tests for model comparisons. Results from Table 5 indicate that Model 2 fit significantly worse than Model 1, DIFFTEST(34) = 132.07, $p < .001$, and Model 3 fit significantly worse than Model 2, DIFFTEST(23) = 404.03, $p < .001$. These results suggest that caution should be warranted when making direct score comparisons across countries.

*Table 4. Fit indices for invariance tests*

| | $\chi^2$ | df | RMSEA | CFI | TLI |
|---|---|---|---|---|---|
| **Model 1:** **Baseline (Configural Invariance)** | 3185.68 | 457 | .04 | .99 | .99 |
| **Model 2:** **Strong Invariance** | 3317.75 | 491 | .04 | .99 | .99 |
| **Model 3:** **Strict Invariance** | 2913.72 | 514 | .03 | .99 | .99 |

*Table 5. Fit indices for model comparisons*

| | $\Delta \chi^2$ | p |
|---|---|---|
| **Model 1 vs Model 2** | 132.07 | <.001 |
| **Model 2 vs Model 3** | 404.03 | <.001 |

## Differential Item Functioning Results

DIF detection through a logistic regression framework follows a general sequence of model building steps as outlined below:

**Model 1:** The total score (matching variable) was entered as a predictor variable.
**Model 2:** The grouping variable was added to Model 1 as a second predictor variable.
**Model 3:** The interaction (i.e., group by total) was added to Model 2 as the third predictor variable.

Chi-square difference testing of Model 1 and Model 3 was performed to test for DIF. The difference in chi-square between Model 2 and Model 1 was examined to test for uniform DIF whereas the chi-square difference between Model 3 and Model 2 was assessed for non-uniform DIF. Different criteria have been suggested to classify items as exhibiting DIF, and there appears to be no clear consensus on a superior approach. In the current study, Zumbo's suggestion was followed in that $p \leq .01$ was used for the chi-square difference test in addition to a significant effect size where the difference in R-squares (Model 3/Model 1) must be at least .035. These recommendations were followed due to the fact that multiple hypotheses were being tested and the sample size was large.

As indicated in Table 6, a number of items appear to be functioning differently across countries according to the p-value and the chosen criterion of $p \leq .01$. However, examination of effect size and given the large sample size, these items may not exhibit DIF. Stated differently, the observed differences may present DIF of sufficiently trivial magnitude, which would indicate that the results are not meaningful in practice. Furthermore, items that are flagged for bias may not represent bias as these items may truly represent differences in group proficiency. Given that flagged items do not necessarily confirm or prove item bias, items would have to be re-reviewed for content by item developers and assessments specialists to ensure that the items are free from bias across countries. If the item content review suggests bias, then items may need to be revised or replaced prior to the next test administration. Furthermore, the following rule of thumb (Raju, 1989) has been suggested in terms of the magnitude of DIF:

- **<10% of Test Items:** Small amount of DIF.
- **10-30% of Test Items:** Medium amount of DIF.
- **>30% of Test Items:** Large amount of DIF.

When a test contains more than 10% of DIF items, closer attention needs to be devoted to the content analysis.

## Solutions and Recommendations

The feasibility of assessing higher-order skills in two different cultures was examined in this case study. Cross-national studies aim to address the question of whether valid test score inferences can be drawn across different nationalities. This case study was an attempt to address bias as a function of the interpretation of test scores rather than an inherent property of the instrument. Test adaptations and translations are prone to introducing bias, such as construct bias, method bias, and item bias. In this feasibility study, translation effects were mitigated through the implementation of

*Table 6. Chi-square difference tests for DIF detection*

| Item | 3 vs. 1 | | | 3 vs. 2 | | 2 vs. 1 | |
|------|---------|---|------|---------|---|---------|---|
| | $\Delta\chi^2$ | $p$ | $\Delta R^2$ | $\Delta\chi^2$ | $p$ | $\Delta\chi^2$ | $p$ |
| 1 | .71 | .70 | .00 | .09 | .77 | .62 | .43 |
| 2 | 9.56 | .01 | .00 | 3.50 | .06 | 6.06 | .01 |
| 3 | 8.95 | .01 | .00 | 3.15 | .08 | 5.80 | .02 |
| 4 | 6.72 | .04 | .00 | 2.46 | .12 | 4.27 | .04 |
| 5 | 66.50 | <.001 | .01 | 8.43 | <.001 | 48.07 | <.001 |
| 6 | 11.10 | .00 | .00 | 9.70 | .00 | 1.40 | .24 |
| 7 | 5.43 | .07 | .00 | .46 | .50 | 4.98 | .03 |
| 8 | 3.34 | .19 | .00 | 2.71 | .10 | .620 | .43 |
| 9 | 8.91 | .01 | .00 | 8.86 | .00 | .043 | .84 |
| 10 | 3.98 | .14 | .00 | .03 | .86 | 3.95 | .05 |
| 11 | 3.27 | .20 | .00 | 1.80 | .18 | 1.47 | .23 |
| 12 | 2.83 | .24 | .00 | 1.02 | .31 | 1.81 | .18 |
| 13 | 5.64 | .06 | .00 | .02 | .89 | 5.62 | .02 |
| 14 | 22.55 | <.001 | .00 | 16.31 | <.001 | 6.24 | .01 |
| 15 | 36.86 | <.001 | .00 | 32.20 | <.001 | 4.17 | .03 |
| 16 | 6.92 | .03 | .00 | 6.80 | .01 | .12 | .73 |
| 17 | 6.87 | .03 | .00 | 2.00 | .16 | 4.88 | .03 |
| 18 | 2.44 | .30 | .00 | .70 | .40 | 1.74 | .19 |
| 19 | 11.78 | .00 | .00 | 1.69 | .19 | 10.09 | <.001 |
| 20 | 21.05 | <.001 | .00 | 8.14 | .00 | 12.91 | <.001 |
| 21 | 140.47 | <.001 | .00 | 26.23 | <001 | 114.25 | <.001 |
| 22 | 108.25 | <.001 | .00 | 49.44 | <.001 | 58.82 | <.001 |
| 23 | 11.63 | .00 | .00 | 2.63 | .11 | 8.99 | .00 |

*Note.* Numbers 21-23 represent the subscales of the Performance Task. Number 21 refers to Analysis and Problem Solving. Number 22 reflects Writing Effectiveness and number 23 represents Writing Mechanics.

a multi-stage translation process. Through the combined effort of colleagues and content-area experts from each country it was possible to specify and examine the similarities in the underlying construct definition of higher-order skills and the alignment of the items with the test blueprint. As part of the adaptation phase, a small pilot study was conducted in Italy to ensure that items on the instrument were functioning as intended. Consequently, it was determined that Italian and

American students appear to associate the same meaning to the definition of higher-order skills and that the items on the instrument were adequately sampled from the domain of higher-order skills. The appropriateness of construct representativeness across countries was confirmed by the results of the CFA analyses. Measurement equivalence at the scale level through the MG-CFA approach indicated that persons ascribed the same meaning to the underlying construct, but the results of the strong equivalence test indicated that there might be a lack of evidence to conduct direct valid score comparisons across countries.

Method bias may be introduced through administration procedures, differences that pertain to the instrument itself, and/or differences in the samples. The test administration platform, for use in Italy, was examined by CAE representatives prior to test administration to ensure comparability of the testing platforms. In order to circumvent problems due to rater effects, specific scoring rubrics and guidelines were developed, and graders underwent rigorous training sessions that were facilitated through the joint efforts of both countries. Heterogeneity of the sample itself, such as differences in motivation, also could impact the outcome of the assessment results. Students in the US who take CLA+ have an independent opportunity to demonstrate their level of higher-order skills compared to other students across the country. CLA+'s matching system is designed to attract students and motivate them to put in their best effort on the assessment. For example, if students score in the top 50% of CLA+ test takers, they are eligible for a badge demonstrating that they achieved the level of proficiency on the test. Furthermore, students can store their test and badge results in Parchment's "vault" and, through Parchment's service, students can share their CLA+ results, transcript, and badge information with prospective employers or use the badge for other purposes. Parchment is a platform that builds a virtual bridge connecting students, educational institutions, and employers who rely on educational credentials.

Students who reach proficiency and/or mastery level also are able to participate in appropriate virtual career fairs where they can meet with prospective employers. Students who participated in Italy do not have these same opportunities/incentives and, thus, motivation could have impacted the assessment results differently for the two samples.

Qualitative approaches to mitigating item bias involved thorough item reviews by content-area experts during the test adaptation phase. Individual items were reviewed in terms of poor translation, complex wording, and whether the items invoke unintended additional abilities. Additionally, cognitive labs were conducted to study the mental processes students use when completing a task. CAE representatives provided ANVUR staff with a protocol for the implementation of cognitive labs. Cognitive labs were carefully designed to guide interviewers in eliciting and recording student responses accurately.

The quantitative analysis included a combination of both DIF analyses at the item level and measurement equivalence at the scale level. Results of the DIF analyses indicated that measurement equivalence, as tested at the item-level, may indeed warrant direct score comparisons across countries. Based on the results, items did not function significantly different between countries. The differences between scale-level and item-level equivalence are in agreement with the findings of B. D. Zumbo (2003), which suggest that scale-level equivalence does not guarantee item-level equivalence or vice versa. These results further strengthen the belief that consideration of only one type of quantitative methodology may yield misleading results regarding whether measurement equivalence has been attained across countries. Furthermore, a mixture of qualitative and quantitative approaches may be necessary to ensure high-quality standards during the test development process. For example, quantitative methods may detect DIF, but review by content-area experts, or cognitive interviewing of persons who responded to items on the instrument, is required to determine why an item is exhibiting DIF.

## FUTURE RESEARCH DIRECTIONS

The concept of assessing higher-order skills will likely grow in importance over the coming decade as these types of skills are in alignment with the demands of careers evolving in the 21st century internationally. Business and political leaders are asking educators worldwide to emphasize career skills, such as critical thinking, problem-solving, creativity, and global aptitude in technology-rich settings (Hart Research Associates, 2006). As education enters a new era through advancements in technology, innovative assessment practices that are enhanced by interactive and/or adaptive scenario-based tasks and simulations are expected to replace traditional paper-and-pencil examinations that elicit the recall of factual knowledge. The remaining challenge regards how to leverage advancements in technology and psychometrics when assessing higher-order skills in complex global environments. More specifically, from a psychometric perspective, measuring competencies within an international framework poses challenges that pertain to test development, scoring, and the validity of score interpretations. Collaborative efforts between measurement scientists, cognitive scientists, and experts within the tertiary education system from various nations will be indispensable in the development of instruments that are within appropriate cultural contexts.

While the analyses presented here refer to score comparisons between two countries, caution needs to be taken when applying MG-CFA procedures to large-scale cross-national data because underlying statistical assumptions are likely not tenable. For example, an assumption when testing for measurement equivalence is that all samples derive from the same population. In particular, when the number of countries increases and, thus, the diversity of groups increases, it becomes evident that analyses may need to be modified to account for arising complexities. A multi-national sample may consist of clusters of countries exhibiting both within-cluster homogeneity and between-cluster heterogeneity. Under these circumstances, the analyses of measurement equivalence may need to be extended to examine whether specific items, nationalities, or a combination of both contribute to an ill-fitting model.

Data for cross-national comparisons inherently follow a nested or hierarchical structure in that individuals are nested within institutions and institutions are nested within countries (Cheung, Leung, & Au, 2006; F. J. Van de Vijver & Poortinga, 2002). Much research in regards to valid cross-national score comparisons has focused on examining psychometric properties at the individual student level, neglecting psychometric properties at the country levels. In the case of large scale cross-national data, statistical procedures that address both the individual (i.e., disaggregated) and the group (i.e., aggregated) levels do exist but rarely have been applied within a cross-cultural comparison context. Consequently, single-level data structures are commonly used to make inferences regarding country-level comparisons. However, failure to account for dependencies in the data may limit the validity of the inferences to be drawn and may lead to distorted results. In order to ensure adequate results, analyses can be conducted at the individual level where students form the unit of analysis or at the country level where countries form the unit of analysis. Student-level analyses examine the extent to which relations among variables within a country are related in a similar manner across countries. Country-level analyses focus on comparisons of means across national groups, without assuming that variable dependencies found across countries hold within each nation.

## CONCLUSION

This chapter outlined a holistic approach to mitigating bias in order to collect evidence for valid cross-national score comparisons. A case study was presented to demonstrate a successful test adaptation and translation process of a computer-based assessment of higher-order skills at the post-secondary school level. Results indicated that higher-order skills were assessed in both countries. However, it is not certain whether measurement equivalence was attained due to the conflicting results between the scale-level and individual item-level analyses. This poses the question of whether valid score inference can be drawn from direct score comparisons of students in different countries. Psychometric evidence exists for providing valid score inferences within each country due to the successful adaptation of CLA+. The findings of this analysis are congruent with other studies that found that the equivalency assumption of comparable results is difficult to attain in cross-national research endeavors, regardless of item type or format (Klein, Zahner, Benjamin, Bolus, & Steedle, 2013; R. Wolf, Zahner, Kostoris, & Benjamin, 2014; Zahner & Steedle, 2014). Thus, caution needs to be taken when score inferences are drawn across countries.

During the last few decades, bias has been predominantly associated with item bias or differential item functioning; methods to address construct and method bias often appear to be neglected. While the importance of addressing item bias is evident in cross-national research, it also is apparent that cross-national comparisons can further be challenged by construct irrelevant sources of variance that go beyond individual items. Perhaps an ongoing effort to include a mixture of qualitative and quantitative approaches could aid in mitigating bias in assessments that attempt to measure higher-order skills at the tertiary education level across nations.

This case study provided empirical support for the recommendation found in the *International Test Commission Guidelines for Adapting Educational and Psychological Tests*, which urges researchers to carry out empirical studies to demonstrate measurement (factor) equivalence of their instrument across language groups and to identify any item-level DIF that may be present (Hambleton & Patsula, 1999; Van de Vijver & Hambleton, 1996).

## REFERENCES

Baker, F. B., & Kim, S. H. (2004). *Item response theory: Parameter estimation techniques* (2nd ed.). New York: Marcel Dekker.

Bentler, P. M., & Wu, E. J. (2005). *EQS 6.1 for Windows*. Encino, CA: Multivariate Software.

Blömeke, S., Zlatkin-Troitschanskaia, O., Kuhn, C., & Fege, J. (2013). *Modeling and Measuring Competencies in Higher Education*. Springer. doi:10.1007/978-94-6091-867-4

Bock, D. R. (1972). Estimating item parameters and latent ability when responses are scored in two or more nominal categories. *Psychometrika*, *37*(1), 29–51. doi:10.1007/BF02291411

Bock, R. D. (1997). A brief history of item theory response. *Educational Measurement: Issues and Practice*, *16*(4), 21–33. doi:10.1111/j.1745-3992.1997.tb00605.x

Bollen, K. A. (1989). A new incremental fit index for general structural equation models. *Sociological Methods & Research*, *17*(3), 303–316. doi:10.1177/0049124189017003004

Byrne, B. M., & Shavelson, R. J. (1987). Adolescent self-concept: Testing the assumption of equivalent structure across gender. *American Educational Research Journal, 24*(3), 365–385. doi:10.3102/00028312024003365

Byrne, B. M., Shavelson, R. J., & Muthén, B. (1989). Testing for the equivalence of factor covariance and mean structures: The issue of partial measurement invariance. *Psychological Bulletin, 105*(3), 456–466. doi:10.1037/0033-2909.105.3.456

Byrne, B. M., & Watkins, D. (2003). The issue of measurement invariance revisited. *Journal of Cross-Cultural Psychology, 34*(2), 155–175. doi:10.1177/0022022102250225

Cai, L. (2013). flexMIRT version 2: Flexible multilevel multidimensional item analysis and test scoring. Chapel Hill, NC: Vector Psychometric Group.

Cai, L., Thissen, D., & du Toit, S. (2011). *IRTPRO for Windows* [Computer software]. Lincolnwood, IL: Scientific Software International.

Camilli, G., & Shepard, L. A. (1994). *Methods for identifying biased test items*. Sage Publications.

Campbell, D. T. (1986). Science's social system of validity-enhancing collective belief change and the problems of the social sciences. In Metatheory in social science: Pluralisms and subjectivities (pp. 108-135). Chicago: University of Chicago Press.

Chang, H. H., Mazzeo, J., & Roussos, L. (1996). Detecting DIF for polytomously scored items: An adaptation of the SIBTEST procedure. *Journal of Educational Measurement, 33*(3), 333–353. doi:10.1111/j.1745-3984.1996.tb00496.x

Cheung, M. W.-L., Leung, K., & Au, K. (2006). Evaluating Multilevel Models in Cross-Cultural Research An Illustration With Social Axioms. *Journal of Cross-Cultural Psychology, 37*(5), 522–541. doi:10.1177/0022022106290476

Cole, J. S., Bergin, D. A., & Whittaker, T. A. (2008). Predicting student achievement for low stakes tests with effort and task value. *Contemporary Educational Psychology, 33*(4), 609–624. doi:10.1016/j.cedpsych.2007.10.002

De Ayala, R. J. (2009). *Theory and practice of item response theory*. Guilford Publications.

Dorans, N. J., & Kulick, E. (1986). Demonstrating the utility of the standardization approach to assessing unexpected differential item performance on the Scholastic Aptitude Test. *Journal of Educational Measurement, 23*(4), 355–368. doi:10.1111/j.1745-3984.1986.tb00255.x

Dorans, N. J., & Schmitt, A. P. (1993). Constructed response and differential item functioning: A pragmatic approach. *Construction versus choice in cognitive measurement*, 135-165.

Edelen, M. O., Thissen, D., Teresi, J. A., Kleinman, M., & Ocepek-Welikson, K. (2006). Identification of differential item functioning using item response theory and the likelihood-based model comparison approach: Application to the Mini-Mental State Examination. *Medical Care, 44*(11Suppl 3), S134–S142. doi:10.1097/01.mlr.0000245251.83359.8c PMID:17060820

Embretson, S. E., & Reise, S. P. (2000). *Item response theory for psychologists*. Psychology Press.

Fidalgo, A. M., & Madeira, J. M. (2008). Generalized Mantel-Haenszel methods for differential item functioning detection. *Educational and Psychological Measurement, 68*(6), 940–958. doi:10.1177/0013164408315265

French, A. W., & Miller, T. R. (1996). Logistic regression and its use in detecting differential item functioning in polytomous items. *Journal of Educational Measurement, 33*(3), 315–332. doi:10.1111/j.1745-3984.1996.tb00495.x

Hambleton, R. (2005). Issues, designs, and technical guidelines for adapting tests into multiple languages and cultures. In R. Hambleton, P. Merenda, & C. Spielberger (Eds.), *Adapting educational and psychological tests for cross-cultural assessment* (Vol. 1, pp. 3–38). Lawrence Erlbaum Associates.

Hambleton, R. K. (1996). *Guidelines for Adapting Educational and Psychological Tests*. Academic Press.

Hambleton, R. K., & Murphy, E. (1992). A psychometric perspective on authentic measurement. *Applied Measurement in Education, 5*(1), 1–16. doi:10.1207/s15324818ame0501_1

Hambleton, R. K., & Patsula, L. (1999). Increasing the validity of adapted tests: Myths to be avoided and guidelines for improving test adaptation practices. *Association of Test Publishers, 1*(1), 1–13.

Hart Research Associates. (2006). *How Should Colleges Prepare Students to Succeed in Today's Global Economy? - Based on Surveys Among Employers and Recent College Graduates*. Washington, DC: Hart Research Associates.

Hirschfeld, G., & von Brachel, R. (2014). Multiple-Group confirmatory factor analysis in R–A tutorial in measurement invariance with continuous and ordinal indicators. *Practical Assessment, Research & Evaluation, 19*(7), 2.

Hocevar, D., El-Zahhar, N., & Gombos, A. (1989). Cross-cultural equivalence of anxiety measurements in English–Hungarian bilinguals. In Advances in test anxiety research (Vol. 6, pp. 223-231). Netherlands.

Holland, P. W., & Thayer, D. T. (1988). Differential item performance and the Mantel-Haenszel procedure. *Test validity*, 129-145.

Holland, P. W., & Wainer, H. (1993). *Differential item functioning*. Psychology Press.

Horn, J. L., & McArdle, J. J. (1992). A practical and theoretical guide to measurement invariance in aging research. *Experimental Aging Research, 18*(3), 117–144. doi:10.1080/03610739208253916 PMID:1459160

Hu, L., & Bentler, P. M. (1999). Cutoff criteria for fit indexes in covariance structure analysis: Conventional criteria versus new alternatives. *Structural Equation Modeling, 6*(1), 1–55. doi:10.1080/10705519909540118

IBM. (2013). *IBM Statistics for Windows. Version 22.0*. Armonk, NY: IBM Corp.

Johnstone, C. J., Bottsford-Miller, N. A., & Thompson, S. J. (2006). *Using the Think Aloud Method (Cognitive Labs) to Evaluate Test Design for Students with Disabilities and English Language Learners*. Technical Report 44. National Center on Educational Outcomes, University of Minnesota.

Jöreskog, K. G., & Sörbom, D. (2014). *LISREL 9.1 for Windows*. Skokie, IL: Scientific Software International.

Kim, S. H., Cohen, A. S., & Park, T. H. (1995). Detection of differential item functioning in multiple groups. *Journal of Educational Measurement, 32*(3), 261–276. doi:10.1111/j.1745-3984.1995.tb00466.x

Klein, S., Zahner, D., Benjamin, R., Bolus, R., & Steedle, J. (2013). *Observations on AHELO's Generic Skills Strand Methodology and Findings*. Council for Aid to Education.

Little, T. D., Card, N. A., Slegers, D. W., & Ledford, E. C. (2007). *Representing contextual effects in multiple-group MACS models*. Academic Press.

Magis, D., Béland, S., Tuerlinckx, F., & De Boeck, P. (2010). A general framework and an R package for the detection of dichotomous differential item functioning. *Behavior Research Methods, 42*(3), 847–862. doi:10.3758/BRM.42.3.847 PMID:20805607

Magis, D., Raîche, G., Béland, S., & Gérard, P. (2011). A generalized logistic regression procedure to detect differential item functioning among multiple groups. *International Journal of Testing, 11*(4), 365–386. doi:10.1080/15305058.2011.602810

Meredith, W. (1993). Measurement invariance, factor analysis and factorial invariance. *Psychometrika, 58*(4), 525–543. doi:10.1007/BF02294825

Miller, T. R., & Spray, J. A. (1993). Logistic discriminant function analysis for DIF identification of polytomously scored items. *Journal of Educational Measurement, 30*(2), 107–122. doi:10.1111/j.1745-3984.1993.tb01069.x

Morales, L. S., Flowers, C., Gutierrez, P., Kleinman, M., & Teresi, J. A. (2006). Item and scale differential functioning of the Mini-Mental State Exam assessed using the differential item and test functioning (DFIT) framework. *Medical Care, 44*(11Suppl 3), S143–S151. doi:10.1097/01.mlr.0000245141.70946.29 PMID:17060821

Muraki, E. (1998). *RESGEN:Item response generator* [Program Manual]. Princeton, NJ: Educational Testing Service.

Muthén, B., & Lehman, J. (1985). Multiple group IRT modeling: Applications to item bias analysis. *Journal of Educational and Behavioral Statistics, 10*(2), 133–142. doi:10.3102/10769986010002133

Muthén, B., & Muthén, L. (2010). *Mplus (version 6.00)* [computer software]. Los Angeles, CA: Muthén & Muthén.

Muthén, B., & Muthén, L. (2010). *Mplus Version 6.1* [Software]. Los Angeles, CA: Author.

Oshima, T., Raju, N. S., & Flowers, C. P. (1997). Development and Demonstration of Multidimensional IRT-Based Internal Measures of Differential Functioning of Items and Tests. *Journal of Educational Measurement, 34*(3), 253–272. doi:10.1111/j.1745-3984.1997.tb00518.x

Penfield, R. D. (2001). Assessing differential item functioning among multiple groups: A comparison of three Mantel-Haenszel procedures. *Applied Measurement in Education, 14*(3), 235–259. doi:10.1207/S15324818AME1403_3

R. (2014). *R: A Language and Environment for Statistical Computing*. Vienna, Austria: R Foundation for Statistical Computing. Retrieved from http://www.R-project.org

Raju, N. S. (1988). The area between two item characteristic curves. *Psychometrika, 53*(4), 495–502. doi:10.1007/BF02294403

Raju, N. S. (1990). Determining the significance of estimated signed and unsigned areas between two item response functions. *Applied Psychological Measurement, 14*(2), 197–207. doi:10.1177/014662169001400208

Raju, N. S., Laffitte, L. J., & Byrne, B. M. (2002). Measurement equivalence: A comparison of methods based on confirmatory factor analysis and item response theory. *The Journal of Applied Psychology, 87*(3), 517–529. doi:10.1037/0021-9010.87.3.517 PMID:12090609

Reckase, M. D. (2009). *Multidimensional item response theory*. Springer. doi:10.1007/978-0-387-89976-3

Rosseel, Y. (2012). Lavaan: An R package for Structural Equation Modeling. *Journal of Statistical Software, 48*(2), 1–36.

Samejima, F. (1997). Graded response model. Handbook of modern item response theory, 85-100.

SAS. (2011). *The SAS system for Windows. Release 9.2.* Carey, NC: SAS Institute Inc.

Selig, J. P., Card, N. A., & Little, T. D. (2008). *Latent variable structural equation modeling in cross-cultural research: Multigroup and multilevel approaches.* Academic Press.

Shealy, R., & Stout, W. (1993). A model-based standardization approach that separates true bias/DIF from group ability differences and detects test bias/DTF as well as item bias/DIF. *Psychometrika, 58*(2), 159–194. doi:10.1007/BF02294572

Stark, S., Chernyshenko, O. S., & Drasgow, F. (2006). Detecting differential item functioning with confirmatory factor analysis and item response theory: Toward a unified strategy. *The Journal of Applied Psychology, 91*(6), 1292–1306. doi:10.1037/0021-9010.91.6.1292 PMID:17100485

Svetina, D., & Rutkowski, L. (2014). Detecting differential item functioning using generalized logistic regression in the context of large-scale assessments. *Large-scale Assessments in Education, 2*(1), 1–17.

Swaminathan, H., & Rogers, H. J. (1990). Detecting differential item functioning using logistic regression procedures. *Journal of Educational Measurement, 27*(4), 361–370. doi:10.1111/j.1745-3984.1990.tb00754.x

Thissen, D. (1991). *MULTILOG user's guide.* Chicago: Scientific Software.

Thissen, D., & Steinberg, L. (1988). Data analysis using item response theory. *Psychological Bulletin, 104*(3), 385–395. doi:10.1037/0033-2909.104.3.385

Thissen, D., Steinberg, L., & Gerrard, M. (1986). Beyond group-mean differences: The concept of item bias. *Psychological Bulletin, 99*(1), 118–128. doi:10.1037/0033-2909.99.1.118

Thissen, D., Steinberg, L., & Wainer, H. (1988). *Use of item response theory in the study of group differences in trace lines.* Academic Press.

Thissen, D., Steinberg, L., & Wainer, H. (1993). *Detection of differential item functioning using the parameters of item response models.* Academic Press.

Tremblay, K., Lalancette, D., & Roseveare, D. (2012). *Assessment of Higher Education Learning Outcomes feasibility study report: volume 1-design and implementation.* Academic Press.

Van de Vijver, F., & Hambleton, R. K. (1996). Translating tests: Some practical guidelines. *European Psychologist, 1*(2), 89–99. doi:10.1027/1016-9040.1.2.89

Van de Vijver, F., & Leung, K. (1997). *Methods and data analysis of comparative research.* Allyn & Bacon.

Van de Vijver, F., & Tanzer, N. K. (2004). Bias and equivalence in cross-cultural assessment: An overview. *Revue Européenne de Psychologie Appliquée. European Review of Applied Psychology, 54*(2), 119–135. doi:10.1016/j.erap.2003.12.004

Van de Vijver, F. J. (1998). Towards a theory of bias and equivalence. *Zuma Nachrichten, 3,* 41–65.

Van de Vijver, F. J., & Leung, K. (1997). *Methods and data analysis for cross-cultural research* (Vol. 1). Sage.

Van de Vijver, F. J., & Poortinga, Y. H. (1997). Towards an integrated analysis of bias in cross-cultural assessment. *European Journal of Psychological Assessment, 13*(1), 29–37. doi:10.1027/1015-5759.13.1.29

Van de Vijver, F. J., & Poortinga, Y. H. (2002). Structural equivalence in multilevel research. *Journal of Cross-Cultural Psychology, 33*(2), 141–156. doi:10.1177/0022022102033002002

Vandenberg, R. J., & Lance, C. E. (2000). A review and synthesis of the measurement invariance literature: Suggestions, practices, and recommendations for organizational research. *Organizational Research Methods, 3*(1), 4–70. doi:10.1177/109442810031002

Werner, O., & Campbell, D. T. (1970). Translating, working through interpreters, and the problem of decentering. In A handbook of method in cultural anthropology (pp. 398-419). New York: American Museum of Natural History.

Wolf, R., Zahner, D., Kostoris, F., & Benjamin, R. (2014). *A Case Study of an International Performance-Based Assessment of Critical Thinking Skills*. Paper presented at the American Educational Research Association, Philadelphia, PA.

Wolf, R. M. (1998). Validity issues in international assessments. *International Journal of Educational Research, 29*(6), 491–501. doi:10.1016/S0883-0355(98)00044-5

Zahner, D., & Steedle, J. (2014). *Evaluating Performance Task Scoring Comparability in an International Testing Program*. Paper presented at the American Educational Research Association, Philadelphia, PA.

Zucker, S., Sassman, C., & Case, B. J. (2004). Cognitive labs. *San Antonio, TX: Harcourt Assessment. Retrieved, 10*(11), 2006.

Zumbo, B., & Thomas, D. (1997). *A measure of effect size for a model-based approach for studying DIF*. Working Paper. Edgeworth Laboratory for Quantitative Behavioral Science.

Zumbo, B. D. (1999). *A handbook on the theory and methods of differential item functioning (DIF)*. Ottawa: National Defense Headquarters.

Zumbo, B. D. (2003). Does item-level DIF manifest itself in scale-level analyses? Implications for translating language tests. *Language Testing, 20*(2), 136–147. doi:10.1191/0265532203lt248oa

Zwick, R., Donoghue, J. R., & Grima, A. (1993). Assessment of differential item functioning for performance tasks. *Journal of Educational Measurement, 30*(3), 233–251. doi:10.1111/j.1745-3984.1993.tb00425.x

## ADDITIONAL READING

Allalouf, A., Hambleton, R. K., & Sireci, S. G. (1999). Identifying the causes of DIF in translated verbal items. *Journal of Educational Measurement, 36*(3), 185–198. doi:10.1111/j.1745-3984.1999.tb00553.x

Allen, J., & Velden, R. K. W. (2012). *Skills for the 21st century: Implications for education: ROA*. Maastricht University School of Business and Economics.

Benjamin, R. (2008). *The Contribution of the Collegiate Learning Assessment To Teaching and Learning*. New York, NY: Council for Aid to Education.

Benjamin, R., Klein, S., Steedle, J. T., Zahner, D., Elliot, S., & Patterson, J. A. (2012). The case for generic skills and performance assessment in the United States and international settings. *CAE - Occasional Paper*. Retrieved from http://www.collegiatelearningassessment.org/files/The_Case_for_Generic_Skills_and_Performance_Assessment_in_the_United_States_and_International_Settings.pdf

Bowman, K. (2010). Background paper for the AQF Council on generic skills: [AQF Council Secretariat].

Byrne, B. M. (2005). Factor analytic models: Viewing the structure of an assessment instrument from three perspectives. *Journal of Personality Assessment, 85*(1), 17–32. doi:10.1207/s15327752jpa8501_02 PMID:16083381

Byrne, B. M. (2008). Testing for multigroup equivalence of a measuring instrument: A walk through the process. *Psicothema, 20*(4), 872–882. PMID:18940097

Byrne, B. M., & Watkins, D. (2003). The issue of measurement invariance revisited. *Journal of Cross-Cultural Psychology, 34*(2), 155–175. doi:10.1177/0022022102250225

Cheung, M. W.-L., & Au, K. (2005). Applications of multilevel structural equation modeling to cross-cultural research. *Structural Equation Modeling, 12*(4), 598–619. doi:10.1207/s15328007sem1204_5

Hambleton, R. K. (2000). Advances in Performance Assessment Methodology. *Applied Psychological Measurement, 24*(4), 291–293. doi:10.1177/01466210022031750

Hambleton, R. K., Hambleton, R., Merenda, P., & Spielberger, C. (2005). Issues, designs, and technical guidelines for adapting tests into multiple languages and cultures. *Adapting educational and psychological tests for cross-cultural assessment*, 3-38.

Hambleton, R. K., & Kanjee, A. (1993). Enhancing the Validity of Cross-Cultural Studies: Improvements in Instrument Translation Methods.

Hambleton, R. K., & Murphy, E. (1992). A psychometric perspective on authentic measurement. *Applied Measurement in Education, 5*(1), 1–16. doi:10.1207/s15324818ame0501_1

Hauptman, A. M., & Kim, Y. (2009). Cost, Commitment, and Attainment in Higher Education: An International Comparison. *Jobs for the future*.

Kline, R. B. (2013). Assessing statistical aspects of test fairness with structural equation modelling. *Educational Research and Evaluation, 19*(2-3), 204–222. doi:10.1080/13803611.2013.767624

Leung, K., & van de Vijver, F. J. (2008). Strategies for Strengthening Causal Inferences in Cross Cultural Research The Consilience Approach. *International Journal of Cross Cultural Management, 8*(2), 145–169. doi:10.1177/1470595808091788

Lim, G. S., Geranpayeh, A., Khalifa, H., & Buckendahl, C. W. (2013). Standard setting to an international reference framework: Implications for theory and practice. *International Journal of Testing, 13*(1), 32–49. doi:10.1080/15305058.2012.678526

Mirazchiyski, P. (2013). Providing School-Level Reports from International Large-Scale Assessments: Methodological Considerations, Limitations, and Possible Solutions. Hamburg: International Association for the Evaluation of Educational Achievement (IEA).

Raju, N. S., Laffitte, L. J., & Byrne, B. M. (2002). Measurement equivalence: A comparison of methods based on confirmatory factor analysis and item response theory. *The Journal of Applied Psychology, 87*(3), 517–529. doi:10.1037/0021-9010.87.3.517 PMID:12090609

Rutkowski, L., & Rutkowski, D. (2010). Getting it 'better': The importance of improving background questionnaires in international large-scale assessment. *Journal of Curriculum Studies, 42*(3), 411–430. doi:10.1080/00220272.2010.487546

Sireci, S. G., & Allalouf, A. (2003). Appraising item equivalence across multiple languages and cultures. *Language Testing, 20*(2), 148–166. doi:10.1191/0265532203lt249oa

Van De Vijver, F. J. (2002). Cross-Cultural Assessment: Value for Money? *Applied Psychology, 51*(4), 545–566. doi:10.1111/1464-0597.00107

Wei, R. C., Cor, K., Arshan, N., & Pecheone, R. (2012). *Can Performance-Based Assessments be Reliable and Valid? Findings From a State Pilot.* Paper presented at the American Educational Research Association, Vancouver, British Columbia.

Wilson, M., Bejar, I., Scalise, K., Templin, J., Wiliam, D., & Torres Irribarra, D. (2010). Draft White Paper 2: Perspectives on methodological issues. *Melbourne: ACTS.*

Zumbo, B. D., & Koh, K. H. (2005). Manifestation of differences in item-level characteristics in scale-level measurement invariance tests of multi-group confirmatory factor analyses. *Journal of Modern Applied Statistical Methods; JMASM, 4*(1), 24.

## KEY TERMS AND DEFINITIONS

**Bias:** Any systematic differences in the meaning of test scores that are associated with group membership.

**CLA+:** A college outcome assessment that purports to measure critical thinking and writing skills.

**Confirmatory Factor Analysis:** Statistical procedure to test whether the data fit a hypothesized measurement model.

**Construct:** A proposed attribute of an individual that often cannot be measured directly, but can be assessed using a number of indicators or manifest variables.

**Differential Item Functioning:** Occurs when individuals from different groups (i.e., gender or ethnicity) with the same ability or skill level have a different probability of giving a certain response on a measurement instrument.

**Item Response Theory:** Theory grounded on the idea that the probability of a correct response to an item on an assessment is a mathematical function of person and item parameters.

**Measurement Equivalence:** Statistical property of measurement that indicates that the same construct is being measured across groups.

**Psychometrics:** Field of study concerned with the theory and technique of educational psychological measurement.

**Structural Equation Modeling:** Statistical technique for testing and estimating causal relationships.

## APPENDIX

### Scenario

You are a staff member who works for an organization that provides analysis of policy claims made by political candidates and makes recommendations to endorse specific candidates.

Pat Stone is running for reelection as the mayor of Jefferson, a city in the state of Columbia. Mayor Stone's opponent in this contest is Dr. Jamie Eager. Dr. Eager is a member of the Jefferson City Council. Dr. Eager made three arguments during a recent TV interview:

First, Dr. Eager said that Mayor Stone's proposal for reducing crime by increasing the number of police officers is a bad idea. Dr. Eager said "it will only lead to more crime." Dr. Eager supported this argument with a chart that shows that counties with a relatively large number of police officers per resident tend to have more crime than those with fewer officers per resident.

Second, Dr. Eager said "we should take the money that would have gone to hiring more police officers and spend it on the Strive drug treatment program." Dr. Eager supported this argument by referring to a news release by the Washington Institute for Social Research that describes the effectiveness of the Strive drug treatment program. Dr. Eager also said there were other scientific studies that showed the Strive program was effective.

Third, Dr. Eager said that because of the strong correlation between drug use and crime in Jefferson, reducing the number of addicts would lower the city's crime rate. To support this argument, Dr. Eager presented a chart that compared the percentage of drug addicts in a Jefferson ZIP Code area to the number of crimes committed in that area. Dr. Eager based this chart on crime and community data tables that were provided by the Jefferson Police Department.

In advance of the debate later this week, your office must release a report evaluating the claims made by Dr. Eager and make a recommendation endorsing either Mr. Stone or Dr. Eager.

### Document Library

1. Memorandum.
2. Newspaper Article.
3. Crime and Drug Statistics.
4. Research Brief.
5. Chart.
6. Online Search Research Abstracts.

### Task

Your task is to write a report evaluating the claims made by Dr. Eager and make a recommendation endorsing either Mr. Stone or Dr. Eager. Make sure to provide an analysis of Dr. Eager's three claims and choose a candidate (either Mr. Stone or Dr. Eager) to support. Your analysis of Dr. Eager's claims should include appropriate and relevant evidence as well as counterarguments from the information given in the document library. Your decision to support either Mr. Stone or Dr. Eager should also be clearly supported using the information in the documents.

There is no "correct" answer. Your report should clearly describe all the details necessary to support your position. Your answers will be judged not only on the accuracy of the information you provide, but also on how clearly the ideas are presented, how thoroughly the information is covered, how effectively the ideas are organized, and how well your writing reflects the conventions of Standard Written English.

While your personal values and experiences are important, please answer all of the questions in this task solely on the basis of the information provided in the Document Library.

# Chapter 19
# Evidence–Centered Concept Map in Computer–Based Assessment of Critical Thinking

**Yigal Rosen**
*Harvard University, USA*

**Maryam Mosharraf**
*Pearson, USA*

## ABSTRACT

*A concept map is a graphical tool for representing knowledge structure in the form of a graph whose nodes represent concepts, while arcs between nodes correspond to interrelations between them. Using a concept map engages students in a variety of critical and complex thinking, such as evaluating, analyzing, and decision making. Although the potential use of concept maps to assess students' knowledge has been recognized, concept maps are traditionally used as instructional tools. The chapter introduces a technology-enabled three-phase Evidence-Centered Concept Map (ECCM) designed to make students' thinking visible in critical thinking assessment tasks that require students to analyze claims and supporting evidence on a topic and to draw conclusions. Directions for future research are discussed in terms of their implications to technology tools in large-scale assessment programs that target higher-order thinking skills.*

## INTRODUCTION

In today's global economy, the need for higher levels of education and thinking skills is large and growing. Proficiency in critical thinking is key not only to unlocking the world of higher education but also in the workplace and in personal, social, and civic life. In light of the importance of critical thinking skills, current large-scale assessment programs such as the Program for International Student Assessment (PISA) and the U.S. National Assessment of Educational Progress (NAEP) have embedded critical thinking in K12 assessment of science, math, and reading, as has the OECD Programme for the International Assessment of Adult Competencies (PIAAC). According to the Partnership for 21st Century Skills (2009) and Assessment and Teaching of 21st Century Skills

DOI: 10.4018/978-1-4666-9441-5.ch019

(Binkley et al., 2012), a set of critical thinking competencies includes skills such as analyzing how parts of a whole interact with each other, synthesizing and making connections between information and arguments, and asking meaningful questions to clarify various points of view. Critical thinking requires the competencies of evaluating the credibility of sources, analyzing the quality of arguments, making inferences using reasoning, and decision-making (see Lai, & Viering, 2012, for a literature review). Measuring complex skills such as critical thinking and other higher-order skills requires designing and developing assessments that address the multiple facets implied by the skill. One of the possible ways to achieve these changes in educational assessment is by providing visible sequences of actions that students have taken by using technology tools. Thinking tools are computer applications that enable students to represent what they have learned and know using different representational formalisms. Studying the role of thinking tools (often called graphic organizers) in computer-based formative assessment of higher-order thinking skills is crucial to determining whether these types of scaffolding tools can bring a real added value into large-scale programs. An interactive Evidence-Centered Concept Map (ECCM) is one of the promising technology tools in making student thinking visible in critical thinking formative assessments (Rosen, 2014; Rosen, & Tager, 2014). When creating an ECCM, students perform a task that no ordinary collection of notes may encompass. ECCM represents a personal visualization of claims and supporting evidence on a topic, as well as relationships between the claims. The tool also represents possible gaps in a student's analysis of the topic and the ability to make a valid and reliable evidence-based conclusion. In this way, concept maps along with feedback system can be used as a formative assessment tool to enhance teaching and learning. This chapter provides a comprehensive overview of ECCM, illustrates a sample task in ECCM-based critical

thinking formative assessment along with the major findings from an international pilot study, and discusses implications for development and further research directions.

## BACKGROUND

People make decisions on very limited evidence and often assert their proposition with great confidence. They tend to believe their current information set is complete and reliable. Kahneman (2011) calls this pattern What You See is All There Is (WYSIATI). Another consequence of WYSIATI is that people evaluate complex topics without considering a wider range of alternatives or trying to get more information that could potentially contradict the decision. The individual may understand in principle that worthless information should not be treated differently from a complete lack of information, but WYSIATI limits the ability to apply this principle. A student that follows WASIATI will achieve high confidence much easier by ignoring what is unknown. Thus, teachers should provide students with practice in a basic understanding of the nature of evidence and well-formed arguments. Analyzing errors addresses the logic, reasonableness, or accuracy of claims; making and defending claims are at the heart of critical thinking instruction and assessment. According to Marzano (2007), students should be taught to identify validity of claims by analyzing their grounds, backing, and qualifiers. The students do not have to understand the technical aspects of grounds, backing, and qualifiers, such as their names and defining characteristics. However, students should be aware that to be valid, claims should be supported by initial evidence (grounds), the sources of the supporting evidence should be identified (warrants), the evidence should be explained and discussed (backing), and exceptions to the claims should be identified (qualifiers). Thus, providing students with opportunities to evaluate the completeness of information across topics and subject areas and providing feedback will promote critical thinking as opposed to the tendency to WASIATI pattern.

There is a notable lack of consensus on whether critical thinking is generalizable or entirely domain-specific. We adopt the intermediate approach (Ennis, 1985; Smith, 2002), according to which some critical thinking skills apply to multiple domains (e.g., analyzing the logics of a claim or evaluating the reliability of evidence source), whereas others are unique to specific subject areas (e.g., experimental inquiry in science or reasoning in math). In our research, an operational definition of critical thinking refers to *the capacity of an individual to effectively engage in a process of making decisions or solving problems by analyzing and evaluating evidence, arguments, claims, beliefs, and alternative points of view; synthesizing and making connections between information and arguments; interpreting information; and making inferences using reasoning appropriate to the situation* (Rosen, & Tager, 2014). In identifying critical thinking skills, this research attempts to incorporate skills identified in other assessment frameworks, such as the Partnership for 21st Century Skills (2009) and Assessment and Teaching of 21st Century Skills (Binkley et al., 2012).

## Assessing Critical Thinking

Critical thinking can be difficult to measure in a valid and reliable manner. First, this is because of the various conceptualizations of critical thinking as domain-general as opposed to domain-specific, as well as because of the differences in the definitions of the construct (Halpern, 1998; Kuncel, & Hezlett, 2010; Moss, & Koziol, 1991; Norris, 1989). A narrower definition in which critical thinking is considered a finite set of specific competencies could provide an optimal platform for measurement purposes. These competencies could be useful for effective decision making for

many (but not all) contexts, while their efficacy is further curtailed by students' specific knowledge demands in the specific context. Second, it is difficult to assess critical thinking because it is an ongoing process rather than a recognizable outcome. The conventional assessment formats limit students' ability to optimally apply their critical thinking and restricts educators' ability to follow students' thinking process (Bonk, & Smith, 1998; Fischer, Spiker, & Riedel, 2009). Among the existing assessments of critical thinking are the California Critical Thinking Skills Test (Facione, 1990), the Cornell Critical Thinking Tests (Ennis, & Millman, 2005), the Ennis-Weir Critical Thinking Essay Test (Ennis, & Weir, 1985), and the Watson-Glaser Critical Thinking Appraisal (Watson, & Glaser, 2008). These assessments use multiple-choice or selected response formats and tend to be general critical thinking assessments rather than subject-specific (Ku, 2009). However, educators advocate using rich performance assessment tasks that make use of authentic, real-world problem contexts (Bonk, & Smith, 1998; Darling-Hammond, & Adamson, 2010; Davey, et al., 2015; Ku, 2009). For example, performance assessments can assess procedural and strategic knowledge, as, for example, when students are required to decide which facts, concepts, and procedures to use when responding to an assessment task. Performance assessments of critical thinking provide adequate collateral materials to support multiple perspectives and include process as well as product indicators. Problems underlying such tasks should use ill-defined structure that often involve multiple goals that are in conflict, have more than one defensible solution, and require students to go beyond recalling or restating learned information (Mayer, & Wittrock, 2006; Moss, & Koziol, 1991). Critical thinking assessment tasks should make student reasoning visible by requiring students to provide evidence or logical arguments in support of judgments, choices, claims, or assertions (Fischer et al., 2009; Norris, 1989).

Making student thinking visible through embedded interactive concept maps in critical thinking performance assessments is one of the promising approaches that should be further explored.

## Concept Maps in Critical Thinking Formative Assessment

Computer technologies such as interactive thinking tools can support intellectual performance and enrich individuals' assessment and learning experience. Thinking tools are computer applications that enable students to represent what they have learned and know by using different representational formalisms. These graphic-verbal representations are constructed by individual or collaborative learners across different situations and environments. There are several classes of thinking tools, including semantic organization tools, dynamic modeling tools, information interpretation tools, knowledge construction tools, and conversation and collaboration tools (Jonassen, 2006; Hyerle, 2009). These tools are now commonplace in schools, colleges, and workplaces around the world. In educational assessment, thinking tools represent processes in which the student is engaged in activities, such as evaluating, analyzing, connecting, elaborating, synthesizing, designing, problem solving, and decision making. Using Perkins's (1993) terminology, the unit of analysis in these assessments is not the student without the technology in his or her environment — the *person-solo* — but the *people plus* — *in this case* the student plus the thinking tool.

Concept mapping as a thinking tool supports, guides, and extends the thinking process of the student. The thinking tool does not necessarily reduce information processing, but its goal is to make effective use of mental efforts of the student to create a *person plus* the technology setting in computer-based formative assessment. To successfully make a decision or solve a multifaceted problem, the student must mentally construct a problem space by analyzing various pieces of information and mapping specific relationships of the problem. Concept maps facilitate the analysis that students conduct and require them to think more deeply about the multifaceted topic being analyzed than they would have without the thinking tool (Novak, & Cañas, 2008). As thinking tools, concept maps help students to examine various questions, such as: To what extent are each of the claims presented in the source materials supported by valid and reliable evidence? How are different claims connected to each other? These mental maps depict complex relationships and can become "blueprints" that make abstract thoughts more visible and concrete. Without the scaffolding provided by a thinking tool, many students simply copy down ideas in static linear form even though the information is hierarchical, causal, or comparative. They have not internalized the static information as active knowledge but instead as a disconnected list. What does not show up in traditional students' response is their thinking pattern and processes of understanding (Rosen, 2014; Rosen, & Tager, 2014). There is a gap between the highly constrained linear representations of information in the students' responses in text block format and the multidimensional mapping of mental models that the brain naturally performs when processing and transforming information into knowledge. Often, students return quick responses without having to organize the information into patterns or they do this patterning in their mind without the capacity to make these patterns visible to the teacher. This ability of concept mapping to capture both the visual-spatial-verbal thinking process and the outcome is the type of assessment that truly informs learning (Jonassen, 1996; Kim, & Olaciregui, 2008). Concept maps have been widely used as thinking tools for teaching, learning, and assessment as a way to help the student think and represent his or her thinking processes (Hoeft et al., 2003; Jonassen, 1996; Kinchin, 2000; McClure, Sonak, &

Suen, 1999; Novak, & Cañas, 2008; Ruiz-Primo, 2004; Weinerth et al., 2014). A concept map is a semi-formal knowledge representation tool visualized by a graph consisting of a finite set of nodes, which depict concepts, and a finite set of arcs, which express relationships between pairs of concepts (Novak, 1998; Novak, & Cañas, 2008). The nodes may represent a single or a multifaceted concept. A linking phrase can specify the kind of relationship between concepts. As a rule, natural language is used to represent concepts and linking phrases. Moreover, the arcs of the graph can have the same weight or different weights. The concept maps comprise concepts and their relationships, often arranged hierarchically according to the importance of the concepts described, with the most general concepts at the top of the map and the more specific concepts below them. Several studies have shown that concept maps lead to better learning achievements compared with the traditional approaches (Kim, & Olaciregui, 2008), making them a valuable pedagogical tool.

Concept maps are used in educational settings in various ways. In the first, students build a concept map on a given topic. The student must decide on the structure and the content of a concept map. Another use of a concept map is "fill-in-the-map" tasks, where the structure of a concept map is given and a student must fill it using the provided set of concepts and/or linking phrases. In the last, students analyze a concept map previously built by an expert. According to Novak and Gowin (1984), new knowledge is optimally constructed based on learners' original cognitive structures so that they can connect existing cognitive structures with new ones to form meaningful learning. Through concept maps, students are able to externalize their original knowledge and combine it with new knowledge for rearranging and internalizing both the original and new knowledge (Lim, Lee, & Grabowski, 2009; Trundle, & Bell, 2010). The advantages of computer-based concept maps include the ease of making corrections, the flexibility of presenting content, automated scoring, and the availability of promoting interactions among teachers and students (Liu, Chen, & Chang, 2010; Shin, Deno, Robinson, & Marston, 2000).

Concept mapping is a cognitively challenging task that requires various higher-order thinking processes, such as assessing and classifying information, recognizing patterns, identifying and prioritizing main ideas, comparing and contrasting, identifying relationships, and thinking logically (Jonassen, 1996; Kinchin, 2000). These processes require the student to elaborate and organize information in meaningful ways, which cannot be realized through simply memorizing facts without understanding their meaning and underlying associations. The thinking processes involved in concept mapping are highly related to critical thinking competency as defined by various assessment frameworks (Binkley et al., 2012; OECD, 2010b; Partnership for 21st Century Skills, 2009). While concept mapping can be used to enhance students' thinking, it also has some challenges. Students in several studies reported that building concept maps is difficult and time-consuming, especially when they first experience it (All, Huycke, & Fisher, 2003; Hsu, 2004). Thus, it is necessary to understand the nature of the task and the thinking skills required while designing a concept map.

Research shows that concept maps are valid and reliable assessment tools (Hibberd, Morris, & Jones, 2004; McClure et al., 1999; Ritchhart, Turner, & Hadar, 2009; Ruiz-Primo, Schultz, Li, & Shavelson, 2001; Schaal, Bogner, & Girwidz, 2010). However, past studies have indicated the practical difficulty of evaluating concept maps by teachers (Wu, Hwang, Milrad, Ke, & Huang, 2012). It typically takes days or weeks for teachers to manually evaluate concept maps developed by their students (Denton, Madden, Roberts, & Rowe, 2008; Hwang, Chu, Shih, Huang, & Tsai, 2010; Ingeç, 2009). This pattern of inability to receive timely feedback not only affects the instructional scope and sequence but also significantly influences the students' learning achievements. Computer-based concept maps offer several advantages in comparison with paper-and-pencil generated concept maps (Erdogan, 2009; Nesbit, & Adesope, 2006). Students can more easily construct, modify, or maintain their concept maps, and real-time feedback on the correctness of student-constructed maps can be delivered by the online system. Also, teachers provide students with facilitation and support based on scored concept maps. Standardized elements in computer-based concept maps make an automatized and objective scoring procedure possible and reduce the time and investments on scoring.

## Scoring Concept Maps

According to Ruiz-Primo and Shavelson (1996), without the following three components, a concept map cannot be considered an assessment task: (a) a task that invites a student to provide evidence bearing on his or her knowledge structure in a domain, (b) a structured format available for the student's response, and (c) a scoring system by which the student's concept map can be accurately and consistently evaluated. Thus, a concept map based assessment is a combination of a task, a response format, and a scoring system. Use of concept maps in assessment varies in task demands (demands made on the students in generating their concept maps), task constraints (restrictiveness of the task; for example, providing the labels for the links between the nodes), and task content structure (intersection of the task demands and constraints with the structure of the subject to be mapped). Also, Ruiz-Primo and Shavelson (1996) have identified three general scoring strategies for concept maps. The first strategy is scoring a student's map components. It focuses on a combination of propositions (i.e., number, accuracy), hierarchy levels, and examples. It may include scored related to the existence of a relation between the concepts, accuracy of the label,

and the correctness of the direction of the arrow. Use of a criterion map is the second strategy. The scoring is based on a comparison of a student's concept map with that of an expert and scores the overlap between them. The assumption in this strategy is that there is an optimal representation of knowledge that best reflects the structure in a domain. This strategy varies in the definition of the expert concept map by using the teacher's map, external experts' map, an average of experts, or an average of top students in the class. A combination of map components scoring and a criterion map is the third strategy.

One example for a manual scoring system of concept maps is the system proposed by Yin and colleagues (2005). In this system, the total proposition accuracy scores are based on an evaluation of the quality of propositions that students constructed in concept map types so-called C and S (Ruiz-Primo, Shavelson, Li, & Schultz, 2001). In the C mapping technique, students are provided with concepts and asked to construct a map using self-created linking phrases. In contrast, the S mapping supplies students with both linking phrases and concept terms, while students need to select and assemble the concepts and linking phrases. The concept maps are scored based on six variables divided into *concept map products* (total accuracy score, individual proposition score, proposition choice, and structure complexity) and *concept map processes* (rate of proposition generation and procedures for generating propositions). Concept map products are based on students' drawn concept maps. The measures include quantitative variables represented by numerical values (total proportion accuracy score and individual proportion accuracy score) and qualitative variables that have categorical values (proposition choice and structure complexity). Concept map process measures are focused on students' inferred cognitive activities during the execution of the concept map, as rated by experts. Similarly to the concept map products, the variables include a quantitative variable (proposition generation rate) and a qualitative variable (proposition generation procedure). A concept map process measure can be created from students' think-aloud protocols while constructing their maps.

A scoring system in the Interactive Concept Map-Oriented Learning System (ICMLS), is one of the examples for automated scoring techniques of concept maps (Wu et al., 2012). The ICMLS has adopted CmapTools (Novak, & Cañas, 2008) as the concept map editing tool with assessment and feedback system. CmapTools enable students to construct concept maps and share them on servers via the Internet. The ICMLS system provides the student with the ability to develop concept maps, store the maps in a database, and assess the database to revise the maps based on feedback and supplementary materials.

The student-created maps are retrieved automatically by the assessment and feedback module for evaluation. The concept maps with higher scores indicate a higher degree of completeness and accuracy. The ICMLS employs an automated concept map scoring mechanism based on the weighted proposition approach proposed by Chang, Sung, Chang, and Lin (2005). A proposition is composed of two concepts and the combination between them. The score for a concept map is derived by comparing each of its propositions with the corresponding proposition in the teacher's concept map. If the two propositions are the same, the weighting of the proposition is added to the accumulated score for the student's concept map. If the two propositions are partially matched, only half of the weighting is added to the accumulated score. The calculation of the final Concept Map Score (CMS) for Student $S_i$ is provided below:

$\text{CMS}(S_i) = (\sum \text{weight value of a student's proposition the accumulated score for } S_i) \div$

$(\sum \text{sum of proposition weightings value in the expert's concept map proposition}) \times 100$

The CMS score is presented to the student along with the hints and supplementary materials concerning the incorrect and incomplete propositions. The feedback includes the score and a set of comments on the structure of concept maps developed by students, such as 'There is a missing notion related to Concept A' or 'There is a missing connection related to Concept A and some other Concept.' On the other hand, the supplementary information is a set of learning materials related to the missing or incorrect concepts and connections.

Generally, the choice of criteria depends on whether it is an additional technique or the only technique used for evaluation of the student's knowledge, the characteristics of a domain where knowledge is to be measured, and the mode of assessment (Strautmane, 2012).

## Evidence-Centered Concept Map

One of the major considerations in adapting technology enabled concept mapping tools to the assessment context is the ability to draw valid and reliable inferences about students' knowledge, skills, and abilities based on independent measures, without introducing construct irrelevant bias (e.g., student technological skills, previous experience with concept maps). In order to enable visibility of a thinking process during students' critical thinking performance, a three-phase concept map has been proposed by Rosen and Tager (2014). The Evidence-Centered Concept Map (ECCM) is designed specifically for formative assessment use to empower the student to analyze various claims and evidence on a topic and to draw a conclusion, as part of critical thinking assessment. The stages of student work with ECCM on an assessment task include: (a) gathering various claims and evidence from the resources provided (some claims and evidence contradict one another); (b) organizing the claims with supporting evidence gathered in the previous phase on ECCM without hierarchical relationships; and

(c) linking claims and specifying the kind of a relationship between claims. By using ECCM in a critical thinking assessment, students are able to construct a well-integrated structural representation of the topic, as opposed to the memorization of fragmentary information. This ability of ECCM to capture both the visual-verbal thinking process and the outcome is in the true essence of formative assessment design. Students are able to go back and revise their knowledge representation by adding new claims and evidence and editing the existing ones. While making the revisions to claims and supporting evidence, new links between the claims start to emerge and the students are able to create these relationships in their ECCM (Rosen, & Tager, 2014). While constructing meaning, students use various processes, skills, and strategies to foster, monitor, and maintain understanding. These processes and strategies are expected to vary with context and purpose as students interact with multiple continuous texts (e.g., newspaper reports, essays, novels, short stories, reviews), non-continuous texts (e.g., lists, tables, graphs, diagrams, advertisements, schedules, catalogues, indexes, forms), mixed text (set of elements in both a continuous and non-continuous format; e.g., email message), audio, and video. The cognitive processes embedded into the ECCM routine are aligned with the current frameworks of reading and writing literacy, such as the OECD-led PISA 2015 (OECD, 2010b) and the U.S. English Language Arts Common Core State Standards (National Governors Association Center for Best Practices & Council of Chief State School Officers, 2010).

The current literacy framework puts a special emphasis on argumentation (i.e., type of text that presents the relationship among concepts or propositions referring to opinions and points of view). In the context of PISA 2015 reading literacy assessment tasks, the students are asked to provide evidence or arguments, assessing the relevance of particular pieces of information or evidence or drawing comparisons. The tasks might require a student to offer or identify alternative pieces of information to strengthen an author's argument or require the student to evaluate the sufficiency of the evidence or information provided in the text. In the Common Core framework for writing literacy, 8th grade students are expected to be able to write arguments to support claims with clear reasons and relevant evidence (see Standard 3 in National Governors Association Center for Best Practices & Council of Chief State School Officers, 2010). This argumentative writing skill includes the ability to introduce claims, acknowledge and distinguish claims from alternate or opposing claims, and organize the reasons and evidence logically, as well as provide a concluding statement or section that follows from and supports the argument presented. The Common Core framework for writing also emphasizes the use of technology, including the Internet, to produce and publish writing and present the relationships between information and ideas efficiently (Standard 6).

The next sections describe the use of ECCM in critical thinking tasks and provide an overview of main findings from an international pilot study.

## Illustration of One Approach: Organic Milk Task

Rosen and Tager (2014) developed a critical thinking assessment task, 'Organic Milk,' that has been administered both in ECCM and Notepad settings to 190 14-year-old students from the United States, the United Kingdom, Singapore, and South Africa. In all, 102 students participated in ECCM mode and 88 participated in Notepad mode. Of the total students who participated, 112 were boys (58.9%) and 78 were girls (41.1%). The ECCM-based assessment task was designed according to concept map assessment characteristics previously mentioned (Ruiz-Primo, & Shavelson, 1996): (a) a task that invites a student to provide evidence bearing on his or her knowledge structure in a domain (in this task, students' understanding of the claims and supporting evidence regarding organic milk), (b) a structured format for the student's response (in this task, ECCM provided a structured form of presenting claims and supporting evidence for and against organic milk), and (c) a scoring system by which the student's concept map can be accurately and consistently evaluated.

In this critical thinking computer-based assessment task, the student was asked to analyze various pros and cons of whether or not to buy organic milk for the school cafeteria and write a recommendation to a school principal. Students who participated in ECCM mode were required to use a concept map during the analysis of web-based pre-determined resources, while students who participated in Notepad mode were able to take notes by using an embedded free text notepad but were not provided any kind of thinking tool. It should be noted that in both conditions the students were not experienced in concept mapping prior to the study. Among the websites that were accessible to the students in both modes were those of the

following causes and organizations: an organic milk company, along with an interview script/ video with the CEO of the organic milk company; an independent organic milk association; dairy farmers of North America; anti-organic milk, along with an interview script/video with the blogger (a past worker for an organic milk company); Disease Control Center; and a news organization. The resources included various content orientations (pros and cons related to the organic milk issue), relevancy, and level of reliability. Due to the exploratory nature of the study, the students were not limited in time-on-task. The task design team consisted of experts in English Language Arts, critical thinking construct, and assessment design. The draft task was shared with participating countries' teachers for content appropriateness.

The following information was presented interactively to the student during the task in ECCM mode (see Figures 1-4):

*Figure 1. Classifying notes into claims and evidence*

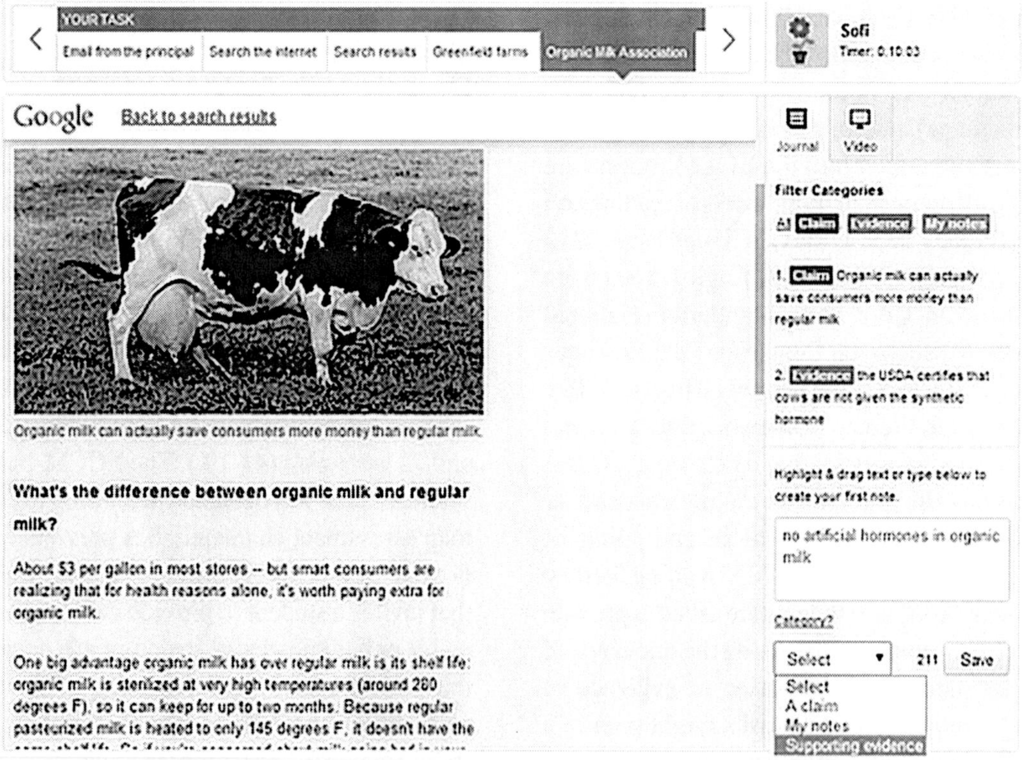

*Figure 2. Sample concept map with no relationships between claims*

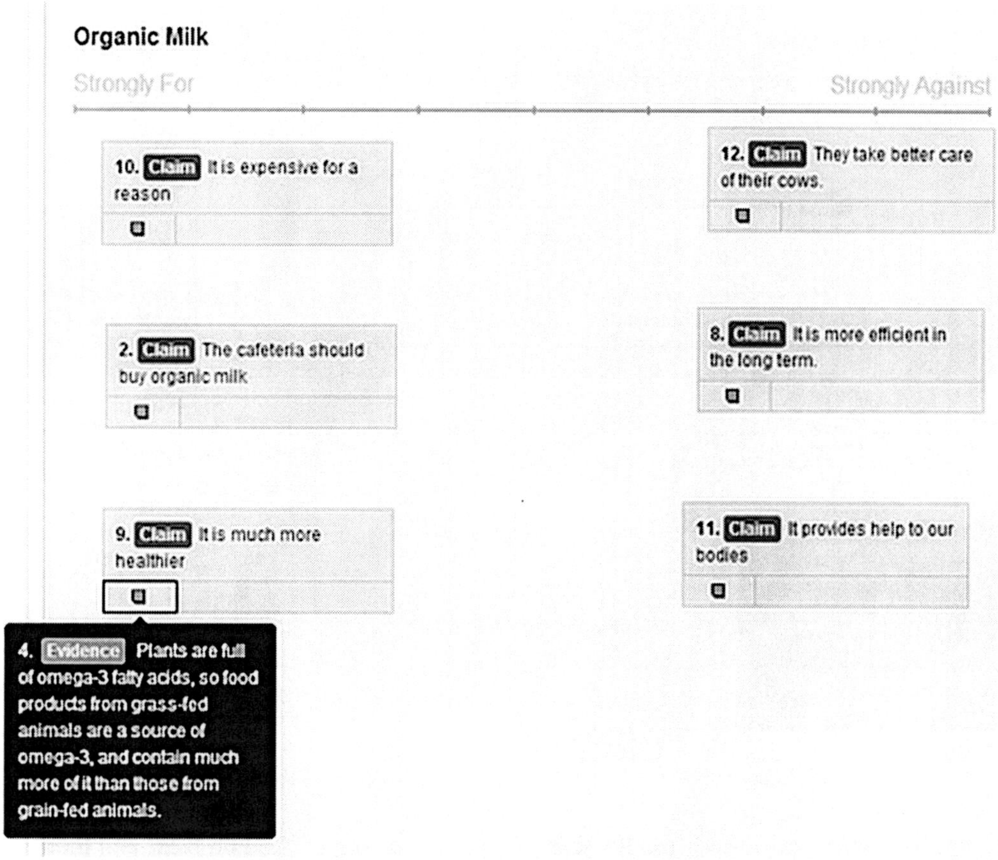

**Episode #1:** The task started by asking the student to provide name and background information and to select the preferred avatar. Then the tool panel and the story panel were introduced to the student. A similar introduction was presented to the students in the second mode of the task, while the notepad replaced the concept map.

**Episode #2:** In both modes, the task was initiated by receiving a request from the principal to conduct research on whether or not to buy organic milk for the school cafeteria:

*From: principal@schoolemail.edu*
*To: me@schoolemail.edu*
*Subject: Organic Milk*

*Mrs. K in the school cafeteria needs your help. She wants to know whether or not to buy organic milk for the cafeteria. Please put on your investigative reporter's hat and research whether or not organic milk should be bought for our cafeteria. Using internet searches you will have to find several sources to support buying either normal milk or organic milk. You will also have the opportunity to interview experts. Take good notes and document your findings in your journal. Be prepared to show how you conducted your research and summarized your findings in your article for the newspaper. You should make a note of any claim made that supports either organic milk or traditional milk and look for evidence that supports these claims.*

*Figure 3. Sample concept map with one relationship between claims*

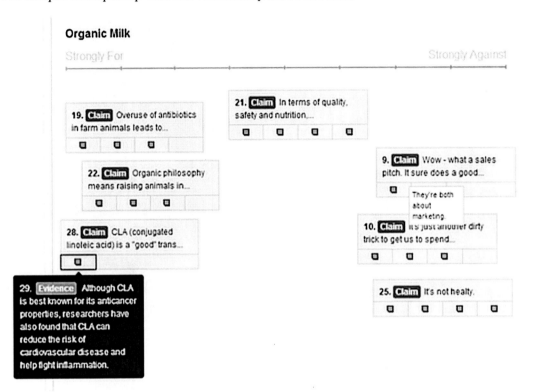

**Episode #3:** The students in both modes were asked to gather various claims and evidence that stand for and against buying organic milk: "You should make a note of any claim made that supports either organic milk or traditional milk and look for evidence that supports these claims." It should be noted that the resources that were provided in both modes were identical. The major area of the screen allowed the student to view the available web-based resources. On the right side of the screen, the student was able to take notes by using drag-and-drop functionality or typing the text. In ECCM mode, the student was able to classify the notes into claims and evidence in preparation for constructing the concept map. *Similar resources* were accessible to the students in both modes. Once the student decided that the resources review was complete, he or she clicked on Next and then proceeded to the concept map construction episode (in ECCM mode) or proceeded directly to the recommendation-writing episode (in Notepad mode).

**Episode #4 (ECCM Mode Only):** In this stage, the student was required to construct a concept map by positioning previously gathered claims and supporting evidence according to whether the claim/evidence was *for* or *against* organic milk. No relationship creation between claims was required at this stage.

**Episode #5 (ECCM Mode Only):** The student was asked to create relationships between claims. These were created by dragging from the link icon on a claim to a second related claim and typing a short description of how they were related.

*Figure 4. Sample concept map with multiple relationships between claims*

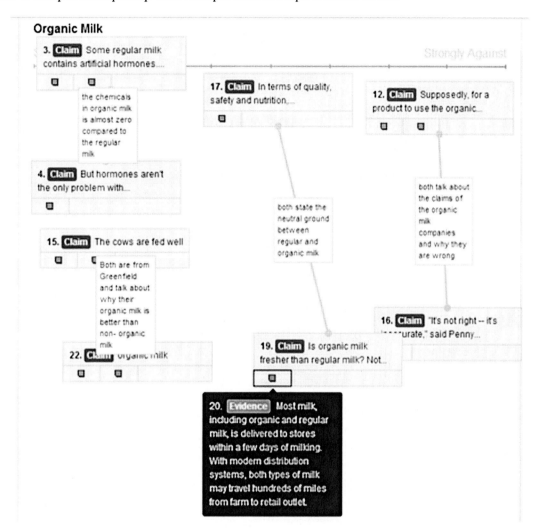

**Episode #6:** The student was asked to write an evidence-based recommendation to a school principal based on the research conducted. Students in ECCM mode were able to view their concept map while typing the recommendation, while students in Notepad mode were able to see the notes previously taken. In both modes of assessment, the student was asked to support the claims with relevant evidence from the resources. Additionally, both modes allowed the student to navigate back and gather more information if needed.

## Scoring Student Performance in Sample Assessment Task

Teachers from the Israel, South Africa, and United States were trained on the Critical Thinking construct definition and were provided with written rubrics. Tables 1-2 show the rubrics that were used to score student concept maps and the relationships created within the concept maps. Following an operational definition of critical thinking in this research (see Background section), the critical thinking score was given based

*Table 1. Scoring rubric for the concept map constructed by a student*

| Point Value | Description |
|---|---|
| 3 | Student concept map captures key points of both sides of the argument and pulls out supporting text. At least 5 valid claims supported by valid evidence were constructed. The claims are positioned correctly according to the 'strongly for' and 'strongly against' scale. |
| 2 | Student response captures a few key points of both sides, but supporting text may be limited or somewhat weak. Three or four valid claims supported by valid evidence were constructed. The claims are positioned correctly according to the 'strongly for' and 'strongly against' scale. |
| 1 | Student response only captures one side of issue and neglects details and key points. One or two valid claims supported by valid evidence were constructed and positioned correctly on the scale OR one valid claim is supported by more than one valid evidence and positioned correctly on the scale OR more than two valid claims supported by valid evidence were constructed but incorrectly positioned on the scale. |
| 0 | Student does not respond or fails to address the task. |

*Table 2. Scoring rubric for the relationships within a concept created by a student*

| Point Value | Description |
|---|---|
| 3 | Student effectively analyzes how parts of a whole interact with each other to produce overall complex dilemma representation system, as it is reflected in the concept map relationships. At least 4 claims are connected and a valid reason for the linkage is provided. |
| 2 | Student analyzes how parts of a whole interact with each other to produce overall complex dilemma representation system, as it reflected in the concept map relationships. At least 3 claims are connected and a valid reason for the linkage is provided. |
| 1 | Student attempts to analyze how parts of a whole interact with each other to produce overall complex dilemma representation system, as it is reflected in the concept map relationships. Two claims are connected and a valid reason for the linkage is provided OR more than two claims are connected but the linkage reasons are limited. |
| 0 | Student does not respond or fails to address the task. |

on the recommendation each student provided on whether to buy organic milk for the cafeteria. The written recommendation represented the capacity of an individual to effectively engage in a process of making decisions by analyzing and evaluating evidence, arguments, claims, beliefs, and alternative points of view; synthesizing and making connections between information and arguments; interpreting information; and making inferences by using reasoning appropriate to the situation. Table 3 shows the rubric that was used to score students' written evidence-based recommendations. There was no correct or incorrect recommendation expected based on the claims and supporting evidence represented in the ECCM. As shown in Table 3, strong critical thinking performance was associated with the ability to provide a clear recommendation on whether or not to use organic

milk in the school cafeteria, while explaining the recommendations based on an analysis of various claims and supporting evidence.

The following two sample recommendations provided by students were each scored as a 3-point response:

*[Sample response #1]: "I have done research online and found the disadvantages and advantages of organic milk. There are many advantages of organic milk and one of them is that there are highly concentrated fatty acids. It is good for the environment too. There is special fat in organic milk that claimed to protect against cancer and other health problems. Scientists say that a cow which is fed grass does not guarantee that its milk will be higher in this special fat. They are also not given antibiotics so none gets in its milk. Research*

*Table 3. Scoring rubric for student written recommendation*

| Point Value | Description |
|---|---|
| 3 | Student provides a recommendation and explains the decision, using supporting text from source material. The recommendation refers to at least 3 of the following dimensions of the topic: health value, animal care, cost, environmental impacts. The student discusses alternative points of view on the topic. |
| 2 | Student provides a recommendation and explains the decision, but may use limited supporting text. The recommendation refers to at least 3 of the following dimensions of the topic: health value, animal care, cost, environmental impacts, but doesn't discuss alternative points of view on the topic. OR the student discusses alternative points of view, but refers to less than 3 of the dimensions. |
| 1 | Student provides a recommendation, but does not explain the decision, OR student explains solution but does not provide a recommendation. The recommendation refers to one of the following dimensions of the topic: health value, animal care, cost, environmental impacts. |
| 0 | Student does not respond or fails to address the task. |

*shows that organically-produced foods have higher amounts of antioxidants and other nutrients. Organic milk often has a 2-month expiration date which is longer than most regular milk in stores. But do not be fooled by all of these advantages as some claims are just lies and is a marketing strategies to have higher sales. Overuse of antibiotics in farm animals leads to the development of dangerous antibiotic-resistant infections. Most companies claimed that organic milk is fresher and healthier than regular milk but there is hardly evidence to prove this statement. Also organic milk is more expensive as companies claimed saying that the cows and milk uses more of the farmers' manpower than regular milk which causes much cheaper than organic milk, which claims are not 100% accurate. As there are more disadvantages than advantages of organic milk, I would prefer that regular milk stays in the cafeteria."*

*[Sample response #2]: "I received your letter, in which you asked for my opinion on what kind of milk you should use in the school cafeteria. In my recommendation, I would go with organic milk. Although people are claiming that it is all the same, and not healthier for you at all, I found evidence declining their beliefs (no persistent pesticides, synthetic fertilizers, antibiotics, GMOs, synthetic growth or breeding hormones are found in organic milk). This is because these cows are fed all natural.*

*They graze on big fields and are much healthier than the ones squished inside of a small indoor area all day long. Those cows are also overfed which can result in sicknesses. Another reason to switch to organic milk is because it saves money. It is sterilized at extremely high temperatures so that you can keep it for up to two months! It is much healthier, it contains no artificial hormones which can make cows sick, and no antibiotics which are drugs that sometimes show up in the milk. This can be helpful, especially in schools because you need money for other things like supplies. If you buy this milk, you don't have to buy new milk every week or so. One last reason why I strongly recommend organic milk is because it contains more vitamins and minerals than regular milk. It has higher concentrations of nutritional desired fatty acids than milk from dairy companies. All this evidence shows how much healthier, and happier this milk will make people, and how much time and money it will save. If we switch to organic milk, more of the kids in the school will probably buy it more often, which will allow you to make more money! Good luck with your decision and have a nice day!"*

## Summary of Preliminary Findings

Similarity in students' backgrounds allowed comparability of students' results in critical thinking assessment tasks between the two modes. Findings from Rosen and Tager's study (2014) showed that students assessed in ECCM mode outperformed their peers in Notepad mode in their critical thinking (M=69.9, SD=27.2 in ECCM mode, compared to M=54.5, SD=19.0 in Notepad mode; ES=.7, t(df=188)=4.7, p<.01). Moreover, it was found that student ability to construct ECCM and the ability to create relationships within ECCM are positively linked to student performance in critical thinking (r=.62, p < .01 and r=.59, p < .01, respectively). The study showed that concept mapping as a thinking tool supports, guides, and extends the thinking process of the student. The goal of concept mapping tool is to make effective use of mental efforts of the student to create a *person plus* the technology in computer-based assessment (Jonassen, 2006; Perkins, 1993). To successfully make a decision or solve a multifaceted problem, the student must mentally construct a problem space by analyzing various pieces of information and mapping specific relationships of the problem. ECCM facilitates the analysis that students conduct and requires them to think more deeply about the multifaceted topic being analyzed than they would have without the thinking tool. Students can see their thinking represented in the ECCM while they make advancements in their analysis and synthesis of claims and supporting evidence on the topic.

The students were asked to report their motivation level during the task through a questionnaire that included 4 items to assess the extent to which students were motivated to work on the task (Rosen, & Tager, 2014). Participants reported the degree of their agreement with each item on a 4-point Likert scale (1 = strongly disagree, 4 = strongly agree). The items, adopted from motivation questionnaires used in previous studies, included (Rosen, 2009; Rosen, & Beck-Hill, 2012): I felt interested in the task; The task was fun; The task was attractive; I continued to work on this task out of curiosity. The results demonstrated that it did not matter for a student's motivation

whether he or she analyzed the dilemma with or without ECCM (M=2.7, SD=.6 in ECCM mode, compared to M=2.6, SD=.6 in Notepad mode; ES=.1, t(df=188)=.9, p=.37). This pattern suggests that the ECCM introduced no motivational obstacles for students in terms of being required to work with a thinking tool. To the degree that students do not give full effort to an assessment test, the resulting test scores will tend to underestimate their levels of proficiency (Eklöf, 2006; Wise, & DeMars, 2005). One may claim that an ECCM-based thinking process in the assessment could be perceived negatively by the students as an additional and unfamiliar requirement and not as an essential tool. Thus, the evidence of equivalent motivational level during both modes of critical thinking assessment is a positive indicator for the use of thinking tools in general and ECCM in particular in computer-based assessments.

Students' perspectives on the ECCM-based critical assessment, presented below, shed light on some of the premises and challenges related to the use of ECCM in critical thinking online assessment.

*[Sample response #1]: "First I did some research on the internet and looked in some sites with different perspectives on the subject. So I collected some evidence and I wrote some notes about the subject. Then I created a map about the subject with bonuses and minuses. I put the evidence and my notes to support the claims. Finally, I wrote and report about the idea. I talked about both of the perspectives and I added the evidence about that subject. I think this test was really fun to do. I don't think it was boring like the usual test we take at schools. I liked that we could use the internet to gather information. And we were allowed to make a map to see the connections between the evidence and the main subjects we found."*

*[Sample response #2]: "In this test I felt like I am on my own and I felt like I am important. The research part was so realistic -almost all informa-*

tion was real. I liked to do the research because I found too much different information. Some parts were saying yes and some parts were saying no but it was also so tricky. I couldn't decide what to do. The concept map helped me to organize my thinking about different perspectives on the topic."

[Sample response #3]: "I liked the fact that the test was very interactive and made me feel like I'm doing something very important. The notes, however, were a bit confusing. I ended up having to make multiple copies of each note with a claim, evidence and note version of each, because I had no idea which one I would need to use. Maybe what you could do is make them just notes, and we can use them in whichever way we want to; for example, using a note for both a claim and supporting evidence for a claim."

[Sample response #4]: "I thought it was a little bit confusing the way the notes, claims, and evidence journal was set up. My overall experience was okay. I feel like I would have done better if the set up was a little more clear and clarified before the test."

[Sample response #5]: "I liked that the concept map was provided so we didn't have to draw it, which would probably waste a lot of time. Also, it helped me organizing my notes, claims, and evidence. It's hard for me to be organized and I'm glad I felt really organized during this test."

[Sample response #6]: "I liked that the task involved a long thinking process and was not like most tests which you can just continually press buttons and finish the whole test."

[Sample response #7]: "What I liked most about this test was that it was hands-on, and entertaining. We didn't just sit there and fill in bubbles; we actually almost set it up ourselves. I loved this because it gave us a little more freedom and it was easier for us to learn using our style. For

example, I am a creative learner so I like to set things out and look at them. I could actually do this with the map, and also, it was excellent for me to be able to organize my evidence, claims, and notes because I felt neat and together. I felt like I knew were everything was and it was much more complex."

[Sample response #8]: "The step by step method makes made it easier for me to concentrate on the task and take notes, claims and evidence on the sidebar gives me a much better visual to what I'm doing."

## FUTURE RESEARCH DIRECTIONS

Future studies need to address the key psychometric issues related to the potential use of ECCM in large-scale accountability assessments. The key questions are related to validity and reliability of ECCM-based assessments. For example: How reliable are ECCM scores across raters? What are the possible future uses of ECCM in accountability reporting? Do concept maps provide a sensible representation of knowledge in a domain as judged by subject-matter experts? Do different mapping techniques provide the same information about a student's knowledge structure? Do different mapping techniques lead to different levels of performance? Although Rosen and Tager's (2014) study reported a promising high inter-rater agreement among teachers in scoring ECCMs, the findings from this study should be interpreted cautiously because of the scoring criteria used, the fact that trained teachers were involved in scoring, and because of the non-representative student and teacher sample used in the study.

Future studies could consider exploring differences in student performance with ECCM in a wide range of problems and decision-making situations in different subject-domains. Research should also focus on the use of ECCMs in classrooms and implications to the design of ECCM-based assessments. Although the ECCMs can be used to enhance teaching and learning, there is a potential for 'teaching to the test' practices. For example, teachers might present an expert ECCM to the students and ask them to memorize it. Also, teachers might test students' ability to memorize the expert ECCM before taking the ECCM-based assessment. These and other challenges should be addressed to promote balanced ways in using ECCMs in teaching, learning, and assessment.

## CONCLUSION

One of the greatest concerns in schools today is how teachers can bring together assessment and learning in a way that is meaningful for students' thinking skills, while focusing on content standards. Better understanding of how different types of technology-based visual and thinking tools can be used for improving classroom teaching and learning, especially across the most challenging areas of performance, is crucial. Using these tools, as forms of graphically and verbally displayed thinking processes, engages students in a variety of higher-level cognitive activities. This chapter describes how concept mapping methodology that is widely used for learning purposes can be adapted to ECCM in assessing higher-order thinking. ECCM facilitates the analysis that students conduct and requires them to think more deeply about the multifaceted topic being analyzed than they would have without the thinking tool. However, learning to construct this visual representation of information appropriately may take considerable time that may not be available in assessment settings. Thinking tools should be in limited use when the formation of verbal generalizations is what is expected from the learner and not necessarily in-depth concept understanding. Therefore, the benefits of using thinking tools in assessment must be weighed against the time invested in creating them and measurement appropriateness.

The "big idea" in this chapter is that if we could embed thinking tools in formative assessments used to help guide teaching and learning of higher-order thinking, and if these assessments had the salutary effect on learning and achievement, then for a relatively small investment (embedding thinking tools) we might experience a substantial impact on learning and achievement for large numbers of students. Thinking tools enable all students to visually and verbally organize complex information and transform information into active forms of understanding beyond the traditional linear structures most often used in educational assessments. However, assessments delivered with or without thinking tools may differ in score meaning and their instructional implications. Each mode of assessment can be uniquely effective for different educational purposes. For example, an assessment program that has adopted a vision of a conceptual change in assessment may consider the *person plus* the thinking tools approach as a more powerful avenue for next generation formative assessment, while the *person-solo* approach may be implemented in more conventional summative settings. While technology tools can promote fundamental improvements in assessment of higher-order thinking skills (Bennett, Persky, Weiss, & Jenkins, 2007; Pellegrino, Chudowsky, & Glaser, 2001; Rosen, 2009), assessment of foundational knowledge, skills, and abilities can rely on more traditional *person-solo* oriented assessment approaches. Thinking tools can enable scaffolding and visibility in the student thinking process while working on complex problem solving or decision-making situations that require mindfulness and thinking beyond WYSIATI (Kahneman, 2011). Similarly to more conventional *person-solo* oriented assessment, students may benefit differently from qualitatively different types of assessment item types or environments.

Thinking tools are a pattern language that is grounded in cognitive processes we use as human beings to make sense of our world (Hyerle, 2009,

Jonassen, 2006). Teachers use the tools to convey, facilitate, and mediate thinking and learning in their classrooms. Thinking tools are also used as a set of graphically and verbally displayed thinking processes for interdisciplinary problem solving and decision making. Embedding computer-based thinking tools in formative assessments and educational technologies is one of the promising approaches that could foster higher-order thinking into today's school systems.

Although ECCM shows promising results in terms of enhancing students' performance in critical thinking tasks, other techniques that make student thinking visible should be explored. This may include online graphic organizers, such as (Bromley, Irwin-De Vittis, & Modlo, 1995; Hyerle, 2009) Compare/Contrast tools, like a Venn diagram (writing details that tell how the subjects are different in the outer circles and how the are alike where the circles overlap) or T-chart (writing details about each thing to be compared in a separate column, then looking for similarities and differences); Cause/Effect fishbone charts (writing the many potential causes for a problem or effect); and Flow charts (writing workflow or process, showing the steps as boxes of various kinds and their order by connecting them with arrows). Some of these graphic organizers were previously adopted for instructional and assessment purposes. Among those techniques are thinking routines studied by Ritchhart, Church, and Morrison (2011). Ritchhart and his colleagues proposed three categories of thinking routines: introducing and exploring ideas (e.g., See Think-Wonder, Think-Puzzle-Explore, The Explanation Game), synthesizing and organizing ideas (e.g., Generate-Sort-Connect-Elaborate: Concept Maps, Connect-Extend-Challenge), and digging deeper into ideas (e.g., Claim-Support-Question, Tug-of-War, What Makes You Say That?). For example, the Claim-Support-Question (CSQ) routine is a thinking routine designed both to identify and to probe claims. CSQ focuses students on evidence

as the arbiter of the validity of a claim. In step one, the idea of a claim is introduced to the students. The topic or the situation is presented to the students individually or in groups, and they are asked to figure out "What is going on here?" The next step is to identify claims, explanations, and interpretations on the topic. In step three, the students are encouraged to seek out supporting evidence for each claim. Raising questions is the next step in CSQ. The students are asked to think beyond the support already offered for the claims and to consider what more might be needed to examine or explain the claims. At the last stage, students are asked to rank the claims on a line of confidence or share their position through writing or a presentation.

Embedding computer-based thinking tools in formative assessments and learning technologies is one of the promising approaches that could foster higher-order thinking into today's school systems. These thinking tools are not just a few more tools for the teacher toolset, but a new foundation for rigorous learning, higher-order thinking, and formative assessment in classrooms (Hyerle, 2009). As shown in this chapter, educators are seeing in practice and in the research that these tools can be used for transforming information into knowledge and for facilitating diverse learners who require individualized learning and higher-order thinking skills. These tools leverage learning and assessment beyond the linear presentation of information that is common in classrooms.

High quality concept maps allow students to illustrate their thinking and provide insights into the structure of their thinking and understanding of certain content (Erdogan, 2009; Lim et al., 2009; Trundle, & Bell, 2010). The concept mapping process involves deep information processing. During concept mapping, students need to identify and classify concepts, clarify relationships between them, and synthesize their understanding into a connected whole. This process requires elaboration and organization of information in meaningful ways, which cannot be achieved through simply memorizing facts without understanding their meaning and underlying relations. Moreover, concept maps constructed by students can provide detailed information about the students' misconceptions and weaknesses. This information allows teachers to have a valuable insight into the mental models of students. Studies showed that concept mapping is a powerful assessment tool (Kinchin, 2000; Novak, & Cañas, 2008; Ruiz-Primo, 2004; Weinerth et al., 2014). The advantages of computer-based concept maps in assessments include the ease of making corrections, providing scoring and feedback, and promoting interactions among teachers and students (Liu et al., 2010; Weinerth et al., 2014). While computer-based concept mapping tools are welcomed, it is necessary that they are valid, reliable, and easy to use. The ECCM tool is designed specifically for formative assessment use to empower the student to analyze various claims and evidence on a topic and to draw a conclusion (Rosen, 2014; Rosen & Tager, 2014). One of the major considerations in ECCM design is the ability to draw valid and reliable inferences about students' knowledge, skills, and abilities, based on independent measures, without introducing construct irrelevant bias (e.g., student technological skills). The three-phase working structure of ECCM is designed to increase the cognitive and measurement interdependency between the distinctive competencies in critical thinking as they are identified in our research. By using ECCM in a critical thinking assessment, students are able to construct a well-integrated structural representation of the topic, as opposed to the memorization of disconnected information. When creating an ECCM, the student performs a task that no ordinary collection of notes may encompass. ECCM represents a personal visualization of claims and supporting evidence on a topic, as well as relationships between the claims. The tool also represents gaps in a student's analysis of the topic and his or her ability to make a conclusion. The ECCM tool acts as a synthesizer of ideas from across the multiplicity of intelligences (Gardner, 1999, 2006). One of the main reasons for difficulty in assessing students' higher-order thinking skills through traditional item formats is that students' abilities reflected in their responses in those item types may not match their thinking abilities. Visual-spatial, linguistic, logical-mathematical, interpersonal, and intrapersonal intelligences are directly supported by ECCM. In this way, concept maps can be used as a tool to enhance teaching and learning and assessment of higher-order thinking skills for diverse learning. Despite the initial evidence, there is still further research needed before we can conclude that ECCM can reliably and validly evaluate students' critical thinking skills, especially in the context of large-scale assessments.

## REFERENCES

All, A. C., Huycke, L. I., & Fisher, M. J. (2003). Instructional tools for nursing education: Concept maps. *Nursing Education Perspectives*, *24*(6), 311–317. PMID:14705401

Bennett, R. E., Persky, H., Weiss, A., & Jenkins, F. (2007). *Problem solving in technology rich environments: A report from the NAEP Technology-based Assessment Project, Research and Development Series (NCES 2007-466)*. Washington, DC: U.S. Department of Education, National Center for Education Statistics.

Binkley, M., Erstad, O., Herman, J., Raizen, S., Ripley, M., Miller-Ricci, M., & Rumble, M. (2012). Defining twenty first century skills. In P. Griffin, B. McGaw, & E. Care (Eds.), *Assessment and Teaching of 21st Century Skills* (pp. 17–66). Dordrecht: Springer. doi:10.1007/978-94-007-2324-5_2

Bonk, C. J., & Smith, G. S. (1998). Alternative instructional strategies for creative and critical thinking in the accounting curriculum. *Journal of Accounting Education, 16*(2), 261–293. doi:10.1016/S0748-5751(98)00012-8

Bromley, K., Irwin-De Vittis, L., & Modlo, M. (1995). *Graphic organizers: Visual strategies for active learning.* New York: Scholastic Professional Books.

Chang, K. E., Sung, Y. T., Chang, R. B., & Lin, S. C. (2005). A new assessment for computer-based concept mapping. *Journal of Educational Technology & Society, 8*(3), 138–148.

Darling-Hammond, L., & Adamson, F. (2010). *Beyond basic skills: The role of performance assessment in achieving 21st century standards of learning.* Stanford, CA: Stanford University, Stanford Center for Opportunity Policy in Education.

Davey, T., Ferrara, S., Holland, P., Shavelson, R., Webb, N., & Wise, L. (2015). Psychometric Considerations for the Next Generation Performance Assessment. Washington, DC: Center for K-12 Assessment & Performance Management, Educational Testing Service.

Denton, P., Madden, J., Roberts, M., & Rowe, P. (2008). Students' response to traditional and computer-assisted formative feedback: A comparative case study. *British Journal of Educational Technology, 39*(3), 486–500. doi:10.1111/j.1467-8535.2007.00745.x

Eklöf, H. (2006). Development and validation of scores from an instrument measuring student test-taking motivation. *Educational and Psychological Measurement, 66*(4), 643–656. doi:10.1177/0013164405278574

Ennis, R. H. (1985). A logical basis for measuring critical thinking skills. *Educational Leadership, 43*(2), 44–48.

Ennis, R. H., & Millman, J. (2005). *Cornell Critical Thinking Test, Level 2* (5th ed.). Seaside, CA: The Critical Thinking Co.

Ennis, R. H., & Weir, E. (1985). *The Ennis-Weir Critical Thinking Essay Test.* Pacific Grove, CA: Midwest Publications.

Erdogan, Y. (2009). Paper-based and computer-based concept mappings: The effects on computer achievement, computer anxiety and computer attitude. *British Journal of Educational Technology, 40*(5), 821–836. doi:10.1111/j.1467-8535.2008.00856.x

Facione, P. A. (1990). *Critical thinking: A statement of expert consensus for purposes of educational assessment and instruction.* Millbrae, CA: The California Academic Press.

Fischer, S. C., Spiker, V. A., & Riedel, S. L. (2009). Critical thinking training for army officers: Vol. 2. *A model of critical thinking. (Technical report).* Arlington, VA: U.S. Army Research Institute for the Behavioral and Social Sciences.

Gardner, H. (1999). *Intelligence reframed: Multiple intelligences for the 21st Century.* New York, NY: Basic Books.

Gardner, H. (2006). *Multiple intelligences: New horizons.* New York: Basic Books.

Halpern, D. F. (1998). Teaching critical thinking for transfer across domains: Disposition, skills, structure training, and metacognitive monitoring. *The American Psychologist, 53*(4), 449–455. doi:10.1037/0003-066X.53.4.449 PMID:9572008

Hibberd, R., Morris, E., & Jones, A. (2004). Use of concept maps to represent students' knowledge of research methods in psychology: A preliminary study. *Journal of Cognitive Education and Psychology, 3*(3), 276–296. doi:10.1891/194589504787382965

Hoeft, R., Jentsch, F., Harper, M., Evans, A. III, Bowers, C., & Salas, E. (2003). TPL-KATS — concept map: A computerized knowledge assessment tool. *Computers in Human Behavior, 19*(6), 653–657. doi:10.1016/S0747-5632(03)00043-8

Hsu, L. L. (2004). Developing concept maps from problem-based learning scenario discussions. *Journal of Advanced Nursing, 48*(5), 510–518. doi:10.1111/j.1365-2648.2004.03233.x PMID:15533089

Hwang, G. J., Chu, H. C., Shih, J. L., Huang, S. H., & Tsai, C. C. (2010). A decision-tree-oriented guidance mechanism for conducting nature science observation activities in a context-aware ubiquitous learning environment. *Journal of Educational Technology & Society, 13*(2), 53–64.

Hyerle, D. (2009). *Visual tools for transformation into knowledge* (2nd ed.). Thousand Oaks, CA: Corwin Press.

Ingeç, S. K. (2009). Analysing concept maps as an assessment tool in teaching physics and comparison with the achievement tests. *International Journal of Science Education, 31*(14), 1897–1915. doi:10.1080/09500690802275820

Jonassen, D. H. (1996). *Computers in the classroom: Mindtools for critical thinking*. Englewood Cliffs, NJ: Prentice-Hall, Inc.

Jonassen, D. H. (2006). *Modeling with technology: Mindtools for conceptual change*. Columbus, OH: Merrill/Prentice-Hall.

Kahneman, D. (2011). *Thinking fast and slow*. New York, NY: Farrar, Strauss and Giroux.

Kim, P., & Olaciregui, C. (2008). The effects of a concept map-based information display in an electronic portfolio system on information processing and retention in a fifth-grade science class covering the Earth's atmosphere. *British Journal of Educational Technology, 39*(4), 700–714. doi:10.1111/j.1467-8535.2007.00763.x

Kinchin, I. M. (2000). Concept mapping in biology. *Journal of Biological Education, 34*(2), 61–68. doi:10.1080/00219266.2000.9655687

Ku, K. Y. (2009). Assessing students' critical thinking performance: Urging for measurements using multi-response format. *Thinking Skills and Creativity, 4*(1), 70–76. doi:10.1016/j.tsc.2009.02.001

Kuncel, N. R., & Hezlett, S. A. (2010). Fact and fiction in cognitive ability testing for admissions and hiring decisions. *Current Directions in Psychological Science, 19*(6), 339–345. doi:10.1177/0963721410389459

Lai, E. R., & Viering, M. (2012, April). *Assessing 21st century skills: Integrating research findings*. Paper presented at the Annual Meeting of the National Council on Measurement in Education, Vancouver, Canada.

Lim, K. Y., Lee, H. W., & Grabowski, B. (2009). Does concept-mapping strategy work for everyone? The levels of generativity and learners' self-regulated learning skills. *British Journal of Educational Technology, 40*(4), 606–618. doi:10.1111/j.1467-8535.2008.00872.x

Liu, P. L., Chen, C. J., & Chang, Y. J. (2010). Effects of a computer-assisted concept mapping learning strategy on EFL college students' English reading comprehension. *Computers & Education, 54*(2), 436–445. doi:10.1016/j.compedu.2009.08.027

Marzano, R. J. (2007). *The art and science of teaching: A comprehensive framework for effective instruction*. Alexandria, VA: Association for Supervision and Curriculum Development.

Mayer, R. E., & Wittrock, M. C. (2006). Problem solving. In P. A. Alexander & P. H. Winne (Eds.), *Handbook of educational psychology* (pp. 287–303). Mahwah, NJ: Lawrence Erlbaum Associates.

McClure, J., Sonak, B., & Suen, H. (1999). Concept map assessment of classroom learning: Reliability, validity, and logistical practicality. *Journal of Research in Science Teaching, 36*(4), 475–492. doi:10.1002/(SICI)1098-2736(199904)36:4<475::AID-TEA5>3.0.CO;2-O

Moss, P. A., & Koziol, S. M. (1991). Investigating the validity of a locally developed critical thinking test. *Educational Measurement: Issues and Practice, 10*(3), 17–22. doi:10.1111/j.1745-3992.1991.tb00199.x

National Governors Association Center for Best Practices & Council of Chief State School Officers. (2010). *Common Core State Standards for English language arts and literacy in history/social studies, science, and technical subjects.* Washington, DC: Authors.

Nesbit, J., & Adesope, O. (2006). Learning with concept and knowledge maps: A meta-analysis. *Review of Educational Research, 76*(3), 413–448. doi:10.3102/00346543076003413

Norris, S. P. (1989). Can we test validly for critical thinking? *Educational Researcher, 18*(9), 21–26. doi:10.3102/0013189X018009021

Novak, J. D. (1998). *Learning, creating, and using knowledge: concept maps as facilitative tools in schools and corporations.* Mahwah, NJ: Lawrence Erlbaum and Associates.

Novak, J. D., & Cañas, A. J. (2008). *The theory underlying concept maps and how to construct them.* (Technical report). IHMC CmapTools, Florida Institute for Human and Machine Cognition. Retrieved from http://cmap.ihmc.us/Publications/ResearchPapers/TheoryUnderlyingConceptMaps.pdf

Novak, J. D., & Gowin, D. B. (1984). *Learning how to learn.* Cambridge, NY: Cambridge University Press. doi:10.1017/CBO9781139173469

OECD. (2010a). *PISA 2012 Field Trial Problem Solving Framework.* Retrieved from http://www.oecd.org/pisa/pisaproducts/46962005.pdf

OECD. (2010b). *PISA 2015 Draft Reading Literacy Framework.* Retrieved from http://www.oecd.org/pisa/pisaproducts/Draft PISA 2015 Reading Framework.pdf

Partnership for 21st Century Skills. (2009). *P21 framework definitions.* Retrieved from http://www.p21.org/storage/documents/P21_Framework_Definitions.pdf

Pellegrino, J. W., Chudowsky, N., & Glaser, R. (2001). *Knowing what students know: The science and design of educational assessment.* Washington, DC: National Academy Press.

Perkins, D. (1993). Person plus: A distributed view of thinking and learning. In G. Salomon (Ed.), *Distributed cognitions* (pp. 88–110). New York: Cambridge University Press.

Ritchhart, R., Church, M., & Morrison, K. (2011). *Making thinking visible: How to promote engagement, understanding, and independence for all learners.* San Francisco, CA: Jossey-Bass.

Ritchhart, R., Turner, T., & Hadar, L. (2009). Uncovering students' thinking about thinking using concept maps. *Metacognition and Learning, 4*(2), 145–159. doi:10.1007/s11409-009-9040-x

Rosen, Y. (2009). Effects of animation learning environment on knowledge transfer and learning motivation. *Journal of Educational Computing Research, 40*(4), 439–455. doi:10.2190/EC.40.4.d

Rosen, Y. (2014). Thinking tools in computer-based assessment: Technology enhancements in assessing for learning. *Educational Technology*, *54*(1), 30–34.

Rosen, Y., & Beck-Hill, D. (2012). Intertwining digital content and one-to-one laptop learning environment. *Journal of Research on Technology in Education*, *44*(3), 223–239. doi:10.1080/1539 1523.2012.10782588

Rosen, Y., & Tager, M. (2014). Making student thinking visible through a concept map in computer-based assessment of critical thinking. *Journal of Educational Computing Research*, *50*(2), 249–270. doi:10.2190/EC.50.2.f

Ruiz-Primo, M. A. (2004). *Examining concept maps as an assessment tool. Concept Maps: Theory, Methodology, Technology. Proceeding of the First International Conference on Concept Mapping*.

Ruiz-Primo, M. A., Schultz, S. E., Li, M., & Shavelson, R. J. (2001). Comparison of the reliability and validity of scores from two concept-mapping techniques. *Journal of Research in Science Teaching*, *38*(2), 260–278. doi:10.1002/1098-2736(200102)38:2<260::AID-TEA1005>3.0.CO;2-F

Ruiz-Primo, M. A., & Shavelson, R. J. (1996). Problems and issues in the use of concept maps in science assessment. *Journal of Research in Science Teaching*, *33*(6), 569–600. doi:10.1002/(SICI)1098-2736(199608)33:6<569::AID-TEA1>3.0.CO;2-M

Ruiz-Primo, M. A., Shavelson, R. J., Li, M., & Schultz, S. E. (2001). On the validity of cognitive interpretations of scores from alternative concept-mapping techniques. *Educational Assessment*, *7*(2), 99–141. doi:10.1207/S15326977EA0702_2

Schaal, S., Bogner, F. X., & Girwidz, R. (2010). Concept mapping assessment of media assisted learning in interdisciplinary science education. *Research in Science Education*, *40*(3), 339–352. doi:10.1007/s11165-009-9123-3

Shin, J., Deno, S. L., Robinson, S. L., & Marston, D. (2000). Predicting classroom achievement from active responding on a computer-based groupware system. *Remedial and Special Education*, *21*(1), 53–60. doi:10.1177/074193250002100107

Smith, G. F. (2002). Thinking skills: The question of generality. *Journal of Curriculum Studies*, *34*(6), 659–678. doi:10.1080/00220270110119905

Strautmane, M. (2012). Concept map-based knowledge assessment tasks and their scoring criteria: An overview. In A. J. Cañas, J. D. Novak, & J. Vabhear (Eds.), *Proceedings of the Fifth International Conference on Concept Mapping*. Valletta, Malta.

Trundle, K. C., & Bell, R. L. (2010). The use of a computer simulation to promote conceptual change: A quasi-experimental study. *Computers & Education*, *54*(4), 1078–1088. doi:10.1016/j.compedu.2009.10.012

Watson, G., & Glaser, E. M. (2008). *Watson-Glaser Critical Thinking Appraisal*. Pearson Education, Inc.

Weinerth, K., Koenig, V., Brunner, M., & Martin, R. (2014). Concept maps: A useful and usable tool for computer-based knowledge assessment? A literature review with a focus on usability. *Computers & Education*, *78*, 201–209. doi:10.1016/j.compedu.2014.06.002

Wise, S. L., & DeMars, C. E. (2005). Low examinee effort in low-stakes assessment: Problems and potential solutions. *Educational Assessment*, *10*(1), 1–17. doi:10.1207/s15326977ea1001_1

Wu, P. H., Hwang, G. J., Milrad, M., Ke, H. R., & Huang, Y. M. (2012). An innovative concept map approach for improving students' learning performance with an instant feedback mechanism. *British Journal of Educational Technology, 43*(2), 217–232. doi:10.1111/j.1467-8535.2010.01167.x

Yin, Y., Vanides, J., Ruiz-Primo, M. A., Ayala, C. C., & Shavelson, R. J. (2005). Comparison of two concept-mapping techniques: Implications for scoring, interpretation, and use. *Journal of Research in Science Teaching, 42*(2), 166–184. doi:10.1002/tea.20049

## ADDITIONAL READING

Ainsworth, S. E. (1999). A functional taxonomy of multiple representations. *Computers & Education, 33*(2-3), 131–152. doi:10.1016/S0360-1315(99)00029-9

Britt, M. A., & Rouet, J.-F. (2012). Learning with multiple documents: Component skills and their acquisition. In M. J. Lawson & J. R. Kirby (Eds.), *The Quality of Learning.* Cambridge University Press. doi:10.1017/CBO9781139048224.017

Chang, K. E., Sung, Y. T., & Chen, I. D. (2002). The effect of concept mapping to enhance text comprehension and summarization. *Journal of Experimental Education, 71*(1), 5–23. doi:10.1080/00220970209602054

Chang, K. E., Sung, Y. T., & Chen, S. F. (2001). Learning through computer-based concept mapping with scaffolding aid. *Journal of Computer Assisted Learning, 17*(1), 21–33. doi:10.1046/j.1365-2729.2001.00156.x

Chmielewski, T. L., & Dansereau, D. F. (1998). Enhancing the recall of text: Knowledge mapping training promotes implicit transfer. *Journal of Educational Psychology, 90*(3), 407–413. doi:10.1037/0022-0663.90.3.407

Ferrario, C. G. (2004). Developing nurses' critical thinking skills with concept mapping. *Journal for Nurses in Staff Development, 20*(6), 261–267. doi:10.1097/00124645-200411000-00005 PMID:15586090

Giudici, H., Rinaldi, C., & Krechevsky, M. (Eds.). (2001). *Making thinking visible: Children as individuals and group learners.* Reggio Emilia, Italy: Reggio Children.

Halpern, D. F. (1989). *Thought and knowledge: An introduction to critical thinking.* Hillsdale, NJ: Lawrence Erlbaum and Associates.

Hwang, G. J., Kuo, F. R., Chen, N. S., & Ho, H. J. (2014). Effects of an integrated concept mapping and web-based problem-solving approach on students' learning achievements, perceptions and cognitive loads. *Computers & Education, 71*, 77–86. doi:10.1016/j.compedu.2013.09.013

Hwang, G. J., Shi, Y. R., & Chu, H. C. (2011). A concept map approach to developing collaborative Mindtools for context-aware ubiquitous learning. *British Journal of Educational Technology, 42*(5), 778–789. doi:10.1111/j.1467-8535.2010.01102.x

Hwang, G. J., Yang, L. H., & Wang, S. Y. (2013). A concept map-embedded educational computer game for improving students' learning performance in natural science courses. *Computers & Education, 69*(1), 121–130. doi:10.1016/j.compedu.2013.07.008

Ifenthaler, D. (2010). Bridging the gap between expert-novice differences: The model-based feedback approach. *Journal of Research on Technology in Education, 43*(2), 103–117. doi:10.1080/15391523.2010.10782564

Ifenthaler, D., & Hanewald, R. (Eds.). (2014). *Digital knowledge maps in education.* New York, NY: Springer. doi:10.1007/978-1-4614-3178-7

Jonassen, D. H. (2009). Externally modeling mental models. In L. Moller, J. B. Huett, & D. Harvey (Eds.), *Learning and instructional technologies for the 21st century. Visions of the future* (pp. 49–74). New York, NY: Springer. doi:10.1007/978-0-387-09667-4_4

Markman, A. B. (1999). *Knowledge representation*. Mahwah, NJ: Lawrence Erlbaum and Associates.

Mislevy, R. J., Behrens, J. T., Bennett, R. E., Demark, S. F., Frezzo, D. C., & Levy, R. et al.. (2010). On the roles of external knowledge representations in assessment design. *The Journal of Technology, Learning, and Assessment*, 8(2), 1–57.

Pirnay-Dummer, P., & Ifenthaler, D. (2010). Automated knowledge visualization and assessment. In D. Ifenthaler, P. Pirnay-Dummer, & N. M. Seel (Eds.), *Computer-based diagnostics and systematic analysis of knowledge* (pp. 77–115). New York, NY: Springer. doi:10.1007/978-1-4419-5662-0_6

Pirnay-Dummer, P., & Ifenthaler, D. (2011a). Reading guided by automated graphical representations: How model-based text visualizations facilitate learning in reading comprehension tasks. *Instructional Science*, 39(6), 901–919. doi:10.1007/s11251-010-9153-2

Pirnay-Dummer, P., & Ifenthaler, D. (2011b). Text-guided automated self assessment. A graph-based approach to help learners with ongoing writing. In D. Ifenthaler, Kinshuk, P. Isaias, D. G. Sampson, & J. M. Spector (Eds.), Multiple perspectives on problem solving and learning in the digital age (pp. 217-225). New York, NY: Springer.

Robinson, D. H. (1998). Graphic organizers as aids to text learning. *Reading Research and Instruction*, 37(2), 85–105. doi:10.1080/19388079809558257

Ruiz-Primo, M. A., Shavelson, R. J., Li, M., & Schultz, S. E. (2001). On the validity of cognitive interpretations of scores from alternative concept-mapping techniques. *Educational Assessment*, 7(2), 99–141. doi:10.1207/S15326977EA0702_2

Spector, M., Merill, M., Elen, J., & Bishop, M. (Eds.). (2014). *Handbook of Research on Educational Communications and Technology*. New York: Springer. doi:10.1007/978-1-4614-3185-5

Tzeng, J. Y. (2009). The impact of general and specific performance and self-efficacy on learning with computer-based concept mapping. *Computers in Human Behavior*, 25(4), 989–996. doi:10.1016/j.chb.2009.04.009

## KEY TERMS AND DEFINITIONS

**Assessment Tasks:** Directions to the test taker about what problem to solve, what product to create, or what performance or process to undertake. Directions to test takers provide information on requirements for responding, including the form or format of the response, and the features on which the response will be scored.

**Claim:** New ideas or assertions. A claim may present information or suggest that a certain action is needed.

**Concept Map:** A graphical tool for representing knowledge structure in a form of a graph whose nodes represent concepts, while arcs between nodes correspond to interrelations between them.

**Critical Thinking:** The capacity of an individual to effectively engage in a process of making decisions or solving problems by analyzing and evaluating evidence, arguments, claims, beliefs, and alternative points of view; synthesizing and making connections between information and arguments; interpreting information; and making inferences using reasoning appropriate to the situation.

**Evidence-Centered Concept Map:** An interactive graphical tool for representing a personal understanding of claims and supporting evidence on a topic, as well as relationships between the claims.

**Performance Assessment:** An assessment activity or set of activities that requires test takers, individually or in groups, to generate products or performances in response to a complex task that provides observable or inferable and scorable evidence of the test taker's knowledge, skills, and abilities (KSAs) in an academic content domain, a professional discipline, or a job. Typically, performance assessments emulate a context outside of the assessment in which the KSAs ultimately will be applied; require use of complex knowledge, skills, and/or reasoning; and require application of evaluation criteria to determine levels of quality, correctness, or completeness.

**Reliability:** The consistency of scores assigned to students' concept maps.

**Scoring System:** A systematic method with which students' concept maps can be evaluated accurately and consistently.

**Thinking Tools:** Computer applications that enable students to represent what they have learned and know by using different representational formalisms. These graphic-verbal representations are constructed by individual or collaborative learners across different situations and environments. There are several classes of thinking tools, including semantic organization tools, dynamic modeling tools, information interpretation tools, knowledge construction tools, and conversation and collaboration tools.

**Validity of Concept Maps:** The extent to which inferences to students' cognitive structures, on the basis of their concept map scores, can be supported logically and empirically.

# Chapter 20

# "Visit to a Small Planet":
## Achievements and Attitudes of High School Students towards Learning on Facebook – A Case Study

**Rikki Rimor**
*Kibbutzim College of Education Technology and the Arts, Israel*

**Perla Arie**
*Kibbutzim College of Education Technology and the Arts, Israel*

## ABSTRACT

*The current chapter deals with the use of Facebook as a social network for learning. Collaborative learning, metacognition and reflectivity are theoretically discussed and assessed in the current Facebook learning environment, as essential skills of the 21st century. The case study presented examines the relationship between attitudes and achievements of high school students learning an English play in the Facebook closed-group environment. Its findings reveal a significant improvement in students' attitudes at the end of the sessions. However, these were not found to correlate with students' final achievements. In addition, low achieving students preferred to study collaboratively, as they did in the Facebook closed group, more than higher achieving students. These findings may indicate the contribution of other factors to achievement in addition to positive attitudes and satisfaction in the Facebook learning environment. A metacognitive analysis of the students' written responses supports and expands the findings of this study.*

## INTRODUCTION

In the last decade the use of Facebook for educational purposes has increasingly become widespread. As a result, various studies have been conducted to examine and characterize students' and teachers' usage habits in educational institutions throughout the world, especially in colleges and universities. The current research studies the relationship between attitudes and achievement of high school students in the Facebook learning environment, and reviews the current trends and controversies in the research literature concerning the use of Facebook as a learning environment for various age groups and subjects. Thirty 12th grade students studied an English play "Visit to

DOI: 10.4018/978-1-4666-9441-5.ch020

a Small Planet" by Gore Vidal, during a period of two and a half months. A blended learning method combining both face to face and virtual learning through Facebook was used in this study. The virtual class took place in a Facebook closed group created exclusively for the EFL (English as Foreign Language) class. The importance of a closed group in Facebook is identified in the literature concerning communities of knowledge which share a common goal, common knowledge and access to resources and communications for creating collaborative products.

This study aims at examining Facebook or, more specifically, the potential of the closed group in Facebook as a formal learning platform for high school students. This examination will be carried out - using both quantitative and qualitative methodologies - by comparing students' attitudes at the beginning and at the end of the learning process and by checking whether there is a relation between these attitudes and their achievement. Students' metacognitive processes will also be analyzed by using a *Tool for Analyzing Metacognitive Thinking of Learners on Facebook* which was designed especially for this research. We aim to obtain richer, more accurate and more reliable findings as a result of using the metacognitive tool.

In addition, this study will present a model for teaching English literature to EFL high school students in a closed group on Facebook. The effectiveness of this model will be tested through three different aspects: attitudes, achievement and metacognition. We assume that attitudes towards learning in the Facebook environment will be improved at the end of the course. We also expect to find a relation between students' attitudes towards studying English literature on Facebook and their achievement in the final test on the play.

The closed group offers the possibility to perform various activities which contribute to collaborative learning (such as, uploading collaborative files, posting on a group wall, messaging the whole group). There are various platforms that allow it, such as Google class and Google doc. Yet the importance and advantage in Facebook is that the environment is part of the daily routine of the students today, and through this activity they get learning experience "anywhere" that is relevant for their life, beside the social media literacy skills.

If Facebook is proved to be effective as a learning environment, it would be possible for teachers to design and implement learning processes that meet professional standards which are not always easy to meet in highly populated traditional classes. The following research questions reflect the above objectives.

## Research Questions

1.  What are the students' attitudes towards learning in the Facebook environment?
2.  Did these attitudes change following the learning process?
3.  Is there a relation between the students' attitudes towards learning on Facebook and their achievement at the end of the learning process?
4.  What can be concluded from the students' metacognitive reflections on their learning experience on Facebook?

The literature review in the following section will include an overview of studies in four domains:

1.  Attitudes, motivations and personality factors in the context of Facebook use.
2.  Facebook as a learning environment.
3.  Formal learning in the Facebook "closed group".
    a.  The pedagogical rationale for using the "closed group" as a collaborative learning environment.
    b.  Collaborative learning and its relation to an online environment: Research results.
4.  Metacognition in a collaborative online learning environment.

## BACKGROUND

Activity on Facebook officially started in 2004 as a closed website intended for students at Harvard University only, and later at other universities. The purpose of its use was primarily for making new friends and keeping in touch with existing ones (Ellison, Steinfeld & Lampe, 2007). In 2005, a new version, adapted for high schools, was launched and in September 2006, the site opened to the public at large with an age restriction of 13 and above. In recent years, educational literature research has focused on the connection between using Facebook and various factors: affective factors (Ellison et al., 2007), patterns and goals of use (Grossek, Bran, & Tiru, 2011; Van Doorn & Eklund, 2013), classroom climate, teacher-student relations (Mazer, Murphy & Simonds, 2007) and the contribution of Facebook to learning processes (Bosch, 2009; Kabilan, Ahmad & Abidin, 2010; Reid, 2011; Cárdenas & Velásquez, 2011; Dunn, 2013).

In recent years, only few studies have examined the connection between use of a social network and academic achievement (Hew, 2011). It is likely that one of the reasons is the difficulty in isolating the variable of usage from other factors that can influence achievement. Studies that examined attitudes towards learning in the Facebook environment concluded that although the Facebook environment was not perceived as one appropriate for formal study, it might be an effective environment for constructivist learning (Parslow, Lundqvist, Williams, Ashton & Evans, 2008; Bosch, 2009; Pempek, Yermolayeva & Calvert, 2009; Grosseck, Bran & Tiru, 2011). These researchers argue that social activity and interaction on Facebook are open to the user's initiative and render it useful as a learning tool.

In this study, we will relate to the four domains mentioned above and elaborate on other factors associated with learning processes on Facebook.

## Attitudes, Motivations and Personality Factors in the Context of Facebook Use

In this section, we will present research data that examine the attitudes of social-network users as well as personality and motivation factors of the participants. Generally speaking, research has been carried out in institutions of higher education among college students rather than high school pupils (Hew, 2011). The purpose of the early studies was to examine attitudes of users as well as their characteristics and patterns of use (Ellison et al., 2007; Mazer et al., 2007).

In a study that examined ninety-two students in early adolescence with regard to their goals in surfing Facebook (Pempek et al., 2009), it was found that 86% of the participants use Facebook mainly to keep in touch with their friends. Other key goals reported by students were: enjoyment (80%) and relief from boredom (71%). A small percentage (0% to 7%) reported using the site to meet new friends or to seek help in learning assignments. Most of these figures are consistent with data from a survey conducted in Israel (Cohen & Eini, 2012, in Hebrew) on 267 students in grades 8-12. It was found that 94% of the participants surveyed had a Facebook profile and that 64% of them had started using Facebook at least two years before the survey. It was also found that the main purpose for using Facebook was to stay in touch with friends (54%), a way to spend their free time or to relieve boredom (58%). Similarly, a significant difference was found between the average surfing time spent by girls (3 hours) compared to the time spent by boys (2:32 hours). Most pupils check their wall (71%) as well as general news feed (51%) at least once a day. The most relevant and interesting finding of that study was that two-thirds of the pupils use Facebook for learning purposes. It is noteworthy that this was not a planned, teacher-guided type of learning but one for receiving updates: main uses were checking with friends about homework, discussing study material for exams, catching up on school and timetable-related matters (36%) as well as uploading/downloading summaries or scanned study material (27%).

The term "social capital" is amply mentioned in the context of social networks (Ellison et al., 2007). On a personal level, "social capital" refers to the resources that the person derives from his relations with other people in his network. These resources are expressed in the ability to obtain useful information, create and maintain social relationships and to organize groups. The data presented in Ellison's study, dealing with motives for using Facebook, indicate a positive correlation between Facebook use and social capital. A positive correlation was also found between frequent Facebook use and social capital among those with low self-esteem and a low level of life satisfaction (Ellison et al., op cit.).

Self-identity formation is another issue that has gained attention in the context of Facebook usage (Pempek, et al., 2009). These researchers studied self-identity formation among college students and indicate it as a crucial stage in the period between adolescence and adulthood. They claim that Facebook offers youngsters at the beginning of their adulthood a unique opportunity to showcase their identity and its components as reflected on Facebook such as: religion, political ideology, occupation as well as hobbies, music, movies and favorite books. This is expressed by updating their profile, uploading pictures and posting links. In addition, getting feedback from friends and strengthening social ties are important components in shaping the identity of young users (op. cit).

Educators and researchers are often preoccupied by the question to what extent instructors should reveal themselves to their students on Facebook. The research findings show mixed results. In their experimental study, Mazer, Murphy and Simonds (2007) examined the connection between

three levels of an instructor's personal exposure through a Facebook account (the independent variable), and motivation, optimal classroom climate and instructor's credibility as perceived by students (the dependent variables). The findings indicate that a great deal of exposure positively correlates with the three levels of the independent variable. In other words, the more the instructor (for whom a fictitious profile was created for research purposes) revealed personal information, including photos and detailed profile updates, the more the students reported that they would like to attend his course to a large extent, and the more they showed a higher level of motivation. On the other hand, research findings on students' attitudes towards friendships between students and teachers on Facebook (Abel, 2005) present a different picture. According to the students interviewed, a relationship of this kind is seen as an invasion of their private space and, in addition, they claimed that lecturers might get wrong impressions of them because profile descriptions are not always congruent with reality. Consequently, they opposed faculty members becoming their Facebook friends.

## Facebook as a Learning Environment

In addition to the affective components of attitudes, motivation and personality involved in Facebook environment as mentioned above, researchers examine whether and to what extent learning can take place or has taken place in practice using Facebook networking, and in what ways its use affects learning processes (Bosch, 2009; Madge, Meek, Wellens & Hooley, 2009; Parslow et al., 2008; Pempek et al., 2009). The data were generally collected by means of surveys, questionnaires, interviews or personal journals. Other studies focus on subjects' attitudes towards Facebook as a learning environment or learning tool (Grossek, Bran & Tiru, 2011; Kabilan, Ahmad & Abidin, 2010; Dunn, 2013). In these studies, the Facebook site was not predefined as a formal learning environment to convey educational content or for achieving specific learning goals. In most studies, the use of Facebook was initiated by the students and not by the lecturers.

Social networks, such as Facebook, can be used as a pedagogical platform which has a positive effect on learning, while adjusted for academic or vocational purposes. (Pempek et al., 2009). Although their research does not examine formal learning in Facebook settings, the researchers suggest different ways in which social networking can be used as a platform for collaborative learning for lecturers and students through discussions and posting of relevant links for the various courses. Both sides could benefit from such use: instructors can get to know the students better and students will be able to develop and better express their intellectual aspect (Pempek et al. op. cit).

Most studies exploring student attitudes towards Facebook as a learning environment (Madge et al., 2009; Kabilan et al., 2010; Grossek et al., 2011; Dunn, 2013) concluded that these attitudes were positive. In Madge et al.'s study (2009) the researchers found that 46% of respondents said they use Facebook to informally discuss academic assignments or study-related issues but 43% reported that they would not like the faculty to use this tool as a formal learning environment and would not like to be friends with their instructors on Facebook. Kabilan et al.'s research (2010) was conducted on 300 students of different science disciplines at a Malaysian university. Learning took place informally through interaction between native and non-native English speakers as well as through various games and activities that the platform offers. Students reported having discovered and learned new words, using them in their authentic context and improving their reading and writing skills. It was found that 78% of respondents reported positive attitudes towards Facebook as a suitable environment for improving English language skills, both in reading and writing, which allowed them to express themselves freely without fear of making mistakes. About 70% reported

that using Facebook can boost their self-esteem and raise their motivation in writing and reading English since they have a chance to communicate in English with native English speakers. Being exposed to a learning environment in the English language, they can express their feelings to their English-speaking friends and can use the language for practical purposes without concern for rules of language structure. 74% agreed that following their participation on Facebook they developed more positive attitudes towards learning English as a foreign language.

Another study which was conducted among 131 university students in Romania (Grossek et al., 2011) indicates positive attitudes towards Facebook as a more comfortable learning environment than ordinary classroom setting. 57% of respondents would prefer to receive their assignments through Facebook messages. 30% reported that Facebook provides an environment in which they feel motivated and comfortable to explore, discover, create and perform learning tasks. These researchers argue in favor of adaptation of the network for learning and concluded that the Facebook environment promotes constructivist learning processes where the users create their own content which others can view, use and critique, Hence, Facebook is viewed as an environment in which social interaction is free, convenient and user-initiated and thus may serve educational objectives. The above findings are aligned with a more recent survey (Dunn, 2013) in which students at the University of Glasgow clearly report positive attitudes towards Facebook as an effective platform for learning. These findings are based on students' perceptions of the desired use of social media to enhance learning though no formal learning actually took place. Some of the key advantages as perceived by the students are:

- Increasing student motivation and engagement with course material.
- Increasing student-to-student collaboration.

- Enhanced interaction between the student and the instructor.
- Accelerated data and information sharing.
- Removing barriers to self-expression and contribution.
- Providing students with 21st century skills which could aide their employability and increase levels of satisfaction.

It seems that students use Facebook to request assistance in learning assignments, to get answers to questions about the material and to share ideas and educational projects. On the other hand, a number of instructors reported using Facebook to ascertain which materials students wish to be taught in the classroom and to forward messages or information to specific students more easily than in the classroom. In some cases through Facebook, it is easier for students to ask questions they may have been too shy to ask in a whole class forum. The central conclusion is that Facebook can be used for both informal and formal learning alike (Bosch, 2010).

## Formal Learning in the Facebook "Closed Group"

The main question regarding the use of Facebook is whether and how teachers in the school system and faculty in teacher education institutions can use it as a platform for formal learning and learning management. Studies dealing with formal learning on Facebook found that teachers play a significant role in this virtual learning environment. They are the ones who decide on the pedagogical content, plan and guide the learning. Many studies in this domain have been conducted in the field of teaching foreign languages, mainly English (Blattner & Fiori, 2009; Kabilan et al., 2010; Cárdenas & Velásquez, 2011; Reid, 2011; Irwin, Ball, Desbrow & Leveritt, 2012; Van Doorn & Eklund, 2013). In these studies, the data were analyzed by means of content analysis of the documented communication among the students themselves or between the students and the instructor.

The use of the social network, in itself offering authentic interaction, makes it possible to create a community of learners which, through asynchronous communication and collaborative learning, enables the students to develop communication strategies that are difficult to acquire when learning a second language in a face-to-face classroom. The key seems to be the use of language for the purpose of authentic communication with a real target audience in the virtual environment of Facebook. The outstanding finding in this case is that, unlike in the case of institutional asynchronous platforms, interaction on Facebook is carried out on a permanent, continuous basis. Learners felt comfortable using Facebook, the environment was familiar to them and they related to it as a tool for improving their language skills and not as a task imposed upon them. A content analysis of the written interactions showed that the students made appropriate use of the new strategies they learned as well as recycling old strategies they had learned in the past.

Cárdenas and Velásquez (2011) also used Facebook as a virtual asynchronous environment in order to promote the process of learning English as a foreign language. The aim of their study was to show how Facebook could be used to upgrade the curricula of teaching English as a foreign language and to teach language strategies related to pragmatics that are difficult to teach using only textbooks. Pragmatic competence is the ability to use language effectively to fulfill intentions and goals. Pragmatic strategies include strategies of compensation such as asking for help during a chat, correcting errors, asking for confirmation that words were correct; strategies for managing negotiations like using expressions that enable a good flow of conversation and make the speakers better conversationalists, as well as rules of politeness like using phrases that soften the expression, using appropriate greetings, apologies, requests. These language strategies are more connected to socio-pragmatics (use of language in a socio-cultural context) rather than to vocabulary or to syntax (op.cit). Various attempts at teaching through Facebook have recently been reported when both educators and researchers propose a plethora of possible uses of the Facebook social network as a learning environment (Irwin et al., 2012; Rotem & Avni, 2012; Van Doorn & Eklund, 2013). Rotem and Avni (2012) present a list of tools and possible applications for learning in the Facebook environment:

- Representing data or topic (dilemma/idea/ attitude), using Facebook's existing representation forms, such as Personal Page, Group Page and Fan Page.
- Managing members' participation in an "open," "closed" or "secret group".
- Discussion, update and dialogue through a dedicated group "Wall" (by subject or educational goal) with application options.
- Collaborative interaction, including sharing and message threading as responses and message updates, including learners' comments as personal feedback in the learning context.
- Online synchronous discussion (chat) between members of a study group for synchronous update in the information construction process.
- Managing messages and real-time updating.
- Marketing and advertising information for a given group of users.
- Managing and sharing documents.
- Managing and advertising events.
- Conducting surveys.
- Uploading pictures, labeling and publishing them in various educational contexts.
- Using pictures, videos, audio for expansion of textual representation.

- Creating pages dedicated to links and references.
- Using feedback tools: comments, "Like," group and personal messages.

## The Pedagogical Rationale for Using the "Closed Group" as a Collaborative Learning Environment

Based on Vygotsky's theory, researchers believe that learning will be more effective in small groups in an environment where "scaffolding" will enable the learner to realize his/her individual potential and where there are clear task instructions. One of the important elements in learning is the learner's metacognitive thinking which involves reflective thinking. Reflective thinking allows learners to monitor their own learning and to realize different points of view. The process of collaborative knowledge construction entails a cyclical process in which, at first, the learner attains understanding on a personal level and then introduces his/her personal perspective regarding the topic of study and, finally, the group develops and elaborates the shared knowledge via group discussion. In challenging tasks, learners use reflective thinking to understand concepts, discuss issues with colleagues and develop common understandings (Rimor & Rosen, 2010, Meishar-Tal, Kurtz & Pieterse, 2012; Kurtz, 2014).

The closed group on Facebook can constitute a platform for collaborative learning which can contribute to knowledge building (Vygotsky, 1978 in Meishar-Tal et al., 2011). Vygotsky emphasized the relationship between cognitive development and interpersonal interactions as well as the role of cultural tools employed in cognitive development (Ealam, 2003). The technological platform of Facebook can be regarded in this context as a cultural-technological, social and cognitive tool which provides a space for collaborative learning and knowledge building. The closed group serves as an environment for creating a community of learners. The importance of creating a closed learning group has been discussed in the literature and relates to building a knowledge community with a shared goal, similar previous knowledge, access to the same resources and mode of communications (Blattner & Fiori, 2009; Cárdenas & Velásquez, 2011).

The development of technological tools and their use in learning contributes greatly to collaborative learning processes in their various stages: in sharing information sources, gathering and processing data, and in creating and assessing learning products. Online media may also decrease the gap between a learner's individual potential and his/her performance level in collaborative learning. It also enables more meaningful learning while forming social contacts, sharing personal experiences and creating new knowledge.

When trying to solve a problem together through the exchange of ideas, a team of learners construct shared meanings that the individual would not have attained alone. The collaborative parameter and the social context of a meaningful learning process are expressed through raising issues for group discussion based on prior knowledge and joint confrontation of the problems, the outcome of which is the ongoing development of thinking. In light of this perception, researchers claim that, on the one hand, one may refer to interpersonal communications that are internalized by the individual and serve personal-cognitive functions, and, on the other, one may refer to joint meaning appropriation (Vygotzky, op.cit).

## Collaborative Learning on Facebook and Its Relation to an Online Environment: Research Results

The addition of the group interface to the Facebook platform gave rise to pioneering studies in the field of learning management and formal learning. (Blattner & Fiori, 2009; Reid, 2011; Shih, 2011; Promnitz-Hayashi, 2011; Meishar-Tal et al., 2012; Wang, Woo, Quek, Yang & Liu, 2012; Marza & Al-Hafizh, 2013; Kurtz, 2014; Rap & Blonder, 2014). A study in the field of foreign language teaching examined the effectiveness of the use of a Facebook closed group in teaching French (Blattner & Fiori, 2009). Similar to Cárdenas and Velásquez (2011), the researchers note the pedagogical potential of Facebook as an appropriate environment for teaching a foreign language as it helps promote high order thinking strategies and construction of knowledge. The interaction between the learners of a foreign language helps develop their awareness of the socio-pragmatic aspects of the language in order to carry out communicative functions such as greetings, apologies, polite requests, expressions of disagreement and the like. These findings seem to corroborate other findings in the field of EFL teaching. Shih's study (2011) for example, offers a unique aspect of the exploration of Facebook use as an educational platform since it is one of the few studies to focus on the relation between Facebook use and achievement. His findings reveal that university students' scores in an English post-test were significantly higher than the pre-test scores. These results support the proposition that the Facebook platform which integrated blended learning for the English writing course was very effective. In addition, it was found that the low score group in the English writing course made the most progress of the three groups tested. Another successful attempt to teach writing to high school students through the closed group was carried out by Marza and Al-Hafizh (2013) who found out that Facebook peer comments had a very positive impact on students' writing. A pioneering study based on students' attitudes examined whether a closed Facebook group could be used as a learning management system at a teacher-training college in Singapore (Wang et al., 2012). The instructor used the closed group to make important announcements on the group wall (and each member was notified via an e-mail alert as well) to share relevant materials for the course (links, photos and video only), to organize weekly training sessions (using the "Create Event" function), and to conduct discussions.

The main conclusion was that the closed group can indeed be used as a substitute for, or an addition to, a learning management system but that it has certain limitations: One could not directly upload PPT and PDF type files and the discussion was not threaded. On the whole, participants expressed satisfaction with the use of the closed group as a learning management system.

A similar conclusion emerges from the research of Meisher-Tal et al. (2012) and Kurtz (2014). In the first study, the researchers present a model of a closed Facebook group which was operated experimentally for a graduate course at the Open University, as a substitute for a learning management system. The closed group interface allows synchronous and asynchronous interactions between the instructor and participants as well as among the participants themselves. It also allows for information sharing of photos, videos and links to websites, etc. When a user starts a Facebook group, all members can send instant messages through a conference group, upload collaborative textual documents (in the Files area), view the list of group members who are on Facebook at any given moment, add content to the group wall and comment on it and send and receive group or individual messages. Kurtz' study (2014) aimed at comparing students' perceptions of two different learning environments: the college-based course website versus the closed group on Facebook. The findings reveal supportive attitudes of the students towards Facebook as an effective virtual environment for discussion and sharing knowledge. Students reported being engaged in interaction and active participation in the Facebook group as well as appreciated its major contribution to their own personal learning experience. In their study in the field of science teaching in high school through the Facebook closed group, Rap and Blonder (2014) identified different types of interaction (social, learning management, links to learning material and sites, etc.) of which 15% was identified as learning discourse. They concluded that the Facebook group was found to foster meaningful

chemistry learning by providing students and the teacher a space where they could ask and answer questions, negotiate, resolve misunderstandings with regard to the learned material and contribute knowledge.

In conclusion, it appears that a closed group on Facebook has several important advantages – whether perceived by students or empirically tested, such as creating a safe and intimate environment, increasing learners' involvement, promoting collaborative learning processes and enhancing learning outcomes.

A review of the literature on the use of Facebook, and the closed group in particular, as a learning environment reveals, so far, a number of possible important advantages:

- Providing a safe, intimate environment in which the participants can confidently express their personal feelings (Parslow et al., 2008; Dunn, 2013; Van Doorn & Eklund, 2013).
- Creating a personal and group identity (Pempek et al., 2009).
- Creating strong interpersonal connections among users who did not previously know one another (Meishar-Tal et al., 2012).
- Affording shy students the opportunity to take an active part in the discussions and learning process (Bosch, 2009; Dunn, 2013; Van Doorn & Eklund, 2013).
- Offering a convenient forum for holding informal discussions on subjects relating to learning tasks or academic topics (Lim, 2010; Dunn, 2013; Van Doorn & Eklund, 2013; Rap & Blonder, 2014).
- Introducing the students to different cultures as well as to different linguistic codes (Blattner & Fiori, 2009; Cárdenas & Velásquez, 2011).
- Raising the students' awareness of the importance of creating an academic network (by means of the social network) (Bosch, 2009).

- Offering "an invisible space that makes people visible" (Reid, 2011; p. 58) and "where students feel safe enough to make their voices heard" (Reid, 2011; p. 69).
- Providing an easily accessible collaborative space where students can create and share knowledge (Promnitz-Hayashi, 2011; Shih, 2011; Rap & Blonder, 2014; Kurtz, 2014).

Along with its numerous advantages, Facebook may also present certain limitations as a learning environment. Some of the users feel that the dynamism and intensiveness of activity in the group has an adverse effect on their routine activities (Lim, 2010; Meishar-Tal et al., 2012). Another disadvantage identified by students in some of the studies is the blurring of social and educational domains (Van Doorn & Eklund, 2013). Some students feel that the social network is not an appropriate space for formal academic learning (Madge et al., 2009). This may also involve a fear of cyber bullying which can decrease intimate and secure feelings in the group. Managing a safe and secure environment requires the construction of rules and agreements as part of the learning process.

From the teachers' perspective, it is understood from the research that more emphasis should be placed on the role of teachers in the Facebook environment in regard to various pedagogical aspects, such as: the planning of tasks, integrating the tasks in the course requirements, providing fast and high quality feedback which has a significant influence on students' motivation. Apparently, Facebook possesses a relatively great potential for learning management but its quality largely depends on the way the facilitator motivates the students and plans discussions as well as providing clear guidelines for the rules in the beginning of the course. Finally, the instructor's evaluation of learning outcomes also serves as a major mechanism to motivate students' learning throughout the course. (Shih, 2011; Meishar-Tal et al., 2012; Irwin et al., 2012; Kurtz, 2014; Rap & Blonder, 2014).

Research has shown that the closed group helps enhance a "sense of community" among students (Reid, 2011) which renders learning more effective and increases motivation (Rovai, 2002). Another advantage found was that students discover the potential of Facebook for their social, academic and personal needs. Shy students feel freer to express themselves in a foreign language on a social network than they do in the classroom. Other studies reveal that the closed group also has a positive influence on teacher-student relations because it helps create an intimate community of learners in which the participants feel secure and are not afraid to take risks (Meishar-Tal et al., 2012; Reid, 2011; Wang et al., 2012).

In addition, the interaction among the participants in an online environment creates an important sense of belonging. Rovai (2002) found a significant relationship existing between classroom community and perceived cognitive learning but only with online learners. He argued that online learners with a perceived sense of community would feel less isolated and have greater satisfaction in their academic work. Vescio, Ross, & Adams' (2008) review of studies in Bissbort, Järvelä, Järvenoja, and Nenniger (2011) indicated some positive links between "developed professional communities" and teaching practice as well as student achievement. However, these findings are claimed by Bissbort et al. (2011) as "student perceptions (in a survey) of their focus and the likely achievement of goals, and therefore are not independently verified measures of learning outcomes." Some researchers claim that personal traits that are essential for collaborative learning, such as a sense of belonging and mutual trust, are lacking when they make the transition to virtual space (Frank, Reich, & Humphreys, 2003; Kreijns, Kirschner, & Jochems, 2003 in Rimor, Rosen &

Naser, 2010; Caspi & Blau (2008). Moreover, research findings show that preference to work collaboratively or individually is a contributor to one's construction of knowledge in the online collaborative learning environment of Google Docs (Rosen & Rimor, 2009, 2013). The researchers found that while more collaboration-oriented participants contributed more to collective knowledge, the individual-oriented participants focused on constructing their own personal knowledge.

## Metacognition in a Collaborative Online Learning Environment

The following review on metacognition in a collaborative learning environment will form the theoretical basis in this study for the evaluation of metacognitive processes in the Facebook environment. The concept of metacognitive knowledge was first brought up by Flavell (1976, 1979, 1987). He discussed the relationship between the development of metacognition for learning and understanding, especially in children. According to his definition, "metacognitive knowledge consists primarily of knowledge or beliefs about what factors or variables act and interact in what ways to affect the course and outcome of cognitive enterprises" (Flavell, 1979). It includes knowledge (explicit and implicit) about ideas, beliefs, perceptions of the self and of others, and the relationship between knowledge and tasks, actions, goals and cognitive strategies. Flavell distinguishes between metacognitive knowledge and metacognitive experiences. The more developed the learner's metacognitive knowledge, the better his/her ability to successfully perform tasks and use the most effective strategies. In his theory on the development of metacognitive knowledge (1978, 1987), he distinguishes between three main metacognitive dimensions: person, task and strategy. Knowledge in the person dimension is defined as acquired knowledge and beliefs relating to the human as a cognitive organism (emotions, motivations, and perceptions). The individual's knowledge and beliefs about himself as a thinker or learner, and what he believes about other people's thinking processes. One's beliefs about himself as a learner may facilitate or impede performance in learning situations. Knowledge in the task dimension informs the individual of the range of possible acceptable outcomes of the task given, and the actions and goals related to its completion. Task difficulty and mental or tangible resources needed are included in this category as well. The metacognitive strategy dimension relates to thinking about how to keep track and monitor one's own cognitive processes, or to examine the appropriate strategies for solving a given task.

Many researchers followed and elaborated Flavell's studies of metacognition in various methods and re-definitions (e.g: Biggs, 1988; Buttler & Winne, 1995; Pintrich, 2002; Huffacker & Calvert, 2003; Papaleontiou-Louca, 2003; Rimor, Reingold & Kalay, 2006; Veenman, Van Hout-Wolters & Affleerbach, 2006). Yet they all agree about the contribution of metacognition to the learning and academic progress. Metacognitive experience is Flavell's second category of metacognition, by which he refers to the subjective internal responses of an individual to his own metacognitive knowledge, goals, or strategies (Flavell, 1979, 1987). Discussing the relationship between metacognition and learning, Efklides elaborates and emphasizes the importance of the affective aspect of Flavell's "metacognitive experience" (Efklides, 2006). According to Efklides' theory, the learning processes inherently involve the combination of cognition and affection. Metacognitive experiences involve emotions (to what extent the task is familiar or difficult, a personal sense of knowledge, confidence and satisfaction), metacognitive assessments (regarding the amount of effort and time to invest) and metacognitive judgment (regarding the required information, the nature of the task and the type of strategies needed). These occur in the working memory and are the product of non-analytical and unconscious processes. These experiences have a decisive impact on decisions, on selected strategies and on learning processes, especially under stressful conditions of uncertainty and inaccessibility to information.

Recent studies claim that collaborative learning is related to higher-order thinking skills, such as critical thinking and metacognition. These 21st century life-skills were studied in online learning environments where learners were involved in complex discussions, reflection on mutual feedback and consequently used higher-order thinking skills (Garrison & Cleveland-Innes, 2005; Akyol & Garrison, 2011; Wadmany, Rimor & Rozner, 2011; Rosen & Rimor, 2013).

In the current research, we examined students' metacognition in a Facebook learning environment. We used a tool for testing metacognition in an online learning environment (Rimor & Kozminsky, 2004). This tool was adapted and elaborated for this research in order to analyze students' reflections regarding their collaborative learning on Facebook environment (see Appendix 3).

In conclusion, the literature review above provides research findings and views concerning attitudes, motivations and learning in the context of Facebook as a learning environment. Our perception is that creating "Closed Groups" in Facebook serves the pedagogical rationale of collaborative learning in a constructivist and situated learning environment. However, there is a noticeable lack of research which proves the cognitive effects of learning in the Facebook environment. Most research deal with the affective variables, such as students' attitudes, motivation and personality factors more than with cognitive variables, such as learning and knowledge construction. Therefore, we focused our study in examining the connection between students' attitudes towards learning on Facebook and their achievement at the end of the learning process.

Since Facebook is perceived here as a collaborative online learning environment, we assumed it was vital to collect information about each student's prior tendencies towards collaborative learning. Such information can be learned through content analysis of students' reflections about their own learning experience on Facebook. These reflections should assist to deepen our understanding beyond the quantified results regarding students' attitudes and achievement. A Tool for the Analysis of Students' Metacognition in the Facebook Learning Environment, was developed for the current research, taking into account the Facebook environment's unique interface, personal attributes and preferences of the learners, as well as their perception of the nature of the tasks, the pedagogical objectives and demands.

## METHODOLOGY

### Population

Thirty twelfth-grade students of EFL on an advanced level in an Israeli high school participated in the study. There were 12 boys and 18 girls in the class. A preliminary survey showed that 64% of the students surf on Facebook six to seven days a week and 32% four to five days; 59% surf three to four hours a day, 37% one to two hours, and 9% surf five hours or more a day.

### The Learning Environment

The intervention in this study took place in a closed group on Facebook in the framework of English literature lessons. The students studied a play for two and a half months, twenty-six hours in total and were given a final test. The play was a social satire wrapped up as a science fiction story which dealt with society and family values against the background of the Cold War in the United States in the 1950s. The main character is an alien in the form of a human who has just "dropped in" for a visit to our small planet from a planet that is light years away and far more advanced for the purpose of amusing himself by playing war games in the world, a hobby of which he is very fond.

In the current study, the thirty twelfth-grade students were randomly divided into seven teams of up to five students each. In order to carry out the collaborative tasks assigned as homework, each team had to upload one shared document for each task to the Wall of the closed class group on Facebook (see Figure 1). The tasks were presented as obligatory homework that would not be graded but only commented on by the teacher. At the beginning of the learning process, the students received a lesson in the computer lab to instruct them how to create and edit shared documents in the Facebook group

Once every two or three weeks, the teacher uploaded one task to Facebook. In all, four different tasks were uploaded, three of which were writing tasks. The first task was to create a picture album that would reflect the socio-cultural background, the setting or the first scene of the play.

The teacher could follow the different stages of editing carried out by members of each team on the shared document.

In this study, interactions on Facebook were carried out both within and among teams; thus, peer learning took place not only between members of the same team who had to submit a collaborative task on file, but also between the different teams by means of their peers' posts and "comments" through which they were able to ask and answer each other. The teacher reacted to the final products in order to state whether the product was satisfactory or needed correction or improvement, to urge students who did not participate in editing the document to add their contribution and to reply to questions asked during the learning process. Rovai (2002), who examined the attitudes and activities of students in an online forum, found that, in such a community, the learners believe

*Figure 1. A shared document in a Facebook group*

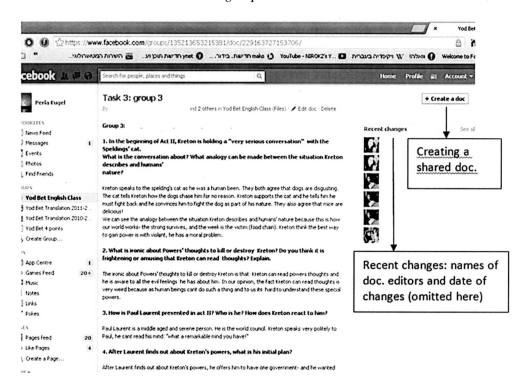

their social collaboration contributes to their own learning experience. For this reason, in order to encourage an effective dialogue among the learners, we divided students into small learning groups.

It seems therefore that, in practice, the Facebook group enables convenient collaborative learning by overcoming limitations of time and space. In order to write a shared document on Facebook, it is not necessary to participate in face-to-face meetings. It also avoids the awkwardness of dividing students into groups in a lesson (in particular when there are classes of thirty-four students) or the need to organize face-to-face meetings after school hours. In addition, pictures, videos and links can be shared in the closed Facebook group. Recently, a number of researchers have emphasized these advantages of the Facebook group which endow it with the potential to serve as a learning management system (Wang et al., 2012; Promnitz-Hayashi, 2011; Shih, 2011; Marza & Al-Hafizh, 2013; Dunn, 2013; Kurtz, 2014; Rap & Blonder, 2014).

The Facebook closed group in this study was created at the beginning of the 11th grade year in the framework of English lessons in this class but only in the twelfth grade was it used for formal structured learning. In the first year, the group was used by the teacher mainly to convey notifications and reminders to the students and to upload links relevant to learning. Most of the students were friends on Facebook and they were all friends of the teacher. In addition, the students felt free to contact the teacher through the system of personal notifications on every subject—personal or study-related. This was clearly indicated by the results of a preliminary online survey. The students were aware of privacy settings existing on Facebook and the possibilities of blocking certain content. Although the teacher stressed the advantages of using special privacy settings in the learning group, very few students blocked pictures and personal posts from the teacher. This demonstrates the relations of respect and trust between the students themselves and between them and the teacher.

## Tools

1. Pre- and post- questionnaires to examine students' attitudes before and after the learning process. The questionnaire included a total of eight statements which were analyzed on Likert scale of 1 to 5 ($\alpha$ Cronbach=0.82).
2. A mastery test: a final paper-and-pencil test on the play studied.
3. A metacognitive tool to analyze students' answers to an open-ended question in the pre- and post- questionnaires.

## Pre- and Post-Attitude Questionnaires Concerning Facebook as a Learning Environment

In order to examine the first and second research questions with regard to the change in students' attitudes towards learning English literature on Facebook before and after the intervention/learning process, a pre- and post- questionnaire was administered at both stages (see Appendices 1 and 2). The questionnaire consists of two parts:

1. Eight statements (quantitative analysis)
2. One open question (qualitative analysis)

The responses to the first eight statements which the students had to rate on a five-point Likert scale ranging from 1 (I do not agree at all) to 5 (I totally agree) mainly related to collaborative learning on Facebook. The obtained data were analyzed quantitatively including average scores, standard deviations and frequency scores. In order to examine whether there was a change in students' attitudes, a t-test for dependent samples was performed. Following are examples of such statements:

"Doing homework on Facebook may improve my grade on the final test" (statement 1); "The collaborative learning on Facebook is likely to improve my ability to analyze the play." (statement

6); I am interested in learning more lessons on the Facebook environment." (statement 8).

The internal consistency of the questionnaire, measured through Cronbach's Alpha was high: α= 0.82 (excluding statement 7 which related to the preference between individual and collaborative learning in general, not necessarily on Facebook.). The questionnaire is partially based on a survey that was carried out in an exploratory study aimed at examining EFL students' perceptions and attitudes concerning pedagogical aspects of Facebook (Grossek, Bran & Tiru, 2001) as well as on a survey carried out among British students in order to assess their opinion on the effectiveness of Facebook versus Blackboard as an educational tool that promotes virtual learning (Parslow et al., 2008).

Before the intervention process in the present study, students were informed about the learning method used to study the play: blended learning consisting of frontal face- to-face lessons and asynchronous collaborative homework tasks to be performed in teams in the closed Facebook group of the class. At that point, the pre-questionnaire was administered. The students were also informed that the questionnaire was anonymous, that their responses would be used only for research purposes and would not affect their final grades or their teacher's evaluation in any way.

At the end of the learning process, which lasted around ten weeks, and following the mastery test on the play, the students were required to fill out the post-questionnaire. This was done before they received their grades in order to avoid bias - positive or negative - in student responses that might result from the level of their personal grades. The pre- and the post- questionnaires are similar except for some slight differences in phrasing (see Appendices 1 and 2).

## Mastery Test on the Play

A mastery test was administered to examine students' understanding of the play which enabled us to deal with the third research question: Is there a connection between the students' attitudes towards learning on Facebook and their achievement at the end of the learning process? Pearson correlation coefficients between the scores in the first part of the post questionnaire (eight first statements) and the students' grades in the mastery test on the play were calculated. The mastery test was a final paper-and-pencil test given at the end of the learning process. It included five questions dealing with analysis of characters, plot and satire. It had two parts: the first consisted of two questions on basic understanding of the play, such as, description of a character and his/her role in the play. The second part consisted of three questions, similar in their difficulty level, dealing with more complex aspects of the play. These questions checked students' deeper understanding, such as, understanding the satire, the irony or the implicit criticism of the playwright towards American values and society in the 1950s. Students had to choose one question in each of the two parts. Fifty points were allotted to each question according to the following breakdown: ten points for language use and forty points for the content of the analysis and its organization. A formal rubric was used to evaluate students' answers. The students were informed about the structure and evaluation of the test beforehand. The test was allotted 90 minutes. Students were required to support their answers with evidence from the play without using any open material. All Questions required mastery of the content and analysis of the play as determined by the teacher according to the instructional objectives of the course.

## A Metacognitive Tool

In order to answer the fourth research question dealing with students' metacognitive reflections on their learning experience on Facebook, a qualitative analysis of their responses to the open-ended question (question 9: "What is your opinion concerning learning English literature on Facebook?") in the attitude questionnaire was carried out. A metacognitive tool was used for content analysis of the students' responses (see Appendix 3). The tool was initially developed by Rimor and Kozminsky (2004) for analyzing metacognitive thinking of online learners. It is based on Flavell's theory (1987) of the three main cognitive dimensions: person, task and strategy. Flavell (1987) defines knowledge of person variables as "the kind of acquired knowledge and beliefs that concern what human beings are like as cognitive (affective, motivational perceptual, etc.) organisms" (p. 22) The second dimension is knowledge of task variables: "The individual learns something about how the nature of the information encountered affects and constrains how one should deal with it" (p. 22). The third dimension, strategy variables, refers to "cognitive strategies or procedures for getting from here to there in order to achieve various goals" (p. 22). These variables also relate to the metacognitive strategies used by the learner to monitor his own cognitive processes or to examine which strategies are most suitable for solving a given problem or achieving a certain goal.

Adapting the metacognitive tool to the present study called for a dynamic elaboration of the original tool for analyzing metacognitive thinking. This process was performed as a result of the content analysis of students' responses, taking into account the Facebook learning environment's unique interface attributes as well as the nature of the tasks and their pedagogical objectives. The tool for analyzing students' reflections in the Facebook learning environment included five measures in the *person* dimension: personal traits, emotions, reference to achievement and motivation, teacher-student relations and group work. The *task* dimension included four measures: availability of internet information sources, problems and difficulties, feasibility of performance and contents. The *strategy* dimension also included four measures: Comparison between learning on

Facebook and learning in a different environment, reaching conclusions or generalizing regarding Facebook characteristics, Requesting help and Offering help. The qualitative analysis process was undertaken by two independent judges. An inter-rater reliability of 89% was achieved.

The contribution of such a qualitative analysis is twofold. Not only does it enable the metacognitive analysis of students' perceptions regarding learning on Facebook it also serves as triangulation and cross-verification of the results from the quantitative analysis of the closed questions in the first part of the questionnaire and the results of the content analysis of students' attitudes as reflected in their responses to the open question ("What is your opinion concerning learning English literature on Facebook?"). As is well-known, the use of a quantitative tool which measures attitude scores on a solely numeric scale (such as the Likert scale) cannot provide data which is sensitive enough to present a full and accurate picture of the situation studied. Therefore, it is important to analyze participants' open responses whose contents are expressed more freely and authentically than indications on a numeric scale (Wadmany, Rimor & Rozner, 2011). In the present study, the integration of both methods is required in order to obtain richer, more accurate and more reliable findings.

## FINDINGS

The first research question examined pre- and post-attitudes towards learning English literature in a closed group environment on Facebook. We found that the mean of the attitudes towards learning on Facebook at the end of the learning process was significantly higher than the mean at the beginning (M = 3.247, SD =0.725; M = 2.861, SD = 0.720); T (df29) = -3.980; p<.001, respectively.

Table 1 presents the distribution of students' attitudes as reflected in the pre- and post- ques-

*Table 1. Distribution of students' attitudes at the beginning and end of the learning process (N=30)\**

| | Pre | | | Post | | |
|---|---|---|---|---|---|---|
| | **1**<br>**Do not**<br>**agree** | **2**<br>**Partially**<br>**agree** | **3**<br>**Agree** | **1**<br>**Do not agree** | **2**<br>**Partially**<br>**agree** | **3**<br>**Agree** |
| 1. Doing homework through Facebook can improve my achievement on the final test. | 50%<br>15 | 30%<br>9 | 20%<br>6 | 13.3%<br>4 | 33.3%<br>10 | 53.3%<br>16 |
| 2. Doing homework on Facebook will increase my motivation to study the play. | 46.5%<br>14 | 43,3%<br>13 | 10%<br>3 | 20%<br>6 | 40%<br>12 | 40%<br>12 |
| 3. Group work on Facebook is more interesting than doing homework individually. | 33.3%<br>10 | 40%<br>12 | 26.7%<br>8 | 20%<br>6 | 23.3%<br>7 | 56.7%<br>17 |
| 4. Doing homework in the group on Facebook seems more effective to me than doing it individually. | 36.7%<br>11 | 40%<br>12 | 23.3%<br>7 | 26.7%<br>8 | 40%<br>12 | 40%<br>12 |
| 5. Group work on Facebook will help me understand the play better than doing homework individually. | 36.7%<br>11 | 26.7%<br>8 | 36.7%<br>11 | 20%<br>6 | 40%<br>12 | 40%<br>12 |
| 6. Group work on Facebook is likely to improve my ability to analyze the play. | 23.3%<br>7 | 30%<br>9 | 46.7%<br>14 | 10%<br>3 | 23.3%<br>7 | 66.7%<br>20 |
| 7. In general, I prefer to study in a group rather than alone. | 53.3%<br>16 | 23.3%<br>7 | 23.3%<br>7 | 56.7%<br>17 | 13.3%<br>4 | 30%<br>9 |
| 8. I am interested in learning more lessons in the Facebook environment. | 40%<br>12 | 26.7%<br>8 | 33.3%<br>10 | 33.3%<br>10 | 40%<br>12 | 26.7%<br>8 |

\*The attitudes on the Likert scale were reduced to 3 levels: 1. do not agree; 2. partially agree; 3. agree.

tionnaires. As it can be seen students significantly improved their attitudes towards learning on Facebook at the end of the process.

A comparison between the attitudes in the post- and the pre-questionnaires showed that at the end of the learning process, more students agreed that preparing homework in the Facebook environment is likely to improve their achievement on the final test (Statement 1), that the group work on Facebook is more interesting than individual work (Statement 3). Group work on Facebook was also found to be more effective (Statement 4), and is more likely to improve their ability to analyze the play (Statement 6). Yet, we found that more than half of the students still prefer to study alone even after learning in the Facebook environment.

An examination of the correlation between students' attitudes towards studying English literature on Facebook and their achievement in the final test on the play (research question 3) did not show any correlation between the two. In order to validate the grades of the final test, a Pearson

Correlation was conducted between the grades on the final test (M= 84.2; Sd=6.880) and the annual grades in English (M=79.7; Sd=7.085). A significant positive correlation was found: Pearson Correlation 0.716\*\* (p<.001) 1-tailed.

An additional statistical analysis revealed a significant negative correlation between the attitudes - pre- and/or post- and the annual grades in English in three of the statements examined in the attitude questionnaire.

Table 2 shows these correlations.

A significant and consistent negative correlation was found between the final grades in English and attitudes in statement 3: students who tend to think that group work on Facebook is more interesting than doing homework individually are those with the lower grades in English. In addition, students with the lower final grades in English expressed a higher level of interest in continuing to learn on Facebook at the end of the process.

In order to examine the fourth research question relating to the metacognitive measures reflected

*Table 2. Correlation between annual grades in English and attitudes expressed in three statements*

| Students' Attitudes | Annual Grades in English -Pre | Annual Grades in English -Post |
|---|---|---|
| **Statement 3:** Group work on Facebook is more interesting than doing homework individually. | Pearson Corr. = -.337* | Pearson Corr. = -.367* |
| **Statement 7:** In general, I prefer to study in a group rather than alone. | Pearson Corr. = -.448** | Pearson Corr. = -.039 |
| **Statement 8:** I am interested in learning more lessons in the Facebook environment. | Pearson Corr. = -.292 | Pearson Corr. = -.385 * |

*(p<0.05), ** (p<0.01)

in the students' attitudes, a content analysis of the open-ended question in the pre- and post-questionnaires was conducted: "What is your opinion about studying English literature (a play/short story) in the Facebook environment?" The analysis was carried out according to the measures of the tool for analysis of metacognitive thinking of learners on the web (Rimor & Kozminsky, 2004), which was elaborated and adapted to the Facebook environment for the purpose of this study (see appendix 3). Nineteen metacognitive measures were used to analyze the content of the students' answers to the open-ended question. The students' reflections were classified in accordance with these measures and their relative frequency was calculated in percentages.

In the content analysis, we related only to those reflections found appropriate for the metacognitive measures: a total of 52 reflections in the pre-questionnaire and 51 in the post-questionnaire. The percentages were calculated from the sum of all the reflections in each questionnaire (in some cases, the same reflection was classified into two or more different measures, so that the total number of reflections belonging to the three dimensions is greater than 51-pre or 52-post).

Table 3 presents the relative frequency of students' reflections in each of the metacognitive measures as they were analyzed in the pre- and post- questionnaires.

Metacognitive level was operationally defined in this study as a function of the relative frequency of the metacognitive measures. An increase in the

dimensions of person, task and strategy indicated that the students were more self-aware as well as being more aware of the task and the strategies needed in the Facebook environment. The data in Table 3 show an increase in the dimension of person (65%, 78%) and in the dimension of strategy (49%, 61%), respectively. At the end of the learning process, the students expressed far fewer objections to learning on Facebook (5.8%, 13%). On the one hand, students expressed more feelings of having felt lost; on the other hand, they expressed a stronger sense of community, greater attention to achievement and motivation (12%, 19.6%), and were more positive towards relations with the teacher (0%, 6%) and to group work (6%, 10%). In the dimension of task, there was a marked decrease in reflection dealing with problems and difficulties (0%, 6%) and a rise in reference to possibilities of performance compared to the beginning of the learning process (6%, 2%). The greatest increase was evident in the students' reflections relating to the Facebook environment as one that promotes the learning processes (17% in the pre-, 37% in the post-).

## DISCUSSION AND CONCLUSION

This study combines quantitative and qualitative methodologies to examine achievement and attitudes of high school students towards learning in the Facebook environment. Recent studies in the area of Facebook as a learning environment have

*Table 3. Relative frequency of the metacognitive measures in the students' reflections*

| Metacognitive Measures | Code | Pre- | Post- |
|---|---|---|---|
| **Person Dimension** | | | |
| 1. Personality traits | PT | (0) 0% | (1) 2% |
| 2. Emotions | | | |
| Expressions of affection, agreement, satisfaction, pleasure, interest | Pa1 | (10) 19.2% | (8) 15.6% |
| Expressions of anger, opposition, reference to need for separation between social & study space | Pa2 | (7) 13% | (3) 5.8% |
| Expressions of community feeling | Pa3 | (0) 0% | (1) 2% |
| Expressions of getting lost, apprehension, frustration | Pa4 | (0) 0% | (1) 2% |
| 3. Reference to achievement and motivation | PP | (6) 12% | (10) 19.6% |
| 4. Teacher-student relations | | | |
| • Positive reference<br>• Negative reference | PR+<br>PR- | (0) 0%<br>(2) 3% | (3) 6%<br>(1) 2% |
| 3. Group work | | | |
| • Positive reference<br>• Negative reference | PG+<br>PG- | (3) 6%<br>(6) 12% | (5) 10%<br>(7) 13.7% |
| Total reflections in person dimension | | (34) 65% | (40) 78% |
| **Task dimension** | | | |
| Reflections on: | | | |
| 1. Accessibility of internet information sources | TZ | (1) 2% | 0% |
| 2. Problems and difficulties | TP | (3) 6% | 0% |
| 3. Possibilities of performing | TF | (1) 2% | 0% |
| Content | CT | | (3) 6% |
| Total reflections in task dimension | | (5) 10% | (3) 6% |
| **Strategy dimension** | | | |
| 1. Comparison between learning on Facebook and learning in another environment | SD | (7) 13% | (6) 11.7% |
| 2. Drawing conclusions, generalizing regarding Facebook characteristics: | | | |
| • As promoting learning processes<br>• As inhibiting or impairing learning processes | SG+<br>SG- | (9) 17.3%<br>(10) 19.2% | (19) 37.2%<br>(4) 8% |
| 3. Requesting assistance from other students | SH1 | (0) 0% | (1) 2% |
| 4. Offering help to others | SH2 | (0) 0% | (1) 2% |
| Total of reflections in the strategy dimension | | (26) 49.5% | (31) 61% |

focused on examining affective aspects (attitudes and perceptions) of learning on Facebook rather than on cognitive aspects (achievement and knowledge), and have been conducted mainly among higher-education students (Blattner & Fiori, 2009; Reid, 2011; Irwin et al., 2012; Meishar-Tal et al., 2012; Wang et al., 2012; Dunn, 2013; Van Doorn & Eklund, 2013). The population of our study consisted of high school students and focused on both affective and cognitive aspects. Our findings reveal positive attitudes towards learning in the Facebook environment, on the one hand, and ambivalence towards collaborative learning in this environment, on the other.

The findings of this study indicate positive attitudes and satisfaction of the students with their learning experience on Facebook as well as a distinct improvement in their attitudes during the learning process. These findings are broadly corroborated by the research literature mentioned above. A relatively large proportion of the students agreed that collaborative work on Facebook is interesting, effective and contributes more to the preparation of homework than individual work, and that by doing homework on Facebook, their motivation to study the play is enhanced and their grades on the final test are likely to improve. They also believed that collaborative work on Facebook contributes to their understanding of the play and improves their ability to analyze it. These attitudes significantly improved after the learning process ended.

On the other hand, positive attitudes towards learning in the Facebook environment were not found to correlate with academic achievement as they were measured in the final test. The lack of correlation between achievement and attitudes can also suggest that, in addition to the interest and pleasure afforded by learning on Facebook, we need to consider and measure other factors which are linked to achievement, such as previous personal tendencies towards collaborative learning, the frequency and quality of teacher's feedback, and the like. One should also note the difference between the format of the final test given on the play and the learning environment of Facebook. The final test was an individual paper-and-pencil test in the classroom, with no access to the internet, and was thus substantially different from the virtual, collaborative and multi-media environment to which the students became accustomed during the learning process. This incongruence between the characteristics of the learning environment and that of the final test format could also explain the lack of correlation between attitudes and achievement. The various activities in which the students participated in the internet environment were not required on the test, such as synchronous and asynchronous interaction between the participants and the teacher, and among students

themselves, the sharing of documents, pictures, videos, links to sites, etc. Students who could use the "like" or "comment" features as part of their activity or could share information in the group were not granted this opportunity during the final test on the play.

Examination of the correlation between the level of achievement in English - as reflected in students' annual grades - and personal preference for collaborative learning on Facebook provided some interesting findings. Students who have lower grades in English tend to think that collaborative work on Facebook is more interesting than doing homework individually. On the other hand, more than half the students with relatively high grades still prefer to study alone even after learning on the Facebook environment. In other words, the lower the final grades in English were, the higher the level of interest in continuing to learn on the Facebook environment. The same trend was found while examining the level of interest expressed by the students in learning additional lessons on the Facebook. Findings revealed that the lower achiever students expressed greater interest in learning more lessons on Facebook than high achiever students

From the above, we might conclude that learning in the Facebook environment is more likely to suit lower achieving students. Apparently, high achieving students have a better ability to study individually and their achievement is less dependent on a supportive environment such as the one in Facebook. A previous study on collaborative knowledge building in an online environment of Google Docs also indicated that individually-oriented students attained higher grades in their personal tasks as compared to collaboration-oriented students (Rosen & Rimor, 2009).

Another conclusion deserving attention is related to the fact that in this experiment, the students were not offered any kind of bonus for participation, neither were they given grades for their homework. It is worth examining a situation where the teacher designs and integrates a clear and transparent evaluation system in the blended teaching, as suggested in various studies (Dunn, 2013; Meishar-Tal et al., 2012). This may result in more active participation of both high and low proficient students and might lead to a correlation between attitudes and achievement.

The results of Vescio et al.'s (2008) review of studies indicated some positive links between "developed professional communities" and teaching practice as well as "student achievement." The reported achievement impacts, however, were likely to be student perceptions (through a survey) of their focus and the likely achievement of goals, rather than independently verified measures of learning outcomes. Indeed, as mentioned in Bissbort, Järvelä, Järvenoja and Nenniger (2011), community feelings of connectedness, cohesion, spirit, trust and independence, which compose Rovai's "sense of community" (2002), do not appear to have a causal relationship to learner performance. It seems that collaborative learning and learning outcomes should be measured as independent and dependent variables, and control other variables contributing to learning, such as personal traits and learning orientation (preference towards individual or collaborative learning), as well as teacher feedback, course design, task demands and transparent evaluation.

A content analysis of the students' answers to the open-ended question provided a rich repertoire of authentic responses and personal perceptions. The findings indicate ambivalent attitudes towards the experience of learning on Facebook, which would not have been expressed in a closed attitude questionnaire (Likert scale). The following quotations are taken from the students' responses which reflect their attitudes towards learning on Facebook. Some examples of quotations follow:

*Studying English Literature on Facebook can be more effective and more interesting than doing it in class face-to-face or than doing the homework alone. This kind of learning makes literature more enjoyable and maybe this way, students will study harder. I personally invested more effort and time here than in the first story we learned in class without Facebook.*

*It is interesting and motivates you to study the play better but it also invades your privacy because everyone sees how you write and your level of knowledge about the play.*

*I definitely support studying English literature on Facebook although there are students who prefer to study alone rather than in a group. But it is also possible to work individually on a play on Facebook, and not necessarily in groups.*

*In my opinion, studying on Facebook is not effective. It gives [the student] a sense of a lack of seriousness and is even a bit irritating.*

*It [studying on Facebook] can also be distracting because of Facebook.*

*On the one hand, when I go into Facebook, I am tempted to look at updates and news about my friends that are not connected to English, and in that way I lose my concentration.*

On the other hand, there are expressions that reflect a sense of community and a positive reference to student-teacher relations:

*It makes you discuss the play with your friends, to think with a friend who knows more about a certain subject. He explains to you and so you can get help from your friends in the group.*

*If you don't understand something, the teacher or a classmate can give you an answer.*

*...and the teacher is online so you can always ask questions about the play in an easy and convenient way if we don't understand something, then the teacher or another student can answer you. It also allows the teacher to better supervise the homework tasks and write comments.*

In conclusion, the content analysis of the students' reflections revealed ambivalence and no consensus between lower and higher achieving students regarding collaborative learning on Facebook. Nonetheless, it added a significant and sensitive range of responses toward collaborative study in the Facebook learning environment far and beyond those that could have been obtained by a quantitative examination of attitudes.

## FUTURE RESEARCH DIRECTIONS

Our findings are aimed at educators and researchers who are interested in better understanding of the potential of social media as a learning environment as well as researchers who are engaged with the concept of computer-based assessment and learning of higher-order thinking, such as metacognition. It is likely that in order to provide a more comprehensive view of Facebook's potential ability to promote learning processes, other parameters besides academic achievement are needed (Hew, 2011).

In the current study, we have developed a metacognitive tool which allows us to learn about students' reflections on their unique learning experience in the Facebook environment. This tool was used here for the first time in the process of content analysis of the students' reflections. We found a rise in the students' awareness of themselves and of their learning process according to the tool's categories. It is highly recommended to apply this tool in further research and in various courses and ages.

The current research also presents a pioneering model for teaching an English play in a EFL class for high school students. This model should be improved pedagogically to include more documented feedback and a transparent evaluation system. If the objective of the learning process in the virtual Facebook group is to enhance achievement, an inherent feedback and evaluation system should be carefully designed, planned and integrated into the model from the beginning. The instructor plays an important role in implementing and maintaining the use of social media for teaching and learning purposes. It requires careful planning and the reasons for adopting Facebook or any social networking in an educational context must be clear and transparent to both parties: educators and learners. Further research should be extended to a wider range of population that would include students with different individual competencies, learning styles and orientation (individual or group orientation). Additional studies in various subject areas which examine and evaluate the nature of educational activities on Facebook as well as the relationship between prior personal tendencies towards collaborative learning and cognitive variables are highly recommended.

Scholars (Blattner & Fiori, 2009; Bosch, 2009; Cárdenas, & Velásquez, 2011; Promnitz-Hayashi, 2011; Meishar-Tal et al., 2012; Kurtz, 2014; Rap & Blonder, 2014) already realize that Facebook can play a vital role in education. It should be kept in mind that if the teaching approach lacks the use of effective pedagogical principles, no matter which social media or technology is used, little or no meaningful learning will take place.

Our findings, along with findings from other research, clearly emphasize the effectiveness of the Facebook group in terms of students' affective attitudes; however, it is still unclear if and how this type of learning can enhance students' academic achievement. Thus, further research is needed involving a systematic analysis of students' cognitive processes and learning outcomes so that educators can better understand the contribution of Facebook to learning outcomes.

# REFERENCES

Abel, M. (2005). Find me on Facebook…as long as you are not a faculty member or administrator. *Esource for College Transitions, 3*(3), 1–2.

Akyol, Z., & Garrison, D. R. (2011). Understanding cognitive presence in an online and blended community of inquiry: Assessing outcomes and processes for deep approaches to learning. *British Journal of Educational Technology, 42*(2), 233–250. doi:10.1111/j.1467-8535.2009.01029.x

Biggs, J. (1988). The role of metacognition in enhancing learning. *Australian Journal of Education, 32*(2), 127–138. doi:10.1177/000494418803200201

Bissbort, D., Järvelä, S., Järvenoja, H., & Nenniger, P. (2011). Advancing conditions for self and shared regulation in collaborative learning settings in higher education. *Proceedings of 36th International Conference 2011- Improving University Teaching.* Bielefeld University.

Blattner, G., & Fiori, M. (2009). Facebook in the language classroom: Promises and possibilities. *International Journal of Instructional Technology and Distance Learning, 6*(1), 17–28. Retrieved from http://www.itdl.org/Journal/Jan_09/Jan_09.pdf#page=21

Bosch, T. E. (2009). Using online social networking for teaching and learning: Facebook use at the University of Cape Town. *Communicatio: South African Journal for Communication Theory and Research, 35*(2), 185–200. doi:10.1080/02500160903250648

Buttler, D. L., & Winne, P. H. (1995). Feedback and self-regulated learning: A theoretical synthesis. *Review of Educational Research, 65*(3), 245–281. doi:10.3102/00346543065003245

Cárdenas, F., & Velásquez, J. (2011). EFL students speaking their minds to the world through Facebook: Curriculum innovation at a language institute in Bogota, Colombia. *Proceedings of World Conference on E-Learning in Corporate, Government, Healthcare, and Higher Education.*

Caspi, A., & Blau, I. (2008). Social presence in online discussion groups: Testing three conceptions and their relations to perceived learning. *Social Psychology of Education, 11*(3), 323–346. doi:10.1007/s11218-008-9054-2

Cohen, A., & Eini, L. (2012). Facebook usage patterns among teenagers and their relation to educational processes. *Proceedings of the 7th Chais Conference for the Study of Innovation and Learning Technologies: Learning In the Technological Era.* Raanana: The Open University of Israel.

Dunn, L. (2013) Using social media to enhance learning and teaching. In *Social Media 2013: 18th International Conference on Education and Technology.* Retrieved November 4, 2014 from http://eprints.gla.ac.uk/89363/

Ealam, G. (2003). The philosophy and psychology of Vygotzky: From cultural to psychological tools. In A. Kozulin & G. Ealam (Eds.), *Lev Vygotzky: Thought and Culture – An Anthology* (pp. 364–374). Jerusalem: Branco-Weiss Institute. (in Hebrew)

Efklides, A. (2006). Metacognition and affect: What can metacognitive experiences tell us about the learning process? *Educational Research Review, 1*(1), 3–14. doi:10.1016/j.edurev.2005.11.001

Ellison, N. B., Steinfield, C., & Lampe, C. (2007). The benefits of Facebook "Friends": Social capital and college students' use of online social network sites. *Journal of Computer-Mediated Communication, 12*(4), 1143–1168. doi:10.1111/j.1083-6101.2007.00367.x

Flavell, J. H. (1976). Metacognitive aspects of problem solving. In L. B. Resnick (Ed.), The nature of intelligence (pp. 231-236). Hillsdale, NJ: Erlbaum.

Flavell, J. H. (1979). Metacognition and cognitive monitoring: A new area of cognitive-developmental inquiry. *The American Psychologist, 34*(10), 906–911. doi:10.1037/0003-066X.34.10.906

Flavell, J. H. (1987). Speculation about the nature and development of metacognition. In F. E. Weinert & R. H. Kluwe (Eds.), *Metacognition, motivation and understanding* (pp. 21–29). Hillsdale, NJ: Erlbaum.

Frank, M., Reich, N., & Humphreys, K. (2003). Respecting the human needs of students in the development of e-learning. *Computers & Education, 40*(1), 57–70. doi:10.1016/S0360-1315(02)00095-7

Garrison, D. R., & Cleveland-Innes, M. (2005). Facilitating cognitive presence in online learning: Interaction is not enough. *American Journal of Distance Education, 19*(3), 133–148. doi:10.1207/s15389286ajde1903_2

Grosseck, G., Bran, R., & Tiru, L. (2011). "Dear teacher, what should I write on my wall?": A case study on academic uses of Facebook. *Procedia: Social and Behavioral Sciences, 15*, 425–1430. doi:10.1016/j.sbspro.2011.03.306

Hew, K. F. (2011). Students' and teachers' use of Facebook. *Computers in Human Behavior, 27*(2), 662–676. doi:10.1016/j.chb.2010.11.020

Huffaker, D., & Calvert, S. (2003). The new science of learning: Active learning metacognition, and transfer of knowledge in E-Learning applications. *Journal of Educational Computing Research, 29*(3), 325–334. doi:10.2190/4T89-30W2-DHTM-RTQ2

Irwin, C., Ball, L., Desbrow, B., & Leveritt, M. (2012). Students' perceptions of using Facebook as an interactive learning resource at university. *Australasian Journal of Educational Technology, 28*(7), 1221–1232. Retrieved from http://ascilite.org.au/ajet/ajet28/irwin.html

Kabilan, M. K., Ahmad, N., & Abidin, M. J. Z. (2010). Facebook: An online environment for learning English in institutions of higher education. *The Internet and Higher Education, 13*(4), 179–187. doi:10.1016/j.iheduc.2010.07.003

Kreijns, C., Kirschner, P., & Jochems, W. (2003). Identifying the pitfalls for social interaction in Computer supported collaborative learning environments: A review of the research. *Computers in Human Behavior, 19*(3), 335–353. doi:10.1016/S0747-5632(02)00057-2

Kurtz, G. (2014). Students' perceptions of using Facebook group and a course website as interactive and active learning spaces. *Proceedings of the 9th Chais Conference for the Study of Innovation and Learning Technologies: Learning In the Technological Era*. Raanana: The Open University of Israel.

Lim, T. (2010). The use of Facebook for online discussions among distance learners. *Turkish Online Journal of Distance Education, 11*(4). Retrieved December 20, 2012 from: http://dergipark.ulakbim.gov.tr/tojde/article/view/5000102541/5000095638

Madge, C., Meek, J., Wellens, J., & Hooley, T. (2009). Facebook, social integration and informal learning at University: "It is more of socializing and talking to friends about work than for actually doing work. *Learning, Media and Technology, 34*(2), 141–155. doi:10.1080/17439880902923606

Marza, L., & Al-Hafizh, M. (2013). Teaching writing recount text to junior high school students by using Facebook peer-comment. *Journal of English Language Teaching*, *1*(2), 683–692. Retrieved from http://download.portalgaruda.org/article.php?article=100265&val=1486

Mazer, J. P., Murphy, R. E., & Simonds, C. J. (2007). I'll see you on "Facebook": The effects of computer-mediated teacher self-disclosure on student motivation, affective learning, and classroom climate. *Communication Education*, *56*(1), 1–17. doi:10.1080/03634520601009710

Meishar-Tal, H., Kurtz, G., & Pieterse, E. (2012). Facebook groups as LMS: A case study. *The International Review of Research in Open and Distance Education*, *13*(4), 1–16.

Papaleontiou-Louca, E. (2003). The concept and instruction of metacognition. *Teacher Development*, *7*(1), 2–9.

Parslow, P., Lundqvist, K. Ø., Williams, S., Ashton, R., & Evans, M. (2008). Facebook & BlackBoard: Comparative view of learning environments. In *SSE Systems Engineering Conference 2008*. The University of Reading. Retrieved January 20, 2012 from: http://centaur.reading.ac.uk/1105

Pempek, T. A., Yermolayeva, Y. A., & Calvert, S. (2009). College students' social networking experiences on Facebook. *Journal of Applied Developmental Psychology*, *30*(3), 227–238. doi:10.1016/j.appdev.2008.12.010

Pintrich, P. R. (2002). The role of metacognitive knowledge in learning, teaching, and assessing. *Theory into Practice*, *41*(4), 219–225. doi:10.1207/s15430421tip4104_3

Promnitz-Hayashi, L. (2011). A learning success story using Facebook. *Studies in Self-Access Learning Journal*, *2*(4), 309-316. Retrieved October 20, 2013 from: http://sisaljournal.org/archives/dec11/promnitz-hayashi

Rap, S., & Blonder, R. (2014). Learning science in social networks: Chemical interactions on Facebook. *Proceedings of the 9th Chais Conference for the Study of Innovation and Learning Technologies: Learning In the Technological Era*. Raanana: The Open University of Israel.

Reid, J. (2011). "We don't Twitter, we Facebook": An alternative pedagogical space that enables critical practices in relation to writing. *English Teaching*, *10*(1), 58–80. Retrieved from http://education.waikato.ac.nz/research/files/etpc/files/2011v10n1art4.pdf

Rimor, R., & Arie, P. (2013). An English play is hosted by Facebook: Students' achievements and attitudes towards studying an English play using the Facebook environment. In L. Gómez Chova, A. López Martinez & I. Cadel Torres (Eds). *Proceedings of ICERI2013 Conference. 6th International Conference of Education, Research and Innovation*. International Association of Technology, Education and Development (IATED).

Rimor, R., & Kozminsky, E. (2004). An Analysis of the Reflections of Students in Online Courses. *EARLI-SIG on Metacognition*. Amsterdam, the Netherlands.

Rimor, R., Reingold, R., & Heiman, T. (2008). Instructor's scaffolding in support of students' metacognition through an online course: Why to promote and how to investigate. In J. Zumbach, N. Schwartz, T. Seufert, & L. Kester (Eds.), *Beyond knowledge: The legacy of competence-meaningful computer-based learning environments* (pp. 43–53). Springer. doi:10.1007/978-1-4020-8827-8_6

Rimor, R., Reingold, R., & Kalay, A. (2006). *The relationship between students' metacognition and instructor's scaffolding in online academic courses*. Paper presented at SIG16 Metacognition: 2nd Biennial Conference, Cambridge, UK.

Rimor, R., & Rosen, Y. (2010). Collaborative knowledge construction in online Learning Environment: Why to promote and how to investigate. In S. Mukerji & P. Tripathi (Eds.), *Cases on Technological Adaptability and Transnational Learning: Issues and Challenges*. IGI-Global. doi:10.4018/978-1-61520-749-7.ch010

Rimor, R., Rosen, Y., & Naser, K. (2010). Are two better than one? A study of social interaction patterns in an online collaborative database environment. IJELLO special series of Chais Conference 2010 best papers. *Interdisciplinary Journal of E-Learning and Learning Objects*, *6*, 355–365.

Rosen, Y., & Rimor, R. (2009). Using a collaborative database to enhance students' knowledge construction. *Interdisciplinary Journal of E-Learning and Learning Objects, 5*, 187-195.

Rosen, Y., & Rimor, R. (2013). Teaching and assessing problem solving in an online collaborative environment. In R. Hartshorne, T. Heafner, & T. Petty (Eds.), Teacher Education Programs and Online Learning Tools: Innovations in Teacher Preparation. Hershey, PA: Information Science Reference, IGI Global. doi:10.4018/978-1-4666-1906-7.ch005

Rotem, A., & Avni, I. (2012). *Facebook in education: Tools and educational applications*. Retrieved April 22, 2013 from http://ianethics.com/wp-content/uploads/2012/01/facebook-in-education-toolsAI.pdf (in Hebrew)

Rovai, A. P. (2002). Building sense of community at distance. *International Review of Research in Open and Distance Learning*, *3*(1). Retrieved from http://www.irrodl.org/index.php/irrodl/article/view/79/152

Shih, R. (2011). Can Web 2.0 technology assist college students in learning English writing? Integrating Facebook and peer assessment with blended learning. *Australasian Journal of Educational Technology, 27*(Special issue, 5), 829-845.

Van Doorn, G., & Eklund, A. A. (2013). Face to Facebook: Social media and the learning and teaching potential of symmetrical, synchronous communication. *Journal of University Teaching & Learning Practice, 10*(1), article 6. Retrieved September 20, 2014 from: http://ro.uow.edu.au/cgi/viewcontent.cgi?article=1268&context=jutlp

Veenman, V. H.-W., Van Hout-Wolters, B. H. A. M., & Afflerbach, P. (2006). Metacognition and learning: Conceptual and methodological considerations. *Metacognition and Learning*, *1*(1), 3–14. doi:10.1007/s11409-006-6893-0

Vescio, V., Ross, D., & Adams, A. (2008). A review of research on the impact of professional learning communities on teaching practice and student learning. *Teaching and Teacher Education, 24*(1), 80–91. doi:10.1016/j.tate.2007.01.004

Wadmany, R., Rimor, R. & Rozner, E. (2011). The relationship between attitude, thinking and activity of students in an e-learning course. *REM – Research on Education and Media, 3*(1), 103-121

Wang, Q., Woo, H. L., Quek, C. L., Yang, Y., & Liu, M. (2012). Using Facebook group as learning management system: An exploratory study. *British Journal of Educational Technology, 43*(3), 428–438. doi:10.1111/j.1467-8535.2011.01195.x

## KEY TERMS AND DEFINITIONS

**Collaborative Online Learning:** Coordinated joint activity online in which two or more learners attempt to construct and maintain a shared conception of a construct, process or a problem through peer interaction and group learning processes on the web. One of the leading fields of research in the context of online collaborative research is the Computer-Supported Collaborative Learning (CSCL).

**Facebook Group:** A Facebook interface added to the regular platform in 2011-2012. Any Facebook member can create a group. It is a private space which allows one to connect with a specific set of friends (workplace, school, campus, hobbies…). A group makes it possible to share information, post updates on the group wall, chat with all members at once, upload/ create and edit a file and more. There are three kinds of groups. 1) Secret (only members can find it and see posts). 2) Closed (Anyone can find it and see who is in it. Only members can see posts). 3) Open (public) (Anyone can see the group, its members and the posts. Anyone can join).

**Metacognition:** The knowledge of one's own cognitive and affective processes and states as well as the ability to consciously and deliberately monitor and regulate those processes and states. The first formal model of metacognition was proposed by Flavell (1979).

**Sense of Community:** Communicative behaviors and attitudes in the community. A sense of community by the learner may be viewed as consisting of four related dimensions: spirit, trust, interaction, and commonality of learning expectations and goals.

**Social Network Sites (SNSs):** Websites that allow individuals to create a public profile, to connect to other users with whom they share a connection or common interest. Through this kind of site, any user can view the list of connections he is connected to and thus create new connections. Facebook is one of the largest and most popular social network sites in the world. Other examples of social network sites are: Twitter, Instagram, Google+ and LinkedIn.

## ENDNOTES

[1]  The tool is theoretically based on Flavell's three metacognitive dimensions (1987). The original tool was developed by Dr. Rikki Rimor and Dr. E. Kozminsky (2002), supported by The Hubert Burda Center for Innovative Communications, Ben-Gurion University, Beersheva. The tool was adapted to the Facebook environment and elaborated for this research

# APPENDIX 1

## Questionnaire 1 (Pre)

As part of my studies in the Technology in Education Department, I am conducting a survey concerning students' attitude towards learning literature on Facebook. Your responses are anonymous and will be used only for research purposes. They will, in no way, affect your grades. It is important that your answers be truthful and reflect your personal attitudes. Thank you very much for your cooperation.

Circle the number which best reflects your attitude towards the following statements (Table 4). (1: Do not agree at all – 5: I agree to a large extent).

*Table 4. Attitudes towards Facebook as a learning environment in literature lessons (Pre)*

| | 1<br>I don' t agree at all | 2<br>I don't agree | 3<br>I partially agree | 4<br>I agree | 5<br>I agree to a large extent |
|---|---|---|---|---|---|
| 1. Doing homework through Facebook may improve my achievement on the final exam. | | | | | |
| 2. Doing homework on Facebook will increase my motivation to study the play. | | | | | |
| 3. Group work on Facebook is more interesting than doing homework individually. | | | | | |
| 4. Doing homework collaboratively on Facebook seems to me more effective than doing it individually. | | | | | |
| 5. Group work on Facebook will help me understand the play better than doing homework individually. | | | | | |
| 6. Group work on Facebook is likely to improve my ability to analyze the play. | | | | | |
| 7. In general, I prefer to study in a group rather than alone. | | | | | |
| 8. I am interested in learning more lessons in the Facebook environment. | | | | | |

9.    Please answer the following question extensively.

What is your opinion concerning learning English literature on Facebook?

................................................................................................................................

................................................................................................................................

................................................................................................................................

................................................................................................................................

.......................................................................

Thank you for your cooperation!
perlitarie@hotmail.com

## APPENDIX 2

## Questionnaire 2 (Post)

As part of my studies in the Technology in Education Department, I am conducting a survey concerning students' attitude towards learning literature on Facebook. Your responses are anonymous and will be used only for research purposes. They will, in no way, affect your grades. It is important that your answers be truthful and reflect your personal attitudes. Thank you very much for your cooperation.

Circle the number which best reflects your attitude towards the following statements (Table 5). (1: Do not agree at all – 5: I agree to a large extent).

*Table 5. Attitude towards Facebook as a learning environment in literature lessons (Post)*

|  | 1<br>I don' t agree at all | 2<br>I don't agree | 3<br>I partially agree | 4<br>I agree | 5<br>I agree to a large extent |
|---|---|---|---|---|---|
| 1. Doing homework through Facebook may have improved my achievement on the final exam. |  |  |  |  |  |
| 2. Doing homework on Facebook has increased my motivation to study the play. |  |  |  |  |  |
| 3. Group work on Facebook was more interesting than doing homework individually. |  |  |  |  |  |
| 4. Doing homework collaboratively on Facebook seems to me more effective than doing it individually. |  |  |  |  |  |
| 5. Group work on Facebook has helped me understand the play better than doing homework individually. |  |  |  |  |  |
| 6. Group work on Facebook has improved my ability to analyze the play. |  |  |  |  |  |
| 7. In general, I prefer to study in a group rather than alone. |  |  |  |  |  |
| 8. I am interested in learning more lessons in the Facebook environment. |  |  |  |  |  |

9. Please answer the following question extensively.

What is your opinion concerning learning English literature on Facebook?

......................................................................................................................................................
......................................................................................................................................................
......................................................................................................................................................
......................................................................................................................................................
...........................................................................................................

Thank you for your cooperation!
perlitarie@hotmail.com

# APPENDIX 3

*Table 6. Tool for analyzing metacognitive thinking of learners on Facebook*

| Metacognitive Dimensions | Code | Description |
|---|---|---|
| **A. Personality Dimension** | | |
| 1. Personal traits | PT | An individual's insight regarding his nature and traits as an online learner |
| 2. Emotions | | Expressions of positive or negative emotions in regard to learning on Facebook |
| Expressions of affection, agreement, satisfaction, pleasure, interest | Pa1 | |
| Expressions of anger, opposition, reference to need for separation between social and learning space | Pa2 | |
| Expressions of community feeling | Pa3 | |
| Expressions of getting lost, apprehension, frustration | Pa4 | |
| 3. Reference to achievement and motivation | PP | Relation to personal achievement, motivation and feeling of progress |
| 4. Teacher-student relations | | An individual's perception of the teacher-student relationship as reflected through the learning process on Facebook |
| Positive reference | PR+ | |
| Negative reference | PR- | |
| 5. Group work | | An individual's perception of the collaborative learning and group work throughout the learning process on Facebook |
| Positive reference | PG+ | |
| Negative reference | PG- | |
| **B. Task Dimension** | | |
| Reflections on: | | |
| 1. Availability of internet information sources | TZ | Monitoring the availability of information sources in relation to search's aim |
| 2. Problems and difficulties | TP | Description of problems and difficulties in the course of carrying the task |
| 3. Feasibility of performance | TF | Monitoring the necessary resources for performing the task such as time, place, communication |
| 4. Contents | CT | An individual's insights on the contents, the information, new ideas, prior knowledge |
| **C. Strategy Dimension** | | |
| 1. Comparison between learning on Facebook and learning in a different environment | SD | An individual's insight on the differences between learning on Facebook and learning face to face in class or doing homework individually. |
| 2. Reaching conclusions, generalizing regarding Facebook characteristics: | | |
| As promoting learning processes | SG+ | Insights concerning the advantages of learning on Facebook. |
| As inhibiting or impairing learning processes | SG- | Insights concerning the disadvantages of learning on Facebook. |
| 3. Requesting help from other students | SH1 | Requesting help from another person in relation to functioning on Facebook |
| 4. Offering help to others | SH2 | Helping another person following a request for help. |

# Chapter 21
# Cross–Border Collaborative Learning in the Professional Development of Teachers:
## Case Study – Online Course for the Professional Development of Teachers in a Digital Age

**Rafi Davidson**
*Kaye Academic College of Education, Israel*

**Amnon Glassner**
*Kaye Academic College of Education, Israel*

## ABSTRACT

*The goal of this chapter is to present a theoretical and practical frame for PD of teachers at the digital age. The main question we ask is how to develop life competencies and skills of teachers in order to change their learning and teaching in a way that enables school graduates to acquire relevant skills for life. The chapter inquires this issue by a qualitative methodology case study . The case is an online course for teachers' professional development. The chapter presents evidence from reflective diaries, interviews and scripts of students' and teachers' discussions, focusing on identification of the effects of the course's learning environments on the development of the teachers' self determination learning and skills. The findings indicate the useful effects of the combination between LMS environments and social media, such as Web 2.0 tools. The conclusions suggest new directions for teachers' professional development that encourage the design of a flexible fractal net which enable fostering teachers' leadership and innovation.*

DOI: 10.4018/978-1-4666-9441-5.ch021

# INTRODUCTION

This chapter addresses the question: How can teachers be trained to advance life competencies and skills? We shall present a case study of an online course for veteran teachers, whose aim is to train teachers to lead pedagogical innovation. We will then propose a model for the professional development of teachers that can adapt to the rapid development of ICT technologies.

The internet has made it possible for accessibility and communication between people across borders, nations, countries, cultures, and lifestyles.

While the education world is undergoing processes of change, and is beginning to adapt to the rapidly developing digital culture, change is still required in the perception and practice of the professional development of teachers, and its adaptation to the schools of tomorrow.

Our book, *The "Arrow Head" and the "Warm Hand"* (Davidson, 2012), discusses a humanistic-constructivist approach to teacher training that mandates rethinking. It discusses questions pertaining to the role of teacher training in engaging in social and emotional elements of online learning, which are of paramount importance at a time when human beings, especially young people, have virtual "friends" on social networks. Classroom doors are increasingly being breached due to the use of cellphones and iPads. Teachers face a situation to which they are unaccustomed, and fear loss of control in their classrooms.

Two major questions arise regarding this changing world:

- How should the teacher training system contend with this new reality?
- How can teachers be trained to be lifelong learners, on the one hand, and to gain the ability train their own students to be lifelong learners, on the other hand?

Learning in the twenty-first century requires the development of new life competencies that did not exist in traditional learning and teaching. Numerous studies demonstrate that teachers are the most important factor in their students' success (McCaffrey, Lockwood, Koretz, & Hamilton, 2003). Our basic premise is that by basing teaching on new pedagogical approaches, teachers will also experience such learning methods.

The underlying approach of teachers should be the premise that learners are capable of individual and collaborative knowledge building (Scardamalia & Bereiter, 2003) provided that the teacher creates conditions that facilitate self-regulated learning.

# BACKGROUND

## A Learning Theory That Contends with the Changes in the Information and Communications Era

The rapid development of ICT technologies in recent years, especially Web 2.0, obliges educators to update prevailing pedagogical approaches and their implementation in the work of teachers (Merchant, 2007).

Concepts such as teaching, learning, knowledge, and understanding require a renewed conceptual frame. Siemens' theory of connectivism attempts to provide an answer to the need for a new pedagogical paradigm (Siemens, 2005). It is challenged by questions such as: What is learning in the internet age? How is personal knowledge created in the individual and collective knowledge in an organization? What elements are required for a paradigmatic change in learning theories and for updating them to the reality of the digital age?

Connectivism views the internet as the primary learning environment in the twenty-first century, and learning as a process of crossing the length and breadth of the network, and utilizing strong and weak connections with human beings and electronic resources to create personal and organizational knowledge (Downes, 2012; Siemens, 2005).

In contrast, the older and more established theory of social constructivism (Brooks & Brooks, 1993; Palincsar, 1998) emphasizes the social aspect of learning, and of the learner being part of a group of learners, but does not provide a sufficient explanation for how human beings learn and how knowledge is built via the network. According to connectivism, the individual's knowledge is distributed and resides not only in his brain, but also in connections with electronic and human components which the learner has developed in the course of his learning. Meaningful learning is a process that requires a network environment that is open to interactions at varying levels of intensity. The significance of intensity of ties for collaborative learning is central to Siemens' theory of connectivism, which views the strength of weak ties created on social networks, blogs, and other Web 2.0 environments, as providing the learner with even more sources for innovation and creativity than his strong ties.

According to connectivism, the distributive nature of learning expands social constructivist pedagogy and adapts it to the internet age. It emphasizes the importance of the learner's reflective and meta-thinking skills, and to a lesser degree the construction of knowledge and the learned content. As stated by Siemens,"The pipe is more important than the content within the pipe. Our ability to learn what we need for tomorrow is more important than what we know today." (Siemens, 2005). According to connectivism, content is constantly changing, and learning is typified by rapid changes and constant updating, and consequently it is important for learning to include development of the life competencies of "lifelong learners". These competencies include

knowing where to look and how to choose relevant information (critical thinking), ability to create new content by means of up-to-date content on the network (creative thinking), maintaining diverse social ties (socio-emotional competencies), drawing conclusions, making decisions, and staying regularly updated. Whereas in the learning process, constructivism emphasizes the ties and collaboration between learners in a group or community jointly constructing common knowledge, connectivism places greater emphasis on learning as an individual, multi-channel, multi-level process, and views the individual as the creator of content who simultaneously forms ties with individuals, groups, or digital tools at his discretion and according to his needs. Anderson and Dron (2011) draw a distinction between these two pedagogical approaches with reference to the types of interaction typifying each theory:

"From the critical role of student-student interaction in constructivism to the student-content interrelationship celebrated in connectivist pedagogies, with their focus on persistent networks and user-generated content." (Anderson & Dron, 2011, p.91).

The advance of ICT has an evolutionary effect on pedagogy. The development of mobile technologies, which include permanent wireless communication in any place and at any time, as well as applications that influence cultural and social changes, ultimately also affect education, its approaches, and teaching and learning methods. The development of Web 2.0 environments has led to development of digital tools with which every individual can express himself. For example, in the online course described below, the personal smartphones and tablets of the learners were used to facilitate communication. Thus, learning is partly self-managed by the learners who maintain contact, and collaboratively write and publish documents on the network. The pedagogical principles adopted by the course lecturers were essentially social-constructivist and connectivist.

They designed network environments that encouraged the learners to use tools for individual and collaborative learning.

Many consider Web 2.0 technological developments a turning point in attitudes to pedagogy and learning methods. These environments enable anyone to be not only a consumer but also a producer of knowledge which opens new possibilities for learning (McLoughlin & Lee, 2008; McLoughlin, 2011).

McLoughlin and Lee (2008) propose a pedagogy model they call "Web 2.0 Pedagogy", which is to a great extent consistent with the way learning took place in the course described below, and consequently we deem it appropriate to quote from it:

"Pedagogy 2.0 also acknowledges that in a networked society, powered by a range of high-speed technologies, learners have access to ideas, resources, and communities to support their learning, are driven by personal needs and choice (personalization), and are able to develop self-regulatory skills. Pedagogies need to engage learners in the social processes of knowledge creation rather than the mere consumption of instructor supplied information (productivity), in addition to scaffolding linkages, dialogue, and connections in and across communities and global distributed networks (participation) for the purposes of idea sharing, inquiry, and problem solving." (McLoughlin & Lee, 2008, p. 15).

## ICT Learning Environments

### Learning Environments: Definitions and Characteristics

This chapter describes a combination between two online learning environments: PLE (Personal Learning Environment) and a LMS (Learning management system) that is for online distance learning. We used in a Moodle (Modular Object-Oriented Dynamic Learning Environment), an open source, online courseware platform, as LMS.

PLEs are communication systems that are controlled by learners rather than teachers, thus increasing the learners' autonomy (Wilson, Liber, Johnson, Beauvoir, Sharples & Milligan, 2007; Chatti, Agustiawan, & Specht, 2010; Dabbagh, & Kitsantas, 2011), such as Facebook groups and Google+ communities.

PLEs environments are typified by:

- Learning through an eclectic collection of free online tools, e.g., Google, Wiki or WordPress services.
- The learner's autonomy and self-determination are more important than structured and ordered organization for which the teacher/lecturer is responsible.
- Accumulated knowledge differs from learner to learner and is adapted to its relevance for each individual.
- The teacher assists in assessment; the learner and his peers take a central part in assessing their learning.
- The learning environments enable learners to be on the network and in interactions with people who are not formally part of the "class", but are relevant for the learner's learning.
- The virtual space is open and has no beginning, middle, or end, and enables distributed learning.

In contrast, LMS environments maintain the boundaries of the traditional classroom and they cannot serve the connectivist learning tools on their own. They enable the teacher to manage the class's learning, but do not contribute to the development of an autonomous learner on the global network (See table 1).

Moodle is a closed system containing a selection of Web 2.0 tools that also facilitate work in a personal environment, such as blogging and Wikis, forums and so forth. However, the Web 2.0 tools on Moodle are closed within the system

*Table 1. Summary of the differences between learning in LMS to learning in PLE*

| PLE | LMS |
|---|---|
| Individual approach | Collectivist approach |
| Based on the connectivist approach | Based on the social constructivist approach |
| Open to any user | Open only to members of the community |
| The learner has full control over the learning (self-control) | The teacher/instructor and the institution have considerable control over the learning |
| Multi-channel and chaotic | Organized structure |
| Requires a high level of ICT literacy and individual and collaborative network learning ability | Enables work at relatively low ICT literacy as well |
| Raises concerns regarding dangers and personal safety | Provides a sense of relative safety (especially for "digital immigrants") |

and do not allow the learners to share with others outside their course. This constitutes good practice and experience in collaboration and interpersonal communication skills, but does not develop the learners' abilities for self-determination and lifelong learning.

Therefore, combination and interaction between tools of social media environments (PLE environments) and tools of the Moodle platform (LMS environment) allow design of a learning environment suitable for developing life and career competencies (Figure 1).

## Life Competencies and Learning Skills in the Digital Age

This chapter focuses on a description and analysis of an online course aimed at developing teachers' technological competencies such as information, media and ICT literacy, creativity innovation and critical thinking, life and career competencies consisting of flexibility, adaptability, initiative, productivity and accountability, as well as leadership

and responsibility (Massachusetts Department of Elementary and Secondary Education, 2008).

## Digital and ICT literacy

Eshet recently updated his model of digital literacy to include the following skills: photo-visual, reproduction, branching, Information, socio-emotional and real-time thinking (Eshet, 2012).

At the center of digital literacy, Steve Wheeler lists skills directly connected with the influences of the internet on competencies required nowadays: social networking, privacy maintenance, identity management, creating content, organizing content, reusing and repurposing, filtering and selecting, self-presentation, and transliteracy (Wheeler, 2012).

Based on the definitions and characteristics of the above skills we decided to classify the life and learning competencies required nowadays according to two dimensions: the learning of the individual and learning as a collaborative social process.

1. The self-determined learner dimension that includes: photo-visual skills, reflective thinking skills, divergent thinking skills, creative thinking skills, critical thinking skills, inquiry thinking skills and real-time thinking.

2. The social-collaborative dimension of the learner includes: interpersonal communication skills using synchronous and asynchronous communication tools; collaborative work skills such as group formation, collaborative writing, reading, and speaking via the network, conflict management and resolution, time management and organization, empowerment and encouragement of collaborative initiative. An important aspect is building trust, making decisions, and creating consensus.

*Figure 1. Combination and interaction between of social media environment tools (PLE environment) and Google tools (LMS environment)*

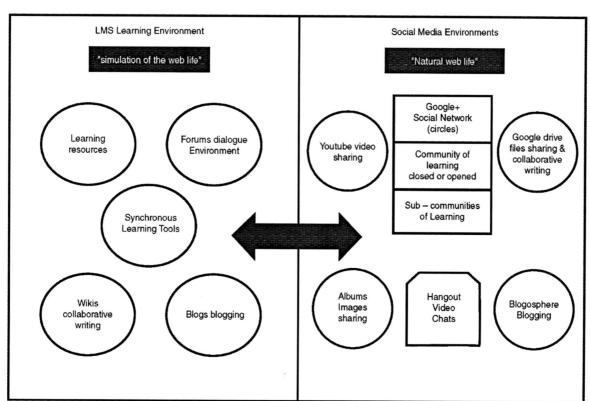

## Social Frameworks for Collaborative Learning

Another feature of learning in a group pertains to the social organization levels of the learning. It can be carried out in small groups (Brindley, Blaschke & Walti, 2009), or in a community of learners whose size can range from several dozen to several thousand participants. The organization of learners in a community differs from the social organization of network learners. The individual learner creates his own learning networks and determines the composition and number of participants. In network learning the number of people is unlimited, there is a high level of flexibility, and the type of people vary according to the learner's needs. In addition, network learning is borderless and requires new skills that can be defined as part of the learner's digital literacy.

## CASE STUDY: AN ONLINE TEACHER TRAINING COURSE

### Background

'Leaders of Up-to-date Pedagogy in Innovative Environments' is a professional development course offered to teachers who are candidates for senior ranks as educators in Israel. The course is held as part of the Ofek Hadash (New Horizon, for elementary school teachers) and Oz Letmura (Courage to Change, for junior high and high school teachers) reforms in Israel's education system. It is an entirely online course, with the exception of two face-to-face meetings, one at the beginning of the course and one at its end.

The following is a description of the course and evidence-based findings collected during it.

## The Course Participants

The forty-two course participants teach a wide range of subjects: Hebrew and Arabic language and expression, mathematics, geography, music, sciences, physical education, educational counseling, and special education. About a quarter of the participants hold positions associated with ICT assimilation in their schools, and some are also homeroom teachers. Some are preschool teachers, while others are elementary, junior high, and high school teachers, in both regular and special education frameworks, in religious, non-religious, Arab, and Jewish schools. All are veteran teachers, some hold leading positions at their schools, and others are teacher educators in their schools or regions. Some hold a BA, and others an MA.

## The Course Lecturers (Instructors)

Four instructors teach the course, two of whom hold a PhD and two who hold an MA, and all are experts, with rich pedagogical and technological experience combined with ICT in the education system. The instructors work in full collaboration (team teaching) (Davidson & Mor, 2005).

All the course participants and instructors are members of a collaborative community of learners. Instruction is provided collaboratively for the whole community, but there is also a division of functions (Davidson & Mor, 2005). Each instructor works with two small groups of learners (4-7 learners per group), and is responsible for providing support, encouragement, and help for the group and individuals in their learning. Throughout the course the instructors meet face-to-face as well as online, to plan, set work assignments, and share reflections (each instructor keeps a reflective notes and documents). The instructors' work method includes exchanging opinions and ideas, working collaboratively to plan the learning activities, design the learning environment (Kalantzis, & Cope, 2010; Miller, 2012) and monitor the progress and

evaluate the learners' learning process. The aim of this method is to provide modeling for teachers who will work in teams in the future.

## Design of the Learning Environment by the Instructors and Learners

*Moodle as LMS System:* The Moodle was designed to include presentation and sharing of learning resources, but especially for the learners' interactive activities. Assignment instructions are posted on the site, but a large proportion of them are prepared by means of collaborative internet tools such as Google Drive. The written assignments include the aims of the activities, the rationale, and instructions on performing each assignment. Additionally, links to online manuals were prepared by means of Google Docs shared documents and instructional video software, and enabled the learners to use them in their work. Online instruction includes instructional videos, written manuals, and interactive tools such as a support forum, use of video chat for group instruction, and synchronous LMSs such as Illuminate.

*Social Media and PLEs:* These are additional environments, designed by the instructors (Miller, 2012) and then collaboratively with the learners, that were used for learning throughout the process. These network environments enable learners, both as individuals and groups, to fully control their learning resources (Dabbagh & Kitsantas, 2011).

At the beginning of the course, a community of learners was opened on Google+ which enabled learning outside Moodle. The decision to open a Google community was based on the fact that it operates at a high level of coherence, with important and convenient internet tools for individual work, sharing, and collaborative learning. It is important to draw a distinction between working on the Google+ social network and working in a Google community. The former is based on PLEs, where each learner has his own PLE, and on the connectivist approach, which is important for the development of life competencies for a lifelong learner with a high level of self-determination. In contrast, the latter environment, a virtual community, is based on the social-constructivist approach, which is important for the development of a social learner with competencies required for working in a group and as part of a collective on the network.

## The Learning Process on the Course

The learning process of the course consisted of two distinct stages. In the first stage (the first semester) the learners experienced working as a community of learners led by the course instructors. The learners acquired collaborative work skills and habits, learned how to manage a group, and improved their ability to work in a Moodle environment, as well as in social media environments (especially Google tools that enable creation of PLEs and a collaborative learning environment). At first the learners also worked as an online internet community comprised of all the participants, who were also split into heterogeneous groups of teachers who knew one another and who learned collaboratively using online resources. The learning activities were guided, and provided the scaffolding for individual and collaborative community learning. The aims of these activities were to improve skills associated with working on the internet, and develop skills associated with personal and professional acquaintance between all the community members on the network. A dialogue was created, as well as the foundation for collaborative work and a common language between the learners themselves and between them and the instructors. The instructors' acquaintance with the learners was also attended by observation and monitoring of their learning using Moodle tools that enable observation and monitoring of participation in discussion forums. The instructors also utilized reports generated by the system for each learner. This is the great advantage of

an LMS over more open environments, since it helps the teacher to obtain a snapshot of each learner's progress, thus facilitating differential teaching adapted to the learners. An additional means of observing the learners' work was each participant's personal electronic portfolio, which included their reflective journals that they shared with the instructors via Google Drive.

The instructors' acquaintance with the learners constituted the basis for dividing the learners into groups later in the first semester. The process of creating and building up the online groups was attended by instruction and reading material on creating effective online work groups. The learners experimented with skills required for creating and building up a group, matching expectations, division of functions, and creating collaborative contracts that include work procedures and each learner's commitment to collaborative learning. Special emphasis was placed on the uniqueness of creating a group that works and maintains contact solely online. The learners received information and guidance from the instructors on publishing their collaborative work products on the community's website on Google+. Each group presented its work products, including the group members' collaborative contracts and a collaborative document in which the learners summarized the characteristics of current pedagogies in network environments from the material they read and their own professional experience. Each participant and group responded to the other groups' products, and discussions were held within the community. In the posts and responses published on the online community page the learners provided feedback on the other groups' products, and wrote how they contributed to them and to improving their own group's work. In the second stage, beginning in the second semester, the learners transitioned to working and learning more autonomously and flexibly in order to further develop life and career competencies, which are typified by the learner's self-regulated learning and behavior in internet environments. In this stage the course was in effect conducted in accordance with the PBL approach, and the aim of the learning was to prepare plans for projects the learners would implement in different frameworks in their schools. This time the learners were asked to choose their project group members themselves, build a team, and decide on their collaborative work method. The work groups were built through dialogue between the learners during which the group chose a subject for their project, defined and formulated work procedures, and in most cases also wrote a work contract that was binding on all its members. The learners also chose and decided on a large proportion of the digital resources they would utilize in their learning. The instructors monitored this process, and whenever difficulties or problems emerged and the learners sought assistance, the instructors helped them overcome the obstacles or encouraged them to resolve the issue themselves.

The learners implemented the learning skills they experienced in the first part of the course, such as creating a group and working collaboratively and harmoniously, division of functions, including a group leader, matching expectations, providing fellow group members with emotional support, planning a project together, and resolving problems that emerge in the group. To this end the groups utilized different means of communication to which they were introduced and experienced during the first semester, such as SMS, WhatsApp, discussion forums, blogs, video chats (Hangouts, Skype), Google+ Circles, chats, and so forth. The life competencies and work skills the learners developed were typified by the requirement for a high level of self-determination (Ryan & Deci, 2002; Zimmerman, 2002), accountability, advancing personal initiative, collaborating with others, and improving their sense of ease and mastery of working on the internet. The findings presented below provide evidence of this.

## Assessment Methods

The assessment criteria described here were proposed and processed together with the learners in a dedicated discussion forum on the course website. In the discussion it was decided that the assessment would comprise two components: (1) Assessment of each learner's learning in the activities he performed on his own, as well as those in which he participated within the group or community of learners. (2) Assessment of collaborative learning – assessment of each group's learning.

### 1. Assessment of Individual Learning

Degree of each individual's development both individually and within the group; the learning processes each learner underwent; performance of individual learning activities as required.

- Personal documentation and reflection throughout the learning process – keeping an online cloud journal.
- Quality of function performance in individual and group assignments; assessment according to the following criteria: responsibility, leadership, initiative, conscientiousness, contribution to advancing the group's work and products, personal time-keeping (not procrastinating).
- Personal progress – assessment according to progress and improvement from the beginning of the course, based primarily on the learner's testimonies. For example, a learner's reflective journal can indicate whether he has noted things he has learned during the course, and which attest to new knowledge he has acquired.

## 2. Assessment of Collaborative Group Learning

The assessment criteria proposed by the learners and instructors during the discussion on the forum:

- The group's general functioning – cohesion, participation, level of collaboration, its contribution to the learning of all community members (peer learning).
- Division of functions and their performance by each group member.
- The group's products: their academic and educational quality, their publication and presentation.
- Meeting schedules.
- Level of collaboration: contribution, content, sharing, creativity, initiative, providing encouragement and support for fellow group members.
- Performing joint learning activities and level of performance.
- Academic quality of the group's end products.
- Contribution to the peer learning of other groups.
- Congruence between the products and aims defined at the start or during the learning.

Two assessment approaches were employed that were consistent with our pedagogical outlook:

- **Formative Assessment:** The assessment process took place throughout the course.
- **Including the Learners in the Assessment:** Peer assessment and self-assessment.

The following assessment tools were employed:

- **Personal and Group Portfolio:** Electronic portfolios (Currant, Haigh, Higgison, Hughes, Rodway & Whitfield, 2010), including reflective journals that the learners shared with the instructors (and with members of their group if they chose to).
- **Indicators:** Related to criteria and performance levels.
- Online LMS database, participation reports, and grades, which are automated features of Moodle.
- **Community Leaders' Reflections and Documentation:** To this end the instructors also kept reflective journals in which they documented their thoughts about the individual and group learning. It is recommended that instructors document the learning process and also note the learners' conduct and performance levels during the learning process.

## FINDINGS

This section presents a variety of course participant testimonies describing the improvement and development of competencies and skills that are important for the careers, work, and learning of human beings in the twenty-first century, as described in the Theoretical Background section. The premise is that the course participants, who are education practitioners and experienced development of these competencies during the course, will encourage the development and advancement of such competencies and skills in their own students as well. And indeed, some of the testimonies we collected indicate that following their experiences on the course, and their recognition concerning the importance of developing these competencies and skills, course participants have already started developing them in their students as well.

The testimonies were collected from discussion forums, blogs, and reflections written during the course as part and independently of the assignments. Additionally, we recently held an in-depth interview with one of the course participants in order to gain a better understanding of the process of developing competencies and skills. The evidence was classified in accordance with the list of competencies and skills hierarchically described in the Theoretical Background section, and are presented accordingly in this section.

## The Personal Aspect

Here we seek to present evidence of the development of a self-regulated autonomous learner's competencies (Zimmerman, 2002).

## Visual Skills

This digital literacy skill is required in order to engage with symbols, icons, and other forms of visual communication, which are occupying an increasingly central place. Working with icons on the course's Moodle website, in Google+ and Drive, as well as in video and audio conferences, Hangouts, and Illuminate, advances the development of visual skills.

Following the introductory activity in which each student chose a picture to represent his professional identity, shared it with the others, and also responded to their pictures, B. writes: 'The activity was very nice and interesting, allowing you to express yourself in a different way, choosing a picture as something that expresses professional identity – activity that enables self-expression not only in words. It's very important to allow different ways for self-expression. I'm considering using a similar activity with my students'.

S. writes: 'The course's Illuminate session just ended. Each time anew I'm excited about this tool that enables everyone to participate: to talk, express an opinion, ask questions, and at the same time watch a presentation and also write'.

The encounter with visual information such as a film, video clip, picture, or using QR code, also provides an opportunity to advance the development of these visual skills.

N. writes in a blog: 'The film watching stage was excellent. First, because of their content.

Second, due to the ability to watch when it was convenient for me, and running them forward and backward according to my needs'.

## Skills for Developing Autonomous, Self-Regulated Learners

N. writes about the transition she experienced on the course compared with other courses: 'From the place of a student accustomed to being led, to a place where it's me who determines the degree of my need for guidance'.

In the development of a self-regulated learner, developing the disposition to experiment through trial and error is of paramount importance; in other words, not to be afraid to make mistakes. A. advances her experimentation and endeavors to understand the importance of making mistakes as an integral and important part of the learning process. She writes: 'I feel that it's only experience that connected me with doing and succeeding... Although I made a lot of mistakes along the way (and I still am), I posted in places I shouldn't have, deleted things, pressed, returned, got confused...'

Y. writes: 'We don't regret the time we invested, because actually we had to learn to cope on our own'.

## Reflective Thinking Skills (Reflecting on and Questioning the Process, the Thinking, the Products, and the Events)

Evidence of the development of reflective skills is expressed by N. in her writing about herself and the group:

*Personal difficulties: not disrupting the group with an unconventional work pace and style. Adapting myself, nonconformist, to group work; but real adaptation, not clipping my wings and non-committal head-nodding.*

*Difficulties outside the classroom: working with inspectors and management who are accustomed to traditional learning, and examining everything in the mirror of achievements. Working with parents who have misgivings about experimenting at their children's expense.*

*Our difficulties with the project: the tension between the desire to soar high with a project free of the bonds of reality, and the desire to initiate a project that has chances of succeeding, a practical project.*

*The decision: at present we're initiating and planning without taking into account whether we'll be able to execute everything, because over-practicality will block creativity at this initial stage. Later we'll examine what's going to be gradually implemented.*

N. asks: 'The film clips demonstrated up to date and innovative practice with elementary and high school students, but did not address the teachers' teaching, an area that some of us are obviously charged with. Are these learning principles valid there too in light of the understanding concerning the difference between pedagogy and andragogy?'

## Creative Thinking Skills

The very challenge of the course's authentic PBL, to identify a real need or a problem in the participants' professional lives and build a project to contend with it, requires and provides an opportunity for creative thinking.

After thinking about what their group project is going to be, N. writes: 'I thought about peer learning between students in different schools via Google Drive and Hangout. A project in which students of the same age group simultaneously learn the same subject and collaborate with each other...'

S. had the idea of using QR code for the transition program (i.e., transition from special education elementary to junior high school).

When a problem emerged in the group, with each group member pulling in a different direction, N. brought up an idea on the group's discussion forum:

*I've just had an idea... Maybe we should do a project that's an inquiry tool in the area of language tools and a different field of knowledge – reading, writing. Each of us will do it in her field.*

Following the distance acquaintance session, T. writes: 'The activity was innovative and interesting and required in-depth thinking at every stage, from choosing the picture, giving it a name, and writing an explanation about my professional identity that's reflected in the picture. All this activity around the pictures enables a variety of points of view and creative expression, since a good picture is worth a thousand words. It was interesting to see the diverse pictures others chose, how each of them creatively interprets and explains his professional identity through them, and how it's expressed in the picture'.

## Critical Thinking Skills

In critical thinking the learner is required to argumentatively justify and establish his words, and to examine and evaluate different alternatives in order to choose one of them.

In one of the groups' discussion forums a need emerged to establish ideas around a project on argumentative writing in an innovative environment. They tried to employ argumentative language at least in the written discussion between them. This kind of discussion enables a more ordered and organized writing of arguments.

In the group forum V. writes:

*I disagree with you. In my response I'll address each argument. First, regarding infringing the students' freedom of choice – the school isn't a democratic institution, the students don't choose the teachers, the subjects, or the teaching method. Consequently, there's no infringement of freedom of choice here. Although I agree on the point that students should be granted the right to choose in some things, and that they should be allowed to participate in decision making, but does freedom of choice specifically have to be on the matter of school dress? I don't believe so.*

*Regarding the third argument: the additional expense is minimal, the cost of a short-sleeved shirt is NIS 10-15 ($3-4), about a third of a simple shirt. The cost of a sweatshirt is higher, but a student can manage with 3-4 sweatshirts per season. Also, in many schools, including ours, assistance is given to needy families to purchase school dress. In summary, in my view, the advantages of a school shirt outweigh the disadvantages... I'm enclosing a link to the minutes of a Knesset committee debate in 2010 on the subject of school dress.*

The course instructors are also required to keep a reflective journal, and following her experience as an instructor on the course one instructor writes on the subject of critical thinking: 'One of the things that came up in the discussions and responses (their reflections) is the need to strengthen critical thinking skills regarding examination of the activity on its conclusion by means of feedback and/or reflection. Proof of this is that I was asked on more than one occasion to "check if there isn't something missing in the assignment..." This request made me think, why are they asking me to check rather than doing it themselves? It could be that this habit (the teacher examines and says what's missing) is still imprinted in them. This phenomenon was also prominent when they wrote feedback for the other groups. There, too, there was no reference to performance level, what was/wasn't performed in the activity and so forth. A sentence that says something like "in this section there was no reference to..."

'This gave me the insight that an indicator should be used for each activity during the course

from the very beginning (from the first activity) that will enable them to examine themselves and refine their critical thinking on performance and requirements. This way their observation will be more critical and constructive'.

## Inquiry Thinking Skills

This refers to the development of digital literacy skills in information activities, such as filtering and sorting, organizing, managing, disseminating, and publishing information on the network.

The students improved and developed inquiry thinking skills of information dissemination and processing through distance learning encounters.

A. writes: 'Following the MOFET Institute's Illuminate encounters on the subject of the "flipped classroom" to which one of the instructors referred us. The encounter was excellent, important, and fascinating. It aroused much more enthusiasm in me than I'd felt before, it opened up a lot of new ideas, reinforced the advantages, and also indicated the difficulties and disadvantages, strengthened the aims, most of which we'd already specified, simply opened up new directions of thinking, and stimulated me to continue thinking about developing this matter. It's also the thinking that addresses the different languages typifying different communication tools on the network, and the importance of addressing these differences when learning through them'.

N. writes: 'Because it's copied from chats, it's somewhat phrased in codes, and I think it should be rephrased in an ordered fashion, exactly what the issue is, so it won't be in fragmented sentences, if you see what I mean'.

G. writes: 'I learned to manage my Google+ account according to my preferences'.

## Real-Time Thinking Skills

These are skills that develop digital literacy in terms of familiarity with the possibilities at the learner's disposal during learning, and his/her ability to use and operate them when the need arises in real time.

Following difficulties with an online distance encounter she initiated and managed, and had to contend with in real time, A. writes: 'In the Hangout meeting I initiated for all the group members with one of the instructors, all the group members responded positively, but for some reason there were technical difficulties beyond our control, and some of the girls felt frustrated and left the meeting. I made great efforts for it to succeed, and repeatedly tried to contact them via chat. This experience constituted meaningful learning, and it can also be part of our project when students encounter this kind of difficulty or problems'.

Note: This also indicates improvement of social-emotional skills, inquiry thinking, and reflective thinking that observes what happens and learns from it.

D. writes: 'Two computers, both of which are giving me problems. In the end I completely removed Java from the computer and reinstalled it, and only then did I manage to connect to the course. After the system started working I noticed I'd forgotten to connect the Madonna (microphone), and the microphone didn't connect, but I was afraid to make changes, because you don't touch what works… So I could listen to the conversation and write on chat if necessary. It was interesting to hear the presentations of the different groups' projects'.

Note: This also attests to practicing inquiry thinking and creative thinking skills.

## The Social/Group Aspect

Here we seek to present evidence of the development of interpersonal and teamwork competencies, which are skills the individual needs in order to advance living together in general and group work in particular. They enable him to join forces with others to construct shared knowledge, solve problems and make decisions by using his peers' knowledge coupled with the knowledge enabled

and accumulated on and off the network. Based on our review in the Theoretical Background section as well, there is no doubt that these social skills are of considerable importance for human beings in the world of work and the society in which they live, for no man is an island. The world of work, too, is undergoing a process of transition from hierarchical to network systems with distributed responsibility and collaboration between diverse and different others.

## Using Synchronous and Asynchronous Communication Tools: Text, Sound, and Multimedia for Interpersonal Dialogue and Discussion

This is a more technical skill set (which also includes visual thinking) of mastering tools that enable interpersonal communication and choosing and adapting tools for communicating with others.

In her reflective journal, N. writes: 'After we coalesced into a group that wants to create an educational project, we decided to open a WhatsApp group that enables instant contact with people who aren't connected to email and Google+'.

D. writes: 'I've learned to operate Google+, share files, work in online groups, and so forth. The learning provided me with new tools for personal and classroom use… I prepare presentations and work with the students, prepare presentations with the students, we search for material on Google and so forth. The students are introduced to the computer, each one according to his abilities, and ICT has become a significant part of learning in the classroom. The new tools enable me to reach additional content, prepare and share files, and use them in additional ways to those I was familiar with. Adding music, film clips, and texts to the lesson, constitute an additional source of motivation for learning, interest, and curiosity. This year we introduced iPad to the classroom, and it serves as an additional communication and learning tool for our students, and the more tools I learn to use on it, I discover that more and more learning tools can be prepared for our students, and include them in the different lessons with the help of new technologies'.

S. raised the idea of using QR code for the transition program: 'I think this kind of program can make a very significant difference to learning at the school, to make the transition more familiar to the students; the film clips can be an essential part of the process for the students. The learning will become meaningful and experiential for them, and that's very important. During the process I met the instructor on the document and we talked on chat. That's a cool feature, that you can see who's going into the document, who's online, and you can see the writing on the document at the same time. I'm already thinking about writing all the documents for next year on Google Drive… because it makes it easier to work together (two teachers) on the same document'.

In her interview, G. describes the decision to use WhatsApp: 'We even created a WhatsApp group, I had apprehensions that it would be just another group with all kinds of pestering, and then a friend said, No, it'll be a professional WhatsApp group. We have to finish the year, there was so much pressure that people didn't know anymore where to communicate, the WhatsApp channel was a dynamic channel'.

The following provides evidence of other skills required to develop collaborative group work competencies.

## Group Formation Skills: Acquaintance, Decision Making

N. writes about her increased familiarity with other members of her group in the course of their work: 'D. is guided by instructions and guidance she receives, and I try to first find myself in the assignment, and only then to execute it. Her hierarchical thinking in contrast with my nonlinear and associative thinking. Additionally, N., who brings her ordered, organized, and clear thinking'.

Y. writes: 'After the idea was raised we exchanged a few mails in order to reach a decision'.

In her reflection on the course's introductory session in which the students chose a picture to represent their professional identity, O. wrote: 'I wish to state that the activity was challenging and very interesting. The requirement to present your professional identity in a creative way by uploading a picture combined with text made me think that it's possible to learn about the personal philosophy of each teacher, and how to create a community of learners from the teachers in an enriching way, with each one learning from the others, by the way each one presents his professional identity. My insights relate to the fact that each one of us is unique, and imparts his values and knowledge in different and creative ways, while remaining congruent with the requirements in the field of knowledge and the differences between our students, for each student thinks and understands what he's learning in his own way, and one way of thinking doesn't resemble another'.

G. writes: 'My experience was that despite the distance learning, the activity created a connection and closeness, interest, and a challenge'.

A. writes: 'A picture is worth a thousand words! It represents the idea that sometimes you don't need to talk a lot and explain, just show, mediate, and every person can take what they understand and want from their understanding, acknowledgement, and acceptance of the differences and similarities between us. The ability to understand, interpersonal communication, respect for the other, are important values and it's important to develop them in our students. In summary: this activity really manages to connect between people who might never have communicated with each other in one way or another, and this is where the advantage of ICT tools is manifested'.

N. writes: 'Activity – professional identity through pictures is interesting and challenging because you can't just choose a picture or image; you have to think deeply about the picture that can really represent you and then verbalize it in a sentence. This activity demanded different and comprehensive thinking from us in order to enable us an alternative for the verbal option, and helps to circumvent the obstacles it entails. It heightens self-awareness, improves self-esteem, and enables emotional expression and communication with others'.

Responding to another person's picture enables expression of inner content, helps to develop interpersonal communication skills, and advances personal and group empowerment.

## Collaborative Writing, Reading, and Speaking Skills

B. writes: 'Each one of us undertook to read articles on the subject and share with the others on the group portfolio, and these articles constituted the theoretical background for us to write the project. It was very important for us to collaborate on this part too, in which the theoretical background serves as a foundation and contributes knowledge'.

A. writes on the forum: 'I shared a document on Google Docs that proposes a model/basis/platform for argumentative writing on any subject that's chosen. Link to the draft: 'Argumentative Writing Platform'. Please comment/remark/respond'.

And R. writes on the forum: 'Articles on emotional intelligence: http://portal.macam.ac.il/Search.aspx?keyType=Subject&itemId=609. Perhaps each of us should read and see which topic she relates to?'

## Conflict Management and Resolution Skills

Y. writes on the forum: 'Good night dear colleagues! I'm sorry to say that after such an inspiring evening in which we managed to come together and significantly advance the project, all the voices have once again fallen silent, not answering emails or phone calls. I'm sorry, I don't want to be the bad cop here, but we won't be able to move forward like this. We need to set objectives for ourselves, assume responsibility, and continue the process. On a personal note I can say that I'm finding it hard to think who to call or mail this evening, because I don't get a response anyway. Please girls! Let's take responsibility together and continue the process'.

In the discussion on the problem that has emerged, S. tries to address it and writes: 'Hi girls, what's happening with our meeting? I think that in light of everything that's been said, perhaps we should have a face-to-face meeting and get to know one another, it could be really nice, what do you think? With regard to opening a WhatsApp group, which is an excellent idea, write what you think, so we can go ahead and open it. Good night'.

## Shared Time Management and Organization Skills

These are division of time skills, especially time utilization, which are facilitated by technology and enable multitasking beyond specific times and places.

In her interview, G. says: 'Each of us was connected not only by computer. For instance, I was with my kids at a climbing wall, and I live in the south of Israel, but I had access through my cell phone, and the fact that I could be in the discussion and be aware of this development, this possibility for dialogue, I think is the greatest experience, because people who didn't participate, who took time out during the Passover holiday, felt disconnected, and I think we also felt that it flowed. It's something in the flow, like our everyday communication. I think one of the life skills is the willingness to be around, not measure it in hours, but in need'. She goes on to say: 'There has to be some kind of flow, there has to be something that simulates everyday dialogue. We're not aware of the extent to which communication is the active facet of our lives'.

In addition to interpersonal communication skills, we wish to emphasize additional skills associated with developing group-learning organizational skills.

## Organizing Peer-Learning

D. writes about learning from the other groups: 'We presented our project, talked, listened, I was exposed to interesting projects the other groups were working on, and we had an idea to upgrade our QR code project to pictures using Layar's image application, which was presented by one of the instructors on the sheet he handed out, scanning pictures can significantly upgrade our project...'

And on the forum, R. writes: 'I'll be posting an additional shared document called 'Roles and Rules' in which we can decide together on procedures and division of functions. I suggest that like the process we had on the course, in the first stage each of us will propose procedures, and then we'll put them to a vote. With regard to division of functions – each one should propose ideas for functions and put herself forward for a particular function. First we need to discuss the subject – emotional intelligence – how each of us relates to it, what appeals to you? I hope you've all read material on the subject, and from the reading we can move on to thinking what do we want to advance in our students in this sphere? What's our need as teachers that hasn't been met? What's the students' need that hasn't gained expression? Once we more or less know our direction, we can redefine the division of functions'.

## Organizing Small Group Learning

N. writes: 'In the Hangout meeting I initiated for all the group members with one of the instructors, all the group members responded positively'.

D. writes: 'I've added a table in the "Thoughts" file: we need to specify the project's execution stages, I've detailed the stages, but the group members may want to add additional stages. I've

processed everything in the "Thoughts" file, transferred it to the project file, completed the editing, and forwarded it to E. for "another pair of eyes"'.

## Work Division by Interests and Strengths

N. writes in her journal: 'We carried out a division of functions between us: group coordinator – N.; language editor – D.; documenter – B.; group liaison – S.; design and editing – G.'

N. writes: 'The team is collaborating and each one is taking part according to their strengths. Y. is sick and I took her seat, not only metaphorically. N. posted the counseling emphases that upgraded the project. Not only mathematics, but also a view of the project in the mirror of the community in which it will be implemented. X. raised important emphases. We met at the school to go over the assignments together, to see what still has to be done, and assign functions'.

In her interview, G. says: 'The division of functions is the responsibility of the whole group, in addition to the function you're responsible for and for which you enlisted. In my case, I was responsible for communication. I think it was a wonderful experience for me. It wasn't self-evident, because in the academic world we're used to working in pairs at most, and for the first time I experienced group work and division of functions. The ability to trust someone you don't even know was also due to the communication we maintained. From the communication between us I don't really know personal details about each group member, but an interpersonal dialogue was established that made me trust them'.

## Leadership Skills

In her interview, G. describes the problems and difficulties sometimes entailed in division of functions, and the need to assume responsibility and display involvement in performing the task: 'If someone hadn't said "I'm doing this" it would have collapsed, because everybody's with their families. Beyond that there has to be sensitivity and willingness, and not only seeing my own function and that's it'.

## Encouraging and Empowering Leadership

In her interview, G. spoke about implementing work in groups based on what she experienced on the course: 'There were students who would turn to me, and I learned from my course instructors that you have to let the group leaders lead and not interfere in their leadership. I learned that the teacher has to demonstrate restraint, because the teacher can intervene and resolve it himself. When students turned to me on Friday, I told them: You remember the rules; and I told them: First of all go to the group leader and see if he has an answer, discuss it together in the group, and the group leader will create a dialogue and you can resolve matters within the group. And it worked in virtually all the groups. That's something I learned on our course. A year ago I would have intervened and resolved everything. I saw how we can manage on our own, and don't always need or have to have the lecturer there'.

Note: There is also evidence here of the development of an autonomous learner. As a practitioner, G. implemented her experience as an autonomous learner with her students so they could practice autonomous learning skills.

## Initiative Development Skills

N. writes: 'It was hard not to be involved in writing the presentation. In the end I couldn't restrain myself and gave it some tweaks. They were a bit upset that they'd worked on it for two hours and in the end I changed it. But we had to be focused for the discussion'.

D. writes: 'I'm urging the group to make progress with the project. I'm adding work progress tables'.

G. writes about initiative beyond the course in the context of her workplace: 'A center for excellence was established this year, PISGA Beersheba, which is in a development process. About a month ago I established a closed community for the team members. From one meeting to the next I manage to expand the circle of users a little'.

In her interview, G. talks about her initiative to implement the practice of work division she experienced in the course in her own classroom: 'On Friday, when I was teaching geometry, I split the students into groups, and in each group I had a group leader, which was clear to me had to be there. I tried to ensure it was a student who is sensitive to weaker others, and can strengthen them. I assigned additional functions, such as being in charge of equipment, because it was second grade and they're still young, but it was clear to me that each student in the group has to find a form of commitment to the group by means of a function'.

When pressed to describe how she created the division of work among her young students, and why in that particular way, G. said: 'Since success is contingent on communication between group members, I chose students who were the most verbal. A student who can encourage a more reserved student, or calm a more impulsive one. For the function of being in charge of equipment I chose a very responsible student who is also very shy, and if I'd assigned him to be a group leader, it would have been beyond his abilities. I created intermediate functions so that everyone felt he belonged to the group'.

## Norms of Membership and Collaboration (Mutual Assistance and Encouragement)

N. attests to G.'s help to the group: 'G. took it upon herself to open a community in Google+, which served as a place for us to communicate and build the project. She even shared a platform with us to help us with learning between different schools. The "Nipagesh" website is a platform G.

recommended. Of course each of us registered on the website in order to familiarize ourselves with it and be a part of it, and moreover, I especially wanted to investigate if it could help us with the project'.

The following conversation takes place in one of the forums. D. asks for help: 'I know some of you shared your portfolios with me, but I can't find the files, how do I get to them?'

A. responds: 'On the Drive toolbar there's "RECENT" where I can see what you've done. Hope this helps'.

N. writes on the forum: 'Hello girls, I've started writing on the flowchart and sent you the file with an editing option. I intentionally didn't erase text boxes and arrows so you can add anything you think is missing. Once you've all responded, I'll erase the redundant boxes and arrows'.

D. writes: 'We're not very expert in the ICT area, we found it difficult in terms of the technological means at the school, the internet didn't come up on cell phones, and so on. Y. and I had never used PowerPoint, although we imagined it wasn't a problem, but it took a bit longer to find everything. In the end we managed to produce a really nice slide, which we sent to N. for proofing, and in minutes/seconds she completely changed everything much more successfully. We don't regret the time we spent on it, because in fact we had to learn to cope on our own. Then we went on to build a summarizing document as our instructor asked, and altogether we were very happy we met because with everything that was hard for me, Y. knew what to do, and vice versa, with things she didn't know how to do I managed to save the day, and if each of us had sat on her own we would probably have been a bit more at a loss'.

These are some of the testimonies we collected in order to demonstrate the development of required life competencies and skills as experienced by the course participants in their writing on their learning. They were not directly asked to write about these skills, but what they wrote definitely indicates their development, or at least progress in their development. The Discussion section will endeavor to link the planning of the course environment components and what facilitated the developments of the competencies and skills described in the Findings sections. The Discussion section will also present principles or guidelines for planning a course that develops the above learning and life skills. We shall also present the difficulties and thoughts entailed in the future development and planning of such courses.

## DISCUSSION

In the Introduction we asked: (1) How can the life competencies and skills required for teachers' learning throughout their professional lives be strengthened? (2) How does the professional development of teachers, as manifested in the course, train teachers to teach their students the required life skills for the digital age?

In the Discussion we shall follow the evidence provided by the course participants regarding development of these skills and competencies, and propose a model that can be appropriate for the professional development of teachers in the present era.

The model is the product of our experiences in the field, and can be suitable for training teacher educators and teachers as the designers of learning environments that encourage a work and learning culture suited to the challenges of the present and the foreseeable future (Kalantzis & Cope, 2010).

### The FLP Model: An Integrated Three-Environments (F2FLE, LMS, PLN)

One of the most important roles of teacher educators engaged in the professional development of teachers is to design learning environments in which learners experience skills relevant for their work and everyday life. In other words, the aim is to reduce the gap between learning culture and work and leisure cultures which have changed and are continually changing. Since work is a culture of constant and ongoing learning through projects, a large proportion of learning in schools should be based on experiencing the production of projects relevant for the learners' needs and interests. Today's work culture mandates a high level of interpersonal communication, teamwork, and willingness for ongoing learning. Work is increasingly networked and less hierarchical, and is based on a combination of creative and critical thinking, leadership, and initiative. Working and learning in diverse ICT environments is natural in this kind of culture since it facilitates empowerment and utilization of the work and leisure cultures developing all over the world. These elements of the work environment should be manifested in the learning environment for young learners to experience in preparation for their life in the future. The simple systems with which learning takes place today do not enable this kind of learning. Learning environments need to be rich, flexible, and distributed on and off the network. Our experience and the data show that one possibility that meets these requirements is designing a learning environment that combines three settings:

(1) LMS – closed online learning management systems, which are usually controlled by the teachers/lecturers and to a much lesser degree by the learners. Their big advantage lies in the possibilities they provide for monitoring and tracking each learner for the purpose of providing feedback. These systems are increasingly being introduced into education systems, and it is important for teachers to experience them; (2) Virtual networks/communities – internet environments that can be used for the collaborative learning of communities of learners, such as Google+ Communities, Facebook groups, or PLNs, which each learner designs and manages himself. In these systems learners can create their network themselves using social media tools. These learning environments encourage learners to be autonomous and develop lifelong learning skills; (3) Face-to-face

learning environments (F2FLE) – physical learning environments. Knowing how to incorporate technology in face-to-face lessons in or outside the classroom is important since face-to-face encounters contribute to the development of life skills required for human beings as social creatures. It is precisely at a time when young people are accustomed to largely conducting their personal and social lives on the network that it is important to develop their abilities to conduct everyday and social life outside the network as well. Another reason for combining the three environments in learning is the development of mobile devices and technologies incorporated into instruments and objects, which has resulted in a blurring between virtual and physical reality, and some life skills include possibilities for simultaneous physical and virtual activity and presence.

Every learning environment possesses its own unique characteristics, and combinations of them can increase motivation to learn and acquire life skills and competencies required for the teaching profession in the twenty-first century. Nowadays, each of these environments includes digital elements. The mobile devices familiar to us today (and soon we will see augmented reality and wearable technology in education as well) enable learning anywhere, anytime, and, simultaneous learning in each of the three environments (Figure 2).

Teachers' professional development programs have to take all this into consideration and teach teachers the characteristics of the learning environments, how to design them, how to work in them, and how to integrate them.

Some of the testimonies we presented indicate that the teachers who participated in the described course recognize the importance and advantage of combining the two online environments for their life in general, and their work as teachers in particular. We propose that pre-service teacher training institutions and in-service teachers' professional development programs develop learning activities that enable teachers to experience being learners in online environments, especially PLNs,

*Figure 2. The FLP model for the professional development of teachers in the twenty-first century*

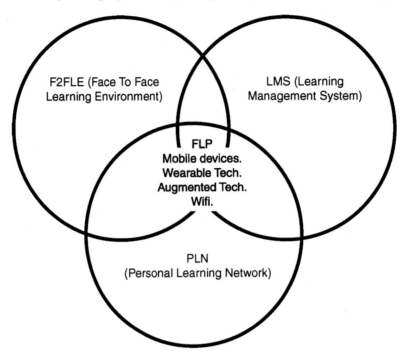

which are still not widespread in teacher training. Teachers should be encouraged to develop skills that will serve them in designing PLEs, and learn to use them to teach their own students, since these skills develop life and teaching competencies that are still manifested to a lesser degree in teacher training. In this chapter we have endeavored to characterize these skills, the competencies deriving from them, and their significance for the professional development of teachers in the twenty-first century.

## The Instruction Method

As indicated by the learners' testimonies on the course structure and learning method, if we want to adapt education institutions to the reality of life today, an essential change is required in the roles of pre-service and in-service teacher educators as well as teachers in the schools. As previously stated, the teacher plays an important role in designing network learning environments as learning designers (Miller, 2012) prior to and during actual learning activities, but the teacher also has other roles, including monitoring, enabling, providing guidance, support, and encouragement, helping with assessment of learning, and modeling. Course instructors play an important role in some of the online learning activities design, i.e., formulating the learning activities so that learners understand their purpose, rationale, and how to perform them. They need to be formulated clearly and provide scaffolding that learners can use to help them in their learning. The activities design should facilitate learning flexibility and their adaptation to the course objectives as they were defined for the learners. The instructors have to define times and directions for the learning activities, but leave room for the learners' decisions regarding their learning process. They need to be aware of different learning styles and paces, be attentive, and respond flexibly to what occurs during the learners' active learning. Learners should have sufficient room for choice in order to afford them autonomy to choose content, locate and collaborate with peers, search for and use sources, and decide on learning methods. Learning should be largely under the learners' rather than the instructors' control. The instructor has to stand behind the learning scenes (Siemens, 2005), but when learners seek his help he has to step out, presence himself, and provide solutions for their needs.

## Developing Self-Determination Skills

The testimonies presented in the Findings section indicate a number of factors that can help to create an environment that encourages learners to become self-determined, such as granting learners the autonomy to learn in the style and pace suited to them (Zimmerman, 2002). Whereas in formal learning an agreed schedule needs to be set for performing activities which the learner has to meet (and thus also develops time management skills), in a network learning environment the learner needs to have sufficient room to perform learning activities in accordance with his own time management.

It is important to allow the learner to experience and get to know himself in diverse individual and collaborative learning situations on the network. The instructors' guidance on how to work individually and in a group enables the learner to get to know himself as a learner in a network environment, and during his learning on the course to choose what suits him. The use we made of diverse network collaborative learning environments, e.g., inviting the learners at the start of the course to join a Google+ Community (other networks can be used, such as Facebook groups), constituted modeling that some of them took with them to their own workplaces. Exposure to Google+ and a community framework within it enabled the learners to experience building a collaborative learning environment via social networks such as Google+, Facebook, or Pinterest.

## Developing the Ability to Function in an Environment Containing Multiple Means of Expression

We recommend using diverse environments and combining texts, multimedia, and sound as part of the learning environment design and experience to develop photo-visual skills (Eshet, 2012). The learners' testimonies show that experiencing use of video clips incorporated into an environment that includes written and spoken dialogue aids learning. In our case, we created a large database of video clips embedded in a blog (which can also be embedded in platforms such as Google+ and Facebook), and discussions on viewed video clips could be held by writing posts. In this way learners also acquire information skills (Eshet, 2012), and experience creating their own content on the network (Wheeler, 2012).

## Developing and Encouraging Interpersonal Dialogue and Communication

Interpersonal communication via the network and encouraging online dialogic learning are highly important components of training learners for collaborative learning. Creating trust within a group is necessary for group members to rely on each other and work synergistically. According to the course participants' testimonies, the interpersonal dialogue on the network was an important component in building trust between group members, especially since they did not meet face to face. Our conclusion is that it is important to incorporate experience with diverse means of communication in the learners' assignments in order to develop their dialogical skills. Dialogue serves as a kind of adhesive that bonds group members for the purpose of performing a joint task. A deliberative dialogue, typified by thinking collaboratively in order to make decisions

(London, 2005), is influenced by the means of communication being used. Video-chats such as Skype, Hangout, or discussion forums are more suited for an online deliberative group dialogue than instant messaging on chats or WhatsApp.

There is evidence that the modeling teachers experience in professional development courses serves them in their own schools, like the teacher who created learning groups in her classroom and gave each group member a function or responsibility. As group leaders she chose students in accordance with their abilities to form interpersonal relationships through dialogue, or in her own words: 'Since success is contingent on communication between group members, I chose students who were the most verbal. A student who can encourage a more reserved student, or calm a more impulsive one'.

## Developing and Encouraging Productive Collaborative Knowledge Building

Many of the sources of knowledge were provided by the learners, who also taught one another how to use different tools, such as mind maps and a social network for schools. Some of the learners attest that fellow group members helped them to acquire network skills, and that meaningful peer learning took place.

Good communication and acknowledging the personal abilities of each group member contribute to the quality of collaborative work. This requires creation of trust, self-assessment abilities, sense of competence, and empathy. In some of the groups the members already knew one another, which made the group-building process easier. In others the group members became acquainted with each other online. The instructor's role is to encourage new acquaintanceships that contribute to the diversity and innovation attending collaborative (peer) learning.

Division of work and functions in a group facilitates effective and efficient collaborative learning. Improving learners' abilities to work in a collaborative online environment also positively influences the overall learning process.

## Developing Proactive Leadership

The learning environments we have described enabled and encouraged expression of the learners' leadership and initiative skills. The testimonies indicate that the openness and flexibility of the learning environment we created and the way the instructors led the course, as members of a community of learners together with the learners, enabled and encouraged the learners' leadership and constituted modeling for their peers.

A professional development course for teachers that enables and encourages learners to develop their own initiatives and share their ideas and remarks with one another is an example of the kind of professional development environment required for up-to-date teacher training. Many learners initiated activities by creating an initial document, sharing it with their group members, and inviting them to add to it, amend and comment on it in order to advance the collaborative work of the whole group.

Leadership in the digital age combines familiarity with and knowledge of using ICT and qualities such as empathy and ability to make decisions that serve the group's common objective. Some of the learners in our course possessed considerable ICT expertise and had led ICT assimilation processes in their schools. Their expertise as veteran teachers combined with leadership skills enabled them to contribute to their peers – they could be called "digital leaders".

In teacher training and the professional development of in-service teachers it is important to emphasize the education process by modeling the flow of knowledge from teacher educator (lecturer, instructor) to in-service teacher, to fellow teachers, to students. However, reverse flow is also important, from the teachers' experience and leadership skills, to their fellow learners, to the instructors. This constitutes optimal utilization of the human capital inherent in the knowledge and experience of learners and instructors alike, and also applies to learning from students' experience and leadership skills in schools.

## Cultural Change in Time Perception and Time Management Skills

The ability of learners to be self-directed partly stems from their time management skills in a flexible environment that does not have the rigid boundaries familiar to us from pre-internet and smartphone culture. The boundaries between private, public, and work/study time have blurred. Time management requires the organization and division of time in accordance with the learner's personal needs. However, if the learner is working collaboratively with other learners, the flow of work is of considerable importance even at the expense of blurring the boundaries between private, public, and work. The success of a group working collaboratively is contingent on its ability to maintain time-flexible communication. Today's technologies influence the way people organize their private, public, and work or study time, and blur the boundaries between them that in the past were very clear. A change in time organization requires ICT skills, as evidenced by some of the testimonies we presented, for example, a learner who describes time in terms of a flow that needs to be properly maintained for collaborative learning to succeed.

## Assessment of Individual and Collaborative Learning

One of the main points that needs to be considered when designing a learning environment in the internet age is the development of new assessment methods.

The main objective of assessment in professional development courses for teachers should be to reflect the learning process and jointly build

tools to improve it. In our view, a verbal assessment is preferable to a numerical one. Assessment can be based on the learner's e-Portfolio (Currant, Haigh, Higgison, Hughes, Rodway & Whitfield, 2010; Bryant, & Chittum, 2013) and his records on intermediate and end products, and examples of contribution via documented online discussions in posts, discussion forums, blogs, and so forth. The learners can choose certain items from their e-Portfolios which they think represent their learning, and share them with the instructor. In teachers' professional development, learners should not be treated in the same way as students in academic institutions who are studying for degrees and diplomas, but rather as practitioners who are lifelong learners. The learners' assessment should primarily be based on their testimonies regarding their part in the learning, and its contribution to their professional development. This assessment can include two components: assessment of individual learning, and assessment of group learning. The instructor's role is to reflect their assessment to the learners both individually and as a group, and the final assessment should include both components.

## Change in the Conceptual Framework of Learning Assessment

Changes in assessment methods also require a change in the conceptual framework of the teaching and learning processes. Concepts such as "products", "processes", "reflection", "immediate feedback", and "assignments" need to change. More room should be provided for the assessment of processes, and less emphasis placed on end products, which is currently the accepted teaching approach. Learners should also be assessed on the intermediate products they have produced throughout the learning process. The term "learning activity" is preferable to "assignment", since the former indicates active, self-regulated learners who assume responsibility for their learning, whereas "assignment" refers to a pedagogical perception wherein the teacher is the center, and it is he who drives and directs the learners' learning – he gives the assignments. The traditional approach of "submitting assignments to the teacher" should be replaced by the teacher's "participation" in the learner's learning. Instead of the objective of "submitting a final paper for examination", emphasis should be placed on "the teacher's participation in the process", i.e., learning should be viewed as "processual". It should be emphasized as a dialogue ("dialogic learning"), and a central place should be accorded to assessing the discourse between the learners, as described in the "assessment of contribution to the discourse" rubric, in the form of "self-assessment" and/or "peer assessment". With the development of massive open online courses (MOOC), the importance of these assessment methods is growing. Learners need to know how to assess each other and themselves. It is important for instructors to be involved throughout the learning processes by the learners sharing their reflective journals with them as they are being written, and not only at the end of the process. This facilitates formative evaluation processes as a central and integral part of the learning process.

## Self-Assessment and Rubrics

The self-assessment rubric described in this chapter is a tool that can enable teachers to assess learners, and if necessary, it can also constitute a grading component. Learners can save messages and responses from discussion forums, blogs, or chats they wrote as part of discussions on learning activities and content as evidence of their contribution to their fellow learners. Other rubrics can be built in accordance with the learning objectives. The teacher can examine the assessments the learners wrote in their e-Portfolios, and use them to provide assessments and grades. According to the learners' testimonies, the rubric helps to improve the standard of discussions on the forums, and promotes the learners' learning and assessment skills.

## Recommendations for New Directions in Teacher Training to Promote Life Skills Required for Their Professional Development

The formal professional development of teachers has remained fairly traditional, and is not keeping pace with the changes our global society is currently undergoing. Many teachers, especially the more veteran ones, find it difficult to change attitudes and behavior due to the requirements and priorities of education systems which have not completely disengaged from the Industrial Era. Systemic changes need to be made that include combination of, and coordination between, numerous factors within the systems and which influence education in different ways.

In many education systems, teachers and the quality of their work, are assessed in accordance with basic assumptions such as: "a good, learning classroom" is a quiet classroom that listens to the teacher most of the time. Another assumption is that there are right and wrong answers, and no room for interpretation and a dialogic discussion. In many cases, discussions are designed to reach the right answer. A good teacher is considered one who meets the demands of conveying content and knowledge items that are stipulated in an outdated curriculum. A good teacher is one whose students' gain high achievements in standardized tests, which are based on repetition and memorization. The assessment methods in education systems are based on assessing only individual, not collaborative work in teams or a community of learners. This is particularly evident in junior high and high school teachers. These requirements constitute a barrier and hindrance to the willingness of teachers to transition from traditional to innovative teaching.

Educational policymakers in various countries are aware of the importance of developing life skills and competencies suited to the present era. For example, the course described in this chapter is supported by and held with the encouragement of the Ministry of Education and the Israeli teachers associations. Our recommendation is that initiatives for planning and developing courses of this kind, or courses with have similar objectives, be increased and encouraged. The operative implications are that the number of courses in which learners experience network learning should be increased. Such courses can reduce the gap between the reality in present-day schools and recognition that this reality needs to change, and adapt schools and make them more relevant to the reality of life around them. It is very important for emphasis to be placed on implementing what is learned in courses in the schools themselves. Room needs to be given in the course to a dialogue within the community of learners on their experience with implementing ideas and learning methods.

With regard to methods for assessing learners, alternative assessment tools should be developed that examine learners' ability to solve problems by forming relevant ties with their surroundings. Current exams that only test the individual learner's declarative knowledge do not enable examination of the learning skills required today. We propose that in the future some of the exams and assessment methods will also be carried out via the network and digital devices that serve to contend with real-life problems and create learning outcomes. External assessment policies (e.g., national and international examinations) also need to be adapted to the assessment of group learning skills, ability to collaborate with peers, ability to solve problems via network sources, and online interpersonal communication.

It is important to formally recognize and allow room for alternative methods for the professional development of teachers and adapt them to the changes of the twenty-first century. One way can be to acknowledge the importance of learning in PLEs on the network as part of the training and professional development of teachers throughout their professional lives. Attempts have been made in recent years to propose new models for the professional development of teachers based on

a combination of social-constructivism and connectivism theories. In this kind of learning, the teachers' combine creating a personal network for learning based on collaborative learning with their peers (McLoughlin & Lee, 2010; Drexler, 2010), LMS environments, and face-to-face meetings.

## Toward a Fractal Network of Learning Communities

During the course described in this chapter, an initiative was developed by five teachers from different schools. Following a process of collaborative learning in the course, which included a dialogue between them, they decided to create a collaborative project. The teachers met face to face as well as online in video chats (Hangout, Skype), in a blog they created, and via additional digital channels. Their idea was to establish an online community network of educators that crosses time and place boundaries and facilitates learning suited to each learner's needs and professional development, and acquisition of skills for work that incorporates ICT. The basic premise of this project was that in the education system's current formal methods of teachers' professional development, teachers have difficulty finding the time required for advanced study due to their extensive work hours in addition to family and other responsibilities.

The model they built is based on an open, flexible network of teachers that affords an opportunity for learning at each participating learner's convenience, and according to each learner's interests and time. The teachers based their learning network on the following elements:

1. **Sharing Human Capital for the Benefit of All:** Peer learning. The information and knowledge are in the hands of the network members, and teachers teach teachers. A short meeting for group learning can take place if there is demand by a few members for a specific learning objective, such as how

to use a particular program for teaching in school. The network uses the knowledge of its participants or ad-hoc temporary users in order to address a particular matter or need.

2. Short learning meetings in small groups (small is beautiful), usually no more than one hour in groups of no more than ten participants (this principle is familiar from the Khan Academy's short films).

3. **Openness to Diverse Possibilities:** Any matter, problem, or need brought up on the network by an individual learner is legitimate; the character of the short meeting is determined by the participants, and can for example be for the purpose of support, learning a pedagogical issue, or introducing and experiencing a digital tool. There are of course no restrictions on creating joint activities on the network for longer periods of time, but this is not a condition for participation.

4. **Voluntary and Free Resources:** Everything is free of charge, participation is voluntary and driven by personal and joint motivation to learn for the purpose of professional development.

5. **Autonomy and Personal Choice:** The choice of time, place, and subject is the responsibility of the network participants who are not committed to a particular level of participation over time.

6. **A Growing Network:** The network can develop and expand, fan-like, into additional connected networks.

The model the teachers built, which was inspired by the course's learning environment, is a fractal network model in which the professional development principles they experienced in the course that functioned as a network of teachers for developing educational leadership (the first network = "the mother network") produced intersections of groups that created their own networks, like the one created by the group of teachers in our course (the second network). Later, a teacher

from the second network initiated a network of students at her school, and thus created a third network. These networks that emerged from others can also connect to the personal networks of each learner who forms his network ties according to his wishes and needs.

Braga describes a study of courses in English reading strategies in which learning was carried out in multi-participant communities that split into small fractal groups and learned autonomously (Braga, 2013). Recent years have seen the development of different types of MOOCs and pedagogical models, such as the Khan Academy and the flipped classroom, but they are still in the process of trial and formulation. Further research and time perspective are needed to understand the significance of the attempts to bring about change in the existing education paradigm. The model presented in this chapter of combining different learning environments and creating open, growing online fractal networks joins the efforts to replace traditional with up-to-date pedagogy from the perspective of teacher training and professional development.

## Future Directions for Research and Development

Our basic premise is that the professional development of teachers should include development of relevant life and learning skills for current reality. We propose conducting further action research to attend professional development programs of this kind which have not yet been tried.

Additional subjects for future research include:

- Studies examining the significance of learning in personal environments for the professional development of teachers and teacher educators.
- Studies on assessment of collaborative learning and knowledge building on the network.

- Studies that will add to our theoretical knowledge on appropriate learning methods for the twenty-first century in educational institutions and organizations of every kind, toward creating a new teaching and learning paradigm that is adapted to reality, and that is influenced by the development of ICT technologies.

Our findings reflect the development of competencies which are required to the real life setting (Shavelson, 2012). Specifically, these are the abilities which should be developed in order to promote in-service teachers to lead up-to-date pedagogy in innovative environments. Similar to the CLA (Collegiate Learning Assessment) assessment model (Shavelson, 2012), the course design was composed from complex tasks which required the integration of skills that cannot be captured when divided into and measured as individual components. As suggested in CLA model, the course tasks were world tasks that are holistic, and drawn from life situations. The teachers were required to cope with the problems of how to design and manage learning environments which use different new technologies and a team work. As opposed to CLA model, we emphasized the importance of assessment as a dynamic process which is constructed together with the students (the teachers) in collaborative thinking and as an integral process of learning. However, for further research in the future and in order to validate the findings of this research, we consider also measuring the results with CLA assessment model tools.

# REFERENCES

Anderson, T., & Dron, J. (2011). Three Generations of Distance Education Pedagogy. *International Review of Research in Open and Distance Learning, 12*(3). Retrieved from http://www.irrodl.org/index.php/irrodl/article/view/890/1663

Braga, J. C. F. (2013). *Fractal groups: Emergent dynamics in on-line learning communities. Revista Brasileira de Linguística Aplicada, 13*(2). doi:10.1590/S1984-63982013000200011

Brindley, J., Blaschke, L., & Walti, C. (2009). Creating Effective Collaborative Learning Groups in an Online Environment. *International Review of Research in Open and Distance Learning, 10*(3). Retrieved from http://www.irrodl.org/index.php/irrodl/article/view/675/1271

Brooks, J. G., & Brooks, M. G. (1993). *In search of understanding: The case for constructivist classrooms.* Alexandria: Association of Supervision and Curriculum Development.

Bryant, L. H., & Chittum, J. R. (2013). ePortfolio effectiveness: A(n ill-fated) search for empirical support. *International Journal of ePortfolio, 3*(2), 189-198. Retrieved from: http://www.theijep.com/pdf/IJEP108.pdf

Chatti, M. A., Agustiawan, M. R., Jarke, M., & Specht, M. (2010). toward a personal Learning Environment Framework. *International Journal of Virtual and Personal Learning Environments, 1*(4), 66–85. doi:10.4018/jvple.2010100105

Currant, N., Haigh, J., Higgison, C., Hughes, P., Rodway, P., & Whitfield, R. (2010). *Designing ePortfolio based learning activities to promote learner autonomy.* Final Report to the Fourth Cohort of the Inter/National Coalition for Research into Electronic Portfolios, University of Bradford. Retrieved from: http://ncepr.org/finalreports/cohort4/University%20of%20Bradford%20Final%20Report.pdf

Dabbagh, N., & Kitsantas, A. (2011). Personal Learning Environments, social media, and self-regulated learning: A natural formula for connecting formal and informal learning. *The Internet and Higher Education, 15*(1), 3–8. doi:10.1016/j.iheduc.2011.06.002

Davidson, R. (2012). Social and emotional aspects of online learning environments. In A. Glassner (Ed.), The arrow head and the warm hand: Narratives concerning ICT and teacher education (pp. 37-72). Tel-Aviv: MOFET Institute. (in Hebrew)

Davidson, R., & Mor, N. (2005, November). Cross-Institutional Team Teaching and Collaborative Learning in an Online Course, In S. Andras, & B. Ingeborg (Eds.), *Lifelong e-learning - bringing e-learning close to lifelong learning and working life: a new period of uptake: proceedings of the EDEN 2005 Annual Conference*. Helsinki: University of Technology, Lifelong Learning Institute TKK Dipoli.

Downes, S. (2012). *Connectivism and connective knowledge: Essays on meaning and learning networks*. National Research Council Canada. Retrieved from: http://www.downes.ca/files/books/Connective_Knowledge-19May2012.pdf

Drexler, W. (2010). The networked student model for construction of personal learning environments: Balancing teacher control and student autonomy. *Australasian Journal of Educational Technology, 26*(3), 369–385. Retrieved from http://www.ascilite.org.au/ajet/ajet26/drexler.html

Eshet, Y. (2012). Thinking in the digital era: A revised model for digital literacy. *Issues in Informing Science and Information Technology,* (9), 267-276. Retrieved from: http://iisit.org/Vol9/IISITv9p267-276Eshet021.pdf

Kalantzis, M., & Cope, B. (2010). The Teacher as Designer: Pedagogy in the new media age. *E-Learning and Digital Media, 7*(3), 200–222. doi:10.2304/elea.2010.7.3.200

London, S. (2005). The Power of Deliberative Dialogue. In R. J. Kingston (Ed.), *Public Thought and Foreign Policy*. Dayton, OH: Kettering Foundation Press.

Massachusetts Department of Elementary and Secondary Education. (2008). *School reform in the new millennium: Preparing all children for 21$^{st}$ century success*. Recommendations from the Massachusetts Board of Elementary and Secondary Education's Task Force on 21$^{st}$ Century Skills.

McCaffrey, D. F., Lockwood, J. R., Koretz, D. M., & Hamilton, L. S. (2003). *Evaluating value-added models for teacher accountability*. Santa Monica, CA: Rand Corporation. doi:10.1037/e658712010-001

McLoughlin, C. (2011). Reinventing the 21st century educator: Social media to engage and support the professional learning of teachers. In G. Williams, P. Statham, N. Brown, & B. Cleland (Eds.), Changing Demands, Changing Directions. Proceedings ascilite Hobart 2011 (pp. 847–851). Retrieved from http://www.ascilite.org.au/conferences/hobart11/procs/McLoughlin-full.pdf

McLoughlin, C., & Lee, M. J. W. (2008). The Three P's of Pedagogy for the Networked Society: Personalization, Participation, and Productivity. *International Journal of Teaching and Learning in Higher Education, 20*(1), 10–27.

McLoughlin, C., & Lee, M. J. W. (2010). Personalised and self regulated learning in the Web 2.0 era: International exemplars of innovative pedagogy using social software. *Australasian Journal of Educational Technology, 26*(1), 28–43.

Merchant, G. (2007). Mind the Gap(s): Discourses and discontinuity in digital literacies. *E-learning, 4*(3), 241–255. doi:10.2304/elea.2007.4.3.241

Miller, A. K. (2012, November 28). *Teacher as learning designer*. Huff Post Education [Web log post]. Retrieved from: http://www.huffingtonpost.com/andrew-k-miller/education-reform_b_2169265.html

Palincsar, A. S. (1998). Social constructivist perspectives on teaching and learning. In J. T. Spence, J. M. Darley, & D. J. Foss (Eds.), *Annual Review of Psychology, 49* (pp. 345–375). Palo Alto, CA: Annual Reviews. doi:10.1146/annurev. psych.49.1.345

Ryan, R. M., & Deci, E. L. (2002). An overview of self-determination theory. In E. L. Deci & R. M. Ryan (Eds.), *Handbook of self-determination research* (pp. 3–33). Rochester, NY: University of Rochester Press.

Scardamalia, M., & Bereiter, C. (2003). Knowledge building environments: Extending the limits of the possible in education and knowledge work. In A. Distefano, K. E. Rudestam, & R. Silverman (Eds.), Encyclopedia of distributed learning. Thousand Oaks, CA: Sage. Retrieved from http://ikit.org/fulltext/2003_KBE.pdf

Shavelson, R. J. (2012). Assessing business-planning competence using the Collegiate Learning Assessment as a prototype. *Empirical Research in Vocational Education and Training, 4*(1), 77–90.

Siemens, G. (2005). Connectivism: A learning theory for the digital age. *International Journal of Instructional Technology and Distance Learning, 2*(1). Retrieved from http://www.itdl.org/Journal/Jan_05/article01.htm

Wheeler, S. (2012). Digital literacies for engagement in emerging online cultures. *eLC Research Paper Series, 5,* 14-25.

Wilson, S., Liber, O., Johnson M.W., Beauvoir, P., Sharples, P. & Milligan, C. (2007). Personal Learning Environments: challenging the dominant design of educational systems. *Journal of e-Learning and Knowledge Society, 3* (2), 27-38.

Zimmerman, B. J. (2002). Becoming a Self-Regulated Learner: An overview. *Theory into Practice, 41*(2), 64–70. doi:10.1207/s15430421tip4102_2

# KEY TERMS AND DEFINITIONS

**Connectivism:** A new learning theory that claims individual's knowledge is distributed and resides not only in his brain, but also in connections with electronic and human components which the learner has developed in the course of his learning. according to the connectivism: Meaningful learning is a process that requires a network environment that is open to interactions at varying levels of intensity.

**Digital Literacy:** A survival skill in the digital era. It constitutes a system of skills and strategies used by learners and users in digital environments. By employing different types of digital literacy, users improve their performance and "survive" a variety of obstacles and stumbling blocks that lie in the way within this special medium. (Eshet 2012).

**Life Competencies:** A cluster of related abilities, commitments, knowledge, and skills that enable a person (or an organization) to act effectively in a life situation. Competence indicates sufficiency of knowledge and skills that enable someone to act in a wide variety of situations.

**Lifelong Learning:** Learning that is pursued throughout life: learning that is flexible, diverse and available at different times and in different places. Lifelong learning crosses sectors, promoting learning beyond traditional schooling and throughout adult life.

**LMS (Learning Management Systems):** Open source learning platform that serves for online distance learning. LMS environments maintain the boundaries of the traditional classroom and they cannot serve the connectivist learning tools on their own.

**Personal Learning Environments:** Communication systems and Social media tools that are controlled by learners rather than teachers, thus increasing the learners' autonomy.

**Social Constructivism:** Sociological theory of knowledge that applies the general philosophical constructivism into the social context. According to this theory reality is constructed through human activity, knowledge is a human product and is socially and culturally constructed, individuals create meaning through their interactions with each other and with the environment they live. (Based on Wikipedia).

**Social Media:** Forms of electronic communication (as Web sites for social networking and microblogging) through which users create online communities to share information, ideas, personal messages, and other content (as videos). (Merriam-Webster Dictionary).

# Section 3

# Automated Item Generation and Automated Scoring Techniques for Assessment and Feedback

*The five chapters in this section address a wide range of technologies for automated scoring, automated item generation and feedback.*

# Chapter 22
# Using Automated Procedures to Generate Test Items That Measure Junior High Science Achievement

**Mark Gierl**
*University of Alberta, Canada*

**Hollis Lai**
*University of Alberta, Canada*

**Syed F. Latifi**
*University of Alberta, Canada*

**Donna Matovinovic**
*CTB/McGraw-Hill, USA*

**Keith A. Boughton**
*CTB/McGraw-Hill, USA*

## ABSTRACT

*The purpose of this chapter is to describe and illustrate a template-based method for automatically generating test items. This method can be used to produce a large numbers of high-quality items both quickly and efficiency. To highlight the practicality and feasibility of automatic item generation, we demonstrate the application of this method in the content area of junior high school science. We also describe the results from a study designed to evaluate the quality of the generated science items. Our chapter is divided into four sections. In section one, we describe the methodology. In the section two, we illustrate the method using items generated for a junior high school physics curriculum. In section three, we present the results from a study designed to evaluate the quality of the generated science items. In section four, we conclude the chapter and identify one important area for future research.*

## INTRODUCTION

Profound global and economic changes are shaping how we develop and deliver educational tests. These changes can be traced to the growing emphasis on knowledge services, information, and communication technologies. To thrive in this new environment, countries require skilled workers who can solve complex problems, adapt to novel situations, and collaborate effectively with others. Educational tests, once developed almost exclusively to satisfy demands for accountability

DOI: 10.4018/978-1-4666-9441-5.ch022

and outcomes-based assessment, are now expected to provide teachers and students with frequent, detailed, feedback to directly support the teaching and learning of these new 21st century skills (Black & Wiliam, 1998, 2010).

Two conditions now exist that, when taken together, will permit us to begin to develop and deliver the kinds of tests that would provide teachers and students with frequent and timely feedback on a diverse range of 21$^{st}$ century knowledge and skills. The first condition stems from the dramatic change in how students' access technology and use the Internet. For example, MediaSmart, a not-for-profit organization that collects and disseminates information about digital literacy in Canada, recently conducted a national survey of 5436 Canadian students from Grades 4 to 11. The report "Life Online: Young Canadians in a Wired World" (Steeves, 2014) provides a comprehensive snapshot of how students access and use technology. Many striking findings were reported. For instance, 99% of the students in the survey accessed the Internet outside of school. The point of access has shifted from desktop home computers, which was the most common method in the MediaSmart 2005 survey, to portable personal computers such as laptops, tablets, and smartphones, which is the most common method today. More than half of the Grade 4 students surveyed said that they accessed the Internet using a portable computer. Twenty-four percent of these students owned their own portable computer. Internet access and portable computer use jumped dramatically as students progressed through school. More than 70% of the Grade 11 students surveyed accessed the Internet using a portable computer. Eighty-five percent of these students owned their own portable devices. These findings demonstrate that Internet access is common, even among elementary students, and that portable computing is viable because many students own their own computers.

The second condition stems from the rapid integration of technology and educational testing. The importance of technology in testing was first described by Bennett more than a decade ago when he claimed that no topic would become more central to innovation and future practice in educational testing than computers and the Internet (see Bennett, 2001). Since Bennett made this claim, there has been a gradual but steady migration from paper- to computer-based testing at both the K-12 and post-secondary education levels as well as among licensure and certification agencies to the point where computerized testing could now be characterized as a common practice. One reason for this migration is feasibility. Simply put, educational testing is no longer feasible when delivered in a paper-based format because it is a resource-intensive process. The printing, scoring, and reporting of paper-based tests require tremendous efforts, expenses, and human interventions. Moreover, as the demand for testing continues to escalate, the cost of developing, administering, and scoring paper-based tests will also increase. The solution that curtails some of these costs is to adopt a computerized testing system. By administering tests on computers over the Internet, educators are liberated from performing the costly and time-consuming administration processes associated with disseminating, scanning, and scoring paper-based tests. Instead, tests can be administered by computers over the Internet and scored automatically.

Another reason for this migration is practicality. Computerized testing offers important benefits to support and promote key principles in formative feedback that are simply not available with paper-based testing (Sadler, 1989; Shute, 2008). For instance, computers permit testing on-demand thereby allowing students to take the test at any time during instruction. Testing on-demand ensures that students can write exams as often as they choose. It also means that students can write exams at different locations due to flexibility of Internet access. Items on computerized tests are scored immediately thereby providing students with instant feedback. Performance on computerized tests can be archived so students, teachers, and parents can review previous assessment outcomes over time as well as within and across courses. Computers support the development of multimedia item types that allows educators to measure more complex performances as well as a broader variety of knowledge and skills. Computers can be used to administer and score diverse item formats including selected-response questions, such multiple choice, as well as constructed-response questions, such as short answer and essays. Computerized Internet testing also supports important instructional concepts such as individualized teaching and learning (i.e., a student progresses through a curriculum at his or her own pace) because feedback can be accessed at any time during course of study.

In short, computerized testing can help educators infuse formative principles into their educational testing practices so that feedback can serve as a rich compilation of information that directs teaching and improves learning on a diverse range of 21st century knowledge and skills. Because Internet access is common and portable computing is feasible, computerized testing translates into an extraordinary opportunity for students and educators alike.

But to truly capitalize on this opportunity, one final condition must be satisfied—educators must have access to large, rich, and diverse sources of assessment content that can be used to measure these 21st century skills in the form of test items. Currently, this condition is not satisfied. In fact, item development or, more specifically, item production is one of the lingering problems that remains to be addressed as we migrate from paper- to computer-based testing (Downing & Haladyna, 2006; Haladyna & Rodriguez, 2013; Schmeiser & Welch, 2006). Thousands, or perhaps, millions of items are needed to develop the banks necessary for computerized testing because items are continuously administered and, therefore, exposed to students. A bank is a repository of test items. These banks must be frequently replenished with new items to ensure that students receive a continuous

supply of unique and content-specific items, while, at the same time, controlling item exposure within the testing environment to maintain security so the process is fair and meaningful for students. Our current test development practices cannot be used to produce the sheer number of test items required to support the type of internet-based, computerized testing we just described. The root of this problem has at least three sources.

First and foremost, our current approach to item development uses the individual item as the unit of analysis. That is, each item is authored, edited, reviewed, formatted, and then revised by content specialists. Drasgow et al. (2006, p. 473) explain:

*The demand for large numbers of items is challenging to satisfy because the traditional approach to test development uses the item as the fundamental unit of currency. That is, each item is individually hand-crafted—written, reviewed, revised, edited, entered into a computer, and calibrated—as if no other like it had ever been created before.*

Second, item development is time consuming and, for some computerized testing situations, expensive.[1] Part of this cost is accrued because content specialist are required to initially create and then transform each individual item as it moves through the creation, editing, and revision process. Because many different specialists are involved and human intervention and manipulation is common, errors can be introduced into the process which further increases the costs associated with creating test items including omissions or additions of words, phrases, or expressions as well as spelling, punctuation, capitalization, item structure, typeface, and formatting problems. Third, traditional item development is not scalable. That is, if more items are required, then more content specialists are needed. But this option may not be economically feasible for scaling item development when thousands of new items are required to create multiple item banks across different content areas and grade levels. It also requires a considerable amount of time to create large banks using the content-specialists approach. Taken together, these important limitations which characterize our current approach to item development suggest that alternative methods are needed.

## PURPOSE OF CHAPTER

One method that may be used to address this item development challenge is to draw on automatic item generation (AIG) (Gierl & Haladyna, 2013; Irvine & Kyllonen, 2002). AIG is the process of using item models to generate test items with the aid of computer technology. AIG was an idea initially described by Bormuth in 1969 that is now gaining renewed interest and attention because it serves as a method for item development that may help address the need to rapidly and efficiently produce large numbers of high-quality, content-specific, test items. The purpose of this chapter is to describe and illustrate a template-based approach to AIG that can be used to produce large numbers of high-quality items both quickly and efficiency. To highlight the practicality and potential feasibility of AIG, we demonstrate the application of this method in the content area of junior high school science. We also describe the results from a study designed to evaluate the quality of the generated items. Our chapter is divided into four sections. In section one, we describe the AIG methodology. In the section two, we illustrate the method using items generated for a junior high school physics curriculum. In section three, we present the results from a study designed to evaluate the quality of the generated science items. In section four, we conclude the chapter and identify one important area for future research.

## 1. OVERVIEW OF AIG METHODOLOGY

Gierl and Lai (2013) recently described a three-step process for generating multiple-choice test items. In step 1, the content for item generation is identified by test development specialists. This content is specified either as elements for an item model or as a cognitive model. Elements identify the variables in an assessment task that can be modified to create new test items. A cognitive model highlights the knowledge, skills, and problem-solving processes students require to answer test questions. In step 2, an item model is developed to specify where the content from step 1 must be placed to generated new items. An item model is like a template that highlights the features in an item that must be manipulated to generate items. The item model specifies both the stem and the options for a multiple-choice item. In step 3, computer-based algorithms place the content specified in step 1 into the item model developed in step 2. Gierl, Zhou, and Alves (2008) demonstrated the use of the computer program IGOR (which is an acronym for *I*tem Generat*OR*) to perform the step 3 assembly task. IGOR is one example of a computer program than can be used for item generation. But any linear programming method can be employed to solve the combinatorial problems found in AIG.

## Step 1: Identify Content for Item Generation

Test development specialists identify the content that will be used to produce new items. Drasgow, Luecht, and Bennett (2006) advised test development specialists to engage in the task of content specification using a combination of design guidelines and principles discerned from experience, theory, and research. They proposed two general approaches: weak and strong theory.

The first approach draws on weak theory. With this approach, design guidelines are used to create item models that generate items by specifying and then manipulating the elements in the model. As a starting point, they suggest identifying a parent item. The parents can be found by reviewing items from previous test administrations, by drawing on an inventory of existing test items, or by creating the parent item directly. The parent item highlights the underlying structure of the model, thereby providing a point-of-reference for creating alternative items. The test developer's task is to then identify and manipulate the content in the elements for the parent that will yield new items. The weak theory approach is well suited to broad content domains where few theoretical descriptions exist on the knowledge and skills required to solve test items (Drasgow et al., 2006). One important drawback of using weak theory is that relatively few elements can be manipulated in the model. When element manipulation is small, the generated items may have the undesirable quality of appearing too similar to one another. Items generated from weak theory are referred to as isomorphs or clones.

The second approach for identify the content is to use strong theory. Drasgow et al. (2006) describe strong theory as the process of using a cognitive model to specify and manipulate elements using a theoretical account of test performance. Cognitive theory helps highlight the examinees' knowledge and skills required to solve problems within specific domains or content areas. Drasgow et al. also claimed that by modeling the interaction between the examinee and the content, it may be possible to predict the psychometric characteristics (e.g., item difficulty) of the generated items. This approach, when successful, has the benefit of yielding a strong inferential link between the examinees' test item performance in a specific content area with the interpretation of the examinees' test score because generation is guided by a strong theoretical approach to item development (Bejar, 2013).

Gierl, Lai, and Turner (2012) introduced the concept of a cognitive model for AIG, as a practical way to implement the strong theory approach. A cognitive model serves as the principled basis for identifying and manipulated those elements that yield generated items using strong theory. Figure 1 contains a generic cognitive model structure. A cognitive model specifies and coordinates the knowledge, skills, and content required to solve

a problem in a specific content area. It contains three panels. The top panel identifies the problem and its associated scenarios. The middle panel specifies the relevant sources of information. The bottom panel highlights the salient features, which includes the elements and constraints, within the relevant sources of information specified in the middle panel. While the methods used to structure and manipulate the elements within a strong theory approach are complex relative to weak theory, it has the benefit of generating heterogeneous test items that do not appear to be cloned. Heterogeneous generated items are often called variants. Strong theory yields variants because the cognitive model draws on a broad range of elements which contain diverse types of content. A cognitive modelling approach can also be used to study the elements that affect the psychometric characteristics of the generated items, such as item difficulty.

Despite the merits of a strong theory approach, the application of this method has focused on the psychology of specific response processes using articulate cognitive models in content areas such as spatial reasoning (Bejar, 1990), abstract reasoning (Embretson, 2002), and mental rotation (Arendasy & Sommer, 2010). Few comparable cognitive theories exist to guide our current item development practices (Leighton & Gierl, 2011) or to account for test performance in broad content areas, typical of those found on most educational achievement tests (Ferrara & DeMauro, 2006; Schmeiser & Welch, 2006). Hence, the applications of strong theory AIG to-date are limited.

## Step 2: Item Model Development

With the content identified and structure in step 1, it must now be positioned within a template that, in turn, will structure the generated items. This template is called an item model. Item models (Bejar, 2002; Bejar, Lawless, Morley, Wagner, Bennett, & Revuelta, 2003; LaDuca, Staples, Templeton, & Holzman, 1986) contain the components in an assessment task that can be manipulated for

*Figure 1. A general cognitive model structure for AIG*

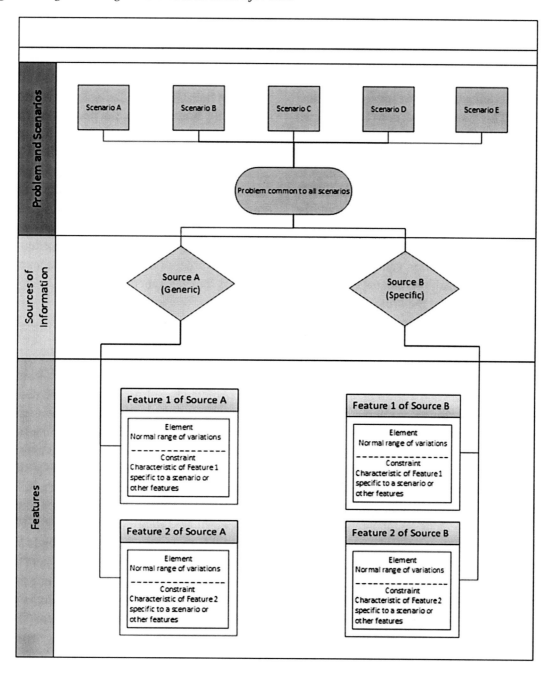

item generation. These components include the stem, the options, and the auxiliary information. The stem contains context, content, item, and/or the question the examinee is required to answer. The options includes a set of alternative answers with one correct option and one or more incorrect options or distracters. Both stem and options are required for multiple-choice item models. Auxiliary information includes any supplementary information, such as graphs, tables, or figures, that contribute to stem and/or options. Auxiliary information is not required for item generation.

## Step 3: Generating Items Using Computer Technology

Once the item models are created and the content for these models has been identified by the test developers, this information is assembled to produce new items. This assembly task must be conducted with some type of computer-based assembly system because it is a complex combinatorial problem. Different types of software have been written to generate test items. For instance, Higgins (2007) introduced *Item Distiller* as a tool that could be used to generate sentence-based test items. Higgins, Futagi, and Deane (2005) described how the software *ModelCreator* can produce math word problems in multiple languages. Singley and Bennett (2002) used the *Math Test Creation Assistant* to generate items involving linear systems of equations. Gütl et al. (2011) outlined the use of the *Enhanced Automatic Question Creator (EAQC)* to extract key concepts from text to generate multiple-choice and constructed-response test items. For this chapter, we describe the use of technology for generating test items using the IGOR software described by Gierl et al. (2008).

IGOR is a JAVA-based program designed to assemble the content specified in an item model, subject to elements and constraints outlined in the cognitive model. Iterations are conducted in IGOR to assemble all possible combinations of elements and options, subject to the constraints. Without the use of constraints, all of the variable content would be systematically combined to create new items. However, some of these items would not be sensible or useful. Constraints therefore serve as restrictions that must be applied during the assembly task so that meaningful items are generated.

To begin, IGOR reads an item model in the form of an XML (Extensible Markup Language) file. The Item Model Editor window permits the programmer to enter and structure each item model. The editor has three panels. The stem panel is where the stem for the item model is specified. The elements panel is used to manipulate the variables as well as to apply the constraints highlighted in the cognitive model. The options panel is used to specify the correct and incorrect alternatives. The options are classified as either a key or a distracter. To generate items from a model, the Test Item Generator dialogue box is presented where the user specifies the item model file, the test bank output file, the answer key file, and the Generator options. The item model file is loaded from the current item model which is specified as an XML file. For the test bank output file, the user selects the desired location for the generated items. The user can also specify Generator options. These options include size of the generated item bank, the order of the options, and the number of options for each generated item.

## Summary

AIG is the process of using item models to generate test items with the aid of computer technology. The template-based AIG approach we described requires three steps. First, the content used for item generation is identified and structured using a cognitive model. Second, item models are created to specify where the content should be positioned within the template-based assessment task. Third, elements in the item model are manipulated with computer-based algorithms to produce new items. Using this three-step method, hundreds of new items can be generated using a single item model. Generated items that are similar to one another are called isomorphs or clones whereas generated items that are different from one another are called variants.

## 2. USING AIG TO CREATE JUNIOR HIGH SCHOOL SCIENCE ITEMS

To illustrate the logic and some of the concepts related to the three-step approach presented in Section 1, we present two examples of how AIG can be used to generate physics items for a junior high school science curriculum. The first example used a weak theory approach where elements in an item model were manipulated to generate new items. The second example used a strong theory approach where a cognitive model were created to guide the item generation method. The examples were developed by two content specialists who were experienced classroom teachers and who also had extensive knowledge, skills, and practice developing items for large-scale educational achievement tests.

The first example focuses on the concept of "molecular mass" using weak theory. The parent item for this example is shown in Box 1. The science concept from the test specification states that "Protons and neutrons have about the same mass and have much more mass than electrons". The associated item model is presented in Box 2. The stem for the item model contains two elements, mass (i.e., <MASS>) and charge (i.e., <CHARGE>). Other weak theory item models could also be created from this parent item. For example, "A certain atom has a mass number of <MASS>, <NEUTRONS> neutrons, and <CHARGE>. How many protons and electrons are in this atom?", "A certain atom has a mass number of <MASS>, <NEUTRONS> neutrons, and <CHARGE>. How many protons are in this atom?", and "A certain atom has a mass number of <MASS>, <NEUTRONS> neutrons, and <CHARGE>. How many electrons are in this atom?".

*Box 1. Parent item for molecular mass*

A certain atom has a mass number of 27 and has no charge. Which of these could represent the number of particles in this atom?

A. 9 protons, 9 electrons, and 9 neutrons
B. 13 protons, 13 electrons, and 14 neutrons*
C. 13 protons, 14 electrons, and 27 neutrons
D. 27 protons, 27 electrons, and 27 neutrons

*-correct option

The options for the item model were created systematically using rules and rationales that yield both the correct solution as well as incorrect solutions based on errors or misconceptions. The incorrect options, also called distractors, are generated using rationales or short description provided by the content specialists that yield wrong answers. The reasoning which underlies each wrong answer is explicitly stated so that distractors can be generated that match each rationale. This method is based on the assumption that algorithms, rules, and procedures can first be articulated by content specialists and then used to create plausible but incorrect answers linked to misconceptions or errors in scientific thinking, reasoning, and problem solving. For instance, a plausible but incorrect option could be generated using the rationale that a student may mistakenly believe that all particle types in an atom have equal mass and contribute to the mass number, even though the mass of an electron is much smaller compared to the mass of a proton or neutron.

IGOR was programmed using the "molecular mass" item model with two elements, along with a set of distractor rationales. In total, 175 items were generated. A random sample of four generated items is presented in Table 1.

The second example focused on the concept of "relationship of unbalanced forces" using strong theory. For this example, a cognitive model representation is required. Figure 2 contains a cognitive model for AIG required to solve problems involving the concept described as the "relationship of unbalanced forces". This cognitive structure outlines the knowledge and skills required to as-

*Box 2. Parent item for molecular mass*

A certain atom has a mass number of <MASS> and has <CHARGE>. Which of these could represent the number of particles in this atom?

*Table 1. A sample of four generated items from the "molecular mass" item model*

---

1. A certain atom has a mass number of 5 and has a charge of -2. Which of these could represent the number of particles in this atom?

A. 3 protons, 5 electrons, and 6 neutrons
B. 5 protons, 3 electrons, and 5 neutrons
C. 5 protons, 3 electrons, and 6 neutrons
D. 5 protons, 7 electrons, and 6 neutrons

---

21. A certain atom has a mass number of 5 and has a charge of -1. Which of these could represent the number of particles in this atom?

A. 4 protons, 5 electrons, and 6 neutrons
B. 5 protons, 4 electrons, and 5 neutrons
C. 5 protons, 4 electrons, and 6 neutrons
D. 5 protons, 6 electrons, and 6 neutrons

---

38. A certain atom has a mass number of 11 and has a charge of -1. Which of these could represent the number of particles in this atom?

A. 10 protons, 11 electrons, and 12 neutrons
B. 11 protons, 10 electrons, and 11 neutrons
C. 11 protons, 10 electrons, and 12 neutrons
D. 11 protons, 12 electrons, and 12 neutrons

---

79. A certain atom has a mass number of 11 and has a charge of -2. Which of these could represent the number of particles in this atom?

A. 11 protons, 9 electrons, and 11 neutrons
B. 11 protons, 9 electrons, and 12 neutrons
C. 9 protons, 11 electrons, and 12 neutrons
D. 11 protons, 13 electrons, and 12 neutrons

---

semble content related to the application of force. The science concept from the test specifications states that "The greater the force acting on an object, the greater will be its change in motion. The greater the mass of an object acted on by a force the less will be its change in motion". To create a cognitive model for this concept, our two science content specialists were provided with the parent item in Box 3. Then, they were asked to describe the knowledge and reasoning skills required to solve this item. The content specialists first began by identifying the problem (i.e., Relationship of Unbalanced Forces) specific to the parent test item. They also identified two scenarios related to that problem [i.e., Balanced State; Greater Force Direction). These outcomes are presented on the top

panel in Figure 2. With a set of related scenarios common to the underlying problem, the content specialists then identified sources of information required to solve the problem. Three sources of information were specified (i.e., Forces; Object; Description). These outcomes are presented in the middle panel in Figure 2. Finally, the content specialists identified one or more feature within each source of information (e.g., Force 1; Force 2; Force Relation; Scenario; Description). Each feature, in turn, contains two nested components. The first nested component for a feature is the element. Elements contain content specific to each feature that can be manipulated for item generation. As an example, for the Force Source of Information, the Force Relation feature had three elements (i.e., Equal; Force 1 greater; Force 2 greater) and two constraints (i.e., Equal for Balanced; Force 1 or Force 2 for Greater Force Movement). These outcomes are presented at the bottom panel in Figure 2. Taken together, Figure 2 serves as a cognitive model structure for AIG because it specifies and coordinates the knowledge, skills, and content required to reason and solve problems involving the relationship of unbalanced forces.

The content presented in the cognitive model structure in Figure 2 can be viewed in two ways. First, it serves as a pragmatic rendering necessary for item generation. The purpose of the rendering is to link the problem (Relations of Unbalanced Forces) and the associated scenarios (Balanced State; Greater Force Direction) in the top panel to the features (Force 1; Force 2; Forces Relation; Scenario; Description) in the bottom panel through the information sources (Forces; Object; Description) in the middle panel. This prescriptive link is used for item generation, as the features can be inserted in their appropriate information sources, as outlined in Figure 2, subject to the elements and their constraints.

Second, Figure 2 serves as an explicit cognitive model where the knowledge and skills required to solve problems about the relationship of unbalanced forces are identified. Because of detailed

*Figure 2. A cognitive model structure for measuring the concept "relationship of unbalanced forces"*

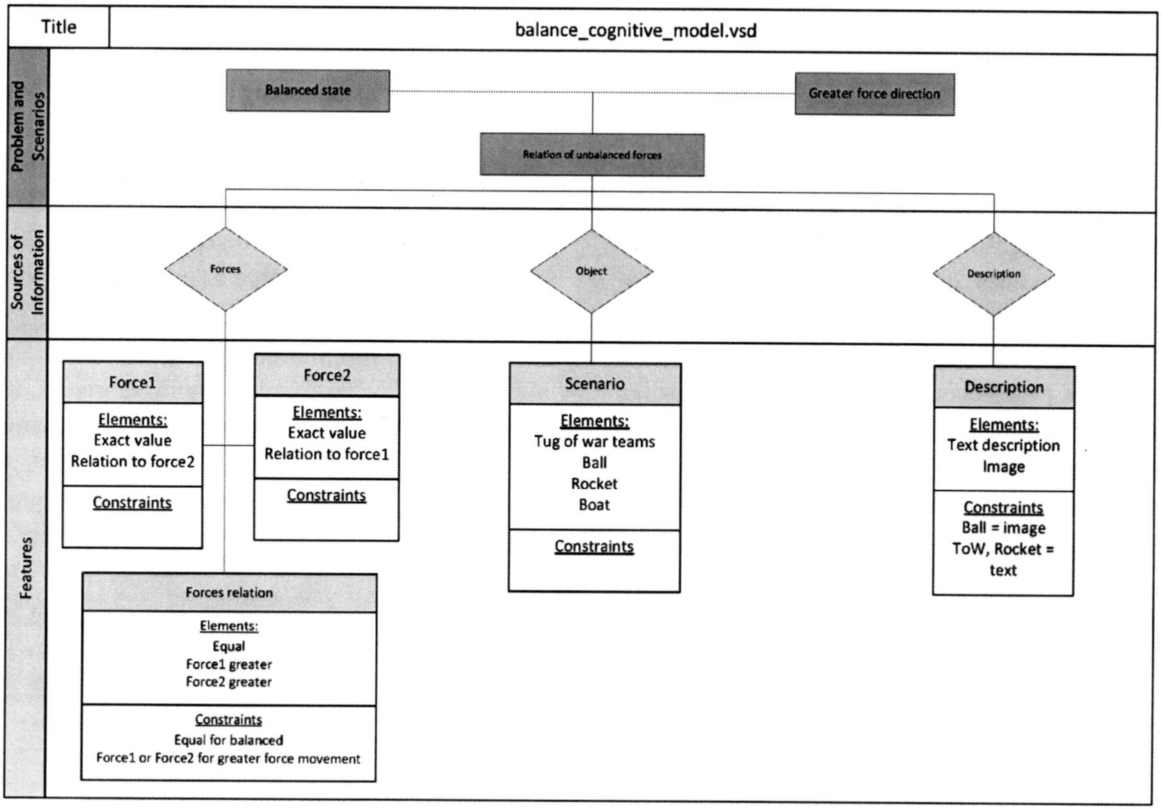

*Box 3. Parent item used to create the "relationship of unbalanced forces" cognitive model*

In a science experiment, students test force and motion by using a spring and two balls, as shown in this picture. One ball has twice the mass of the other ball.

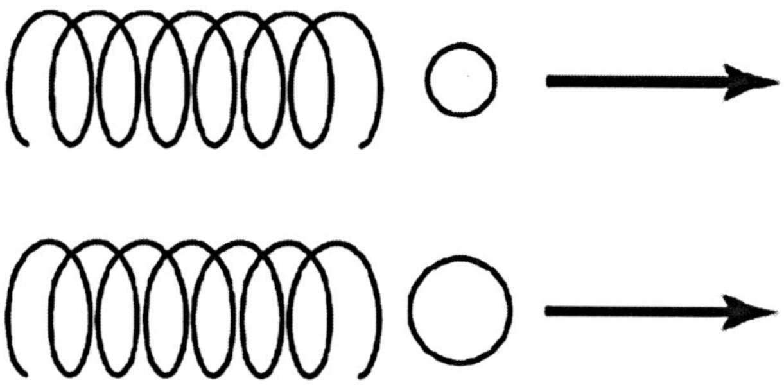

The springs push both balls with equal force. Which of these is true about the motion of the balls after they are pushed by the springs?

A. The ball with less mass will have greater acceleration.*
B. The ball with more mass will have greater acceleration.
C. The balls will both stop when the force moving them is exhausted.
D. The speed of the balls is the same because they are pushed with the same force.

*-correct option

representation for this task, both the number and types of variables specified for this task can be manipulated leading to different kinds of generated items. The quality of the representations can also be evaluated. In our example, the features and information sources, along with their organization as specified by the elements and the constraints, form the cognitive model for reasoning about the relationship of unbalanced forces. These representations can be evaluated by other content specialists. These representations can be evaluated by having examinees think aloud as they solve sample problems to validate the number, type, and organization of the cognitive components specified in the model. These representations can also be compared to alternative models developed for item generation or to models described in the literature on scientific reasoning. Cognitive models for AIG should be validated, in some way, to ensure that the reasoning and problem-solving skills provide an accurate representation of how examinees think, reason, and solve problems. These three evaluation methods—content specialist review, think aloud protocols, and competing model comparisons—serve as examples of possible validation strategies.

IGOR was programmed using the "relationship of unbalanced forces" cognitive model, as presented in Figure 2, along with a set of distractor rationales. In total, 113 items were generated. A random sample of four generated items is presented in Table 2.

*Table 2. A sample of four generated items from the "relationship of unbalanced forces" cognitive model*

| |
|---|
| 1. Team A and B have a tug of war. Team A pulls a rope with a force greater than Team B. As a result the teams will<br><br>A. stay stationary on their side of the line<br>B. move back and forth on their side of the line<br>C. move across the tug of war line in the direction of Team B<br>D. move across the tug of war line in the direction of Team A |
| 11. The weight of a boat is equal to the buoyancy. As a result the boat will<br><br>A. stay on the surface because the forces are equal<br>B. become submerged because the forces are equal<br>C. stay on the surface because there are two applied forces<br>D. become submerged because the buoyancy is greater than the boat's weight |
| 84. The thrust of a rocket engine when placed on the ground is 1000 N and the rocket's weight is 500 N. As a result the rocket will<br><br>A. take off because the engine thrust is less than the rocket's weight<br>B. take off because the engine thrust is greater than the rocket's weight<br>C. stay on the ground because the rocket's weight is less than the engine thrust<br>D. stay on the ground because the engine thrust is greater than the rocket's weight |
| 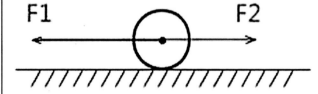<br><br>129. In the diagram above, force F1 is greater than force F2. As a result, the ball will move in the direction of<br><br>A. force F1 because force F1 is less than force F2<br>B. force F2 because force F2 is less than force F1<br>C. force F1 because force F1 is greater than force F2<br>D. force F2 because force F1 is greater than force F2 |

## Summary

The three-step AIG described in Section 1 was used to generate item using a weak and strong theory approach in Section 2. Weak theory was used by two content specialists to identify the elements within an item model. IGOR was used to manipulate the elements in order to generate test items. Strong theory was used by the same two content specialists to specify a cognitive model. IGOR was used to manipulate the elements within the cognitive model to generate test items. The incorrect options or distractors for the weak and strong theory approaches were based on algorithms, rules, and procedures first identified by the content specialists and then used to create plausible but incorrect alternatives. IGOR generated 175 weak theory items and 113 strong theory items. The weak theory items were similar to one another and, hence, could be considered isomorphs (see Table 1). Conversely, the strong theory items were different from one another and would be called variants (see Table 2).

## 3. EVALUATING THE QUALITY OF THE GENERATED ITEMS

### Evaluating the Comparability of Generated Items Using a Statistical Measure

Once the items are generated, they must be evaluated. Two different approaches for evaluating item quality are presented next. The first approach focuses on the similarity of the generated items. Recall, generated items produced from weak theory are often characterized as isomorphs because they are similar to one another. Alternatively, generated items produced from strong theory are often characterized as variants because they are dissimilar to one another. Unfortunately, there are few empirical methods available for quantifying the similarity of generated test items and, hence,

similarity is often established more subjectively using judgments from test development specialists. To overcome this limitation, we describe one measure of item similarity that can be used to evaluate the comparability of the generated items. We quantify similarity using the cosine similarity index (CSI). The CSI is a measure of similarity between two vectors of co-occurring texts. It is computed using the cosine of the angle between the two vectors in a multidimensional space of unique words. In other words, the CSI provides a global summary of the text similarity in a sample of the generated items. The CSI is given as

$$\cos(\theta) = \frac{A \cdot B}{\|A\|\|B\|},$$

where A and B are two items expressed in a binary vector of word occurrences. For example, if A is a list of three words (e.g., dog, walk, talk) and B is a list of three words (e.g., cat, walk, furry), then the length of both binary vectors is the number of unique words used across both lists (i.e., dog, walk, talk, cat, furry). To place A and B in a vector format so the words can be compared, the occurrence of each word in the vector list is quantified with a value of 1. The resulting vectors for A and B in our example are [1,1,1,0,0] and [0,1,0,1,1]. The CSI has a minimum value of 0, meaning that no word overlapped between the two vectors, and a maximum of 1, meaning that the words represented by the two vectors are identical.

To illustrate the use of the CSI in our chapter, a random sample of 100 items from each example in Section 2 was selected and analyzed. The CSI outcomes can be used as evidence to decide whether an item model has generated isomorphs (i.e., high mean CSI and low standard deviations) or variants (i.e., low mean CSI and high standard deviation). Because fewer elements are manipulated with the "molecular mass" model compared to the "relationship of unbalanced forces" model, similarity should be higher for the items generated with the weak theory approach. The "molecular mass" model produced an overall CSI mean of 0.66 and a standard deviation of 0.10. Because the CSI ranges from 0 (no similarity) to 1 (perfect similarity), a high mean for this model indicates that the generated items are quite similar to one another while the low standard deviation reveals the items are relatively homogeneous. By comparison, the "relationship of unbalanced forces" model produced a lower overall CSI mean of 0.45 and a higher standard deviation of 0.31. These results allow us to conclude that the "relationship of unbalanced forces" model produce more heterogeneous and diverse items compared to the items generated from "molecular mass" model using a measure of text similarity.

## Evaluating the Comparability of Generated Items Using Substantive Judgments

Item quality can also be evaluated using judgments from content specialists where the guidelines, conventions, and standards of practice for creating multiple-choice items form the basis of scrutinizing the items. A sample of the items generated in Section 2 was evaluated by content specialists in two ways. First, a panel of science content specialists rated the quality of items created using both traditional and AIG practices. Second, a predictive accuracy study was conducted where the same content specialists were asked to identify those items developed using AIG in a blind review (see Gierl, Latifi, Lai, Matovinovic, & Boughton, 2014). These outcomes help determine if AIG yields items that meet appropriate standards of quality required for science achievement testing relative to items created using a more traditional approach.

To compare the quality of multiple-choice items developed using traditional and AIG item development approaches, an experimental design was implemented. To begin, a random sample of 16 items were drawn from the bank of traditional

items at a large testing company. These items are described as "traditional" because they were developed using a one-item-at-a-time content-specialist method that met the content standards and item development requirements for a junior high school science curriculum. These items were created over many item-writing sessions by groups of content specialists who had practical as well as item development experience. The items, once developed, were edited and then reviewed by a validation committee of content specialists to ensure that they met content and item development principles, standards, and guidelines. The items in our sample were drawn from eight different content areas in Physics. Two items from each of the eight content areas were randomly selected and included in the traditional item set to form a subtest of 16 items.

Next, two content specialists, who contributed to the creation of the items in the traditional bank, received a workshop on AIG. During this workshop the principles and practices of AIG were presented and illustrated. Once the workshop was completed, the content specialists used the three-step AIG process described Section 2 of our chapter to produce the generated items described in Section 3. In total, 9823 items were generated. From this set, two items from each of the eight content areas were randomly selected to form a subtest of 16 items. The items from the traditional and the AIG subtest were combined and their order in the form randomized to create the evaluation test used in this study.

Next, a three-member panel of science content and test development specialists was convened. The panel included content specialists who had a range of test development experiences. The panelists represented three different science areas (Earth Sciences, Life Sciences and Ecology, General Science) with a range of teaching (0-5 years) and test development (4-10 years) experiences.

The panelists, who were blind to the outcomes of the process used to create the items for the evaluation test, rated each item on a 4-point scale:

1-Item is fine (no changes needed), 2-Minor revisions (item requires minor revisions, revisions can be made in-house), 3-Major revisions (item requires major revisions, return to item developer for changes), 4-Reject (item is flawed, reject item outright). The panelists were also asked to provide a justification for their rating. A single, 4-point, scale was selected because we wanted a succinct but relevant indicator of item quality given that AIG may warrant the review of large numbers of items. Based on our discussions with test development practitioners and psychometric researchers, items in the development cycle are typically classified into two categories—acceptable or unacceptable. Items judged to be outright acceptable meet the content and item development conventions required for operational administration. Item that require minor revisions can be quickly modified to meet these content and item development standards. Hence, item judged to be either acceptable or requiring minor revisions are seen as acceptable because they require little or no additional work. Conversely, item that require major revisions warrant a considerable amount of time and extra work. Items that are rejected have no value for an operational testing program because they fail to meet the content and item development standards. As a result, these two categories of items are unacceptable. We used these two categories—acceptable or unacceptable—to help characterize and compare the traditional and generated items. After the panelists completed their item evaluation,

they we debriefed on the purpose of this study. They were also given a shortened version of the AIG workshop that was initially delivered to the two content specialists who developed items for the AIG condition. Then, the panelist were asked to independently review each item and identify which were developed using a traditional approach and which were created using AIG.

The first analysis focused on the indicator of multiple-choice item quality. An independent samples *t*-tests was conducted where the item quality indicator, which ranged from 1-Accept to 4-Reject, served as the dependent variable and item type (Traditional vs. AIG) served as the independent variable. A lower mean score indicates higher item quality. The means for the Traditional and AIG condition were 2.33 and 2.12, respectively, which were not statistically different from one another, $t(94) = 1.17$, $p=0.25$. Hence, the overall rating by the panelists indicates that the traditional and AIG items were of comparable quality.

Next, the rating for each item quality indicator was evaluated by item type as a function of the three panelists (see Table 3). Fifty-two percent (or 25 of the 48 ratings) of the traditional items were judged to be acceptable (i.e., rating of 1 or 2) while 65% (31 of 48) AIG items were considered acceptable. Conversely, 48% (23 of 48) of the traditional item were found to be unacceptable but only 35% (17 of 48) of the AIG items were rated as unacceptable. It is interesting to note that across the three panelists, almost half of the

*Table 3. Item quality rating for the 3-member science panel*

| Panelist | Rating | | | | | | | |
|---|---|---|---|---|---|---|---|---|
| | 1-Acceptable | | 2-Minor Revision | | 3-Major Revisions | | 4-Reject | |
| | Traditional | AIG | Traditional | AIG | Traditional | AIG | Traditional | AIG |
| 1 | 3 (19%) | 5 (31%) | 2 (13%) | 6 (38%) | 11 (69%) | 5 (31%) | 0 (0%) | 0 (0%) |
| 2 | 3 (19%) | 4 (25%) | 5 (31%) | 5 (31%) | 5 (31%) | 7 (44%) | 3 (19%) | 0 (0%) |
| 3 | 4 (25%) | 4 (25%) | 8 (50%) | 7 (44%) | 4 (25%) | 3 (30%) | 0 (0%) | 2 (20%) |
| Overall Rating | 10 (21%) | 13 (27%) | 15 (31%) | 18 (38%) | 20 (42%) | 15 (31%) | 3 (6%) | 2 (4%) |

traditional items were judged to be unacceptable despite the extensive development, review, and revision process that items in the bank must first undergo. It is also important to note that the overall inter-rater agreement across the three panelists was low, as Fleiss' kappa reveals. Kappa was only 0.12, which is considered to show "slight agreement" across the three panelists (Landis & Koch, 1977). Taken together, the outcomes from the item quality analyses indicate that the traditional and AIG item-sets were considered, overall, to be of comparable quality. The item-level agreement among the panelists found to be very low.

The second analysis focused on the predictive accuracy of the panelists. Once the panelists were debriefed on the purpose of the study and provided with a AIG workshop, they reviewed all 32 items with the goal of differentiating the traditional from the AIG items. Table 4 contains the proportion of correctly and incorrectly identified traditional and AIG items, as a function of panelist. The panelists correctly identified the AIG items, on average, 73% of the time. But they also incorrectly identified the AIG items (i.e., mistook traditional items for AIG items), on average, 58% of the time. When taken together, the three panelists correctly identified 57% of the items, but incorrectly identified 43% of the items. The item-level reliability across the three raters was low, with a Krippendorff's alpha of 0.13. These outcome suggests that the panelists could not consistently distinguish the AIG from the traditional items. It also reveals that there was little item-level agreement on which items were created using traditional methods relative to those items produced using AIG.

## Summary

Despite the feasibility and potential usefulness of using the AIG methodology to generate test content, the quality of the generated items must also be considered. We illustrated how item quality can be evaluated using a statistical approach like the CSI so that the text similarity among the generated items can be determined. The CSI is a measure of similarity between two vectors of co-occurring texts. It is computed using the cosine of the angle between the two vectors in a multidimensional space of unique words thereby providing a global summary of the text similarity in a sample of the generated items. We demonstrated how the CSI outcomes can be used as evidence to decide whether an item model has generated isomorphs (i.e., the "molecular mass" model produced an overall CSI mean of 0.66 and a standard deviation of 0.10) or variants (i.e., the "relationship of unbalanced forces" model produced a lower overall CSI mean of 0.45 and a higher standard deviation of 0.31).

We also illustrated how item quality can be evaluated using substantive judgments from content specialists. Two indicators were used. The first indicator was based on item quality where a panel of science content specialists who rated the quality of items created using both traditional and AIG practices. The second indicator was based predictive accuracy where the same panelists were asked to identify those items developed using AIG in a blind review. Three outcomes were reported. The items produced using traditional and AIG processes were of comparable quality. The predictive accuracy of the panelists for predicting whether an

*Table 4. Predictive accuracy for the 3-member science expert panel*

| Panelist | Accuracy | | | |
|---|---|---|---|---|
| | Correct | | Incorrect | |
| | Traditional | AIG | Traditional | AIG |
| 1 | 38% | 69% | 63% | 31% |
| 2 | 44% | 56% | 56% | 44% |
| 3 | 44% | 94% | 56% | 6% |
| Overall Accuracy | 57% | | 43% | |

item was created using a generative or traditional item development process was only 57%. There was considerable inconsistency among the panelists' item-level ratings on, both, the measure of item quality and predictive accuracy. From these results we conclude that the generated items do not contain systematic differences that permit content experts to consistently differentiate the outcomes between traditional and AIG item development.

## 4. CONCLUSION

Four key ideas were described in this chapter. First, we provided a context for one line of research that is now being conducted in educational testing as it relates to formative feedback and technology-enhanced assessment. We assert that educators are now in the position to change their testing practices for the betterment of teachers and students by combining fundamental concepts in formative assessment with dramatic changes in how students access and use technology to develop a rich feedback system that improves teaching and promotes learning. Computerized testing can be used to promote formative assessment by permitting testing on-demand, by providing students with instant feedback, by supporting the development of new item types and testing formats, and by fostering instructional concepts such as individualized teaching and learning. The most pressing challenge facing educators who want to implement formative feedback is the availability of test content. Our current item development processes are slow, expensive, and unscalable. As a result, the large number of test items required to implement technology-enhanced assessment are not currently available.

Second, we introduced a method for developing test items called automatic item generation (AIG).

AIG is the process of using item models to generate test items with the aid of computer technology. We described a three-step process for generating multiple-choice test items. In step 1, the content for item generation is identified by test development specialists, either in the form of elements in an item model or as a cognitive model. In step 2, an item model is developed to specify where the content from step 1 must be placed to generated new items. In step 3, computer-based algorithms place the content specified in step 1 into the item model developed in step 2. We demonstrated the use of the computer program IGOR for performing the step 3 assembly task.

Third, we used the three-step AIG to generate junior high school physics item using a weak and strong theory approach. Weak theory was employed by two content specialists to identify the elements within an item model. IGOR was then used to manipulating the elements in order to generate test items. Strong theory was implemented by the same two content specialists to specify a cognitive model. IGOR manipulated the elements within the cognitive model to generate test items. IGOR produced 175 weak theory items and 113 strong theory items as part of our demonstration of the AIG method.

Fourth, we evaluated the quality of the generated items using a statistical measure of item similarity called the Cosine Similarity Index as well as substantive judgments of item quality from content specialists. We demonstrated how the CSI outcomes can be used as evidence to decide whether we generated items considered to be similar to one another (i.e., isomorphs) or different from one another (i.e., variants). We also showed that generated items could be created that are relatively indistinguishable from items produced using a more traditional item development approach.

## Future Research

We claimed in the introduction to this chapter that profound global and economic changes are shaping how we develop and deliver educational tests because of the growing emphasis on knowledge services, information, and communication technologies. Countries require skilled workers who can think, reason, communicate, collaborate, and adapt. If educational testing is to contribute to the development of this new global workforce, then our assessments must also be produced in multiple languages. We demonstrated how AIG could be used to generate multiple-choice items in English. But many countries require exams in two or more languages. Hence, a truly universal item development system must produce multilingual test items.

One way to address this problem is to apply the three-stage AIG approach to each language group. That is, an item model is developed for each required language group. Another way to address this problem is to develop a generalized approach that allows for multilingual AIG. To generalizing AIG from one language to multiple languages *n-layer item modelling* is required (Gierl & Lai, 2012). The goal of AIG using n-layer modeling is to generate items by manipulating a relatively large number of elements at two or more levels in the model simultaneously. 1-layer item modeling is constrained to a linear set of generative operations using a small number of elements at a single level. n-layer item modeling permits manipulations of a nonlinear set of generative operations using elements at multiple levels. The concept of n-layer item generation is adapted from the literature on syntactic structures of language where sentences are organized in a hierarchical manner (e.g., Jurafsky & Martin, 2009). The use of an n-layer item model is a flexible template for expressing different syntactic structures thereby permitting the development of many different but feasible combinations of embedded elements. The n-layer structure can be described as a model with multiple layers of elements, where each element can be varied simultaneously at different levels to produce different items.

A comparison of the 1-layer and n-layer item model is presented in the top of Figure 3. For this example, the 1-layer model can provide a maximum of four different values for element A. Conversely, the n-layer model can provide up to 64 different values by embedding the same four values for elements C and D within element B. Because the maximum generative capacity of an item model is the product of the ranges in each element, the use of an n-layer item model will always increase the number and type of items that can be generated relative to a 1-layer structure.

By adding language as an element, n-layer item modeling can be used to generate multilingual items (see bottom of Figure 3). A 1-layer item model can be used to generate multilingual items, but a new model is required for each language group because different languages require different grammatical structures and word orderings. A 1-layer item model cannot accommodate this type of linguistic variation because the generative operations are constrained to those elements at a single level. Hence, the linguistic content must be created specific to each item model. However, with the use of an n-layer item model, the generative operations are expanded dramatically to include a large number of elements at multiple levels. Language, therefore, can serve as an additional layer that is manipulated during item generation thereby permitting multilingual AIG. Research should now be undertaken in an attempt to implement our claim that n-layer item modeling can produce items in multiple languages simultaneously and

*Figure 3. A comparison of the elements in a 1-layer and n-layer item model using 1 and 2 languages*

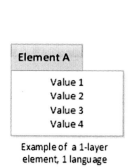

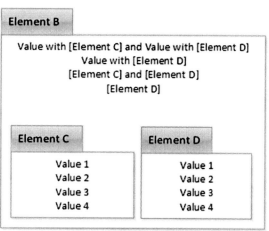

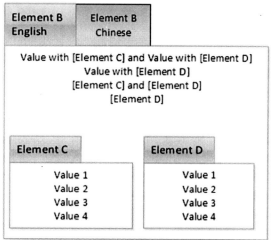

evaluate the quality of the items generated using the n-layer approach. The ability to generate items in multiple languages would not only enhance the applicability of the AIG method but it would also yield large numbers of content-specific test items *in multiple languages* thereby providing educators with an enormous pool of items across multiple language groups that can be used to support a more robust feedback system in educational testing.

## ACKNOWLEDGMENT

The authors would like to thank Michael Frontz and Andrina Aragon from CTB/McGraw-Hill for their help developing the item models. However, the authors are solely responsible for the methods, procedures, and interpretations expressed in this study. Our views do not necessarily reflect those of CTB/McGraw-Hill.

# REFERENCES

Arendasy, M. E., & Sommer, M. (2010). Evaluating the contribution of different item features to the effect sixe of the gender differences in three-dimensional mental rotation using automatic item generation. *Intelligence, 38*(6), 574–581. doi:10.1016/j.intell.2010.06.004

Bejar, I. I. (1990). A generative analysis of a three-dimensional spatial task. *Applied Psychological Measurement, 14*(3), 237–245. doi:10.1177/014662169001400302

Bejar, I. I. (2002). Generative testing: From conception to implementation. In S. H. Irvine & P. C. Kyllonen (Eds.), *Item generation for test development* (pp. 199–217). Hillsdale, NJ: Erlbaum.

Bejar, I. I. (2013). Item generation: Implications for a validity argument. In M. J. Gierl & T. Haladyna (Eds.), *Automatic item generation: Theory and practice* (pp. 40–55). New York: Routledge.

Bejar, I. I., Lawless, R., Morley, M. E., Wagner, M. E., Bennett, R. E., & Revuelta, J. (2003). A feasibility study of on-the-fly item generation in adaptive testing. *Journal of Technology, Learning, and Assessment, 2*(3). Available from http://www.jtla.org

Bennett, R. (2001). How the internet will help large-scale assessment reinvent itself. *Education Policy Analysis Archives, 9*(0), 1–23. doi:10.14507/epaa.v9n5.2001

Black, P., & Wiliam, D. (1998). Assessment and classroom learning. *Assessment in Education: Principles, Policy & Practice, 5*(1), 7–74. doi:10.1080/0969595980050102

Black, P., & Wiliam, D. (2010). Inside the black box: Raising standards through classroom assessment. *Phi Delta Kappan, 92*(1), 81–90. doi:10.1177/003172171009200119

Downing, S. M., & Haladyna, T. M. (2006). *Handbook of test development*. Mahwah, NJ: Erlbaum.

Drasgow, F., Luecht, R. M., & Bennett, R. (2006). Technology and testing. In R. L. Brennan (Ed.), *Educational measurement* (4th ed.; pp. 471–516). Washington, DC: American Council on Education.

Embretson, S. E. (2002). Generating abstract reasoning items with cognitive theory. In S. H. Irvine & P. C. Kyllonen (Eds.), *Item generation for test development* (pp. 219–250). Mahwah, NJ: Erlbaum.

Ferrara, S., & DeMauro, G. E. (2006). Standardized assessment of individual achievement in K-12. In R. L. Brennan (Ed.), *Educational measurement* (4th ed.; pp. 579–621). Westport, CT: National Council on Measurement in Education and American Council on Education.

Gierl, M. J., & Haladyna, T. (2013). *Automatic item generation: Theory and practice*. New York: Routledge.

Gierl, M. J., & Lai, H. (2012). *Using automatic item generation to create items for medical licensure exams*. Paper presented at the annual meeting of the National Council on Measurement in Education, Vancouver, BC.

Gierl, M. J., & Lai, H. (2013). Using automated processes to generate test items. *Educational Measurement: Issues and Practice, 32*, 36–50.

Gierl, M. J., Lai, H., & Turner, S. (2012). Using automatic item generation to create multiple-choice items for assessments in medical education. *Medical Education, 46*, 757–765. doi:10.1111/j.1365-2923.2012.04289.x PMID:22803753

Gierl, M. J., Latifi, F., Lai, H., Matovinovic, D., & Boughton, K. (April, 2014). *Evaluating the quality of items generated using automatic processes*. Paper presented at the annual meeting of the National Council on Measurement in Education, Philadelphia, PA.

Gierl, M. J., Zhou, J., & Alves, C. (2008). Developing a taxonomy of item model types to promote assessment engineering. *Journal of Technology, Learning, and Assessment, 7*(2). Retrieved from http://www.jtla.org

Gütl, C., Lankmayr, K., Weinhofer, J., & Höfler, M. (2011). Enhanced Automatic Question Creator – EAQC: Concept, development and evaluation of an automatic test item creation tool to foster modern e-education. *The Electronic Journal of e-Learning, 9,* 23-38.

Haladyna, T. M., & Rodriguez, M. C. (2013). *Developing and validating test items.* Routledge.

Higgins, D. (2007). *Item Distiller: Text retrieval for computer-assisted test item creation. Educational Testing Service Research Memorandum* (RM-07-05). Princeton, NJ: Educational Testing Service.

Higgins, D., Futagi, Y., & Deane, P. (2005). *Multilingual generalization of the Model Creator software for math item generation. Educational Testing Service Research Report (RR-05-02).* Princeton, NJ: Educational Testing Service.

Irvine, S. H., & Kyllonen, P. C. (2002). *Item generation for test development.* Hillsdale, NJ: Erlbaum.

Jurafsky, D., & Martin, J. H. (2009). *Speech and language processing: An introduction to natural language processing, computational linguistics, and speech recognition* (2nd ed.). Upper Saddle River, NJ: Pearson.

LaDuca, A., Staples, W. I., Templeton, B., & Holzman, G. B. (1986). Item modeling procedures for constructing content-equivalent multiple-choice questions. *Medical Education, 20*(1), 53–56. doi:10.1111/j.1365-2923.1986.tb01042.x PMID:3951382

Landis, J. R., & Koch, G. G. (1977). The measurement of observer agreement for categorical data. *Biometrics, 33*(1), 159–174. doi:10.2307/2529310 PMID:843571

Leighton, J. P., & Gierl, M. J. (2011). *The learning sciences in educational assessment: The role of cognitive models.* Cambridge, UK: Cambridge University Press. doi:10.1017/CBO9780511996276

Rudner, L. (2010). Implementing the Graduate Management Admission Test Computerized Adaptive Test. In W. van der Linden & C. A. W. Glas (Eds.), *Elements of adaptive testing* (pp. 151–165). New York, NY: Springer.

Sadler, R. D. (1989). Formative assessment and the design of instructional systems. *Instructional Science, 18*(2), 119–144. doi:10.1007/BF00117714

Schmeiser, C. B., & Welch, C. J. (2006). Test development. In R. L. Brennan (Ed.), *Educational measurement* (4th ed.; pp. 307–353). Westport, CT: National Council on Measurement in Education and American Council on Education.

Shute, V. J. (2008). Focus on formative feedback. *Review of Educational Research, 78*(1), 153–189. doi:10.3102/0034654307313795

Singley, M. K., & Bennett, R. E. (2002). Item generation and beyond: Applications of schema theory to mathematics assessment. In S. H. Irvine & P. C. Kyllonen (Eds.), *Item generation for test development* (pp. 361–384). Mahwah, NJ: Erlbaum.

Steeves, V. (2014). Young Canadians in a Wired World, Phase III: Life Online. Ottawa: MediaSmarts.

## KEY TERMS AND DEFINITIONS

**Automatic Item Generation:** A process of using item models to generate test items with the aid of computer technology.

**Cognitive Model:** A representation that highlights the knowledge, skills, and problem-solving processes students require to answer test items.

**Cosine Similarity Index:** A measure of similarity between two vectors of co-occurring texts computed using the cosine of the angle between the two vectors in a multidimensional space of unique words.

**Elements:** Variables in the item model that can be modified to create new test items.

**Formative Assessment Principles:** Includes any assessment-related activities that yield constant and specific feedback to modify teaching and improve learning—can include testing on-demand, providing students with instant feedback, permitting testing in different locations and at different times.

**Isomorphs:** Generated items produced from the same item model that appear similar to one another.

**Item Model:** A template, a mould, or a rendering that highlights the features in an item that must be manipulated to generate new items.

**Variants:** Generated items produced from the same item model that appear different from one another.

## ENDNOTE

[1] Rudner (2010) claimed that items created for high-stakes computerized exams using the current content specialist approach cost between $1,500-$2,500 USD *per item*. Comparable costs for low-stakes computerized exams, to our knowledge, have not been presented in the literature.

# Chapter 23
# Automated Scoring in Assessment Systems

**Michael B. Bunch**
*Measurement Incorporated, USA*

**David Vaughn**
*Measurement Incorporated, USA*

**Shayne Miel**
*LightSide Labs, USA*

## ABSTRACT

*Automated scoring of essays is founded upon the pioneer work of Dr. Ellis B. Page. His creation of Project Essay Grade (PEG) sparked the growth of a field that now includes universities and major corporations whose computer programs are capable of analyzing not only essays but short-answer responses to content-based questions. This chapter provides a brief history of automated scoring, describes in general terms how the programs work, outlines some of the current uses as well as challenges, and offers a glimpse of the future of automated scoring.*

## INTRODUCTION

Automated scoring of written essays and other types of student responses has been a dream of educators, educational assessment specialists, and computer scientists for over 50 years. Educators have looked for ways to teach more efficiently; assessment specialists have looked for objective ways to produce scores for examination types that have historically been considered quite subjective; and computer scientists have viewed automated scoring as a field ripe for exploiting the power of the computer. In this chapter, we explore the history of automated scoring and examine the development of systems before turning our attention to current applications and challenges. We conclude with a look to the future.

## A BRIEF HISTORY OF AUTOMATED SCORING

Automated scoring has a rich history, dating back to *Natural Language and the Computer*, edited

DOI: 10.4018/978-1-4666-9441-5.ch023

by Paul Garvin (1963). That book contained an overview and 16 essays on various aspects of solving natural language problems with high-speed computers. The tone of the book, as well as a clue to its application to automated essay scoring, is clearly expressed in the chapter by L. C. Ray (1963, p. 95):

*These new tools are important in research because they promise significant economies, especially in terms of time, in operations involving massive paperwork. They are equally important in that they can be utilized to carry out tasks that are not now being done because other means cannot accomplish the job or cannot do it in time for the results to be of use.*

Garvin's book was an outgrowth of the artificial intelligence (AI) movement sparked by British mathematician (and famed wartime codebreaker) Alan Turing. In the years following World War II, Turing and others turned their attention from the narrow task of codebreaking to the more general application of artificial intelligence to a host of problems. The transition from decoding secret messages to deconstructing and reconstructing prose was a natural one.

Although the term "automated essay scoring," or AES, did not appear formally in the research lexicon until Shermis & Burstein's 2003 publication of *Automated Essay Scoring: A Cross-Disciplinary Perspective*, the computer scoring of student essays traces its origins to the pioneering work of Ellis Batten Page (1924–2005). Page, widely acknowledged as the father of automated essay scoring, was a pioneer in the application of the computer to the scoring of student essays. His focus was specifically on writing quality, as opposed to correctness of content (e.g., the communicative effectiveness of a five-paragraph essay as opposed to the historical accuracy of an exposition on the Treaty of Ghent). Page (1966) reported on an early effort to understand how human graders applied evaluation criteria to student essays and to recreate those criteria in a computer program. That program, Project Essay Grade, or PEG®, was designed to score student essays using mainframe computers in the 1960s.

Dr. Page and his colleagues coined two new terms: *trin* and *prox*. A trin is an intrinsic characteristic of writing, such as diction or style. A prox is a quantifiable approximation of that intrinsic characteristic. For example, a prox for diction might be the proportion of words in a fifth grader's essay found on word lists for sixth grade and above. A prox for style might be the number of times the word "because" appears in an essay, as such words are proxies for complex sentences with subordinate clauses. These terms have since been replaced by "features," and there is no practical distinction between intrinsic and objectified features.

In their initial experiment, the PEG team had four human judges (English teachers) read 276 essays written by high school students. Dr. Page and his colleagues then translated several trins into 31 proxes—predictors of overall essay quality. All essays were keypunched, and PEG calculated their scores on the 31 proxes and then correlated those scores with the overall quality scores assigned by human judges. The multiple R for the initial run was .71, with shrinkage to .65. PEG had produced total score estimates that correlated with scores assigned by humans about as well as individual human graders' scores correlated with one another. Documenting PEG's early and somewhat startling results, Page wrote, "The results of our first data run, read at 11 p.m. one night last May, were truly stunning, so much so that my colleagues and I spent the next hours in champagne and excited talk" (Page, 1966, p. 241).

Although the experiment was a huge success, it left the team with some questions.

1.  What about input? Who is going to transcribe all those handwritten essays?
2.  What about the gifted student who is offbeat and original?

3. Shouldn't we instead begin with easier matters like punctuation and grammar?
4. What about content (like history or science)?
5. Won't this grading system be easy to con?
6. Shouldn't this focus on correction rather than grading?
7. Isn't this just one more step in the mechanization of modern life?

Page solved the grading problem with the tools available to him as an English teacher turned psychometrician; namely, a deep understanding of the intrinsic qualities of good writing (*trins*) and the ability to translate those qualities into objective units (*proxes*) to which the power of multiple regression could be applied. Page continued his research on PEG through the end of the 1990s and began to search for an outlet for its commercial exploitation. In 2002, he approached Measurement Incorporated (MI), a company with an established record of handscoring essays, and completed the sale of PEG to MI by the end of 2003. MI continued to refine and engineer PEG to meet the demands of 21st century assessments.

Others solved the problem with different tools and methods, most notably, latent semantic analysis (Landauer, Foltz, & Laham, 1998), natural language processing (Burstein, 2003), neural networks (cf. Burstein et al., 1998), and Bayesian approaches (cf. Rudner & Liang, 2002). By the turn of the 21st century, there were several computer programs designed specifically to apply one of these systems to evaluating essays.

Valenti, Neri, & Cucchiarelli (2003) analyzed 10 such programs. These programs could be classified into four primary categories plus a hybrid category:

- **Multiple Regression:** PEG.
- **Natural Language Processing:** Educational Testing Service I, Automark, Schema Extract Analyze and Report (SEAR), Paperless School Free-Text Marking Engine (PS-ME), Conceptual Rater (C-Rater).
- **Bayesian:** Bayesian Essay Test Scoring sYstem (BETSY).
- **Neural Networks:** Intelligent Essay Marking System (IEMS).
- **Hybrids:** Intelligent Essay Assessor (IEA) (latent semantic analysis and natural language processing), E-Rater (multiple regression and natural language processing).

Each program had its strengths and weakness. Some were quite general in their applications, while others were designed for more narrowly defined purposes. C-Rater and Automark, for example, focused specifically on correct response to short-answer questions. Some had been commercialized, and others had not.

By the time Valenti et al. (2003) published their paper, technological advances had just about caught up with the vision of automated scoring. With the advent of personal computers in the early 1980s and the emergence of graphical user interfaces and word processing applications, question #1 above (What about input?) was becoming moot—students could now enter their own essays, so there was no need to transcribe or keypunch anything. The rest of the questions were close to solution, but #7 (mechanization), more philosophical than empirical, will never be subject to scientific methods.

As the notion of automated scoring gained momentum, product vendors and educational assessment companies joined the pursuit of scoring student essays, notably Educational Testing Service (ETS), Measurement Incorporated (MI), Pearson, Vantage Learning, and others. In each instance, the goal of programmers was to create a program that would read and score student essays as reliably as human judges could. MI, for example, modified PEG extensively; in fact, by

2010, PEG no longer fit neatly into the multiple regression category, but was more of a hybrid.

In 2012, the William and Flora Hewlett Foundation sponsored an event to which all vendors of automated scoring programs were invited (Morgan, Shermis, Van Deventer, & Vander Ark, n.d.). The competition consisted of a set of student essays spanning multiple grades and genres. The goal was to score those essays by computer as reliably as human scorers had done. In a second round of the competition, student responses to short-answer, content-based questions were introduced, and the objective was the same—to score them as reliably as human judges could. The results were somewhat surprising, indicating the potential of automated scoring.

The Hewlett Foundation invited nine vendors of automated scoring of student essays (eight companies and one university) to participate in the first phase of the Automated Scoring Assessment Prize (ASAP) competition. The competition included essays written to eight different prompts by students in various grade levels. Each essay had been scored by two professionally trained judges. Their scores were used to "train" the automated scoring programs. All such programs "learn" by reading digitally entered essays and their associated scores and by drawing conclusions about how essay content leads to a given score.

After providing sample essays for vendors to train their programs, the Hewlett Foundation sent 4,000 more essays for the vendors to score within three days. Dr. Mark Shermis, a recognized authority on automated essay scoring, then checked the work of each vendor, comparing their results to scores previously given to the same essays by trained (human) judges. He also computed agreement indices for pairs of human judges.

The agreement index the ASAP competition used (quadratic weighted kappa or QWK) was more stringent than simple agreement in that it did not give credit for chance agreement. For example, on a four-point scale, it would be possible to agree one-fourth of the time by chance. The QWK index has been used for the past 50 years and is well documented. After computing an agreement index for each of the eight essay prompts for each vendor, it is also possible to average over all eight prompts to produce a single score for each vendor. The results are shown in Figure 1.

Measurement Incorporated's PEG achieved the highest agreement index, as Figure 1 shows. In addition, five programs (PEG and those for vendors A–D) had higher agreement indices than human judges had with one another (as shown by the dashed line at .75). The dashed line near the bottom of the graph shows the agreement that could be achieved simply by estimating each essay's score based on the number of words it contained (word count).

Phase 1 included a public competition for independent researchers willing to share their open-source solutions. This segment of the competition awarded a total of $100,000 in prizes. The first-place team (winners of the $60,000 prize) consisted of Stephan Henß, Jason Tigg, and Momchil Georgiev, none of whom had a background in education or English (Morgan et al., n.d.).

Phase 2 of the competition focused on short-answer responses of about 150 words. Student responses were drawn from three different state testing programs across three grade levels (7, 8, and 10) and a range of subjects (English, general science, and biology). Different scoring criteria had been used in arriving at the original scores. The rules for the competitors were the same as in Phase 1, with quadratic weighted kappa agreement between the competitor's scores and the original scores as the criterion.

One hundred and fifty teams competed in Phase 2. Measurement Incorporated joined forces with the third-place winner of the Phase 1 open-source competition and outperformed all other teams. Four individuals and one team shared $100,000 in prize money. Measurement Incorporated, as a closed-source vendor, was not eligible for prize money.

*Figure 1. Results of ASAP phase 1: commercial vendors*

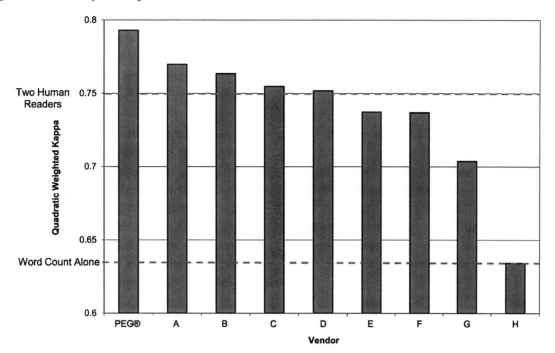

The ASAP competition represents the first time these widely used programs have been compared to one another under controlled, objectively refereed conditions. The results demonstrate conclusively the viability of automated scoring.

## The Members of the Winning Team of ASAP

As more and more large-scale assessments have moved online, automated scoring has become less of an academic curiosity and more of an economic necessity. Understandably, competitors in the ASAP competition, as well as others in the assessment field, have come forward to meet the demand. The Partnership for Assessment of Readiness for College and Careers (PARCC) and the Smarter Balanced Assessment Consortium (Smarter Balanced) have created open-ended test items that they plan to have scored by computer. The Smarter Balanced proposal, for example, calls

for computer scoring of extended constructed-response (ECR) items and performance tasks (PTs) with 10% teacher read-behind within two weeks (Smarter Balanced Assessment Consortium, 2010). Smarter Balanced conducted pilot tests in association with the 2014 field test to determine which constructed-response items could be scored by computer, and the results were encouraging enough to continue to consider automated scoring for 2015 and beyond.

Today, there are more than a dozen corporations and institutions offering automated scoring on a commercial basis. The field has matured in much the same way that machine scoring of multiple-choice test items did between 1959 and 1989. Automated scoring is big business. As such, it is guided by commercial objectives: grow, improve, and serve a larger audience. To meet these objectives, automated scoring requires systems.

As these systems have proliferated, the need for objective evaluation of their effectiveness has become increasingly apparent. Williamson, Xi, and Breyer (2012) provided a set of simple and logical criteria. Using scores assigned by human readers as the standard by which all automated scores would be judged, Williamson et al. (2012) offered these guidelines:

- Quadratic weighted kappa: minimum value of .70.
- Difference between human-machine kappa and human-human kappa: maximum value of .10.
- Standardized mean difference between human-based scores and machine-based scores: maximum value of .15.

The choice of .70 for QWK corresponds to the expectation that score sets correlate .70 or higher (though QWK and correlation are acknowledged not to be the same thing), approximating 50% shared variance. Williamson et al. (2012) referred to the difference between human-human QWK and human-machine QWK as degradation. Even if the machine scoring achieves a QWK of .70, the model would be considered flawed if human-human QWK exceeded that value by .10. In other words, agreement is a relative term, and if humans can apply a scoring rubric reliably, a machine should be able to learn to apply the same rubric nearly as well. A difference of .10 in terms of QWK is considerable. Finally, agreement should not be the only criterion. Scores should have roughly the same mean. Perfect correlations are possible even when there are mean shifts. It is possible to have fairly high values of QWK and still have significant mean shifts. Therefore, Williamson et al. (2012) established the .15 standardized mean difference as a mechanism for flagging scoring algorithms that systematically assign scores that are significantly higher or lower overall than those assigned by humans. These criteria have proved quite useful and are being employed currently in work being performed for the Smarter Balanced Assessment Consortium in the evaluation of scoring models for short-answer and extended-response items.

## Development of an Automated Scoring System

As noted in the previous section, there are many different ways to build automated assessment systems. Early automated scoring systems used standard linear regression to "read" surface features of key-entered text such as word length, sentence length, vocabulary, and other quantifiable features and compare those features to scores assigned by human judges. The latest systems now measure incredibly large numbers of features, both surface and complex, and employ a range of linear and non-linear algorithms to correlate those features with scores. Given enough scored sample texts, automated scoring systems can discover relationships between features and scores and predict scores of subsequent texts with similar features. The more texts sampled, the more precise the prediction can be. As with other prediction systems, of course, the increase in precision will never reach perfection, short of inclusion of every text to be scored, which would defeat the purpose of automated scoring.

Critical to this prediction process are the consistency and accuracy of the scores provided by the human judges. The data for training scoring programs must be an accurate representation of both the skill range and variety of student responses in the general population. This section focuses on the following key aspects:

- **Model Building:** Representations, feature generation, dimensionality reduction, learning, and ensembling.
- **Evaluation Metric:** Method for defining scoring accuracy.
- **Integration with Scoring System:** Making the automated scoring program

perform in a way that facilitates interoperability with a variety of computer-based testing components.

The process is described primarily from the point of view of PEG, but the steps described may be generalized to most automated scoring programs.

*Model building.* Page's insight, which sparked the field of automated essay scoring, was that there are certain features of a written text that can be measured by a computer and which can serve as indicators of the quality of that text (Page, 1966). Page's original formulation of PEG measured only 31 features and has been criticized for dealing only with surface features of the text (Ben-Simon & Bennett, 2007). PEG also used standard linear regression, which cannot provide a good fit for the sort of non-linear features sometimes found in writing.

There has been a great deal of research done over the past few decades in the fields of natural language processing, text analytics, and machine learning. It is now possible for researchers to introduce new algorithms and techniques quickly and easily, ensuring that the system is able to stay at the cutting edge of automated scoring technology. If a new component does not increase the accuracy with which the model scores student responses and predicts human scores, it is automatically excluded from the final model. This self-correcting feature highlights the philosophy that the authority on whether a particular piece of writing embodies the writing construct being measured resides with the human scoring experts and rubric creators, rather than with the engineers of any particular piece of technology.

PEG's approach to measuring the writing construct begins with the assumption that the goal of the model-building process is to generate an algorithm (or model) that faithfully mimics the scoring done by the expert human judges who scored the training set. Rather than try to identify ahead of time the optimal features to measure

and algorithms to use in correlating scores with features, automated scoring engines allow the data to drive the process, automatically finding those features and algorithms that best minimize the error rate on the training data. In order to jumpstart the process, PEG linguists and engineers have worked together to create thousands of handcrafted features. These features measure the elements of writing that expert judges and teachers look for when scoring student responses, as well as those elements of the text that researchers have found commonly correlate with high- and low-scoring responses.

This extrinsic feature set is then extended with a vast set of intrinsic features that can be automatically extracted from the training set corpus. These are created in a number of ways, but some of the commonly used methods involve n-grams of characters, words, parts of speech, and phrases; similarity measures; and various matrix manipulations on the underlying intrinsic and extrinsic features.

If these features correlate with the scores given by the expert human judges, then they can be encoded into the model without being directly observed by the researchers. In many cases it would not be possible to observe them explicitly, because they are too complex.

These concepts are fairly commonplace for researchers in the machine learning community. They are the same tools used to route mail, recommend movies on Netflix, and detect cancer. However, to researchers in the field of education, they may seem like a black box. What follows is a simplified explanation of some of these concepts, in hopes of fostering understanding and shining a little light inside the box. While the example is based on PEG, most of the features described are common to all or most automated scoring programs.

When designing PEG's modular structure, it has been helpful to divide these concepts into six broad categories: representations, features, local aggregates, dimensionality reduction, learners, and ensembles. Note that the examples listed in the categories below are meant to give a sense of the category, rather than provide an exhaustive list of what is happening inside the PEG engine or any other automated scoring program.

- **Representation:** A representation is simply a transformed version of a student response to a test item. Some simple examples of representations that PEG has used include a spell-corrected version of the response, or the response transformed to lowercase with common words removed. More complex transformations borrowed from the field of computational linguistics, such as those involving word frequencies and dependency parsing, are also implemented as needed.

- **Feature:** As discussed above, a feature is any element of a response that can be measured with a numeric value. These can range from very simple (i.e., surface features) to very complex linguistic features. Some examples from PEG include length of the response, the average number of sentences per paragraph, where the student has made errors, the number of times a particular phrase occurs (e.g., "Brooklyn Bomber" in an essay about Babe Ruth), the response's rank in the list of responses returned from a search of the most frequent non-trivial words in the training set, and so on. Any given feature can be measured on multiple representations of the response, giving rise to multiple features. In addition, features can be combined with other features using nonlinear transformations that give rise to new features that can be even more predictive than the sum of their parts.

- **Local Aggregates:** A local aggregate is a structure used to collect meaningful statistics about a set of responses. It is often useful to measure something about a response

in comparison to the other responses in the training set. For instance, one could measure a response's deviation from the average response length, using the global average of all responses to all questions. But it may be more informative to measure, for a particular response, its deviation from the average length of only the other responses to that particular question. In order to measure that feature, PEG must first compute statistics about the mean and standard deviation of the response lengths in the training set for that question. That information is stored in a local aggregate. Some other examples of local aggregates include the list of all non-trivial words in the training set, the list of the top-10 occurring proper noun sequences in the training set, and so on.

- **Dimensionality Reduction:** Due to either the computational complexity or the nature of the algorithm, some of PEG's prediction methods perform poorly when the feature space is massive. In order to reduce that space, PEG has a number of dimensionality-reduction algorithms that can perform feature selection and/or feature extraction on the data. Feature selection is the process of choosing a subset of features in order to optimize a particular constraint. PEG generally tries to find the features that prove most useful in predicting the score. Feature extraction is the process of performing transformations on the feature space (e.g., matrix operations) in order to reduce the size. This creates a new set of implicit features that are functions of the original features. Principal component analysis (PCA) and random indexing (RI) are but two examples of dimensionality reduction algorithms. In addition to reducing the complexity of the feature space, these methods can also be viewed as a means of filtering out noise from the data.

- **Learner:** Also called hypothesis, classifier, or regressor, a learner is an algorithm that takes as input a set of features for all of the responses in the training data and infers a function (i.e., a formula) that predicts the most likely score for a response, given its features. Common examples include linear regression, decision trees, and artificial neural networks. Most learning algorithms have several parameters that need to be adjusted (e.g., maximum allowable decision tree depth). These are commonly referred to as *hyper-parameters*. When searching for the best predictive model, PEG will optimize over a large space of possible learner and hyper-parameter combinations.

- **Ensemble:** An ensemble is similar to a learner, except that it takes as input multiple score predictions (i.e., the outputs of multiple learners) and combines them to produce a single, final score prediction. This is roughly analogous to a committee of judges suggesting scores for a response so that an authoritative final score can be determined by averaging over all the judges. Machine learning research has shown that building a model that blends predictions in this way consistently outperforms any of the individual prediction models (Rokach, 2010). Analogous to learners, ensembles can take zero or more hyper-parameters (i.e., parameter families or sets).

*Evaluation metric.* Also called the objective, error, or cost function, the evaluation metric is the formula that an automated scoring program is trying to minimize or maximize when building a model. PEG searches over all of the combinations of representations, features, local aggregates, dimensionality-reduction algorithms, learners, and ensembles and attempts to find the particular combination that predicts scores that are close to the scores given in the training data (i.e., those supplied by human judges and considered to be

"true" scores). The measure of how close the predictions are to the true scores is called the metric. Some common examples of metrics include Cohen's kappa (in its various forms, including quadratic weighted kappa), Pearson's r, perfect/adjacent agreement, and so on. While certain learners may use a particular objective function (for instance, linear regression algorithms often use mean squared error), when PEG is making decisions between models, it will use the metric supplied. This is the self-correcting nature of the system alluded to earlier. If a particular component does not lead to a model that scores well with the given metric, it will be discarded from the model-building process.

PEG takes all of these components, the best algorithm generated by the learners and ensembles, as well as the representations, features, local aggregates, and dimensionality-reduction algorithms used to transform a response into a score, and stores them in a model. Once the model has been saved, new responses can be run through the model to generate a score for that response. While model-building is a lengthy process, taking anywhere from 2 to 24 hours, depending on the average length of the response and the number of samples in the training data, using the model to produce a score on a new response is relatively quick, on the order of minutes or seconds. When being used in a formative context, PEG generally operates with a reduced set of the aforementioned components, so that response times can remain at only a few seconds. This constraint is merely a logistical one, however, put in place to ensure that students are able to receive feedback quickly.

PEG's data-driven approach lends itself equally well to many different item types. The resulting models might look very different, but the PEG engine can learn to score anything from multi-page essays with trait-based rubrics all the way down to single-word answers, regardless of the subject matter. In order to build a model that can score the content of what was written (i.e., how well the student's response answers a particular question or prompt), PEG simply needs a training set that has been scored for the construct being tested. Likewise, to build a model that will score for style, organization, mechanics, etc., a training set that has been scored for each trait is required. PEG has performed equally well on both source-based and non-sourced items in subject matters as diverse as reading comprehension, writing, mathematics, and science.

In the same way that *what* PEG can score is driven by the construct being measured in the human-scored training data, *how well* PEG can score is also heavily dependent on the quality of the training data. It is important that the training set be representative of the testing population, be reliably scored by human judges, and provide good coverage of the answer space to the item. Because proper coverage of the answer space is dependent on the complexity of the item, it is difficult to provide a general recommendation for the required size of the training set, although it is always the case that more training data will lead to more accurate models. Also, as with training of human readers, it is helpful to have a good mix of clear examples of each score point as well as examples of borderline responses.

Complexity of the test item can also have an effect on the reliability of the human scores on the training data, as measured through inter-rater reliability. Therefore, the success of a PEG model may best be measured by its ability to meet or exceed the human inter-rater reliability (within a certain threshold such as those defined above; e.g., QWK equal to or greater than .75). When developing test items to be scored, a good rule of thumb is that if it is difficult for humans to score, it will be difficult for computers to score as well.

*Integration with scoring system.* Typical automated scoring systems are parts of larger systems that include test administration, objective (e.g., multiple-choice) scoring, information management, and score reporting routines. Moreover, data moving into and out of the larger system may take on a variety of forms and formats. The automated scoring portion of the system must therefore be capable of taking in data from several sources, producing score metrics that are compatible with reporting routines, and directing scores to a variety of reporting programs. Thus, the architecture of the automated system is of necessity driven in large measure by the larger goals of the full system. Specifying all the features of the full system, and the role of the automated scoring program within it, are necessary first steps. PEG interacts with a variety of other programs in both in-house and commercial applications, some of which are described in the next section.

## Current Applications

While the viability of automated scoring has been established for high-stakes summative assessments, its greatest utility may be in interim and formative assessments. For the teaching of writing in particular, automated scoring presents an opportunity for teachers to make multiple writing assignments that are scored by computer, with scores and annotations added to student portfolios. Here, we return to Page's (1966) questions 2–6:

2. What about the gifted student who is offbeat and original?
3. Shouldn't we instead begin with easier matters like punctuation and grammar?
4. What about content (like history or science)?
5. Won't this grading system be easy to con?
6. Shouldn't this focus on correction rather than grading?

*Gifted students (question 2).* Gifted students often think and write outside the box. Their inspired essays may not have the same characteristics as more pedestrian essays that follow all the rules. This particular question does not seem to have attracted a great deal of attention. To date, research has focused on the general population, which contains a handful of truly gifted writers who may or may not follow the same rules as everyone else. What is needed is a study specifically of gifted writers. What characterizes their writing? Is all of it good, or can gifted writers also produce rubbish, just like everyone else? The likely outcome of such research would be a subset of specific rules for an automated scoring system to apply when certain criteria are met; that is, a branch off the main program triggered by the presence of certain key features that characterize essays by gifted writers, if those features exist.

*Punctuation and grammar/correction (questions 3 and 6).* Automated essay scoring has come a long way since 1966. Virtually every computer with a word processor has spell-check and grammar-check. Students in school today are generally oblivious to the fact that these features have not always been there. But these tools didn't just appear; they are the result of the pioneering work done by Page and others in the 1960s, 1970s, and 1980s, and they operate on the same principles that Page and others expounded.

Applied to the larger effort of essay scoring, however, punctuation and grammar checkers are now incorporated into student feedback and instruction. PEG Writing, for example, highlights misspelled words and grammar errors. Moreover, the PEG scores and highlighting can be programmatically linked to exercises designed to help students develop greater spelling and grammatical skills. Thus, a student receives not only an overall evaluation of the essay just submitted but an opportunity to study his or her mistakes (not only in grammar and spelling but in syntax, word choice, and other features of good writing), review helpful resources, and try again.

It is at this juncture that Dr. Page's vision of the computer as teaching assistant has been most fully realized. Using PEG Writing as an example, let us look in on a fairly brief encounter and follow-up of a sixth-grade student working on an essay assignment. This particular assignment is based in the Common Core State Standards, so it is writing in response to reading. Specifically, the student is

to read one or more texts and then write an essay that extends, evaluates, or synthesizes the text(s) just read. The scenario unfolds as follows:

1. The student reads stimulus text(s) online.
2. The student logs into a writing practice site and constructs an outline.
3. The student moves to the writing site, drafts an essay, and submits it for scoring.
4. PEG Writing scores the essay on six traits of writing (Organization, Development, Language/Style, Conventions, Word Choice, and Sentence Structure) and provides feedback on grammar and spelling.
5. The student reads the feedback, checks the trait scores, and clicks on one of the suggested tutorials.
6. The student completes the tutorial, clicks back to the writing site, revises the original essay, and submits it.
7. The student invites fellow students to review the revised essay.
8. Other students review the essay and provide feedback.
9. The student reviews feedback from fellow students, completes another tutorial, and revises the essay one more time, submitting it for PEG scoring and teacher review.
10. The teacher reviews the trait scores and spelling and grammar feedback and then provides additional feedback to the student.

Steps 5–8 could be repeated any number of times, and the teacher could become involved at any step. The net result, however, is that the student gets to write and revise numerous times, obtain quick and focused feedback, and grow as a writer in the process. This was Ellis Page's original goal. In this genuinely formative context, the stakes are low and there is no incentive to con the system.

*Scoring for content (question 4).* The second ASAP competition focused on short-answer questions. These were short responses to a content-based prompt or question, and for the 5,100 responses in the test set, which was used to compare teams, they averaged 42 words in length, with a standard deviation of 26 words (Morgan et al., n.d.). While the computer programs failed to reach the level of agreement that two human judges reached, they came very close for most items. Specifically, the winning program achieved a quadratic weighted kappa of about .78, while the (expert) human judges achieved a kappa coefficient closer to .89. While interpretation of quadratic weighted kappa is subjective, in general anything over 0.75 is considered to be excellent agreement (Fleiss, Levin, & Paik, 2013). In acknowledging this result, Morgan et al. (n.d.) suggested that machine scores could be used as a supplement to human scores in situations requiring second readings to assure score reliability.

Since the ASAP competition, automated scoring of content has continued to improve. Both Smarter Balanced and PARCC have included short-answer items in their interim and summative assessments, administered operationally for the first time in spring 2015. In the summer of 2013, Smarter Balanced conducted a pilot test of several thousand items, including short-answer items in mathematics (equations) and English language arts (McGraw-Hill Education, 2014). Machine-human agreement (in terms of QWK) was comparable to that of human-human. Results for these short-answer items are shown in Table 1 (summarized from Table 5.2 of that report).

*Table 1.*

|  | **English Language Arts** | **Mathematics** |
|---|---|---|
| Items Evaluated | 343 | 56 |
| QWK > .70 for Human-Human | 241 | 44 |
| QWK > .70 for Machine-Human | 269 | 46 |

Liu et al. (2014) performed an extended study of the effectiveness of ETS's c-rater for scoring science content. They examined scoring for four specific science short-answer items posing the following questions (p. 21):

1. Can holistic scoring rubrics be transformed to concept-based analytic scoring rubrics for automated scoring?
2. Can concept-based automated scoring accurately score science explanation items with rubrics representing multiple levels of understanding?
3. What are the main sources of disagreement in developing automated scores for explanation items?

Their findings were somewhat less encouraging than those of the second ASAP Competition:

- None of the four items produced a QWK of .70 (values ranged from .46 to .64).
- Two of the items had QWK values within .10 of the human-human QWK values (differences ranged from .09 to .41).
- Two of the items met the standardized mean difference criterion of .15.

A primary difference between the Liu et al. (2014) study and the second ASAP Competition results was that the latter permitted tweaking of systems to maximize QWK, while c-rater followed fixed rules with limited numbers of variables. The answer to question 4, therefore, appears to be that it depends on the content being assessed and the flexibility of the model-building paradigm.

*Conning the system (question 5).* On learning of the results of the first ASAP competition, Massachusetts Institute of Technology (MIT) Professor Les Perlman famously lambasted automated scoring systems for favoring the complex over the simple and for failing to recognize gibberish.

He submitted several essays with significant portions omitted or obfuscated to ETS's e-rater and received consistently high scores for papers he would have given failing scores (Winerip, 2012). Consider the following:

*In the Middle Ages, the University of Paris grew because it provided comfortable accommodations for each of its students, large rooms with servants and legs of mutton. Although they are expensive, these rooms are necessary to learning. The second reason for the five-paragraph theme is that it makes you focus on a single topic.*

There is more, but this should suffice. Professor Perlman has discovered a weak spot in the automated scoring system and has exploited it to the amazement and amusement of countless online followers.

Most students in elementary, middle, or high school, and likely in college, are hardly as skilled at writing as a college English professor would be. And frankly, it takes quite a bit of skill to write the kind of gibberish Professor Perlman produced for e-rater to score. Therefore, the probability of such an occurrence is considered rather low, but that does not mean it is trivial. Nevertheless, automated scoring programs have to assume "good faith" and some degree of motivation on the part of the author. A "good faith" essay is one that reflects the writer's best efforts to respond to the assignment and the prompt without trickery or deceit. A "motivated" writer is one who genuinely wants to do well and for whom the assignment has some consequence (a grade, a factor in admissions or hiring, etc.).

PEG currently conducts screening for a variety of anomalies, including excessively short responses, excessive repetition (such as a paragraph copied and pasted several times), repeated use of vulgarities, and excessive misspellings. In addition, PEG can conduct off-topic detection, but this requires training for each item. Other screening that is underway includes all capital letters, many non-ASCII characters, too many proper nouns, plagiarism, "kitten on the keys" (words like "asdfjkl" and "sdakfdask"), abuse, and refusal.

## Specific Applications: Summative Assessments

Since 2009, the Utah State Office of Education has successfully used PEG as the sole scoring method on the statewide summative Direct Writing Assessment in Grades 5 and 8. PEG has scored 344,000 student responses on Utah's six-trait rubric. PEG was also used in 2013 as the second reader on the Connecticut SBAC Aligned Practice Assessment (APA), providing scores for 90,000 student responses.

PEG is also being used in several pilot and field testing applications of automated scoring, including the Australian Curriculum, Assessment and Reporting Authority's pilot program to score their yearly NAPLAN assessment, in addition to the Smarter Balanced field test described above.

## Specific Applications: Formative Assessments

PEG has also been used to provide tens of millions of scores to students in formative writing assessments, via the PEG Writing family of practice sites, with over three million essays scored in the last year alone. In addition to providing real-time scores, PEG also adds value when used in a formative context by providing response-specific feedback to the students on the grammar and spelling errors found in their essays, as well as offering targeted instructional feedback on how to improve their writing skills. In order to facilitate the automated flagging of grammar and spelling errors, MI has developed a custom computer language, similar to regular expressions, that allows our linguists to easily write and test rules that look for complex syntactic patterns in the student response.

PEG is in widespread use as an automated scoring engine for formative writing practice websites, including Educational Records Bureau's Writing Practice Program (WPP), Utah State Office of Education's Utah Compose, North Carolina's NC Write, Learning Express Advantage, and PEG Writing.

## Challenges

A critical challenge actually emerges from the recent successes of computer scoring when compared to human scoring. In the head-to-head competitions, the single criterion of success has been reliability, as measured (most often) by quadratic weighted kappa. Scoring programs are being adjusted to maximize kappa, sometimes at the expense of explanatory power. In short, reliability is trumping validity. We have gotten better and better at replicating scores of humans, but we can't always explain what the scores mean. Replicating scores of human judges is not enough; developers of automated scoring programs need to pay more attention to a theory of action underlying the scores.

Automated writing evaluation, as an extension of machine learning and natural language processing into the educational realm, is well established as an assessment tool. Its use in an instructional context, however, presents particular challenges for the industry. Numerical scores as feedback are useful to students in the sense that they provide a target toward which the student can strive in every submission and revision of an essay. The current level of targeted, non-score feedback that is given does not yet approach the kind of feedback offered by an attentive teacher. This, like many challenges in machine learning, is partially one of data collection—given the appropriate data about what types of feedback teachers would give to a set of responses, it should be possible to build systems that can learn when and how to offer that feedback.

For a similar reason, being able to score content-based items in a formative setting presents a challenge for the industry. As Common Core moves us toward content-based essay rubrics and source-based items, it becomes difficult to build models that generalize across tasks. As noted above, in order to build a model for a content-based item, PEG requires a training set that has been scored for that item. Unless the item is being used in a high-volume setting, as is usually the case in summative scoring, the cost of collecting sufficient training data can outweigh any cost savings made available by automated scoring. In a formative context, items are often administered on a per-class basis, making it difficult to build enough demand for any one item. Research is now underway that will involve teachers in the creation of training data for the items they wish to use, so that we can still offer formative scoring at a reasonable price.

The real benefit of automated writing evaluation in an instructional context will not be realized until these systems can move beyond the kind of feedback that a teacher would give when grading a stack of papers, and instead offer the students a rich interactive environment that gently guides them toward improvement, as a teacher might in a one-on-one setting. In order to do this, our systems will have to learn as they go, adding another layer of complexity.

## The Future of Automated Scoring

The future of automated scoring seems secure. In fact, the work of the past 50 years seems merely a prelude to the real advances to come. Major corporations have commercialized automated scoring, the ASAP competition has legitimized it, and the adoption by both PARCC and Smarter Balanced has institutionalized it. Automated scoring has emerged from the laboratory and is in full view of the educational community, if not the whole world.

Most of Ellis Page's (1966) questions have been answered or are being addressed. Students have nearly universal access to computers with which to enter their essays. Computer programs provide feedback for both evaluation and instruction, for content, and for style. Automated scoring is now fully integrated with online instruction. Work on identifying bad faith compositions is underway. The two major assessment consortia are poised to use automated scoring of interim and summative assessments in the 2014–15 school year.

In the beginning, the primary challenges to automated scoring were technological. As technology has advanced rapidly over the past 50 years, the challenges for the future are practical, logistical, social, and even political. Indeed, the most pressing challenges seem to be rejection of computer-generated scores, which may be indistinguishable from scores conferred by humans, simply because they are computer generated. Many people strongly object to computer scoring of essays simply because the computer is not human.

The recording industry has faced a similar challenge for more than a hundred years. No matter how good recording became or how faithfully it reproduced the sound of the human voice (or instruments played by humans), people objected, simply because it was not human. An iconic set of television ads in the 1980s asked, "Is it live, or is it Memorex?" Today, having moved from cylinders to wax to vinyl to 8-track to mini-cassette to CDs to MP3 formats and beyond, few people care whether the sound they are hearing is live or a recording. They don't care because they know they can listen to their music in some form wherever they go. They can't do that with live music. Convenience, cost, and fidelity have won.

In the same way, we will eventually embrace automated scoring of essays, not because automated scoring is so superior to human scoring but because it can provide instantaneous and reliable scores. Humans can't do that. Or if they could, it would be terribly expensive to do so. Once again, convenience, cost, and fidelity will win.

As the field of automated writing evaluation continues to evolve, it is important for both researchers and practitioners to remember that the goal of automated scoring is not to replace teachers, but to assist them. When calculators were invented, replacing tedious long-hand arithmetic with the press of a few buttons, engineers did not lose their jobs *en masse*. Instead, their field flourished, and they were free to spend their time on higher level cognitive tasks. Likewise, as machine learning has risen to the challenge of detecting cancer from a patient's medical data (Cruz & Wishart, 2007), physicians are able to spend more time on their core mission of treating the patients. Nobody cares whether the cancer detection algorithm is doing the same thing the doctor does when she diagnoses a patient. Of course it doesn't. All that matters in this situation is whether the algorithm is making a correct diagnosis. For teachers and those invested in the education of children, the core mission is not assessment. Automated scoring and feedback can be a tool that allows teachers to do what they do best: teach.

## REFERENCES

Ben-Simon, A., & Bennett, R. E. (2007). Toward More Substantively Meaningful Automated Essay Scoring. *Journal of Technology, Learning, and Assessment, 6*(1). Retrieved from http://files.eric.ed.gov/fulltext/EJ838611.pdf

Burstein, J. (2003). The E-rater(R) Scoring Engine: Automated Essay Scoring with Natural Language Processing. In M. D. Shermis & J. Burstein (Eds.), *Automated Essay Scoring: A Cross-Disciplinary Perspective* (pp. 113–122). Mahwah, NJ: Lawrence Erlbaum Associates.

Burstein, J., Braden-Harder, L., Chodorow, M., Hua, S., Kaplan, B., Kukich, K., & Wolff, S. (1998). *Computer Analysis of Essay Content for Automated Score Prediction: A Prototype Automated Scoring System for GMAT Analytical Writing Assessment Essays. Research Bulletin RR-98-15*. Princeton, NJ: Educational Testing Service.

Cruz, J. A., & Wishart, D. S. (2007). Applications of machine learning in cancer prediction and prognosis. *Cancer Informatics*, 2, 59–67. PMID:19458758

Fleiss, J. L., Levin, B., & Paik, M. C. (2013). *Statistical methods for rates and proportions.* John Wiley & Sons.

Garvin, P. L. (1963). *Natural Language and the Computer.* New York: McGraw-Hill.

Landauer, T. K., Foltz, P. W., & Laham, D. (1998). Introduction to Latent Semantic Analysis. *Discourse Processes*, 25(2-3), 259–284. doi:10.1080/01638539809545028

Liu, O. L., Brew, C., Blackmore, J., Gerard, L., Madhok, J., & Linn, M. C. (2014). Automated scoring of constructed-response science items: Prospects and obstacles. *Educational Measurement: Issues and Practice*, 33(2), 19–28. doi:10.1111/emip.12028

McGraw-Hill Education. (2014). *Smarter Balanced Pilot Automated Scoring Research Studies.* Olympia, WA: Smarter Balanced.

Morgan, J., Shermis, M. D., Van Deventer, L., & Vander Ark, T. (n.d.). *Automated Student Assessment Prize: Phase 1 & Phase 2: A Case Study to Promote Focused Innovation in Student Writing Assessment.* Retrieved 9/1/14 from http://gettingsmart.com/wp-content/uploads/2013/02/ASAP-Case-Study-FINAL.pdf

Page, E. B. (1966). The imminence of…grading essays by computer. *Phi Delta Kappan*, 47(2), 238–243.

Ray, L. C. (1963). Programming for natural language. In P. L. Garvin (Ed.), *Natural Language and the Computer.* New York: McGraw-Hill.

Rokach, L. (2010). Ensemble-based classifiers. *Artificial Intelligence Review*, 33(1–2), 1–39. doi:10.1007/s10462-009-9124-7

Rudner, L., & Liang, T. (2002). Automated essay scoring using Bayes' theorem. *The Journal of Technology, Learning, and Assessment*, 1(2), 1–21.

Shermis, M. D., & Burstein, J. (Eds.). (2003). *Automated Essay Scoring: A Cross-Disciplinary Perspective.* Mahwah, NJ: Lawrence Erlbaum Associates.

Smarter Balanced Assessment Consortium. (2010). *Race to the Top Assessment Program Application for New Grants: Comprehensive Assessment Systems CFDA Number 84.395B. Proposal submitted by Washington State on Behalf of the Smarter Balanced Assessment Consortium.* Olympia, WA: Author.

Valenti, S., Neri, F., & Cucchiarelli, A. (2003). An overview of current research on automated essay grading. *Journal of Information Technology Education*, 2, 319–330.

Williamson, D., Xi, X., & Breyer, J. (2012). A framework for evaluation and use of automated scoring. *Educational Measurement: Issues and Practice*, 31(1), 2–13. doi:10.1111/j.1745-3992.2011.00223.x

Winerip, M. (2012, April 22). Facing a Robo-Grader? Just Keep Obfuscating Mellifluously. *New York Times.* Retrieved from http://www.nytimes.com/2012/04/23/education/robo-readers-used-to-grade-test-essays.html?_r=0

# Chapter 24
# Automated Scoring of Multicomponent Tasks

**William Lorié**
*Questar Assessment, Inc., USA*

## ABSTRACT

*Assessment of real-world skills increasingly requires efficient scoring of non-routine test items. This chapter addresses the scoring and psychometric treatment of a broad class of automatically-scorable complex assessment tasks allowing a definite set of responses orderable by quality. These multicomponent tasks are described and proposals are advanced on how to score them so that they support capturing gradations of performance quality. The resulting response evaluation functions are assessed empirically against alternatives using data from a pilot of technology-enhanced items (TEIs) administered to a sample of high school students in one U.S. state. Results support scoring frameworks leveraging the full potential of multicomponent tasks for providing evidence of partial knowledge, understanding, or skill.*

## INTRODUCTION

Assessment of real-world skills increasingly requires development and efficient scoring of test items that go beyond standard multiple-choice and open-response formats. There are long-acknowledged limitations on what can be tested with the former. Developing, field testing, administering, and scoring the more interesting open-ended items involves costly training and marking, even when some or all of the scoring is eventually handled through the application of machine learning algorithms. Open-ended test items have also been criticized – rightly or not – for their "subjectivity" and the inter-rater variance they introduce and which contributes to test score unreliability.

An assessment middle ground has emerged which promises a higher level of (at least) face validity while at the same time avoiding the costs and criticisms associated with open-ended items. This chapter addresses that middle ground, which consists of test items with constrained responses that can be enumerated and ordered a priori in terms of quality. Thus, they can be scored automatically.

Interaction-based problems in the Problem Solving exam from the Organisation for Economic Cooperation and Development (OECD) Programme for International Student Assessment (PISA), simulations in the American Institute of CPA (AICPA) Uniform CPA Examination, vignettes in the National Council of Architectural Registration Boards (NCARB) Architect Regis-

DOI: 10.4018/978-1-4666-9441-5.ch024

tration Examination, and multi-select and other new item types in the National Council of State Boards of Nursing (NCSBN) National Council Licensure Examination (NCLEX) are just a handful of examples of these kinds of assessment items in real-world skills exams.

The extent to which these tasks are superior to either multiple-choice or open-response formats for real-world skills assessment is a critical question beyond the scope of this chapter. The answer depends on the degree to which salient aspects of the environments in which the target skills are exhibited can be modeled in terms of constrained choices among enumerable alternatives. Many real-world skills seem to have these features: There are a limited number of actions that can be taken by pilots to respond to a particular set of readings on an airplane dashboard, by nurses in response to given specific symptoms presented by a patient, and by hotel reservation agents when a request is made for a block of rooms with special requirements for specific individuals. Contexts like these are most amenable to assessment through the types of items discussed here.

This chapter presents a framework for scoring these types of items, or parts of them. The framework examines the relationship between the response space of a test item (that is, all of the different ways in which one may respond to the item) and the evaluation function that transforms that space to yield a qualitative ordering of responses from worst to best. This general, abstract approach extends beyond what is required for standard multiple choice test items, simple open-ended items, and most other tasks the responses to which are evaluated through human scoring or machine learning algorithms that mimic human scoring. For these more typical tasks, either (a) the response space is small and the evaluation function is binary (as with multiple choice items), (b) the response space is large but most of it can be ignored (as with items requiring the examinee to supply a word, a number, or the like), or (c)

the evaluation function is non-deterministic but rendered more reliable through training (as with human or machine scoring of essays).

In contrast, the item formats discussed here feature expanded (but finite) response spaces that potentially carry a great deal of information about response quality – an important reason test developers make use of them to begin with. Introducing human judgments into the evaluation functions for these items is not optimal – not only because of the possibility of introducing inconsistencies in the scoring of identical responses, but also because of the time and expense associated with collecting and modeling such judgments.

Thus, a different approach is needed. This chapter introduces the general concept of a multicomponent task, and illustrates how several recently popular test item types, such as "drag-and-drop," "hot spot," and "select all that apply," are simple examples of multicomponent tasks. These simple tasks form the foundation for more complex tasks that are, in turn, featured in assessments of real-world skills.

Essential topics for understanding multicomponent tasks include the maximum and optimal sizes of the evaluation space (in other words, how many points the item can or should support), logical dependencies between components, the role of the default response state, and the information content of real responses to multicomponent items.

This chapter takes as its point of departure a psychometric perspective in covering these topics, providing background on attempts to model responses to related tasks within the framework of item response theory. After distinguishing multicomponent tasks from other types of complex item formats, principles for an effective response coding schema for various simple multicomponent tasks are proposed. Task types, their parameters, and response spaces are described. Response evaluation functions for one type of multicomponent task are proposed and their relative merits discussed. Three alternative scoring criteria – two of them representing extreme cases of scoring stringency (on the one hand) and detail (on the other) – are the subject of an empirical evaluation of evaluation functions, based upon data from four different end-of-course examinations administered to high school students as part of a pilot program of multicomponent technology-enhanced items (TEIs) in a U.S. state. The findings support evaluation functions consistent with the multicomponent task schema presented, which leverages multicomponent task potential for providing evidence of partial knowledge, understanding, or skill.

## BACKGROUND

### Types of Complex Assessment Tasks

Complex assessment tasks are those for which responses entail more than one interaction or stage. Complex tasks are usually defined by what they are not, rather than what they are: There is general agreement than traditional multiple-choice items are not complex assessment tasks. The main driver of complex tasks in assessment is the frequent call for freedom from multiple-choice test formats, and toward more authentic, real-world assessment tasks that are presumed to yield more valid assessment (e.g., Lane & Stone, 2006).

Drasgow, et al. (2006) discuss three types of assessment tasks that more faithfully reflect those that examinees may encounter in academic and work settings. The first class of tasks can be scored via a simple match between key and response. Examples include the selection of a point of insertion for a particular sentence in a test-supplied paragraph or longer passage, or by clicking the appropriate point on a number line. Drasgow, et al. also includes "problems that call for ordering values by dragging and dropping them into slots" in this first class of tasks. Responses to such problems, however, may carry important information about examinee skills that would be lost if a simple match between key and response

were always employed. As will be shown later in this chapter, there is a distinction between tasks supporting only two states of scoring – correct and incorrect – and those which can support more, but which for other reasons are scored dichotomously. To this end, the author will present and discuss responses to a problem calling for ordering elements through a drag-and-drop procedure, and demonstrate how – when the door to partial-credit is opened – evaluation of responses to this sort of item requires more than a simple match to a key.

The second type of assessment task discussed by Drasgow, et al. (2006) "consists of static problems for which the responses are too complex to be graded by a simple match." (p.497). This chapter concerns itself chiefly with this second class of tasks. Examples cited by Drasgow, et al. include the scoring of step-by-step solutions to algebra problems, graphs sketched on a coordinate plane, computer programs, and concept maps.

This second class of assessment tasks encompasses automatic scoring of essays and computer-aided design drawings, two domains in which scoring approaches can be usefully contrasted. Increasingly, scoring of essays has relied heavily on machine learning methods. Such artificial intelligence approaches aim to mimic human scorers' scoring or classification of responses by applying statistical models to human-identified features (such as presence of certain vocabulary, sentence length or structure, etc.). The scoring of computer-aided drawings in responses to vignettes for the Architect Registration Exam on the National Council of Architect Registration Board, on the other hand, is based on a "scoring tree" (Katz, 2014) in which features of drawings are checked sequentially and scored based on assigned weights. The more essential the feature (lack of dead-end corridors, instance), the greater the weight. This analytic manner of automated scoring also aims to mimic the judgments of expert scorers, but by virtue of its more principled approach, results are more reproducible. They are also free of (human) error variance.

The most complex assessment tasks that resemble real-world tasks are those that change as a consequence of examinee actions. Simulations and games exemplify this arena of assessment. So-called "serious games" (or games for learning), such as *SimCityEDU: Pollution Challenge!* (GlassLab, 2013), *Lifeboat to Mars* (PBS Kids Go, 2011), and *Papers, Please* (Pope, 2013) balance narrative structure with interactivity to engineer environments in which user actions are assessed in reference to some overarching goal. Serious games are developed with a learning outcome in mind; engagement in the game is intended to bring about that outcome.

This chapter does not deal directly with assessment in this vast landscape. However, elements of some of these games and simulations may be amenable to the techniques presented in this chapter. For example, a student of landscape design engaged in a simulation-based assessment on fulfilling a client project may be required to compile a list of plant species, from the inventory of a contracted supplier, meeting climate and site constraints. That phase of the assessment can be modeled as a multicomponent selection task.

## Multicomponent Tasks and Automated Scoring

As the name implies, a multicomponent task is an assessment task that can be broken down into components, each of which supports a finite number of possible responses. Those responses can be coded as binary variables, the values of which can in turn be summarized to produce a task score. Because all possible responses are known ahead of time, responses to multicomponent tasks can be scored automatically if all potential responses are covered by the rules for scoring such tasks.

According to Drasgow, et al. (2006), automated scoring can be decomposed into feature extraction, feature evaluation, and feature accumulation, the three of these processes being subcomponents of evidence identification in the evidence-centered design (ECD) assessment framework. The collection of evidence, for or against assessment-based claims about examinee knowledge, skills, or abilities, is precisely what automated scoring must accomplish in order to be effective.

For multicomponent tasks, the three processes of automated scoring can be applied straightforwardly. Feature extraction is the process by which the scorable units of a task are identified. In the case of multicomponent tasks, this entails isolation of the components. The components are obvious for some multicomponent tasks, but much less so for others. Once the components are identified, they must be evaluated and accumulated. As will be discussed later in this chapter, this entails the application of an evaluation function particular to the type of multicomponent task and how that type is treated within a scoring framework. Individual components are treated as binary values (present or not present), and they are summarized according to the accumulation rules for a particular item type. If all possible responses are taken into account within the scoring framework for a particular task type, including the possibility of omissions, multiple markings, and other errors, then automated scoring can be programmed for the task.

## Multicomponent Tasks as Collections of Interdependent Items

By definition, responses to multicomponent tasks can be expressed in terms of a finite set of binary variables. Given that strings of right and wrong answers are the basic data of most applications of modern test theory, it is natural to turn to psychometrics in attempting to understand how to make sense of responses to multicomponent tasks. The psychometric approach to modeling responses to several related items or tasks helps to inform how scores to multicomponent tasks might best be scored and analyzed. And, since psychometrics treats all tasks as parts of larger collections of test items (item banks or test forms), the relationships among the components of multicomponent tasks are best evaluated in the context of this larger collection that operationally represents the knowledge, ability, or skill being measured.

Wainer and Kiely (1987) define a "testlet" as "a group of items related to a single content area that is developed as a unit and contains a fixed number of predetermined paths that an examinee may follow" (p. 190). By this definition, the concept of a testlet is closely related to a multicomponent task because both share three critical features. Both ideas refer to an interrelated group of item (or components), developed as a unit and measuring a single content area, and permitting a finite number of possible responses.

Thissen, Nelson, Rosa, and McLeod (2001) explain that although the testlet concept finds initial utility in the arena of computerized adaptive testing (CAT), it is more generally a solution to the problem of local item dependence, as discussed by Yen (1993). Local item dependence (LID), a central topic of psychometric research, is best understood in the context of item response theory (IRT). IRT statistically models the probability of a certain level of response to an item (for example, getting a 2 on a 4-point essay) as a function of one or more parameters describing the examinee (such as his or her ability), one or more parameters describing the item (such as its difficulty), and nothing else. Thus, by definition, responses to different items are assumed to be independent once examinee parameters are known. Put differently, in IRT, the examinee parameters are assumed to carry all of the relevant information about examinee standing on whatever construct is being measured. LID occurs when the joint probability, conditioned on ability, of an examinee's response to two or more test items is not the product of that examinee's individual item response probabilities, each also conditioned on ability. As Yen (1993) notes, LID means that knowing a person's standing on the ability being measured by a test is not enough to explain his or her pattern of right and wrong answers. A discovery of significant LID calls into question the very model used to explain examinee and test characteristics. When LID is present, a test is measuring a mixture of constructs, some of which are unknown and most likely unintentional, and no assurances can be made about the validity of inferences and decisions based on test scores.

But a small amount of LID is not detrimental and may even be expected in some situations. An example often cited is a reading comprehension test in which several text passages are each followed by a few questions pertaining to comprehension of the passage. The questions for a given passage explicitly refer to the passage, and performance on those questions presumably depends on comprehension of that specific passage. The text passages in such a test will have varying levels of readability and cover a range of topics, and there is likely to be dependence among responses to a given passage due to factors not modeled, such as examinee interest in or familiarity with the content of reading passage. This is reflected in larger-than-expected correlations among responses to questions for a given passage, even after an IRT model is applied. Depending on the magnitude of those correlations, it may be more appropriate to treat the questions to a passage as a unit, to remove the influence of factors not related to the construct of interest: reading comprehension of a representative sample of texts, which can be modeled as a unidimensional construct if the passages are treated as units (see, for example, Min & He, 2014).

Encapsulating related test items into higher level units whose parameters can be modeled is a general solution to those cases in which LID emerges due to a failure to account for variance unique to sets of items within a larger whole. This is precisely what testlet response models do (Bradlow, Wainer, & Wang, 1999; Li, Bolt, & Fu, 2006; Wainer, Bradlow, & Du, 2000; Wainer, Bradlow, & Wang, 2007). Appropriately, each item continues to be treated as an independent measure, with the modification that now its independence is conditional on its nesting within its respective testlet. This is important in the context of multicomponent tasks, where it might occur to test developers that responses to the components themselves can be modeled as conditionally independent, their association with the task being the conditioning variable.

It is instructive to note here that the testlet response model is formally equivalent to what is known in the factor analytic literature as a second-order model, and that the testlet / second-order model is in turn a restricted bi-factor model (Rijmen, 2011). For present purposes, these model equivalences allow referring to psychometric approaches for handling nested relationships within ability or achievement domains simply as bi-factor modeling.

Thus, it would seem that psychometric theory is well-equipped to directly handle multicomponent tasks assessing real-world skills – specifically, by applying bi-factor models and treating individual components within tasks as independent items. Complex, multicomponent tasks of the kinds surfacing in novel measures of real-world skills are not all amenable to bi-factor modeling, however. This places limitations on attempts to score them under the assumptions of bi-factor models, which treat test items as independent units contributing independently to a total score by a straightforward adding up of points.

The reason for the failure of bi-factor models in some complex test items is that even when such tasks can be analyzed into components, in many cases responses to those components retain dependencies that are not statistical, but logical. These logical dependencies among items within a unit are of three kinds: (1) dependencies with respect to the response space of the unit as a whole, (2) dependencies (of questionable construct relevance) with respect to the measured construct, and (3) dependencies due to explicit referencing of responses to other items within the unit. The last of these is fairly common for modularized tasks in which items "build upon" the work done in previous items within the module. In the U.S. Common Core State Standards, "paired items" are used by major publishers and assessment consortia to assess English language arts / literacy standards in which students are required to support their conclusions – one item to register their answer in response to a question about a passage, the next one to elaborate further or indicate appropriate supports for their conclusion (see, e.g., PARCC, 2014, pp 2-3 and 9-10). Such paired items are interdependent in this third sense. The other logical dependencies will be covered in more depth in a later section.

Unlike logical dependencies, statistical dependencies are the result of stratification or clustering within the domain being assessed. Stratification can be explicit and intentional. For example, a mathematical skills test might be composed of a mixture of two kinds of items – one group testing computational skills and another assessing mathematical reasoning – each of which is considered a separate skill by the test designers, but both constitutive of mathematical skills as a target construct. Or, stratification in a set of item responses might be uncovered through factor analysis or structural equation modeling. The same is true for clustering, which would be unsurprising for items that share common stimulus materials, but might also surface across seemingly unrelated items. Structural modeling and model fit assessments, as well as theory-based arguments, can inform test developers and researchers as to the exact nature of statistical dependencies in a particular testing context.

Depending on the composition of the tests in which they appear, multicomponent tasks amenable to bi-factor modeling may or may not require such modeling for successful scoring. The usual treatment of reading comprehension test items as sufficiently statistically independent of their passages to warrant single-factor modeling, even in high-stakes contexts, illustrates that in practice it is a matter of judgment as to whether a simpler model might be robust enough. The same will be true of those multicomponent tasks the components of which exhibit logical dependencies.

## The Implications of Component Interdependency for Scoring Approach

To connect the issue of component interdependency with scoring, three general approaches to scoring multicomponent tasks are described here, and summarized in Table 1.

Dichotomous scoring, the first approach, credits a response to a multicomponent task when and only when the response is in perfect agreement with the key. Otherwise, the response is scored as incorrect.

The second approach is componential scoring. It is dichotomous scoring applied at the level of the component, rather than the whole multicomponent task. Componential scoring treats each component as an independent item.

The third scoring approach, polytomous, treats each multicomponent task as capable of supporting more than one scoring level. As will be discussed, polytomous scoring requires a careful analysis and classification of the task in order to understand how levels of increasing response quality can be defined and quantified.

## AUTOMATED SCORING OF MULTICOMPONENT TASKS

### Preliminary Considerations regarding Multicomponent Task Types

In the discussion to follow, some multicomponent task types will be introduced, but a more complete taxonomy is reserved for the section dedicated to multicomponent task types. The taxonomy presented there is based primarily upon scoring considerations, so in some sense the latter precedes taxonomy. Nonetheless some preliminary considerations will help illuminate this chapter's approach to "item types," prior to a discussion of how they might be scored.

Although descriptions such as "multi-select item," "drag and drop," "matching," "table completion," and "hotspot" describe many item types that fit the general rubric of multicomponent task as defined here, these item type labels are too ambiguous to serve the purposes of scoring. Thus, a more generalized taxonomy will be presented, which requires an understanding of the types of examinee interactions that are and are not allowed by an item. For example, suppose a "drag and drop" item has four objects and four targets, and the act of dragging one object into a target fills the

*Table 1. Three scoring approaches for multicomponent tasks*

| Sample Application | Scoring Approach | Description | Implications of Component Interdependency |
|---|---|---|---|
| A multiple choice item is scored as right or wrong | Dichotomous | Each task is scored 0 or 1 | None. All independent information from each task's components is ignored |
| A point is assigned to correctly conducting each step of a four-step chemical equation balancing problem. Each step is considered a separate test item | Componential | Tasks are not scored directly – only their components. Each component is scored 0 or 1 | Potentially significant. All association between a component and its associated task is ignored, potentially introducing task-specific factors that distort scores |
| As above, but the points are added to obtain a total score on the problem, ranging from 0 to 4 | Polytomous | Tasks are scored according to a rule for combining the component scores. Each task can have a score from 0 to the maximum number of levels supported by that task | None. Component interdependencies within task are eliminated in the evaluation function that translates component scores to task scores |

target completely but causes an identical object to replace the dragged object in the latter's original location. This item is a "composite selection task." Consider on the other hand an identical item except that copies of dragged objects do not reappear to replace them. This item is a "mapping task."

The distinction is not readily apparent without consideration of each item's "components" and "response spaces," which are in turn intimately related to scoring. These more fundamental concepts are introduced prior to a discussion of the types, but here is a less formal description of the three elementary multicomponent tasks to aid in the discussion of scoring.

1. Selection tasks, as the name implies, are those in which the primary interaction made by an examinee is to pick out one or more objects / choices from a list of available objects / choices. The traditional multiple choice item is a selection task in which the examinee is informed that only one of the (typically four) objects / choices provided may be selected.

2. Ordering tasks are those in which examinees must place objects / choices in ordinal relations to each other. Simple examples include placing numbers in order from least to greatest, and drawing arrows between pictures of organisms to designate predator-prey relationships in a food web.

3. Mapping tasks require examinees to specify relations between elements in two sets of objects. This is an abstract type that is applicable to cases beyond the obvious one of matching entries in two columns.

An item can be a "composite" of one or more elementary tasks. This use of "composite" is not to be confused with the "components" making up elementary tasks.

## Response and Evaluation Spaces for Multicomponent Tasks

The size of the response space of a multicomponent task – that is, the number of different possible responses – is an important consideration in designing / planning for scoring of responses to multicomponent tasks because there are usually many different possible responses and the scoring of each one needs to be determined and justified ahead of time. For definiteness, a response space includes all the different ways in which a test delivery system allows a person to respond to an item. This includes omissions and multiple markings, both of which are normally scored as "incorrect" in operational settings.[1]

To illustrate a response space, this section will discuss a type of multicomponent task called a selection task, which will be defined more formally together with other basic task types in the section on multicomponent task types. More specifically, the selection task discussed here is one in which an examinee is informed of how many options to select out of a given set of options.

Consider an electronically-delivered test item prompting an examinee to select three out of five possible options, in which the delivery system allows users to select and de-select options but does not allow the selection of more than three options at a time, has a response space size of

$$1 + \binom{5}{1} + \binom{5}{2} + \binom{5}{3} = 26$$

The first term is the number of ways in which an examinee can omit the item (1), the second is the number of ways an examinee can make one selection (5), the third term is the number of ways two options can be selected (10), and the last term is the number of ways three options can be made (10).

It is possible to write out all possible responses in the response space, but it is not necessary to do so for the purposes of this discussion. Of greater importance is how those 26 responses can and should be ordered from worst to best, and what number should be assigned to each.

It may be that for some test items similar to this one, selecting one particular incorrect response represents a greater error than selecting other incorrect responses, or conversely that leaving blank one of the correct responses is more serious than leaving another one blank. If a differential weighting scheme of this kind is put in practice, then the multicomponent item is not analogous to the traditional selected response item, in which all incorrect options to a particular item are given the same "weight" – that is to say, if the answer to a selected response item is "C", then it makes no difference to a person's score if s/he selects "A" instead of "B". That does not mean that differential weighting may not be justified or appropriate in some settings. An item on a physician's assistant licensure exam might give a greater negative weight to an option that would definitely harm the patient under their care. Or, more sophisticated psychometric models that grade response options from worst to best (such as the graded response model, Samejima, 1969) might be applied for some constructs. Items employing this type of option weighting cannot be analyzed directly using the tools of this chapter.

To make assumptions explicit, the multicomponent items under consideration here have the following properties relevant to evaluating responses: (a) a correct option (or component) is like any other correct option and equally no meaningful distinction can be made among incorrect components; (b) selecting an incorrect component represents the same error as leaving blank a correct component. These two assumptions will be referred to as equal option weighting and symmetrical error weighting, respectively. As

will be shown, these two assumptions simplify the evaluation space immensely and are also much easier to communicate to examinees than other alternatives.

Under these assumptions, it can be shown that the aforementioned select-three-out-of-five item cannot support 26 levels or scores. Instead, the number of supportable levels must be a function of just one value which can be derived from any response: the number of options correctly selected (if they should have been selected) or left blank (if they should have been left blank). This value is just the number of options for which the person's response (select or omit) matches the key. For this item, this value – call it $n$ – will be between zero and five.

It is useful to carry this example forward to derive the number of supportable levels for this type of item, which will be called a "Select $H - 3$ out of 5" item, abbreviated "Sh3(5)", with "Select $H$" defined as "a selected-response item where the number of possible selections is constrained to be no more than the number of keyed options, which are themselves greater than one but less than the number of options."

One peculiarity of many multicomponent tasks, this one included, is that they present a scorable default state. What this means is that when the item is presented, it already contains some options that are correct by default – namely, those which should remain deselected. This does not occur with typical selected-response items, for which an omission is never correct. The score represented by the default state always needs to be considered when scoring a multicomponent item, however. In the case of Sh3(5), two options are correct by default. To prevent awarding credit for a response in which an examinee simply leaves all options blank, an adjustment must be made when scoring this item. The adjustment that comes to mind is the number of options minus the number of keyed options, or $5 - 3 = 2$. This is an adjustment made to the number of options for which the person's response matches the key (that is, $n$ as defined above).

The problem with this adjustment is that it awards credit at the other extreme of "test gaming," which is when an examinee selects all options in the hopes of obtaining credit without attempting to sincerely respond to the item. This possibility can become a threat to test validity. Of course, the delivery system in this hypothetical example prevents such gaming because it allows only three options to be selected. In general, however, the system might not have such safeguards. Setting aside for the moment questions concerning the comparability of scores on this task for paper-and-pencil versus computerized administration modes, consider administering this task on paper, where no mechanism prevents an examinee from attempting to score points by responding to all options. There, if an examinee selects all options, the resulting score under the adjustment just proposed would be one point: 3 (the number of responses matching the key) – 2 (the adjustment) = 1. To avoid this situation, a different scoring rule needs to be in place for items of type Sh$H(N)$ when they meet the condition in which $H$, the number of keyed

options, exceeds ½ of $N$, the number of options. The adjustment in this "inverted" condition is just $H$. Thus, to score an item of type Sh3(5) requires counting up the number of options in which the response matches the key ($n$), subtracting the number of keyed options ($H$), and replacing any negative result with zero.

From this, it can be shown that an examinee leaving the item blank will get a zero, one selecting all options will also get a zero, one whose response perfectly matches the key will get two points, and any other response will result in either a zero or one point. The rule for Sh3(5) can be applied to any multicomponent task for which the underlying response space is identical to a straightforward select-three-out-of-five test item.

Recall that for tasks of type Sh$H(N)$, the proposed adjustments to $n$, the number of options in the response matching the key, are $N-H$ for $H \leq \frac{1}{2} N$, and $H$ when $H \geq \frac{1}{2} N$. Table 2 illustrates how scoring would work for a sample of responses to three tasks of type Sh$H(N)$. The "coded response" is the result of matching the sample response to the sample key using a logical XNOR operation (1 where there is a match, zero otherwise), and $n$ is the count of ones in the coded response.

*Table 2. Scoring of sample responses to three ShH(N) tasks*

| Task Type | H | N | Sample Key | Sample Response | Coded Response | n | n-(N-H) | n-H | Score |
|---|---|---|---|---|---|---|---|---|---|
| Sh2(4) | 2 | 4 | ●○●○ | ●○●○ | 1111 | 4 | 2 | N/A | 2 |
| Sh2(4) | 2 | 4 | ●○●○ | ●○○○ | 1101 | 3 | 1 | N/A | 1 |
| Sh2(4) | 2 | 4 | ●○●○ | ○●○● | 0000 | 0 | -2 | N/A | 0 |
| Sh2(4) | 2 | 4 | ●○●○ | ○○○○ | 0101 | 2 | 0 | N/A | 0 |
| Sh3(5) | 3 | 5 | ○○●●● | ○○●●● | 11111 | 5 | N/A | 2 | 2 |
| Sh3(5) | 3 | 5 | ○○●●● | ●○○●● | 01011 | 3 | N/A | 0 | 0 |
| Sh3(5) | 3 | 5 | ○○●●● | ○○○●● | 11011 | 4 | N/A | 1 | 1 |
| Sh3(5) | 3 | 5 | ○○●●● | ○○○○○ | 11000 | 2 | N/A | -1 | 0 |
| Sh2(5) | 2 | 5 | ○○●●○ | ○○●●○ | 11111 | 5 | 2 | N/A | 2 |
| Sh2(5) | 2 | 5 | ○○●●○ | ○○●○○ | 11101 | 4 | 1 | N/A | 1 |
| Sh2(5) | 2 | 5 | ○○●●○ | ●○○○● | 01000 | 1 | -2 | N/A | 0 |
| Sh2(5) | 2 | 5 | ○○●●○ | ○○○○○ | 11001 | 3 | 0 | N/A | 0 |

## Evaluation Spaces and Evaluation Functions

The example of how an Sh3(5) task might be scored illustrates the concepts of evaluation spaces and evaluation functions for multicomponent tasks. In this section, those concepts are made more explicit. A multicomponent task's evaluation space is the set of consecutive integers, beginning with zero, and ending with one less than the number of distinct score levels an item will support (under the assumptions of equal option weighting and symmetrical error weighting).

A traditional multiple-choice (or selected-response) item has two levels with evaluation space $\{0, 1\}$. The integers in an evaluation space are usually treated as "points" which can be tallied to obtain a raw score on an exam. When test scoring is not done directly through a raw score – for example, when latent scores are estimated via maximum-likelihood of a response pattern – the relevant characteristics of the response space are that they are ordered and that there are a specific number of them. These, and not the actual numerical values, are the most important characteristics of response spaces in all cases. It may be that the policy of a testing program is such that some items count twice as much as other items, in which case the possible scores are 0 and 2. What is preserved regardless of policy, however, is that the item supports only two levels and that one level is greater than the other. This principle generalizes to evaluation spaces of multicomponent tasks.

Unlike the evaluation spaces of traditional selected-response items, however, in general the size of multicomponent item evaluation spaces can be reduced. If the size of the evaluation space of a multicomponent item is greater than two, it can be reduced to any number between two and one less than its current size. In other words, the number of levels of an item can be brought down to some desired target. The recommended transformation is one that always assigns the perfect response to the maximum level. This can be achieved by multiplying each value of the evaluation space by the new desired maximum, dividing by the old maximum, and rounding down to the nearest integer. This results in a collapsing of two or more levels. Evaluation spaces can and should be reduced whenever an item supports more levels than test designers believe should be awarded for a correct response, in light of points awarded on other test tasks. Note that although reduction of the response space is meaningful, expansion is less so, since this will only change some of the values in the evaluation space, without affecting the number of levels. It will also introduce one or more gaps in the distribution of item scores.

## Evaluation Spaces and Task Scores

The concept of evaluation spaces is more general than that of task or item scores. Often test scores are weighted, and in some cases this weighting is reflected in the maximum number of points associated with a test item. It is difficult to make sense of differences in points assigned to tasks without some consideration of evaluation spaces. This is because a task's evaluation space establishes a limit to how many distinct levels a response to that task can support. The two-level limit of a traditional multiple-choice item's evaluation space means that whenever more than one point is assigned to such an item, these are "all-or-none", and do not represent the number of real distinctions that can be made regarding the quality of a response. Whether or not the evaluation space of a task is used directly in score point assignments, the former expresses the psychometric information limit contained in any response to that item. It is always possible to meaningfully reduce this limit in the translation to score points, but any expansion of it only serves to give the task greater weight with respect to other items on the assessment.

## Multicomponent Task Types

### Selection Tasks

A multi-response test item prompting examinees to select a specific number of options, greater than one, is a natural generalization of the traditional multiple choice item. It can be shown that applying the Sh$H(N)$ evaluation function to the response space of Sh1$(N)$, $N \geq 2$, will always yield the evaluation space $\{0, 1\}$, with the 1 assigned when and only when a response perfectly matches the key. Thus, traditional multiple-choice test questions fit the framework of this chapter.

An extension of Sh$H(N)$ is an item or task type in which the examinee is not told how many options to select, but is freely allowed to "select all that apply," a common direction to this type of item. Because the size of the key is not communicated to the test taker, here the constant $H$ is replaced with the variable $X$, and this type of item is referred to as Sx$X(N)$, or "Select $X$ out of $N$".

Not all tasks of this type appear as "select all that apply" items followed by a series of statements. Sx$X(N)$ tasks generalize to more innovative assessment tasks. The difference lies in the context. Consider a simulation in which participants must select objects from a vault before they embark on a journey. Carrying too much comes with increased encumbrance and a substantial risk of not completing the mission on time, thus incentivizing participants to put effort into their decision-making during the object-selection stage. If game designers know ahead of time the optimal collection of objects for this scenario, then this "assessment" is essentially an Sx$X(N)$ task.

The evaluation function for responses to Sx$X(N)$ tasks is identical to that for responses to Sh$H(N)$, replacing the $H$ with $X$. Communicating the size of the key to an examinee should make a difference in the item's overall difficulty (typically making it easier). In theory, an Sx$X(N)$ task may be configured so that none of the options should

be selected, per the key, or alternatively that all of them should be selected. Applying the evaluation function to such a task will always yield zero, however, and if such tasks are possible in an exam a different procedure must be used to score them. Designing such tasks, especially the first (a key size zero task), is ill-advised. First, the correct response to a key size zero task is indistinguishable from an omission. One might be able to secure an answer to the question of whether the examinee attempted the task and judged that all options should be left blank, but this would have to be a response to a different item, and so scoring would have to depend on another item, which is also subject to test gaming. Second, applying the "inverse condition" evaluation function to Sx$X(N)$ when $X = N$ (a key size $N$ task), yields zero for the perfect response. Again, the inverse condition evaluation function is established to prevent test gaming at the other extreme – where examinees seek to secure some credit by selecting everything indiscriminately.

There may be cases in which test developers will want to include multi-select tasks in which all responses are correct answers, but they should carefully review the expected score across tasks for hypothetical persons who may select all options, compare this to guessing levels on traditional multiple choice tests, and assess whether selecting all options is related to other variables, such as risk taking behavior, that are not the intended target of assessment. At least one high stakes assessment program, the *GRE®* revised General Test (ETS, 2014), containing Sx$X(N)$ items indicates to students that a key size of $N$ is possible. Whether or not multi-select tasks on a test may legitimately have key size zero or key size $N$, it is important to communicate to examinees any special response conventions, especially in high stakes situations.

Sh and Sx tasks, collectively called "selection tasks" here, are related to a multiple choice item format called a "Type K" item (Hubbard, 1978), in which particular combinations of primary options (but not all possible combinations) are presented for the examinee to choose from. The examinee selects only one such combination. Type K items are a restricted form of selection tasks.

## Ordering and Mapping Tasks

A surprising variety of novel assessment items can be modeled as selection tasks. This is not to detract from assessment developers' claims regarding the cognitive complexity or real-world authenticity of these tasks, only to point out that responding to them essentially boils down to making a selection of one or more options among given alternatives. As such, a compelling case can be made that scoring rules (or more broadly evaluation functions) for these tasks should be consistent with whatever other rules are established for selection tasks.

Not all multicomponent tasks are amenable to modeling this way, however. There are two other major groups of tasks – those which require examinees to order elements and those the responses to which result in some sort of mapping between sets of objects. When tasks require ordering, such as ordering numerical values from least to greatest, partial credit can be awarded for the relative ordering of elements, even when, for example, the first element in the response is not literally the first element in the key. When tasks require mapping (such as matching from a "column A" to "column B"), special constraints play into the complexity of the response space, including whether more than one mapping can be made from or to a given object, whether mappings have a meaningful sense or a direction (a "from" and a "to"), and how many mappings the item requires.

As with selection tasks, the underlying task type for ordering or mapping tasks might not even be apparent from the surface features of the item. There are several equally valid answers to the drag-and-drop portion of this task, where the six blank boxes in three stacks of two indicate the drop targets. Partial credit is possible on this task, per

the test designers: According to its scoring rubric, credit is to be awarded for each unit fraction in the key which the respondent assembles. These fractions are 3 slices / 1 person, $6.50 / 1 pizza, and 1 pizza / 6 slices. No credit is awarded for an inverted fraction. The five boxes on the left are the drag objects. As required by this item, these objects are not exhausted when they are dragged – that is, another one of the same kind appears in its place once it is moved into a target box. Approaching this task in selection terms yields an unwieldy structure. A more elegant solution is to organize it as a directed match from one set to another identical set, both consisting of those elements in the shaded boxes. In this case the direction is from numerator to denominator. An evaluation function counts up the number of successful matches made, and maps these directly to the evaluation space {0, 1, 2, 3}. The open-ended box above "Answer" can be evaluated automatically by computationally assessing whether the user-entered content is equivalent to 117.

As indicated earlier, there is an important distinction to be drawn between tasks supporting only correct/incorrect scoring and those which can support partial credit, but are scored dichotomously for other reasons, such as an assessment program sponsor's requirement that all items be equally weighted regardless of their inherent complexity. Moreover, it is useful here to demonstrate how some of the simplest assessment tasks described by Drasgow et al. (2006) (those scored through a simple match between response and key) appear to cross the boundary into the next class of tasks when the interest is in supporting an assessment of partial knowledge.

Consider a task calling for ordering elements using a drag-and-drop procedure. There are many possibilities for scoring a problem like this one. At one end is the extreme of providing credit only for responses showing each element in its correct position. This dichotomous approach is fine insofar as communicating scoring rules to examinees and in simplifying test result interpretation, but it fails to acknowledge that students may have some knowledge of the relative degree of democracy in various key forms of government, yet not all.

Given an interest in capturing partial knowledge, one may attempt to score the item as a selection task, but roadblocks eventually emerge. First, a partially correct response may show correct relative ordering the four most democratic forms of government, yet place the fifth one at the wrong end, resulting in all objects misaligned with their targets. A binary evaluation of the contents of each target results in a score of zero. Two other issues with modeling this task as a selection task are less obvious but similarly problematic. They will be dealt with in more detail in the section on logical dependencies. Since the objects are exhausted as they are placed in their targets, there is only one object and one target remaining after four are placed; hence the response space has a reduced degree of freedom for all practical purposes. Along these lines, each successive placement constrains the remaining selections, inducing such interdependency among the "components" that the appropriateness of evaluating them one by one is called into question.

It is thus necessary to introduce another type into the taxonomy of multicomponent tasks. Like the selection task this new type – the ordering task – has several variants. Of immediate interest is the sort of ordering task in which the elements to be ordered are given and not initially located in the response area. (Elements initially located in the response area present a default ordering, and hence potentially induce a non-zero default score for the task overall, a situation that can be addressed in a manner analogous to non-zero default score states for selection tasks.) Whether response areas are initially empty or populated the general goal in awarding partial credit is to do so to the extent that the response mirrors the key.

The critical question is: What are the components to be scored? One might begin by consider-

ing the number of pairwise orderings that coincide in the response the key. If there are $n$ elements to be ordered, then there are $n(n+1)/2$ pairwise orderings in the key, and depending on how many elements an examinee places into the response area (omits are always possible), there may be just as many pairwise orderings in the response. For a task with five elements to be placed in order, there would be as many as 15 pairwise orderings to compare between the response and the key. On the face of it, these are too many comparisons. Moreover, the 15 pairwise orderings constitute a redundant set because of the transitivity of the order relationship: If A precedes B and B precedes C, then A precedes C, and there is no meaningful distinction between awarding credit for obtaining all three rather than "just" the first two. On the other hand, it is not immediately clear which relationships to check in the response, which might correctly register that A precedes C but only one of the other two correct relations, or none of them (recall that omits are possible).

Without claiming that what follows is the best solution to this task evaluation problem, a proposal here is to simplify the matter by evaluating only the correctness of *successive* pairs of elements in the response. These then would be the components to be scored. Correctness is evaluated in terms of whether the ordering of any given successive pair of elements in the response also appears in the complete set of $n(n+1)/2$ correct pair relations in the key. One virtue of this approach is that only up to $n$-1 evaluations need be made for each response; another is that $n$-1 is also the maximum score obtainable under this approach, which is consistent with the reduced degrees of freedom of this task. It can be shown moreover that this maximum score is only obtainable through a perfect response.

Table 3 shows the scoring of a five-element ordering task identical in structure. The objects are represented with the letters A through E for

*Table 3. Scoring of sample responses to a five-element ordering task*

| Response* | Evaluation 1 | Evaluation 2 | Evaluation 3 | Evaluation 4 | Score |
|-----------|--------------|--------------|--------------|--------------|-------|
| ABCDE | ?(A<B) | ?(B<C) | ?(C<D) | ?(D<E) | 4 |
| xxxxx | - | - | - | - | 0 |
| BxDAE | ?(B<D) | ?(D<A) | ?(A<E) | - | 2 |
| ACBDE | ?(A<C) | ?(C<B) | ?(B<D) | ?(D<E) | 3 |
| AxxxE | ?(A<E) | - | - | - | 1 |
| EDCBA | ?(E<D) | ?(D<C) | ?(C<B) | ?(B<A) | 0 |
| EABCD | ?(E<A) | ?(A<B) | ?(B<C) | ?(C<D) | 3 |
| AEBCD | ?(A<E) | ?(E<B) | ?(B<C) | ?(C<D) | 3 |
| xxxAB | ?(A<B) | - | - | - | 1 |

*Note. The key is ABCDE and "x" represents an omission.

simplicity, and the key is ABCDE. Each successive pair, regardless of whether there are omissions in between them, is evaluated in turn. The result of each evaluation is coded to zero if false and one if true, and the response score is just the sum of these evaluation codes.

If the proposed procedure is not appropriate for a task in which elements are to be ordered, then it is most likely because the quality of a response inheres in more than just the relative ordering of the elements. An example is a language comprehension task in which examinees are asked to order the sentences of a five-sentence paragraph. The quality of a response to this sentence-ordering task would presumably involve more than just the relative positioning of elements; some sentences may need to be immediately after other sentences to avoid interruptions to the logic of the text or to make sense of transitional markers. This requirement implies a more complex evaluation function than what can be provided by one attending to relative ordering alone. To determine if in a particular case the simple evaluation function is appropriate, one might apply it to various partially correct responses and solicit from subject matter experts an informed judgment as to whether the responses do indeed reflect partial knowledge.

## Assessing Evaluation Functions

The preceding discussion regarding the scoring of examples of selection, ordering, and mapping tasks outlined a few considerations relevant to assessing the appropriateness of evaluation functions for a given situation, and proposed a simple test to check for appropriateness. In this section, the matter of evaluating such functions is addressed more generally.

### Contextual Factors

The desirability of employing particular evaluation functions for the multicomponent tasks in a given testing program depends greatly on the context of the program. In general, high-stakes settings require simpler approaches to scoring, because these are the easiest to communicate to stakeholders. The non-obviousness of scoring for multicomponent tasks in general render them more difficult to defend as parts of high-stakes testing program, but in recent years the trend has been toward greater inclusion. As previously illustrated in the case of the *GRE®* program, clear instructions to examinees indicating that a dichotomous scoring rule is being adopted on multicomponent tasks shows that it is possible to include these types of items in a high-stakes program, at least if a simple scoring rule is adopted.

Although is not clear yet to what extent more complex rules such as those awarding partial credit can successfully be implemented for high-stakes testing programs, these rules seem naturally suited to skill acquisition contexts. Because formative environments for testing allow greater flexibility to make subtler distinctions along the road to mastery, the possibilities are greater there for implementing more informative evaluation functions.

### Logical Interdependencies among Components

In the discussion on the psychometric treatment of test units with multiple components, it was noted that unlike traditional interrelated items, multicomponent items can exhibit interdependencies that are not merely statistical. These logical dependencies could be of three kinds: (1) dependencies with respect to the response space of the unit as a whole, (2) dependencies (of questionable construct relevance) with respect to the measured construct, and (3) dependencies due to explicit referencing of responses to other components within the unit.

The third of these was discussed in the context of serialized tasks in which responses to later questions "build upon" responses to previous questions.

The first type of dependency is present in tasks with an underlying one-to-one mapping structure. A simple example is a task calling for matching terms in one column with definitions in another. If the number of terms is the same as the number of definitions, then there is no real distinction between getting all of the components correct, and getting all but one correct.

The second form of logical dependency, one of questionable construct relevance, can be illustrated as follows. Consider a high school mathematics task in which students are asked to allocate a "true" or "false" to twelve cells of a table in which each

of three column headers shows a pair of equations, each describing a line in the Cartesian plane, and four row headers are statements regarding the relationship between two lines. Each statement may be true or false when applied to each pair of equations, and this is what the respondent is asked to ascertain for each statement-equation pair combination. Suppose further that these are the statements: (1) the lines are parallel, (2) the lines are perpendicular, (3) the lines intersect in Quadrant II, and (4) both lines are functions.

Regardless of the pairs of equations presented, a "true" on the first statement implies a "false" on the second and third, a "false" on the first implies a "true" on the second, and a "true" on either the second or third statement implies a "false" on the first. Finally, the third statement cannot be true about a pair of lines if the second is false. These dependencies may be desirable or they may be problematic, depending on the intended measurement goal for the task. What is clear, however, is that treating each of the twelve components as if they were independent sources of evidence on how well a student can evaluate the geometric relationship between two specific lines is muddied by the presence of these dependencies and a potential awareness of them on the part of the respondent.

Thus, some types of evaluation functions should be avoided when logical dependencies are at play – in particular, any evaluation functions which skip the "feature accumulation" step and treat responses to multicomponent tasks as responses to separate items. (These "componential" approaches are explored further in the next section on assessing evaluation functions in the context of an actual testing program.) A principle reason for not treating logically dependent items as separate items is that many modern approaches to test analysis (such as IRT) assume that items are independent variables. If they are not independent in practice, however, then correlations among some items will be artificially inflated or deflated, causing problems for psychometrics models. It may be that in some cases, test scores are "robust" to these dependencies; this would need to be demonstrated to support working from an assumption that cannot otherwise be defended.

### Empirical Criteria

On an assessment consisting of multicomponent tasks, it is nearly always possible to study the effects of different evaluations functions using real data. If the response data are collected at the component level, then a set of evaluation functions can be applied to the data and standard psychometric analyses conducted. Distribution of task scores and raw scores can be examined for reasonableness; these distributions should be relatively unimodal, free of gaps, and not excessively skewed, for example. In general, the extremes of the raw score distributions should not have a piling up of cases at the minimum or maximum possible score.

The average percent-correct score on an item (sometimes called difficulty although it is actually a measure of easiness) and the correlation between an item's score and the total score on a test (called discrimination) are useful measures because when they are in a certain range (for difficulty) or above a certain value (for discrimination), they contribute positively to test score reliability. High reliability is desirable because it is the proportion of variance in test scores that can be attributed to real differences in knowledge, skill, or achievement.

Aside from the "classical" statistics, various other empirical measures of the appropriateness of a scoring scheme can be obtained through the application of modern psychometric techniques such as IRT. Fit to IRT models is of particular relevance not only because of the near-ubiquity of IRT modeling in operational testing programs, and because poor fit helps identify tasks exhibiting scoring or other problems.

All of these metrics are best assessed in terms of values they take on under different conditions, rather than on their own. This implies that evaluation functions should be assessed in relation to other evaluation functions, preferably applied to the same data whenever feasible. In the next section, three evaluation functions are evaluated in this manner.

## An Empirical Assessment of Evaluation Functions for Multicomponent Tasks

As previously discussed, empirical criteria can play an important role in evaluating or assessing the appropriateness of certain evaluation functions for multicomponent tasks. The collection of these evaluation functions constitutes a scoring framework. At the most general level, scoring frameworks can adopt one of three approaches to multicomponent tasks, briefly mentioned earlier: dichotomous, componential, or polytomous. One of these – polytomous – takes full advantage of the partial credit possibilities of these tasks *and* treats the individual components within a multicomponent task as part of a larger whole. The polytomous approach acknowledges the possibility that those components may have logical interdependencies, recommending against their being treated as independent measures, even under bi-factor modeling assumptions.

The outlines of a scoring framework adopting a polytomous approach were presented in the earlier discussion concerning proposals for scoring responses to selection, ordering, and mapping tasks. In a study to assess the performance of a polytomous scoring framework applied to multicomponent tasks, response data from eight test forms (two in each of four content areas) in a pilot exam were scored in three ways (including the polytomous approach), analyzed, and summarized along key statistics of traditional importance in assessing the quality of data from tests. This section describes the three scoring approaches, the procedures of the study, and results.

## Three Alternative Scoring Approaches

Responses to multicomponent test items can be scored using one of three general approaches, as noted earlier. The first scoring approach, dichotomous, credits a response to a multicomponent item with a point when and only when the response is in perfect agreement with the key. The second approach, componential scoring, in general increase the effective length (item count) of a test with multicomponent tasks because it breaks each of these out according to its separate components, treating each component as a separate test item. The third scoring approach, polytomous, treats each multicomponent item as capable of supporting more than one scoring level. Under a polytomous scoring approach, a scoring framework is applied to the responses to each multicomponent task according to the task's underlying type. The evaluation function for that type is used to compute the polytomous score.

## Data Preparation and Methodology

A scoring framework developed by Questar Assessment, Inc. was used in scoring multicomponent tasks for the eight test forms of this study: two in Algebra, two in English, two in Biology, and two in Government. All forms were composed of a mixture of traditional items and "technology-enhanced items" (TEIs). Most TEIs were classifiable as some type of multicomponent task (selection, ordering, or mapping), or combination of these types. For the purposes of this study, multiple choice items and constructed-response items scored by human readers or raters were considered to be traditional item types.

Forms varied in length from 18 to 21 items, and were administered to high-school students from 35 districts of one U.S. state. The students had completed relevant coursework for the content area in which they took the exam, and were thus part of the intended population for these pilot exams. Depending on the test form, complete data from between 337 to 428 students was available. The percentages per form of TEIs classifiable as multicomponent tasks ranged from 48% (Algebra Form A) to 85% (Government Form B). Scoring of these items was influenced by scoring approach; the other items (standard multiple choice or human-scored constructed response items, for the most part) were scored the same regardless of scoring approach.

For polytomous scoring, scores on any multicomponent task supporting more than four points were rescaled so that the maximum score was four. This was done to prevent any item from having too large a scoring weight in relation to other items, thereby biasing overall test scores too greatly toward performance on that one item. For dichotomous scoring, a simple transformation of polytomous scores to $\{0, 1\}$ was applied, with the "1" assigned only to perfect responses. For componential scoring, the separate components of each multicomponent task were broken, and each one was scored dichotomously. This resulted in three separate data sets for the same common set of items. Each set was analyzed separately and results compared across the three.

## Classical Item and Test Form Statistics

Table 4 summarizes the raw score distributions for the eight forms in the study. Consistently and as expected, dichotomous scoring gave the smallest possible range of scores. Componential scoring yielded the highest range because the polytomous scoring was capped at four points per item, whereas a multicomponent task might have 10 or more components, and componential scores were not adjusted for the number of components per item.

The total number of units, or items, for the dichotomous and polytomous scoring approaches are the same as the total number of items for the form. However, the total number of units, or components, for the componential scoring approach can be much greater. Table 5 shows the effect of this increase for the tests under consideration.

*Table 4. Raw score statistics by form and scoring approach*

| Form | # of Cases | Scoring Approach | Max. Possible | Min. | Mean | Max. | SD |
|---|---|---|---|---|---|---|---|
| Algebra A | 409 | Dichotomous | 24 | 0 | 8.8 | 22 | 4.8 |
| | | Componential | 64 | 13 | 35.7 | 61 | 9.9 |
| | | Polytomous | 46 | 4 | 21.2 | 43 | 8.1 |
| Algebra B | 337 | Dichotomous | 29 | 1 | 8.9 | 26 | 5.2 |
| | | Componential | 92 | 28 | 51.2 | 84 | 10.8 |
| | | Polytomous | 60 | 9 | 26.4 | 53 | 8.7 |
| English A | 382 | Dichotomous | 28 | 3 | 13.5 | 23 | 4.1 |
| | | Componential | 106 | 39 | 72.4 | 95 | 10.9 |
| | | Polytomous | 57 | 16 | 34.7 | 49 | 6.6 |
| English B | 424 | Dichotomous | 28 | 2 | 13.0 | 25 | 4.7 |
| | | Componential | 95 | 29 | 62.8 | 90 | 13.0 |
| | | Polytomous | 54 | 13 | 31.2 | 49 | 7.7 |
| Biology A | 377 | Dichotomous | 29 | 0 | 15.6 | 25 | 4.8 |
| | | Componential | 73 | 18 | 50.4 | 69 | 10.5 |
| | | Polytomous | 56 | 10 | 36.2 | 51 | 8.3 |
| Biology B | 399 | Dichotomous | 27 | 1 | 12.4 | 22 | 4.1 |
| | | Componential | 81 | 24 | 53.3 | 75 | 10.0 |
| | | Polytomous | 56 | 13 | 34.6 | 51 | 7.7 |
| Government A | 390 | Dichotomous | 34 | 0 | 11.2 | 28 | 5.5 |
| | | Componential | 81 | 17 | 45.9 | 74 | 10.3 |
| | | Polytomous | 66 | 9 | 34.0 | 60 | 9.2 |
| Government B | 428 | Dichotomous | 36 | 0 | 8.9 | 25 | 5.2 |
| | | Componential | 104 | 24 | 57.9 | 89 | 13.0 |
| | | Polytomous | 68 | 8 | 30.9 | 55 | 9.7 |

Separating items into their components caused forms to triple or quadruple in number of points. This increase in maximum point total helps to contextualize the higher componential scoring form reliabilities (alpha).

Average item or unit p-values (or percent correct) are also displayed in Table 5, as are mean point-biserial correlation coefficients. The p-value for a polytomously-scored is equivalent to the average item score, divided by the maximum score possible for the item. An item's point-biserial correlation is the correlation between the score on an item and total test score (with the item included). Extreme item p-values and low point-biserial

correlations were flagged and the counts of these flags tallied. Note that all items are included in these statistics, not just the multicomponent items. This inclusion acknowledges that the composition of items on a test changes the composition of the total score, which in turn affects the relationship between each item and the total score, regardless of item type.

As noted previously, reliabilities should increase and greater statistical flagging should occur as a result of having more units to flag. However, the increases in reliability for componential scoring compared to polytomous or dichotomous scoring were less than one would expect from such

*Table 5. Classical statistics by form and scoring approach*

| Form | # of Items | Scoring Approach | # of Units | Test FormAlpha | Mean P-Value | Mean Pt. Biserial | Units Flagged for Difficulty* (Percent of Units) | Units Flagged for Discrimination* (Percent of Units) |
|---|---|---|---|---|---|---|---|---|
| Algebra A | 18 | Dichotomous | 18 | 0.78 | 0.35 | 0.45 | 4 (22) | 5 (28) |
| | | Componential | 59 | 0.87 | 0.57 | 0.34 | 1 (2) | 9 (15) |
| | | Polytomous | 18 | 0.82 | 0.47 | 0.51 | 0 (0) | 0 (0) |
| Algebra B | 21 | Dichotomous | 21 | 0.78 | 0.29 | 0.40 | 6 (29) | 4 (19) |
| | | Componential | 84 | 0.84 | 0.58 | 0.25 | 4 (5) | 31 (7) |
| | | Polytomous | 21 | 0.80 | 0.43 | 0.45 | 0 (0) | 1 (5) |
| English A | 20 | Dichotomous | 20 | 0.72 | 0.47 | 0.39** | 3 (15) | 3 (15) |
| | | Componential | 87 | 0.85 | 0.69 | 0.26 | 15 (17) | 27 (31) |
| | | Polytomous | 20 | 0.75 | 0.62 | 0.41 | 2 (10) | 1 (5) |
| English B | 19 | Dichotomous | 19 | 0.77 | 0.45 | 0.42 | 1 (5) | 1 (5) |
| | | Componential | 74 | 0.90 | 0.67 | 0.33 | 11 (15) | 13 (18) |
| | | Polytomous | 19 | 0.81 | 0.59 | 0.48 | 0 (0) | 0 (0) |
| Biology A | 20 | Dichotomous | 20 | 0.75 | 0.50 | 0.40 | 1 (5) | 2 (10) |
| | | Componential | 68 | 0.88 | 0.69 | 0.35 | 7 (10) | 8 (12) |
| | | Polytomous | 20 | 0.79 | 0.63 | 0.45 | 0 (0) | 2 (10) |
| Biology B | 18 | Dichotomous | 18 | 0.66 | 0.37 | 0.38** | 6 (33) | 3 (17) |
| | | Componential | 80 | 0.86 | 0.66 | 0.29 | 7 (9) | 21 (26) |
| | | Polytomous | 18 | 0.73 | 0.58 | 0.41 | 2 (11) | 3 (17) |
| Government A | 20 | Dichotomous | 20 | 0.57 | 0.38 | 0.37** | 3 (15) | 1 (5) |
| | | Componential | 73 | 0.86 | 0.60 | 0.30 | 6 (8) | 13 (18) |
| | | Polytomous | 20 | 0.73 | 0.58 | 0.42 | 0 (0) | 0 (0) |
| Government B | 20 | Dichotomous | 20 | 0.70 | 0.31 | 0.43** | 1 (5) | 0 (0) |
| | | Componential | 96 | 0.89 | 0.59 | 0.30 | 3 (3) | 23 (24) |
| | | Polytomous | 20 | 0.82 | 0.51 | 0.49 | 0 (0) | 0 (0) |

*p-value ≤ 0.10 or p-value ≥ 0.90; pt. biserial ≤ 0.20

**One or more dichotomously scored item has a p-value of zero, so the pt. biserial could not be calculated. Therefore, items with p-values of zero were not included when calculating the mean pt. biserial.

large increases in the number of possible points, and the rate of flagging per unit was much higher for componential scoring compared to the other two approaches.

Consistently, and as suggested by the pattern of mean item p-values across the three approaches for each form, dichotomous scoring resulted in the most difficult items and componential resulted in the easiest. It should not be surprising that dichotomous scoring resulted in more difficult items since credit is awarded only for a fully correct response. The more components a TEI has, the more severe the effect of the conjunctive rule governing dichotomous scoring (i.e., the need for all components of an item to be correct in order to obtain credit for that item).

The high level of per-unit discrimination flagging for dichotomous scoring appears to be the result of low item p-values since extreme p-values are mathematically linked to low point-biserial correlations. However, this may not be the sole reason for the high level of discrimination flagging of units under componential scoring, since discrimination flagging of componential scoring units occurred along the range of p-values. To better understand the pattern of discrimination flagging, it is helpful to examine the relationship between difficulty and discrimination for a sample of multicomponent items, across the three scoring approaches, as follows.

## The Effect of Evaluation Function on the Statistics of a Multicomponent Item

Figure 1 plots difficulty and discrimination separately for the ten TEIs in Algebra, Form A. Each plot shows one point for the dichotomously scored item, one for the polytomously scored item, and several for the componentially scored units within the item. The statistical flagging zone corresponding to that in Table 5 is overlain on each plot (indicated by the shaded regions). The scatterplots are arranged roughly according to the relative dichotomous difficulty-by-discrimination position of each multi-component TEI.

As shown, a dichotomous evaluation function consistently makes a multicomponent item more difficult and less discriminating than a polytomous evaluation function. Four of the multicomponent items are within or very near the flagging zone when scored dichotomously. The items "created" by componential scoring tend to be easier than either of the other two approaches. These items are nearly all less discriminating than their polytomously-scored counterparts, and several of them are close to or within the statistical flagging zone. In theory, the corresponding statistics for multiple-choice items would be unaffected by scoring approach, but to the extent that specific multiple-choice items correlate with TEI performance, some of the multiple-choice point-biserial

correlations could increase or decrease, because the total test score is defined differently for each approach.

## Fit to Standard Item Response Theory (IRT) Models

Another measure of the appropriateness of an evaluation function is the degree to which it facilitates the construction of a unidimensional test scale. Granted, this criterion is not always applicable, as there is no a priori reason that all tests should measure a unidimensional construct. In many cases, however, unidimensional measurement is indeed a goal because the alternative poses special challenges for score interpretation. The simplest (and most widely used) IRT models assume scales of one dimension, and deviations from this assumption show up in fit statistics generated when an attempt is made to scale multidimensional data using these models, assuming the items have no other problems, like incorrect scoring keys or multiple right answers.

To explore dimensionality, each form was calibrated using IRT models appropriate for the items and coding used. All dichotomous items were calibrated to the Rasch model, which models the probability of a correct response to an item $i$ as a logistic function of student ability $\theta$, with the position of the logistic function determined by the difficulty $b_i$ of the item:

$$P(i = 1 \mid \theta) = \frac{e^{\theta - b_i}}{1 + e^{\theta - b_i}}$$

The naturally polytomous items (i.e., the human-scored constructed response items) and the polytomously-scored multicomponent items were calibrated to Masters' (1982) partial credit model, an extension of the Rasch model that takes into account the difficulty of the item, parameters called "level thresholds" that quantify how dif-

*Figure 1. ITEM difficulty and discrimination across three scoring approaches to ten TEIs*

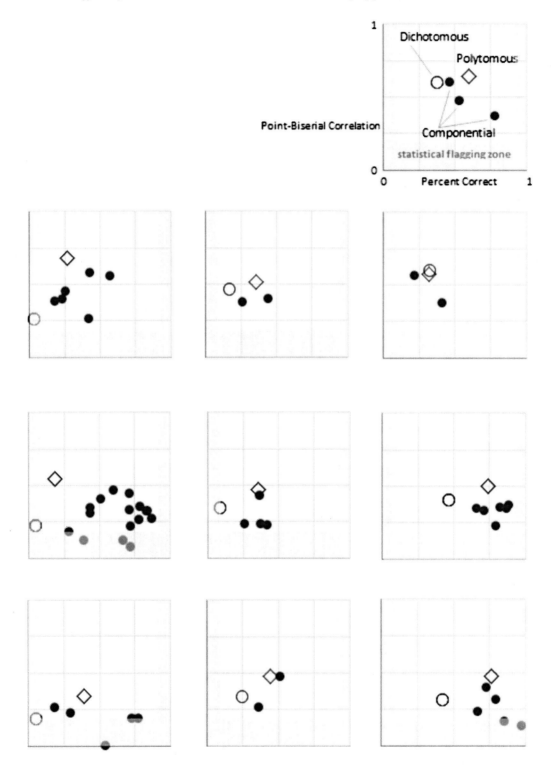

ficult it is to perform at a given level of the item, and the student's ability. The partial credit model expresses the probability of getting a given score on a given item, rather than just getting it right or wrong. All calibrations were conducted using the Winsteps® (Linacre, 2012) program.

The fit to IRT calibrations was evaluated using a Winsteps®-provided measure, outfit mean square (OMNSQ), a conventional chi-square statistic divided by its degree of freedom. OMNSQ should be 1 for units whose response data fit the IRT model well. Values greater than 1 indicate under-fit and values less than 1 indicate over-fit. For purposes of evaluation, however, only values less than 0.7 and values greater than 1.3 were flagged for over-fit and under-fit, respectively. Table 6 tallies these flags.

In general, IRT calibrations were more successful for English, Biology, and Government forms than for Algebra forms. This was due to the greater number of over-fitting items or units on Algebra. In the context of multiple-choice items,

*Table 6. Item fit statistics from Rasch IRT calibrations*

| Form | Scoring Approach | # of Units Used in Calibration | Under-Fitting* (Percent of Units) | Over-Fitting* (Percent of Units) | Total Mis-Fitting (Percent of Units) |
|---|---|---|---|---|---|
| Algebra A | Dichotomous | 18 | 4 (22) | 5 (28) | 9 (50) |
| | Componential | 59 | 3 (5) | 12 (20) | 15 (25) |
| | Polytomous | 18 | 4 (22) | 4 (22) | 8 (44) |
| Algebra B | Dichotomous | 21 | 3 (14) | 3 (14) | 6 (29) |
| | Componential | 84 | 9 (11) | 15 (18) | 24 (29) |
| | Polytomous | 21 | 5 (14) | 3 (14) | 8 (38) |
| English A | Dichotomous | 20 | 2** (10) | 2 (10) | 4 (20) |
| | Componential | 84 | 0 (0) | 1 (1) | 1 (1) |
| | Polytomous | 20 | 1 (5) | 0 (0) | 1(5) |
| English B | Dichotomous | 19 | 1 (5) | 1 (5) | 2 (11) |
| | Componential | 74 | 3 (4) | 6 (8) | 9 (12) |
| | Polytomous | 19 | 1 (5) | 0 (0) | 1 (5) |
| Biology A | Dichotomous | 20 | 2 (10) | 0 (0) | 2 (10) |
| | Componential | 68 | 2 (3) | 7 (10) | 9 (13) |
| | Polytomous | 20 | 3 (15) | 0 (0) | 3 (15) |
| Biology B | Dichotomous | 18 | 7** (39) | 0 (0) | 7 (39) |
| | Componential | 80 | 6 (8) | 2 (3) | 8 (10) |
| | Polytomous | 18 | 2 (11) | 0 (0) | 2 (11) |
| Government A | Dichotomous | 20 | 1** (5) | 0 (0) | 1 (5) |
| | Componential | 73 | 2 (3) | 3 (4) | 5 (7) |
| | Polytomous | 20 | 1 (5) | 0 (0) | 1 (5) |
| Government B | Dichotomous | 20 | 3** (15) | 1 (5) | 4 (20) |
| | Componential | 96 | 4 (4) | 0 (0) | 4 (4) |
| | Polytomous | 20 | 4 (20) | 0 (0) | 4 (20) |

*Under-fitting items are those with an OMNSQ greater than 1.3, and over-fitting items are those with an OMNSQ less than 0.7.

**Includes items that could not be calibrated due to having a dichotomous p-value of zero. There was one such item in English A, two in Biology B, one in Government A, and one in Government B.

over-fitting happens when there are fewer instances than expected of careless errors (i.e., high-ability students getting easy items incorrect) or guessing (i.e., low-ability students getting hard items correct). This can occur when there are incorrect answer options that tend to draw students away from the correct answer. This may have occurred more often on the Algebra forms than on the other tests. However, over-fitting is not considered as serious a problem as under-fitting, which indicates a greater-than-expected instance of careless errors or guessing – that is, too much "noise" in the data relative to the Rasch model.

The under-fit results are mixed. In two out of the eight cases, dichotomous scoring produced the fewest under-fit counts; it was tied for first in two other cases. Componential scoring also produced the fewest counts of under-fit in two cases; it was tied for first in one other case. By under-fit counts, polytomous scoring was favored in only one instance, and it was tied for first in two. The fit results are generally inconclusive in terms of which scoring approach results in a better fit to a Rasch model, with one exception: dichotomous scoring has the greatest probability of resulting in items with p-values of zero, which will fit no model because there is no variation in the responses.

It may be that less restrictive IRT models could provide better fit results, and possibly different models are appropriate for the different scoring approaches. To explore this, units from the Algebra and English forms were assigned to one of three different IRT models depending on their characteristics, and calibrations were conducted for each form-by-scoring approach combination using the PARSCALE (Scientific Software International, Inc., 2003) program. A combination of three-parameter logistic (3PL), two-parameter logistic (2PL), and partial credit (GPCM, Muraki, 1992) models was used for each form, depending on how many levels an item or unit supported and whether including a pseudo-guessing parameter

was justified. (Including this parameter is justified for units, such as multiple-choice items, in which students might make a correct selection by chance, without having the requisite knowledge measured by the unit.) The Rasch model can be considered a special case of the more general 3PL model:

$$P(i = 1 \mid \theta) = c_i + \frac{(1 - c_i)e^{a_i(\theta - b_i)}}{1 + e^{a_i(\theta - b_i)}}$$

The 3PL model includes two additional parameters to account for differences in discrimination ($a_i$) and pseudo-guessing probabilities ($c_i$) among units. If all the discriminations are set to 1 and all the pseudo-guessing probabilities are set to zero, the equation above becomes the Rasch equation. If only the pseudo-guessing probabilities are set to zero, the 2PL model results.

With the exception of human-scored constructed response items, all units in the dichotomously scored forms were calibrated to a 3PL model, with pseudo-guessing parameters estimated for each item. Any dichotomous human-scored constructed response item was calibrated to a 2PL model. Items allowing more than one point were calibrated to a partial-credit model.

These mixed IRT model calibrations were conducted with a convergence criterion set to 0.0001 logit on the location parameters and 200 Newton cycles. This condition was relaxed for calibrations of the componential data, which generally did not converge in 200 cycles unless the convergence criterion was increased to 0.001 logit. In any of the calibration runs, if one item was consistently exhibiting the highest location difference between cycles and the program failed to converge, the item was removed and the calibration was run again.

The metrics of interest in these IRT calibrations were (1) the number of items lost due to the inability to calibrate the data for those items and (2) the number of items exhibiting poor fit, again being defined as a chi-square statistic exceeding a particular threshold. Table 7 presents the results of the PARSCALE calibration runs for the Algebra and English forms.

In general, the mixed IRT model calibrations were more successful on the English forms than on the Algebra forms. In Algebra, there was no calibration in which all units calibrated and none were flagged for fit. However, such completely successful calibrations occurred once for each of the English forms, which were both polytomously scored. In general, calibrations of the polytomously-scored data had the fewest items flagged for fit. In none of those runs were items unable to calibrate, nor did any fail to converge. Indeed, on these more flexible IRT calibrations of the data, the polytomously scored tests compared well to the alternative scoring approaches. Several units (in one case representing nearly half of the entire exam) failed to converge under the componential calibration runs, suggesting that when multicomponent tasks are broken down into components, these do not easily conform to a 3PL model.

## Discussion and Conclusion

Comparing the results across the three scoring methods supports the appropriateness of applying evaluation functions based on a scoring framework modeled on a polytomous approach. On the whole, multicomponent tasks are best treated as units supporting multiple levels, rather than one complex task supporting just two (right or wrong) levels, or many separate items that can each be right or wrong.

Key findings supporting this conclusion are:

1.  Items (or components in the case of componential scoring) are most difficult when scored dichotomously and are easiest when scored by component.
2.  Point-biserial correlations are lower for dichotomous and componential scoring than for polytomous scoring.
3.  Test form reliabilities are highest for componential scoring but do not correspond with the numbers of scorable units in com-

*Table 7. Item fit statistics from mixed IRT model calibrations*

| Form | Scoring Approach | # of Units Used in Calibration | Calibrated & Not Flagged for Fit (Percent of Units) | Calibrated but Flagged for Fit* (Percent of Units) | Unable to Calibrate or Non-Converging (Percent of Units) |
|---|---|---|---|---|---|
| Algebra A | Dichotomous | 18 | 17 (94) | 1 (6) | 0 (0) |
| | Componential | 59 | 47 (80) | 10 (17) | 2 (3) |
| | Polytomous | 18 | 15 (83) | 3 (17) | 0 (0) |
| Algebra B | Dichotomous | 21 | 8 (38) | 9 (43) | 4 (19) |
| | Componential | 84 | 42 (50) | 38 (45) | 4 (5) |
| | Polytomous | 21 | 15 (71) | 6 (29) | 0 (0) |
| English A | Dichotomous | 20 | 19 (95) | 0 (0) | 1 (5) |
| | Componential | 84 | 72 (86) | 12 (14) | 0 (0) |
| | Polytomous | 20 | 20 (100) | 0 (0) | 0 (0) |
| English B | Dichotomous | 19 | 15 (79) | 2 (11) | 2 (11) |
| | Componential | 74 | 52 (70) | 16 (22) | 6 (8) |
| | Polytomous | 19 | 19 (100) | 0 (0) | 0 (0) |

*The PARSCALE fit index is a likelihood-ratio chi-square statistic, and the flag was set to $p \leq 0.05$.

ponentially scored test forms. Polytomously scored test form reliabilities are higher than their dichotomously scored counterparts.

4. IRT calibrations of polytomously scored test forms have the fewest convergence and item non-fit problems, while componentially scored test forms have the most.

Each of these scoring approaches results in a different statistical profile to the tests, with some notable patterns. The dichotomous approach yielded very difficult tests and many items with poor statistics, and componentially scored tests yielded the widest range of scores but at the cost of many poorly functioning items. Applying evaluation functions based on a partial-credit scheme and supported by a scoring framework to address the special features of multicomponent tasks gave the best results overall, with the highest per-item contribution to test reliability and item survival rates.

## Summary and Recommendations

The practice of assessment has moved beyond multiple-choice testing, not by abandoning it but by opening up to new task formats. This expansion of the assessment horizon to encompass complex tasks with similar underlying structures has brought with it a need to be systematic about how to score these tasks automatically, in a manner analogous to the treatment of scoring in the relatively simple case of multiple-choice testing. Many complex tasks in real world assessments can be analyzed and characterized as multicomponent tasks, defined as tasks all possible responses to which can be modelled as finite sets of binary elements. Simply put, these are tasks which have a limited and pre-determined set of possible responses. Responses to these tasks are capable of showing gradations of knowledge, skill, or understanding and thus they can be ranked and scored to indicate greater or lesser quality. This in turn allows them to be scored automatically.

Responses to multicomponent tasks can be treated using standard psychometric methods, but it is especially important to be aware of the statistical and logical interdependencies among components. When components are treated separately, the logical interdependencies can render even bi-factor modeling unsuited to proper analysis of the resulting data. This chapter showed that it is possible to score multicomponent tasks using a principled approach in which partial credit is awarded according to the underlying task type. As was demonstrated in the empirical section of this chapter, assessment response data scored using a polytomous scoring approach, consistent with the recommendation here for scoring multicomponent tasks, exhibit better psychometric characteristics than alternative approaches.

Proper application of a scoring framework for multicomponent tasks entails that assessment program developers and sponsors address the context for assessment, and make an informed decision about what scoring approach to use in light of the purpose of the assessment program and available resources. If these considerations support polytomous scoring for multicomponent tasks, the next step is to survey the response space of the more complex assessment tasks and determine if they, or parts of them, can be modeled as multicomponent tasks. To classify those tasks as involving selection, ordering, or mapping requires determining the underlying task structure despite the surface appearance of the item.

Developing and applying a comprehensive scoring framework ensures that tasks with similar underlying task structures are scored in a consistent manner. Moreover, many pitfalls can be avoided by building such a framework into the task development process itself, where it can be made clear to task authors what configurations of task parameters (such as the number of answers relative to the number of choices, for selection task) allow for supporting greater or fewer scoring levels. Finally, a scoring framework assists in proper communication to examinees, especially in high-stakes contexts. Depending on the intended test use, it may be critical that examinees, long accustomed to the script of traditional testing and scoring, be informed about how their responses to multicomponent tasks are being scored.

## FUTURE RESEARCH DIRECTIONS

It is difficult to overstate the central role of the multiple-choice test item in the history of research on assessment. Enabling technologies, together with a demand for more complex assessment tasks, are bringing alternative forms of automatically scorable assessment into the testing arena, and these will need to be researched to be better understood. Following are several directions that research on multicomponent tasks can take.

1.  Identifying multicomponent tasks as elements of more complex tasks. Multicomponent assessment tasks remain largely unidentified as such because assessment participants generally are not accustomed to seeing them in standardized testing. One direction of research, then, is that of identifying complex tasks, or parts of them, as multicomponent tasks in disguise. These tasks are likely deeply embedded in simulations, games, and other novel forms of assessment without developers' or other participants' awareness of their presence.

2.  Building best practices for developing multicomponent tasks. Just as there is plenty of research informing how best to author multiple-choice test items, there should be a parallel strand to deal with best practices for multicomponent tasks. This research could attend to the special features of these tasks, and can focus on topics such as minimizing logical interdependencies among components and manipulating default configurations of elements so that they support the most information about respondent knowledge, skill, and understanding.

3.  Modeling and validation of multicomponent tasks. The field of psychometrics has paid little attention to modeling multicomponent tasks largely because of their relative scarcity in more formal assessment settings. This might change as a result of a greater representation of such tasks in practice. Do standard IRT models work well with multicomponent tasks? Is bi-factor modeling useful for some types of multicomponent items, and which ones? Do such tasks deliver on the promise of more information and validity, without compromising the efficiency of automated scoring? Although the findings of this chapter point to affirmative responses to the first and third of these questions, they are only initial answers based on one context for multicomponent tasks and one specific scoring framework.

4.  Assessing evaluation functions for multicomponent task. Unlike traditional test items, multicomponent tasks do not come equipped with an obvious scoring approach. Alternative proposals to scoring selection, ordering, and mapping tasks may be advanced and evaluated. Perhaps there is a different way to classify and describe multicomponent tasks that leads towards a more unified understanding of item types featuring finite response spaces.

5.  Communicating information about partial knowledge, skill, and understanding. If a multicomponent task is in some ways a mini-assessment capable of revealing, when it is present, less than perfect mastery, then how is that information to be conveyed to stakeholders? What sort of statistics and reporting on multicomponent task performance is most useful to educators and students?

6. Multicomponent tasks and cognitive diagnostic modeling (CDM). When task components are identified systematically, their relationship to specific examinee knowledge, skills, and abilities can be made more explicit and the evidentiary models for uncovering these skills can be articulated. Viewed the other way around, multicomponent tasks intentionally designed to elicit evidence of the interrelated skills that are subject of CDMs may provide the ideal scenario for implementing componential scoring successfully. Of course, the goal of such assessment would be directly to make claims about examinee mastery states, rather than to locate their relative standing on an underlying continuum. What seems needed for the former is repeated testing of variations in a specific domain, and multicomponent tasks with many components can provide these very conditions.

These avenues and no doubt others will surface if multicomponent tasks occupy a greater role in the script of testing. Just as the emergence of constructed-response tasks ushered in new methods to deal with the problem of rater consistency and severity, as well as debate about the relative merits of human-scored open-ended test items over those which already provide the right answer, but require the respondent identify it, so too can multicomponent tasks add to the conversation about the best ways to test.

## CONCLUSION

Assessment of real-world skills increasingly requires development and efficient scoring of test items that go beyond standard multiple-choice and open-response formats. There are long-acknowledged limitations on what can be tested in the case of the former. But developing, testing and scoring the more interesting open-ended items involves labor intensive training and scoring by humans.

This chapter addressed an emerging middle ground of assessment, which consists of test items with constrained responses that can be enumerated and ordered a priori in terms of quality, and that are thereby automatically scorable. Many assessments feature these multicomponent tasks either in a directly identifiable form, or as part of more complex tasks, such as interaction-based problems and games.

The outlines of a framework for scoring these types of items was laid out based on an analysis of the response space of any test item with a finite set of possible responses, how those response might be ordered from worst to best, and how they might be combined into ordered groups representing increasing knowledge, skill, or understanding on the part of the respondent. This general, abstract approach went beyond what is required for standard multiple choice test items, simple open-ended items, and other exam tasks evaluated through human scoring or algorithms designed to model or predict human scoring. The multicomponent task formats discussed here feature expanded (but finite) response spaces that potentially carry a great deal of information about response quality – an important reason test developers make use of them to begin with, and the framework presented in this chapter is designed to capture that information.

Because multicomponent items are defined as collections of more fundamental binary elements, this chapter covered the psychometrics of attempts to model responses to related tasks within the framework of item response theory. After distinguishing multicomponent tasks from other types of complex item formats, principles for an effective response coding schema for various simple multicomponent tasks were proposed. Response evaluation functions for one type of multicomponent task (selection tasks) were proposed and their relative merits discussed. Three alternative scoring criteria – two of them representing extreme cases of scoring stringency (on the one hand) and detail (on the other) – were the subject of an empirical evaluation based upon data from four different end-of-course exams administered to high school students as part of a pilot program of multicomponent technology-enhanced items (TEIs) in a U.S. state. The findings support evaluation functions consistent with the multicomponent task schema presented, which leverages multicomponent task potential for providing evidence of partial knowledge, understanding, or skill.

## REFERENCES

Board of Certification for the Athletic Trainer (BOCAT). (2014). *BOC™ sample exam questions* [Sample examination questions]. Retrieved from http://www.bocatc.org/candidates/exam-preparation-tools/sample-exam-questions/

Bradlow, E. T., Wainer, H., & Wang, X. (1999). A Bayesian random effects model for testlets. *Psychometrika, 64*(2), 153–168. doi:10.1007/BF02294533

Drasgow, F., Luecht, R. M., & Bennett, R. E. (2006). Technology and testing. In R. L. Brennan (Ed.), *Educational measurement* (4th ed.; pp. 471–515). Westport, CT: Praeger Publishers.

Educational Testing Service (ETS). (2014). *GRE® revised General Test: Quantitative Reasoning question types* [Sample examination questions]. Retrieved from http://www.ets.org/gre/revised_general/about/content/quantitative_reasoning/

GlassLab. (2013). *SimCityEDU: Pollution Challenge!* [Computer software]. Retrieved from http://www.simcityedu.org/

Hubbard, J. P. (1978). *Measuring medical education: The tests and experience of the national board of medical examiners* (2nd ed.). Philadelphia: Lea & Febiger.

Katz, M. (2014). *How the ARE is Scored* [Web log post]. Retrieved from http://blog.ncarb.org/en/2014/April/HowAREScored.aspx

Kids Go, P. B. S. (2012). *Lifeboat to Mars* [Computer software]. Retrieved from http://pbskids.org/lifeboat/

Lane, S., & Stone, C. (2006). Performance assessment. In R. L. Brennan (Ed.), *Educational measurement* (4th ed.; pp. 387–431). Westport, CT: Praeger Publishers.

Li, Y., Bolt, D. M., & Fu, J. (2006). A comparison of alternative models for testlets. *Applied Psychological Measurement, 30*(1), 3–21. doi:10.1177/0146621605275414

Linacre, J. M. (2012). Winsteps® (Version 3.75.0) [Computer software]. Beaverton, OR: Winsteps.com.

Masters, G. N. (1982). A Rasch model for partial credit scoring. *Psychometrika, 47*(2), 149–174. doi:10.1007/BF02296272

Min, S., & He, L. (2014). Applying unidimensional and multidimensional item response theory models in testlet-based reading assessment. *Language Testing, 31*(4), 453–477. doi:10.1177/0265532214527277

Muraki, E. (1992). A generalized partial credit model: Application of an EM algorithm. *Applied Psychological Measurement, 16*(2), 159–176. doi:10.1177/014662169201600206

Partnership for Assessment of Readiness for College and Career (PARCC). (2014). *Grade 8 Sample Items* [Sample examination questions]. Retrieved from http://parcconline.org/sites/parcc/files/Grade%208%20Sample%20Item%20Set-Revised%204-25-14.pdf

Pope, L. (2013). *Papers, Please.* [Computer software]. Retrieved from http://papersplea.se/

Rijmen, F. (2010). Formal relations and an empirical comparison among the bi-factor, the testlet, and a second-order multidimensional IRT model. *Journal of Educational Measurement, 47*(3), 361–372. doi:10.1111/j.1745-3984.2010.00118.x

Samejima, F. (1969). *Estimation of latent ability using a response pattern of graded scores (Psychometric Monograph No. 17)*. Richmond, VA: Psychometric Society.

Scientific Software International, Inc. (2003). *PARSCALE, version 4.1.2328.4* [Computer software]. Skokie, IL: Publisher.

Thissen, D., Nelson, L., Rosa, K., & McLeod, L. D. (2001). Item response theory for items scored in more than two categories. In D. Thissen & H. Wainer (Eds.), *Test scoring* (pp. 141–186). Mahwah, NJ: Lawrence Erlbaum Associates.

Wainer, H., Bradlow, E. T., & Du, Z. (2000). Testlet response theory. An analog for the 3-PL useful in testlet-based adaptive testing. In W. J. van der Linden & C. A. W. Glas (Eds.), *Computerized adaptive testing: Theory and practice* (pp. 245–270). Boston, MA: Kluwer Academic Publishers. doi:10.1007/0-306-47531-6_13

Wainer, H., Bradlow, E. T., & Wang, X. (2007). *Testlet response theory and its applications*. New York, NY: Cambridge University Press. doi:10.1017/CBO9780511618765

Wainer, H., & Kiely, G. L. (1987). Item clusters and computerized adaptive testing: A case for testlets. *Journal of Educational Measurement, 24*(3), 185–201. doi:10.1111/j.1745-3984.1987.tb00274.x

Yen, W. M. (1993). Scaling performance assessments: Strategies for managing local item dependence. *Journal of Educational Measurement, 30*(3), 187–214. doi:10.1111/j.1745-3984.1993.tb00423.x

## KEY TERMS AND DEFINITIONS

**Bi-Factor Model:** A psychometric model in which there are two levels of test-related factors contributing to examinee responses – an overall factor measured by all items on a test, and a specific factor measured by groups of items.

**Complex Task:** In the context of assessment, any task the response to which entails more than one interaction or stage.

**Componential Scoring:** A scoring approach in which responses to a multicomponent task are treated as responses to separate items, one for each component, with each response scored correct or incorrect.

**Dichotomous Scoring:** A scoring approach in which the response to an item or task is always scored as either correct or incorrect, regardless of the task's inherent complexity or any indication of partial knowledge or understanding in the response.

**Item Response Theory (IRT):** A psychometric framework which models the probability of observing specific responses to items as functions of latent respondent and item parameters.

**Mapping Task:** A multicomponent task whose underlying response structure involves constructing a correct mapping between the elements of given finite sets.

**Multicomponent Task:** Or multicomponent item, a task all possible responses to which can be modelled as a finite set of binary elements.

**Ordering Task:** A multicomponent task requiring placing elements from a finite set in a correct order.

**Polytomous Scoring:** In the context of scoring multicomponent task, the scoring of responses to these in such a way as to potentially award partial credit in accordance with the application of an evaluation function appropriate for the underlying task type.

**Scoring Framework:** A set of specifications for scoring different types of items or tasks on a test, including multicomponent tasks.

**Selection Task:** A multicomponent task entailing the selection of one or more elements from a finite set.

**Technology-Enhanced Item (TEI):** Computer-delivered complex tasks associated with assessments aligned to the U.S. Common Core State Standards.

**Testlet:** According to Wainer and Kiely (1987, p.190), "a group of items related to a single content area that is developed as a unit and contains a fixed number of predetermined paths that an examinee may follow."

## ENDNOTE

[1]  Computerized delivery systems are usually configured to prevent multiple markings, and can also prompt the user to respond before proceeding on an exam. In general, this chapter does not assume that responses are validated to prevent multiple markings or omissions – scoring procedures are meant to apply regardless of the presence of such response validation mechanisms. Many multicomponent tasks can be implemented on paper and pencil, where there are no response validation mechanisms present. (The comparability of multicomponent tasks with and without validation mechanisms is an interesting question beyond the scope of this chapter.)

# Chapter 25
# Advances in Automated Scoring of Writing for Performance Assessment

**Peter W. Foltz**
*Pearson, USA & University of Colorado – Boulder, USA*

## ABSTRACT

*The ability to convey information through writing is a central component of real-world skills. However, assessing writing can be time consuming, limiting the timeliness of feedback. Automated scoring of writing has been shown to be effective across a number of applications. This chapter focuses on how automated scoring of writing has been extended to assessing and training of real-world skills in a range of content domains. It illustrates examples of how the technology is used and considerations for its implementation. The examples include 1) Formative feedback on writing quality, 2) scoring of content in student writing. 3) improving reading comprehension through summary writing, and 4) assessment of writing integrated in higher-level performance tasks in professional domains.*

## WRITING FOR PERFORMANCE ASSESSMENTS

Writing is the ability to create meaning through symbols (e.g., Kellogg, 1999) and to communicate that meaning to others. Communicating information through writing is considered one of the key 21st Century skills and has been incorporated as a critical component in many national standards (e.g., Ananiadou & Claro, 2009; OECD, 2013). For example, the U.S. Common Core State Standards require students to develop more rigorous writing skills with a stronger emphasis on the ability to

synthesize and summarize informational text, formulate arguments, as well as respond appropriately to source documents. This puts greater emphasis on writing for a purpose, with students linking ideas to texts and argumentation and writing across the curriculum. With the advent of information technologies, writing also plays a more central role in everyday communication. Information can be readily published on the web and communication via writing has become more ubiquitous through email, chat, and other collaborative tools. Thus, within an information economy, writing is not just an academic pursuit, it is the primary conduit for

DOI: 10.4018/978-1-4666-9441-5.ch025

effective transmission of the vital information. As such, writing is a crucial skill across almost all career paths.

Educational practice has also recognized that writing is not just a matter of teaching compositional writing skills. Training of writing typically occurs both through more domain general means, such as in language arts classes and as integrated components within particular curricula to train domain specific writing skills. Over the past few decades, greater emphasis has been placed in training writing across the curriculum (e.g., McCleod, 1992), by emphasizing that students are not just learning to write, but by embedding writing in curricula, they are writing to learn. Indeed, over half of U.S. higher education institutions have formal programs where writing is integrated across the curriculum (Thaiss & Porter, 2010). Thus, writing activities must occur within natural performance tasks in order to promote the abilities that will be needed and used in and out of the classroom.

Learning to write well is a multi-faceted ability. It requires language, organization and expression skills as well as domain knowledge, and it develops slowly over a person's educational career. It is a well-known adage that in order to become a good writer, one needs to do a lot of writing. However, while time on task is typically a strong predictor of performance gains in reading and writing, receiving timely feedback is critical (e.g., Black & William, 1998; Hattie & Timperley, 2007; Shute, 2008). Meta-analyses of studies of formative writing (e.g., Graham, Harris, & Hebert, 2011; Graham & Hebert, 2010; Graham & Perin, 2007) have shown that instructional practices can have strong effects on helping students with learning to write. For example, supporting students with feedback had an effect size of 0.77, and providing students with instruction in strategies for planning, revising and editing their compositions had an effect size of 0.82 (Graham & Perin, 2007), indicating that each instructional practice can be highly valuable. Other findings from these studies indicate that having teachers actively monitor a

student's writing progress and teaching students to monitor their own writing also significantly improve student performance. Thus, it is not good enough to just tell students to write more or write more often. The writing must be monitored and the students need to receive timely feedback and instruction for it to be most effective.

However, a key limitation of implementing increased writing instruction is the amount of time that instructors need to review, edit, and comment on student writing. Typically a teacher can only review student essays after a class period and even then, students may not receive the feedback on their writing a day or a week later. This limits learning since students learn best when receiving timely feedback (e.g., Anderson et al., 1990). Automated scoring of student writing provides the potential to give students specific, immediate, feedback that addresses both the content of their writing, as well as the quality of the written expression. As such, it can give students increased opportunities to practice writing skills and use the feedback to improve writing. Given the need for greater performance assessments for real-world skills, it is critical to have computer-based tools that can support formative processes in writing and be general enough to support types of writing that people perform in real-world tasks. These tools can do more than just *automate* existing educational processes for formative writing. They can also *enhance* and *change* these processes to be more effective for students and teachers. This chapter provides some illustrations of how the technology supports this change.

## Automated Scoring of Writing

Automated scoring of writing, or Automated Essay Scoring (AES), provides the ability to analyze student writing and score writing instantly. AES has become increasingly accepted with multiple systems available for implementing the scoring of writing (e.g., Shermis & Burstein, 2013; see also Bunch et al., this volume; Wilson & Andrada, this volume). Studies of AES systems have shown that they can be as accurate as human scorers (e.g., Burstein, Chodorow, & Leacock, 2004; Landauer, Laham & Foltz, 2001; Shermis & Hamner, 2012), can score on multiple traits of writing (e.g., Foltz et al., 2013), can be used for feedback on content (Beigman-Klebanov et al., 2014; Foltz, Gilliam, & Kendall, 2000), and can score short responses (e.g., Higgins et al., 2014; Thurlow, et al., 2010). AES is now being used operationally in a number of high stakes assessments (e.g., GED, and various state k-12 assessments), placement tests (e.g., Pearson Test of English, ACCUPLACER), and for writing practice (e.g., Criterion, WriteToLearn). AES is therefore becoming more widely accepted as part of educational and assessment practice. While there is a great deal of ongoing research and validation on AES, the purpose of this chapter is not to focus on validation of these approaches, but to explore where it can be used in additional areas of real-world skill building for both summative assessment and formative feedback.

## AUTOMATED SCORING APPLIED TO REAL-WORLD SKILL BUILDING

In this chapter we explore four examples of how automated writing scoring can be applied to real-world skill building. The goal is to illustrate from these examples how the technology can be used and considerations for its implementation. The examples are: 1) Formative feedback on writing quality, 2) scoring of content in student writing, 3) improving student comprehension through summary writing, and 4) assessment of writing integrated in higher-level performance tasks in professional domains. All four examples use a single underlying scoring approach and technology, although different aspects are used in each to achieve the specific applications. A brief overview of the general approach is first described.

## Overview of Automated Scoring with IEA

The automated scoring approaches used for the examples in this chapter are based on the use of the Intelligent Essay Assessor (IEA). It should be noted that there are a number of other scoring engines that can also be used for similar applications (see Bunch et al., this volume; Burstein & Shermis, 2013; Hearst, 2001; Shermis & Hamner, 2012). The IEA uses a combination of language analysis and machine-learning techniques to learn how to score writing based on the collective wisdom of trained human scorers. The original scoring technology was developed and first implemented in the 1990s (e.g., Foltz, 1996; Foltz, et al., 1999; Landauer et al., 2001), and has been subsequently refined and developed over the intervening years and implemented across a number of operational applications (Foltz et al., 2013). IEA learns to assess writing through a training process. Training IEA involves first collecting a representative sample of essays that have been scored by human raters. IEA extracts features from the essays that measure aspects of student performance, such as the student's expression of knowledge and command of vocabulary and linguistic resources. Then, using machine-learning methods, IEA examines the relationships between both the scores provided by the human scorers and the extracted features in order to learn how the human scorers weigh and combine the different features to produce a score. The resulting representation is referred to as a "scoring model". Thus, a scoring model learns to generate the scores and/or types of feedback that an instructor would provide for the essay topic. This section provides details of the scoring features used in IEA, how the features are combined to score different aspects of writing, and considerations for building and evaluating the performance of scoring models.

## Scoring Features

A student's written text can be characterized by a range of features that measure the student's expression and organization of words and sentences, the student's knowledge of the content of the domain, the quality of the student's reasoning, and the student's skills in language use, grammar and the mechanics of writing. In developing analyses of such features, the computational measures extract aspects of student performance that are relevant to the constructs for the competencies of interest (e.g., Hearst, 2000; Williamson et al., 2010). For example, a measure of the type and quality of words used by a student provides an effective and valid measure of a student's lexical sophistication. However, a measure that simply counts the number of words in an essay, although it will likely be highly correlated with human scores for essays, does not provide a valid measure of writing sophistication, in that it is not actually assessing the construct of interest. Thus, multiple language features are typically measured and combined to provide a score. IEA uses a combination of features that measure aspects of the content, lexical sophistication, grammar, mechanics, style, organization, and development within essays. Figure 1 illustrates some of the features used in IEA and how they relate to specific constructs of student writing performance.

## Scoring Content and Form in IEA

As shown in Figure 1, there are a range of features that can contribute to an essay's score. Often when writing is assessed, there is a distinction in scoring the *form* of the essay (e.g., the quality of the expression and organization) and the *content* (e.g., the quality of ideas and student knowledge). While most automated scoring has focused on scoring of the form, the IEA was designed to score both and can do so either as combined scores or independently. This provides an ability to assess and provide feedback on not just students' ability to express language, but also whether they are expressing the correct meaning appropriate for the topic.

Scoring of *content* within IEA is performed by deriving features using a statistical semantic technique called Latent Semantic Analysis (LSA) (Deerwester, et al., 1988; Landauer & Dumais, 1997). LSA derives semantic models of English (or any other language) from an analysis of large volumes of text. For essay scoring applications, the system typically uses a collection of texts that is equivalent to the reading a student is likely to have done over their academic career. LSA builds a co-occurrence matrix of words and their usage in paragraphs and then reduces the matrix by Singular Value Decomposition (SVD), a technique similar to factor analysis. The output of this analysis is a several hundred dimensional semantic space in which every word, paragraph, essay or document is represented by a vector of real numbers to represent its meaning. The semantic similarity between words, paragraphs and essays can be determined by computing the cosine between the vectors of two units of text. For example, the sentence "Surgery is often performed by a team of doctors" has a high semantic similarity to "On many occasions, several physicians are involved in an operation" even though they share no words in common. Although the technique is based on the statistics of how words are used in ordinary language, its analysis is much deeper and more powerful than simple frequency, co-occurrence, or keyword counting and matching techniques that have sometimes been used in traditional Natural Language Processing (NLP) techniques.

The underlying LSA method has been broadly used in many applications in many languages, including Internet search, psychological diagnosis, signals intelligence, educational and occupational assessment, intelligent tutoring systems, and in basic studies of collaborative communication and problem solving. The accuracy of the mean-

*Figure 1. Sample features used in the IEA*

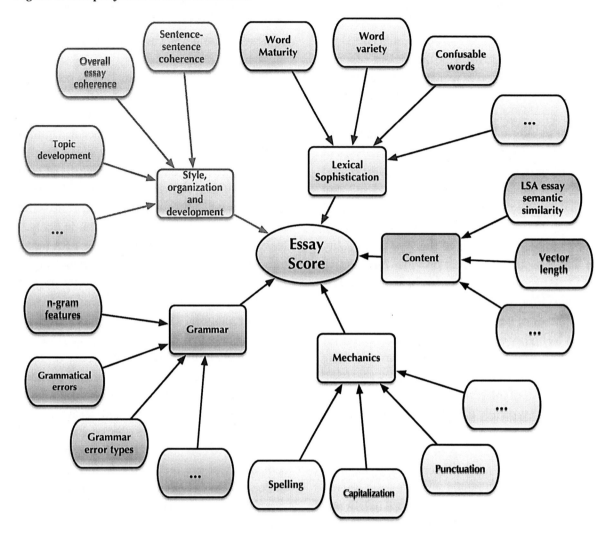

ing representation has been empirically tested in many ways. After training on domain corpora from which humans learned or might have learned, LSA-based simulations have passed multiple choice vocabulary tests and textbook-based final exams at student levels (Landauer, Foltz & Laham, 1998). In rating the similarity of meaning between pairs of paragraphs and the similarity of meaning between pairs of words, LSA measures the similarity of meaning 90% as well as two human raters do when agreeing with each other about word and paragraph meanings (Landauer et al.,, 1998). LSA has been found to measure coherence of text in

such a way as to predict human comprehension as well as sophisticated psycholinguistic analysis, while measures of surface word overlap fail badly (Foltz, Kintsch & Landauer, 1998).

Within IEA, LSA is used as one of the approaches to derive measures of content, organization, and development-based features of writing. For example, a k-nearest neighbor measure compares the semantic similarity of a student essay against a set of training essays of known quality. A content score is assigned to the essay based on the scores of the most similar essays, weighted by their semantic similarity. This correlates highly with human scores of essays (see Landauer, Laham & Foltz, 2001; 2003; Rehder et al., 1998). LSA-based measures are also used to compare the content of individual sentences to each other to compute measures of coherence (see Foltz, Kintsch & Landauer, 1998), as well as to computing semantic similarity of the content of sentences or paragraphs against gold standard samples (see Foltz, 1996; Foltz, Gilliam & Kendall, 2000). Finally, it can measure the degree to which a student has stayed on topic and flag an essay for a teacher to review if it appears to have been written either on a different topic or in a manner inappropriate for an assignment (Foltz et al., 2013).

In order to measure the *form* of student writing, a range of automatically computed measures are used to score lexical sophistication, grammatical, mechanical, stylistic, and organizational aspects of essays. These measures can be calibrated against both the training set of essays and national norms of writing. Measures of lexical sophistication, include measuring the developmental maturity of the words used (see Landauer, Kireyev & Panaccione, 2011) and the variety of types of words used. Grammar and mechanics measures use natural language processing (NLP)-based approaches to analyze specific linguistic features of the writing. For grammar, such measures detect run on sentences, subject-verb agreement, sentence fragments use of possessives, among others. For assessing mechanics, measures are used that examine appropriate spelling, punctuation, and capitalization.

The assessment of stylistic and organizational aspects of essays are evaluated using a combination of LSA-based measures to analyze coherence in the essay, as well as NLP-based measures that assess aspects of the organization, flow and development across the essays. In addition, for specific essay types, additional features are incorporated which assess aspects of topic development, such as the strength of an introduction, use of support-ing arguments, and the quality of the conclusion. However, unless explicitly called for by a test design and documented for users, measures based on raw counts of words, sentences or paragraphs are not included (e.g., counting words, adjectives, number of occurrences of "therefore"). While these measures do tend to be predictive of writing quality, students can be easily coached to exploit such measures.

## Building a Scoring Model

A scoring model is built by first obtaining a sample of student responses that represent the full range of student responses and scores. Typically the set of essays should represent a normal distribution, while ensuring that there are sufficient (e.g., at least a minimum of 10-20) examples at each score point. During training of the system, the responses should be 100 percent double-scored by human scorers and also receive resolution scores for non-adjacent agreement. By having scores from multiple human scorers, IEA can be trained on something closer to the true score (e.g., the average of multiple human raters) rather than the scores of an individual rater. The goal is to have as much and as accurate information as possible about the range of possible responses and how those responses should be evaluated. Generally, essay sets that are not as accurately scored by human raters will result in less accurate automated scoring models (e.g., Foltz, Lochbaum, Rosenstein & Davis, 2012).

Using the sample of responses, the IEA is then trained to associate the extracted features in each essay to scores that are assigned by human scorers. A machine learning-based approach is used to determine the optimal set of features and the weights for each of the features to best model the scores for each essay. From these comparisons, a prompt and trait-specific scoring model can be derived to predict the scores that the same scorers would assign to any new responses. Based on this scoring model, new essays can be immediately scored by analysis of the features weighted according to the scoring model

The number of responses typically required to train the scoring engine varies depending on the type of prompt and expected use of the response. For general formative and content-based scoring, 200-300 essays are required to train the scoring engine. For an essay prompt in a high stakes assessment, a sample of about 500-1000 student responses is preferred, while for a short-answer prompt 1000 responses are recommended for best performance (see Foltz et al., 2013). These numbers allow for using part of the data to train the scoring engine while holding out the other part for testing and validation.

## What Kinds of Writing Can Be Scored?

Human scorers are able to score essays for different traits within essays by focusing on different features of the essays in their evaluation. For example, to score an essay on conventions, a human scorer might focus on a student's grammar, spelling, and punctuation. Similarly, IEA can generalize to scoring different traits by choosing and weighting different combinations of features. A subset of the features can be used in the training, for example just choosing features related to conventions if scoring a convention trait. By training IEA on human scores, it learns to associate the features within the IEA set that best model judgment on a specific trait. IEA has been used to accurately score a range of traits including:

- Overall writing quality;
- Content and Ideas;
- Development;
- Response to the prompt;
- Effective Sentences;
- Focus & Organization;
- Grammar, Usage, & Mechanics;
- Word Choice;

- Development & Details;
- Conventions;
- Coherence;
- Reading comprehension;
- Progression of ideas;
- Style;
- Point of view;
- Critical thinking;
- Appropriate examples, reasons and other evidence to support a position;
- Sentence structure;
- Skilled use of language and apt vocabulary.

## Evaluation of Scoring Performance

In scoring writing, a scoring engine's performance can be evaluated by how well the scores match human scoring, but a better criterion should be how well the scores align with the constructs of interest (e.g., Williamson et al., 2012). The most common benchmark of performance is to compute the reliability of the scoring engine by examining the agreement of a scoring engine's predicted scores to human scorers, as compared to the agreement between human scorers. Metrics for computing the reliability include correlation, kappa, weighted kappa, and exact and adjacent agreement. Using "true scores" (e.g., the average of multiple scorers or the consensus score) for the comparison can provide more accurate measures of an engine's accuracy. However, human agreement is seldom sufficient as a means to evaluate performance. Performance can be compared against external variables that provide a measure of the validity of the scoring, including comparison of engine scores with scores from concurrent administrations of tests with a similar construct, agreement with scores from subsequent tests, predicting student age or grade level, agreement to scorers with different levels of skill, and tests of scoring across different population subgroups.

There have been a number of studies which have tested and validated the performance of automated scoring methods using the evaluation approaches described above. While this chapter does not focus on the evaluation of the performance of the scoring models for IEA in the examples described below, each has been validated and been shown to provide accurate levels of assessment and these evaluations have been described elsewhere.

## SCORING AND FEEDBACK ON WRITING QUALITY

While much focus has been placed on the accuracy of automated scoring, on the types of essays that can be scored and its use for summative scoring (e.g., Shermis & Hamner, 2012), AES has wide applicability to improving writing skills through formative feedback. Indeed, a first major market for automated essay scoring was for formative assessment of writing skills in English Language Arts (ELA). As a component of a formative tool, AES can provide instantaneous feedback to students and support the teaching of writing strategies based on detecting the types of difficulties students encounter. For example, when incorporated into classroom instruction, students are able to write, submit, receive feedback and revise essays multiple times over a class period. Given that teachers typically assign an average of 3 to 4 essay assignments a semester due to the load of hand-scoring required, a computer-delivered automated scoring provides the opportunity to submit essays, receive instant feedback and then revise and resubmit, thereby allowing greater writing practice.

When scoring is used in formative contexts the focus of evaluation is no longer on just whether the system can provide accurate scores. Evaluation of its performance should then be considered within a framework of measuring learning gains. As students receive formative feedback, revise their essays and resubmit, automated scoring can be evaluated in how well it improves students'

content knowledge, reading skills (e.g., Franzke, et al., 2005) and writing abilities (e.g., Foltz, Lochbaum & Rosenstein, 2011).

WriteToLearn provides an example of the use of AES with formative feedback. WriteToLearn is a web-based writing environment that provides students with exercises to write responses to narrative, expository, descriptive, and persuasive prompts and write summaries of texts in order to build reading comprehension. Students use the software as an iterative writing tool in which they write, receive feedback and then revise and resubmit their improved essays. The automated feedback provides an overall score and individual trait scores such as ideas, organization, conventions, word choice, and sentence fluency. Supplemental educational material can also be viewed by the student to help them with understanding the feedback, as well as indicating approaches to improve their writing. In addition, grammar and spelling errors are flagged. Figure 2 below shows a portion of the system's interface, in this case illustrating the scoring feedback resulting from a submission to a high school persuasive prompt about whether schools should have cameras in the classroom. Students can use the scores from the system as well as click on particular pieces of feedback in order to receive additional training. For example, in figure 2, the student scored a 2 out of 4 on "organization" and could click on the word "Improve" to receive additional training on how to improve the organization of his or her essay. Evaluations of WriteToLearn have shown significantly better reading comprehension and writing skill in middle school students from two weeks of use (Landauer, Lochbaum, & Dooley, 2009) and has validated the system scores as being as reliable as human raters.

In a formative writing system, all student writing is done online and automatically scored and recorded. Thus, there is a record of all the students' work, the actions they took and all feedback they

*Figure 2. Essay feedback scoreboard*

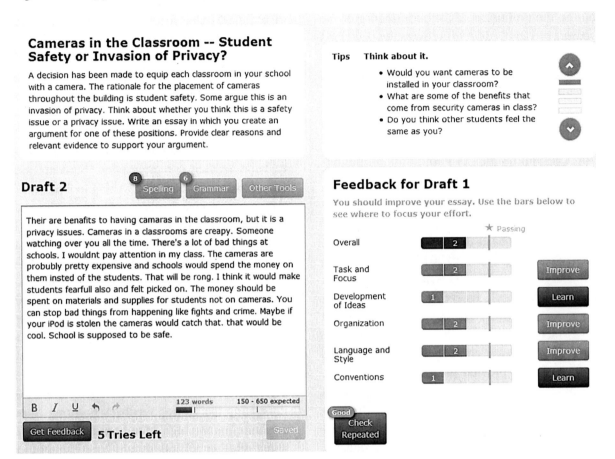

received. This archive permits continuous monitoring of performance changes in individuals and across larger groups of students, such as classes or schools. Teachers can scrutinize the progress of each student in a class and intervene when needed. For example, Figure 3 shows a class's performance on an essay. The system keeps the teacher informed of how well each student is writing as well as letting the teacher know which aspects of writing are proving most difficult for individual students, and the class as a whole. In this example, the class is scoring lowest on organization and voice. The score reports also allow teachers to see how much time each student is spending writing and how many drafts they have attempted. By clicking on any student, the teacher can pull up a portfolio of the student's complete writing and can write his or her own comments on the essay.

The above interface allows teachers to monitor all of the students' writing and stay involved in assessing and giving feedback to the students. At the same time, students are able to work on their own time and receive instantaneous feedback. This allows students more time for writing practice while not increasing the load on the teacher for scoring each essay. For example, one teacher who uses the WriteToLearn automated scoring system has 120 students annually who produce 25,000 revisions to essays and summaries in the school year.

*Figure 3. Sample teacher feedback screen*

In evaluating students writing in response to prompts, one large study examined a state-wide implementation of WriteToLearn. Based on an analysis of 21,137 students writing to 72,051 assignments (an average of almost four assignments per student), students generated over a quarter million essays in the course of four months. For each submission, students received feedback and scores on their overall essay quality, as well on six different writing traits. An analysis of the administration (Foltz, Lochbaum & Rosenstein, 2011; Foltz & Rosenstein, 2013) showed that, on average, students would revise an assignment four times. This represents more revision practice than could or would occur in a conventional classroom with teacher grading. Over the revisions, students on average improved their scores by one grade point out of a total of six. The results further showed not just improvement for basic writing skills such as grammar, but also for traits like the quality of their ideas, and organization. Similar results have been found using other automated scoring systems that provide feedback. For example, Wilson & Andrada (2013) showed that a significant portion of students who were initially identified as at-risk, were able to move out of the at-risk classification when they made 5 or more revisions while receiving feedback.

## Automated Scoring and Feedback of Paragraphs

While providing overall scores on writing traits can help students improve on specific aspects of writing, automated scoring is not as optimized to always pinpoint what needs to be fixed within each paragraph. One example of an approach used within a grammar and writing curriculum program includes automated evaluation and feedback on each individual paragraph as they build toward a complete essay. Students receive paragraph feedback on features such as:

- **Topic Focus:** How well the sentences in the paragraph support the topic, as well as listing of those sentences that do not.
- **Topic Development:** How well developed the ideas in the paragraph are.
- Variety of sentence length, sentence beginnings, and sentence structure.
- Transitions, vague adjectives, repeated words, pronouns, spelling, grammar, and redundancy.

A sample of feedback that analyzes an introductory paragraph of an essay is shown in Figure 4.

## FEEDBACK ON CONTENT IN WRITING

In the above examples on scoring writing quality, some of the trait feedback was provided on aspects such as the quality of the ideas, and the topic focus and development. In each of these cases, a holistic feedback score was given, (either on a 1-4 or 1-3 scale). More directed feedback can also be provided by using IEA's semantic features to match particular content in an essay against exemplars of content that should be covered. In Figure 5 below (see Foltz, Gilliam & Kendall, 2000), undergraduate students were asked to write an essay describing McClelland and Rumelhart's interactive activation model and explain how it accounts for the word superiority effect. The system provided a holistic score on a scale of 0-100, while also measuring specific semantic content within the essay. If particular information was missing

*Figure 4. Writing coach feedback for paragraphs*

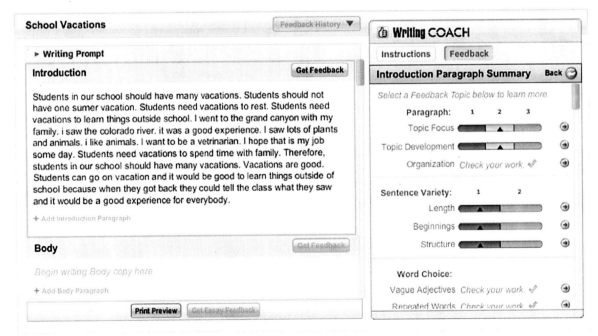

*Figure 5. Content based feedback*

On a scale of 0-100, the estimated grade you would get is: **64**

In comparison to undergraduates in PSY 301, your grade would correspond to an **D**.

**Suggestions and comments**

**Your essay does not appear to focus enough on the following issue(s)**

○ What are the primary assumptions made by the model?
○ The processing occurs at three different levels, what are they?
○ Does the processing occur serially or in parallel?
○ Provide more of a description of the interactions among the levels

Describe McClelland and Rumelhart's Interactive Activation model of word recognition. How does it account for the Word Superiority Effect?

Please make any changes you want below, then resubmit the essay to have it graded again.

How would you like your results outputted?
○ Simple (grade only, takes about 5 seconds)
● Extended (grade and suggestions. Note:- this takes 20-30 seconds to complete, DEFAULT)

```
    In interactive activation model of visual word recognition shows that a
letter is easier to recognize in the context of a word.  The test of the
model you would have people look at a fixation point, then a word is flashed
(work) or only the "k" is flashed.  The people would have to identify
whether or not they saw a certain letter.  The word superiority effect would
be that if the person was asked what letter was flashed that they would
more easily see the K in the word work.  If just the letter was flashed it
would be harder because there was no word to help process the features of
the letter  so it would be harder to recognize.  This is a reason for word
superiority effect.  It is clear that is easier to remember specific things
like letters in the context of word than not in the context of a word.  So
this is a top-down and bottom-up process because we have word knowledge
```

or incorrect in the essay, the system prompted the student with questions that would cause the student to go back and review the material and rewrite the essay. For example, if the student did not describe the architecture of the interactive activation model, it would prompt the student with: "The processing occurs at three different layers. What are they?" Students who used the system in class wrote an average of three revisions of their essays and average class grades on the essay moved from a B to an A. Similar results have been found with related automated scoring methods for content domains. For example, Attali & Powers (2008, 2010) provided immediate feedback to students writing short response for GRE subject tests in Biology and Psychology. Students receiving feedback significantly improved the correctness of their responses and increased their scores.

## SCORING SUMMARIES

Explicitly and systematically teaching students how to summarize texts allows students to practice both reading comprehension and writing across content areas. Summarizing has also been shown to be highly effective at improving writing and reading skills (Graham & Perin, 2007). Automatic evaluation of summaries enables students to participate in a read, write, and revise cycle that encourages them to re-read, re-think and re-express those parts of the text that they have not yet fully understood. Like the content analysis described above, the IEA summary evaluation process measures how well a student's summary covers the content of each major section of a reading by calculating the semantic similarity between the summary and each section of the text. Other automated summarization assessment approaches have used feature-based classifiers that use a rubric of skills associated with summarization ability (e.g., Madnani et al., 2013). The overall approach to assessing summaries expands the role of writing across the curriculum by automatically evaluating written summaries of informational texts in disciplines other than language arts, such as science, social studies, and history.

In a typical summarization process, a student first reads a passage such as a book chapter, or short information passage. Next, the student writes a summary of the passage that was just read. After submitting the passage for scoring, feedback is provided in the *scoreboard*. Figure 6 shows an example of the scoreboard for a student summary of a passage on populations from a geography textbook. The feedback on a summary includes an assessment of how well the student covered the content in each major section of the reading, hints for how to improve content coverage in a particular section, and feedback on length, unimportant content, redundant content, and direct copying from the original text. Students can get additional help in understanding what they need to cover for any section by clicking on "hints", as well as going back to any section of the text. Students are encouraged to reread the sections on which they are not doing well and revise their summary to push the score bars for each section over the passing threshold shown between Fair and Excellent. Scoring is accomplished by analyzing both the passage sections and summary for their holistic meanings, not by looking for particular key words.

*Figure 6. Sample feedback on a student summary of a chapter on population growth*

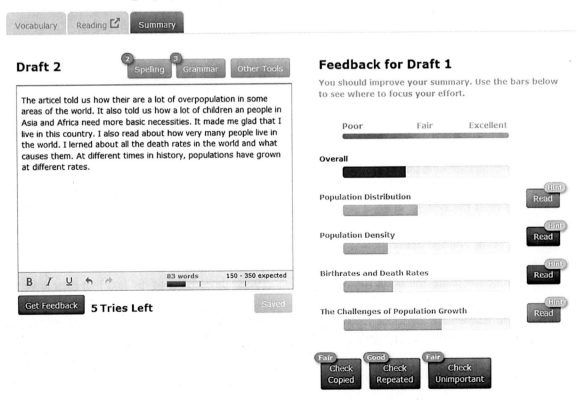

## Evidence for Improving Reading and Writing Skills through Summary Writing

Studies that have examined the effects of automated feedback for summary writing within the classroom have shown that the approach is quite effective. These studies have examined feedback in summary writing for improving both reading comprehension and writing skill. In one study, four eighth grade classes received four weeks of training on summarization. Half of the students received automated summary feedback, while the other half (control group) received the same training but did their summary writing on word processors, without feedback (Franzke et al., 2005). Students receiving feedback improved their summary writing by an overall effect size of $d = 0.9$ compared to the control students. (An effect size of 1.0 corresponds to approximately a one-grade difference, e.g., from eight to ninth grade). Mid-level students (those scoring at the fiftieth percentile) improved their writing performance with more difficult materials to the eighty-second percentile. The low- and medium-ability students (those in the lower 75 percent of the distribution) showed an effect size to $d = 1.5$ for the most difficult materials.

Another study conducted a large evaluation of 2,851 students in grades 5-9 across nine Colorado schools districts over two years (Caccamise, et al., 2009). Classes of students were assigned to either use the summarization tools of WriteToLearn or to receive traditional teacher-provided summarization instruction. Each group summarized approximately six texts in a year. Results showed that students receiving automated summarization feedback were superior to the control groups over both years of the study. Improvement in summarization was also highly related to the number of texts a student studied during the year, as well as the amount of time students spent using the tool. While the results showed that the tools sup-ported summarization skills, tests using the Test of Reading Comprehension (TORC) also showed significant effects of improvement based on the number of texts that students summarized.

## WRITING IN PERFORMANCE TASKS

The ability to automatically evaluate content enables scoring of complex tasks, such as responding to scenarios. In a scenario-based tasks, students are typically provided an overarching purpose for reading thematically related texts in which they then must complete a higher level task, such as write a recommendation based on a set of documents (e.g., Sabatini et al., 2014). Such tasks require application and synthesis of complex knowledge either already possessed by the learner or gained experientially by taking a vocational or academic course. Performance tasks can require students to integrate information from multiple sources, reason from the information and then convey it in a form appropriate for that domain (e.g., email, report). The tasks provide a means for students to practice their skills within a domain and for teachers and employers to assess those skills. We illustrate three such performance tasks below.

### Email Writing Task

As part of the E^Pro professional language assessment, candidates must demonstrate their writing ability using email in relatively formal, work-related settings. Candidates are presented with a short description of a situation and must write an email in response to the situation. Possible functions which candidates might encounter include, but are not limited to: giving suggestions, making recommendations, requesting information, negotiating a problem, giving feedback, and reporting an event. Each email situation contains several elements:

- The setting or place of work where the correspondence takes place.
- The addressee or audience for whom the email is to be written, and the relationship between the candidate and the addressee.
- The goal or functional purpose of the email.
- Three themes (e.g. suggestions, reasons, or recommendations) which the candidate should address in his/her response.

For example:

*You work for a restaurant. The restaurant's manager, Ms. Johnson wants to reward her employees for working hard but can't afford to increase salaries at this time. Write an email to her suggesting three other ways she could reward her staff.*

*Your suggestions must come from the following three themes:*

- *free lunch*
- *employee discount*
- *vacation days*

*You should include all three themes. Provide supporting ideas for each of your suggestions.*

Candidates are not dependent on their own creativity when responding as the themes to address are provided for them. However, they are required to construct elaborations, supporting ideas or reasons for each of the themes that they address. In order to fulfill the task, candidates must understand the situation presented, relate it to their existing background knowledge, and synthesize and evaluate the information such that an appropriate response can be composed. Thus, they must be conscious of the purpose of the email, address each of the themes, and understand the relationship between themselves as the writer and the intended recipient of the email. Their writing must further be constructed an informative, organized, succinct response with appropriate tone, word choice, and grammatical accuracy. The system then scores them on subscales of Grammar, Vocabulary, Voice & Tone, Organization, and Reading Comprehension. A validation of the automated scoring showed that split-half reliability achieved or exceeded that of human scorers and with correlations to human scorers ranging from 0.9 to 0.98 for different writing subscales (see http://eproexam.com/pdfs/epro_validation_report.pdf).

## Scenario-Based Responses

A second performance-based scoring example comes from the Collegiate Learning Assessment (CLA), an assessment that is scored automatically. One task type involves presenting students with a scenario and a variety of information sources and asking the student to synthesize the information in a written response. An example of such an item is shown in Table 1. Students must read multiple

*Table 1. CLA sample scenario-based prompt*

| Prompt | You advise Pat Williams, the president of DynaTech, a company that makes precision electronic instruments and navigation equipment. Sally Evans, a member of DynaTech's sale force, recommends that DynaTech buy a small private plane (a SwiftAir 235) that she and other member of the sales force could use to visit customers. Pat was about to approve the purchase when there was an accident involving a SwiftAir 235. |
| --- | --- |
| Resources: Document Library | *Newspaper article about the accident*<br>*Federal Accident Report on in-flight breakups in single engine planes*<br>*Internal Correspondence (Pat's email to you and Sally's e-mail to Pat)*<br>*Charts relating to SwiftAir's performance characteristics*<br>*Excerpt from magazine article comparing SwiftAir 235 to similar planes*<br>*Pictures and descriptions of Swiftair Models 180 and 235* |

documents, synthesize the information and then turn it into a memorandum with recommendations. Automated scoring performance on these types of items has an average Pearson correlation of 0.88 with the human consensus score, whereas the human-human correlation was 0.79.

## Automated Assessment of Diagnostic Skills

A final example of automated assessment of performance tasks comes from a study performed with the National Board of Medical Examiners where IEA was used to rate a physician evaluation in simulations in which doctors examine and diagnose actors posing as patients feigning diseases. A sample patient note produced by a doctor in this evaluation is shown in Table 2 below. The note is divided into separate text sections by patient's history, the findings of the doctor's physical examination of the patient, the potential diagnoses, and the additional diagnostic tests to be performed. IEA was used to score the notes and its scores correlated more highly with the ratings of expert physicians than other physicians agreed with each other (Swygert et al., 2003).

The three examples above all illustrate that scoring can be applied in complex performance tasks. Other examples include work with the military studying automated assessment of "Think Like a Commander" scenarios in which officers are presented with a scenario and asked to write a response detailing their approach to the scenario and the steps they would take. Automated scoring performance on such scenarios was shown to match that of the expert military evaluators (Lochbaum, Psotka, & Streeter, 2002). The approach has also been used to assess learning and performance in online collaborative work environments (See Foltz & Martin, 2008; Streeter et al., 2007) to automatically monitor online discussion groups to alert the instructor to discussion drift; to assess relative contributions of participants; to enhance the value of the discussion by automatically placing expert commentary into the discussion based on assessing the quality of the student discussion (LaVoie et al, 2010). Finally, it has been used in psychiatric settings as a means of assessing clinical disorders to predict depression and schizophrenia from retelling familiar stories or from analysis of transcribed psychiatric interviews in which the patient describes routine daily tasks (Elvevåg, et al., 2007).

## CONCLUSION

Automated scoring of writing is often viewed as being geared towards scoring the standard composition essays seen in grade school and

*Table 2. Sample patient note response*

| History | L-upper arm dull pain upon exertion (walking x2 weeks, each episode lasting <5 minutes, one episode at rest last night. 2. No associated chest pain, shortness of breath, numbness, parasthesia, weakness/paralysis, dizziness, syncopal episodes. 3. Past medical history of hypertension. 4. Post-menopausal, no hormone replacement therapy. Occupational history, social history, social history negative for activities that may contribute to arm strain. |
|---|---|
| **Physical Examination** | 1. No focal tenderness, erythema, warmth. 2. L-upper extremeity exam with normal pulse, capillary refill, motor/sensory function, reflexes. |
| **Differential Diagnosis** | Tendonitis<br>Bursitis<br>Angina Pectoris |
| **Diagnostic Workup** | EKG<br>CBC<br>Plain film x-ray L-upper extremity |

language arts classes. The goal of this chapter was to illustrate the utility of automated scoring for performance tasks in content areas rather than just for compositional writing. The kinds of skills needed for real-world success require practice in content domains. Learning comes through having students writing frequently, encountering topics and texts across the curriculum, while receiving feedback. Students can perform realistic tasks in which they must argue, persuade, summarize, synthesize, or diagnose using the forms of communication associated with different professions.

Technology is often conceived as a way of *automating* existing processes. In one sense, automated scoring can be thought of as just doing what was formerly done by human scorers. However, integrating automated scoring is more than simple automation. It provides the potential to *enhance* and *change* educational processes. With automated scoring, students can now receive rapid, timely feedback that was not formerly possible. This feedback can be scaffolded to allow students to adjust their learning in realtime, both improving their expression of writing and the depth of their content knowledge. At the same time, instructors are able to monitor the learning of whole classes and intervene with individual students as needed. Additional research will continue to be needed to expand automated assessment and feedback into new content domains and to improve the effectiveness of the feedback to further improve student learning. However, in its current state, the technology has great potential for inclusion into more technologies for teaching, supporting and assessing real-world skills.

## REFERENCES

Ananiadou, K., & Claro, M. (2009). 21st century skills and competences for new millennium learners in OECD countries. *OECD Education Working Papers, 41*.

Anderson, J. R., Boyle, C. F., Corbett, A. T., & Lewis, M. W. (1990). Cognitive modeling and intelligent tutoring. *Artificial Intelligence, 42*(1), 7–49. doi:10.1016/0004-3702(90)90093-F

Attali, Y., & Powers, D. (2008). *Effect of immediate feedback and revision on psychometric properties of open-ended GRE Subject Test items* (ETS Research Report No. RR-08-21, GRE Research Report No. GREB-04-05). Princeton, NJ: Educational Testing Service.

Attali, Y., & Powers, D. (2010). Immediate feedback and opportunity to revise answers to open-ended questions. *Educational and Psychological Measurement, 70*(1), 22–35. doi:10.1177/0013164409332231

Beigman-Klebanov, B., Madnani, N., Burstein, J. C., & Sumasundaran, S. (2014). Content importance models for scoring writing from sources. *Proceedings of the 52 Annual Meeting of the Association for Computational Linguistics.* doi:10.3115/v1/P14-2041

Black, P., & William, D. (1998). Assessment and classroom learning. *Assessment in Education: Principles, Policy & Practice, 5*(1), 7–74. doi:10.1080/0969595980050102

Burstein, J., Chodorow, M., & Leacock, C. (2004). Automated essay evaluation: The Criterion Online writing service. *AI Magazine, 25*(3), 27–36.

Caccamise, D. J., Snyder, L., Allen, C., Oliver, W., DeHart, M., & Kintsch, E. (2009). *Teaching comprehension via technology-driven tools: a large scale scale-up of Summary Street.* IES.

Deerwester, S., Dumais, S. T., Furnas, G. W., Landauer, T. K., & Harshman, R. (1990). Indexing by Latent Semantic Analysis. *Journal of the American Society for Information Science, 41*(6), 391–407. doi:10.1002/(SICI)1097-4571(199009)41:6<391::AID-ASI1>3.0.CO;2-9

Elvevåg, B., Foltz, P. W., Weinberger, D. R., & Goldberg, T. E. (2007). Quantifying incoherence in speech: An automated methodology and novel application to schizophrenia. *Schizophrenia Research, 93*(1-3), 304–316. doi:10.1016/j.schres.2007.03.001 PMID:17433866

Foltz, P. W. (1996). Latent Semantic Analysis for text-based research. *Behavior Research Methods, Instruments, & Computers, 28*(2), 197–202. doi:10.3758/BF03204765

Foltz, P. W., Gilliam, S., & Kendall, S. (2000). Supporting content-based feedback in online writing evaluation with LSA. *Interactive Learning Environments, 8*(2), 111–129. doi:10.1076/1049-4820(200008)8:2;1-B;FT111

Foltz, P. W., Kintsch, W., & Landauer, T. K. (1998). The measurement of textual coherence with Latent Semantic Analysis. *Discourse Processes, 25*(2&3), 285–307. doi:10.1080/01638539809545029

Foltz, P. W., Laham, D., & Landauer, T. K. (1999). The Intelligent Essay Assessor: Applications to Educational Technology. *Interactive Multimedia Education Journal of Computer Enhanced Learning, 1*(2).

Foltz, P. W., Lochbaum, K. E., & Rosenstein, M. (2011). *Analysis of student writing for a large scale implementation of formative assessment.* Paper presented at the National Council for Measurement in Education, New Orleans, LA.

Foltz, P. W., & Martin, M. J. (2008). Automated Communication Analysis of Teams. In E. Salas, G. F. Goodwin, & S. Burke (Eds.), *Team Effectiveness in Complex Organizations and Systems: Cross-disciplinary perspectives and approaches.* New York: Routledge.

Foltz, P. W., & Rosenstein, M. (2013). Tracking student learning in a state-wide implementation of automated writing scoring. *Proceedings of the Neural Information Processing Systems (NIPS) Workshop on Data Driven Education.* Retrieved from http://lytics.stanford.edu/datadriveneducation/

Foltz, P. W., Streeter, L. A., Lochbaum, K. E., & Landauer, T. K. (2013). Implementation and applications of the Intelligent Essay Assessor. In M. Shermis & J. Burstein (Eds.), *Handbook of Automated Essay Evaluation* (pp. 68–88). New York: Routledge.

Franzke, M., Kintsch, E., Caccamise, D., Johnson, N., & Dooley, S. (2005). Summary Street ®: Computer support for comprehension and writing. *Journal of Educational Computing Research, 33*(1), 53–80. doi:10.2190/DH8F-QJWM-J457-FQVB

Franzke, M., Kintsch, E., Caccamise, D., Johnson, N., & Dooley, S. (2005). Summary Street: Computer support for comprehension and writing. *Journal of Educational Computing Research, 33*(1), 53–80. doi:10.2190/DH8F-QJWM-J457-FQVB

Graham, S., Harris, K. R., & Hebert, M. (2011). *Informing Writing: The Benefits of Formative Assessment. A Report from Carnegie Corporation of New York.* Carnegie Corporation of New York.

Graham, S., & Hebert, M. (2010). *Writing to read: Evidence for how writing can improve reading: A report from Carnegie Corporation of New York.* Carnegie Corporation of New York.

Graham, S., & Perin, D. (2007). A meta-analysis of writing instruction for adolescent students. *Journal of Educational Psychology, 99*(3), 445–476. doi:10.1037/0022-0663.99.3.445

Hattie, J., & Timperley, H. (2007). The power of feedback. *Review of Educational Research, 77*(1), 81–112. doi:10.3102/003465430298487

Hearst, M. A. (2000). The debate on automated essay grading. *Intelligent Systems and Their Applications, 15*(5), 22–37. doi:10.1109/5254.889104

Higgins, D., Brew, C., Hellman, M., Ziai, R., Chen, L., Cahill, A., … Blackmore, J. (2014). *Is getting the right answer just about choosing the right words? The role of syntactically-informed features in short answer scoring.* arXiv: 1404.0801,v2.

Kellogg, R. T. (1999). *The psychology of writing.* Oxford, UK: Oxford University Press.

Landauer, T., Lochbaum, K., & Dooley, S. (2009). A New Formative Assessment Technology for Reading and Writing. *Theory into Practice, 48*(1), 44–52. doi:10.1080/00405840802577593

Landauer, T. K., & Dumais, S. T. (1997). A solution to Plato's problem: The Latent Semantic Analysis theory of the acquisition, induction and representation of knowledge. *Psychological Review, 104*(2), 211–240. doi:10.1037/0033-295X.104.2.211

Landauer, T. K., Foltz, P. W., & Laham, D. (1998). An introduction to Latent Semantic Analysis. *Discourse Processes, 25*(2&3), 259–284. doi:10.1080/01638539809545028

Landauer, T. K., Kireyev, K., & Panaccione, C. (2011). Word Maturity: A New Metric for Word Knowledge. *Scientific Studies of Reading, 15*(1), 92–108. doi:10.1080/10888438.2011.536130

Landauer, T. K., Laham, D., & Foltz, P. W. (2001). *Automated essay scoring. IEEE Intelligent Systems.* September/October.

LaVoie, N., Streeter, L., Lochbaum, K., Wroblewski, D., Boyce, L. A., Krupnick, C., & Psotka, J. (2010). Automating Expertise in Collaborative Learning Environments. *Journal of Asynchronous Learning Networks, 14*(4), 97–119.

Madnani, N., Burstein, J., Sabatini, J., & O'Reilly, T. (2013). Automated Scoring of a Summary-Writing Task Designed to Measure Reading Comprehension. In *Proceedings of the North American Association for Computational Linguistics Eighth Workshop Using Innovative NLP for Building Educational Applications.*

McLeod, S. H. (1992). *Writing Across the Curriculum: An Introduction. Writing Across the Curriculum: A Guide to Developing Program.* Newbury Park, CA: Sage Publications.

OECD. (2013). *OECD Skills Outlook 2013. First results from the survey of adult skills.* Retrieved from http://skills.oecd.org/skillsoutlook.html

Rehder, B., Schreiner, M., Laham, D., Wolfe, M., Landauer, T., & Kintsch, W. (1998). Using latent semantic analysis to assess knowledge: Some technical considerations. *Discourse Processes, 25*(2-3), 337–354. doi:10.1080/01638539809545031

Sabatini, J., O'Reilly, T., Halderman, L., & Bruce, K. (2014). Broadening the scope of reading comprehension using scenario-based assessments: Preliminary findings and challenges. *International Journal of Topics in Cognitive Psychology, 114,* 693–723.

Shermis, M., & Hamner, B. (2012). *Contrasting state-of-the-art automated scoring of essays: Analysis.* Paper presented at Annual Meeting of the National Council on Measurement in Education, Vancouver, Canada.

Shermis, M. D., & Burstein, J. (2013). *Handbook of Automated Essay Evaluation: Current Applications and Future Directions.* New York: Routledge.

Shute, V. J. (2008). Focus on formative feedback. *Review of Educational Research, 78*(1), 153–189. doi:10.3102/0034654307313795

Streeter, L., Lochbaum, K., LaVoie, N., & Psotka, J. (2007). Automated tools for collaborative learning environments. In T. Landauer, D. McNamara, S. Dennis, & W. Kintsch (Eds.), *Latent Semantic Analysis: A Road to Meaning.* Mahwah, NJ: Lawrence Erlbaum.

Thaiss, C., & Porter, T. (2010). The State of WAC/WID in 2010: Methods and Results of the U.S. Survey of the International WAC/WID Mapping Project. *College Composition and Communication, 61*(3), 524–570.

Thurlow, M., Hermann, A., & Foltz, P. W. (2010). *Preparing MSA Science Items for Artificial Intelligence (AI) Scoring.* Paper presented at the Maryland Assessment Group Conference, Ocean City, MD.

Williamson, D., Xi, X., & Breyer, J. (2012). A framework for evaluation and use of automated scoring. *Educational Measurement: Issues and Practice, 31*(1), 2–13. doi:10.1111/j.1745-3992.2011.00223.x

Williamson, D. M., Bennett, R., Lazer, S., Bernstein, J., Foltz, P. W., … Sweeney, K. (2010, June). *Automated Scoring for the Assessment of Common Core Standards.* Retrieved July 1 2014 from http://www.ets.org/s/commonassessments/pdf/AutomatedScoringAssessCommonCoreStandards.pdf

Wilson, J., & Andrada, G. N. (2013, April). *Examining patterns of writing performance of struggling writers on a statewide classroom benchmark writing assessment.* Paper presented at the presented at that annual meeting of the American Educational Research Association, Classroom Assessment SIG, San Francisco, CA.

# Chapter 26
# Using Automated Feedback to Improve Writing Quality:
## Opportunities and Challenges

**Joshua Wilson**
*University of Delaware, USA*

**Gilbert N. Andrada**
*Connecticut State Department of Education, USA*

## ABSTRACT

*Writing skills are essential for success in K-12 and post-secondary settings. Yet, more than two-thirds of students in the United States fail to achieve grade-level proficiency in writing. The current chapter discusses the use of automated essay evaluation (AEE) software, specifically automated feedback systems, for scaffolding improvements in writing skills. The authors first present a discussion of the use of AEE systems, prevailing criticisms, and findings from the research literature. Then, results of a novel study of the effects of automated feedback are reported. The chapter concludes with a discussion of implications for stakeholders and directions for future research.*

## INTRODUCTION

In the 21st century, writing skills are essential for academic success, college acceptance and completion, and stable gainful employment. Writing skills support the development of academic skills such as reading ability and higher-level thinking (Graham & Hebert, 2010; Langer & Applebee, 1987), and writing skills are frequently relied upon as a means for evaluating learning in content area classrooms (Graham, Capizzi, Harris, Hebert, & Morphy, 2014; Kiuhara, Graham, & Hawken,

2009). In addition, writing skills are regarded as one of the best predictors of college success (ACT, 2005; Noeth & Kobrin, 2007; Norris, Oppler, Kuang, Day, & Adams, 2006), and they serve as a "gatekeeper" in the workplace—weak writing skills prevent applicants from being hired and employees from being promoted (National Commission on Writing for America's Families, Schools, and Colleges, 2004, 2005).

Despite the importance of writing skills in each of these contexts, in the United States more than two-thirds of students in grades four, eight,

DOI: 10.4018/978-1-4666-9441-5.ch026

and twelve fail to achieve grade-level proficiency in writing (National Center for Educational Statistics, 2012; Persky, Daane, & Jin, 2002) and an estimated 6-22% of school-age students meet diagnostic criteria for specific learning disabilities in the area of written expression (Hooper et al., 1993; Katusic, Colligan, Weaver, & Barberesi, 2009). Present K-12 academic reform efforts in the United States aim to change these outcomes. The adoption of the Common Core State Standards (CCSS, 2010) and its associated assessment systems—those developed by the Partnership for the Assessment of College and Career Readiness and Smarter Balanced Assessment Consortia—are intended to serve as levers to raise writing achievement by requiring educators to focus greater instructional resources on improving writing skills. For example, the CCSS expects students to compose well-organized texts in multiple genres for multiple purposes (i.e., to persuade, to inform, to narrate); to engage in the processes of planning, revising, editing, and rewriting; to use writing to gather information and build understanding about topics; and, to use technology while completing independent and collaborative writing projects. Technology applications in writing instruction include, but are not limited to, the use of word processing programs, the use of the internet to gather information and publish texts, and the use of automated essay evaluation (AEE) systems as learning tools to support revising and editing processes. It is this latter application which comprises the focus of the current chapter.

## PURPOSE OF THE PRESENT CHAPTER

Recent reform efforts have moved writing instruction, and the application of technology within instruction, to the forefront of stakeholders' minds in a way hitherto unseen in the 21st century. Consequently, AEE systems are increasing their visibility and adoption as learning tools within school settings. However, there are mixed findings from empirical research on the effects of automated feedback on writing quality. Thus, to aid stakeholders interested in the use of AEE and automated feedback for improving writing skills, the remainder of this chapter will:

1.  Describe AEE and automated feedback, the underlying theory associated with their use, and praise and criticisms of this technology.
2.  Review results of previous studies of automated feedback on writing quality and report results of a novel study by the chapter authors of a formative AEE system called Project Essay Grade (PEG™) for scaffolding improvements in the writing quality of students in grades 4-8.
3.  Discuss results of the present study in light of previous research and theory, discuss implications for stakeholders, and discuss areas of future research for the field.

## AUTOMATED ESSAY EVALUATION (AEE) AND AUTOMATED FEEDBACK

AEE is a term used to describe any number of computerized essay evaluation programs designed for use in educational settings. Such programs have been in continuous development since the pioneering work of Ellis Page and colleagues during the late 1960's. While AEE is beginning to be applied outside of the domain of educational testing companies, the state-of-the-art of this technology is represented by systems developed by such companies. Widely known examples of such systems are ETS's *e-Rater* and *Criterion* system (Attali & Burstein, 2006; Burstein, 2003; Burstein, Chodorow, & Leacock, 2004), Pearson's *Intelligent Essay Assessor* (IEA; Landauer, Laham, & Folz, 2003) and *Summary Street* systems (Franzke, Kintsch, Caccamise, Johnson, & Dooley, 2005; Wade-Stein & Kintsch, 2004), and Measurement Incorporated's *Project Essay Grade* system (PEG;

Page, 1966, 1994). Other AEE systems include Vantage Learning's *Intellimetric*, Pacific Metrics' *CRASE®*, CTB McGraw Hill's *Mosaic™*, Meta-Metrics' *Lexile® Writing Analyzer*, American Institutes for Research's *AutoScore*, and LightSide Labs' open-source AEE platform *LightSide*.

AEE systems employ unique and proprietary algorithms for analyzing and evaluating text. For example, E-rater and Criterion use a technique known as natural language processing (NLP) to model human ratings. Burstein (2003) explains that e-rater's scoring model is built by using a corpus-based approach. A sample of essay responses is analyzed using three NLP modules which analyze syntax, discourse, and topical-features. These modules extract linguistic features at each of these levels of language which are combined in regression algorithms to predict human ratings of writing quality. IEA and Summary Street use a different technique, known as latent semantic analysis (LSA; Landauer & Dumais, 1997) which uses statistical analyses to evaluate the semantic similarity of words and phrases within and between texts. PEG uses a syntactic text parser to measure hundreds of text variables which serve as approximations, or "proxes," for intrinsic characteristics of high quality writing, or "trins" (Page, 1994; Page, Poggio, & Keith, 1997). These methods are far more advanced than legacy analytic schemes—e.g., keyword searches, straight word counts, syllable counts, comma counts, etc. Those depended upon easily quantifiable correlates to good writing, but did not themselves evidence good writing which the modern AEE systems attempt to do. Readers interested in learning more about the techniques used in NLP, LSA, and syntactic text parsing, may consult the resources suggested in the "Additional Readings" section of this chapter.

## Praise for AEE

While AEE systems differ in terms of their method for analyzing text, a common function is their ability to analyze text in a manner which is (a) highly predictive of human ratings of writing quality (Landauer et al., 2003; Shermis & Hammer, 2012) and (b) of equal or greater reliability than scoring conducted by pairs of human raters (Clauser, Swanson, & Clyman, 2000; Shermis, 2014; Shermis & Hammer, 2012). In addition, AEE systems report scores free of intra-rater variability; that is, unlike human-raters AEE systems will score an essay the same way every time (100% consistency). Finally, these systems are designed to provide immediate scoring capabilities across a number of dimensions of writing ability (i.e., holistic and analytic writing quality scores). For instance, while human raters typically require a minimum of 1-2 minutes to score a single trait of writing quality (Huot, 1990), PEG requires only a single second to score up to two essays for six traits of writing quality and to provide specific feedback for improving a text (T. Martin, personal communication, September 5, 2014).

The reliability and efficiency of AEE systems has made them ideal for use in summative assessment contexts, which is their most common application. For example, several states have contracted with AEE vendors to facilitate the scoring of state-level achievement tests used for accountability purposes (e.g., IN, WV). Currently, AEE systems are being developed to score short- and extended constructed-response items for the new PARCC and SBAC English Language Arts assessments (U.S. Department of Education, 2012a, 2012b). AEE systems are also used to score writing components of entrance examinations, such as the Graduate Record Exam (GRE), the Graduate Management Admissions Test (GMAT), the Medical College Admissions Test (MCAT), the Test of English as a Foreign Language (TOEFL); and college writing placement examinations, such as the College Board's Accuplacer and ACT's COMPASS e-Write placement tests (Shermis, Burstein, & Leacock, 2006).

However, a burgeoning application of AEE is in formative assessment contexts; that is, contexts in which AEE is utilized as a learning tool to support the development of students' writing skills. This is accomplished via the provision of instantaneous and reliable feedback in the form of essay ratings (quantitative feedback) and individualized suggestions for improving writing quality (qualitative feedback). Collectively, this quantitative and qualitative feedback, when provided by AEE systems, is referred to as *automated feedback*. For students, the instructional benefit of automated feedback systems, as compared to human-only feedback, is manifest in the immediacy with which this feedback can be returned. This effectively accelerates the practice-feedback loop (Kellogg & Whiteford, 2009), which in turn promotes increased opportunities to practice writing skills and internalize the feedback.

As a learning tool, AEE appears to support teachers' instructional processes and students' motivational processes related to writing. A qualitative study conducted by Warschauer & Grimes (2008) on the use of automated feedback systems in four middle and high schools reported that teachers, principals, and students held favorable attitudes towards the use of AEE to support writing instruction. Teachers, in particular, valued AEE because it freed up time to devote to other aspects of instruction and to be more selective regarding the aspects of students' text on which they provided feedback. Teachers also liked that the AEE systems emphasized revision, and some of the teachers attempted to integrate the use of AEE within the process model of writing instruction. However, teachers expressed two main concerns: (a) that AEE may not be appropriate or effective for students with weak reading skills, and (b) the inability to embed teacher-created writing prompts deterred usage of the AEE system. A subsequent study by Grimes and Warschauer (2010) confirmed prior results and expanded on students' perceptions of AEE, specifically of Vantage Learning's AEE program called *My Access!* Three-fourths of teachers agreed or strongly agreed that students were more motivated to write when using My Access! than with a basic word processor. Results

of a student survey indicated favorable attitudes towards My Access! in terms of its ease of use, likeability, and its helpfulness for improving writing. Students also tended to agree that they revised their writing more when using the AEE program than without it.

## Criticisms of AEE

The use of AEE for formative, instructional purposes is praised for several things: efficiency, reliability, usability, and acceptability. Yet, as AEE evolves from its principal role in summative assessment contexts to address the unique opportunities and challenges of the classroom context, a number of criticisms must be addressed. For instance, AEE has been criticized as being a black box due to the proprietary nature of the scoring algorithms; and for being easily fooled to assign high scores to essays which are long, syntactically accurate, and replete with sophisticated words. Others fear that AEE and automated feedback systems will replace the teacher as a reader of student text. While these criticism have some validity, it is important to understand that these criticisms are not unique to AEE. Some of these same criticisms also can be leveled against methods of human-scoring of essays, such as holistic and analytic scoring.

## AEE as a Black Box

AEE algorithms are typically not subject to public scrutiny since they are proprietary information. Therefore, the public is often uncertain of the text features that an AEE system is evaluating and what weights it assigns to those features when calculating the essay score(s). This has led some to question the validity of inferences drawn from automated scores. However, to some degree, this criticism can also be leveled at rubric-based scoring methods conducted by human raters. While published rubrics appear to make transparent the process of rating and evaluating written text, the rubric is not the same thing as the rating. It is ultimately the individual rater who selects how they weight and apply the rubric features. Even with the use of rubrics and strict rater training, there will always be some inter- and intra-rater variability. Indeed, studies have found substantial variation in the way raters apply rubric criteria (Eckes, 2008; Engelhard, 1994; Goldberg & Roswell, 2000; Wiseman, 2012; Wolfe, 1997; 2005).

Furthermore, the design of rubrics is an inexact science. Olinghouse and colleagues (Olinghouse, Wilson, O'Shea, Jagaiah, & Troia, 2014) developed a framework to evaluate the content (i.e., the constructs) of writing ability assessed within and across performance levels of writing rubrics. In an analysis of 132 rubrics spanning grades K-12 and post-secondary writing, they found lack of consistency in measured constructs across performance levels, substantial variation across rubrics with regard to the number and type of writing constructs assessed, and frequent overlap in the content of analytic rubrics (i.e., lack of discriminant validity). In sum, due to rater-effects and lack of guidance related to the design of rubrics, the use of published rating criteria does not itself ensure transparency in the scoring of written text.

## AEE Is Easily Fooled

Given that AEE has most often been used in summative assessment contexts, a serious concern has been its susceptibility to "gaming," a form of cheating which results in the assignment of high scores to essays a human rater would flag as low quality. Indeed, some studies have found that essays with greater than average length, high syntactic complexity, and liberal use of sophisticated vocabulary receive high scores even if there are errors in content (Bejar, Flor, Futagi, & Ramineni, 2014; Higgins & Heilman, 2014; Powers, Burstein, Chodorow, Fowles, & Kukich, 2002). Findings such as these lead to broader concerns about construct validity: critics fear that AEE privileges superficial aspects of the text that are non-central to the construct of writing quality.

However, it is important to recall four points. First, AEE is not a static technology; it is continually advancing and increasing its capabilities. AEE systems have begun integrating algorithms that can detect gamed responses—see Lochbaum, Rosenstein, Foltz, & Derr (2013) for a discussion of such methods used by Pearson's IEA.

Second, the issue is not that AEE systems can be fooled and human raters cannot. Human raters are not immune to the influence of superficial aspects of the text non-central to the construct of writing quality. Indeed, human raters frequently provide higher scores to texts written with neater handwriting and which contain fewer spelling and grammar mistakes (see Graham, Harris, & Hebert, 2011 for review).

Third, AEE systems are validated on their degree of approximating human scores (Keith, 2003). Thus, the variables that an AEE system privileges are also privileged in human raters. While much is made of the criticism of text length, syntactic accuracy, and low-frequency vocabulary being highly predictive of AEE scores (Perelman, 2012), these features are also highly predictive of human scores (Olinghouse, Santangelo, & Wilson, 2012). Furthermore, as Shermis & Burstein (2003) point out, it often takes a good writer to produce nonsensical, intelligent sounding text to begin with. To do so requires command over syntax, grammar, cohesion, word choice, and mechanics. For those concerned with the writing of struggling writers and students with disabilities, it would be a small victory if they were able to demonstrate command over these component skills, even if there were errors in content. Indeed, this population of students demonstrates marked weaknesses in these areas (Berninger, Abbott, Whitaker, Sylvester, & Nolen, 1995; Dockrell, Lindsay, Connelly, & Mackie, 2007; Houck & Billingsley, 1989).

Lastly, the application of AEE within instructional contexts is meant to complement, not replace, a teacher's evaluation (Kellogg, Whiteford, & Quinlan, 2010). Thus, faked scores are not a problem in instructional contexts because they will not get past a human's evaluation for content adequacy.

## AEE Will Replace the Teacher as Reader

The involvement of AEE systems in evaluation and feedback has led to concerns that the computer is replacing the teacher as reader, and that students will come to internalize the values of a computer audience rather than a teacher audience (Drechsel, 1999; Ericcson & Haswell, 2006; Herrington & Moran, 2001). Aware of this possibility, Warschauer and Grimes (2008) examined whether the use of AEE and automated feedback replaced the teachers as instructors or readers. Instead, they found that the technology freed up teachers' time and did not deteriorate the quality of their instruction.

Moreover, it is disingenuous to claim that this criticism is only applicable to AEE. Human holistic scoring was also criticized for replacing reading-for-meaning with a form of general-impression-reading more akin to matching—i.e., matching the quality of the text with pre-established rubric criteria or benchmark papers (Elbow & Yancey, 1994; Huot, 1990). A similar criticism could also be applied to any type of evaluation method aimed at achieving high inter-rater reliability. To some extent, the goal of achieving high inter-rater reliability is antithetical to the very subjectivity which some theories of reading suggest is essential for creating meaning (e.g., Elbow & Yancey, 1994). Thus, couching the criticism as a dichotomy between AEE and human-evaluation obscures the more nuanced reality: different AEE systems process text in different ways, and just because a human rater is reading the text does not mean they are processing the text at a deep level. Indeed, studies of human feedback have found that teachers typically provide comments on surface (i.e., spelling, punctuation, grammar), rather than

substantive, aspects of student text (Clare, Valdés, & Patthey-Chavez, 2000; Matsumara, Patthey-Chavez, Valdés, & Garnier, 2002).

## THEORY UNDERLYING THE USE OF AUTOMATED FEEDBACK TO IMPROVE WRITING SKILLS

To understand why we should expect an AEE learning tool that offers automated feedback to make a difference in students' learning experience, it is first necessary to understand elements of two learning theories that undergird and support this relationship: cognitive theories of writing, and Vygotsky's theory of socially mediated learning and the zone of proximal development (ZPD).

### Cognitive Theories of Writing

Cognitive theories of writing describe writing as a complex problem-solving activity (Bereiter & Scardamalia, 1987; Flower & Hayes, 1980; Hayes, 1996, 2012). Writing requires authors to leverage component writing skills (e.g., handwriting, spelling, grammar, idea development, organization), topic and discourse knowledge, and metacognitive resources to solve several rhetorical problems, such as: (a) conceptualizing the purpose, task, and audience of the writing assignment; (b) identifying and structuring relevant topic and discourse knowledge; (c) translating and transcribing linguistic information into grammatically and mechanically accurate text; and (d) reading, diagnosing, and repairing errors in grammar, usage, mechanics, content, organization, and style. Each of these problems serves as a constraint on the cognitive resources of the writer. Proficient writers are those who, through substantial practice, have learned to manage these constraints with a minimum of cognitive effort.

It is the importance of practice which, from the perspective of cognitive writing theories, supports the use of automated feedback systems for scaffolding improvements in writing skills. Unfortunately, current instructional practices in the U. S. do not afford these opportunities. Elementary-grade students in the U. S. typically spend less than 25 minutes/day practicing writing skills, and the majority of this time is spent completing short answer items—journal writing, response to reading, worksheets, note-taking, summarizing, and listing—rather than composing extended text (Cutler & Graham, 2008; Gilbert & Graham, 2010; Graham, Harris, Fink-Chorzempa, & MacArthur, 2003). These findings are also consistent with studies of instructional practices in middle and secondary schools (Applebee and Langer, 2006; 2009; Kiuhara et al., 2009). Teachers indicate that a central barrier to increasing writing practice is the time-costs associated with grading (Graham et al., 2014). A way of overcoming this barrier is to offload some of the grading and evaluation responsibilities to AEE systems.

In addition, cognitive theories of writing suggest that practice must be complemented with instructional feedback related to writing quality and accuracy of written language skills (Hayes, 1996). Indeed, recent research reviews and meta-analyses support the use of instructional feedback for improving writing outcomes (Graham et al., 2012; Graham, Harris, Hebert, 2011; Graham, Hebert, & Harris, under review; Hattie & Timperley, 2007; Shute, 2008). However, for feedback to be effective, the gap between practice and feedback must be sufficiently narrow in order to support a continuous cycle of deliberate practice (Kellogg & Whiteford, 2009). This is difficult to achieve when relying solely on teacher- or peer-provided feedback. In contrast, automated feedback systems are able to provide immediate instructional feedback on a number of aspects of writing quality. This effectively closes the practice-feedback loop (Kellogg & Whiteford, 2009) and may thereby accelerate the development of writing skills.

## Vygotsky's Theory of Socially Mediated Learning and the (ZPD)

In this theory, Vygotsky (1978) posits that the process of interacting with, and receiving feedback from, more experienced peers and adults leads to the activation of an individual's zone of proximal development (ZPD). Vygotsky (1978) describes the ZPD as "the distance between the actual developmental level as determined by independent problem solving and the level of potential development as determined through problem solving under adult guidance or in collaboration with more capable peers" (p. 87). A key point is that the ZPD is only activated in a social environment. It is only through collaboration or the receipt of feedback that an individual is able to internalize new skills. Hence, this theory has been referred to as socially mediated learning. From the perspective of socially mediated learning, engagement with automated feedback systems can be viewed as a form of guided participation (Rogoff, 1990) which activates an individual's ZPD, enabling them to gradually internalize the knowledge and strategies needed to achieve higher levels of independent performance. This notion of internalization is also consistent with constructivist views on learning and pedagogy (e.g., Duffy & Jonassen, 1992).

In a sense, the AEE system represents the collective knowledge and expertise of a vast culture of writers. AEE systems are developed by collecting and analyzing thousands of writing samples representing the collective experience of thousands of writers. AEE systems are then able to distill this experience into constituent components that can be measured and assessed in essays submitted for evaluation and feedback. Furthermore, the AEE system is able to demarcate levels of quality within this collective experience so that an individual is able to regulate his or her own behavior to increase their ranking relative to the norms of the culture of writers upon which the

AEE system was developed. Thus, when a student receives automated feedback from an AEE system, they are effectively engaging in a form of socially mediated learning which activates their ZPD. With repeated exposure, a student gradually internalizes this feedback and is able to independently compose texts of higher quality.

# PRIOR RESEARCH ON AUTOMATED FEEDBACK AND WRITING QUALITY

As stated earlier, there is substantial variation in AEE systems due to the nature of their method for processing text and their specific capabilities. Consequently, it is important to contextualize a discussion of the effects of automated feedback on writing quality within the specific AEE system used to provide feedback. Hence, the following literature review begins with a discussion of studies of e-Rater and Criterion, Summary Street, and Project Essay Grade (PEG).

## Studies of E-Rater and Criterion

A study by Shermis and colleagues (Shermis, Burstein, & Bliss, 2004) used random assignment to assign 1,072 tenth graders to either a business as usual condition or a Criterion condition, in which students would respond to seven pre-packaged essay questions across the 20 weeks of the study. Groups were subsequently compared with regard to their performance on the Florida state writing assessment (FCAT). No statistically significant differences in performance were noted, though students in the Criterion condition showed evidence of growth in their writing scores, increases in text length, and decreases in the percent of errors relative to text length. However, only 112 of 537 treatment students completed all seven essays, most only completed 4-5 essays. This highlights the point that automated feedback is only effective if it is used.

A later study by Shermis, Wilson Garvan, and Diao (2008) on the use of e-Rater and Criterion studied growth in student writing measures in a sample of 11,685 essays completed across a school year by students in grades six through eight, and grade ten. Specific research questions examined patterns of growth and whether growth patterns differed by grade-level. The authors used generalized linear mixed modeling to assess growth across final drafts of seven subsequent essays. Dependent measures were the e-Rater holistic score, essay length (measured in total words written), and five specific error variables (grammar, usage, mechanics, style, and organization). The authors found positive effects for all grades in the expected direction—i.e., increasing quality and text length concomitant with decreasing error scores. However, as this study did not control for alternative explanations for the growth of writing quality, there is no causal evidence to support the inference that engagement with e-Rater and Criterion was responsible for these improvements. Furthermore, since the study solely examined growth across final drafts of essays, there is no way to determine whether the provision of automated feedback was associated with improvements in writing performance across drafts of an essay.

A final study of e-Rater and Criterion by Kellogg et al. (2010) varied exposure to automated feedback to evaluate whether frequency of feedback was associated with differential gains in the writing performance of 59 college freshmen. Students were assigned to a continuous feedback group in which they received feedback on three practice essays, an intermittent feedback group in which they received feedback on only the second of three practice essays, and a no-feedback condition. Essays completed two weeks after the practice period assessed transfer effects. Dependent measures included the e-rater holistic quality score, and the number of errors of grammar, usage, mechanics, and style. Results indicated that all students improved from their practice essays regardless of the amount of feedback they received. No evidence of transfer effects was noted for the overall quality measure. However, students in the continuous feedback condition produced lower errors scores compared to the no-feedback condition across drafts of the practice essays and in the transfer essay.

## Studies of Summary Street

In the first of two studies evaluating the effects of automated feedback from the Summary Street program, Wade-Stein & Kintsch (2004) sampled two sixth-grade classrooms in a single middle school in Colorado. The classes each received instruction in how to write a summary, and then created a summary of a non-fiction text. Their summary was submitted to the Summary Street program for evaluation and feedback. Then students were assigned to receive feedback either from Summary Street or a limited feedback program that solely gave feedback about length and spelling. The following week, students completed a second summary and were assigned to the alternative feedback condition from the prior week. Summaries were scored by human-raters for content adequacy, and by Summary Street for holistic quality. Results indicated that students assigned to the Summary Street condition spent statistically significantly more time working on their summaries and received higher content scores. However, no effects were found on holistic quality after controlling for the effect of feedback on the content-adequacy score. Thus, as with the studies of e-rater and Criterion, the effect of automated feedback was limited to a specific aspect of the domain of writing ability, not the full domain. However, some evidence of transfer was noted. Students who engaged with Summary Street in the first week maintained their scores in the following week when they were assigned to the limited feedback condition. This occurred concomitant with students making improvements in their content scores in the second week.

A subsequent study of Summary Street (Franzke, Kintsch, Caccamise, Johnson, & Dooley, 2005) used a similar design. Eighth-grade students ($n = 111$) assigned to receive feedback from Summary Street outperformed students receiving feedback only on spelling and text length in terms of holistic quality, organization, content, sparing use of detail, and style. However, the authors did not perform a similar analysis as the earlier study (Wade-Stein & Kintsch, 2004) to determine whether the gains in holistic quality were explained by gains in content scores, the most proximal measure given the nature of feedback from Summary Street. Transfer effects were noted for students in the Summary Street condition who composed increasingly difficult texts over a four-week period. They maintained the quality of their summaries despite having to summarize increasingly more complex texts. Findings from Franzke et al. (2005) were confirmed in a subsequent study (Caccamise, Franzke, Eckhoff, Kintsch, & Kintsch, 2007 [study 1]) of students in grades seven through nine. In contrast to a control group, students who had used Summary Street independently created higher quality summaries than their peers.

## Studies of PEG

Wilson, Olinghouse, and Andrada (2014) studied the effects of automated feedback from PEG in a sample of 955 students in grades 4-8 who completed a minimum of two revisions to an essay prompt. Growth in overall writing performance, as measured by the PEG Overall Score—a combined measure of six individual trait scores [range: 6-36]—was first examined across revisions to a single essay. Then, evidence of transfer effects was examined in two ways: (a) unaided transfer—a comparison of first draft performance from an initial essay to a transfer essay, and (b) aided transfer—a comparison of the growth slopes when revising an initial essay to the growth slopes of revising a transfer essay with the aid of automated feedback from PEG. Additional research questions explored whether differential effects of automated feedback were noted for students of different levels of prior writing achievement, gender, grade-level, and socio-economic status.

Hierarchical linear modeling was used to address these research questions. A three-level model was posited in which revision attempts (level-1) were nested within students (level-2) who were nested within schools (level-3). For both prompts a quadratic model displayed the best fit to the data with students growing at an average rate of 0.55 points per revision and decelerating at a rate of -0.02 points per revision. No evidence of grade-level effects was found, but this may have been due to the small sample of students in grades 4-5. Gender and prior writing achievement were statistically significant predictors of the intercept, but not the slope parameters. The only statistically significant predictor of the slope for the first prompt was socio-economic status, measured as eligibility for free or reduced lunch (FRL). However, FRL was no longer a significant predictor in the growth model for the transfer prompt. While growth was noted in the overall AEE score—a novel finding compared to prior research on other AEE systems—there was no evidence of transfer to improved first draft performance on the transfer prompt (unaided transfer) or accelerated growth when revising the transfer prompt with the aid of feedback from PEG (aided transfer).

## In Conclusion

Studies report mixed findings on the effects of automated feedback on writing quality. When an effect is reported it is generally of small magnitude and limited to specific component writing skills versus the full construct of writing quality. In addition, there is mixed evidence regarding whether AEE has differential effects for students of different grade-levels (c.f., Shermis et al., 2008; Wilson et al., 2014). If there are differential effects, this would suggest that AEE may not be appropriate for all grade-levels. Second, teachers

in the study reported by Warschauer and Grimes (2008) reported two obstacles to the use of AEE: students' reading skills and the inability to embed teacher-created prompts within the AEE system. Previous research has yet to explore whether there are differential effects of AEE for students of differing reading ability levels and for whether students derive equal benefit from automated feedback when it is applied to system-created and teacher-created prompts. Finally, though both cognitive and socially-mediated theories of writing detail processes by which automated feedback supports transfer, evidence is mixed on this point (c.f., Franzke et al., 2005; Wilson et al., 2014).

To further explore these unanswered questions we report results of a novel study of the effects of automated feedback from PEG on the writing quality of students in grades 4-8. We asked the following research questions: (1) Do students demonstrate growth in writing quality across revisions to a single writing prompt? (2) Are there differential effects of automated feedback on writing quality as a result of students' grade-level, socio-economic status, prior reading or writing ability, or whether they responded to system-created or teacher-created writing prompts? (3) Is there evidence of unaided or aided transfer effects when students composed a follow-up writing prompt?

## METHODS

### Project Essay Grade (PEG)

Data from the present study came from a sample of students in grades 4-8 who utilized Project Essay Grade (PEG) as part of a non-compulsory state-provided assessment and instructional resource. Students participated in the assessment by logging-on to a web-based application via the state department of education website and inputting their ID and password. Then, students selected a prompt, or responded to one selected for them by their teacher, and were given up to 60 minutes to type and submit their response. Writing prompts were either system-created or teacher-created. System created prompts were developed for argumentative, informative/explanatory, and narrative text. These prompts also were designed to tie-in to different academic subjects. System-created prompts tended to provide a brief 1-3 sentence scenario followed by the specific question students were asked to respond to. Prompts also provided students with reminders about important elements of writing in the specific genre.

PEG also allowed teachers to create their own prompts. PEG did not provide direct guidance to teachers for creating writing prompts. Consequently, there was greater variability in these prompts compared to the system-created prompts. Some were very brief: just a single statement or question. While others had more information and reminders about the key genre-elements to include. More so than the system-created prompts, teacher-created prompts appeared to be closely aligned with a specific teacher's curriculum. As such, these prompts more heavily relied on students' content knowledge rather than general background knowledge, experience, or ability to identify information from provided stimulus materials.

Once completed and submitted, PEG immediately scored the essay for six traits of writing quality, each on a 1-5 scale: overall development, organization, support, sentence structure, word choice, and mechanics. PEG also reported an Overall Score, formed as the sum of the individual trait scores (range: 6-30). PEG provided qualitative feedback in the form of individualized suggestions for revision related to each of these traits. Students could then revise and resubmit their essay as many times as they wished, each time receiving feedback to scaffold the subsequent revision.

## Participants

During the period of January 1, 2014 and June 20, 2014 a total of 6,663 students in grades 4-8 from 52 schools submitted a total of 38,985 essay attempts (first-drafts and revisions) for evaluation by PEG. Collectively, these students responded to 423 different prompts, of which 38% were argumentative, 42% were informative/explanatory, and 19% were narrative. The majority of these prompts were teacher-created (72%). Though students completed a wide range in their number of revisions (range: 0-51), the majority of submissions were first-drafts (28% of the sample), with decreasing percentages of submissions being single revisions (22%), two revisions (17%), and three revisions (12%), and so forth.

## The Present Sample

A sample was selected for the present study in the following manner. First, because three time points is the minimum needed for growth modeling, we identified all students who completed at least two revisions to their first-draft ($n = 3,134$). Then, we selected a random sample of 1,000 students whose data would be analyzed in the current study. The process of data screening led to the removal of 64 students, resulting in a final sample that included 913 students from 15 school districts and 27 schools. To estimate transfer effects we retained students who completed a follow-up prompt and at least two revisions to that prompt ($n = 349$). The process of data screening led to the removal of 20 students, resulting in a final sample of 329 students from 12 school districts and 21 schools.

Demographic and achievement characteristics for both samples are presented in Table 1. Chi-square tests were used to assess statistically significant differences across the two samples in demographic variables and school classification. *T*-tests were conducted to compare the means of each sample with regards to prior writing achievement, prior reading achievement, and students per instructional computer (described below). In all but two comparisons the null hypothesis was retained. The second sample had higher proportions of students in grades four and eight, and smaller proportions of students in grades six and

*Table 1. Demographic and descriptive information for successive samples*

| | Sample A | Sample B |
|---|---|---|
| Total Students (*n*) | 913 | 329 |
| Total Districts (*n*) | 15 | 12 |
| Total Schools (*n*) | 27 | 21 |
| Grade (%) | | |
| 4 | 9.7 | 13.4 |
| 5 | 19.2 | 19.5 |
| 6 | 25.5 | 21.3 |
| 7 | 25.0 | 20.1 |
| 8 | 20.6 | 25.8 |
| Race (%) | | |
| Hispanic | 10.4 | 7.3 |
| American Indian/Alaskan Native or Native Hawaiian/Pacific Islander | 0.2 | 0.3 |
| African American | 5.1 | 6.4 |
| Asian | 5.5 | 4.9 |
| White | 77.4 | 78.4 |
| Two or More Races | 1.3 | 2.7 |
| Free or Reduced Lunch (%) | 18.8 | 14.6 |
| Special Education (%) | 6.5 | 6.4 |
| English Language Learner (%) | 2.4 | 1.5 |
| Prior Writing Achievement (*M, SD*) | 267.94 (40.32) | 269.75 (40.02) |
| Prior Reading Achievement (*M, SD*) | 264.41 (37.54) | 265.34 (37.94) |
| School Classification Code (%) | | |
| 1 = Excelling | 23.7 | 27.1 |
| 2 = Progressing | 53.9 | 58.4 |
| 3 = Transitioning | 22.5 | 14.6 |
| Students per Instructional Computer (*M, SD*) | 2.35 (0.90) | 2.34 (0.83) |

*Note.* Sample A was used to estimate a growth model for Prompt 1. Sample B was comprised of students retained from Sample A who also completed a first-draft and a minimum of two revisions to a follow-up prompt (Prompt 2). Prior Writing Achievement was based on students' scale score (range: 100-400) from the 2013 administration of the state writing test used for accountability purposes. Prior Reading Achievement was based on students' scale score (range: 100-400) from the 2013 administration of the state reading test used for accountability purposes.

seven ($\chi^2 = 10.26$, $df = 4$, $p = .04$), and had fewer students from transitioning schools ($\chi^2 = 9.35$, $df = 2$, $p = .009$).

## Design and Data Analysis

Data analysis was conducted using a three-level longitudinal hierarchical linear model (HLM; Raudenbush & Bryk, 2002; Singer & Willett, 2003). Repeated observations of the outcome variable (level-1) were nested within students (level-2) who were nested within schools (level-3). As this was a post-hoc analysis, we did not control for the time students spent between revisions, or the number of revisions they completed. Some students completed several revisions within an hour, while others completed their revisions across several days. In addition, the number of revisions students completed varied substantially (range: 2-52), though the majority of students (roughly 20% of each sample) completed the minimum necessary to be selected (i.e., 2 revisions). We therefore elected to analyze a trimmed dataset that included data from the number of revisions completed by 95% of participants, 10 revisions. All analyses were conducted using HLM V.7 (Raudenbush, Bryk, & Congdon, 1988) and estimated using Full Information Maximum Likelihood (FIML). All estimated models converged without error.

## Measures

### Outcome Variable

As in our earlier study, we selected the PEG Overall Score as the outcome variable. This measure ranged from 6-30, and was formed as the sum of individual ratings of six traits of writing quality each on a 1-5 scale.

### Level-1 Variables

Two level-1 variables were entered into the model: *Time*, a variable counting each revision, and *Time²*, a variable formed by raising *Time* to the second power. Each variable was centered such that 0 represented students' first-draft attempt.

### Level-2 Variables

Student-level measures included two demographic variables: (a) *Grade-level*, a variable centered such that 0 represented fourth grade; and (b) *Free or Reduced Lunch (FRL)*, a measure of socio-economic status (0 = not FRL, 1 = FRL). In addition, we included data on students' prior reading and writing achievement as measured by the 2013 state accountability assessments. Both tests were scored on a 100-400 scale. Both achievement measures were re-centered by subtracting 100 from each score to set the range equivalent to 0-300, and entered into HLM models using grand mean centering. Finally, we examined whether growth trajectories differed as a result of responding to system-created or teacher-created writing prompts.

### Level-3 Variables

The present study examined two school-level variables. The first variable, *School Classification* was a measure of school performance developed by the state department of education. Multiple indicators were combined to yield a school classification system with five categories: 1 = Excelling, 2 = Progressing, 3 = Transitioning, 4 = Review (including Focus Schools), and 5 = Turnaround. For data analysis, School Classifications was recoded to a 0-4 scale, with 0 = Excelling and 4 = Turnaround. The second measure, *Students per Instructional Computer (SPIC)* was a proportion which measured the availability of computers within each school relative to the size of the student population. An SPIC of 1.0 indicated that there were equal numbers of students and computers. Data was drawn from the most recent data available, the 2012-2013 school year.

## RESULTS

### Prompt 1

Table 2 presents results of the unconditional means model, unconditional quadratic growth model, and final conditional model for students' growth across revisions to their first prompt. Intra-class correlations calculated from the unconditional means model indicated that 10.78% of the variance in PEG Overall Score was within students (level-1), 67.40% of the variance was between students within schools (level-2), and 21.82% was between schools.

*Table 2. Results of models estimating initial performance and growth across revisions for prompt 1*

| | | Unconditional Means Model | | Unconditional Quadratic Growth Model | | Final Conditional Model | |
|---|---|---|---|---|---|---|---|
| | | Coefficient (S.E.) | t (df) | Coefficient (S.E.) | t (df) | Coefficient (S.E.) | t (df) |
| **Fixed Effects** | | | | | | | |
| Initial Status, $\pi_{0i}$ | Intercept | 20.49*** (0.43) | 47.52 (26) | 19.72*** (0.45) | 44.22 (26) | 18.32*** (0.43) | 42.94 (25) |
| | Grade | | | | | 0.99*** (0.15) | 6.68 (828) |
| | Prior Writing Achievement | | | | | 0.03*** (0.00) | 7.68 (828) |
| | Prior Reading Achievement | | | | | 0.02*** (0.00) | 6.60 (828) |
| | Teacher-Created | | | | | -1.09*** (0.27) | -3.99 (828) |
| | School Classification | | | | | -0.87*** (0.27) | -3.99 (828) |
| Rate of Change, $\pi_{1i}$ | Intercept | | | 0.60*** (0.10) | 6.16 (26) | 0.61*** (0.10) | 6.11 (26) |
| Deceleration, $\pi_{2i}$ | Intercept | | | -0.06*** (0.01) | -3.83 (26) | -0.06*** (0.02) | -3.81 (26) |
| **Variance Components** | | | | | | | |
| Level-1 (time) | Within-person | 2.10 | | 0.77 | | 0.78 | |
| Level-2 (students) | In initial status | 13.12*** | | 15.08*** | | 12.13*** | |
| | In rate of change | - | | 0.75*** | | 0.76*** | |
| | In deceleration | - | | 0.01*** | | 0.01*** | |
| Level-3 (schools) | In initial status | 4.25*** | | 4.49*** | | 1.61*** | |
| | In rate of change | - | | 0.19*** | | 0.20*** | |
| | In deceleration | - | | 0.00*** | | 0.01*** | |
| **Goodness-of-fit Statistics** | | | | | | | |
| | Deviance | 18802.66 | df = 4 | 16871.56 | df = 16 | 16598.94 | df = 21 |
| | AIC | 18810.66 | | 16903.56 | | 16640.94 | |
| | BIC | 18829.93 | | 16980.63 | | 16742.09 | |
| | SBIC | 18817.22 | | 16929.78 | | 16675.35 | |
| $\chi^2$ Difference Test | | - | | 1931.10***, df = 12 | | 272.63***, df = 5 | |

*Note. \*p < .05; \*\*p < .01; \*\*\*p < .001.*

Like our previous study, the quadratic model proved to be the best fit to the data, yielding a 63% reduction in level-1 variance. Based on this model the PEG Overall Score for a first draft was approximately 20 points. With each successive revision students increased their Overall Score by 0.60 points and decelerated at a rate of -0.06 points multiplied by the respective values for each time variable. The saturation point was reached after five revisions. In a quadratic function, the point at which growth slows to 0 and after which turns negative is called the saturation point, and it was estimated using the equation $[(-1*\pi_{1i})/(2*\pi_{2i})]$ (Singer & Willett, 2003). After five revisions, the PEG Overall Score grew from 19.72 points to 21.30 points.

The final conditional model, presented in the final column of Table 2, revealed that the influence of level-2 and level-3 predictors was restricted to the intercept (i.e., students' initial performance). None of the predictors had a statistically significant effect on the slope terms. Compared to the unconditional quadratic growth model, the contribution of the four level-2 variables resulted in a 20% reduction in between-student variance

in the intercept. The contribution of the single level-3 variable resulted in a 64% reduction in between-school variance in the intercept.

## Prompt 2

Student performance on a follow-up prompt was analyzed for evidence of transfer effects to either improved first-draft performance (unaided transfer) or accelerated growth on a follow-up prompt when using automated feedback to revise (aided transfer). Table 3 reports results of the unconditional means model, the unconditional quadratic

*Table 3. Results of models estimating initial performance and growth across revisions for prompt 2*

| | | Unconditional Means Model | | Unconditional Quadratic Growth Model | | Final Conditional Model | |
|---|---|---|---|---|---|---|---|
| | | Coefficient (S.E.) | $t$ (df) | Coefficient (S.E.) | $t$ (df) | Coefficient (S.E.) | $t$ (df) |
| **Fixed Effects** | | | | | | | |
| Initial Status, $\pi_{0i}$ | Intercept | 19.92*** (0.67) | 29.64 (20) | 19.16*** (0.66) | 28.87 (20) | 19.22*** (0.62) | 31.03 (11) |
| | Prior Writing Achievement | | | | | 0.02*** (0.01) | 3.95 (264) |
| | Prior Reading Achievement | | | | | 0.02*** (0.01) | 3.86 (264) |
| Rate of Change, $\pi_{1i}$ | Intercept | | | 0.57*** (0.11) | 4.88 (20) | 0.57*** (0.12) | 4.93 (20) |
| Deceleration, $\pi_{2i}$ | Intercept | | | -0.05* (0.02) | -2.46 (20) | -0.05* (0.02) | -2.52 (20) |
| **Variance Components** | | | | | | | |
| Level-1 (time) | Within-person | 2.66 | | 1.23 | | 1.24 | |
| Level-2 (students) | In initial status | 10.41*** | | 12.84*** | | 10.84*** | |
| | In rate of change | - | | 0.85*** | | 0.84*** | |
| | In deceleration | - | | 0.01*** | | 0.01*** | |
| Level-3 (schools) | In initial status | 8.15*** | | 7.71*** | | 6.76*** | |
| | In rate of change | - | | 0.12*** | | 0.12*** | |
| | In deceleration | - | | 0.00** | | 0.00*** | |
| **Goodness-of-fit Statistics** | | | | | | | |
| | Deviance | 6833.88 | df = 4 | 6485.83 | df = 16 | 6419.69 | df = 18 |
| | AIC | 6991.00 | | 6517.83 | | 6455.69 | |
| | BIC | 7006.07 | | 6578.56 | | 6524.02 | |
| | SBIC | 6993.36 | | 6527.72 | | 6466.81 | |
| $\chi^2$ Difference Test | | - | | 497.06***, df = 12 | | 66.14***, df = 2 | |

*Note.* \*$p < .05$; \*\*$p < .01$; \*\*\*$p < .001$.

growth model, and the final conditional model for students' follow-up prompt. Intra-class correlations calculated from the variance components of the unconditional means model indicated that 12.54% of the variance was within students (level-1), 49.06% of the variance fell between students (level-2), and 38.40% of the variance fell between schools (level-3).

The quadratic growth model again displayed the best fit to the data, explaining 54% of the level-1 variance in the unconditional means model. Based on this model, students responding to a follow-up prompt scored 19.16 points for their first-drafts. With each subsequent revision their score improved at a rate of 0.57 points and decelerated at a rate of -0.05 points. The saturation point for this model was reached after 5.5 drafts; however, since students completed only full drafts, this can be interpreted as meaning that effort expended after five drafts yielded diminishing returns. After five revisions, the PEG Overall Score grew from 19.16 points to 20.70 points.

*T*-tests were used to test for evidence of transfer effects by comparing the fixed-effects parameters of the unconditional quadratic growth model for the first and second prompts. In each case the null hypothesis was retained. Thus, consistent with our previous study, we found that while students increased their scores in response to automated feedback, the experience of revising a single writing prompt multiple times did facilitate unaided or aided transfer.

The final random coefficients model for prompt 2—presented in the final column of Table 3—indicated that only prior writing achievement and prior reading achievement were statistically significant predictors of students' first-draft performance. Similar to the final model for Prompt 1, none of the level-2 or level-3 predictors explained variance in between-student or between-school growth rates.

## DISCUSSION

### Study Findings

### Shape and Rate of Growth

Consistent with our previous study, a quadratic function best explained students' growth across revisions. This suggests that students were able to benefit from automated feedback with each successive revision up to a point (five drafts), but completing subsequent revisions yielded diminishing returns. The instructional implications of this finding is that teachers should encourage students to engage with the automated feedback system multiple times (up to five times), but not ad infinitum. Growth in writing skills would be best supported by completing fewer revisions to multiple prompts, rather than completing extensive revisions to a single prompt. However, additional research is needed to confirm this point, as it is possible that this finding is a result of a self-selection bias: students who completed five drafts may have been qualitatively different from students who completed fewer drafts.

Students were shown to grow at a modest rate of approximately 0.5 points per revision, with a deceleration of -.05 points per revision. This rate of growth was consistent across demographic, achievement, and school-level variables. This was an encouraging finding, as it suggests that students did not derive differential benefit due to prior reading or writing achievement, or as a function of their socio-economic status or school classification. However, this finding also suggests that educators should be cautioned against solely relying on automated feedback as a method for accelerating the performance of low-achieving students. By itself, it does not appear to help these students close the gap. That said, the intent of formative applications of AEE and PEG is for it to be used *in conjunction* with teacher-led instruction, not to supplant it.

## Grade-Level

Our previous study did not find an effect of grade-level on initial-performance or growth across revisions, but the sample used in that study was unbalanced. Greater proportions of students came from middle-grades versus upper-elementary grades. In the present study, with a more balanced sample, an effect of grade-level was found, though it was limited to influencing first-draft performance on Prompt 1. Grade-level was not a statistically significant predictor of the growth slopes for either prompt. While the current findings must be interpreted with caution due to differences in the samples for Prompt 1 and Prompt 2, it is encouraging that students of different grade-levels derived equal benefit from automated feedback. Indeed, growth was consistent across grades, regardless of initial performance on the first-draft of Prompt 1.

## Reading Ability

It is logical that reading ability may moderate the effects of automated feedback on writing because students must read, interpret, and apply the feedback they receive. However, previous studies had not examined whether this is the case. Present findings suggest that reading ability is a statistically significant predictor of independent performance (i.e., first-draft performance), but not of growth. This finding was consistent across Prompts 1 and 2, and suggests that less-skilled readers derived equal benefit from automated feedback as their more-skilled peers.

## Teacher-Created vs. System-Created Prompts

The present study was the first of its kind to examine whether students experienced differential effects of automated feedback as a function of responding to teacher- or system-created writing prompts. While PEG is validated on a specific set of writing prompts (system-created prompts), it also can be applied to teacher-created prompts. In this way, its scoring system is prompt-independent. In both our previous study and the present study, teachers took advantage of this function. Indeed, the majority of the prompts students responded to were teacher-created. Findings from the present study support this practice. For Prompt 1, students scored lower on their initial performance on teacher-created prompts, but still grew at an equivalent rate as peers who responded to system-created prompts. For prompt 2, there was no difference in initial performance or growth when responding to teacher- versus system-created prompts. Thus, PEG appears to facilitate the same rate of growth in writing skills regardless of who created the prompt. This affords teachers substantial flexibility in integrating AEE with existing instruction.

## Evidence of Transfer Effects

Consistent with our previous study, and others in the literature, no evidence of transfer effects was found. However, this may be less a function of the limitations of automated feedback, and more a function of study design. In this and other studies, students engaged in intensive exposures to automated feedback in narrow timeframes (Kellogg et al., 2010; Wilson et al., 2014; Wilson & Andrada, this chapter), or infrequent exposure across a longer timeframe (Shermis et al., 2008; Shermis et al., 2004). No study has examined transfer effects by utilizing intensive exposure (i.e., multiple revisions to multiple prompts) over an extended timeframe (e.g., 3-6 months). Given the complexity of writing, and the amount of practice needed to achieve proficiency, transfer effects are more likely to be obtained in such conditions.

## Implications for Stakeholders

Stakeholders interested in the instructional opportunities afforded by AEE systems should be encouraged by the present findings, and those in the literature. Modest but statistically significant effects on measures of writing quality are associated with the use of automated feedback. In addition, teachers and students report positive attitudes towards such systems (Roscoe & McNamara, 2013; Warschauer & Grimes, 2008; Grimes & Warschauer, 2010).

However, stakeholders should be aware that not all automated feedback systems are equal. Just as establishing validity evidence for a single test of reading comprehension does not support the validity of score inferences for all tests of reading comprehension, nor lack of validity evidence for one test invalidate all others, so too must stakeholders view the field of AEE. Decisions on whether to adopt an automated feedback system must be made in light of the instructional goals of the school district and the specific capabilities of the system in question. Thus, continued independent research on automated feedback systems is essential for aiding in this decision-making process.

In addition, successfully integrating AEE with teacher-led instruction depends on sufficient availability of technological resources. Though the present study found no effect of the proportion of students per instructional computer in schools, this may have been due to our sample selection procedure. Students were included in the sample only if they completed a minimum of two revisions to their initial draft. This likely resulted in pre-selecting students from schools with sufficient technological resources to support repeated use of PEG. Students who had infrequent access to computers or the computer lab were less likely to engage in this form of repeated use. Given that the real benefits of AEE arise from its ability to accelerate the practice-feedback loop and support internalization of feedback, it is essential that schools possess necessary technological resources to facilitate such usage.

Finally, and most importantly, stakeholders must understand that automated feedback systems are not a panacea. The benefits of automated feedback are derived up to a point, but then diminish; and low-achieving students do not close the gap with their higher-achieving peers. Just as a calculator or spreadsheet can provide technological assistance to persons learning math or science, AEE systems are learning tools that provide similar support for writing. The calculations (for math and science) and attending to the scored elements from an AEE (for writing) certainly provide foundational support for learning, but both require the kind of higher-level (application, analysis, synthesis, and evaluation) instruction to achieve the kind of learning that is intended. Therefore, the key will be developing effective ways for teachers to utilize AEE at each stage of the instructional process. This implies that AEE should be integrated with effective teacher-led instruction.

## AREAS OF FUTURE RESEARCH

Results of the study reported here, and those in prior research report that automated feedback yields modest gains across revisions, averaging slightly less than one point increase. This raises the practical question of whether students' effort would yield a greater return on investment if they responded to multiple forms of feedback: automated, teacher, and peer. It also raises the question of how much within and across grade writing growth should be expected. To address these questions, future research should adopt rigorous experimental and quasi-experimental designs to support more precise causal inferences of the magnitude of the effect of automated feedback on writing outcomes. Such studies should pay particular attention to issues of fidelity of implementation. For example, in our studies, due to the post-hoc nature of the analyses, we did not control for the amount of time students spent engaged in automated feedback or the number of revisions they conducted. Some students completed several revisions within an hour, sometimes averaging a minute or less on their revision attempts. Other students completed their revisions across several hours, days, or weeks. These variations in implementation are important as they may indicate variations in the cognitive processes students were engaged in, be it reviewing and revising, or editing. Longer elapsed times between drafts may indicate revision processes, while shorter elapsed times more likely indicate editing processes. Whereas, revision is shown to have stronger effects on writing quality (see MacArthur, 2009), editing has a smaller effect. Consequently, variations in PEG implementation may have affected what cognitive processes students engage in when responding to automated feedback, and thus, in part, may explain the results of the present study. Hence, tighter control on the conditions which teachers and students engage with AEE systems will be essential for improving stakeholder understanding of the effects of automated feedback.

Moreover, the issue of transfer should be a greater focus in future research. Theoretical frameworks supporting the use of automated feedback posit mechanisms—practice, metacognitive awareness, and internalization—by which students can transfer learning to improved independent performance. This is an important aspect of the overall validity argument for the use of AEE as learning tools in instructional settings. If students make gains, but only do so when they depend on automated feedback, are students truly learning to be better writers? Previous research, including the study presented in this chapter, has found minimal evidence of transfer effects. However, this may, in part, be due to the use of study designs that provide students with intense exposures to automated feedback over a brief timeframe—e.g., several revisions to a single prompt—or mild exposures over a longer timeframe—e.g., one revision to multiple prompts. Writing is a complex multicomponent skill which develops slowly as a result of substantial practice (Kellogg & Whiteford, 2009). Thus, future research interested in transfer effects should seek to combine intense exposure to AEE systems with longer timeframes. These conditions are more likely to document evidence of transfer.

Finally, to date, much of the research on the effects of automated feedback systems has focused on their use as a parallel or independent curriculum, separate from teacher-led curriculum. This is an essential first step, and additional research is needed in this area, as suggested above. However, researchers should continue to seek innovative ways of integrating AEE with teacher-led instruction. To this end, future research must explore a number of questions: What features of the technology and the classroom environment make it feasible to achieve this integration? What kinds of supports do teachers require to use AEE effectively? How do students understand and apply automated feedback? Does an integrated, technology-enhanced writing curriculum lead to greater improvements in students' writing skills than typical teacher-led writing instruction? Answering these questions will be the responsibility of the next wave of research on AEE.

## CONCLUSION

Educational reform initiatives in the United States emphasize that students should possess strong writing skills. At the same time, AEE technology is experiencing rapid advances. With each passing year, these systems display greater flexibility, refine their scoring and feedback capabilities, and incorporate new features. For example, PEG now features a peer review component which enables students to engage in blinded or un-blinded peer review with classmates. Thus, opportunities abound to incorporate AEE as learning tools in the classroom. We believe this is a positive development. AEE has the potential to support teacher instruction, increase the amount of writing practice students complete, and increase student motivation and writing skills. The challenge will be moving beyond the use of AEE as an independent or parallel writing curriculum. Testing companies, educators, and researchers should illustrate models of successfully integrating AEE with curricular content and pedagogical best practices. When this is achieved, the benefits of AEE systems for improving students' writing quality will become increasingly manifest.

# REFERENCES

ACT. (2005). *Crisis at the core: Preparing all students for college and work.* Iowa City, IA: ACT. Retrieved from: http://www.act.org/research/policymakers/reports/crisis.html

Applebee, A. N., & Langer, J. A. (2006). *The state of writing instruction in America's schools: What existing data tell us.* Albany, NY: Center on English Learning and Achievement.

Applebee, A. N., & Langer, J. A. (2009). What is happening in the teaching of writing? *English Journal, 98*(5), 18–28.

Attali, Y., & Burstein, J. (2006). Automated Essay Scoring with e-rater V.2. *Journal of Technology, Learning, and Assessment, 4*(3). Retrieved from http://www.jtla.org

Bejar, I. I., Flor, M., Futagi, Y., & Ramineni, C. (2014). On the vulnerability of automated scoring to construct-irrelevant response strategies (CIRS): An illustration. *Assessing Writing, 22,* 48–59. doi:10.1016/j.asw.2014.06.001

Bereiter, C., & Scardamalia, M. (1987). *The psychology of written composition.* Hillsdale, NJ: Lawrence Erlbaum Associates.

Berninger, V. W., Abbott, R. D., Whitaker, D., Sylvester, L., & Nolen, S. B. (1995). Integrating low- and high-level skills in instructional protocols for writing disabilities. *Learning Disability Quarterly, 18*(4), 293–309. doi:10.2307/1511235

Burstein, J. (2003). The E-rater® scoring engine: Automated essay scoring with natural language processing. In M. D. Shermis & J. Burstein (Eds.), *Automated essay scoring: A cross-disciplinary perspective* (pp. 113–122). Mahwah, NJ: Lawrence Erlbaum Associates.

Burstein, J., Chodorow, M., & Leacock, C. (2004). Automated essay evaluation: The *Criterion* online writing service. *AI Magazine, 25*(3), 27–36.

Caccamise, D., Franzke, M., Eckhoff, A., Kintsch, E., & Kintsch, W. (2007). Guided practice in technology-based summary writing. In *Reading comprehension strategies: Theories, interventions, and technologies* (pp. 375–396). Mahwah, NJ: Erlbaum.

Clare, L., Valdés, R., & Patthey-Chavez, G. G. (2000). *Learning to write in urban elementary and middle schools: An investigation of teachers' written feedback on student compositions* (Center for the Study of Evaluation Technical Report No. 526). Los Angeles: University of California, Center for Research on Evaluation, Standards, and Student Testing (CRESST).

Clauser, B. E., Swanson, D. B., & Clyman, S. G. (2000). A comparison of the generalizability of scores produced by expert raters and automated scoring systems. *Applied Measurement in Education, 12*(3), 281–299. doi:10.1207/S15324818AME1203_4

Common Core State Standards Initiative. (2010). *Common core state standards for English language arts & literacy in history/social studies, science, and technical subjects.* Retrieved from http://www.corestandards.org/assets/CCSSI_ELA%20Standards.pdf

Cutler, L., & Graham, S. (2008). Primary grade writing instruction: A national survey. *Journal of Educational Psychology, 100*(4), 907–919. doi:10.1037/a0012656

Dockrell, J. E., Lindsay, G., Connelly, V., & Mackie, C. (2007). Constraints in the production of written text in children with specific language impairments. *Exceptional Children, 73*(2), 147–164. doi:10.1177/001440290707300202

Drechsel, J. (1999). Writing into silence: Losing voice with writing assessment technology. *Teaching English in the Two-Year College, 26*(4), 380–387.

Duffy, T. M., & Jonassen, D. H. (Eds.). (1992). *Constructivism and the technology of instruction: A conversation.* Hillsdale, NJ: Lawrence Erlbaum Associates.

Eckes, T. (2008). Rater types in writing performance assessments: A classification approach to rater variability. *Language Testing, 25*(2), 155–185. doi:10.1177/0265532207086780

Elbow, P., & Yancey, K. B. (1994). On the nature of holistic scoring: An inquiry composed on Email. *Assessing Writing, 1*(1), 91–107. doi:10.1016/1075-2935(94)90006-X

Engelhard, G. (1994). Examining rater errors in the assessment of written composition with a many-faceted rasch model. *Journal of Educational Measurement, 31*(2), 93–112. doi:10.1111/j.1745-3984.1994.tb00436.x

Ericcson, P. F., & Haswell, R. J. (Eds.). (2006). *Machine scoring of student essays: Truth and consequences.* Logan, UT: Utah State University Press.

Flower, L. S., & Hayes, J. R. (1980). The dynamics of composing: Making plans and juggling constraints. In L. W. Gregg & E. R. Sternberg (Eds.), *Cognitive processes in writing* (pp. 3–29). Hillsdale, NJ: Lawrence Erlbaum Associates.

Franzke, M., Kintsch, E., Caccamise, D., Johnson, N., & Dooley, S. (2005). Summary Street®: Computer support for comprehension and writing. *Journal of Educational Computing Research, 33*(1), 53–80. doi:10.2190/DH8F-QJWM-J457-FQVB

Gilbert, J., & Graham, S. (2010). Teaching writing to elementary students in grades 4-6: A national survey. *The Elementary School Journal, 110*(4), 494–518. doi:10.1086/651193

Goldberg, G. L., & Roswell, B. S. (2000). From perception to practice: The impact of teachers' scoring experience on performance-based instruction and classroom assessment. *Educational Assessment, 6*(4), 257–290. doi:10.1207/S15326977EA0604_3

Graham, S., Bollinger, A., Booth Olson, C., D'Aoust, C., MacArthur, C., McCutchen, D., & Olinghouse, N. (2012). Teaching elementary school students to be effective writers: A practice guide (NCEE 2012- 4058). Washington, DC: National Center for Education Evaluation and Regional Assistance, Institute of Education Sciences, U.S. Department of Education. Retrieved from http://ies.ed.gov/ncee/wwc/publications_reviews.aspx#pubsearch

Graham, S., Capizzi, A., Harris, K. R., Hebert, M., & Morphy, P. (2014). Teaching writing to middle school students: A national survey. *Reading and Writing, 27*(6), 1015–1042. doi:10.1007/s11145-013-9495-7

Graham, S., Harris, K. R., Fink-Chorzempa, B., & MacArthur, C. (2003). Primary grade teachers' instructional adaptations for struggling writers: A national survey. *Journal of Educational Psychology, 95*(2), 279–292. doi:10.1037/0022-0663.95.2.279

Graham, S., Harris, K. R., & Hebert, M. A. (2011). *Informing writing: The benefits of formative assessment: A Carnegie Corporation Time to Act report*. Washington, DC: Alliance for Excellent Education.

Graham, S., Hebert, M., Sandbank, M. P., & Harris, K. (in preparation). *Assessing the writing achievement of young struggling writers: Application of generalizability theory*.

Graham, S., & Hebert, M. A. (2010). *Writing to read: Evidence for how writing can improve reading. A Carnegie Corporation Time to Act Report*. Washington, DC: Alliance for Excellent Education.

Graham, S., Hebert, M. A., & Harris, K. (under review). *Formative Assessment and Writing: A Meta-analysis with Implications for Common Core*.

Grimes, D., & Warschauer, M. (2010). Utility in a fallible tool: A multi-site case study of automated writing evaluation. *The Journal of Technology, Learning, and Assessment, 8*(6), 1–44. Retrieved from http://www.jtla.org

Hattie, J., & Timperley, H. (2007). The power of feedback. *Review of Educational Research, 77*(1), 81–112. doi:10.3102/003465430298487

Hayes, J. R. (1996). A new framework for understanding cognition and affect in writing. In R. B. Ruddell & N. J. Unrau (Eds.), *Theoretical models and processes of reading* (5th ed.; pp. 1399–1430). Newark, DE: International Reading Association.

Hayes, J. R. (2012). Modeling and remodeling writing. *Written Communication, 29*(3), 369–388. doi:10.1177/0741088312451260

Herrington, A., & Moran, C. (2001). What happens when machines read our students' writing? *College English, 63*(4), 480–499. doi:10.2307/378891

Higgins, D., & Heilman, M. (2014). Managing what we can measure: Quantifying the susceptibility of automated scoring systems to gaming behavior. *Educational Measurement: Issues and Practice, 33*(3), 36–46. doi:10.1111/emip.12036

Houck, C. K., & Billingsley, B. S. (1989). Written expression of students with and without learning disabilities: Differences across grades. *Journal of Learning Disabilities, 22*(9), 561–568. doi:10.1177/002221948902200908 PMID:2809408

Huot, B. (1990). The literature of direct writing assessments: Major concerns and prevailing trends. *Review of Educational Research, 60*(2), 237–263. doi:10.3102/00346543060002237

Katusic, S. K., Colligan, A. L., & Barbaresi, W. J. (2009). The forgotten learning disability: Epidemiology of written-language disorder in a population-based birth cohort (1976-1982), Rochester, Minnesota. *Pediatrics, 123*(5), 1306–1313. doi:10.1542/peds.2008-2098 PMID:19403496

Keith, T. Z. (2003). Validity and automated essay scoring systems. In M. D. Shermis & J. C. Burstein (Eds.), *Automated essay scoring: A cross-disciplinary perspective* (pp. 147–167). Mahwah, NJ: Lawrence Erlbaum Associates, Inc.

Kellogg, R. T., & Whiteford, A. P. (2009). Training advanced writing skills: The case for deliberative practice. *Educational Psychologist, 44*(4), 250–266. doi:10.1080/00461520903213600

Kellogg, R. T., Whiteford, A. P., & Quinlan, T. (2010). Does automated feedback help students learn to write? *Journal of Educational Computing Research*, *42*(2), 173–196. doi:10.2190/EC.42.2.c

Kiuhara, S. A., Graham, S., & Hawken, L. S. (2009). Teaching writing to high school students: A national survey. *Journal of Educational Psychology*, *101*(1), 136–160. doi:10.1037/a0013097

Kolowich, S. (2014, April 28). Writing instructor, skeptical of automated grading, pits machine vs. machine. *The Chronicle of Higher Education*. Retrieved from http://chronicle.com/article/Writing-Instructor-Skeptical/146211/

Landauer, T. K., & Dumais, S. T. (1997). A solution to Plato's problem: The latent semantic analysis theory of acquisition, induction, and representation of knowledge. *Psychological Review*, *104*(2), 211–240. doi:10.1037/0033-295X.104.2.211

Landauer, T. K., Laham, D., & Foltz, P. W. (2003). Automated essay scoring and annotation of essays with the Intelligent Essay Assessor. In M. D. Shermis & J. C. Burstein (Eds.), *Automated Essay Scoring: A cross disciplinary perspective* (pp. 82–106). Mahwah, NJ: Lawrence Erlbaum Associates.

Langer, J. A., & Applebee, A. N. (1987). *How writing shapes thinking: A study of teaching and learning.* NCTE Research Report No. 22. Urbana, IL: National Council of Teachers of English.

Lochbaum, K. E., Rosenstein, M., Foltz, P. W., & Derr, M. A. (2013, April). *Detection of gaming in automated scoring of essays with the IEA.* Paper presented at the National Council on Measurement in Education Conference (NCME), San Francisco, CA.

MacArthur, C. A. (2009). Evaluation and revision. In V. W. Berninger (Ed.), *Past, present, and future contributions of cognitive writing research to cognitive psychology* (pp. 461–483). New York, NY: Taylor and Francis.

Matsumara, L. C., Patthey-Chavez, G. G., Valdés, R., & Garnier, G. (2002). Teacher feedback, writing assignment quality, and third-grade students' revision in lower- and higher-achieving urban schools. *The Elementary School Journal*, *103*(1), 3–25. doi:10.1086/499713

National Center for Education Statistics. (2012). *The Nation's Report Card: Writing 2011 (NCES 2012–470).* Washington, DC: Institute of Education Sciences, U.S. Department of Education.

National Commission on Writing for America's Families, Schools, and Colleges. (2004). *Writing: A ticket to work…or a ticket out. A survey of business leaders.* Iowa City, IA: The College Board.

National Commission on Writing for America's Families, Schools, and Colleges. (2005). *Writing: A powerful message from state government.* Iowa City, IA: The College Board.

Noeth, R. J., & Kobrin, J. L. (2007). *Writing changes in the nation's K-12 education system. Research Notes-34.* Iowa City, IA: The College Board.

Norris, D., Oppler, S., Kuang, D., Day, R., & Adams, K. (2006). *The College Board Sat® writing validation study: An assessment of predictive and incremental validity.* New York, NY: The College Board.

Olinghouse, N. G., Santangelo, T., & Wilson, J. (2012). Examining the validity of single-occasion, single-genre, holistically-scored writing assessments. In E. Van Steendam, M. Tillema, G. Rijlaarsdam, & H. Van den Bergh (Eds.), *Measuring writing. Recent insights into theory, methodology and practices* (pp. 55–82). Leiden, The Netherlands: Brill. doi:10.1163/9789004248489_005

Olinghouse, N. G., Wilson, J., O'Shea, K., Jagaiah, T., & Troia, G. A. (2014, February). *A framework to evaluate the writing assessment episode.* Paper presented at the meeting of the International Society for the Advancement of Writing Research, Paris, France.

Page, E. B. (1966). The imminence of grading essays by computer. *Phi Delta Kappan, 48,* 238–243.

Page, E. B. (1994). Computer grading of student prose, using modern concepts and software. *Journal of Experimental Education, 62*(2), 127–142. doi:10.1080/00220973.1994.9943835

Page, E. B., Poggio, J. P., & Keith, T. Z. (1997, March). *Computer analysis of student essays: Finding trait differences in student profile.* Paper presented at the annual meeting of the American Educational Research Association, Chicago, IL.

Persky, H. R., Daane, M. C., & Jin, Y. (2002). *The Nation's Report Card: Writing 2002. (NCES 2003-529).* Washington, DC: National Center for Education Statistics, Institute of Education Sciences. U. S. Department for Education.

Powers, D. E., Burstein, J. C., Chodorow, M., Fowles, M. E., & Kukich, K. (2002). Stumping *e-rater*: Challenging the validity of automated essay scoring. *Computers in Human Behavior, 18*(2), 103–134. doi:10.1016/S0747-5632(01)00052-8

Raudenbush, S. W., & Bryk, A. S. (2002). *Hierarchical linear models: Applications and data analysis methods* (2nd ed.). Thousand Oaks, CA: Sage.

Raudenbush, S. W., Bryk, A. S., & Congdon, R. T. (1988). *HLM: Hierarchical linear modeling.* Chicago: Scientific Software International, Inc.

Rogoff, B. (1990). *Apprenticeship in thinking: Cognitive development in social context.* New York, NY: Oxford University Press.

Roscoe, R. D., & McNamara, D. (2013). Writing Pal: Feasibility of an intelligent writing strategy tutor in the high school classroom. *Journal of Educational Psychology, 105*(4), 1010–1025. doi:10.1037/a0032340

Shermis, M. D. (2014). State-of-the-art automated essay scoring: Competition, results, and future directions from a United States demonstration. *Assessing Writing, 20,* 53–76. doi:10.1016/j.asw.2013.04.001

Shermis, M. D., & Burstein, J. (Eds.). (2003). *Automated essay scoring: A cross-disciplinary perspective.* Mahwah, NJ: Lawrence Erlbaum Associates.

Shermis, M. D., Burstein, J., & Leacock, C. (2006). Applications of computers in assessment and analysis of writing. In C. A. MacArthur, S. Graham, & J. Fitzgerald (Eds.), *Handbook of Writing Research* (pp. 403–416). New York, NY: Guilford.

Shermis, M. D., Burstein, J. C., & Bliss, L. (2004, April). *The impact of automated essay scoring on high stakes writing assessments.* Paper presented at the annual meeting of the National Council on Measurement in Education, San Diego, CA.

Shermis, M. D., & Hammer, B. (2012). *Contrasting state-of-the-art automated scoring of essays: Analysis.* Retrieved from ASAP: http://www.scoreright.org/NCME_2012_Paper3_29_12.pdf

Shermis, M. D., Wilson Garvan, C., & Diao, Y. (2008, March). *The impact of automated essay scoring on writing outcomes.* Paper presented at the annual meeting of the National Council on Measurement in Education, New York, NY.

Shute, V. J. (2008). Focus on formative feedback. *Review of Educational Research, 78*(1), 153–189. doi:10.3102/0034654307313795

Singer, J. D., & Willett, J. B. (2003). Applied longitudinal data analysis: Modeling change and event occurrence. New York, NY: Oxford. doi:10.1093/acprof:oso/9780195152968.001.0001

U. S. Department of Education, Office of the Deputy Secretary, Implementation and Support Unit. (2012a). *Race to the Top assessment: Partnership for Assessment of Readiness for College and Careers year one report.* Washington, DC: Author. Downloaded from: http://www2.ed.gov/programs/racetothetop-assessment/performance.html

U. S. Department of Education, Office of the Deputy Secretary, Implementation and Support Unit. (2012b). *Race to the Top assessment: Smarter Balanced Assessment Consortium year one report.* Washington, DC: Author. Downloaded from: http://www2.ed.gov/programs/racetothetop-assessment/performance.html

Vygotsky, L. S. (1978). *Mind in society: The development of higher psychological processes.* Cambridge, MA: Harvard University Press.

Wade-Stein, D., & Kintsch, E. (2004). Summary Street: Interactive computer support for writing. *Cognition and Instruction, 22*(3), 333–362. doi:10.1207/s1532690xci2203_3

Warschauer, M., & Grimes, D. (2008). Automated writing assessment in the classroom. *Pedagogies, 3*(1), 22–36. doi:10.1080/15544800701771580

Wilson, J., Olinghouse, N. G., & Andrada, G. N. (2014). Does automated feedback improve writing quality? *Learning Disabilities (Weston, Mass.), 12,* 93–118.

Wiseman, C. S. (2012). Rater effects: Ego engagement in rater decision-making. *Assessing Writing, 17*(3), 150–173. doi:10.1016/j.asw.2011.12.001

Wolfe, E. W. (1997). The relationship between essay reading style and scoring proficiency in a psychometric scoring system. *Assessing Writing, 4*(1), 83–106. doi:10.1016/S1075-2935(97)80006-2

Wolfe, E. W. (2005). Uncovering rater's cognitive processing and focus using think-aloud protocols. *Journal of Writing Assessment, 2,* 37–56.

## ADDITIONAL READING

Attali, Y., & Burstein, J. (2006). Automated essay scoring with e-rater® V.2. *The Journal of Technology, Learning, and Assessment, 4*(3), 1–31. Retrieved from http://www.jtla.org

Burstein, J. (2003). The E-rater® scoring engine: Automated essay scoring with natural language processing. In M. D. Shermis & J. Burstein (Eds.), *Automated essay scoring: A cross-disciplinary perspective* (pp. 113–122). Mahwah, NJ: Lawrence Erlbaum Associates.

Graham, S., Harris, K. R., & Hebert, M. A. (2011). *Informing writing: The benefits of formative assessment: A Carnegie Corporation Time to Act report.* Washington, DC: Alliance for Excellent Education.

Hattie, J., & Timperley, H. (2007). The power of feedback. *Review of Educational Research, 77*(1), 81–112. doi:10.3102/003465430298487

Keith, T. Z. (2003). Validity and automated essay scoring systems. In M. D. Shermis & J. C. Burstein (Eds.), *Automated essay scoring: A cross-disciplinary perspective* (pp. 147–167). Mahwah, NJ: Lawrence Erlbaum Associates, Inc.

Landauer, T. K., & Dumais, S. T. (1997). A solution to Plato's problem: The latent semantic analysis theory of acquisition, induction, and representation of knowledge. *Psychological Review, 104*(2), 211–240. doi:10.1037/0033-295X.104.2.211

Page, E. B. (1994). Computer grading of student prose, using modern concepts and software. *Journal of Experimental Education, 62*(2), 127–142. doi:10.1080/00220973.1994.9943835

Page, E. B. (2003). Project Essay Grade: PEG. In M. D., Shermis, & J. Burstein (Eds.), Automated essay scoring: A cross-disciplinary perspective (pp. 39-50). Mahwah, NJ: Lawrence Erlbaum Associates. General resources on automated essay scoring and automated essay evaluation

Shermis, M. D. (2014). State-of-the-art automated essay scoring: Competition, results, and future directions from a United States demonstration. *Assessing Writing, 20*, 53–76. doi:10.1016/j.asw.2013.04.001

Shermis, M. D., & Burstein, J. (Eds.). (2003). *Automated essay scoring: A cross-disciplinary perspective*. Mahwah, NJ: Lawrence Erlbaum Associates.

Shermis, M. D., & Burstein, J. (Eds.). (2013). *Handbook of automated essay evaluation: Current applications and new directions*. New York, NY: Taylor & Francis.

Shute, V. J. (2008). Focus on formative feedback. [Additional information about PEG]. *Review of Educational Research, 78*(1), 153–189. doi:10.3102/0034654307313795

Yang, Y., Buckendahl, C. W., Juskiewicz, P. J., & Bhola, D. S. (2002). A review of strategies for validating computer-automated scoring. [Additional information on the benefits of instructional feedback for writing]. *Applied Measurement in Education, 15*(4), 391–412. doi:10.1207/S15324818AME1504_04

## KEY TERMS AND DEFINITIONS

**Analytic Scoring:** A method of evaluating written text that assigns individual scores to separate aspects of writing quality, such as organization, ideas, sentence structure, word choice, and mechanics.

**Automated Essay Evaluation:** A term used to describe any number of computerized essay evaluation programs designed for use in educational settings.

**Automated Feedback:** Information provided to a learner from a computerized source (e.g., software program) about the learner's task performance.

**Feedback:** Information provided to a learner regarding specific aspects of his/her task performance or conceptual understanding.

**Holistic Scoring:** A method of evaluating written text that assigns a single score based on the overall quality of the text.

**Process Model of Writing Instruction:** A method of writing instruction characterized by teaching writing in multiple stages—planning, drafting, revising, editing, and publishing—using mini-lessons to teach skills and strategies for engaging in each stage of writing.

**Prompt:** An item used as a stimulus to elicit a writing sample from a student or test-taker.

**Rubric:** A scoring tool that defines evaluation criteria, and which demarcates levels of quality for those criteria.

# Section 4

# Analysis, Interpretation, and Use of Learning and Assessment Data from Technology Rich Environments

*This section introduces tools for analysis, interpretation and use of learning and assessment data in technology environments.*

# Chapter 27
# Assessing Problem Solving in Technology-Rich Environments:
## What Can We Learn from Online Strategy Indicators?

**Jean-Francois Rouet**
*University of Poitiers, France*

**Zsofia Vörös**
*University of Poitiers, France*

**Matthias von Davier**
*Educational Testing Service, USA*

## ABSTRACT

*The spread of digital information system has promoted new ways of performing activities, whereby laypersons make use of computer applications in order to achieve their goal through the use of problem solving strategies. These new forms of problem solving rely on a range of skills whose accurate assessment is key to the development of postindustrial economies. In this chapter, we outline a definition of problem solving in technology-rich environment drawn from the OECD PIAAC survey of adult skills. Then we review research studies aimed at defining and using online indicators of PS-TRE proficiency. Finally, we present a case study of one item that was part of the PIAAC PS-TRE assessment.*

## INTRODUCTION

The spread of digital information networks over the past decades has raised new societal challenges worldwide. An increasing number of everyday activities inside and outside the workplace can and sometimes must be performed through a computer and an Internet connection. Such activities might include online shopping or banking as well as accessing public services and information pertaining to various domains (health, law, regulations, and so forth).

Assuming they have access to computers and a connection to the Internet, do laypersons possess the skills needed to use these tools in order to fulfill their needs? What are the cognitive demands of

DOI: 10.4018/978-1-4666-9441-5.ch027

problem solving in the context of digital technologies, and how can they be assessed? In this chapter we examine the use of online indicators of proficiency, based on the available research literature and on the study of adult skills conducted by the OECD (Program for the International Assessment of Adult Competencies, or PIAAC; OECD, 2013a; OECD, 2013b). The PIAAC study examined three domains of skills, namely reading literacy, numeracy, and problem solving in technology-rich environments (PS-TRE). In the first part of the chapter, we outline the conceptual underpinnings of the latter domain. Then we discuss the use of various types of online indicators. Finally, we present a case study of one of the items included in the PIAAC PS-TRE study, to illustrate the potential of simple and more complex indicators.

## PROBLEM SOLVING IN TECHNOLOGY-RICH ENVIRONMENTS (PS-TRE)

People are said to face a problem whenever they cannot routinely fulfill their purposes. Problem solving has been a prominent subject of investigation in cognitive science ever since the advent of the "cognitivist" paradigm (e.g., Newell & Simon, 1972). Problem solving typically involves a series of cognitive steps and operations: One must understand the nature of the problem (i.e., "problem finding"; Getzels, 1979); plan a set of subgoals and actions that can lead to the resolution of the problem (or "problem shaping"); and unfold the plan until a solution is reached, unless an impasse or another obstacle forces them to reconsider their plans. Problem solving plays a central part in a large number of activities—from the simplest everyday issues, to schooling, to post-secondary training, to the most complex professional occupations. Accumulated experience, knowledge, and one's ability to articulate goals and plans are essential to successful problem solving (Chi, Glaser, & Rees, 1982 Funke, 2010; Mayer, 1992; Sweller, 1998).

Problems vary according to a number of dimensions. The openness of the problem space or the amount of information needed to come to a solution (a continuum sometimes construed as the "information-lean" vs. "information-rich" problem dichotomy) are two of the dimensions along which problems may vary. In recent decades, there has been a growing interest in problems that require people to make use of large amounts of information. The phrase "information problem solving" (Eisenberg & Berkowitz, 1990; Moore, 1995) was proposed to denote this category of problems. Brand-Gruwel, Wopereis, and Vermetten (2005) define information problems as "tasks or assignments that require [students] to identify information needs, locate corresponding information sources, extract and organize relevant information from each source, and synthesize information from a variety of sources." Early studies found that even simple information problems can be challenging for students from grade school (Kobasigawa, 1983; Moore, 1995; Rouet, 1990) to college and beyond (Brand-Gruwel, Wopereis, & Walraven, 2009; Rouet, Favart, Britt & Perfetti, 1997; see also Lazonder & Rouet, 2008).

Most activities involving the use of digital devices may qualify as information problem solving, since digital devices are primarily meant to support the production, dissemination, and access to various types of information. Digital environments require the use of specific tools, such as computer desktops and icons, e-mail systems, electronic text processing software, menu frames, index tables, search engines, and so forth. In general, software applications are operated by selecting functions in menus, clicking on specific icons or links displayed on a screen, using the scroll bar, or entering semantic information with the help of computer peripheries. Procedural knowledge of operating a keyboard and a mouse; opening up, moving, and closing windows; selecting and launching applications; as well as understanding computer features and functionalities are necessary to successfully interact with digital devices.

Although human-computer interaction is accomplished through simple actions, it often takes place in the context of non-routine activities. Indeed, the use of digital devices often requires case-based reasoning and self-regulatory processes (Azevedo, Moos, Johnes, & Chauncey, 2010; Lazonder & Rouet, 2008; Naumann, Richter, Christmann, & Groeben, 2008; Brand-Gruwel et al., 2009; OECD, 2009; Shapiro & Niederhauser, 2004; Zimmerman, 2008). Therefore, to perform computer-supported tasks—such as searching for information on the Internet, organizing folders, extracting information from large data sets, or shifting across software applications and windows—generalized and sometimes complex problem solving skills are required to be employed in addition to more basic computer skills.

Interacting with computers always involves the comprehension of symbolic information. Users have to decode and understand menu names or graphical icons in order to follow the appropriate chain of actions to reach a goal. In many cases, problem solving also includes the localization of information, the comprehension of larger digital texts, or the synthesis of textual information from different sources or web pages. Researchers have been providing more and more empirical evidence proving that reading practices of electronic documents rely on capacities that are not involved in the same way in printed text comprehension. The challenges that readers face using digital information systems was hallmarked by the phenomena of disorientation and cognitive overload in the early literature (Conklin, 1987; Foss, 1988 Kim & Hirtle, 1995). Recent studies have confirmed the high cognitive load associated with hypertextual learning (Amadieu & Tricot, 2006; DeStefano & LeFevre, 2007; Rouet, 2006; Zumbach & Mohraz, 2008). Research has elicited three main factors of cognitive load:

- Factors related to the surface features of information;

- Factors associated with the intrinsic structure of information; and

- Factors related to the operation of electronic information systems.

The digitalization of texts changes the way readers access and process information. Digital content is mostly hidden "behind" a dynamic screen. Earlier studies compared electronic text to printed text reading by comparing their surface features. For example, it was found that reading from a screen is slower than reading from high quality print (Dillon, 1994; Smedshammar, Frenckner, Nordquist, & Romberger, 1989). Furthermore, reading speed decreases with screen size (de Bruijn, de Mul, & van Oostendorp, 1992). Since then, digital technologies have been continuously developing both on hardware and software levels. Hardware improvements such as larger screens, better definition, or touchpads make the devices more user-friendly while new applications ensure better system usability and adjustment of the content to the display window size. Interface design standards also have been forming gradually, allowing users to activate schemas when navigating within and across information windows (Nielsen, 1999).

Parallel to the development and dissemination of the technology, cognitive theories have attempted to account for the complex and dynamic processes of information selection, evaluation, and integration. General models such as the Information Foraging theory (Pirolli & Card, 1999) have been proposed to account for how people search for information in complex environments. Semi-computational approaches (e.g., Collides: Kitajima, Blackmon, & Polson, 2000; Collides+: Juvina & van Oostendorp, 2008; SNIF-ACT: Pirolli & Fu, 2003) attempt to predict navigation in online environments. Cognitive theories address the processes at work when solving complex problems (e.g., Funke, 2010). Other conceptual frameworks describe the steps involved in managing information search tasks (e.g., the IPS-I model by Brand-Gruwel et al., 2005; or the MD-TRACE theory by Rouet & Britt, 2011). Theories of text comprehension and representation in memory (e.g., Kintsch, 1998) are being supplemented by new approaches that consider the integration of information from multiple texts (e.g., the "Documents Model" framework: Perfetti, Rouet, & Britt, 1999; or the CSI Model of textual conflict resolution by Stadtler & Bromme, 2013). Studies exploring readers' memory of multiple texts suggest that source information sometimes plays a part in forming coherent content representations (Braasch, Rouet, Vibert, & Britt, 2012; de Pereyra, Britt, Braasch, & Rouet, 2014).

Research also indicates that the formal representation of information influences online navigation behavior and decision making. By signaling the relationship between semantic contents, concept maps were shown to ease the cognitive charge of learning from multimedia documents, producing more efficient navigation and promoting the comprehension on a macrostructural level. (For a recent review, see Amadieu & Salmerón, 2014.) It was also found that users generally prefer the links displayed toward the top of search engine results (Pan et al., 2007; Salmerón, Kammerer, & García-Carrión, 2013). The spatio-temporal context of digital reading events was proved to be stored in users' episodic memory (Vörös, Rouet, & Pléh, 2011) as well. Moreover, social cues such as user ratings citation figures seem to influence link selection (Skov, Le Bigot, Vibert, de Pereyra, & Rouet, 2014).

Overall, research is exploring ways to characterize people's behavior when dealing with complex information presented in digital environments, in order to achieve specific, non-trivial purposes. A key challenge is to develop techniques to determine online indicators of proficiency, based on the collection and analysis of timed events such as function use, link selection, and their combination into more elaborate second-order indicators.

# ONLINE INDICATORS OF INFORMATION PROBLEM SOLVING PROFICIENCY

For the past two decades, researchers have attempted to come up with accurate predictors of online navigation efficiency. Rouet and Passerault (1999) reviewed some of the online methods used in text comprehension research and discussed their application in the then-emerging hypermedia interaction research area. They listed reading time, concurrent verbal protocols, secondary tasks, memory probing, and event-related potentials as major techniques used to study the cognitive processes at work during text comprehension. In regards to the analysis of hypermedia usage, they proposed categorizing online indicators as a function of the "grain size" of the observation. Coarse-grain indicators include the total time or total number of actions spent performing a task. Medium-grain indicators are derived from the grouping of observable actions into chunks, or the selection of key actions (for instance, a user visiting a specific page). Fine-grain indicators make use of all observable actions—for instance, to compare an actual sequence of page visits to a template representing the most effective route. Further research has confirmed the value of online measures at each of these levels of "grain" as well as the potential of deriving more complex indicators from "first-order" variables that can be directly derived from a raw log of observable actions. In this section, we review some studies devoted to the online analysis of navigation proficiency (that is, an ability to get to relevant information efficiently and effectively) and other studies more specifically devoted to the prediction of content comprehension.

## Navigation Proficiency

This section reviews research attempts to characterize navigation proficiency through the use of online indicators. Some studies have focused on the use of first-order metrics, that is, measures that can be directly derived from a set of observable actions, whereas others have sought to derive meaningful second-order indications that combine several simpler measures.

In one of the first comprehensive studies of Web navigation indicators, Juvina and van Oostendorp (2006) identified several navigational indices and styles predicting user characteristics and task outcomes. In their study, university students were instructed to perform tasks involving information search, personal life planning, problem solving, and personal decision making. Actions performed while navigating, task outcomes (both objective and subjective), and a number of individual characteristics were recorded. Several first-order metrics, such as path length, time spent per page, or the number of visits per page, were calculated from navigational log files. Two combined metrics, "reading time" and "semantic similarity," between the titles of pages visited and instructions were computed. Reading time was a linear combination of several first-order measures of reading time. Latent Semantic Analysis (LSA, a statistical method to determine the semantic distance between text units; see Foltz, Kintsch, & Landauer, 1998) was used to calculate the degree of semantic resemblance between page titles and the task instructions. In addition, a factor analysis performed on 19 first-order metrics resulted in four factors interpreted as "navigation styles." Second-order metrics were found to be better predictors of task outcomes than first-order metrics. For instance, a "flimsy navigation style" was associ-

ated with higher perceived disorientation. Higher path adequacy resulted in higher task efficacy. In addition, Juvina and van Oostendorp 2006, found that Internet expertise, spatial ability, working memory, episodic memory, trust propensity, and general interest can be estimated based on the navigational behavior. In short, task outcomes were better predicted with a model including not only complex navigational measures but also context factors such as user and interface characteristics.

In another landmark study, the NAEP Technology-Based Assessment Project (Bennett, Persky, Weiss, & Jenkins, 2007), science was used as a content topic to evaluate the computer usage, search, and digital comprehension skills of approximately 1,000 8th grade students. Students were required to locate and synthesize information from a simulated World Wide Web environment.

Students' scientific inquiry and computer skills were evaluated separately and combined. Scientific inquiry skills referred to the ability to efficiently find relevant content ("inquiry exploration" skills), understand and synthesize information, and communicate a coherent interpretation ("inquiry synthesis" skill). Scientific inquiry skills were assessed based on the following observable navigation and outcome variables (Table 1).

Computer skill indicators captured the usage of computer features from a technical aspect. A "computer skills score" was obtained from the following process indicators:

- Use of bookmarking to save pages.
- Degree of use of Help (*).
- Consistency of use of Back button.

*Table 1. Types of skills and online indicators used in the NAEP Study (Bennett et al., 2007)*

| Scientific Inquiry Exploration Skill | Scientific Inquiry Synthesis Skill |
|---|---|
| - Average relevance of pages bookmarked<br>- Average relevance of hits to motivating problem<br>- Proportion of relevant pages to total pages bookmarked<br>- Degree of use of relevant search terms<br>- Percentage of relevant pages among the pages visited<br>- Number of searches for relevant hits | - Number right on multiple-choice questions<br>- Accuracy/completeness of constructed-response questions |

- Degree of use of Tips for searching (*).
- Use of hyperlinks to dig down.
- Use of deletion for unwanted filed pages.
- Use of advanced search techniques.

(* These indicators were dropped because they had no or very little effect on overall performance.)

Observed indicators were evaluated on a two-, three-, or four-point scale (except for the use of deletion for unwanted filed pages, which was dichotomous). The combined scores were calculated using a Bayesian model. Scientific inquiry skill was found to be positively associated with the relevance of the pages visited or bookmarked, the quality of the constructed response, and the degree of use of relevant search terms. Students with higher computer skill used hyperlinks, the Back button, and the bookmarking tool more frequently overall and found relevant information with fewer searches. The findings also suggest that computer and inquiry skills are distinct, but not totally independent, indices. Students whose behavior was more efficient at a technological level also tended to reach better scores on learning outcome and inquiry exploration.

Just like the study by Juvina and van Oostendorp (2006), the NAEP study suggests that combining first-order indicators into more complex indicators is an effective way to describe users' problem solving behavior. The statistical combination of different metrics assessing the usage of diverse computer features or characterizing the navigational pattern in terms of time and actions facilitates the evaluation of solution processes.

In the study by Vaughan and Dillon (2006), undergraduate participants performed browsing and information-seeking tasks over five sessions, either in a genre-conforming or in a genre-violating news website condition. The experimental website consisted of a home page, category nodes, and story pages. Navigation performance was assessed by using three measures: time on task, path length, and path breadth. The length was calculated as the total number of page visits. The path breadth was computed as the number of category nodes visited at least once. With those measures, the authors were able to show that exploration became more comprehensive and the information-seeking efficiency was improving over time. A between-group difference showed that genre-conforming sites encourage users toward broader exploration and support more efficient searching. The time on the information-seeking task was also shorter in the genre-conforming group condition and decreased over time.

McDonald and Stevenson (1998) studied the effect of prior knowledge on text topic and navigational aids—lists and spatial maps of page titles—on navigation performance. Participants were instructed to read the hypertext and then look for answers to specific questions. The level of disoriented reader actions were captured by the number of different pages visited and the number of pages visited more than once. In general, higher prior knowledge yielded better navigation efficiency, except in the map condition, where the low and high prior knowledge subjects' performance was equivalent. During the reading period, participants in the map condition opened more pages than subjects in the contents list condition, who visited more nodes than subjects in the no-aid condition. The map condition also resulted in fewer repeated visits than the two other conditions. During the searching phase, the lack of navigation aid produced fewer correct answers, slower response time, and more disoriented navigation.

Other studies have found that not all page revisits derive from disorientation. Ahuja and Webster (2001) came to a conclusion contradicting the results of McDonald and Stevenson (1998). In an experiment, they explored the effect of diverse hypertext structures and prior knowledge levels on information search tasks using the same indices. About 200 graduate and undergraduate students were instructed to look for answers on a website by using the most direct route. Perceived and measured disorientation were only weakly correlated. Moreover, perceived disorientation was more related to search outcome (as assessed by the number of correct answers) than the more objective measure of disorientation .

Dørum and Garland (2011) investigated the effect of three types of metaphors on information search and retrieval from a website. University students completed structurally identical search tasks in a website whose layout was compared to that of a house (i.e., pages were compared to rooms), a town (i.e., pages as typical places in a town) or a social group (i.e., pages as typical roles). Participants' navigational behavior was characterized by the task response time and disorientation, in terms of proportion of nodes revisited (number of different nodes visited divided by the total number of node visits). The house metaphor resulted in significantly faster task times than the social metaphor. No effect of metaphors on disorientation was revealed. According to the authors, the house metaphor was both spatial and familiar, which may have faciliated the navigational charge of information searching.

In the study by Herder (2005), graduate and undergraduate students were browsing through websites about the field of personal finance and an online store with the aim of finding answers to specific questions. The following process indicators were used to capture users' actions:

- Perceived Disorientation,
- Page revisit ratio,
- Percentage of Back button clicks among the navigational actions,
- Average number of times that a page was revisited (Return rate),
- Average length of a path between connected pages (Average connected distance),
- Median view time of pages.

The percentage of pages visited more than once, or revisit ratio, was 38% on average, but this ratio was higher for the tasks on the personal finance websites than for the online store. The Back button usage was most likely to be linked to

structural and design differences between pages. A small site with a clear menu system resulted in less frequent Back button usage. The return rate inversely correlated with disorientation, indicating that revisiting a page is more a strategic decision than a result of disorientation. The revisit ratio did not correlate with the perceived disorientation. A higher level of perceived disorientation was linked to higher median view time and lower average connected distance. Subjects with a higher working memory and who were in an active mood were more likely to lengthen their navigational cycles, i.e., their average connected distance was higher. The author concluded that the average connected distance together with some other metrics is a good predictor of disorientation.

McEneaney (2001) adapted the metrics of compactness and stratum described by Botafogo et al. (1992) to evaluate navigational paths. Compactness indicates the connectedness of the path. Stratum reveals the degree of linearity of a navigational sequence. The index of stratum is derived from a distance matrix of the navigational path. If it is possible to navigate from page i to page j, the $C_{ij}$ element of the matrix is equal to the minimum number of steps between i and j pages. If not, $C_{ij}$ is set to $\infty$. Compactness is based on a converted distance matrix, where $\infty$ is replaced by the number of different pages visited during the navigation (n). In one study, subjects were instructed to answer as many questions as possible within 15 minutes using an electronic student-advising handbook. Print-reading ability, computer experience, path length (i.e., number of page visits), the number of different pages viewed, the number of consultations of the content table, and the two path metrics (path compactness and path stratum) were taken into consideration as independent variables in a correlation analysis to explain the variables behind task outcome differences. The outcome correlated significantly with print reading ability, both path metrics, and the computer experience. Successful learning was correlated with high compactness and low stratum.

In contrast to the results of McEneaney (2001), Shih, Mate, Sanchez, and Munoz (2004) found that high prior e-learning experience subjects' navigation paths were more linear and less connected (high stratum and low compactness). According to Gwizdka and Spence (2007), search success is also linked to lower values of compactness and higher stratum value.

In summary, disorientation seems difficult to characterize, as page revisits or repeated actions do not reliably represent the degree of being lost. Returning to certain pages—such as the homepage, overview, or index pages—supports the orientation, and the revisiting of certain pages can be a result of a strategic decision. Therefore, in the case of complicated hypertext structures and browsing tasks, complex indices—such as average connected distance, stratum, and compactness—that capture the structural features and the shape of the navigational path may predict the task outcome with higher efficiency. Nevertheless, it also seems that the direction of relationship between those measures and the outcome depends on the task and hypertext layout characteristics.

Other researchers take into account not only the number and frequency of page visits but also the relevance of pages visited. Padovani and Lansdale (2003) compared university students' navigation performance in structurally identical websites embedded either in a spatial or a non-spatial metaphor. Participants performed information search tasks and path retrieval tasks. Results showed that spatial metaphors engendered more efficient searches in terms of time spent on tasks, total number of screens visited with or without repetition, proportion of screens accessed by the Back button, and navigation redundancy (repeated visits/total visits). The direction of correlation was negative with the usage of the Back button and with the redundancy measure and positive with the other indices. During the retrieval phase, the spatial metaphor condition also generated less time on tasks, lower number of pages and unnecessary pages visited, and higher navigation efficiency

(calculated as the proportion of the targets reached multiplied by the number of pages on optimal retrieval route divided by the total page visits). More target pages were reached and re-accessed by subjects in the spatial metaphor condition.

Smith (1996) proposed a "Lostness" indicator to assess the level of disorientation during hypertext consultation:

$$L \text{ (Lostness)} = (N/S - 1)2 + (R/N - 1)2$$

where R = the number of nodes that need to be visited to complete a task; S = the total number of nodes visited while searching; and N = the number of different nodes visited while searching. In case of a perfect search, L equals zero; L increases as lostness increases.

Smith (1996) did not correlate her measure to other navigation indices or task outcomes. However, using Smith's measure, Larson and Czerwinski (1998) proved that different hypertext structures can cause different levels of disorientation.

Otter and Johnson (2000) developed Smith's measure by taking into consideration the importance of links used during navigation. Associative links were weighted by one quarter, taxonomic links by one half, sequential links by three quarters, and annotational links by one. In their experiment, participants carried out information search tasks on a website. The weighted and unweighted measures of lostness were correlated. The weighted measure varied more tightly with the perceived disorientation, but none of them was significant. The lostness measures positively correlated with the subjects' self-reported effort to keep mental note of where they were in the system and negatively correlated with the perceived easiness of returning to specific pages and the helpfulness of the start page.

By applying a sequence alignment algorithm, Gwizdka and Spence (2007) also assessed the level of homogeneity between the performed and the optimal navigational paths. Their results show that, in general, the similarity measure is a better predictor of both the outcome and the disorientation than the stratum and compactness. However, in the case of some tasks, when for example the optimal path is not clear, the correlation between the outcome and the structural measures of the navigational graph is the strongest

Finally, Zoanetti (2010) introduced a tool aimed at estimating student computer-based problem-solving proficiency through the collection and analysis of online indicators. In the study, various problem-solving profile variables were identified through literature review and linked to observable variables derived from logged interaction data. A Bayesian Network was applied to map observable process values of about 900 students from grades three to eight onto profile variables. However, no result on links between task outcome and process indicators was published.

The above research indicates that taking into account the relative or absolute amount of relevant and irrelevant information reached during the search activity appears to be a better approach than considering only the number of actions and repeated actions to assess disorientation. For goal-oriented tasks with an apparent optimal solution path, indicators based on whole path relevancy— i.e., the similarity between the optimal and the performed path—seem to be the most likely to be related to task outcome and perceived disorientation. Moreover, relevancy measures also assess the efficiency of actions carried out.

## Online Correlates of Content Comprehension

In some studies, comprehension measures are simply based on the number of task-relevant pages visited, i.e., the amount of relevant information acquired. In an experiment by Naumann et al. (2008), undergraduate students received either cognitive, metacognitive, or no strategy training. The participants were then asked to read a hypertext on the psychology of old age and write an essay about a related question. Subjects were also assessed

on their print reading skill and working memory capacity. Process efficiency was calculated as the number of task-relevant pages accessed. According to the results, comprehension scores were linked to navigational efficiency. Moreover, high reading skill or high working memory readers could benefit from the strategy training in terms of their navigation behavior, which had a positive impact on their comprehension, while low reading skill and low memory capacity readers' performance was impaired by the training. The authors concluded that the impact of trainings and reading skill on hypertext comprehension was mediated through the navigational behavior.

In another study by Naumann, Richter, Flender, Christmann, and Groeben (2007), university students learned form a hypertext either rich or poor in dynamic overviews and hyperlinks showing conceptual relationships between text contents on different nodes. The navigational behavior was captured by four indices:

- Total number of page visits;
- Number of visits to task-relevant pages;
- Number of two-step linear sequences, i.e., a step on the same page; and
- Number of three-step backtrack sequences (page1 →page2 →page1; i.e, going back to the previous page after a trial ending in error).

The navigational pattern indices showed that learners' navigation was more efficient in the hyperlink-rich environment. Participants relied less on trial-error sequences and showed more thorough study behavior (higher number of two-step linear sequences). However, the total number of page visits and number of task-relevant pages visited were equal in the two conditions. In addition, the number of visits to task-relevant pages and the number of linear sequences positively correlated with the learning scores. The total number of page visits, task relevant pages visited, and backtrack sequences had positive correlations with print reading skill. However, the relationship between those navigational measures and reading skill was much stronger and more systematic in the restricted hypertext condition.

In PISA 2009 (OECD, 2011), some tasks required students to construct a navigational path through several pages in order to identify the location of certain information or integrate information from several nodes. Three measures were developed to characterize test takers' navigational behavior:

- Number of page visits and revisits;
- Number of visits and revisits to task-relevant pages; and
- Number of relevant pages visited.

Each of the three indices correlated positively with the digital reading performance across countries. The connection was the strongest for the number of relevant pages visited. The effect of number of page visits and relevant page visits on digital comprehension was less clear because of the massive variance between countries. Higher navigational efficiency was also associated with higher print reading scores. However, that relationship was much weaker than the association between digital reading scores and the navigational behavior indicators. Accounting for the effect of print reading comprehension scores, all three navigational measures were still significant predictors of the learning outcome: the impact of the number of relevant pages visited was still strong, but the print reading proficiency was comparatively the stronger predictor of the two other measures.

Lawless and Kulikowich (1996) used combined indicators to show the influence of navigational steps. Based on the result of a cluster analysis of several indices derived from static measures—like the number of task-relevant pages visited—they distinguished between "knowledge seekers," "feature explorers," and "apathetic users." While navigating through a hypertext environment, knowledge seekers tended to spend more time on

task-related documents, whereas feature explorers seemed to be more interested in technical features (like videos and maps) and apathetic users visited few pages and chose links randomly. The authors found that the first group scored the highest in the comprehension test.

Other studies originate the classification of the subjects not in discrete processing steps but in the semantic consistency of the whole navigational path (Protopsaltis, 2008; Salmerón, Cañas, Kintsch, & Fajardo, 2005; Salmerón, Kintsch, & Cañas, 2006, Salmerón, Kintsch, & Kintsch, 2010). Latent Semantic Analysis (LSA) is often used to compute the coherence between text units of the visited hypertext pages.

Salmerón et al. (2010) asked university students to navigate a hypertext environment where each node contained a text unit and two links. One link drove the readers to the node of the text section with the highest coherence, while the other link pointed to the unit with the lowest coherence with the previously read text. At the end of the navigation phase, participants responded to open-ended, text-based, and inference questions at the situation model level. Participants also self-reported their link selection criteria. The self-reported use of the coherence strategy was associated with the following of pages in a semantically based order and resulted in higher comprehension scores for the inference questions, especially in the case of low prior knowledge readers. The default screen position strategy correlated with the continuous selection of the link presented at the top of screens. This strategy impaired learning outcomes the most.

In two other experiments (Salmerón et al., 2005), university undergraduates navigated freely in a hypertext system with the aim to retrieve as much information as they could. After the navigation session, they answered text-based and inference questions. The results prove that the number of different nodes influences the comprehension at the text-based level, while the reading order affects the reading outcome at the situation model level. Low prior knowledge participants needed to visit more content pages and follow the links in a coherent order to reach higher comprehension outcome (see Kintsch, 1998), whereas high prior knowledge learners could follow other strategies to reach high performance. That was explained by the active processing stimulated by the lack of coherence between text units.

The results of the above studies suggest that the amount of relevant information directly influences the low-level comprehension, while the reading order affects the reading outcome on a higher level. Research also reveals that acquiring more germane information in a semantically coherent order is more important for low prior knowledge learners. Moreover, the sequential measure of linear movements was also shown to positively correlate with digital learning outcome.

## A CASE STUDY OF ONLINE PROBLEM-SOLVING PROFICIENCY INDICATORS

The OECD PIAAC study provided a rich set of data to further investigate the use of online indicators as predictors of laypersons' digital problem solving proficiency. In this section, we present a case study based on one representative task included in the PS-TRE domain of PIAAC (see OECD, 2013a for more information on the PIAAC study).

The target population of PIAAC included the whole non-institutionalized population, aged 16–65 years, residing in the given country at the time of data collection. The participating countries used a multi-stage sampling design with a probability sample representative of the target population. At least 95% of the target population was covered in each country. However, since PS-TRE was a computer-based assessment, respondents had to go through a screening procedure and agree to taking the test on a computer. Depending on the participating country, between 8% and close to 50% of the participants either failed the screening or opted

out of the computerized procedure. As a result, the population represented in the PS-TRE domain can be seen as the computer-literate subset of the general population (see for more details: OECD, 2013a). In total, data from more than 20,000 test takers from 16 countries were analyzed. All the participants whose PS-TRE data were available at the start of the present analyses (January 2013) were taken into account for the purpose of this study. The data were provided by the Educational Testing Service (Princeton, USA).

The PS-TRE cognitive assessment was based on a framework designed by an international expert group (OECD, 2009). The materials consisted of 14 tasks divided into two modules. Each test taker was randomly assigned to one or both modules. The tasks took place in diverse, sometimes multiple, electronic environments. All tasks appeared on a simulated computer desktop, and their solution involved the manipulation of either a mail client, a word processor, a spreadsheet, a web browser, or the combination of those environments. All these applications were simulated. They implemented only a small subset of the functions normally included in authentic applications. Thus, the test takers could learn the computerized testing environment quite easily. Materials used for the tasks embraced the computer-specific surface and structural features of the information presentation as well as some of the new sub-activities of digital text comprehension (e.g., evaluation of source reliability). Task goals could be reached through clicking on specific icons or links displayed on the screen, using the scroll bar, opening up windows, or entering semantic information with the help of roll-down menus and computer peripherals.

For the purpose of this study, we chose one task: implementing an online shopping incident scenario. Participants had to proceed through a shopping website and an email client to exchange a lamp that they received because it was the wrong color. The website consisted of a relatively large number of pages and involved high navigational charge, as the instructions did not mention explicitly what the return procedure was. Participants needed to locate the information about how to exchange a product and complete a return form containing the reason and the aim of the transaction as well as a return authorization number. The return authorization number was requested by test takers via the site and was received in an email. Thus, to solve the task, participants had to utilize both the web and the mail environments. The task was actually taken by 23,340 participants, and the estimated difficulty level was easy/medium. The optimal solution path contained 16 steps, of which 14 were actually logged by the system (Table 2).

We conducted a series of exploratory analyses to address the following research questions: Is the number of actions related to the task outcome? Do people who start with some exploration of the environment (as opposed to going straight to the task-relevant page) have a higher chance of success? Do people who generally follow the "optimal" path to the solution have more chances to achieve?

The following three pieces of information had to be correctly entered on a return authorization

*Table 2. Optimal solution path for PIAAC PS-TRE task U23 "Lamp return"*

| No. | Optimal Actions |
|-----|-----------------|
| 1 | Go to customer service page |
| 2 | Click on "obtain a return authorization number link" |
| 3 | Go to return form |
| 4 | Click on "obtain number" |
| 5 | Click pop-up "ok" |
| 6 | Go to the e-mail environment |
| 7 | Open the e-mail from KE-lamp store |
| 8 | Return to the web platform |
| 9 | Back to customer service |
| 10 | Back to return form |
| 11 | Choose "wrong item shipped"* |
| 12 | Choose "exchange for correct item" |

*= Due to technical problems, this action was not logged.

form to fully solve the task: reason for return, requested transaction, and authorization number. Partial results were appraised by giving a point for each piece of information above. About 33% of the sample typed in all three, 12% completed two, and another 2% entered one piece of information correctly. The correct response rate of the return authorization number was about 8–10% lower than the proportion of right answers for the other two questions. This is probably because that information was more difficult to acquire (i.e., the participant had to go to the e-mail environment) than other information stated in the task instructions.

*Number of actions and achievement.* We examined the relationship between the total number of actions (including task-relevant and irrelevant actions) and the probability to get partial or full credit (as a function of how many of the requested pieces of information were actually entered). The sample was divided into three groups based on their total number of actions: Low (average number of actions = 4.00, n = 8025); Medium (average number of actions = 14.22, n = 7260), and High (average number of actions = 32.28, n = 8055). Since the Low group performed less than the minimum required number of actions, they could not possibly get full credit on this task. However, a comparison of the Medium and the High action groups showed that more actions were associated with a higher chance of getting full credit (estimated percentages of 62% vs. 44%, respectively). Not surprisingly, the analysis of time-on-task data resulted in similar conclusions: longer completion times were positively associated with a successful outcome. In other words, faster and more parsimonious participants were often those who "gave up" as opposed to persisting to arrive at a correct outcome. (For the sake of brevity, detailed statistical analyses are not reported in this chapter. The specifics are available upon request to the authors.)

*Exploring and achievement.* As an estimate of how much participants "explored" the environment before undertaking task-relevant actions, the sample was split into three groups based on the number of actions participants took before requesting an authorization number (step 2 in the optimal path shown in Table 1). The Low group (n = 7484) had an estimated average of 0 exploratory actions, the Medium group (n = 8373) had 3 actions, and the High group (n = 7483) had 19 actions on average. We found that exploring more pages before getting to the authorization number (step 2) was associated with a higher success probability (estimated percentages of 56% vs. 42%, respectively; Wald F (3, 15.838) = 29.10, p = 0).

*Optimal path and achievement.* The actual path of each test taker was compared to the optimal path described in Table 1 through an "Optimal path efficiency" index (OPE). OPE is based on the relative number of the optimal actions compared to the total number of actions taken and the total number of actions that should have been taken to fulfill the task. It shows how efficiently the actions were planned and how strictly the chosen optimal path was followed. The maximum value of the efficiency measure is 1, and it decreases to 0 along with the declining of efficiency, i.e., when there are more erroneous steps carried out. The maximum value is reachable only with a perfect solution path without erroneous actions. The sample was split into three groups based on the distribution of OPE values. The Low group (n = 7751) had an estimated average OPE of .11, the Medium group (n = 7801) had an OPE of .60, and the High group (n = 7788) reached .87. A logistic regression showed that higher OPE categories are linked to higher odds of arriving at a better outcome. The probability of getting full credit was .80, .24, and .002 in the High, Medium, and Low groups, respectively.

In total, this simple case study suggests that both first-order and more complex indicators can be linked to the probability of successfully completing a digital problem-solving task. In the context of the PIAAC study, more time on task and more actions were generally associated with successful outcomes. Especially interesting is the finding that some initial exploration of the environment(s) can have positive consequences. However, the analysis also found that people whose actual route in the environments complied with the optimal path had better chances of achieving. The latter finding suggests that visiting irrelevant pages may not have the same meaning depending on when these visits take place in the course of problem solving.

## CONCLUSION AND PERSPECTIVES

As computers and the Internet are being increasingly used worldwide, a large number of personal, social, and economic activities have shifted toward computer-mediated environments. Human-computer interactions involve low-level ICT skills and also more abstract problem solving skills. Carrying out tasks with computers always implies the processes of low-level comprehension of symbolic information, and in many cases, the localization of information and the comprehension and synthesis of larger digital texts are also included.

Timed interaction data captured in log files enables the analysis not only of the outcome of the activity but also the processes performed. The impact of computer function usage—such as the Home or Back button, bookmarking, extent of usage of hyperlinks and advanced search techniques—on task outcome, disorientation, or navigational style is often estimated by qualitative or quantitative combined indicators (Bennett et al., 2007; Juvina & van Oostendorp, 2008; Zoanetti, 2010). The effect of frequency of backtracking is studied as a first-order metric as well, but there is no consensus as to its interpretation. Juvina and van Oostendorp (2008) linked it to flimsy and laborious navigational styles. Padovani and

Lansdale (2003) demonstrated that the usage of the Back button negatively correlated with the search outcome, while that association is positive according to the NAEP project (Bennett et al., 2007). In the study by Naumann et al. (2007), the number of three-step backtracking did not have any effect on the digital learning outcome. Finally, Herder (2005) concluded that the frequency of Back button usage is linked to the structural and design features of websites.

Online activity during information problem solving can be analyzed more precisely through simple first-order indicators based on the number of actions, page visits, and revisits. The number of page visits and revisits were successfully employed by some studies (McDonald & Stevenson, 1998; Padovani & Lansdale, 2003; Vaughan & Dillon, 2006) to assess web search efficiency in different navigational conditions. A more efficient search was associated with fewer page revisits. In addition, participants spent less time on searching. However, other research did not arrive at the same conclusion (Ahuja & Webster, 2001; Dørum & Garland, 2011 and implied that not all page revisits derive from disorientation, especially in the case of more browsing-like tasks (Herder, 2005). Returning to certain pages can support the orientation within the hypertext virtual networks, and revisiting of some pages can be a strategic decision or simply inevitable due to structural features.

It may be suggested that for the assessment of navigational activities in restricted environments and in the case of goal-oriented tasks (e.g., there is a solution path that must be performed or a single information should be reached efficiently), simple measures based on action, repeated and relevant action count, or duration may be successfully used. In other cases, complex indices capturing the structural features of the navigational path—for example, average connected distance, stratum, compactness, and semantic proximity of the pages viewed—are more likely to be related

to the outcome (McEneaney, 2001; Gwizdka & Spence, 2007; Herder, 2005; Juvina & van Oostendorp, 2008; Salmeron et al. 2010; Shih et al., 2004). The simple case study presented in the last part of this chapter tends to support this view.

Taking into consideration the relevancy of actions, page visits, or the whole navigational path is an effective approach to evaluate searching behavior in different conditions (Larson & Czerwinski, 1998; Padovani & Lansdale, 2003) or to estimate the degree of disorientation (Gwizdka & Spence, 2007; Otter & Johnson, 2000). The similarity between the applied and the optimal solution paths seems to be a good predictor of the outcome and the disorientation for tasks with a well-defined optimal action chain (Gwizdka & Spence, 2007). Measures based on action relevance were also found to be related to complex problem solving task outcomes (Bennett et al., 2007). Furthermore, research on learning ascertains that the amount of relevant information reached influences the comprehension (Bennett et al., 2007; Lawless & Kulikowich, 1996; Naumann et al., 2007; Naumann et al., 2008; OECD, 2011), especially on a low level (Salmerón et al., 2005).

In conclusion, measures based on time, number of actions, repeated and relevant actions, computer or hypertext feature usage, and sequential path characteristics may predict the task outcome as well as disorientation, navigational style, and users' characteristics. Nonetheless, studies often arrived to contradictory results, and interactions between those measures and outcome indicators seem to depend on task and material features. Task-specific relevancy indices along with complex indicators assessing the structural features of the navigational path and combined measures were used the most successfully to show the impact of interactions on task outcome.

The logged interaction data also enable the assessment of the cognitive processes carried out and their relationship with the outcome measures. In general, digital problem solving task accomplishment involves the application of a complex hierarchy of cognitive and metacognitive processes in addition to computer skills. Some or all of the cognitive and metacognitive skills of goal setting, planning, and monitoring as well as selecting, accessing, understanding, evaluating, organizing, and communicating information are implied by navigational, searching, digital learning, and other problem-solving tasks. Log-files give a unique opportunity to analyze those abilities separately. Further research should address the assessment of underlying skills behind task performance as well, as different measures can be related to different skills and sub-tasks of the information problem.

## REFERENCES

Ahuja, J., & Webster, J. (2001). Perceived disorientation: An examination of a new measure to assess web design effectiveness. *Interacting with Computers*, *14*(1), 15–29. doi:10.1016/S0953-5438(01)00048-0

Amadieu, F., & Salmerón, L. (2014). Concept maps for comprehension and navigation of hypertexts. In R. Hanewald & D. Ifenthaler (Eds.), *Digital Knowledge Maps in Education* (pp. 41–59). New York: Springer. doi:10.1007/978-1-4614-3178-7_3

Amadieu, F., & Tricot, A. (2006). Utilisation d'un hypermedia et apprentissage: Deux activités concurrentes ou complémentaires? [Hypermedia usage and learning: two competing or complementary activities?]. *Psychologie Française*, *51*(1), 5–23. doi:10.1016/j.psfr.2005.12.001

Azevedo, R., Moos, D., Johnes, A., & Chauncey, A. D. (2010). Measuring Cognitive and Metacognitive Regulatory Processes During Hypermedia Learning: Issues and Challenges. *Educational Psychologist*, *45*(4), 210–223. doi:10.1080/00461520.2010.515934

Bennett, R. E., Persky, H., Weiss, A. R., & Jenkins, F. (2007). *Problem solving in technology-rich environments: A report from the NAEP Technology-Based Assessment Project (NCES 2007-466)*. Washington, DC: National Center for Education Statistics, US Department of Education. Retrieved August 25, 2011, from http://nces.ed.gov/pubsearch/pubsinfo.asp?pubid=2007466

Botafogo, R. A., Rivlin, E., & Shneiderman, B. (1992). Structural analysis of hypertexts: Identifying hierarchies and useful metrics. *ACM Transactions on Information Systems*, *10*(2), 142–180. doi:10.1145/146802.146826

Braasch, J. L. G., Rouet, J. F., Vibert, N., & Britt, M. A. (2012). Readers' use of source information in text comprehension. *Memory & Cognition*, *40*(3), 450–465. doi:10.3758/s13421-011-0160-6 PMID:22086649

Brand-Gruwel, S., Wopereis, I., & Vermetten, Y. (2005). Information problem solving by experts and novices: Analysis of a complex cognitive skill. *Computers in Human Behavior*, *21*(3), 487–508. doi:10.1016/j.chb.2004.10.005

Brand-Gruwel, S., Wopereis, I., & Walraven, A. (2009). A descriptive model of information problem solving while using internet. *Computers & Education*, *53*(4), 1207–1217. doi:10.1016/j.compedu.2009.06.004

Chi, M. T. H., Glaser, R., & Rees, E. (1982). Expertise in problem solving. In R. Sternberg (Ed.), *Advances in the psychology of human intelligence* (Vol. 1, pp. 7–76). Hillsdale, NJ: Erlbaum.

Conklin, J. (1987). Hypertext: An introduction and Survey. *IEEE Computer*, *20*(9), 17–41. doi:10.1109/MC.1987.1663693

De Bruijn, D., de Mul, S., & van Oostendorp, H. (1992). The influence of screen size and text layout on the study of text. *Behaviour & Information Technology*, *11*(2), 71–78. doi:10.1080/01449299208924322

De Pereyra, G., Britt, M. A., Braasch, J. L. G., & Rouet, J. F. (2014). Reader's memory for information sources in simple news stories: Effects of text and task features. *Journal of Cognitive Psychology*, *24*(2), 187–204. doi:10.1080/2044 5911.2013.879152

DeStefano, D., & LeFevre, J.-A. (2007). Cognitive load in hypertext reading: A review. *Computers in Human Behavior*, *23*(3), 1616–1641. doi:10.1016/j.chb.2005.08.012

Dillon, A. (1994). *Designing Usable Electronic Text: Ergonomics Aspects of Human Information Usage*. London: Taylor and Francis. doi:10.4324/9780203470343

Dørum, K., & Garland, K. J. (2011). Efficient electronic navigation: A metaphorical question? *Interacting with Computers*, *23*(2), 129–136. doi:10.1016/j.intcom.2010.11.003

Eisenberg, M., & Berkowitz, R. (1990). *Information problem solving: The big six skills approach to library & information skills instruction*. Norwood, NJ: Ablex.

Foltz, P. W., Kintsch, W., & Landauer, T. K. (1998). The measurement of textual coherence with latent semantic analysis. *Discourse Processes*, *25*(2-3), 285–307. doi:10.1080/01638539809545029

Foss, C. L. (1988). Effective browsing in hypertext systems. In *Proceedings of the Conference on User-Oriented Content-Based Text and Image Handling (RIAO'88)*, (pp. 82–98). Academic Press.

Funke, J. (2010). Complex problem solving: A case for complex cognition? *Cognitive Processing*, *11*(2), 133–142. doi:10.1007/s10339-009-0345-0 PMID:19902283

Getzels, J. W. (1979). Problem finding: A theoretical note. *Cognitive Science*, *3*(2), 167–172. doi:10.1207/s15516709cog0302_4

Gwizdka, J., & Spence, I. (2007). Implicit measures of lostness and success in web navigation. *Interacting with Computers*, *19*(3), 357–369. doi:10.1016/j.intcom.2007.01.001

Herder, E. (2005). Characterizations of User Web Revisit Behavior. In *Proceedings of Workshop on Adaptivity and User Modelling in Interactive Systems*, (pp. 32-37). Academic Press.

Juvina, I., & van Oostendorp, H. (2006). Individual differences and behavioral metrics involved in modeling web navigation. *Universal Access in the Information Society*, *4*(3), 258–269. doi:10.1007/s10209-005-0007-7

Juvina, I., & van Oostendorp, H. (2008). Modeling semantic and structural knowledge in web navigation. *Discourse Processes*, *45*(4-5), 346–364. doi:10.1080/01638530802145205

Kim, H., & Hirtle, S. C. (1995). Spatial metaphors and disorientation in hypertext browsing. *Behaviour & Information Technology*, *4*(4), 239–250. doi:10.1080/01449299508914637

Kintsch, W. (1998). *Comprehension: A paradigm for cognition*. New York: Cambridge University Press.

Kitajima, M., Blackmon, M. H., & Polson, P. G. (2000). A Comprehension-based Model of Web Navigation and Its Application to Web Usability Analysis. *People and Computers*, *XIV*, 357–373.

Kobasigawa, A. (1983). Children's retrieval skills for school learning. *The Alberta Journal of Educational Research*, *29*(4), 259–271.

Larson, K., & Czerwinski, M. (1998). Web page design: Implications of memory, structure and scent for information retrieval. In *CHI '98 Proceedings of the SIGCHI conference on Human factors in computing systems* (pp. 25–32). New York, NY: ACM.

Lawless, K. A., & Kulikowich, J. M. (1996). Understanding hypertext navigation through cluster analysis. *Journal of Educational Computing Research, 14*(4), 385–399. doi:10.2190/DVAP-DE23-3XMV-9MXH

Lazonder, A. W., & Rouet, J.-F. (2008). Information problem solving instruction: Some cognitive and metacognitive issues. *Computers in Human Behavior, 24*(3), 753–765. doi:10.1016/j.chb.2007.01.025

Mayer, R. E. (1992). *Thinking, problem solving, cognition* (2nd ed.). New York: Freeman.

McDonald, S., & Stevenson, R. J. (1998). Effects of text structure and prior knowledge of the learner on navigation in hypertext. *Human Factors, 40*(1), 19–27. doi:10.1518/001872098779480541

McEneaney, J. E. (2001). Graphic and numerical methods to assess navigation in hypertext. *International Journal of Human-Computer Studies, 55*(5), 761–786. doi:10.1006/ijhc.2001.0505

Moore, P. (1995). Information problem-solving: A wider view of library skills. *Contemporary Educational Psychology, 20*(1), 1–31. doi:10.1006/ceps.1995.1001

Naumann, J., Richter, T., Christmann, U., & Groeben, N. (2008). Working memory capacity and reading skill moderate the effectiveness of strategy training in learning from hypertext. *Learning and Individual Differences, 18*(2), 197–213. doi:10.1016/j.lindif.2007.08.007

Naumann, J., Richter, T., Flender, J., Christmann, U., & Groeben, N. (2007). Signaling in expository hypertexts compensates for deficits in reading skill. *Journal of Educational Psychology, 99*(4), 791–807. doi:10.1037/0022-0663.99.4.791

Newell, A., & Simon, H. A. (1972). *Human problem solving.* Englewood Cliffs, NJ: Prentice-Hall.

Nielsen, J. (1999). *Designing Web Usability: The practice of simplicity.* Indianapolis: New Riders.

OECD. (2009). *PIAAC Problem Solving in Technology-Rich Environments: a conceptual framework* (OECD Education Working Paper No. 36.). Paris, France: OECD. 10.1787/220262483674

OECD (2011). *PISA 2009 Results: Students on Line: Digital Technologies and Performance (Volume VI).* Paris, France: OECD. 10.1787/9789264112995-en

OECD. (2013a). *OECD Skills Outlook 2013: First Results from the Survey of Adult Skills.* Paris, France: OECD Publishing. doi:10.1787/9789264204256-en

OECD. (2013b). *Technical Report of the Survey of Adult Skills (PIAAC).* Paris, France: OECD. Retrieved February 17, 2015 from www.oecd.org/site/piaac/_Technical%20Report_17OCT13.pdf

Otter, M., & Johnson, H. (2000). Lost in hyperspace: Metrics and mental models. *Interacting with Computers, 13*(1), 1–40. doi:10.1016/S0953-5438(00)00030-8

Padovani, S., & Lansdale, M. (2003). Balancing search and retrieval in hypertext: Context-specific trade-offs in navigational tool use. *International Journal of Human-Computer Studies, 58*(1), 125–149. doi:10.1016/S1071-5819(02)00128-3

Pan, B., Hembrooke, H., Joachims, T., Lorigo, L., Gay, G., & Granka, L. (2007). In Google we trust: Users' decisions on rank, position, and relevance. *Journal of Computer-Mediated Communication, 12*, article 3. Retrieved from http://jcmc.indiana.edu/vol12/issue3/pan.html

Perfetti, C. A., Rouet, J.-F., & Britt, M. A. (1999). Towards a theory of documents representation. In H. van Oostendorp & S. R. Goldman (Eds.), *The Construction of Mental Representations During Reading* (pp. 99–122). Mahwah, NJ: Lawrence Erlbaum Associates.

Pirolli, P., & Card, S. K. (1999). Information Foraging. *Psychological Review, 106*(4), 643–675. doi:10.1037/0033-295X.106.4.643

Pirolli, P., & Fu, W.-T. F. (2003). SNIF-ACT: a model of information foraging on the world wide web. In *Proceedings of the Ninth International Conference on User Modeling*. Berlin: Springer Verlag. doi:10.1007/3-540-44963-9_8

Protopsaltis, A. (2008). Reading strategies in hypertexts and factors influencing hyperlink selection. *Journal of Educational Multimedia and Hypermedia, 17*, 191–213.

Rouet, J.-F. (1990). Interactive text processing by inexperienced (hyper-) readers. In A. Rizk, N. Streitz, & J. André (Eds.), *Hypertexts: Concepts, systems, and applications* (pp. 250–260). Cambridge, UK: Cambridge University Press.

Rouet, J.-F. (2006). *The skills of document use: From text comprehension to Web based learning*. Mahwah, NJ: Lawrence Erlbaum.

Rouet, J.-F., & Britt, M. A. (2011). Relevance processes in multiple document comprehension. In M. T. McCrudden, J. P. Magliano, & G. Schraw (Eds.), *Text Relevance and Learning from Text* (pp. 19–52). Greenwich, CT: Information Age Publishing.

Rouet, J.-F., Favart, M., Britt, M. A., & Perfetti, C. A. (1997). Studying and using multiple documents in history: Effects of discipline expertise. *Cognition and Instruction, 15*(1), 85–106. doi:10.1207/s1532690xci1501_3

Rouet, J.-F., & Passerault, J.-M. (1999). Analyzing Learner-hypermedia interaction: An overview of online methods. *Instructional Science, 27*(3/4), 201–219. doi:10.1023/A:1003162715462

Salmerón, L., Cañas, J. J., Kintsch, W., & Fajardo, I. (2005). Reading strategies and hypertext comprehension. *Discourse Processes, 40*(3), 171–191. doi:10.1207/s15326950dp4003_1

Salmerón, L., Kammerer, Y., & García-Carrión, P. (2013). Searching the Web for conflicting topics: Page and user factors. *Computers in Human Behavior, 29*(6), 2161–2171. doi:10.1016/j.chb.2013.04.034

Salmerón, L., Kintsch, W., & Cañas, J. J. (2006). Reading strategies and prior knowledge in learning from hypertext. *Memory & Cognition, 34*(5), 1157–1171. doi:10.3758/BF03193262 PMID:17128614

Salmerón, L., Kintsch, W., & Kintsch, E. (2010). Self-regulation and link selection strategies in hypertext. *Discourse Processes, 47*(3), 175–211. doi:10.1080/01638530902728280

Shapiro, A., & Niederhauser, D. (2004). Learning from hypertext: Research issues and findings. In D. H. Jonassen (Ed.), *Handbook of research on educational communications and technology* (pp. 605–620). Mahwah, NJ: Lawrence Erlbaum Associates.

Shih, P.-C., Mate, R., Sanchez, F., & Munoz, D. (2004). *Quantifying user navigation patterns: a methodology proposal*. Paper presented at the 28th International Congress of Psychology. Retrieved August 15, 2011, from http://www.uam.es/personal_pdi/psicologia/pei/download/Shih2004quantifying_ICP.pdf

Skov, O., Le Bigot, L., Vibert, N., de Pereyra, G., & Rouet, J.-F. (2014). *The Role of Popularity Cues in Students' Selection of Scholarly Literature Online*. Paper presented at the EARLI SIG2 Conference, Rotterdam, The Netherlands.

Smedshammar, H., Frenckner, K., Nordquist, C., & Romberger, S. (1989). *Why is the difference in reading speed when reading from VDUs and from paper bigger for fast readers than for slow readers?* Paper presented at WWDU 1989, Second International Scientific Conference, Montreal, Canada.

Smith, P. A. (1996). Towards a practical measure of hypertext usability. *Interacting with Computers*, *4*(4), 365–38. doi:10.1016/S0953-5438(97)83779-4

Stadtler, M., & Bromme, R. (2013). Multiple document comprehension: An approach to public understanding of science. *Cognition and Instruction*, *31*(2), 122–129. doi:10.1080/07370008.2013.771106

Sweller, J. (1998). Cognitive load during problem solving: Effects on learning. *Cognitive Science*, *12*(2), 257–285. doi:10.1207/s15516709cog1202_4

Vaughan, M., & Dillon, A. (2006). Why structure and genre matter to users of digital information: A longitudinal study with readers of a web-based newspaper. *International Journal of Human-Computer Studies*, *64*(6), 502–526. doi:10.1016/j.ijhcs.2005.11.002

Vörös, Z., Rouet, J.-F., & Pléh, C. (2011). Effect of high-level content organizers on hypertext learning. *Computers in Human Behavior*, *27*(5), 2047–2055. doi:10.1016/j.chb.2011.04.005

Zimmerman, B. J. (2008). Investigating self-regulation and motivation: Historical background, methodological developments, and future prospects. *American Educational Research Journal*, *45*(1), 166–183. doi:10.3102/0002831207312909

Zoanetti, N. (2010). Interactive computer based assessment tasks: How problem-solving process data can inform instruction. *Australasian Journal of Educational Technology*, *26*, 585–606.

Zumbach, J., & Mohraz, M. (2008). Cognitive load in hypermedia reading. *Computers in Human Behavior*, *24*(3), 875–887. doi:10.1016/j.chb.2007.02.015

# Chapter 28
# Analyzing Process Data from Technology–Rich Tasks

**Lisa Keller**
*University of Massachusetts – Amherst, USA*

**April L. Zenisky**
*University of Massachusetts – Amherst, USA*

**Xi Wang**
*University of Massachusetts – Amherst, USA*

## ABSTRACT

*A key task emerging in item analysis is identification of what constitutes valid and reliable measurement information, and what data support proposed score interpretations. Measurement information takes on many forms with computerized tests. An enormous amount of data is gathered from technology-based items, tracing every click and movement of the mouse and time stamping actions taken, and the data recorded falls into two general categories: process and outcomes. Outcomes are traditional scored answers that students provides in response to prompts, but technology-based item types also provide information regarding the process that students used to answer items. The first consideration to the practical use of such data is the nature of the data generated when learners complete complex assessment tasks. The chapter we propose serves to discuss some possible methodological strategies that could be used to analyze data from such technology-rich testing tasks.*

## INTRODUCTION

As assessment increasingly moves toward computerization, technology-rich items are being evaluated to measure academic outcomes that are historically challenging to assess with traditional test formats, such as critical thinking skills. Technology-rich items typically involve one or more of the following elements such as digital media, electronic resources (authoritative literature, websites, etc.), a range of tasks and varied response actions, and high interactivity. Large-scale implementation of these items depends on the capabilities of computer technology to seamlessly deliver such items to examinees given high-levels of administration requirements, and beyond that, a key task

DOI: 10.4018/978-1-4666-9441-5.ch028

emerging in item analysis is the identification of what constitutes valid and reliable measurement information. With technology-rich items, a great deal of data can be generated, but the challenge remains as to what data support proposed score interpretations, and what is, quite simply, noise.

Measurement information can take on many forms with technology-rich items administered via computer. Truly, an enormous amount of data is available for collection with many technology-based item formats, tracing every click and movement of the mouse and time stamping actions taken. The data typically available for recording falls into two general categories: *process* and *outcomes*. Outcomes are traditional scored answers that students provides in response to prompts, but technology-based item types potentially also provide information regarding the *process* that students used to answer items. This process-related information can be used as an element in the scoring of the item, or to provide diagnostic and formative information to educators *and* test developers. The challenge that is emerging with these tasks is distilling the *useful* information from such items; again, separating signal from noise.

Since traditional item types typically do not provide process information, the literature on strategies to analyze and use such data effectively is in its infancy, and thus peer-reviewed guidance is limited. Where such documentation exists is primarily in the form of technical reports advanced by testing agencies specific to particular innovative testing initiatives, and as such is sporadic in nature. Recent work has detailed some of the analyses undertaken in the context of the assessment of critical thinking, while a number of other studies have focused on additional data mining strategies (Almond, Deane, Quinlan, Wagner, & Sydorenko, 2012; Carr, 2013; Bouchet, Harley, Trevors, & Azevedo, 2013; Kinnebrew, Loretz, & Biswas, 2013; Kerr & Chung, 2012). Reflecting on this nascent body of literature, it is possible to identify certain emerging trends relevant to the present work.

The first consideration to the practical use of such data is the nature of the data generated when learners complete complex assessment tasks. At present, the proverbial "anything" is theoretically *possible* but operationally challenging. Technology allows testing programs to gather a vast amount of data during test administration, and this data takes on many forms. It can include records of mouse position, display time of on-screen materials, mouse clicks, drag and drop movements, deletions, drafts, and submitted final products, among other data elements. For operational testing programs, however, collection within this universe of data possibilities presents two issues. First, the data to be gathered must be operationally defined and its purposes articulated. This is necessary because this kind of formal reflection serves as the basis of the technical specification for the data collection mechanism, which must be programmed into the test administration system so as to provide the data miners with the data in a usable (or at least transformable) format. The other issue to be resolved here is that depending on what data is collected and what format it takes, the individual records for any one test session may be quite extensive, to the extent that across examinees the data storage requirements may be substantial and perhaps prohibitive for larger testing programs absent clear goals and plans for the data.

To this end, while process information has potential to be pedagogically quite interesting, techniques to capture and effectively use such data have not been well developed. These data have been characterized as "semi-amorphous" (Scalise, 2013), a term which seems to aptly captures both the challenge and the promise that characterizes innovations in assessment task formats This chapter presents some possible methodological strategies that could be used to analyze data from such technology-rich testing tasks. First, a synthesis and evaluation of the approaches that have been used is presented. The strengths and limitations of the methodologies will be noted, along with the context under which the methods have been employed, and done so successfully. Following this synthesis and overview, an illustrative example using data from a specific type of technology-rich scenario with multiple component tasks will be provided. A description of both the scenario itself as well as the resulting data that is captured is included here. Various analytic techniques used to capture potential information for the scenario are described and illustrated, along with commentary regarding the feasibility of completing the analyses in an operational setting. Lastly, some information regarding the generalizability of methodology and findings across parallel scenarios and tasks is discussed.

## BACKGROUND

### Mining the Click-Stream of Technology-Rich Test Tasks

As noted above, technology-rich assessments provide the opportunity to collect not only outcome data but also process data. Outcome data is nothing new, but these process data can potentially provide useful and actionable formative and diagnostic information to teachers, as well as potentially contribute to the final score of the student, or examinee in the case of credentialing. Due to the emerging nature of this type of data, the literature on strategies to analyze complex assessment data from the angle of process rather than outcome (and to connect such process information to inform instruction) is limited, attention is drawn to technical reports from testing programs that are out there in the field, and operationally using these types of assessments. The advantage to using technical reports is that the approaches summarized are those used with actual technology rich tasks, and as such provide practical guidance, rather than just theoretically satisfying processes.

The first consideration to the practical use of such data is the nature of the data generated when learners complete complex assessment tasks. Technology allows testing programs to gather a vast amount of data during test administration, and this data takes on many forms. It *can* include records of mouse position, display time of on-screen materials, mouse clicks, drag and drop movements, deletions, drafts, and submitted final products, among other data elements. These types of semi-amorphous data can then be analyzed in a variety of ways. Typically, these analytic techniques are exploratory in nature, where patterns of data are extracted from the observed actions collected in the assessment process. These patterns are then analyzed using a variety of statistical techniques, allowing inferences to be drawn about examinees that exhibit certain patterns. This approach is in stark contrast to how outcome data are typically analyzed.

Taking a broad overview, in a traditional testing scenario, outcome data are of primary interest. In these cases, constructs are well defined and measurements/assessments are constructed to measure these constructs. The result is variables (test items, test scores) whose meaning is fully rooted in a theoretical perspective and can be clearly understood based on that frame. The clarity of the meaning of the data leads to clarity in the best ways to analyze the data, and well-established procedures exist. When considering process data, a similar process of data collection and analysis could be implemented if the processes involved in solving problems were well understood and could be codified. Such approaches have been investigated in the realms of automatic item generation (Gierl & Haladyna, 2012) and cognitive diagnostic modeling (Rupp, Templin, & Henson, 2010; de la Torre, 2011).

At present, there has been limited success in being able to fully specify cognitive processes used in solving even some basic problems. For this reason, at this stage in many operational settings it might well be quite difficult to actually create well-defined models that represent the construct of interest with the process data currently gathered.

Computer technology can assist by capturing process information but this can be set to occur without a full understanding of *why* it is being collected or of what the data might mean.

Given this, one task ahead in this area is for data (within specific applications, as well as across testing programs) to be examined and analyzed to attempt to develop some theories of problem solving for specific task types. The resulting theories will not likely rest in the realm cognitive psychology at first, but might be more linked to a sequence of observable actions, that lead to specific outcomes. It may take time to develop the cognitive theory to explain why these specific actions result in specific outcomes, but the information gained in the meantime may still provide useful information for educators.

Below are provided overviews of several recent efforts to mine such data for measurement and instructional goals.

This section provides a review of the work done. Following the description of the methods and findings of each study, some comments regarding the strengths and potential limitations of the methodology for operational testing programs are provided. These comments are not meant to be evaluation of the quality of the research, but rather a discussion of the potential value of the methods presented in the research to other testing scenarios.

The studies can be classified in two different groups. In the first group, the researchers defined process variables *a priori*, and coded them in their data sets from the start. These variables were then subjected to statistical analysis. In the second group, a data mining approach was undertaken. In these cases, the full log of events, or some portion of the log of events, recorded during the assessment was subjected to a more machine learning type of algorithm. In these cases, patterns in the data were uncovered in a statistical way that is devoid of expert judgment. Once these patterns are identified, they are classified in some way to make conclusions about the processes used by the students. The first group of studies are conducted in more traditional assessments contexts, while the second group of studies were conducted in less structured, more novel environments.

## EXAMPLES WITH EXPERT DEFINED VARIABLES

### Study 1: Writing Assessment

A recent research report involving a writing task on the CBAL Writing assessment focused on potential strategies for analyzing keystroke log data (Almond, Deane, Quinlan, Wagner, & Sydorenko, 2012). In this study, researchers reviewed the assessment data records from 79 middle school students who participated in a pilot of the CBAL Writing test development (for a variety of technical reasons, the final data set included 68 sets of essays and keystroke logs). The writing task was structured such that the students were asked to read some quantity of source material, respond to a few basic comprehension questions, and then complete an essay task. In terms of data collection, a keystroke logger was employed, which maintained record of keys pressed and time spent *between* keystrokes.

Almond, et al. (2012) noted that a "major challenge in making use of keystroke logs is defining meaningful summaries that can then be input into scoring algorithms or factor analyses" (p. 2). The purpose of this study was exploratory in nature and aimed at developing definitions of potential summary variables, establishing algorithms for extraction of those variables from the logs, and testing those algorithms with student data. This study was framed in the context of understanding critical thinking as evidenced by completion of a writing task, so the summary variables to be derived from the keystroke logs were those that the researchers identified as being part of the writing process (referencing the specific model proposed by Deane, 2012). The specific details of the writing model of interest underlying the Almond, et al. research is beyond the scope of the present chapter, but their study is relevant in terms of devising a conceptual framework and creating a data collection system and analysis strategy to model data effectively based on that framework.

The main element of data analysis undertaken in Almond, et al. (2012) was to categorize events in the keystroke log according to what was happening when the event was logged, to create a narrative of logical events and thereby recreate the logic of the examinee throughout the course of the task, using observable data. The keystroke logger implemented here compared current and revised versions of the student work every 5 milliseconds, and where difference were found, logged an event. The log entry consisted of the time of the event, the position of the change, and the added and removed text. From there, an event classification schema was applied to the data, using timing data to categorize events into the following possible states:

- Pause between letters within a word.
- Pause between words.
- Pause between sentences.
- Pause between paragraphs.
- Pause before an editing operation (e.g., single or multiple backspaces).
- Pause before cut, paste, or replace operation; or before using a mouse to navigate to a different part of the essay.

The main research finding that emerged from this study concerned the distribution of most of the pauses, which was identified by the researchers as being consistent with data generated from a mixture of lognormal distributions, which the authors noted lent itself to the use of mixture models and suggested that some pauses are simply part of typing while others are more involved cognitively (the data "corresponds to a cognitive model of text production in which several different processes are operating") (Almond, et al., 2012, p.

49). Positive correlations were also found between these timing features and student scores; while the authors noted this could be due to limited sample sizes, it bears repeating that a priority here was the exploration of data mining strategies which can be applied to larger data sets to further evaluate the robustness of any observed patterns.

## Commentary on the Methodology Presented

As noted by the authors, the methodological advance that emerged from this study was to identify strategies for translating keystroke logs into summary data for use in the analysis. The work done by these authors provides a starting point for future researchers, since the variables have been identified and could be used in other writing assessments. The type of data collected in this study could be obtained in other computer-based writing assessments. Given the small sample size, the results should be replicated in future work, and this work provides a practical framework for other testing programs.

## Study 2: Science Experiments

Development work on the next generation of NAEP's Science assessments has likewise sought to advance measurement of process (Carr, 2013). In this study, students were given hands on tasks (HOTs) where students perform simulations of science experiments on the computer. The students are provided with options of tasks to perform, and they can click on the task they would like to carry out. The sequence of tasks that a student completes provides information that the student can then use to answer the question(s) posed. Interestingly, this research has made a conceptual distinction between the task (which is typically performance-based and interactive) and the evidence types (described as automatically-captured data aimed at process and outcome). In reflecting on process, one possible strategy to be employed is the identify *efficient* processes and *systematic* processes, as in the former there are little or no unnecessary steps and in the latter problem-solving is methodological and logically sequenced. To this end, the data that is collected is a) what is clicked; b) order of clicks; c) number of clicks; and d) timing of clicks. This trail of actions allows the test developers to reconstruct the problem-solving process, characterize strategies, and try to link such strategies to underlying cognitions. Modeling the click-stream in Carr (2013) was carried out by creating a two dimensional grid of systematic and efficient actions, where action sequences can be modeled as shown in Figure 1.

The solutions (i.e. sequences of actions) produced by student were placed into this plane, and could be categorized as low or high on either axis (efficient and systematic). This would result in patterns being classified into one of four categories: (1) low systematic, low efficiency, (2) low systematic, high efficiency, (3) high systematic, low efficiency, and (4) high systematic, high efficiency. The most valued process is one in which

students are using strategies that are at once both highly efficient and systematic. Using this classification, it is possible to identify areas where students may be having problems in solving the tasks, and remediation can be developed. In the study presented, the majority of the strategies employed by the study participants were classified as low efficiency, low systematic, meaning students engaged in too many steps that weren't necessary, and the process was not logical. The author suggested that this information has application in helping to inform teachers of where the process is breaking down for their students.

## Commentary on the Methodology Presented

The methodology presented in this study was quite interesting, and certainly provides a promising area for how to construct tasks with the idea of process embedded into the task itself. In the previous example (Almond, et al., 2012) the process data was created through the definition of

*Figure 1. Modeling action sequences in NAEP Science ((Two dimensional grid example)*

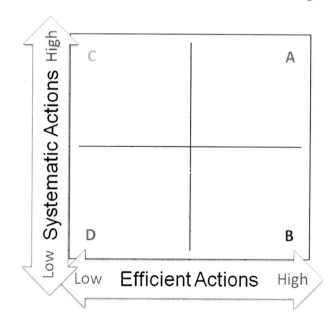

variables using keystroke information. In the Carr (3013) study, however, the process information was explicitly made part of the item. Being able to include process information in the item was possible in large part because of the type of item that was used: a science experiment. This type of task is very process-oriented, so building in the process piece into the data collection is more straightforward. This type of information cannot be built into all kinds of tasks, but this is a great example of making the process data explicit in the task. One issue that emerged in this study was that the classification of the solution onto the two dimensional grid was not clearly defined, and may require a lot of labor from subject matter experts to classify the works. Looking for ways to classify the responses in an automatic way would be necessary for implementation in a large-scale context, but could be done for smaller-scale (e.g. classroom) applications.

## DATA MINING STRATEGIES

### Study 1: Computer Based Learning Environment

The context for a study by Kinnebrew, Loretz, and Biswas (2013) is a little different than a traditional assessment setting, in that instead of being an assessment, it is more of a learning environment that is shaped by the students' interaction with the material. Students explored a science concept within "Betty's Brain," an online learning tool in which the students use various sources to access science content (and then themselves learn by teaching the concepts to "Betty", the virtual 'teachable agent'),. As the learning progresses, questions can be asked and answered based on the input provided by the students. It is a complex system that would require space beyond this chapter to summarize. The result is a large stream of data collected through the interaction between the teachable agent and the student. This string

of information can then be subjected to a data mining approach to identify patterns of behaviors exhibited by students.

Many of the data mining algorithms look for patterns of behavior that occur frequently. In many cases, this can still result in a large number of patterns that are difficult to then categorize. The statistical methodology employed here by Kinnebrew, Loretz, and Biswas (2013) draws on differential sequence mining techniques, which transforms raw data logs into coherent sequences of actions through action abstraction to filter out irrelevant actions/information and combine similar items. Patterns observed are them compared across user-created groups of students, to identify both differences and similarities. Instead of just identifying frequent patterns of responses, they looked for patterns that were different between specified groups of students, such as high performers and low performers, looking for behaviors that differentiate groups. It is important to note that the Kinnebrew, Loretz, and Biswas (2013) work also sought to analyze these data in terms of productive and counterproductive phases of activity, analogous to the efficient/systematic conceptualization of click-stream actions advanced by Carr (2013). Here, productive actions are defined as those that yield correct decisions/answers to the questions in the system. Once identified within each group, comparisons of the two groups are made, to determine which behaviors are different between groups. After the differential patterns of behavior are determined, they are examined to ascertain the cognitive and meta-cognitive behaviors represented by these patterns of behavior in the learning system.

### Commentary on the Proposed Methodology

In the context of this study, a computer based learning environment, it is not possible to predefine the variables since the data are much more amorphous. In that sense, it makes sense to use a data mining approach, to be sure to capture information and patterns that might be impossible to be identified by humans. it is expected that these types of exploratory approaches will find greater use as less structured experiences are utilized for assessment purposes. However, there is room for such techniques to be applied to more structured settings such as those presented in the first group of studies. The strength of this approach is that experts are not required to determine what variables might be important, because that is the task of the data mining algorithm to detect patterns and report the analysis results. In that context, variables that experts might not consider could be identified as important process variables. This method also had the strength of looking at what types of patterns pre-identified groups of students used in an attempt to gain insight into how to evaluate the patterns detected.

## Study 2: Video Games

Kerr and Chung (2012) applied data mining procedures to data captured from video games. The authors were interested in viewing video games as assessment opportunities but capturing the key features of student performance is not as obvious in that context, when compared to more traditional assessment contexts. The log files from the video game were examined and actions that were not attempted at least five times were determined to be arbitrary and eliminated as possible actions for further analysis. Once the list of consequential actions was obtained, a matrix of zeros and ones was constructed where for each student, where a "1" was recorded if the student took an action and a "0" if not. This matrix of zeros and ones was then subjected to a cluster analysis. The cluster analysis was done at the feature level, rather than the student level, so the resulting clusters are clusters of actions and not people. The strings of actions then have to be named, and applied to the people, based on their string of actions. While this process is very laborious (as noted by the authors), it provides a

different way of looking at the data at the feature level rather than the student level. A process like this could be coded into data collection in future applications, limiting the intensity of the labor.

## Commentary on the Proposed Methodology

This case is similar to the Kinnebrew, Loretz, and Biswas (2013) study, where the environment is much less structured, and the definition of variables would be difficult. Unlike the previous example, however, a less sophisticated, and more labor-intensive process was used to code the data for analysis. The advantage is that there is less statistical expertise required to implement the methodology, although it would be necessary to automate the coding of the data to make this a practical technique.

## Summary of Examples

Looking across these examples of creative strategies to extract data, it is clear that great possibilities for data analysis are contained in the data collected through innovative computer-based task environments, but there also remains much room for methodological exploration. These examples provide useful starting points for how to think about examining process data resulting from complex computer-based tasks. A key variable in choosing a methodology should be whether the features/actions that are captured in the process are defined a priori, or whether all possible features/ actions are captured and subjected to a machine learning algorithm. Both scenarios have their advantages and disadvantages and the choice often comes down to practical considerations such as memory requirements and analytic expertise. An illustrative example of a technology-rich task is presented next, along with attempts to analyze the process data. This example would be classified into the first group of studies, where the variables are defined *a priori*.

## A New Analysis: The Case of "Organic Milk"

The following illustrative example is an actual task that has been developed for use in an operational testing context. Pilot data have been collected on the task, and lre used for the analysis presented here. A brief description of the task that the students were presented with is given first, as well as a description of the type of data that were collected during the administration of the task. In this case, all actions made by a student in the course of completing the full simulated task were captured.

## Description of the Task

This technology-based task, termed "Organic Milk", is delivered through the computer and is designed to measure critical thinking skills (Rosen & Tager, 2014). The scenario first requires that students complete a tutorial regarding the interface of the item, as well as review an overview of what the item will entail. Once the student is ready to begin, they click on a button to start the actual scenario. The student is then presented with an introduction to the actual measurement scenario.

The scenario begins with the frame story that the student "receives an email" from the principal of their school asking them to help conduct some research and make a recommendation relative to an issue facing the school. [In this context, the task is to determine whether the school should provide organic milk in the cafeteria.] This email outlines the four key tasks required of the student within the scenario, as follows:

- Internet search.
- Interviewing experts.
- Taking notes.
- Making a recommendation in the form of a persuasive essay that provides evidence for the position taken.

At this point, a sequence of actions is presented to the student. The four key tasks that students must progress through are described in greater detail below.

1.  **Internet Search and Interviews:** They are then prompted to begin an internet search. The student is presented with a 'Google' search screen (which is actually a facsimile of a search engine built to operate only within the scenario, rather than the full, unfiltered Internet). The student then carries out an internet search using keywords of their own choosing. As part of the deliberately controlled nature of the scenario, the results of the search are standardized across all students, regardless of the search term(s) supplied by the student. The limited number of search results returned by this simulated internet search intentionally vary in terms of their relevance and reliability.

Students are instructed to take notes from the websites. This can be done by either typing notes directly into the "journal" space provided, or by highlighting and dragging text to that journal space. When text is entered into the journal, they are asked to classify it as a note, a claim, or evidence. It should also be noted that all search results must be visited to move forward.

2.  **Interviewing Experts:** At two of the search result websites, the students are prompted to generate questions and type them into text boxes. In one case, questions are directed to the CEO of a company that produces organic milk, and in the other it is for a blogger with opinions about organic milk. Once any question(s) are submitted by the student to each of these personas, the student is presented with a video in which the person is answering some of the commonly asked

questions. It should be noted that in addition to the text-based evidence that could be put in the journal spaceStudents can capture portions of this video into their journal to use in their final recommendation.

3. **Concept Map:** After this note-taking experience, the student is asked to construct a concept map to organize their ideas before making their recommendation. This activity requires students to drag and drop their notes into a region of the screen to organize their accumulated data. Students are provided some general guidance on how to place their notes into the concept map. It should be noted that only claims and evidence can be placed onto the map. They are also instructed that they have the capability to go back to the websites to gather more information if they choose to do so. Once the map is created, the student is given the functionality to draw connections between claims that are related. They are also provided with a pop-up box to explain why they think the claims are related.

4. **Completing the Recommendation:** After connections are made between claims, the student is asked to enter their recommendation in a text box as a persuasive essay, formatted as a letter. They are allowed to enter text freely and also to drag and drop claims from the concept map that they have created.

More detail regarding the nature of the task and its validity for measuring critical thinking can be found in Rosen and Tager (2014).

## Scoring the Task: Outcome Variables

Students receive several scores when they complete all the tasks in the scenario, corresponding to the different component tasks of the scenario. Teachers are used to score each of the tasks on a 0-3 point scale. It should also be noted that the total

score is a weighted composite of these subscores. The specific weighting of the scores is as follows:

- **Google Search:** 5% (Task 1).
- **Concept Map:** 35% (Task 3).
- **Anti-Organic Milk Score:** 10% (Task 4).
- **Concept Map Link Score:** 10% (Task 3).
- **Recommendation:** 40% (Task 4).

## Description of Data Captured

During the completion of the task, all actions that the student performs are recorded along with the time spent on each task. The result is an extensive amount of click-stream data, along with the traditional performance data. The click-stream information is indeed "semi-amorphous" per Scalise (2013). To provide a comprehensive list of all possible variables difficulties not productive, because the nature of the raw data is such that it does not lend itself to simple categorization, and the potential derivative variables are numerous but not necessarily purposeful (and, therefore, perhaps not meaningful, either). As stated earlier, the study described here is exploratory in nature, to identify data analysis strategies that may help to identify strategies to mine the students' data records and provide stakeholders with ways to describe students' critical thinking skills, both in the context of this specific task and perhaps (in the future, with the analysis of other, similar tasks) across other similarly-constructed critical thinking activities. Informed by the work of Almond, et al. (2012), specific variables were chosen to use in the analysis, rather than subject all the data to a machine learning type of analysis. Since the data were not collected with an eye toward particular analyses, or with particular variables in mind to capture, the format of the data capture was very dense. The specific variables studied here were in part determined by the potential to extract the variable from the data capture, and also in part by the conceptual value of the variable. That is to say, there were some variables that we may have liked to use but were impossible to isolate from the nature of the data capture.

## PROCESS VARIABLES USED IN ANALYSES

The variables extracted from the data captured on each student as he/she proceeded through the task that were not used for scoring purposes are referred to as process variables in the remainder of the chapter. This is to differentiate from the outcome variables that were the scores that the students received. Although different analyses used different process variables, the complete list of process variables used across analyses is provided here.

- **Total Number of Notes Taken by the Student:** This variable is the number of notes that the student placed into the journal. Since all notes are not the same by the student, this variable was further broken down into
  ○ Number of notes labeled as claims;
  ○ Number of notes labeled as evidence;
  ○ Number of notes labeled only as notes, not claims or evidence.

This breakdown of the types of notes is essential, because only claims and evidence can be placed into the concept map. Additionally, a student's proficiency at recognizing what constitutes a claim and what constitutes evidence may serve as an indicator of the student's critical thinking ability. It is worth noting that the note was understood to be a claim or piece of evidence based on the student's designation as such, and the quality of this designation was not investigated.

- **Percent of Evidence and Claims in the Notes That Were Taken:** Because students took different numbers of notes, the absolute number of claims and evidence is not necessarily indicative of the *quality* of the information gathered. To adjust for differing numbers of total notes, the percent of notes labeled as evidence and claims was also computed and used in the analysis

- **Number of Notes Used in the Concept Map:** One perspective that can be taken is that the value of notes lies in the fact that they can be used in the concept map. For this reason, the number of notes used in the map was included as a piece of evidence to determine if using more notes resulted in a higher score.

- **Percent of Notes Used in the Concept Map:** As described above, because the total number of notes that students collected varied, looking at the percent of those that ended up in the concept map was likewise investigated. This variable could also signify the student's ability to take notes purposefully, and to not make note of information that was irrelevant in the completion of the concept map and essay tasks.

- **Number of Minutes Taken to Complete the Note-Taking and Concept Map Construction:** It was not clear whether or not the amount of time taken would relate to the quality of the work. Since the rate of work varies so greatly among students, there was no expectation that there would be a relationship between the time spent and the total score. Given the exploratory nature of the study, and the interest in determining if and how response time may have value in this context, these data were included in the study.

## ANALYSIS

Since task scores were available for the each of the major tasks in this assessment experience, the primary goal in this study was to investigate the relationship between possible process-related variables to these outcome measures. To put this study in the context of previous work in this area, features or actions were identified *a priori* to use in the analyses, rather than use a machine learning type of data mining. This approach was also chosen in part to examine methodologies that were accessible and that could be reasonably conducted by those engaged in test development.

### Previous Research on Organic Milk Task

Rosen and Tager (2014) analyzed the pilot data of the Organic Milk task with the goal of determining whether engaging in "thinking tools" would enhance their critical thinking skills. Using data from 190 students from 4 countries, what they found was that students that engaged in using the concept map scored higher on a critical thinking assessment than students that did not use a concept map. Further, students who scored higher on the critical thinking assessment were more able to create the connections in the concept map, indicating a better understanding of the relationships among the information gathered in the research process. This study provides evidence that the Organic Milk task does appear to measure critical thinking, and that the use of thinking tools such as a concept map can enhance the students' critical thinking ability. In ths current study, several different analyses were conducted and descriptions and rationales for each analysis are provided next.

### Analysis 1: Relationship of Process and Outcome Variables

Because the approach used here was to select variables and designate them as process variables

at the outset, the first step in this study was to determine whether the variables selected could actually be considered process variables. To examine this issue, the relationship between the process variables and the total score was examined. If there was no relationship between the process and outcome, then that was an indication that the selected variable might not be a good indicator of process.

Unfortunately, due to a data capture problem, many student records in the dataset were incomplete (in that they did not have a score on the anti-organic milk task), and no students received a score on the CEO task. To ensure that the scores were comparable among the students, the total score was recomputed for all students without those tasks. The weights were adjusted so that each component was still represented in the same proportion as was originally intended. The following correlational and regression analyses are based on this re-computed total score.

Additionally, to ensure these analyses are based on a typical sample, outliers were deleted; in this dataset two student records were deleted as outliers. Outliers were determined as students whose scores were beyond two standard deviations of the mean score.

As described above, the process variables investigated include number of notes labeled as claims (Claim), number of notes labeled evidence (Evidence), number of notes not labeled claim or evidence (MyNotes), percent of claim and evidence in the total number of notes (Note structure), number of notes used in the map (Map Notes), percent of notes used in the map construction (Percent Notes in Map), and task time. The outcome variable of interest was total score.

The first results of interest looked at the correlations observed between the process variables and the final total score. The results of this analysis are presented in Table 1. The process variables referenced in Table 1 are defined as follows:

- Claim = number of notes labeled as claims;

*Table 1. Correlation of process variables to the total score*

| Process Variables | Correlation with Total Score | Sample Size | *p*-value |
|---|---|---|---|
| Claim | .455** | 129 | 0.000 |
| Evidence | .337** | 129 | 0.000 |
| MyNotes | .209* | 129 | 0.017 |
| Total Notes | .426** | 129 | 0.000 |
| Note Structure | 0.054 | 129 | 0.545 |
| Map Notes | .556** | 129 | 0.000 |
| Percent Notes in Map | .214* | 129 | 0.015 |
| Task Time | .447** | 128 | 0.000 |

* Correlation is significant at the 0.05 level (2-tailed), ** Correlation is significant at the 0.01 level (2-tailed).

- Evidence = number of notes labeled as evidence;
- MyNotes= number of notes labeled only as notes, not claims or evidence;
- Total Notes= total number of notes taken by the student;
- Note Structure = percent of claim and evidence in the notes that were taken;
- Map Notes= number of notes used in the concept map;
- Percent Notes in Map = percent of notes used in the concept map;
- Task Time=Number of minutes taken to complete the note-taking and concept map construction.

As can be observed in the correlation results presented above, there is a significant correlation between most of the variables and the total score. A Bonferroni correction was included to adjust for type one error given the number of correlations examined. Only the process variable of 'Note Structure' did not have a significant correlation with the total score. Not surprisingly, students who took more notes (as denoted by 'MyNotes'), regardless of the designation of the notes as claim, evidence or neither, had higher scores. Similarly, students with more notes in the concept map ('Map Notes') also got higher scores. Interestingly, the percent of notes that were categorized as evidence or claim did not have a significant relationship with total score ('Note Structure'). This suggest that students who categorized notes as evidence or claim more often ('Note Structure'), rather than just as notes, did not have higher scores than those who might have had many notes, none of which were claims or evidence. This is surprising since it was hypothesized that students who might be more purposefully thinking of the notes that they take as claims or evidence - rather than as just general information - may be exhibiting higher levels of critical thinking that those that had many unclassified notes. Though the students are prompted to classify each note as they take it, the actual process of classifying notes may be less strategic for some students.

## Analysis 2: Relationship of Process Variables to One Another

The next analysis was to look at the intercorrelations among those variables that did have a relationship to the total score. The goal of this analysis was to determine whether or not the individual variables provided unique information or whether they were just measures of the same thing. The expectation is that many of the variables would be correlated, but hopefully would not be entirely redundant to each other. The correlation matrix is provided in Table 2.

*Table 2. Correlations among process variables with relationship to total score*

|  | Claim | Evidence | Total Notes | Map Notes | Task Time |
|---|---|---|---|---|---|
| Claim | 1 | .661** | .838** | .718** | .361** |
| Evidence | .661** | 1 | .779** | .762** | .276** |
| Total Notes | .838** | .779** | 1 | .756** | .383** |
| Map Notes | .718** | .762** | .756** | 1 | .402** |
| Task Time | .361** | .276** | .383** | .402** | 1 |

**all p-vlaues were 0.000, significant at the p<.01 level

As is evident from the correlation matrix above, total number of notes taken by a student is highly correlated with the process variables of 'Claim', 'Evidence', and 'Map Notes', which is not surprising. Students with a large number of notes also had a large number of 'Claims' and a large number of notes labeled 'Evidence'. Further, students with more notes also had more notes in their maps ('Map Notes'). These high correlations are not surprising, though these results do likewise provide some insight. This suggests that students do appear to be designating notes as claims and evidence, and not merely taking more notes without rhyme or reason. Further, students who are taking more notes are using them in their maps and these students are getting higher scores. These data together indicate that students do not seem to be taking large numbers of notes that are irrelevant. Also, not too that he correlations among the other variables are not very high, indicating that there is unique information being captured in several of these variables.

Scatterplots of the data were also examined to further characterize the nature of the relationship between these process variables, and to help select variables to use in the linear regression. 'Note Structure', 'MyNotes', and 'Percent of Notes Used' in the map did not have an obvious linear relationship with the total score, so the choice was made to focus on number of claims ('Claim'), number of pieces of evidence ('Evidence'), 'Total Notes', 'Map Notes', and 'Task Time' for the following analyses.

## Analysis 3: Predictive Nature of the Variables

Once it was ascertained that there was a significant relationship between the process variables and the outcome variable of total score, and also that there was unique information captured by the process variables themselves, the investigation turned to the nature of the predictive relationship between the process variables and the outcome variable. A linear regression was performed to determine which *combinations* of process variables were most related to the total score. The individual correlations provide insight into how individual variables are related, but the linear regression can take into account intercorrelations among the individual variables, and provide evidence regarding a set of variables that can explain the variability in the scores. The regression model was constructed based on the results in the first two analyses. The variables that were correlated with the total score, but not highly correlated with each other, were chosen for inclusion in the model. Furthermore, independent variables that were correlated above 0.80 were not placed into the model together. The goal of this analysis was to identify the variables that would best predict the total score, to help understand what process factors most impact the total score. Again, by illuminating these relationships, the intent is to gain insight into the processes of the students that result in higher critical thinking scores as measured by this scenario/set of tasks.

Using information about the nature of the relationships between the variables chosen for analysis as well their statistical connection to the total score, a linear regression model was built to see if the combination of variables that was most related to the total score could be found. The individual correlations provide evidence of which individual pieces are related, but this analysis can be provide insight into which combination of variables is most important.

Despite the high intercorrelation of the variables, all of the variables were entered into the regression and found only 'Map Notes' and 'Task Time' to be significant. The interaction of these two variables was added to the model as well, and non-significant predictors were removed from the model. Table 3 provides the model summary, and Table 4 provides the estimates of the regression coefficients.

This regression model explains about 40% of the variability in total scores, which is quite high considering it contained only three variables. This result indicates that the number of notes used in the map and the time it took the students to complete the task are very strong predictors of the total score, with students who took longer scoring higher than those who took less time.

As is evident from the regression coefficients, both variables independently have a positive relationship with the total score, as was found earlier. The strange result obtained concerns the interaction effect, where the coefficient is so small that for all intents and purposes it is zero. It was hypothesized that 'Task Time' could be moderateing the relationship between predictors and the total score, and so to get deeper insight into the role of time in this analysis, task time was dummy coded into two groups. Foe each study participant, 'Task Time' was coded as *0* if the student's time was below the median task time (60 minutes) and *1* if task time was at or above the median time. Regression analyses were then performed for each time group separately, and the correlation among variables for each group was examined separately.

Table 5 presents the model summary for the two regressions carried out. It is clear that there is a difference between the two models relative to their predictive power.

*Table 3. Model summary for linear regression*

| Model[a] | R | R Square | Adjusted R Square | Std. Error of the Estimate |
|---|---|---|---|---|
| 1 | .629[a] | .396 | .381 | .391 |

a. Predictors: (Constant), Map Notes by Time, time to complete the site review and map construction in minutes, Map Notes.

*Table 4. Regression coefficients from linear regression model*

| Model[a] | Unstandardized Coefficients | | Standardized Coefficients | t | p. |
|---|---|---|---|---|---|
| | B | Std. Error | Beta | | |
| (Constant) | .439 | .152 | | 2.891 | .005 |
| Map Notes | .072 | .017 | .888 | 4.257 | .000 |
| Time | .009 | .002 | .489 | 4.048 | .000 |
| Map Notes by Time | .000 | .000 | -.580 | -2.264 | .025 |

a. Dependent variable: total score excluding the anti-organic milk task score

*Table 5. Model summary for two regression models: data split on 'task time'*

| Time_group | R | R Square | Adjusted R Square | Std. Error of the Estimate |
|---|---|---|---|---|
| Below median | .623[a] | .388 | .378 | .332 |
| At or Above median | .401[a] | .161 | .148 | .446 |

a. Predictors: (Constant), Map Notes

The model for shorter-time group (below median) explains more variability (38.8%) than that for the longer-time group (at or above median) (16.1%). It is worth noting that the two groups were approximately the same size. The below-median group consisted of 65 students, while the at or above-median group consisted of 69 students. Students below the median received lower scores (mean score was 1.17, SD = 0.42) than those above the median (mean score was 1.58, SD=0.48). Table 6 below provides the regression coefficients for the two models.

As can be seen here, the relationship between the Map Notes and the dependent variable is stronger for shorter-time group as well.

When the complete correlation matrix was recomputed for these two subgroups, there were no large differences in the correlations, although a systematic pattern did emerge. The correlations between variables and the total score are systematically smaller for the at or above-median group, as compared to the below-median group. Given

the relatively small sample sizes, it is doubtful that these differences are significant. However, due to the systematic nature of these results, it is worthy of exploration.

## Analysis 5: Note Taking Patterns

As noted above in the description of the task, students were permitted and encouraged to return to the Google search documents to take more notes when the time came to construct the concept map. Because different note taking patterns might lead to different scores, there was interest in examining note-taking patterns as an indication of the process that students were using. Upon hand-review of the raw data, six different note-taking patterns were coded as described below.

- **0:** Do not go back to the websites when constructing the map. Use only notes taken in the initial note-taking activity.
- **1:** Go back to the website and gather more notes before constructing the concept map.
- **2:** Go back to the website but do not take notes from the websites before constructing the concept map.
- **3:** Type in own notes before creating the concept map.
- **1,3:** Both go back to take notes and create own notes before creating the concept map.
- **2,3:** Go back to websites without taking notes, but create own notes before creating the construct map.

*Table 6. Regression coefficient for two linear regression models: Data split on time on task*

| Time_group | Model[a] | Unstandardized Coefficients | | Standardized Coefficients | t | Sig. |
|---|---|---|---|---|---|---|
| | | B | Std. Error | Beta | | |
| Below median | (Constant) | .779 | .075 | | 10.349 | .000 |
| | MapNotes | .054 | .009 | .623 | 6.222 | .000 |
| At or Above median | (Constant) | 1.246 | .111 | | 11.225 | .000 |
| | MapNotes | .030 | .009 | .401 | 3.501 | .001 |

a. Dependent Variable: total score

For each note-taking pattern, the number of students engaging in that pattern was counted. Further, descriptive statistics on students' scores for each note-taking strategy were computed.

The summaries of the number of students engaging in each strategy as well as their scores on the various tasks are provided below. Also given is the mean and standard deviation for the full group of participants.

From the descriptive statistics for students with different notes-taking patterns, it is clear that students who went back to the websites and created some notes by themselves before creating the concept map (students using strategy 1,3) received this highest score overall, and this was also the most common strategy (though not by a large margin). Students who constructed the concept map directly after the site view (strategy 0) received the lowest overall scores on average. In reflecting on students who went back to the website - which is those students using strategy 1, 2, (1,3), or (2,3) – it appears that students who gathered some notes from the website tend to have better performance. It is important to note here that the goal is not to try to dictate an optimal strategy, but for educators to try to understand that first, these different note-taking strategies did seem to yield different scores, and then, naturally, *why* this

was the case. It could be useful, for example, to identify students using less optimal strategies and help them to refine their strategies.

## Analysis 6: Qualitative Analysis of Note Taking Strategies

In addition to looking quantitatively at the note-taking strategies, a qualitative analysis of the notes was also undertaken. The thought was that students who go back into the websites to gather more notes might do so for various reasons. Two potential reasons are (1) to gather additional evidence for the claims that they are making and (2) to gather new claims and evidence for the concept map, but of course there may be additional reasons. However, in terms of measurement, going back to the websites for additional information is only valuable if new information is gathered. Therefore, for the students who engaged in strategy 1 ($n=30$), both the initial and subsequent notes were examined qualitatively. Themes were obtained by examining the notes for content. Once the themes were identified, the notes from both note-taking sessions were coded, and the number of themes, and number of notes related to the themes were tabulated. These variables were then examined relative to student scores to determine if higher scoring students used any specific note-taking strategies.

The content analysis of the notes collected at both time points (initially and then returning to web sites) revealed 14 themes in the notes that they took. These 14 themes were identified as having the following components, in order of most to least frequent:

*Table 7. Descriptive statistics of task scores for different note-taking patterns*

| Notes Taking Pattern | N | Mean | Standard Deviation |
|---|---|---|---|
| Overall | 129 | 1.38 | 0.48 |
| 0 | 30 | 1.17 | 0.52 |
| 1 | 31 | 1.38 | 0.43 |
| 2 | 8 | 1.29 | 0.49 |
| 3 | 21 | 1.47 | 0.57 |
| 1,3 | 32 | 1.54 | 0.46 |
| 2,3 | 7 | 1.37 | 0.45 |

1. Hormones/antibiotics
2. Pesticides
3. Health fats
4. Shelf life
5. Cost

6.  Animal care
7.  Farm practices
8.  Nutrition/nutrients
9.  Trustworthiness
10. Bacteria
11. Regulations
12. Environment
13. Genetically modified ingredients
14. Marketing

The notes were coded relative to the count how often each theme was present in the notes. Scores for students were compared relative to the number of themes present in their notes. The number of themes that were included in the notes taken by the students initially was counted. The number of themes ranged from 2 to 12, with an average of 5.2 themes per student.

When compared with the total score of the student, there was a significant correlation between the number of themes in the initial note-taking and the total score of the student. The correlation between these was 0.53 and this was significant at the $p<.05$ level. When the group was split on the number of themes, the two groups were characterized as "many themes" (greater than 3) and "few themes" (less than 3). THe results indicated that when the scores for these two groups were compared, there were significant differences in their test scores. These results are summarized in Table 8. It is clear that the students had more themes present in their notes had higher total scores than the students whose notes reflected a smaller

*Table 8. Descriptive statistics of total test score by number of themes in notes*

| Group | N* | Mean | SD |
|---|---|---|---|
| Few Themes | 15 | 1.17 | 0.31 |
| Many Themes | 15 | 1.58 | 0.47 |
| | p-value: .009 | | |

\* The group was not intentionally split to lead to groups of equal size. This is just a coincidence.

number of themes. This is not surprising, since the more themes that were present, the richer the recommendation was likely to be.

## Summary of Findings

The findings presented here indicate that it was possible to identify process variables that both related to the total scores of the students *and* also differentiated amongst the students. This process information could potentially have instructional value for providing feedback and diagnostic information to teachers, and other stakeholders. The process variables chosen in this example were shown to have a relationship with the total score obtained by the student. When conceptualized as outlined here, the evidence presented suggests that these variables may well have meaning from a measurement perspective. The variables themselves did show some differentiation, in that they were not totally redundant when considered relative to each other, and showed very good predictive power in predicting the total score. Further, it was observed that the note-taking patterns of students did have a relationship with the total outcome score. This indicates that students of higher critical thinking ability seem to have used different strategies than those with lower abilities. And lastly, students that had more themes present in their note taking had higher scores as well.

## Generalizability of Results

The broader value of these findings of course depends on the extent that they are generalizable to other tasks. This has been and remains a challenge for data mining innovative task types, to identify methods and results that are informative widely. In the context of the present study, it should be noted that a parallel task to the Organic Milk scenario, called the Dolphin Dilemma task, was developed as another measure of critical thinking. There were some data limitations that prevented the extent to which the full set of analyses carried out on Organic Milk could be replicated on Dolphin Dilemma, most notably the lack of scores for the completed student work. However, it was possible to look at two areas of comparability: first, the intercorrelations of the process data, and second, the note-taking strategies employed.

The intercorrelations of the process variables for both tasks are presented in Table 9.

The patterns of correlations observed were fairly similar across the two tasks, with some notable exceptions. Most interesting in this respecet were the correlations of task time with (1) the percent of notes labeled as evidence (2) notes labeled as my notes, and (3) the total number of notes. These three correlations were significant for the Organic Milk task, but not for the Dolphin Dilemma task, although this could be due in part to the differences in sample size. Additionally, the correlation between the percent of notes labeled as evidence and percent of notes labeled as claims was noticeably smaller in the Dolphin Dilemma task as compared to the Organic Milk task, but again this could be attributable to the difference in sample sizes. However, the overall pattern of the relationships was fairly similar, indicating similar relationships across tasks.

When examining the note-taking strategies of the students, different patterns of behavior were noted across the two tasks. Recall that the strategies were labeled as:

- **0:** Do not go back to the websites when constructing the map. Use only notes taken in the initial note-taking activity.
- **1:** Go back to the website and gather more notes before constructing the concept map.
- **2:** Go back to the website but do not take notes from the websites before constructing the concept map.
- **3:** Type in own notes before creating the concept map.
- **1,3:** Both go back to take notes and create own notes before creating the concept map.
- **2,3:** Go back to websites without taking notes, but create own notes before creating the construct map.

Table 10, and Figure 2 provide the distribution of students across these strategies for each task.

The table and the figure clearly indicate that the strategy most preferred for students doing the Dolphin Dilemma task included strategy 1, which involved going back into the websites before

*Table 9. Correlation among variables: Both tasks*

|  |  | Claim | Evidence | Total Notes | My Notes | Task Time |
|---|---|---|---|---|---|---|
| Claim | Organic | 1 | .66** | .84** | .33** | .36** |
|  | Dolphin | 1 | .40** | .71** | .38** | .41** |
| Evidence | Organic | .66** | 1 | .78** | .33** | .28** |
|  | Dolphin | .40** | 1 | .71** | .31** | .13 |
| Total Notes | Organic | .84** | .78** | 1 | .70** | .38** |
|  | Dolphin | .71** | .71** | 1 | .83** | .17 |
| My Notes | Organic | .33** | .33** | .70** | 1 | .27** |
|  | Dolphin | .38** | .31** | .83** | 1 | -.022 |
| Task Time | Organic | .36** | .28** | .38** | .27** | 1 |
|  | Dolphin | .41** | .13 | .17 | -.02 | 1 |

Note: the N for the Organic Milk Sample was approximately 180 across the analyses, and for the Dolphin Dilemma was approximately 90.

** Correlation is significant at the 0.05 level (2-tailed).

*Table 10. The proportion of students using each strategy for both tasks*

| | 0 | 1 | 2 | 3 | 1,3 | 2,3 |
|---|---|---|---|---|---|---|
| Organic Milk | 0.254 | 0.231 | 0.060 | 0.164 | 0.239 | 0.052 |
| Dolphin Dilemma | 0.156 | 0.389 | 0.044 | 0.078 | 0.311 | 0.022 |

*Figure 2. Comparison of note-taking strategy in two tasks*

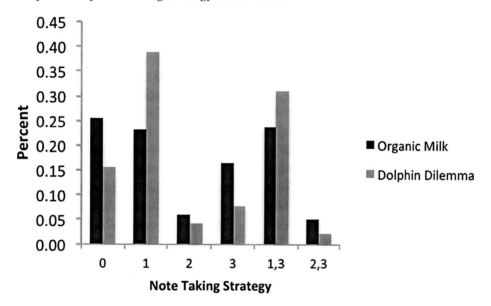

constructing the map, while very few employed strategy 0, where they did not go back into the website. This pattern is in contrast to those in the Organic Milk task, where over a quarter of the students employed strategy 0, and fewer employed strategy 1 than strategy 0. It should also be noted that strategy 3, which included typing in self-generated notes before completing the map, was used with much greater frequency in the Organic Milk task than the Dolphin Dilemma task.

Given the fairly sizable differences in these patterns, a deeper investigation revealed that the directions given to the students were different across the two tasks. For Organic Milk, students were *required* to make notes before clicking through to the Concept Map creation task. In contrast, for Dolphin Dilemma, students could click through to the Concept Map task without making any notes, then click back to make notes once they had seen the task. These differences in implementation may well have resulted in different strategies used by the students under the two different scenarios. Given the differences observed in the note taking strategies, it is thus critically important to understand that the instructions students are given directly impact the strategies employed by students. Without the outcome data, it is difficult to ascertain how the different strategies were ultimately related to the final scores, yet the presence of differences as observed are interesting, and with further study could provide useful insight into the role of note taking strategies on the ultimate performance.

While no strong conclusions can be made about the generalizability of the findings presented to this point from the Organic Milk scenario, there is some evidence that the relationships among the process data are stable across scenarios, making them potentially important process indicators. Although the administration protocols varied by scenario, there were large differences observed in note taking strategies among the students in both Organic Milk and Dolphin Dilemma, indicating that this process element might be particularly useful in identifying the strategies that students of various ability levels are using.

## How to Use Process Data

The analyses above provided evidence that the variables that were selected and coded provide useful evidence regarding the processes that were used by students. There was also considerable variability in the response processes used by different students, and some evidence was found that some strategies, or processes, resulted in higher scores on the task than other strategies. But, what has not yet been discussed is what information these variables have provided about what students know and can do, or whether these data could be used to help inform instruction, or the extent to which they offer any useful diagnostic feedback. Statistical analysis alone does not provide substantive meaning or guidance on the appropriate use of data. So how can these data be used, and used wisely? The ideas presented here are not specific to the particular variables selected in the illustrative example presented earlier, and hopefully can be generalized to process data and its analysis more broadly.

First, it is necessary to determine goals for analyzing process data. New item types, such as those presented here, along with computerized delivery allows agencies to collect so much *more* data, as well as so much more varied data. Of course it is hoped that that data could be used to provide more meaningful information, especially when the tasks take a long time to complete. What type of information is sought, and how can it actually be put to use? Process data can be used to help understand how different students approach the task, and certainly, some strategies may be more beneficial than others. Suppose it were possible to identify different strategies that produced different outcomes, what benefit would that serve? It depends on whether or not the strategies can be linked to actionable information. For example, in the Organic Milk scenario, the number of notes used was related to the total score: the more notes taken led to higher scores. Clearly, that relationship does not mean that students should be instructed to simply take more notes for the sole purpose of having more notes in the scenario's electronic "journal". The mere existence of more notes would not likely lead to higher scores. What is important, is that students who scored higher also took more notes, but the imperative question to ask is why this is. It could be related to the fact that these students with high numbers of notes had more themes present in their notes. Students that had more themes in their notes, also had more notes. This information could be actionable. Also, lower-scoring students may have focused on only one aspect of why organic milk was better than conventional milk, while higher scoring students focused on multiple aspects. By identifying this type of information, students could be encouraged and instructed in looking at multiple reasons for a recommendation rather than a single reason. Critical thinking skills require looking at an issue from multiple viewpoints, and these data might be indicators of the ability to do so.

Another example of actionable evidence from our illustrative example is the note-taking strategies. In the Organic Milk task higher performing students utilized different note-taking strategies than the strategies used by lower performing students. In particular, students that went back into the website to gather additional information when constructing their concept maps scored higher than those that did not do so. Again, students should not just be instructed to go back into the site to get more notes without purpose, since that would not likely lead to higher scores. However, it is possible that those that scored higher on the task (and hence higher in critical thinking) may have had the skills to self-identify gaps in their concept maps, which they then remedied by going back into the search results to find additional, relevant information with which to fill those gaps. While not all students can do that at the same level of proficiency, all students can be taught the fundamental basic strategy of going back and looking for different information that supports their position or argument, especially in terms of referencing multiple points of evidence.

Other goals for identifying process information might also exist, apart from diagnostic information. For example, specific strategies may have been part of the instructions provided on how to create a concept map. Students may have been instructed to go back into the website once the map was constructed to gather new evidence. In this case, the process evidence could serve also as outcome evidence: which students are utilizing the strategies taught in class, and which are not? Also, it is likewise evident that the differences between the strategies can be evaluated. Suppose a teacher instructed students to go back into the website, but no relationship between that process and the outcome was detected in analysis: this provides important instructional information for the teacher.

In a similar example, classifying notes as claims or evidence might have been a focus of instruction. In the example of Organic Milk explained earlier, the results indicated that there was no different in results concerning whether students classified more notes as claims and/or evidence. The implication of this finding is that either the measurement of this classification was not very good, that it was not a meaningful designation to the students, or the instruction was not very successful. Either way, information is provided back to the teacher regarding the efficacy of this strategy, and changes can be made to either the strategy, or the measurement of the strategy.

The full, detailed analysis of the process data described in our illustrative example is provided here as a way to use these data. In the next section, some recommendations for Teaching and Pedagogy and for Data Analysis based on the analysis of Organic Milk Task are provided.

## RECOMMENDATIONS

The findings of this study suggest that there are indeed some strategies that students use in the area of critical thinking assessment that might lead to higher scores (and thus be indicative of higher levels of critical thinking skills). By understanding the elements of a good solution, teachers can help students gain the skills that they need to become more proficient at this type of critical thinking task. First, students need to have enough content accessible (for example, as notes in an online "journal") to be able to construct a good concept map and ultimately make a good argument. This idea was recurring through several types of variables and analyses: the number of notes a student collected, the number of themes present in the students' notes, and going back to do additional note-taking all were related to higher final scores. It is unlikely that taking more notes in and of itself is a good strategy, because the skill of being able to focus on a more complex web of ideas, rather than a few simplistic thoughts, takes on greater importance. Also, having enough evidence to support those claims is necessary. Not surprisingly then, students need to have the skills to obtain quality content. This starts with the more basic skills of how to actually carry out a web search and evaluate the results for reliability, then how to read the content for important ideas, and lastly to select those ideas. Being able to classify the ideas as claims/evidence are critically important skills as well.

Similarly, understanding that going back into the notes and obtaining additional information (if necessary) is an important step is essential. Not all students did this, even though the directions prompted them to. Teachers can use this opportunity to teach students how to evaluate what they have, and decide if they need more: more claims, more evidence or both. These skills would be essential to all students, since even though some students did go back into the data to gather more notes, they did not necessarily use that opportunity to fill gaps into their concept maps. Oftentimes, redundant information was gathered.

One factor to consider in examining the results is that some skills depend on other skills. In this sense, some skills might be thought of as lower-order (e.g. Google search and anti-organic milk) and some might be higher-order (concept map, concept map link, recommendation), in that they require the successful completion of the lower-order tasks. Teachers should evaluate which of these skills their students are most deficient in independently of the measurement task, since there is a dependence among the tasks as presented here. If a student cannot do the lower order tasks, they do not have the data to do the higher order tasks well. As an example, suppose a student cannot take good notes. It follows that it would be impossible for that student to get a good score on the concept map since he/she would not have the raw data to do so. An alternative, and one that is perhaps differently informative, involves presenting all students with standardized, high-quality notes to make a map, after completing the note-gathering task on their own. In this way, they are graded on their note-taking proficiency, and then, also be graded on the extent to which they can build a quality concept map (in, other words, can a student make the map and see the connections if they have good notes at the outset?).

The final recommendation to come from this analysis regards the classification of notes as either (1) note (2) claim or (3) evidence. Each time the student takes a note, he/she is prompted to classify it. It is not understood from this study how accurate the students' classifications of those notes are, but because it is a fundamental aspect of the task, more analysis is needed. In terms of instruction, helping students to understand the

difference between these categories and to help them appropriately classify the notes would be a valuable skill that may lead to better scores, or at the minimum help them produce - potentially - more efficient work.

## Recommendations for Data Analysis

While this study investigated some of the possible ways to analyze the data for process information, it is of course quite limited in some significant ways. First, the analyses presented here are entirely and purposefully largely descriptive in nature, and the number of additional analyses that could be conducted is large. This section does not attempt to look at the potential other analyses that could be done, but rather what analyses are immediately suggested by the findings here.

First, the idea of the labeling of notes as claims/ evidence/note may well be a future direction of interest. In this study the students' designation of the notes that they took was taken at face value, and there was no way of knowing if students were good at classifying the notes appropriately or not. Given that the task is designed to measure critical thinking, this might be an avenue worthy of further exploration, as it is likely that some students were more proficient at this than others. Methodologically speaking, exploring ways of quantifying the successful labeling of notes would be important. While having experts rate the quality of the labeling for each individual student record would be one approach, it is likely too time consuming for this to be done in operational practice at the large-scale level. Because the web search is artificial, and standardized for all students, the information returned to all students is the same regardless of search terms entered. It could be possible to *a priori* identify key claims and evidence that could be used to evaluate the student's ability to classify notes as claims and evidence. However, it may not be possible to classify all possible pieces of information, and so it may be necessary to identify be key pieces of information that could be denoted as such. The percent of these pieces evident in the students' notes and their proper labeling could be measured.

The second recommendation concerns the idea that there might be higher/lower order skills measured by the different tasks. If this is a correct interpretation, then a deeper look into the pattern of performance of students might be fruitful. For example, if a student gets low score on the lower order tasks, does that mean he/she gets a low final score? Or a low score on the higher order tasks? What are the relationships between the scores on these tasks? The sores are correlated, so there is a relationship, but the pattern of scores for these different types of students is not yet known. Similarly, for students obtaining high scores on the higher order tasks, did they necessarily get high scores on the lower order tasks or higher score overall? The correlations suggest yes, but a deeper dive into the data might illuminate some these issues.

Lastly, one of the primary issues with any performance task is the problem of task specificity. Will the patterns of performance on this task on organic milk translate to the same type of task that uses a different context? While there was some limited data to investigate the generalizability of these results, the findings were mixed and incomplete due to issues with the data, but this is a condition that is easily enough fixed for other studied with other datasets. Validating these analyses using a different context will provide valuable evidence regarding the utility of the findings observed here.

## CONCLUSION

Scenarios like Organic Milk and Dolphin Dilemma are examples of an exciting new task type that is being used in standardized testing. The promise of such task families is great. The experiences are more authentic and engaging, and hopefully measure skills that were not easily measured with more traditional item types like multiple choice items, or even essay questions. Since they take longer than traditional items, from a measurement perspective it is necessary to get more data about student performance out of these task families beyond traditional outcome scores. Through computer-based delivery of such tasks, the potential is high to capture a wide range of information for analysis, and such data may yet yield insight into process information. With traditional items and test administration conditions, the only information that was typically garnered was outcomes in the form of scores.

However, regardless of the type of information, information for information's sake is not useful. In fact, teachers, schools, parents, and educators at all levels are inundated with information. It is critically necessary for the purpose of *use* that this information be distilled into actionable information. To be actionable, the purpose of collecting the information must be determined beforehand, so that when the data arrive, their format is understood and can be translated into something accessible. This chapter has provided but one example rooted in the emerging area of understanding process data from large-scale assessments, as well as some thoughts about how that process data might be used. The implications and recommendations that can be made on the basis of that process data are numerous. As these types of tasks become more common, new methodologies to analyze and extract data will become more available, and it is hoped that the full promise of these items can be realized.

## REFERENCES

Almond, R., Deane, P., Quinlan, T., Wagner, M., & Sydorenko, T. (2012). *A preliminary analysis of keystroke log data from a timed writing task (Research Report, ETS RR-12-23)*. Princeton, NJ: Educational Testing Service.

Bouchet, F., Harley, J. M., Trevors, G. J., & Azevedo, R. (2013). Clustering and profiling students according to their interactions with an intelligent tutoring system fostering self-regulated learning. *Journal of Educational Data Mining*, *5*(1), 104–145.

Carr, P. (2013, September). *NAEP innovations in action: Implications for the next generation science standards.* Presentation at the Invitational Research Symposium on Science Assessment, Washington, DC.

de la Torre, J. (2011). The generalized DINA model framework. *Psychometrika*, *76*(2), 179–199. doi:10.1007/s11336-011-9207-7

Gierl, M. J., & Haladyna, T. M. (2012). *Automatic item generation: Theory and practice.* New York, NY: Routledge.

Kerr, D., & Chung, G. K. W. K. (2012). Identifying key features of student performance in educational video games and simulations through cluster analysis. *Journal of Educational Data Mining*, *4*(1), 144–182.

Kinnebrew, J. S., Loretz, K. M., & Biswas, G. (2013). A contextualized differential sequence mining method to derive students' learning behavior patterns. *Journal of Educational Data Mining*, *5*(1), 190–220.

Rosen, Y., & Tager, M. (2014). Making student thinking visible through a concept map in computer-based assessment of critical thinking. *Journal of Educational Computing Research*, *50*(2), 249–270. doi:10.2190/EC.50.2.f

Rupp, A., Templin, J., & Henson, R. (2010). *Diagnostic measurement: Theory, methods, and applications.* New York: Guilford.

## KEY TERMS AND DEFINITIONS

**Computer-Based Test:** Any test that is delivered on a computer, as opposed to a paper and pencil test.

**Concept Map:** A diagram that relates concepts to one another by connecting related ideas with lines.

**Data Mining:** The process of searching for patterns in data without a theoretical framework.

**Higher Order Skills:** Skills that are beyond recall of facts or definitions, such as analyzing data.

**Outcome:** The result of taking a test, or an assessment.

**Performance Task:** A task that requires students to complete an activity that is open-ended, and without a prescribed correct answer.

**Process Data:** The steps students takes to solve a problem.

# Chapter 29

# Analyzing Process Data from Problem-Solving Items with N-Grams:
## Insights from a Computer-Based Large-Scale Assessment

**Qiwei He**
*Educational Testing Service, USA*

**Matthias von Davier**
*Educational Testing Service, USA*

## ABSTRACT

*This chapter draws on process data recorded in a computer-based large-scale program, the Programme for International Assessment of Adult Competencies (PIAAC), to address how sequences of actions recorded in problem-solving tasks are related to task performance. The purpose of this study is twofold: first, to extract and detect robust sequential action patterns that are associated with success or failure on a problem-solving item, and second, to compare the extracted sequence patterns among selected countries. Motivated by the methodologies of natural language processing and text mining, we utilized feature selection models in analyzing the process data at a variety of aggregate levels and evaluated the different methodologies in terms of predictive power of the evidence extracted from process data. It was found that action sequence patterns significantly differed by performance groups and were consistent across countries. This study also demonstrated that the process data were useful in detecting missing data and potential mistakes in item development.*

## INTRODUCTION

Computer-based assessments (CBAs) are used for more than increasing construct validity (e.g., Sireci & Zenisky, 2006) and improving test design (e.g., van der Linden, 2005). They also provide new insights into behavioral processes related to task completion that cannot be easily observed using paper-based instruments (Goldhammer, Naumann, & Keßel, 2013). In CBAs, a variety of timing and process data accompanies test performance data. This means that much more than data is available

DOI: 10.4018/978-1-4666-9441-5.ch029

besides correctness or incorrectness. The analyses of these types of data are necessarily much more involved than those typically performed on traditional tests.

This study draws on process data from log files recorded in a computer-based large-scale program, the Programme for International Assessment of Adult Competencies (PIAAC; cf. Schleicher, 2008), to address the question of how sequences of actions recorded in problem-solving tasks are related to task performance. As shown in the following, by analyzing the process data produced by test takers in different performance groups, we were able to obtain insights into how these action sequences are associated with different ways of cognitive processing and to identify key actions that lead to success or failure. These results can be useful for test developers, psychometricians, and instructors to help them better understand what distinguishes successful from unsuccessful test takers and may eventually contribute to improved task and assessment design.

## Problem-Solving Items in PIAAC

Large-scale survey assessments of skills and knowledge targeting student and adult populations have often been at the forefront of innovations in test design and the use of analytic methodologies (Rutkowski, Gonzalez, von Davier, & Zhou, 2014; von Davier, Sinharay, Oranje, & Beaton, 2006; von Davier & Sinharay, 2014). PIAAC is no exception. PIAAC, whose first results were released by the Organisation for Economic Co-operation and Development (OECD) in October 2013, is an assessment of literacy skills among adult populations that provides important comparative information to government leaders and policy makers worldwide.

Of significance here, it is the first international household survey of skills predominantly collected using information and communications technology (ICT). The use of computers as the delivery platform enables data collection not just on whether respondents are able to solve the tasks but how they approach the solution and time their efforts.

Three constructs are measured in PIAAC—literacy and numeracy, which are both available in both computer-based and paper-based modes—and problem solving in technology-rich environments (PSTRE), which involves more interactive item types and is available only on computer. The PSTRE items that we focus on in this study are used to assess the skills required to solve problems for personal, work, and civic purposes by setting up appropriate goals and plans, and accessing and making use of information through computers and networks (OECD, 2009).

The construct behind the PSTRE items describes skillful use of ICT as collecting and evaluating information for communicating and performing practical tasks such as organizing a social activity, deciding between alternative offers, or judging the risks of medical treatments (OECD, 2009). To give a response in the simulated computer environments that form the PSTRE tasks, participants are required to click buttons or links, select from dropdown menus, drag and drop, copy and paste, and so on. Two example items are shown in Figure 1 and in Figures 2-4. The layout of the first item (Figure 1) is rather simple. To solve this problem, test takers are required to fill in the box by performing calculations based on the table provided. The second item (Figures 2-4) is more complex as three environments are involved in a Web searching task. In this item, test takers are required to access and evaluate information in the context of a simulated job search. As shown in the item directions, located on the left side of the screen, test takers must find and bookmark one or more sites that do not require users to register or pay a fee.

## Action Sequences as Process Data

In CBAs, the processing power of modern-day information technology by far surpasses the data

*Figure 1. An example item with a single environment used in the PIAAC PSTRE test (OECD, 2012)*

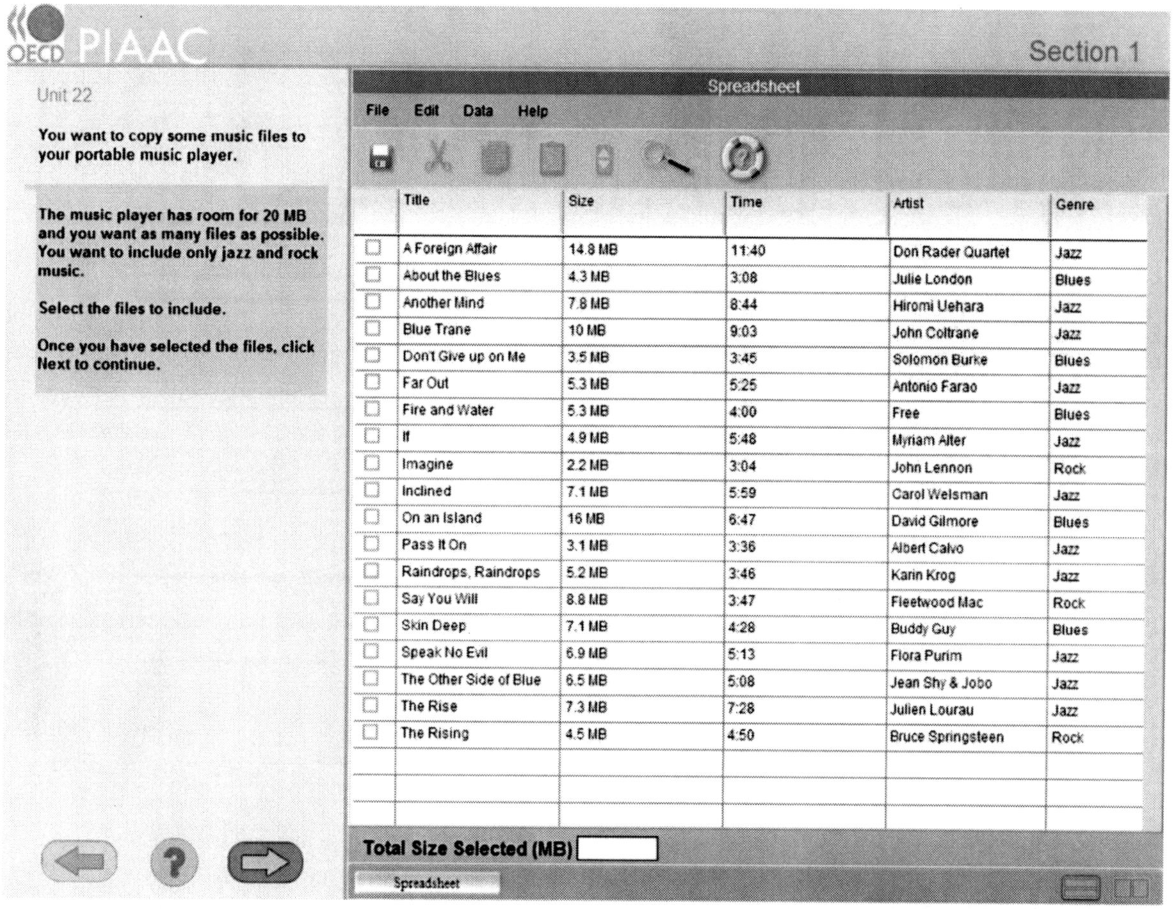

stream coming in from keystrokes and mouse clicks produced by the test taker. The dynamic records of actions generated during the item-response process form a distinct sequence that is derived from test taker input. Following and analyzing these sequences can facilitate the understanding of how individual's plan, evaluate, and select operations to achieve the problem-solving goal.

Sequences are an important type of data that occur frequently in many scientific, medical, security, business, and other applications. For example, sequences can be used to capture how individuals behave in various activities, such as by producing blogs and customer purchase histories. They are also often used in natural language processing (NLP) techniques as a proxy for capturing linguistic information. Typical applications are in the field of information retrieval (e.g. Su, Yang, Lu, & Zhang, 2000; Lin & Wilbur, 2009) as well as speech recognition and dialog system (e.g., Schatztnann, Stuttle, Weilhammer, & Young, 2005; Hara, Kitaoka, & Takeda, 2010). Furthermore, DNA or RNA sequences encode the genetic makeup of all species, and protein sequences describe the amino acid composition of proteins and encode the structure and function of proteins (Dong & Pei, 2007); sequences of actions can be analyzed with techniques borrowed from bioinformatics used on DNA and RNA sequences (Sukkarieh, von Davier & Yamamoto, 2012). The availability of process log data sequences from educational learning systems such as intelligent

*Figure 2. An example item with multiple environments used in the PIAAC PSTRE test (OECD, 2012). This is the opening screen of a job search task (see other screens in Figures 3 and 4).*

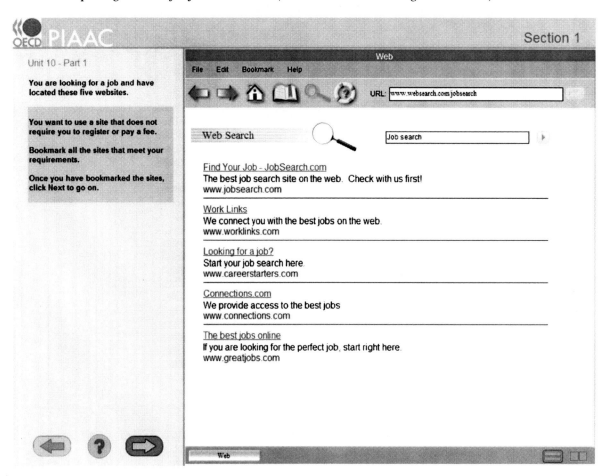

tutors and computer-based assessments stimulated interest in education research (e.g., Graesser et al., 2004; Sonamthiang, Cercone, & Naruedomkul, 2007; Goldhammer et al., 2014) and appears promising. However, research that uses analytic methodologies to explore sequence patterns in the field of educational assessment, with the goal of evaluating the utility of action sequences for explaining test takers' cognitive task performance, is only at a preliminary stage.

## Sequential Mining in Process Data

Identifying sequential patterns in process data can be useful for discovering, understanding, and ultimately scaffolding student learning and problem-solving behaviors. Some researchers have employed sequential pattern mining to inform student models for customizing learning to individual students (e.g., Corbett & Anderson, 1995; Amershi & Conati, 2009). Other researchers have employed sequential pattern mining to better understand learning behavior in particular conditions of groups (e.g., Martinez, Yacef, Kay, Al-Qaraghuli, & Kharrufa, 2011; Zhou, Xu, Nesbit, & Winne, 2010; Anderson, Gulwani, & Popovic, 2013). Ideally, these patterns provide a basis for generating models and explaining how students learn, solve problems, and interact with the environment. Algorithms for mining sequen-

*Figure 3. A website where relevant information regarding fees and registration can be found but is not shown (secondary screen for item shown in Figure 2).*

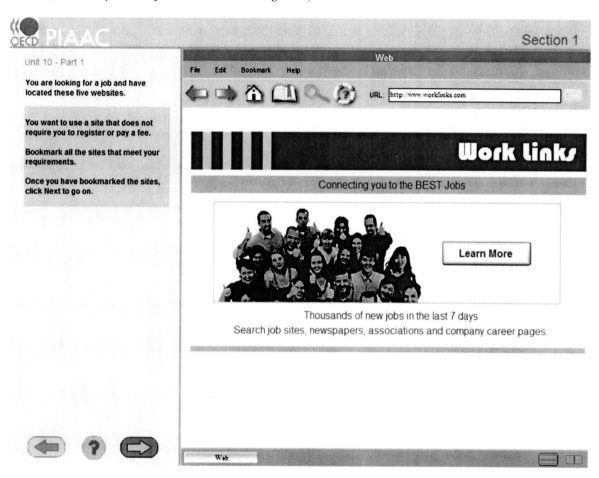

tial patterns generally associate some measure of pattern frequency to rank identified patterns. Investigation of the frequency with which a pattern occurs over time can reveal additional information for interpretation. Further, these changes in pattern occurrence may help identify more important patterns, which occur only at certain times or become more or less frequent, rather than patterns that occur frequently but uniformly over time (Kinnebrew, Mack, & Biswas, 2013).

Sequential pattern mining in process data can be conducted via a variety of approaches. For instance, Biswas, Jeong, Kinnebrew, Sulcer, & Roscoe (2010) used hidden Markov models (HMMs; Rabiner, 1989; Fink, 2008) as a direct probabilistic representation of the internal states and strategies. This methodology facilitated identification, interpretation, and comparison of student learning behaviors at an aggregate level. Like students' mental processes, the states of an HMM are hidden, meaning they cannot be directly observed but produce observable output (e.g., actions in a learning environment).

Kinnebrew, Loretz et al. (2013) employed a piecewise linear segmentation algorithm in concert with the differential sequence mining algorithm to identify and compare learning behaviors during productive and nonproductive periods (where productive periods are characterized by increasing performance in constructing the correct map).

*Figure 4. Second page of the website shown in Figure 3. Details on fees and registration are located in the directions for the form.*

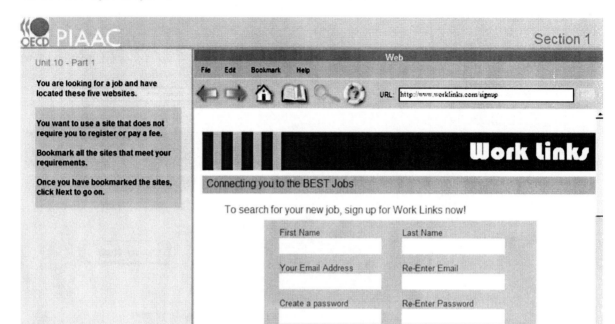

They applied exploratory data mining methodologies to learning interaction trace data gathered during a Betty's Brain study in a middle school classroom. (Betty's Brain is a software environment used to promote student understanding.) The results illustrated their methodology's potential for identifying learning activity patterns relevant to the investigation of cognitive and metacognitive learning behaviors and strategies. One of the weak points of this approach might exist in a strict linear regression model with parameter settings.

Perera et al. (2009) performed mining of data collected from students who were working in teams and using an online collaboration tool in a software development project, supporting learning group skills in the context of a standard state-of-the-art tool. They applied clustering to find groups of both similar teams and individual members. Sequential pattern mining was used to extract sequences of frequent events. The clustering patterns can be easily visualized through this approach. However, a further validation of the clustering model is recommended to ensure the generalizability of the model to different subpopulations.

Gobert Sao Pedro, Raziuddin, and Baker (2013) measured students' science inquiry performance by using log data from an online inquiry intelligent tutoring system. The transformation from log files to assessment metrics was conducted in a two-step process. In the first phase, the text replay tagging was allocated to the students' log data; an educational data mining model was subsequently deployed in the second phase, which combined the text replay data and machine-distilled features of student interactions in order to produce an automated means of assessing the inquiry skill in question. This approach featured integrating various information in process data as well as text data, though it is a bit complex for general application in large-scale assessments. For a review of data mining in educational application and methods in sequential pattern mining, refer to Romero & Ventura (2010) and Dong & Pei (2007).

## Goals of the Present Study

The purpose of this study is twofold: first, to extract and detect robust sequential action patterns that are associated with success or failure on a PSTRE item, and second, to compare the extracted sequence patterns among selected countries.

We investigated the utility of behavioral process data for predicting differences in task performance in the PIAAC PSTRE domain. More specifically, we separated the database into two performance groups (correct and incorrect) in a sample item, extracted action sequences, and identified the key action sequences that were significantly associated with task completion. For our comparative study, we chose the United States, the Netherlands, and Japan as exemplary countries from three continents (North America, Europe, and Asia) among the group of participating countries. This selection allowed for a broad range of country performances, as Japan and the Netherlands performed at a high level in all three domains in PIAAC, while the US was a relatively low-performing country (OECD, 2013). This selection also provided us countries with high percentages of individuals using computers among their subpopulations, a necessary element to get relatively valid results for the PSTRE domain, which required test takers to be familiar with computers and have prior experience with them either in work or daily life.

## METHOD

## Sample

For this study, data from the PSTRE domain collected during the 2012 PIAAC main study were used. The PIAAC sample was representative of the population of adults with the age range of 16 to 65 years old who had prior experience with computers. People who never used computers before were excluded from the problem-solving section; the task for this scale was by default (and by definition of the construct) assessed only on a computer-based testing platform.

A total of 3,926 test takers who completed the PSTRE items in the PIAAC assessment were included in the present study. Of these, 1,340 test takers were from the US, 1,508 from the Netherlands, and 1,078 from Japan. There were 2,025 female test takers (51.6%) and 1,901 male test takers (48.4%). The average age was 39.6 years (SD=14.0). A plurality (1,812) of this sample had an educational level above high school (46.2%), with 1,493 reporting a high school degree (38.0%), 615 reporting less than high school (15.7%) and four cases recorded as missing (0.1%). Detailed demographic information of this sample is listed in Table 1.

To get more accurate population estimates, we took sampling weights into account in the calculations. We standardized the weights to a sum of 5,000 in each country[1] to ensure that each country contributed equally (for details in PIAAC sample design and weighting standards, refer to OECD, 2010). With this sum normalization, the range of sampling weight is within [0.15, 3.69], [0.39, 2.54] and [0.30, 2.53] for the samples from the US, the Netherlands and Japan, respectively. In addition, we conducted the same analyses without using sampling weights as well. Only marginal differences were found between the two conditions with and without sampling weights.

*Table 1. Sample characteristics*

| Characteristics | Total | US | Netherlands | Japan |
|---|---|---|---|---|
| N | 3,926 | 1,340 | 1,508 | 1,078 |
| Gender | | | | |
|   Female | 2,025 | 629 | 711 | 526 |
|   Male | 1,901 | 711 | 629 | 552 |
| Age (years) | | | | |
| Mean (S.D.) | 39.6 (14.0) | 39.2 (14.0) | 40.9 (14.3) | 38.4 (13.5) |
| Educational level | | | | |
|   Less than high school | 615 | 124 | 401 | 90 |
|   High school | 1,493 | 534 | 590 | 369 |
|   Above high school | 1,812 | 680 | 513 | 619 |
|   Missing | 6 | 2 | 4 | 0 |

## Instrumentation

A total of 14 PSTRE items were administered in the PIAAC main study. We focused on the sequence data resulting from the task requirements of one item. This item consists of two environments: a spreadsheet environment (that serves as the stimulus) that contains a database with the information required to solve the task, and an email environment to provide the response. The task is to identify the ID number of a specified club member (e.g., "David Smith")[2] and email it to a correspondent. On the spreadsheet (SS) page, four pieces of information for each club member are provided by columns: ID number, name, number of activities this year, and years as a member. There is a checkbox on each line to facilitate flagging the potential correct answer. On the email (E) page, test takers are required to enter the ID number into an email to a correspondent.

An interim score was evaluated based on the email responses only. It meant that an empty or a wrong answer on the email page led to an incorrect result even though the participant might have correctly identified the specified person on the SS page.

The task for this item is situated in a simulated office environment that included tools and functionality similar to those found in Microsoft Excel and email applications, that is, clickable buttons for saving, searching, sorting, sending email and help; clickable dropdown menus; clickable buttons for switching between the SS and E environments; and so on. The opening page presents the task description on the left side and is always displayed. The working part is on the right side of the screen, which switches upon change in task environment.

## Analytic Strategy

To explore the relationship between action sequences and task completion, we divided the sample into two groups: correct and incorrect. It resulted in 2,754 individuals (70.1%) in the correct group, including 882 from the US, 1,104 from the Netherlands and 768 from Japan, and a total of 1,172 people (29.9%) in the incorrect group, consisting of 458 test takers from the US, 404 from the Netherlands, and 310 from Japan. The rate of correctness in the US, the Netherlands, and Japan was 65.8%, 73.2%, and 71.2%, respectively.

The data analysis was undertaken in two phases. First, we explored the relationship between sequence patterns and binary classification (i.e., correct and incorrect groups) by decomposing the complete sequences into smaller units (*n*-grams) and extracting the most robust units to distinguish the two groups. Secondly, we conducted a comparative study among the three countries to examine whether the action sequence patterns differed across countries. As Fink (2008) pointed out, the development and growth in use of sequential models was closely related to the statistical modeling of texts as well as to the restriction of possible sequences of word hypotheses in automatic speech recognition. Motivated by the methodologies and applications in NLP and text mining (e.g., He, Veldkamp, & de Vries, 2012; He, Glas, Kosinski, Stillwell, & Veldkamp, 2014), we used the *n*-gram representation model and chi-square feature selection algorithm (Oakes, Gaizauskas, Fowkes, Jonsson, & Beaulieu, 2001) in analyzing the process data in this study.

## N-Gram Representation of Sequence Data

*N-grams.* In NLP, textual data is usually encoded via a data representation model. Namely, each document is generally represented as a vector of (possibly weighted) word counts (Manning & Schütze, 1999). The simplest and most commonly used data representation model is the "bag of words" (BOW), where each word in a document collection acts as a distinct feature. As an extension of BOW, *n*-grams that consider the interaction effect of two, three, or more consecutive words are proposed as a way to expand the standard unigram representation model (e.g., Bekkerman & Allan, 2003; Tan, Wang, & Lee, 2002). For instance, in the sentence "I cry because I am frightened.", taking the punctuation into account, there are seven unigrams (e.g., "I", "cry", etc.), six bigrams (e.g., "I cry", "cry because," etc.), and five trigrams (e.g., "I cry because," "cry because I," etc.).

Analogous to textual data, action sequences collected in computer-based performance tasks can be decomposed into *n*-grams. That is, the unigrams are defined as "bags of actions," where each single action in a sequence collection represents a distinct feature. Moving away from unigrams, which are not informative about transitions between actions, we looked at *n*-grams. Specifically, we considered bigrams and trigrams, which are defined as action vectors that contain either two or three ordered adjacent actions, respectively. The following is an example of an action sequence decomposed by *n*-grams for the item that we focused on in the present study (Box 1).

This action sequence can be interpreted as follows: A test taker started this item ("START") by clicking on the spreadsheet page ("SS") and then typed in the full name of the specified person to

*Box 1.*

| | Action sequence: STRT, SS, SS_Type_FN, E, E_S, Next, Next_OK, END |
|---|---|
| Unigrams (8) | "START", "SS", "SS_Type_FN", "E", "E_S", "Next", "Next_OK", "END" |
| Bigrams (7) | "START, SS", "SS, SS_Type_FN", "SS_Type_FN, E", "E, E_S", "E_S, Next", "Next, Next_OK", "Next_OK, END" |
| Trigram (6) | "START, SS, SS_Type_FN", "SS, SS_Type_FN, E", "SS_Type_FN, E, E_S", "E, E_S, Next", "E_S, Next, Next_OK", "Next, Next_OK, END" |

execute the search ("SS_Type_FN"). Afterward, the person switched to the email environment ("E") to fill in the answer and then send the email out ("E_S"). Finally, the test taker clicked on the arrow button to continue to the next item ("Next"), confirmed approaching to the next item ("Next_OK") and finalized the current item ("END"). For a more efficient coding system, we subsequently combined the actions that always concurrently appear in the same order into one code. For instance, the action "END" is always preceded by "Next_OK", hence, we recoded "Next_OK,END" into one code "FINALENDING".

*Term weight.* In information retrieval, raw term frequency usually suffers from a critical problem: All terms are considered equally important when assessing relevancy on a query. In fact, certain terms have little or no discriminating power in determining relevance. During the analysis of action sequences from PIAAC PSTRE items we encountered a similar problem: The actions such as "START" and "FINALENDING" occurred in all the test takers' processing sequences and provided little information in distinguishing the correct and incorrect groups. To solve this problem, a term for a weighting mechanism in text mining—inverse document frequency (IDF; Spärck Jones, 1972)—was applied for attenuating the effect of actions or action vectors that occurred too often in the collection to be meaningful.

In this study, we renamed the IDF to speak about inverse sequence frequency (ISF). To scale the weight to each action, we denoted the total number of sequences in the collection by $N$ and defined the ISF of an action $i$ as $\text{ISF}_i = \log(N / \text{sf}_i) \geq 0$, where $N$ indicates the total number of sequences in the collection, namely, the total number of test takers (3,926 in this study) and $\text{sf}_i$ is the number of sequences where the action $i$ appears. Thus, the ISF of a rare action is high, whereas the ISF of a frequent action is low. The ISF of an action that occurs in all the sequences namely, used by all the test takers, is zero. Therefore, the low-informative actions such as START or FINALENDING were eliminated from further analyses. This can be compared to the removal of frequent words (i.e., stop words) in textual responses such as "an," "a," and "the" (Manning & Schütze, 1999).

Another concern about term frequency is about clustering at the individual level. The importance of an action that is taken multiple times by one individual should be different from that when the action is taken once each by multiple individuals. It is similar to the issue occurred in natural language processing: a word that occurs multiple times in one document plays a different role than a word that occurs only once but in multiple documents. NLP provides a commonly used solution to the problem by dampening the term frequency by a function $f(\text{tf}) = 1 + \log(\text{tf})$, $\text{tf} > 0$ because more occurrences of a word indicate higher importance, but not as much relative importance as the undampened count would suggest (Manning & Schütze, 1999). We applied rescaling of frequencies in the current study. For example, we used $1 + \log 3$ to slightly dampen the importance of an action with three occurrences in a single respondent sequence than the count of 3 itself. Such a sequence is somewhat more important than a sequence with one occurrence under the rescaling, but not 3 times as important.

Analogous to the weighting scheme in NLP, an action's term frequency $\text{tf}_{i,j}$ (action $i$ in sequence $j$) and its ISF was further combined into a single weight as follows:

$$\text{weight}(i,j) = \begin{cases} [1 + \log(\text{tf}_{i,j})] \log(N / \text{sf}_i) & \text{if } \text{tf}_{ij} \geq 1 \\ 0 & \text{if } \text{tf}_{ij} = 0 \end{cases}$$

$$(1)$$

where $N$ is the total number of sequences. The first clause applies to actions occurring in the same sequence, whereas for actions that do not appear ($\text{tf}_{i,j} = 0$), we use $\text{weight}(i, j) = 0$.

A total of 36 actions (i.e., unigrams) were defined for this item and are listed in the first column of Table 2. The interpretation corresponding to each action is presented in the second column. The frequency of sequences (SeqFreq) that contain the action by each row is shown in the third column, following by the raw frequency of actions (Act-Freq) in the fourth column. Note that the SeqFreq and ActFreq are not always equal, because an action may occur several times in one sequence, which results in an increment for ActFreq but not SeqFreq. The last four columns of Table 2 present the raw and weighted frequency of actions in correct and incorrect groups, respectively. To ensure the reliability of calculation, actions (i.e., unigrams) and action vectors (i.e., bigrams and trigrams) that occurred fewer than 5 times or had zero ISF weights (i.e., used by all test takers) were deducted from further analyses. As a result, 27 unigrams, 144 bigrams and 257 trigrams were included in the present study.

## Chi-Square Selection Model

To answer the question regarding which actions or action vectors are the key factors that lead to success or failure in the problem-solving process, we applied a commonly used tool in NLP—the chi-square feature selection model (Oakes et al., 2001)—to identify robust classifiers. Robust classifiers are generally defined as the "best" features with high information gain in the NLP (Joachims, 1998), thus the use of *robust classifier* here is different from the meaning of the term in statistics. The chi-square feature selection model is recommended for use in textual analysis due to its high effectiveness in finding robust keywords and for testing the similarity between different text corpora (e.g., Manning & Schütze, 1999; He et al., 2012; He et al., 2014; for more feature selection models, refer to Forman, 2003). Because of the structural similarity between textual and process data, it appears appropriate to apply this

*Table 2. Raw and weighted frequency of actions (unigrams) defined in a sample PSTRE item*

| Action Code | Interpretation | Seq Freq | Act Freq | Freq in Correct | | Freq in Incorrect | |
|---|---|---|---|---|---|---|---|
| | | | | Raw | Wgt | Raw | Wgt |
| E | Switch to Email page | 3533 | 7164 | 5721 | 434.02 | 1443 | 117.93 |
| E_S | Send email | 1676 | 1814 | 1384 | 1102.00 | 430 | 324.69 |
| **FINALENDING** | **Finalize the item** | **3926** | **3926** | **2755** | **0.00** | **1171** | **0.00** |
| **Next** | **Continue to the next item** | **3926** | **4662** | **3109** | **0.00** | **1553** | **0.00** |
| Next_C | Cancel to continue to the next item | 564 | 736 | 354 | 591.45 | 382 | 651.29 |
| SS | Switch to Spreadsheet page | 1976 | 3047 | 2683 | 1446.51 | 364 | 198.93 |
| SS_H | Use "Help" on Spreadsheet page | 120 | 161 | 116 | 336.44 | 45 | 125.63 |
| SS_Save | Save results on Spreadsheet page | 169 | 186 | 119 | 350.33 | 67 | 201.63 |
| SS_Se | Start searching engine on Spreadsheet page | 883 | 952 | 808 | 1135.39 | 144 | 199.74 |
| SS_So | Start sorting engine on Spreadsheet page | 445 | 578 | 486 | 905.03 | 92 | 168.65 |
| SS_So_1_0 | Sort by null in the first choice | 11 | 12 | 9 | 58.39 | 3 | 11.60 |
| SS_So_1A | Sort by 1ˢᵗ column (ID number) in the first choice | 41 | 43 | 32 | 149.11 | 11 | 48.52 |
| SS_So_1B | Sort by 2ⁿᵈ column (Name) in the first choice | 573 | 581 | 518 | 910.56 | 63 | 107.67 |
| **SS_So_1C** | **Sort by 3ʳᵈ column (#Activities this year) in the first choice** | **2** | **2** | **1** | **7.58** | **1** | **7.58** |

*continued on following page*

*Table 2. Continued*

| Action Code | Interpretation | Seq Freq | Act Freq | Freq in Correct | | Freq in Incorrect | |
|---|---|---|---|---|---|---|---|
| | | | | Raw | Wgt | Raw | Wgt |
| **SS_So_1D** | **Sort by 4th column (Year as a member) in the first choice** | **1** | **1** | **0** | **0.00** | **1** | **8.28** |
| SS_So_2_0 | Sort by null in the second choice | 7 | 7 | 5 | 24.76 | 2 | 8.29 |
| SS_So_2A | Sort by 1st column (ID number) in the second choice | 56 | 57 | 50 | 191.09 | 7 | 24.81 |
| SS_So_2B | Sort by 2nd column (Name) in the second choice | 51 | 52 | 40 | 165.67 | 12 | 39.25 |
| **SS_So_2C** | **Sort by 3rd column (#Activities this year) in the second choice** | **1** | **1** | **1** | **8.28** | **0** | **0.00** |
| **SS_So_2D** | **Sort by 4th column (Year as a member) in the second choice** | **2** | **2** | **1** | **7.58** | **1** | **7.58** |
| **SS_So_3_0** | **Sort by null in the third choice** | **2** | **2** | **0** | **0.00** | **2** | **15.16** |
| SS_So_3A | Sort by 1st column (ID number) in the third choice | 9 | 9 | 7 | 43.12 | 2 | 9.96 |
| SS_So_3B | Sort by 2nd column (Name) in the third choice | 20 | 20 | 15 | 68.60 | 5 | 23.79 |
| **SS_So_3C** | **Sort by 3rd column (#Activities this year) in the third choice** | **2** | **2** | **2** | **15.16** | **0** | **0.00** |
| SS_So_3D | Sort by 4th column (Year as a member) in the third choice | 6 | 6 | 3 | 15.59 | 3 | 14.27 |
| SS_So_C | Cancel sorting | 88 | 95 | 69 | 234.10 | 26 | 90.59 |
| SS_So_OK | Click "OK" after setting sorting conditions | 596 | 735 | 649 | 1052.88 | 86 | 129.43 |
| SS_Type_FN | Type in full name for searching | 462 | 686 | 569 | 1022.24 | 117 | 208.84 |
| SS_Type_GN | Type in given name for searching | 85 | 154 | 136 | 357.31 | 18 | 59.76 |
| SS_Type_null | Type in null for searching | 25 | 28 | 21 | 113.90 | 7 | 36.02 |
| SS_Type_PGN | Type in partial given name for searching | 7 | 12 | 5 | 43.38 | 7 | 36.39 |
| SS_Type_PSN | Type in partial surname for searching | 9 | 16 | 12 | 61.66 | 4 | 23.65 |
| SS_Type_SM | Typing with spelling mistakes in searching | 115 | 283 | 237 | 585.57 | 46 | 100.38 |
| SS_Type_SN | Type in surname for searching | 433 | 644 | 572 | 1041.88 | 72 | 124.06 |
| SS_Type_UM | Typing with understanding mistakes in searching | 25 | 40 | 30 | 104.14 | 10 | 35.47 |
| **START** | **Start the item** | **3926** | **3926** | **2755** | **0.00** | **1171** | **0.00** |

*Note*. SeqFreq indicates the frequency of sequences that contain the action by each row, i.e., the number of test takers who used the action by each row. ActFreq represents the frequency of actions that occur in the whole collection. Raw and Wgt indicate the raw and weighted frequency of each action that occurs in the correct and incorrect groups, respectively. Actions that occur fewer than five times (ActFreq<5) or are used by all the test takers (N=3,926) were deducted from the further analysis, which are highlighted in the bold font.

approach to detect those actions or action vectors that are highly informative for distinguishing the two performance groups.

To apply the chi-square feature selection algorithm, the joint frequencies of presence versus absence of each action or action vector crossed by the correctness or incorrectness of the response were arranged into a 2-by-2 contingency table as shown in Table 3. The (weighted) number of action occurrences in two groups $C_1$ (i.e., correct group) and $C_2$ (i.e., incorrect group) is indicated by $n_i$ and $m_i$, respectively. The sum of the weighted action occurrences in each group is defined as the group length $len(C)$. The idea behind this method is to test whether occurrence

*Table 3. 2-by-2 contingency table for action $i$ in chi-square score calculation*

| | $C_1$ | $C_2$ |
|---|---|---|
| action $i$ | $n_i$ | $m_i$ |
| ¬ action $i$ | $\text{len}(C_1) - n_i$ | $\text{len}(C_2) - m_i$ |

*Note.* $C_1$ and $C_2$ represent the two study groups (e.g., correct and incorrect). $n_i$ and $m_i$ indicate the weighted frequency of the action $i$ occurs in $C_1$ and $C_2$, respectively. $\text{len}(C)$ indicates the sum of the weighted action occurrences in each group.

and nonoccurrence of actions and correctness are independent. Thus, the method compares two groups to determine how far $C_1$ departs from $C_2$ in terms of action frequencies.

Under the null hypothesis the two collections are randomly equivalent, so their distribution of actions is proportional to each other. A chi-square value is computed to evaluate the departure from this null hypothesis. For a 2-by-2 contingency table, the chi-square value is computed as

$$\chi^2 = \frac{M(O_{11}O_{22} - O_{12}O_{21})^2}{(O_{11} + O_{12})(O_{11} + O_{21})(O_{12} + O_{22})(O_{21} + O_{22})},$$ 
(2)

where $M$ is the total number of actions in the collection, and $O_{ij}$ represents the weighted counts in each cell in the matrix (see more in Bishop, Fienberg, & Holland, 1975; Agresti, 1990). The weighted counts $O_{11}$ and $O_{12}$ are the number of occurrences of an action (vector) in the correct and incorrect group, respectively, while $O_{21}$ and $O_{22}$ are the number of nonoccurrences of this action in the two performance groups.

The actions with higher chi-square scores are more discriminative in classification (Manning & Schütze, 1999). Therefore, we ranked the chi-square score of each action in a descending order. The actions ranked at the top were defined as the

robust classifiers. Using a 95% confidence interval, that is, if the chi-square score was greater than 3.84, we could be 95% confident that the action occurred more frequently in one of the two performance groups. Further, if the ratio $n_i / m_i$ was larger than the ratio $\text{len}(C_1) / \text{len}(C_2)$, the action was defined as more typical of group $C_1$ (as a "positive indicator"); otherwise, it was more typical of group $C_2$ (as a "negative indicator") (for more details, refer to Oakes et al., 2001).

## Across and Within Country Analyses

As described above, the first set of analyses used the extracted actions and action sequences jointly from all three countries selected for this study. The goal of this joint analysis was to examine whether there are features (actions and action sequences) that could distinguish correct and incorrect groups on an aggregate level. However, in order to examine whether the same features would be detected as robust classifiers for each country as well, we conducted separate analyses by country. Figure 5 provides a representation of this approach using the chi-square selection algorithm. Each country is represented by a separate layer. Within each country slice, a 2-by-2 contingency table associated with actions and performance groups is displayed, which corresponds to that presented in Table 3.

*Figure 5. The strategy of extracting classifiers by performance and by country using chi-square selection algorithm. Note: NL=Netherlands; JP=Japan; $a_i$, $b_i$, $c_i$ and $d_i$ correspond to the cells in Table 3, respectively.*

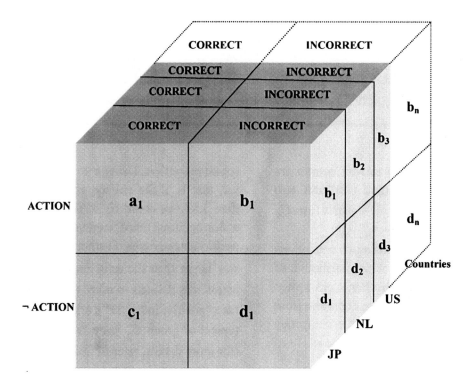

The second set of analyses was conducted to contrast countries by examining whether there was country dependency of the feature (actions and action sequences) distribution. The analysis was analogous to the preceding one, except that the definition of categories $C_1$ and $C_2$ in Table 3 was changed to selected country and remaining countries, respectively. For example, in the analysis of extracting features that distinguish the sample of Japan, we defined Japan as the selected country and the Netherlands and US as the remaining countries, that is, $C_1 = $ JP and $C_2 = $ NL+US.

## RESULTS

### Robust Classifiers by Performance Groups

*Performance groups on an aggregate level.* The first set analysis of feature extraction was conducted by performance groups. Table 4 presents the "best" eight features (actions and action sequences) that distinguished the correct and incorrect group based on an aggregated sample. The top eight classifiers of *n*-grams that typically represent each performance group are listed in a descending order according to their chi-square

*Table 4. Eight robust features of actions and action sequences distinguishing correct and incorrect group*

| | Unigrams | | Bigrams | | Trigrams | |
|---|---|---|---|---|---|---|
| | Actions | $\chi^2$ | Actions | $\chi^2$ | Actions | $\chi^2$ |
| Correct | SS | 70.72 | E, SS | 229.99 | E, SS, E | 272.49 |
| | SS_Type_SN | 68.04 | SS, E | 191.18 | START, E, SS | 226.42 |
| | SS_So_OK | 64.58 | SS_So_OK, E | 153.90 | SS, E, E_S | 211.37 |
| | SS_So_1B | 59.66 | SS_So_1B, SS_So_OK | 122.49 | SS_So_OK, E, SS | 150.25 |
| | SS_Se | 22.53 | SS_Type_SN, E | 120.56 | SS_So_1B, SS_So_OK, E | 137.53 |
| | SS_So | 12.84 | SS_Se, SS_Type_SN | 98.21 | SS, E, SS | 133.85 |
| | SS_Type_SM | 12.58 | SS_So , SS_So_1B | 84.43 | SS_Se, SS_Type_SN, E | 108.55 |
| | SS_So_2A | 9.76 | START, SS_Se | 70.03 | SS_Type_SN, E, SS | 108.20 |
| Incorrect | Next_C | 892.80 | START, Next | 2416.20 | START, Next, FINALENDING | 2420.26 |
| | SS_Save | 98.90 | Next, Next_C | 521.74 | Next, Next_C, Next | 478.16 |
| | SS_Type_PGN | 33.19 | Next_C, Next | 504.22 | START, E, Next | 399.02 |
| | SS_H | 15.75 | E_S, E_S | 492.26 | Next_C, Next, FINALENDING | 392.59 |
| | SS_So_3D | 14.56 | E_S, E | 364.66 | E_S, Next, Next_C | 374.83 |
| | SS_So_C | 13.23 | E_S, SS | 299.74 | E, E_S, E_S | 353.88 |
| | E_S | 7.91 | Next_C, E | 232.94 | E_S, E_S, Next | 349.52 |
| | SS_Type_PSN | 3.27 | SS_Type_FN, Next | 196.80 | E, E_S, E | 338.26 |

scores. Note that due to space limitation, we only present the top eight features as examples to illustrate the results of feature selection. The raw frequency of each action and action sequence in Table 4 was within the range from 12 to 3,047.

Among the unigrams, the actions related to using tools to find clues on the spreadsheet page, such as searching or sorting approaches (e.g., "SS_Type_SN", "SS_So_OK", "SS_So_1B", "SS_Se", "SS_So") were found to be robust classifiers in the correct group. This matches our expectation, as the use of searching or sorting tools plays an important role in simplifying the problem-solving process and facilitates success on this item. Conversely, classifiers that were most

salient indicators of the incorrect group involved breakoff actions such as canceling a started sequence (e.g., "Next_C", "SS_So_C"). These cancel actions suggested that the test takers in the incorrect group were unsure about decisions during the response process and may have decided to cancel what they started as a result. Furthermore, the actions that potentially led to wrong answers (e.g., "SS_So_3D") were also found to be robust indicators for the incorrect group. For instance, the action "SS_So_3D", meaning sorting the fourth column (year as a member) in the third choice in the spreadsheet page, was not helpful in identifying the specified person as required. The use of robust classifiers such as "SS_Save" and "SS_H" (seeking for help), that is, actions that did not directly relate to the shortest path to success, also suggested that test takers in the incorrect group did not fully understand how to solve the problem. Hence, they frequently sought help and aimlessly saved the results on the server.

The extracted classifiers of bigrams and trigrams further supported the initial findings based on unigrams. We noticed that the action sequences identified as typical behaviors in the correct group showed that the test takers had clear subgoals in different environments and well understood how to achieve these goals. For example, the correct group usually chose a tool (searching or sorting) at the very beginning to solve the item (e.g., "START, SS_Se"). On the contrary, the robust $n$-gram-based incorrect indicators suggested that the first actions taken by test takers in the incorrect groups were more likely to be clicking on "Next" (e.g., "START, Next") or directly switching to the email page (e.g., "START, E, Next"). Further inspection of the robust indicators of incorrect responses showed that some action sequences led to wrong answers due to careless mistakes. For instance, some participants in the incorrect group followed the action sequence "SS_Type_FN, Next", meaning they found the unique result from the search engine that was probably correct in the spreadsheet environment; unfortunately they then clicked on "Next" and either forgot—or maybe were unaware of the need—to enter this result in the email. The robust incorrect indicators such as "Next, Next_C" and "Next_C, Next" provided additional evidence of the breakoff behavior in the incorrect group, which is consistent with the results obtained based on unigrams.

In addition, we noticed that the process data of action sequences could also be used as indicators of missing data. For instance, the most robust trigram in the incorrect group, "START, Next, FINALENDING", was found 321 times in the dataset, which implied that these 321 participants (which correspond to 8.18% in the whole sample)

simply skipped this item. For better precision, they should be labeled as missing rather than as incorrect responses.

*Performance groups within each country.* To investigate whether the features (actions and action sequences) extracted by performance groups on an aggregate level were consistent across countries, we further explored the data by conducting separate analyses within each country. Specifically, we applied the chi-square selection method on each country layer in Figure 3 and compared the extracted $n$-gram classifiers among three countries. Table 5 presents the consistency rate of each performance group between the top eight classifiers extracted within each country and those extracted on an aggregate level as shown in Table 4. For instance, the consistency rate is as high as 88% in the first cell under the column of US. It suggested that seven out of the top eight classifiers extracted from the correct group in the US sample matched the classifiers extracted from the correct group of the aggregate sample. The consistency rate of classifiers in the correct group was within a range of [63%, 88%], with an average of 79%. These results suggested that the

*Table 5. Consistency rate of extracted classifiers by performance groups compared between country level and aggregate level*

| | US | Netherlands | Japan |
|---|---|---|---|
| **Correct** | | | |
| Unigrams | 0.88 | 0.88 | 0.63 |
| Bigrams | 0.75 | 0.88 | 0.75 |
| Trigrams | 0.75 | 0.88 | 0.75 |
| **Incorrect** | | | |
| Unigrams | 0.63 | 0.63 | 0.63 |
| Bigrams | 0.63 | 0.88 | 0.88 |
| Trigrams | 0.75 | 0.63 | 0.75 |

*Note.* The calculation is based on the comparison between top eight robust classifiers extracted by performance groups within each country and those extracted on an aggregate level as shown in Table 4.

extracted classifiers within each country were generally consistent with the features detected from a joint sample. Comparatively, the consistency rate of classifiers in the incorrect group was a bit lower but still acceptable. The range was [63%, 88%], with an average of 71%. The reason for a relatively low consistency rate in the incorrect group was probably the diversity of mistakes that led to wrong actions.

## Robust Classifiers by Countries

A second set of analysis focused on exploring country differences in the process of solving PSTRE items. Table 6 presents the top five robust

actions and action sequences extracted across the three selected countries: US, the Netherlands and Japan. The *n*-grams that most typically represented each country are listed in a descending order according to their chi-square scores. It was noticed that in the panel for the US, the chi-square scores of unigrams were fairly low within a range of [6.22, 20.40]. This suggests that there were no unique actions that set the US sample apart. However, from the robust classifiers in bigrams and trigrams, it was clear that the US test takers were more likely to multiply click on the email page (e.g., "E, E" and "E, E, E"). The test takers in the Netherlands group were more likely to identify information in the spreadsheet by typing

*Table 6. Five robust features of actions and action sequences across countries*

| | Unigrams | | Bigrams | | Trigrams | |
|---|---|---|---|---|---|---|
| | Actions | $\chi^2$ | Actions | $\chi^2$ | Actions | $\chi^2$ |
| US | Next_C | 20.40 | E, E | 261.08 | E, E, E | 309.01 |
| | SS_Type_FN | 15.64 | START, Next | 39.82 | E, E, Next | 278.87 |
| | E | 13.25 | Next, E | 39.28 | SS, E, E | 132.21 |
| | SS_Type_PGN | 10.14 | START, E | 38.97 | START, E, E | 85.14 |
| | SS_Save | 6.22 | SS_So_C, SS_Type_FN | 37.63 | SS_Type_FN, E, E | 54.23 |
| NL | SS_Type_FN | 315.30 | SS_Se, SS_Type_FN | 252.93 | START, SS_Se, SS_Type_GN | 226.67 |
| | SS_Type_GN | 232.93 | SS_Type_FN, SS_Type_FN | 249.97 | START, SS_Se, SS_Type_FN | 212.73 |
| | SS_Se | 60.88 | SS_Type_FN, E | 203.30 | SS_Type_FN, E, Next | 193.03 |
| | SS_So_3B | 31.59 | SS_Se, SS_Type_GN | 202.10 | SS_Type_FN, SS_Type_FN, E | 162.64 |
| | SS_So_2A | 16.15 | START, SS_Se | 117.42 | SS_Se, SS_Type_FN, SS_Type_FN | 161.06 |
| JP | SS_Type_SM | 383.58 | SS_Type_SM, SS_Type_SM | 308.58 | SS_Type_SM, SS_Type_SM, SS_Type_SM | 248.84 |
| | SS_Type_null | 123.49 | SS_Type_SM, SS_So | 166.12 | E_S, Next, Next_C | 149.25 |
| | SS_Type_UM | 70.75 | E_S, E_S | 137.22 | SS_Type_SM, SS_So, SS_So_1B | 149.21 |
| | Next_C | 47.37 | SS_Se, SS_Type_SM | 116.73 | SS_Type_SM, SS_Type_SM, SS_So | 140.96 |
| | SS_Type_PSN | 44.68 | SS_Type_SM, E | 115.33 | SS_Type_SM, SS_Type_SM, E | 116.15 |

in full names ("SS_Type_FN") or given names ("SS_Type_GN") of the specified person in a searching strategy. The Netherlands group also featured action sequences associated with double checking. For instance, repetitive actions such as "SS_Type_FN, SS_Type_FN" were found to be robust classifiers to distinguish the Netherlands from the other two countries.

An unexpected finding was that the most discriminative action that distinguished Japan from the Netherlands and US was an apparent typing mistake in the searching strategy ("SS_Type_SM"). This action appeared as a key element and repeatedly occurred in the bigrams and trigrams as well. To explore the possible reasons for this issue, we took a further look into the Japanese process data as well as the pilot item in the Japanese version. It was noticed that, in the spreadsheet of Japanese version, there was a space between individuals' given names and surnames. However, such a space is optional and may or may not appear in daily use in Japanese writings. The optional space caused an increase in repeated searching actions, because a number of test takers did not notice the presence of the space in the table. However, this issue didn't seem to have a major impact on the response probabilities or on the overall proficiency level of the Japan group, which is the highest performing PIAAC country. A closer examination of the bigrams and trigrams showed that a substantial number of successful test takers switched to a second strategy (sorting) (e.g., "SS_Type_SM, SS_Type_SM, SS_So") or revised their search to include the space between the given names and surnames, matching the display in the spreadsheet (e.g., "SS_Type_SM, E") after trying the spelling without the space. Although more steps and longer processing time might have occurred in the Japan group, the final performance scores were not significantly influenced.

We conducted the whole set of analyses without sampling weights as well. The results were only marginally different from identifying robust classifiers when weights were used. However, the ranking order of classifiers was slightly different. This agreed with our expectations as the range of weights was not large, hence, we did not expect a substantial difference in results obtained with or without sampling weights.

In addition, we compared the results under the condition of whether or not term frequency adjustment was used in an individual level, that is, whether an adjusted lower weight $(1 + \log(\text{tf}))$ or a full weight $(\text{tf})$ was given to actions that occurred multiple times in one sequence. The results showed a marginal change in identification of unigram classifiers but little impact on the identification of bigrams and trigrams.

## DISCUSSION

Computer-based assessments provide new sources of evidence to study cognitive abilities and underlying processes by measuring not only the outcome of a task but also behavioral process data that can be interpreted in terms of cognitive processes happening throughout task completion (Goldhammer et al., 2013). This is of interest especially in action-driven items, such as PSTRE items in large-scale assessments.

The goal of this study was to explore associations between action sequences and task completion within and across countries. Motivated by the methodologies from NLP and text mining, we chose the *n*-gram representation method and the chi-square feature selection model to extract action sequence patterns that facilitate differentiation between performance groups. It was found that actions related to using tools such as sorting and searching occurred significantly more often in the group of respondents that produced a correct response, while actions suggesting hesitative behaviors such as repeatedly clicking the cancel button were found more often in the incorrect group. Further, among these robust indicators we noticed that the correct group had a better understanding of the subgoals of different environments and were more likely to recover from initial errors in the problem-solving process. Conversely, respondents in the incorrect group appeared to have only a relatively vague idea about what was expected in the item and were more likely to use the help function.

These observed result patterns based on the aggregate level were subsequently also found in performance groups analyzed by country. In the study aimed at country comparisons, the US group showed a comparably high rate of repetitive clicking on the email page, while the Netherlands group was characterized by a comparably high rate of using full names or given names in the search. While an issue with spelling variations in search patterns was identified in the Japanese version of the task, this did not significantly alter the results. In fact, this spelling variation, which can be remedied in future versions of the assessment, demonstrated how process data can inform our interpretation of respondent behaviors. Overall, the analyses and results reported here illustrate the potential of process data that become available through computer-based assessment. The methodology presented in this study shows promise in analyzing process data and extracting robust information about how performance groups differ in terms of their interaction with a complex task.

The present study also demonstrates that process data can be useful in detecting nonresponse due to low engagement of test takers. This may be a valuable source of information for item developers. For instance, in the current study, the action sequence "START, Next, FINALENDING" was identified quite frequently in the data. This sequence may be taken as an indicator of low engagement that led to respondents avoiding interaction with the item. For better precision, the responses of test takers who followed such an action sequence should be labeled as missing data instead of incorrect, because they simply skipped the item without trying to solve the task. Further,

process data can be used as a method to examine items, which is especially useful in pre-testing and field-testing situations. For example, if something unusual is found in the process data of an item, such as rapid repetition of a single action, or many instances of a short overall sequence length indicating a tendency to avoid engaging with the item, or a majority of test takers choosing the wrong problem-solving path, we may be able to find out whether the item is technically flawed or it is hard to engage meaningfully with the content, and we can detect where the potential error occurred. As a consequence, by examining the process data before the main study data collection, based on field test log files, we can help ensure that all items function as expected in the main study and respondents are able to engage with the content to provide meaningful performance data.

Besides the positive results, some limitations also merit discussion. First, the present study focused on extracting action sequence patterns by different performance groups without taking background characteristics into consideration. For example, background variables such as gender, educational level, working status, and familiarity with computer might be important factors in the problem-solving process and will likely be associated with performance on the PSTRE items as well. For example, cultural differences may be associated with how respondents interact with the items, and hence process data collected from culturally diverse samples may show such differences. This effect may be even more salient than item-score by population interactions (DIF – differential item functioning), so the distribution of action sequence patterns may differ noticeably from country to country. For example, test takers from the Netherlands were more likely to identify the information in the spreadsheet by using the search engine, while those from the US were more likely to sort or scroll down the spreadsheet to scan the information row by row. This leads to new research questions and future studies: for instance, whether test takers from different cultural backgrounds or different countries adopt the same solution to a complex task, and whether the differences in strategies have an association with test takers' responses in tradition (correct/incorrect) item-scores or in responses to questionnaire items given along with the test. Therefore, we believe that process data will play an important role in providing a new angle to explore the cultural diversity. It would be interesting to include these and other variables as controls in future studies to further explore the interaction effects of process data and background variables on complex task performance.

Secondly, although the timing and process data could be simultaneously extracted from log files, it was not easy to combine the utilization of these two sources in one study. Evidence has shown that timing is highly correlated with the problem-solving process and performance (e.g., Goldhammer et al., 2014). Thus, it might be interesting to develop a model that can take advantage of both timing and process data in an integrative analytic approach.

Future studies will provide more information about the predictive power of feature extraction models. More specifically, action sequences harvested across multiple tasks should be related to proficiency estimates based on scored task responses from the same as well as other proficiency scales that were assessed simultaneously. In addition, future studies will benefit from the explorations presented here and will be able to scale up analyses to include more data from a larger variety of countries.

Problem-solving tasks as used in the present study require higher-order thinking, finding new solutions, and sometimes interaction with a dynamic environment (Klieme, 2004; Mayer, 1994; Goldhammer et al., 2013). Solving such a complex task requires developing a plan consisting of a set of properly arranged subgoals and performing corresponding actions to attain the goal. This differs from solving logical or mathematical problems, where complexity is determined by

reasoning requirements but not primarily by the information that needs to be accessed and used (Goldhammer et al., 2013). Consequently, with the help of process data from computer-based assessments, more problem-solving items may be developed, which increasingly use information technology-based features of assessing, integrating, and managing information.

The use of process data to detect likely failure or disengagement will provide valuable information for tailored tests in an adaptive environment. For instance, when repetitive action sequences are captured in process data, such as repeatedly typing in a wrong keyword or making spelling mistakes in the searching engine ("SS_Type_SM, SS_Type_SM"), the system may generate a hint (e.g., present the correct spelling) to help test takers solve the task, essentially adjusting task difficulty based on process data. Although the hint can lower the item difficulty due to the involvement of more clues, it would be helpful to encourage test takers to continue trying to solve the problem, especially in a dynamic learning environment. To build up an action-based adaptive testing system would be a further step. Unlike the proficiency-based computerized adaptive testing (CAT; Wainer et al., 1990; van der Linden & Glas, 2000), the action-based CAT would make item selections based on test takers' previous actions. That is, if a test taker follows a correct path of problem solving, a set of more challenging tasks might be allocated for the subsequent steps. On the contrary, a set of easier tasks or clues may be given to test takers who do not follow a correct path tracked in the process data.

In conclusion, with increasing use of computer-based assessments, process data play an increasingly important role in tracking test takers' thinking and action sequences. This pilot study presented what we think is a promising method to analyze process data and extract robust sequence features that are informative for differentiating between performance groups. However, the research regarding process data is still nascent in educational assessments. The benefits that process data can bring and how we can use it are questions waiting to be fully understood. For future studies, we recommend including background characteristics and timing data in the analysis of process data to further explore their interaction effects on performance. In addition, explorations of how process data may inform adaptive testing appear to be a potential valuable research direction. This could be realized by taking ideas developed in the context of user modeling and integrating them into adaptive testing environments.

# REFERENCES

Agresti, A. (1990). *Categorical data analysis*. New York, NY: John Wiley & Sons, Inc.

Amershi, S., & Conati, C. (2009). Combining unsupervised and supervised classification to build user models for exploratory learning environments. *Journal of Educational Data Mining*, *1*(1), 18–81.

Anderson, E., Gulwani, S., & Popovic, Z. (2013). A trace-based framework for analyzing and synthesizing educational progressions. In *Proceedings of the Special Interest Group on Computer-Human Interaction (SIGCHI) Conference on Human Factors in Computing Systems*, (pp. 773–782). doi:10.1145/2470654.2470764

Bekkerman, R., & Allan, J. (2003). *Using bigrams in text categorization* (Technical Report IR-408). Retrieved April 13, 2012 from the Center for Intelligent Information Retrieval, University of Massachusetts website: http://ciir.cs.umass.edu/pubfiles/ir-408.pdf

Bishop, Y. M. M., Fienberg, S. E., & Holland, P. W. (1975). *Discrete multivariate analysis: Theory and practice*. Cambridge, MA: MIT Press.

Biswas, G., Jeong, H., Kinnebrew, J., Sulcer, B., & Roscoe, R. (2010). Measuring self-regulated learning skills through social interactions in a teachable agent environment. *Research and Practice in Technology-Enhanced Learning*, *5*(2), 123–152. doi:10.1142/S1793206810000839

Corbett, A. T., & Anderson, J. R. (1995). Knowledge tracing: Modeling the acquisition of procedural knowledge. *User Modeling and User-Adapted Interaction*, *4*(4), 253–278. doi:10.1007/BF01099821

Dong, G., & Pei, J. (2007). *Sequence data mining*. New York, NY: Springer.

Fink, G. A. (2008). *Markov models for pattern recognition*. Berlin, Germany: Springer.

Forman, G. (2003). An extensive empirical study of feature selection metrics for text classification. *Journal of Machine Learning Research*, *3*, 1289–1305.

Gobert, J. D., Sao Pedro, M., Raziuddin, J., & Baker, R. (2013). From log files to assessment metrics: Measuring students' science inquiry skills using educational data mining. *Journal of the Learning Sciences*, *22*(4), 521–563. doi:10.1080/10508406.2013.837391

Goldhammer, F., Naumann, J., & Keßel, Y. (2013). Assessing individual differences in basic computer skills: Psychometric characteristics of an interactive performance measure. *European Journal of Psychological Assessment*, *29*(4), 263–275. doi:10.1027/1015-5759/a000153

Goldhammer, F., Naumann, J., Selter, A., Toth, K., Rolke, H., & Klieme, E. (2014). The time on task effect in reading and problem solving is moderated by task difficulty and skill: Insights from a computer-based large-scale assessment. *Journal of Educational Psychology*, *106*(4), 608–626. doi:10.1037/a0034716

Graesser, A. C., Lu, S., Jackson, G. T., Mitchell, H., Ventura, M., Olney, A., & Louwerse, M. M. (2004). AutoTutor: A tutor with dialogue in natural language. *Behavior Research Methods, Instruments, & Computers*, *36*(2), 180–193. doi:10.3758/BF03195563 PMID:15354683

Hara, S., Kitaoka, N., & Takeda, K. (2010). Estimation Method of User Satisfaction Using N-gram-based Dialog History Model for Spoken Dialog System. In *Proceedings of International Conference on Language Resources and Evaluation*, (pp. 78–83).

He, Q., Glas, C. A. W., Kosinski, M., Stillwell, D. J., & Veldkamp, B. P. (2014). Predicting self-monitoring skills using textual posts on Facebook. *Computers in Human Behavior*, *33*, 69–78. doi:10.1016/j.chb.2013.12.026

He, Q., Veldkamp, B. P., & de Vries, T. (2012). Screening for posttraumatic stress disorder using verbal features in self-narratives: A text mining approach. *Psychiatry Research*, *198*(3), 441–447. doi:10.1016/j.psychres.2012.01.032 PMID:22464046

Joachims, T. (1998). Text categorization with Support Vector Machines: Learning with many relevant features. *Machine Learning: ECML-98. Lecture Notes in Computer Science*, *1398*, 137–142. doi:10.1007/BFb0026683

Kinnebrew, J. S., Loretz, K. M., & Biswas, G. (2013). A contextualized, differential sequence mining method to derive students' learning behavior patterns. *Journal of Educational Data Mining*, *5*(1), 190–219.

Kinnebrew, J. S., Mack, D. L., & Biswas, G. (2013). Mining temporally-interesting learning behavior patterns. *Proceedings of the 6th International Conference on Educational Data Mining*, (pp. 252–255).

Klieme, E. (2004). Assessment of cross-curricular problem-solving competencies. In J. H. Moskowitz & M. Stephens (Eds.), *Comparing learning outcomes: International assessments and education policy* (pp. 81–107). London: Routledge.

Lin, J., & Wilbur, W. J. (2009). Modeling actions of PubMed users with n-gram language models. *Information Retrieval*, *12*(4), 487–503. doi:10.1007/s10791-008-9067-7 PMID:19684883

Manning, C. D., & Schütze, H. (1999). *Foundations of statistical natural language processing*. Cambridge, MA: MIT Press.

Martinez, R., Yacef, K., Kay, J., Al-Qaraghuli, A., & Kharrufa, A. (2011). Analysing frequent sequential patterns of collaborative learning activity around an interactive tabletop. In *Proceedings of the 4th International Conference on Educational Data Mining*, (pp. 111–120).

Mayer, R. E. (1994). Problem solving, teaching and testing for. In T. Husen & T. N. Postlethwaite (Eds.), *The international encyclopedia of education* (2nd ed.; Vol. 8, pp. 4728–4731). Oxford, UK: Pergamon Press.

Oakes, M., Gaizauskas, R., Fowkes, H., Jonsson, W. A. V., & Beaulieu, M. (2001). A method based on chi-square test for document classification. *Proceedings of the 24th Annual International ACM SIGIR Conference on Research and Development in Information Retrieval* (pp. 440–441). New York, NY: ACM. doi:10.1145/383952.384080

Organisation for Economic Co-operation and Development. (2009). *PIAAC problem solving in technology-rich environments: A conceptual framework (OECD Education Working Paper No. 36)*. Paris, France: Author.

Organisation for Economic Co-operation and Development. (2010). *PIAAC technical standards and guidelines*. OECD Publishing. Retrieved May 16, 2014, from http://www.oecd.org/site/piaac/PIAAC-NPM(2010_12)PIAAC_Technical_Standards_and_Guidelines.pdf

Organisation for Economic Co-operation and Development. (2012). *Literacy, numeracy and problem solving in technology-rich environments: Framework for the OECD Survey of Adult Skills*. OECD Publishing. 10.1787/9789264128859-en

Organisation for Economic Co-operation and Development. (2013). *Technical Report of the Survey of Adult Skills (PIAAC)*. OECD Publishing. Retrieved August 13, 2014, from http://www.oecd.org/site/piaac/_Technical%20Report_17OCT13.pdf

Perera, D., Kay, J., Koprinska, I., Yacef, K., & Zaiane, O. R. (2009). Clustering and sequential pattern mining of online collaborative learning data. *IEEE Transactions on Knowledge and Data Engineering, 21*(6), 759–772. doi:10.1109/TKDE.2008.138

Rabiner, L. (1989). A tutorial on hidden Markov models and selected applications in speech recognition. *Proceedings of the IEEE, 77*(2), 257–286. doi:10.1109/5.18626

Romero, C., & Ventura, S. (2010). Educational data mining: A review of the state of the art. Systems, Man, and Cybernetics, Part C: Applications and Reviews. *IEEE Transactions on Systems, Man, and Cybernetics, 40*(6), 601–618. doi:10.1109/TSMCC.2010.2053532

Rutkowski, L., Gonzalez, E., von Davier, M., & Zhou, Y. (2014). Assessment design for international large-scale assessments. In L. Rutkowski, M. von Davier, & D. Rutkowski (Eds.), *Handbook of international large-scale assessment* (pp. 75–95). Boca Raton, FL: Taylor & Francis.

Schatztnann, J., Stuttle, M. N., Weilhammer, K., & Young, S. (2005). Effects of the user model on simulation-based learning of dialogue strategies. In *Proceedings of IEEE Workshop on Automatic Speech Recognition and Understanding*, (pp. 220–225). doi:10.1109/ASRU.2005.1566539

Schleicher, A. (2008). PIAAC: A new strategy for assessing adult competencies. *International Review of Education, 54*(5-6), 627–650. doi:10.1007/s11159-008-9105-0

Sireci, S. G., & Zenisky, A. L. (2006). Innovative item formats in computer-based testing: In pursuit of improved construct representation. In S. M. Downing & T. S. Haladyna (Eds.), *Handbook of test development* (pp. 329–347). Mahwah, NJ: Erlbaum.

Sonamthiang, S., Cercone, N., & Naruedomkul, K. (2007). Discovering Hierarchical Patterns of Students' Learning Behavior in Intelligent Tutoring Systems. In *Proceedings of IEEE International Conference on Granular Computing*, (pp. 485–489).

Spärck Jones, K. (1972). A statistical interpretation of term specificity and its application in retrieval. *The Journal of Documentation, 28*(1), 11–21. doi:10.1108/eb026526

Su, Z., Yang, Q., Lu, Y., & Zhang, H. (2000). WhatNext: A prediction system for Web requests using n-gram sequence models. In *Proceedings of the First International Conference on Web Information Systems Engineering*, (vol. 1, pp. 214–221).

Sukkarieh, J. Z., von Davier, M., & Yamamoto, K. (2012). *From biology to education: Scoring and clustering multilingual text sequences and other sequential tasks*. (ETS Research Report No. RR-12-25). Princeton, NJ: Educational Testing Service.

Tan, C. M., Wang, Y. F., & Lee, C. D. (2002). The use of bigrams to enhance text categorization. *Information Processing & Management*, *38*(4), 529–546. doi:10.1016/S0306-4573(01)00045-0

van der Linden, W. J. (2005). *Linear models for optimal test design*. New York, NY: Springer. doi:10.1007/0-387-29054-0

van der Linden, W. J., & Glas, C. A. W. (2000). *Computerized adaptive testing: Theory and practice*. Boston, MA: Kluwer Academic Publishers. doi:10.1007/0-306-47531-6

von Davier, M., & Sinharay, S. (2014). Analytics in international large-scale assessments: Item response theory and population models. In L. Rutkowski, M. von Davier, & D. Rutkowski (Eds.), *Handbook of international large-scale assessment* (pp. 155–174). Boca Raton, FL: Taylor & Francis.

von Davier, M., Sinharay, S., Oranje, A., & Beaton, A. (2006). Statistical procedures used in the National Assessment of Educational Progress (NAEP): Recent developments and future directions. In C. R. Rao & S. Sinharay (Eds.), Handbook of statistics (Vol. 26): Psychometrics. Amsterdam, Netherlands: Elsevier.

Wainer, H., Dorans, N. J., Flaugher, R., Green, B. F., Mislevy, R. J., Steinberg, L., & Thissen, D. (1990). *Computerized adaptive testing: A primer*. Hillsdale, NJ: Lawrence Erlbaum Associates.

Zhou, M., Xu, Y., Nesbit, J. C., & Winne, P. H. (2010). Sequential pattern analysis of learning logs: Methodology and applications. Handbook of educational data mining, 107–121.

## ADDITIONAL READING

Agrawal, R., & Srikant, R. (1995). Mining sequential patterns. In *Proceedings of the Eleventh IEEE International Conference on Data Engineering (ICDE)*, pp. 3–14. doi:10.1109/ICDE.1995.380415

Ahuja, J., & Webster, J. (2001). Perceived disorientation: An examination of a new measure to assess web design effectiveness. *Interacting with Computers*, *14*(1), 15–29. doi:10.1016/S0953-5438(01)00048-0

Aleven, V., McLaren, B. M., & Sewall, J. (2009). Scaling up programming by demonstration for intelligent tutoring systems development: An open-access website for middle-school mathematics learning. *IEEE Transactions on Learning Technologies*, *2*(2), 64–78. doi:10.1109/TLT.2009.22

Azevedo, R. (2005). Using hypermedia as a metacognitive tool for enhancing student learning? The role of self-regulated learning. *Educational Psychologist*, *40*(4), 199–209. doi:10.1207/s15326985ep4004_2

Baker, R., & Yacef, K. (2009). The state of educational data mining in 2009: A review and future visions. *Journal of Educational Data Mining*, *1*(1), 3–16.

Bennett, R. E., Persky, H., Weiss, A. R., & Jenkins, F. (2007). *Problem solving in technology-rich environments: A report from the NAEP technology-based assessment project* (NCES Report 2007–466). Washington, DC: U.S. Department of Education, National Center for Education Statistics.

Bennett, R. E., Persky, H., Weiss, A. R., & Jenkins, F. (2010). Measuring problem solving with technology: A demonstration study for NAEP. *The Journal of Technology, Learning, and Assessment*, *8*(8), 1–43.

Biswas, G., Leelawong, K., Schwartz, D., Vye, N., & Vanderbilt, T.The Teachable Agents Group at Vande. (2005). Learning by teaching: A new agent paradigm for educational software. *Applied Artificial Intelligence*, *19*(3), 363–392. doi:10.1080/08839510590910200

Blair, K., Schwartz, D., Biswas, G., & Leelawong, K. (2006). Pedagogical agents for learning by teaching: Teachable agents. *Journal of Educational Technology & Society*, *47*(1), 56.

Botafogo, R. A., Rivlin, E., & Shneiderman, B. (1992). Structural analysis of hypertexts: Identifying hierarchies and useful metrics. *ACM Transactions on Information Systems*, *10*(2), 142–180. doi:10.1145/146802.146826

Bouchet, F., Harley, J. M., Trevors, G. J., & Azevedo, R. (2013). Clustering and profiling students according to their interactions with an intelligent tutoring system fostering self-regulated learning. *Journal of Educational Data Mining*, *5*(1), 104–146.

Brand-Gruwel, S., Wopereis, I., & Walraven, A. (2009). A descriptive model of information problem solving while using Internet. *Computers & Education*, *53*(4), 1207–1217. doi:10.1016/j.compedu.2009.06.004

Breslow, L., Pritchard, D. E., DeBoer, J., Stump, G. S., Ho, A. D., & Seaton, D. T. (2013). Studying learning in the worldwide classroom: Research into edX's first MOOC. *Research & Practice in Assessment*, *8*, 13–25.

Comeaux, P. (2005). *Communication and collaboration in the online classroom*. Boston, MA: Anker.

Davidson, C. (2012). *What can MOOCs teaching us about learning?* Retrieved April 5, 2014, from http://hastac.org/blogs/cathy-davidson/2012/10/01/what-can-moocs-teach-us-about-learning

Glogger, I., Holzäpfel, L., Kappich, J., Schwonke, R., Nückles, M., & Renkl, A. (2013). Development and evaluation of a computer-based learning environment for teachers: Assessment of learning strategies in learning journals. *Education Research International*, *12*. doi:10.1155/2013/785065

Gwizdka, J., & Spence, I. (2007). Implicit measures of lostness and success in web navigation. *Interacting with Computers*, *19*(3), 357–369. doi:10.1016/j.intcom.2007.01.001

Hadlock, F. (1988). Minimum detour methods for string or sequence comparison. *Congressus Numerantium*, *61*, 263–274.

Herder, E. (2005). Characterizations of user web revisit behavior. In *Proceedings of Workshop on Adaptivity and User Modelling in Interactive Systems*, 32–37.

Hirschberg, D. S. (1975). A linear space algorithm for computing maximal common subsequences. *Communications of the ACM*, *18*(6), 341–343. doi:10.1145/360825.360861

Hirschberg, D. S. (1977). Algorithms for the longest common subsequence problem. *Journal of the ACM*, *24*(4), 664–675. doi:10.1145/322033.322044

Huang, X., & Miller, W. (1991). A time-efficient, linear-space local similarity algorithm. *Advances in Applied Mathematics*, *12*(3), 337–357. doi:10.1016/0196-8858(91)90017-D

Juvina, I., & van Oostendorp, H. (2008). Modelling semantic and structural knowledge in web navigation. *Discourse Processes*, *45*(4-5), 346–364. doi:10.1080/01638530802145205

Katz, S., Albacete, P., Ford, F., Jordan, P., Lipschultz, M., Litman, D., & Wilson, C. (2013). Pilot test of a natural-language tutoring system for physics that simulates the highly interactive nature of human tutoring. In *Proceedings of the 16th International Conference on Artificial Intelligence in Education (AIED)*, pp. 636–639, Memphis, TN. doi:10.1007/978-3-642-39112-5_77

Katz, S., & Albacete, P. L. (2013). A tutoring system that simulates the highly interactive nature of human tutoring. *Journal of Educational Psychology*, *105*(4), 1126–1141. doi:10.1037/a0032063

Kintsch, W. (1998). *Comprehension: A paradigm for cognition*. New York, NY: Cambridge University Press.

Landauer, T. K., McNamara, D. S., Dennis, S., & Kintsch, W. (2007). *Handbook of latent semantic analysis*. Hillsdale, NJ: Lawrence Erlbaum Associates.

Larson, K., & Czerwinski, M. (1998, April). Web page design: Implications of memory, structure and scent for information retrieval. In *Proceedings of the SIGCHI Conference on Human Factors in Computing Systems (CHI '98)*. New York, NY: ACM Press/Addison-Wesley, 25–32. doi:10.1145/274644.274649

Lawless, K. A., & Kulikowich, J. M. (1996). Understanding hypertext navigation through cluster analysis. *Journal of Educational Computing Research*, *14*(4), 385–399. doi:10.2190/DVAP-DE23-3XMV-9MXH

Lazonder, A. W., & Rouet, J. F. (2008). Information problem solving instruction: Some cognitive and metacognitive issues. *Computers in Human Behavior*, *24*(3), 753–765. doi:10.1016/j.chb.2007.01.025

McDonald, S., & Stevenson, R. J. (1998). Effects of text structure and prior knowledge of the learner on navigation in hypertext. *Human Factors*, *40*(1), 19–27. doi:10.1518/001872098779480541

McEneaney, J. E. (2001). Graphic and numerical methods to assess navigation in hypertext. *International Journal of Human-Computer Studies*, *55*(5), 761–786. doi:10.1006/ijhc.2001.0505

Mislevy, R. J., Behrens, J. T., Dicerbo, K. E., & Levy, R. (2012). Design and discovery in educational assessment: Evidence-centered design, psychometrics, and educational data mining. *Journal of Educational Data Mining*, *4*(1), 11–48.

Naumann, J., Richter, T., Christmann, U., & Groeben, N. (2008). Working memory capacity and reading skill moderate the effectiveness of strategy training in learning from hypertext. *Learning and Individual Differences*, *18*(2), 197–213. doi:10.1016/j.lindif.2007.08.007

Naumann, J., Richter, T., Flender, J., Christmann, U., & Groeben, N. (2007). Signaling in expository hypertexts compensates for deficits in reading skill. *Journal of Educational Psychology*, *99*(4), 791–807. doi:10.1037/0022-0663.99.4.791

Otter, M., & Johnson, H. (2000). Lost in hyperspace: Metrics and mental models. *Interacting with Computers*, *13*(1), 1–40. doi:10.1016/S0953-5438(00)00030-8

Padovani, S., & Lansdale, M. (2003). Balancing search and retrieval in hypertext: Context-specific trade-offs in navigational tool use. *International Journal of Human-Computer Studies*, *58*(1), 125–149. doi:10.1016/S1071-5819(02)00128-3

Protopsaltis, A. (2008). Reading strategies in hypertexts and factors influencing hyperlink selection. *Journal of Educational Multimedia and Hypermedia*, *17*, 191–213.

Salmerón, L., Cañas, J. J., Kintsch, W., & Fajardo, I. (2005). Reading strategies and hypertext comprehension. *Discourse Processes*, *40*(3), 171–191. doi:10.1207/s15326950dp4003_1

Salmerón, L., Kintsch, W., & Cañas, J. J. (2006). Reading strategies and prior knowledge in learning from hypertext. *Memory & Cognition*, *34*(5), 1157–1171. doi:10.3758/BF03193262 PMID:17128614

Salmerón, L., Kintsch, W., & Kintsch, E. (2010). Self-regulation and link selection strategies in hypertext. *Discourse Processes*, *47*(3), 175–211. doi:10.1080/01638530902728280

Seaton, D. T., Bergner, Y., Chuang, I., Mitros, P., & Pritchard, D. E. (2014). Who does what in a massive open online course? *Communications of the ACM*, *57*(4), 58–65. doi:10.1145/2500876

Shapiro, A. M., & Niederhauser, D. (2004). Learning from hypertext: Research issues and findings. In D. H. Jonassen (Ed.), *Handbook of research on educational communications and technology* (pp. 605–620). Mahwah, NJ: Lawrence Erlbaum.

Shih, P.-C., Mate, R., Sanchez, F., & Munoz, D. (2004). Quantifying user navigation patterns: A methodology proposal. Poster presented at the *28th International Congress of Psychology*. Retrieved April 5, 2014 from Smith, P. A. (1996). Towards a practical measure of hypertext usability. *Interacting with computers, 4*, 365-38.

Spärck Jones, K. (1972). A statistical interpretation of term specificity and its application in retrieval. *The Journal of Documentation*, *28*(1), 11–21. doi:10.1108/eb026526

Tavangarian, D., Leypold, M. E., Nölting, K., Röser, M., & Voigt, D. (2004). Is e-learning the solution for individual learning? *Electronic Journal of e-Learning, 2*(2), 273–280.

Vaughan, M., & Dillon, A. (2006). Why structure and genre matter to users of digital information: A longitudinal study with readers of a web-based newspaper. *International Journal of Human-Computer Studies*, *64*(6), 502–526. doi:10.1016/j.ijhcs.2005.11.002

Winne, P. H., & Baker, R. (2013). The potentials of educational data mining for researching metacognition, motivation and self-regulated learning. *Journal of Educational Data Mining, 5*(1), 1–8.

Winne, P. H., & Hadwin, A. F. (1998). Studying as self-regulated learning. In D. J. Hacker, J. Dunlosky, & A. C. Graesser (Eds.), *Metacognition in educational theory and practice* (pp. 277–304). Mahwah, NJ: Lawrence Erlbaum Associates.

Zimmerman, B. J. (2002). Becoming a self-regulated learner: An overview. *Theory into Practice*, *41*(2), 64–70. doi:10.1207/s15430421tip4102_2

Zimmerman, B. J. (2008). Investigating self-regulation and motivation: Historical background, methodological developments, and future prospects. *American Educational Research Journal*, *45*(1), 166–183. doi:10.3102/0002831207312909

## KEY TERMS AND DEFINITIONS

**Computer-Based Assessment (CBA):** Assessment built around the use of a computer (or smart phone or tablet) to collect response data.

**Frequency:** Term (action) frequency captures how salient an action is within a sequence. Sequence frequency refers to the number of sequences that contain a certain action.

**Natural Language Processing (NLP):** A field of computer science, artificial intelligence, and linguistics concerned with the interactions between computers and human (natural) languages.

***N*-Gram:** A contiguous sequence of *n* items from a given sequence of text or speech in the fields of computational linguistics and probability. Items can be phonemes, syllables, letters, words, or actions depending on the application.

**Problem Solving in Technology Rich Environments (PSTRE):** In PIAAC, it refers to the ability to use technology to solve problems and accomplish complex tasks in a contextualized setting (buying concert tickets, organizing multiple work-group meetings using web-based tools, etc.). PSTRE items generally involve interactive item types and are available only on computer.

**Process Data:** Data (often stored in log files) that captures respondents' interactions with the computer separated into discrete (typically time-stamped) actions while working on a computer-based task.

**Sequence Feature Selection:** A process to select the informative ("good") features from a set of potential features that will be further used in data analytic tasks.

**Sequential Pattern Mining:** A type of data mining related to finding statistically relevant patterns between data examples where values are delivered in a sequence.

**Text Mining:** The process of deriving information from text using data analytic techniques.

## ENDNOTES

[1]   Approximately 5,000 people in each country participated in PIAAC, which consists of three constructs: literacy, numeracy, and PSTRE. Only those who had experiences in using computers and agreed to use the computer-based tests participated in the PSTRE session. Hence, the realized sample size for PSTRE is, on average, a quarter of the total sample in each country.

[2]   The name of the specified club member differs by language versions.

# Chapter 30
# Assessment of Task Persistence

**Kristen E. DiCerbo**
*Pearson, USA*

## ABSTRACT

*Task persistence is defined as the continuation of activity in the face of difficulty, obstacles, and/or failure. It has been linked to educational achievement, educational attainment, and occupation outcomes. A number of different psychological approaches attempt to explain individual and situational differences in persistence and there is mounting evidence that interventions can be implemented to increase persistence. New technological capabilities offer the opportunity to seamlessly gather evidence about persistence from individuals' interactions in digital environments. Two examples of assessment of persistence in digital games are presented. Both demonstrate the ability to gather information without interruption of activity and the use of in-game actions as evidence. They also both require consideration of the student/player model, task model, and evidence models. A design pattern outlining each of these elements is presented for use by those considering assessment of persistence in digital environments.*

## INTRODUCTION

Task persistence is most simply defined as continuing with a task despite obstacles, difficulty, and/or failure. In the cognitive literature, persistence is generally classified as an element of executive function and thought to be related to self-regulated attention and response inhibition (Schmeichel, 2007). In the temperament literature, persistence is viewed as a biologically-based tendency to persevere in conditions of partially reinforced behavior, resisting extinction (Cloninger, Svrakic, & Przybeck, 1993). In personality literature, it is described as an aspect of conscientiousness (Shute

& Ventura, 2013), related to but not identical to grit (Duckworth, Peterson, Matthews, & Kelly, 2007). In the motivation literature, persistence is related to mastery goals and a growth mindset in which failure is viewed as an opportunity to learn, rather than evidence of personal shortcomings (Dweck, 2006).

It could be argued that persistence in not a "new" skill in the 21st century workplace, given that there was a historical review of the literature on measurement of persistence written in 1939 (Ryans, 1939). However, it is often enumerated in lists and discussions of 21st century skills and attributes (Fadel, 2011; Pellegrino & Hilton, 2012),

DOI: 10.4018/978-1-4666-9441-5.ch030

because jobs in the 21st century are increasingly complex, requiring sustained application of effort to complete multifaceted tasks (Andersson & Bergman, 2011).

Task persistence is of particular interest and importance because it has been shown to be predictive of many academic and employment outcomes, including adult educational attainment, income, and occupational level (Andersson & Bergman, 2011). The relationship between persistence and academic achievement has been repeatedly documented (Boe, May, & Boruch, 2002; Deater-Deckard, Petrill, Thompson, & DeThorne, 2005; McClelland, Acock, Piccinin, Rhea, & Stallings, 2013). It is hypothesized that willingness and ability to persist or persevere increases an individual's opportunities to learn from the environment (Sigman, Cohen, Beckwith, & Topinka, 1987).

This chapter will begin with a review of definitions of task persistence from multiple theoretical perspectives. The second section will explore the relationship between task persistence and educational and occupational outcomes. A third section will examine evidence for interventions that impact an individual's persistence.

The fourth section will review methods of assessment of persistence, focusing on how new technological capabilities allow us to gather evidence about persistence seamlessly from individuals' interactions in digital environments. It will specifically explore two projects that used log file data from game play to assess persistence, leading to a discussion of issues related to game-based assessment. Games potentially provide a means to assess 21$^{st}$ century skills that are difficult to assess via traditional means. A final section will propose a design pattern for the assessment of persistence in digital environments that can help those interested in creating performance-based measures of persistence consider the important elements of definition, tasks, and evidence.

# DEFINITION OF PERSISTENCE

Given a fairly simple definition of persistence as the continuation of an activity in the face of difficulty or failure, it is interesting to note the number of different conceptualizations and explanations for its presence or absence. This section will review explanations of persistence from cognitive, temperament, personality, and motivational perspectives.

## Cognitive Perspective

From a cognitive perspective, persistence is related to executive control and self-regulation. Persisting at a task requires executive control processes including focusing attention, inhibiting the impulse to give up, and updating working memory to meet the requirements of a task (Schmeichel, 2007). Executive control processes are theorized to control the selection, initiation, execution, and termination of tasks (Logan, 1985; Meyer & Kieras, 1997; Shiffrin & Schneider, 1977). In the cognitive perspective, persistence is closely linked with sustained attention, or the ability to engage attention on a task for an extended period of time despite distracting external or internal stimuli. Research suggests that ability to sustain attention is related to broad executive control measures rather than individual working memory or response inhibition measures by themselves (Unsworth, Redick, Lakey, & Young, 2010).

Interestingly, research suggests that the capacity for executive control is not constant and that prior efforts requiring significant levels of executive control can reduce the ability to exercise those resources in the immediate future (Schmeichel, 2007). For example, people who forced themselves to eat radishes rather than chocolate chip cookies subsequently quit faster on unsolvable puzzles than those who did not have to resist eating the cookies (Baumeister, Bratslavsky, Muraven, &

Tice, 1998). This research suggests that variations in persistence might be due not only to individual differences in executive functioning, but also recent deployment of those resources.

## Temperament Perspective

Much modern research on childhood temperament stems from the work of Thomas, Chess, and colleagues (Thomas & Chess, 1977). Researchers in this tradition most often espouse a nine-dimension model of temperament that emerged from clinical observation: activity, adaptability, approach/withdrawal, distractibility, emotional intensity, mood, rhythmicity, threshold, and persistence (Thomas, Chess, & Birch, 1968). Empirical efforts to verify these dimensions have had mixed results (Presley & Martin, 1994), however the construct of task persistence has repeatedly emerged. In Presley & Martin's (1994) factor analysis of temperament items, the items that fell on the factor they labeled task persistence related to giving up quickly when faced with difficulty and working on projects until they are complete.

Cloninger and colleagues (Cloninger et al., 1993) proposed a psychobiological theory of temperament and character with four dimensions of temperament and three dimensions of character. Extensive work with their Temperament and Character Inventory has yielded continued support for persistence as one of the four temperament dimensions (along with reactions to reward, avoiding aversive stimuli, and novelty seeking). In this work, persistence is operationalized as persevering with partially reinforced behavior and resistance to extinction of past conditioning. In other words, persistent individuals are those who continue a behavior even when it is not reinforced. Cloninger views temperament as an individual difference in heritable traits while character is less biologically based. Support for a biological foundation for persistence is found in a functional MRI study that revealed a correlation between high persistence scores and activity in a specific brain circuit related to reward seeking behavior (Gusnard et al., 2003).

The study also suggested that persistence may be related to the ability to generate and maintain arousal and motivation internally, in the absence of immediate external reward. The authors speculate, based on the location of the brain circuits activated, that persistence may serve to moderate between the emotion-driving limbic system and the rational prefrontal cortex by holding incentive information in memory when there is a delay in goal achievement. In this psychobiological view temperament and character together account for some (but not all) personality characteristics (Cloninger, 2003).

## Personality Perspective

In personality literature, descriptions of taxonomies begin with the Five Factor Model of personality: openness, conscientiousness, extraversion, agreeableness, and neuroticism (McCrae & Costa, 1987). There is extensive research and debate about facets that make up each of these larger factors. Work on the conscientiousness factor has yielded a number of attempts to delineate facets of conscientiousness, each coming to somewhat different conclusions (MacCann, Duckworth, & Roberts, 2009). Initial work often included the narrow trait of achievement, which included adopting high standards for performance and working to accomplish goals (Dudley, Orvis, Lebiecki, & Cortina, 2006). This trait is generally defined in ways that contain the idea of continuing action to complete a task but generally also include elements of standards of performance (Hough, 1992; Perry, Hunter, Witt, & Harris, 2010) and often do not explicitly include the idea of working in the face of frustration.

More recently, using factor analytic techniques on full sentence items (instead of adjective lists) with adolescents, one group of researchers (Mac-

Cann et al., 2009) has posited a separate narrow facet of conscientiousness that they name perseverance made up of items such as "I give up easily." Interestingly, this factor had a correlation of .68 with conscientiousness but also -.55 correlation with Neuroticism.

## Grit

There has been significant interest recently around the construct of grit, defined as "perseverance and passion for long term goals" (Duckworth et al., 2007) It involves continually pursuing a goal despite failure and sustained commitment in the face of adversity. The key element of grit, however, is the pursuit of a goal *over the long term*. This is apparent in self-report instruments developed to measure grit like the Short Grit Scale (Duckworth & Quinn, 2009) which contains items such as "I have achieved a goal that took years of work," and "My interests change from year to year." The short-term task persistence discussed in this chapter could be viewed as a necessary but not sufficient component of grit. It captures the continued effort on a given task when faced with difficulty. Grit would require repeated examples of task persistence along with consistency of interest.

## Motivation Perspective

An alternative to the view that persistence is a personality trait is the view that persistence is a result of motivation (Elliott & Dweck, 1988), and related mindsets (Dweck, 2006). Motivation research has revealed two different classes of goals: learning goals (sometimes called mastery goals), in which an individual seeks to master something new, and performance goals, in which an individual seeks to gain favorable evaluations of their competence (or avoid negative evaluations) (Elliott & Dweck, 1988). In this framework, persistence is more likely to occur in combination with learning goals, which are aligned with interest in a task and enjoyment of an effort, rather than

with performance goals, in which effort in the face of uncertainty about eventual achievement is aversive. For someone with a goal of appearing intelligent (or not appearing less intelligent), failures or challenges are viewed as threatening due to the potential impact of making errors on others' views of their competence. Alternately, those with learning/mastery goals are more likely to enjoy challenging tasks and sustain involvement in learning (Ames & Archer, 1988).

Dweck describes two mindsets: fixed and growth. Those with a fixed mindset believe that their basic qualities, such as intelligence, talents, aptitudes, and temperament are stable or fixed. Those with a growth mindset believe that these things can be changed through effort and experience. In this model, those with a fixed mindset see challenges and failure as signs of low ability, something that cannot be changed, so there is nothing to be gained by continuing to try to solve the difficult problem. In this mindset, intelligence is an entity, and challenging tasks can be seen as a threat to the perception of one's intelligence (Yeager & Dweck, 2012). Effort is seen as a signal that one lacks natural intelligence. Alternately, those with a growth mindset see struggle as a necessary part of advancement, so continuing to work on difficult problems is viewed as a path to improvement. In the growth mindset, intelligence is viewed as incremental and challenges are seen as being helpful and offering the opportunity to improve (Yeager & Dweck, 2012).

Based on this approach, researchers at the Carnegie Foundation developed the concept of productive persistence, which they define as students continuing to put forth effort during challenges and using effective strategies when they do so (Silva & White, 2013). The addition of the second aspect of using effective strategies makes this a somewhat different concept than task persistence described here. However, in their aim to develop interventions to improve the success of developmental math students, they have identified primary drivers of productive persistence as: 1) having skills, habits, and know-how to succeed in college, 2) feeling socially tied to peers, faculty, and the course, 3) believing the course has value, 4) believing they are capable of learning math, and 5) faculty supporting students' skills and mindsets. Researchers on the project are developing interventions in these five areas that they believe will change productive persistence, and thereby improve course completion and achievement. Further discussion of interventions to impact persistence will be discussed later in the chapter.

Different types of mindset have been suggested to play a role in cultural difference in classrooms across countries. Stevenson and Stigler (1994) gave an impossible math problem to American and Japanese students. They reported that the American students worked on it less than 30 seconds on average while the Japanese students worked for an hour. Through further research, they attribute this difference to differences in belief about effort and struggle. They found that students in Japanese culture learn that continuing in the face of difficulty is a chance to demonstrate their ability to persevere to eventual success while students in American culture believe that struggle may be a sign that they lack the ability to learn.

A different conceptualization of mindset has been offered by Gollwitzer and colleagues in describing how individuals progress in the process of achieving goals (Gollwitzer & Bayer, 1999). They propose the concepts of a deliberative and an implemental mindset and posit that individuals move back and forth between them as they work towards a goal. They break activities down into a predecisional phase, in which a person is choosing a goal from among various possible goals, and a postdecisional phase when the goal has been decided upon and planning and execution towards that goal are underway. The deliberative mindset should be dominant in the predecisional phase as it is characterized by an open-mindedness to available information, systematic, objective analysis of the chances of meeting a goal, and

the estimation of the desirability of reaching a goal. In the postdecisional phase, the implemental mindset should dominate as it is characterized by creating plans for action, an overrepresentation of the desirability of a goal, and a more positive perception of a goal's feasibility.

In this framework, the feasibility and desirability of goals is the important determinant of persistence. In an experiment to determine the effects of implemental and deliberative mindsets on persistence, Brandstätter and Frank (2002) created conditions in which goals were feasible but not desirable or desirable but not feasible. They then induced either deliberative or implemental mindsets in individuals by framing the task as predecisional or postdecisional. Those in the implemental mindset persisted longer on the tasks than those in a deliberative mindset, suggesting perceptions of desirability and feasibility common in the implemental mindset may be an explanation for persistence.

## PERSISTENCE AND OUTCOMES

Interest in persistence is high because of its positive relationship to many educational and occupational outcomes, including adult educational attainment, income, and occupational level (Andersson & Bergman, 2011). The relationship between persistence and academic achievement has been repeatedly documented (Boe et al., 2002; Deater-Deckard et al., 2005; McClelland et al., 2012). Boe et al. (2002) examined whether cross-national differences in math and science achievement on the Third International Mathematics and Science Study (TIMMS) could be partially explained by task persistence. They created a persistence measure by examining the number of background questions answered on the TIMSS. Approximately 53% of variability in math achievement across nations, 22% of variability between classrooms within nations, and 7% of variability between students within classrooms could be attributed to persistence scores. Similar results were seen for science, making this persistence measure one of the strongest predictors of national differences in math and science achievement.

In a longitudinal study, Andersson & Bergman (2011) analyzed the relationship between teachers' ratings of student persistence at age 13 and educational and occupational outcomes at age 43. They report that for men, higher levels of task persistence were related to higher income and occupational level, after controlling for multiple other variables, including educational attainment. In women, educational attainment mediated the effect of persistence on income and occupational level. In other words, once adult educational attainment was taken into account, persistence at age 13 no longer had a significant effect on occupational outcomes for women. For both women and men, persistence at age 13 was related to grades at age 16, to the extent that a one standard deviation increase in persistence resulted in a .19 standard deviation increase in GPA, the equivalent of another year of schooling.

It is not just persistence with academic tasks that predicts persistence with other academic tasks. Two-year-olds who spent more time trying to open a plexiglass box containing a toy were found to have fewer behavior problems and were more likely to complete school work at age 5 (Sigman et al., 1987). McClelland et al. (2012) used parents' ratings of their children at age 4 on five items relating to attention span-persistence to predict educational outcomes. The items centered mostly on play, for example, "Plays with a single toy for long periods of time" and "With a difficulty toy, child gives up easily." They report that parents' ratings of their children's persistence with difficult toys predicted reading and math skills at age 21 and odds of college completion by age 25. Being rated one standard deviation higher on early attention span-persistence at age 4 increased the odds of completing college at age 25 by 48.7%.

These effects were not mediated by achievement at age 7, suggesting a direct relationship between persistence and later educational outcomes.

It is hypothesized that willingness and ability to persist or persevere increases an individual's opportunities to learn from the environment (Sigman et al., 1987). Interestingly, Teng (2011) attempted to relate personality characteristics to flow. Flow is generally defined as the state of total concentration that occurs when all of an individual's attentional resources are devoted to a task, creating a feeling of total absorption (Nakamura & Csikszentmihalyi, 2002). In the flow state, action seems effortless, even when a great deal of physical or mental energy is exerted. Using a measure associated with Cloninger's factors and a self-report measure of flow, Teng reports a significant relationship between persistence and flow. Although the links between flow and learning are still being developed (Shernoff & Csikszentmihalyi, 2009), this is one path that may contribute to the relationship between persistence and learning.

It should be noted that some cross-sectional studies have found the relationship between persistence and academic achievement to be curvilinear (Carrier & Williams, 1988; Goldman, Hudson, & Daharsh, 1973), indicating that there may be a point at which continuing to persist on a task is detrimental. For example, in the Carrier and Williams (1988) study, participants were placed in four groups based on their persistence in an introductory activity. Following an instructional intervention, scores on a post-test were compared. Both the lowest and highest persistence groups performed worse on the post-test than the two middle groups. In addition, while research on the relationship between persistence and psychological disorders revealed that high persistence is related to a decrease in mood disorders, it is also related to an increase in anxiety disorders (Cloninger, Zohar, Hirschmann, & Dahan, 2012). High persistence appears to increase positive constructs such as happiness, enthusiasm, attention, and activity at the same time it is related to an increase in negative feelings of distress, fear, guilt, and shame. We should be aware that more persistence is not always better.

## INTERVENTION TO INCREASE PERSISTENCE

Given the differing conceptualizations of persistence described above, an interesting question becomes whether persistence can be changed. Is persistence a personality trait that is relatively immutable or is it something we can target with intervention to bring it toward levels associated with good educational and occupational outcomes? Results of efforts to increase persistence have so far been mixed. Ostrow, Schultz, and Arroyo (n.d.), for example, examined the effects of messages meant to target mindset on persistence in an intelligent math tutor with 765 students. They presented both general attribution messages and messages following incorrect answers in six different ways. General attribution messages included things like, "Did you know what when we practice to learn new math skills our brain grows and gets stronger?" Methods of delivery included various combinations of pedagogical agents, static images, sound, and text. Messages following incorrect answers included statements such as, "Making a mistake is not a bad thing. It's what learning is all about!" None of the conditions improved student persistence over the control for the overall sample. However, struggling students showed an increase in persistence when given the messages. The dependent measure of the study was number of problems completed, which is different from the time spent on difficult or impossible problems that many studies use. Therefore, it may be that participants in the study overall were not experiencing sufficient challenge to get a good assessment of their persistence. That said, the impact on struggling students is consistent with

previous research showing warnings given to students indicating that they did not appear to be giving their best efforts improved test performance (Wise, Bhola, & Yang, 2006).

Kamins & Dweck (1999) hypothesized that feedback type would impact persistence. Specifically, they theorized that person- or trait-related feedback would encourage learners to measure themselves by their performance, encouraging a fixed mindset, likely resulting in lowered persistence. Alternately, process feedback focused on strategy or effort should foster a more growth mindset with learning/mastery goals, and therefore greater persistence. In two randomized control trials examining the impact of different feedback types on persistence, the researchers had 67 and 64 kindergarten children respectively role-play a task (using a doll as themselves) on which they either failed (study 1) or succeeded (study 2). After each task, the children received one of three types of feedback: person (e.g., "I'm very disappointed in you"), outcome ("That's not the right way to do it"), or process ("The blocks are all crooked"). The students were then asked whether they would try the task again and whether they could generate new strategies for success. The researchers found that children who received person-centered feedback demonstrated lower persistence than those in the process feedback group on the subsequent task. That is, those with process feedback were more likely to try a failed problem again and generate strategies for overcoming a setback. A number of studies have found similar links between praise, mindset, persistence, and ultimately performance (Gunderson et al., 2013; Mueller & Dweck, 1998; Shute, 2008).

Apart from feedback received from others, learners may also receive feedback from the frequency of their own successes. Kennelly, Dietz, and Benson (1985) examined the effects of three different success-failure schedules on learners' persistence with 35 male special education students aged 9-15 years. They manipulated success schedules on mathematics problems such that students were successful 100%, 76.9%, or 46.2% of the time. Only the 76.9% condition increased the attribution of failures to lack of effort and improved persistence on later tasks when faced with failure. The authors hypothesize that learners are likely to attribute an infrequent event (like failing 24% of the time) to an unstable cause (lack of effort) but attribute frequent events (like failing more than half the time) to stable causes (like lack of ability). This research would suggest that the experience of the learner should be considered when measuring persistence and could be manipulated to increase persistence.

The introduction of technology offers the opportunity to control praise, challenge, and success levels in real time as students interact with digital environments. Researchers modified an educational puzzle game called Refraction in an attempt to increase persistence through messaging aimed at mindset (O'Rourke, Haimovitz, Ballweber, Dweck, & Popović, 2014). They created a reward system in the game called Brain Points that rewarded effort, use of strategy, and incremental progress. Children earned Brain Points while they are working to solve levels. Researchers used a combination of four metrics to define behaviors that earned points. The new hypothesis metric captured each new idea tried. The board cleared metric was triggered by actions that indicated the player stepping back to consider the puzzle from a fresh perspective. The math metric captured progress using new mathematical procedures. Finally, the moves metric was triggered each time the player made ten distinct moves. When Brain Points were earned, they triggered an animated brain with messages such as, "Hey, did you know when you work hard and struggle, your brain gets smarter and stronger?" The researchers also added an adaptive level progression such that players would be faced with difficult or challenging tasks, necessary to measure persistence. Persistence was measured by the amount of time spent playing the game and the number of levels played. Data were gathered from 15,491 anonymous players,

half in the control condition (Refraction without Brain Points) and half with the experimental Brain Points. Children in the condition with the Brain Points both played the game longer and completed more levels. It therefore appears promising that technological interventions can be used to impact persistence.

While the evidence of intervention to increase persistence looks promising, it is also clear that there are a number of different methods for measuring persistence, which may affect both the results of research and future efforts to implement intervention programs. The studies reviewed here used measures including: time spent on a task, attempting a task, levels played, and problems completed. The remainder of this chapter addresses issues of the assessment of persistence.

## ASSESSMENT OF PERSISTENCE

### Traditional Measures

There is a long history of assessing psychological constructs via rating scales. In various studies, researchers who rely on survey measures of persistence included questions such as "fails to finish things" and "cannot concentrate or pay attention for long" (Deater-Deckard et al., 2005), "Child persists at a task until successful, "Child gives up easily when difficulties are encountered" and "With a difficult toy, child gives up quite easily" (McClelland et al., 2012), and "When I fail at something, I am willing to try again and again forever" (Lufi & Cohen, 1987). There is a long history of measuring persistence through rating scales. Those from the temperament approach can look to Cloninger's Temperament and Character Inventory (Cloninger, 2003). Those who have a personality-based approach can select items from the International Personality Item Pool. Of course rating scale items are subject to many human biases in making decisions under uncertainty (Tversky & Kahneman, 1982). In addition, cultural factors can impact responses through things like acquiescence and extreme response styles that vary by culture (Van Herk, Poortinga, & Verhallen, 2004).

An alternative to rating scales is direct observation. When directly observing behavior, some have counted the number of times a task was attempted (Foll, Rascle, & Higgins, 2006) while others measured the amount of time during which a child exhibits task-directed behavior (Sigman et al., 1987). While these methods are appropriate for research studies, they are not scalable to assess persistence in a large sample or population. In important contrast between rating scales and observation lies in the use of deduction versus induction. Rating scale measurement of persistence focuses on persistence broadly, across challenging tasks in general. That requires generalizing from a broad measure to specific situations to predict persistence, or deduction. Direct observation of persistence focuses on specific tasks and situations, which requires generalizing from specific situations to other situations, or induction.

## Invisible Assessment

A major affordance of technology is its ability to capture data from individuals as they interact in digital environments without interrupting the natural activity of the individual (DiCerbo & Behrens, 2012; DiCerbo & Behrens, 2014). With its relatively straightforward behavioral operationalization, persistence is a prime candidate for measurement via invisible or stealth assessment. Shute coined the term stealth assessment to describe the process of using information from learners' actions with digital learning environments to make inferences about their knowledge, skills, and attributes (Shute, 2011). Rather than intrusive assessments that are not connected to the learning environment, stealth assessment unobtrusively gathers data from students' everyday interactions with the instructional environment. Proponents of stealth assessment argue that it allows for the assessment of skills that are difficult

to assess with traditional assessment tools, reduces time spent on assessment at the expense of other activity (particularly in learning environments), and direct observation of behavior in context. Two independent examples of the assessment of persistence in games using a stealth assessment approach can be found in DiCerbo (2014) and Ventura & Shute (2013).

## Persistence toward a Goal: Poptropica

DiCerbo (2014) investigated player persistence in Poptropica® (www.poptropica.com), a virtual world in which players explore "islands" with various themes and overarching quests that players can choose to fulfill. Players choose which islands to visit and navigate the world by walking, jumping and flipping. The quests generally involve 25 or more steps, such as collecting and using items, usually completed in a particular order. For example, in Vampire's Curse Island, the player must rescue her friend Katya who has been kidnapped by Count Bram. In order to do this, she must navigate to the Count's castle (eluding wolves on the way), discover the potion for defeating the vampire, identify and mix the potion ingredients, hit the vampire with a potion-tipped arrow from a crossbow, and then find Katya. Apart from the quests, players can talk to other players in highly scripted chats, play arcade-style games head-to-head and spend time creating and modifying their avatar. The game is designed for children ages 6-14.

The backend of the game captures time-stamped event data for each player. Events include, for example, the completion of quest-related steps, modifying avatars, collecting objects, and entering new locations. On an average day 350,000 players generate 80 million event lines. Players can play the game anonymously and for free or, with purchase of a membership, and gain access to premium features such as early access to new quests.

In Poptropica, fewer than 10% of those beginning quests go on to complete them and the number of YouTube walkthroughs and hint pages published by players suggest that the quests are challenging to solve. Therefore, the requirement of having difficult or frustrating tasks was met. In order to measure the response to this difficulty, a number of potential indicators were considered.

In seeking to create a measure of persistence, researchers examined log files of 892 players aged 6-14 years. Data were from anonymous players visiting the site so no information was available about the environment in which they were playing (for example school versus home), limiting generalization of the results of this study to other players. Initial investigations presented an obstacle to the researchers as the potential indicators did not seem to correlate as expected. Examination of the log files and discussions with the game designers led to the realization that different players of the game likely had differing goals. This yielded the key insight that persistence implies the pursuit of a goal. Research by Bartle (Bartle, 1996) on Multi-User Dungeons identified four different types of player goals: achievement (reaching game goals), exploration (finding out as much as they can about how the virtual world works), socializing (interacting with other players), and imposition on others (disrupting play of others).

These various goals influence how different observed behavior might be interpreted. For example, Sabourin and colleagues (Sabourin, Rowe, Mott, & Lester, 2011) describe off-task behavior as "spending too much time in a location irrelevant to the task" (p. 2). However, if a student's goal is exploration of the entire space, this may not be irrelevant to their perceived task, and perhaps would be classified as on-task behavior. Even if the goal of a game is clearly defined for players, they may choose to adopt their own goals. If the interest is in using evidence from the game to assess constructs such as persistence, caution should be taken so as not to identify a student as lacking persistence when in fact they were very

persistently pursuing a different goal. As learning environments become more open and attempts to make inferences about more player characteristics from these free-flowing activities become more common, it becomes more important to be able to identify players' goals.

Therefore, before pursuing further definition of the indicators of persistence, DiCerbo and Kidwai (2012) used classification and regression tree analysis to develop rules by which to classify players by their goals. Then, a sample of players who were pursuing the goal of completing quests (as opposed to enhancing their avatar or socializing with friends) was selected for further analysis.

Once a more homogenous sample (at least in terms of goal) was established, selection of indicators of persistence proceeded more smoothly. Four potential indicators from each quest were investigated: time spent on quest events, number of quest events completed, maximum time spent on an individual quest event successfully completed, and time spent on the last event prior to quitting the island (unsuccessful quest event). Data was not captured in the game in a way that would allow for a count of number of attempts after failure; this could be inferred only based on the time from the completion of one event to the completion of the next event. Following analysis of relationships between variables, two indicators per quest, the total time spent on quest-related events and the number of quest events completed, were selected as evidence of persistence. These indicators were computed from the log files for each of the three quests each player attempted to "seriously" complete.

A confirmatory factor analysis was run in order to evaluate whether there a common factor explained variance across quest indicators and across quests. A model was specified with the two indicators of persistence from each of the three islands loading onto a single factor. The error terms for the pairs of indicators from the same island were each correlated because these measures are not independent (completing more events requires more time). Good fit was achieved for the model with the original sample and a separate sample.

Using this factor structure, factor scores can be computed for individuals, resulting in a persistence score. The internal consistency reliability of these scores, as measured by alpha, was .87. In addition, there was a general upward trend in scores across grades, rising from first grade to ninth grade, for a change of .72 deviations across the nine grades, as would be expected over the ages spanned by these grades (Hartshorne, May, & Maller, 1929; Lufi & Cohen, 1987).

## Persistence Validated: Physics Playground

While the above example demonstrates evidence of internal consistency, the anonymous nature of Poptropica play prevented validation of the persistence measure with external measures of persistence. Such a validation was accomplished by Ventura and Shute (Ventura & Shute, 2013) using a game called Physics Playground (http://www.empiricalgames.org/projects.html#). Physics Playground is a two-dimensional computer-based game that requires the player to guide a green ball to a red balloon. The player uses the mouse to draw simple machines (levers, ramps, pendulums, and springboards) on the screen. The objects "come to life" once the machine is drawn and the solution is tested to see if the machine drawn gets the ball to the balloon. Students have the opportunity to redraw over and over until they are successful. Everything obeys the basic rules of physics relating to gravity and Newton's three laws of motion. Difficulty of the problems depends on the position of the ball and balloon, obstacles in the way, and the number of machines required to solve the problem.

The game captures a variety of information about each attempt, including: time spent on the level in seconds, number of "restarts" of the level, total number of objects used in a solution attempt, whether it was ultimately solved, and trajectory of the ball in X,Y coordinate space. Each of these variables provides useful information about students' gameplay behaviors which can then be used to make inferences about how well they are doing in the game, their persistence, their creativity, and their current understanding of qualitative physics. For example, if most players use a springboard and ramp to get the ball to the balloon, but a small group uses a lever, the assessment authors might use that as evidence to estimate players' level of creativity. In addition, physics knowledge, as estimated by the completion of problems using fewer than three machines, was related to physics knowledge as measured by a paper-and-pencil test. Playing the game for four hours across 1.5 weeks led to improved understanding of physics, demonstrating how both learning and assessment took place in the same activity by the learner.

In order to measure persistence in the game, Ventura and colleagues (Ventura, Shute, & Zhao, 2013; Ventura, Shute, & Small, 2014) focused on two indicators: time spent on solved problems and time spent on unsolved problems in samples of 70 8th and 9th graders and 102 undergraduate students. As opposed to the anonymous play of the Poptropica sample, students in both samples were aware they were participating in a research study by taking a variety of assessments and playing a game. Players completed performance-based measures of persistence, self-report measures, and played the game. The total amount of time spent on unsolved problems, the total amount of time spent on solved problems with "Silver" solutions (solved but not optimally), and the total amount of time spent on "Gold" solutions (optimally solved) were computed.

They compared scores from the game-based measure of persistence to an external performance-based measure and also to a self-report of persistence. The external measure consisted of anagrams and picture comparisons, with seven easy tasks and seven impossible tasks. In the impossible anagram tasks the letters of the anagram did not form a word while in the impossible picture comparison task, the participants were told to find four differences between pictures when there were only three. The score for the task is the amount of time spent on impossible items. In addition eight self-report Likert-type items intending to measure persistence were taken from the International Personality Item Pool.

The performance-based measure of persistence correlated with the time spent on unsolved and silver solution problems, which were combined with the reasoning that both represented attempts that were not completely successful. Interestingly, the time spent on gold solution problems was not related to the performance-based measure of persistence. In part, this may be because for those achieving gold solutions the problems were not challenging enough to elicit persistence. The authors report that the relationship between the game-based measure and the performance-based measure was stronger among players who achieved fewer gold and silver solutions. It may be that the game called for persistence among this group more than it did among the higher achieving group.

The performance-based and game-based measures of persistence were correlated with post-game physics knowledge even after controlling for pre-game knowledge, game experience, gender, and enjoyment of the game. However, the self-report of persistence was not correlated with either the performance-based or game-based measure of persistence, nor was it correlated with post-game physics knowledge. This may not be surprising given the existing research on differences between self-report and behavioral observation (McCroskey, 2009), but deserves consideration regarding why there is a difference between self-perception and behavioral observation.

As outlined in the *Standards for Educational and Psychological Testing* (American Educational Research Association, American Psychological Association, National Council for Measurement in Education, 2014), establishing validity requires multiple sources of evidence: content coverage, response processes, internal structure, relations

to other variables, and consequences. It is important to note that validity is a property of the interpretation for use of an assessment, not of the assessment itself. In the case of both Poptropica and Newton's Playground, the use of the assessment is as a low-stakes, formative measure. Both games have evidence based on internal structure from the factor analysis, suggesting a single factor accounts for significant shared variance among the indicators. Unlike many academic constructs, persistence is a relatively simple construct, so content coverage requires mostly repeated measures of continued effort in response to failure. Both Poptropica and Physics Playground appear to have this, but a common method of verifying this is independent expert review, which has not yet been done. Newton's Playground adds evidence from relations to other variables, including other measures of persistence and measures of learning. Interestingly, the use of existing measures of the same construct can present a challenge to game-based assessment. Proponents of game-based assessment argue that it can assess constructs that are difficult to assess in other ways, meaning they would expect the results to be different from existing measures. If the correlations were high, there would not be the need for new measures. In this case, we might expect moderate correlations with measures of the same construct, and look at patterns of relationships with other related constructs. If those correlations with other constructs are in the pattern hypothesized, that would provide further validity evidence.

## Game-Based Assessment

A major challenge in game-based assessment arises from creating what Evidence-Centered Design (ECD; Mislevy, Steinberg, & Almond, 2002) refers to as the measurement model. ECD is a framework that seeks to define the claims we wish to make with an assessment, the behaviors that would provide evidence for those claims, and the tasks or activities that would elicit those behaviors. Assessment design requires the specification of a student model, specifying the constructs of interest, a task model, specifying the activity to be performed, and an evidence model to link the two. The evidence model consists of two parts: the scoring model and the measurement model. Both present new challenges in game-based assessment.

The scoring model specifies which elements of a work product should be extracted and what rules applied to create observable evidence. In a multiple choice test, this is a simple task. Extract the selected response and apply the simple rule, "If the selected answer equals the correct answer in the key, then correct, otherwise incorrect." In a game log, it is much less obvious what information should be extracted and the rules do not involve being correct or incorrect. In the example of persistence and many 21$^{st}$ century skills, we are interested in levels of behavior, not correctness of a response. If a game is designed from scratch as an assessment, these considerations should be part of the design process. The complexity increases when a game and accompanying data structures already exist and a scoring model is being retrofitted to them. In the case of the Poptropica work, the model was retrofitted. As an example of the challenge this created, it would have been ideal to have a record of each failed attempt at a task, but the data definitions only recorded successful attempts. Therefore, rather than extract counts of failure from the log, the researchers had to extract time between successes. Time in digital environments always contains some error from individuals doing multiple tasks, for example, leaving to check email or instant message. The definition of these observations is key to valid assessment.

Once the scoring model is created, it is then often necessary to create measurement models to aggregate the observable evidence in ways that tell us about latent constructs. The Poptropica work employed factor analysis to do this. Game data present many challenges to traditional assessment models, such as Item Response Theory (Hamble-ton, Swaminathan, & Rogers, 1991), because the evidence pieces are not independent from each other and are often related to multiple constructs. In addition, many of these models were initially created around binary evidence (present versus not present, correct versus incorrect). As a result, many researchers have turned to Bayesian Networks (BN; Pearl, 1988) as a method for accumulating data from games (Mislevy et al., 2014; Shute & Ventura, 2013). BNs are flexible in the kinds of relationships that can be modeled and allow for rapid updating of beliefs about the constructs of interest as evidence arrives, as might be required for making real time decisions in game play. They require categorical indicators, but not necessarily binary, so evidence like counts of activities and time taken can be included in the models.

Measurement models determine the ways we make inferences about constructs. For example, the Poptropica model described above used standardized measures as inputs and yield a factor score that can be interpreted only in relation to the mean and standard deviation of the score, the performance of others. Alternately, BNs can be used to identify the probability that a learner is at a particular level of mastery of a construct or at a given level of a learning progression (Mislevy et al., 2014). For example, if there are three levels of a progression, probability tables are constructed to estimate the likelihood that learners at different levels will display various behaviors. Then, when these behaviors are observed, they can be used to update the probabilities that learners are at a given level of the learning progression. In the case of persistence, there are not clear qualitative categories. This could be addressed by creating generic "high," "medium," and "low" designations, but there is no research to support how these would be defined, so the BN approach was not used in this case. Ventura and Shute (2013) created a continuous measure based on accumulated time. This is actually an observed metric and does not attempt to make an inference to a latent construct.

Once the scoring and measurement models are designed, concerns about psychometric rigor deserve to be examined in further detail. To quote Samuel Messick (1994), "such basic assessment issues as validity, reliability, comparability, and fairness need to be uniformly addressed for all assessments because they are not just measurement principles, they are social values that have meaning and force outside of measurement wherever evaluative judgments and decisions are made" (p. 13). As described above, evidence for validity in game-based assessment can fairly easily follow the validity evidence already established by measurement experts. The same is not true for measures of reliability. Many of the techniques for measuring reliability have been developed in the context of high stakes assessment, consisting of discrete items specifically designed to assess a single construct, scored as correct or incorrect. As a result, in many cases, the models and techniques for estimation of particular types of reliability and validity evidence will need revision in order to be applicable for new types of activity and data.

For example, the traditional notion of test-retest reliability is that if test scores are stable, the measure should yield the same result when given multiple times under similar conditions. Therefore, a common method of assessing reliability is to give the same test on multiple occasions, often 30 or 60 days apart, and compute the correlation between the scores. Most descriptions of test-retest reliability caution that testing must be done on individuals who are not expected to change on the trait under measurement, since the goal is to see if the assessment produces the same result. However, as a student plays through a game, they are provided with feedback and tasks specifically designed to increase their skill. The second time they play through the game, we would expect higher scores. To complicate matters further, in many digital environments, the learner will have a different experience on a second attempt due to adaptivity resulting from their differing responses. Therefore, traditional measures and methods of assessing test-retest reliability need to be reconsidered, examining, for example, the potential of adding a learning parameter to the analysis. Similarly, generalizability theory, which seeks to quantify the error associated with various elements of the assessment situation (items, raters, occasions), requires learners to take either the same items or the same forms (sets of items), neither of which may happen in a game setting. Overall, many of the psychometric methods used to define reliability need translation for application in game-based assessment.

The lack of standardization in the presentation activities in classroom-based formative assessments makes it difficult to ensure students are actually reaching desired skill levels. In addition, it is difficult to assess many 21st century skills with traditional paper-and-pencil methods. Game-based assessments can address both of these concerns, controlling presentation, responses, and scoring across classrooms, schools, and districts. They also can provide problems in a variety of contexts and the ability to collect a wide variety of observations of student activity. As noted above, work remains to be done in addressing the psychometric rigor of these assessments, including the development of new methods for assessing some types of validity and reliability constructs. Given this state of the research, they are best used in a low-stakes, formative manner. Information from a game-based assessment can be used by parents, teachers, and students, combined with their own observations, as guidance for classroom-based intervention.

# A DESIGN PATTERN FOR ASSESSMENT OF PERSISTENCE

Technology enables us to assess constructs such as persistence in new ways. Rather than relying on rating scales, which are always subject to bias, or in-person observations, which are not scalable, we can gather data from large numbers of individuals and automatically extract and score evidence. This type of assessment requires thinking in different ways (Behrens & DiCerbo, 2013). For example, rather than think about individual items that might be rated, we can think in terms of assessment activity. Rather than being constrained about the type of responses that can be easily scored, we can focus on designing activities that are most likely to elicit behaviors of interest. However, just because we can gather data seamlessly from digital interactions does not mean that we will be able to make inferences about persistence from any given digital activity. We still need to design activities specifically so that they will elicit evidence that will allow for those inferences.

One way to focus and define the claims, evidence, and activities for assessment of a particular skill or attribute is through the use of design patterns (Mislevy et al., 2003). Design patterns in this context are tightly aligned with the ECD framework. A design pattern is a way to formally specify, and potentially make a template of, the assessment argument (the link between claims and evidence) to allow both for its examination and reuse. It is meant to be a narrative representation of the argument, rather than a technical or mathematical one. The three main components of a design pattern are: 1) definition of the knowledge, skills, and attributes under consideration, 2) description of characteristic features of a task, and 3) identification of potential observations. This lines up with the Conceptual Assessment Framework described in ECD that contains student model, task model, and evidence model.

The details of design patterns were originally laid out with specific examples in Mislevy et al. (2003), a paper resulting from the Principled Assessment Designs for Inquiry project. SRI International was a leader on that project and has continued to make iterations to the generic design pattern template. The design pattern below contains headings and subheadings suggested by SRI International researchers working on the Analytics for Learning project.

## Student Model

### Focal Construct

Task persistence is defined as the continuation of a challenging activity in pursuit of a goal despite difficulty, failure, or obstacles.

### Additional Knowledge, Skills, and Attributes

This section of the design pattern is meant to enumerate other constructs that may confound the measurement of the focal skill or introduce construct irrelevant variance. For persistence, *content knowledge* of an individual will confound the measurement of persistence because it will impact the level of challenge the activity presents. *Skill in manipulating the user interface* and familiarity with the activity type can also similarly introduce either unexpected difficulty or easiness into a task that will impact the persistence required to complete it. Finally, *interest in the task* itself is likely to impact persistence. In the Poptropica example above, each of the 30 islands has a different theme, ranging from game shows to vampires to ghosts to art mysteries. Interest in these islands varies in some predictable ways based on demographic characteristics (for example, boys play Superpower Island more than girls), but there are likely also individual differences in interest. A player is probably more likely to persist on an island if they are intrinsically interested in the topic of the island.

## Task Model

### Characteristic Features of the Task

If someone wishes to assess persistence, these characteristic features are required in order to elicit evidence of persistence. *The task must present a difficult problem in which success or failure can be judged by the learner and with an allowance for multiple attempts and/or a significant amount of time for student completion.* It may seem obvious, but if an activity does not indicate to the learner that he/she has not been successful, they will not have a reason to try again or continue trying. Similarly, if an activity (like many assessment activities) only allows for one attempt, we cannot observe whether they make multiple attempts after failure. An alternative to multiple attempts is an activity like the impossible tasks described by Ventura and Shute (2013) above, where the failure is actually the inability to complete the task, and is also apparent to the learner.

## Variable Features of the Task

Variable features are aspects of an activity that can be intentionally varied to impact the levels of persistence required. In assessment of more traditional skills, these are things that make a problem more difficult. For example, when assessing knowledge of how to compute the area of a shape, asking about irregular shapes is more difficult than asking about rectangles. In assessing persistence, the following task elements can be varied in ways that will require more or less persistence of the learner:

- **Task Requirements:** Requirements such as finding a solution to a problem (how to get by a wolf in a game) and comparing two figures require different cognitive processes that may impact the expression of persistence.
- **Content Area:** Content area will interact with individuals' own content knowledge and impact persistence measure.
- Repetitiveness of task.
- **Reinforcement for Task Completion:** The schedule of reinforcement should be considered, even when the incentive is only the completion of the problem itself.
- Difficulty of task for student.

- **Expectation of Success in the Environment:** Messages about whether effort is likely to result in successful outcomes in this context will likely impact persistence.
- **Attractiveness of Alternatives to the Task:** Persistence will likely differ in situations where there is embarrassment associated with quitting versus situations in which quitting lets the individual engage in interesting other activities.
- **Importance/Relevance of the Task:** One way to identify importance or relevance is alignment with an individual's goals.

Note that this is likely not an exhaustive list. Given the number of theoretical approaches to understanding persistence, it is likely there are other features that a given approach might indicate that is not named here.

## Work Products from the Task

Work products describe the things a student produces while engaged in a task. They contain the evidence that will be described in the next section. In the assessment of persistence, the work product should capture the initiation of any attempt, the time spent on the attempt, and the success or failure of the attempt.

### Evidence Model

### Potential Observations

Observations are the elements we will extract from the work product and use to make inferences about persistence. There are two basic pieces of evidence to use to measure persistence: *number of attempts* after failure or without success and *time spent* on the activity after failure or without success.

## Scoring Considerations

It is fairly clear that more time spent and more attempts made after failure are indications of more persistence. However, interpretation of the amount of time or number of attempts requires context. It will need to be determined whether a norm-referenced or criterion-referenced measure is desired. The Poptropica work resulted in a norm-referenced measure after normalizing all of the indicators. However, cut scores could also be used. For example, the minimum amount of persistence required to be successful at learning a new concept or skill could be determined and that used as a cut score. More complex statistical models, for example Bayesian Networks, might be employed to combine evidence such as time and number of attempts that do not fall into our traditional assessment models of "correct" and "incorrect."

## FUTURE RESEARCH DIRECTIONS

The above discussion reveals that there are a number of open research questions to be addressed. First, in relation to the use of design patterns, there are not well-developed examples of a group picking up a design pattern created by a research group and implementing those concepts in an operational testing program. That is, while the effort of design pattern creation is often a good exercise in helping its creators define the key student, task, and evidence models, their promise as a template has yet to be realized. It is not clear if the design pattern for persistence outlined here would result in either more consistency across assessments of persistence or a more common language by which to discuss differences.

Second, the elements called out as variable task features require further research. Uncovering more variable task features is a needed path of research. In addition, it is not clear how the features named here interact amongst themselves.

For example, how does a repetitive task with attractive alternatives compare to a nonrepetitive task with attractive alternatives compare in terms of how much persistence is required? Traditional assessment gives us concepts such as the difficulty parameter arising out of Item Response Theory. It is unclear if the concept of difficulty could be adapted to this non-cognitive task, but it seems conceivable. It might be that we could specify something along the lines of an item characteristic curve that indicates the probability that individuals with a certain level of persistence will in fact persist on the activity. We could then examine how this curve shifts when features of the task are varied.

Third, the search for interventions that impact persistence is required in order to impact learning outcomes of individuals. The researchers associated with views of mindset appear to have done the most in this area, likely because their theoretical framework is more geared toward viewing persistence as mutable. Evaluation of these interventions should not stop only with increasing persistence, but should test the logic model that the intervention increases persistence and the increased persistence results in improved learning or occupational outcomes. The evaluations must look for these relationships both within the system (for example, intervention and results in a game environment) and outside the system (the extent that the effects transfer to other contexts).

Finally, looking at not just persistence, but a variety of 21st century skills, continued research into invisible assessment generally and game-based assessment particularly should center on development of methods for establishing reliability and other psychometric concerns. This will require an examination of the intent of our existing methods and translation of those to the types of data obtained from game-based assessment. For example, the intent of test-retest reliability measures is to understand the stability of the scores and inferences over time. Translation of this to game-based assessment may require the acknowledgement that the level of the construct may change over time, so stability must take that change into account. In addition, expansion of traditional measurement models to accommodate new types of data and/or development of new models will expand our ability to use new types of evidence to estimate constructs of interest.

## CONCLUSION

As jobs in the 21st century become increasingly complex, requiring sustained application of effort to complete multifaceted tasks, task persistence becomes more important. It is clear that it is related to both academic and occupational outcomes. Although there are a variety of approaches to understanding task persistence, there is general agreement that it is defined as the continuation of an activity despite difficulty, obstacles, and/or failure. Due to this relatively simple operational definition, task persistence is a good candidate for invisible assessment. That is, digital activities can be designed such that they can gather information that can be used as evidence to make inferences about individuals' level of persistence without interrupting the experience of interacting with the digital activity (be it a game, an intelligent tutor, or other activity).

This type of invisible assessment still requires careful design of both activities and data. The activities must present challenge for the individual in order for persistence to be required. Multiple attempts and/or allowance for time to spend solving the problem must be available. That is, the continued effort of the individual must be visible. Finally, the technology system must collect information to observe the evidence of persistence. If a system does not retain all attempts, for example, there will be no record of the behaviors to be used as observations.

Technology also allows us to examine new interventions to increase persistence. If engaging activities such as games can be instrumented with incentive systems that reinforce mastery goals and growth mindset in ways that increase persistence in and out of the game, the ability to intervene with learners will be able to scale in previously unattainable ways. Given the consistent evidence of the positive relationship between persistence and educational and occupational outcomes, it appears that efforts to validly assess it and effectively intervene to increase it should receive continued attention.

## REFERENCES

American Educational Research Association. American Psychological Association, & National Council for Measurement in Education. (2014). Standards for educational and psychological testing. Washington, DC: American Educational Research Assn.

Ames, C., & Archer, J. (1988). Achievement goals in the classroom: Students' learning strategies and motivation processes. *Journal of Educational Psychology*, *80*(3), 260–267. doi:10.1037/0022-0663.80.3.260

Andersson, H., & Bergman, L. R. (2011). The role of task persistence in young adolescence for successful educational and occupational attainment in middle adulthood. *Developmental Psychology*, *47*(4), 950–960. doi:10.1037/a0023786 PMID:21639622

Bartle, R. (1996). Hearts, clubs, diamonds, spades: Players who suit MUDs. *Journal of MUD Research*, *1*(1), 19.

Baumeister, R. F., Bratslavsky, E., Muraven, M., & Tice, D. M. (1998). Ego depletion: Is the active self a limited resource? *Journal of Personality and Social Psychology*, *74*(5), 1252–1265. doi:10.1037/0022-3514.74.5.1252 PMID:9599441

Behrens, J. T., & DiCerbo, K. E. (2013). *Technological Implications for Assessment Ecosystems: Opportunities for Digital Technology to Advance Assessment.* Princeton, NJ: The Gordon Commission on the Future of Assessment.

Boe, E. E., May, H., & Boruch, R. F. (2002). *Student Task Persistence in the Third International Mathematics and Science Study: A Major Source of Acheievement Differences at the National, Classroom, and Student Levels.* Retrieved from http://www.eric.ed.gov/ERICWebPortal/content-delivery/servlet/ERICServlet?accno=ED478493

Brandstätter, V., & Frank, E. (2002). Effects of deliberative and implemental mindsets on persistence in goal-directed behavior. *Personality and Social Psychology Bulletin, 28*(10), 1366–1378. doi:10.1177/014616702236868

Carrier, C. A., & Williams, M. D. (1988). A test of one learner-control strategy with students of differing levels of task persistence. *American Educational Research Journal, 25*(2), 285–306. doi:10.3102/00028312025002285

Cloninger, C. R. (2003). Completing the psychobiological architecture of human personality development: Temperament, character, and coherence. In U. M. Staudinger & U. E. R. Lindenberger (Eds.), *Understanding Human Development: Dialogues with Lifespan Psychology* (pp. 159–181). Springer. doi:10.1007/978-1-4615-0357-6_8

Cloninger, C. R., Svrakic, D. M., & Przybeck, T. R. (1993). A psychobiological model of temperament and character. *Archives of General Psychiatry, 50*(12), 975–990. doi:10.1001/archpsyc.1993.01820240059008 PMID:8250684

Cloninger, C. R., Zohar, A. H., Hirschmann, S., & Dahan, D. (2012). The psychological costs and benefits of being highly persistent: Personality profiles distinguish mood disorders from anxiety disorders. *Journal of Affective Disorders, 136*(3), 758–766. doi:10.1016/j.jad.2011.09.046 PMID:22036800

Deater-Deckard, K., Petrill, S. A., Thompson, L. A., & DeThorne, L. S. (2005). A cross-sectional behavioral genetic analysis of task persistence in the transition to middle childhood. *Developmental Science, 8*(3), F21–F26. doi:10.1111/j.1467-7687.2005.00407.x PMID:15819750

DiCerbo, K., & Behrens, J. (2012). Implications of the digital ocean on current and future assessment. In R. Lissitz & H. Jiao (Eds.), *Computers and their impact on state assessment: Recent history and predictions for the future* (pp. 273–306). Charlotte, NC: Information Age.

DiCerbo, K. E. (2014). Game-based assessment of persistence. *Journal of Educational Technology & Society, 17*(1), 17–28.

DiCerbo, K. E., & Behrens, J. T. (2014). *Impacts of the Digital Ocean on Education.* London: Pearson. Retrieved from https://research.pearson.com/digitalocean

DiCerbo, K. E., & Kidwai, K. (2013). *Detecting "Serious" Intent in Game Play.* Presented at the Sixth International Conference on Educational Data Mining, Memphis, TN.

Duckworth, A. L., Peterson, C., Matthews, M. D., & Kelly, D. R. (2007). Grit: Perseverance and passion for long-term goals. *Journal of Personality and Social Psychology, 92*(6), 1087–1101. doi:10.1037/0022-3514.92.6.1087 PMID:17547490

Duckworth, A. L., & Quinn, P. D. (2009). Development and validation of the Short Grit Scale (GRIT-S). *Journal of Personality Assessment, 91*(2), 166–174. doi:10.1080/00223890802634290 PMID:19205937

Dudley, N. M., Orvis, K. A., Lebiecki, J. E., & Cortina, J. M. (2006). A meta-analytic investigation of conscientiousness in the prediction of job performance: Examining the intercorrelations and the incremental validity of narrow traits. *The Journal of Applied Psychology, 91*(1), 40–57. doi:10.1037/0021-9010.91.1.40 PMID:16435937

Dweck, C. (2006). *Mindset: The new psychology of success*. Random House LLC.

Elliott, E. S., & Dweck, C. S. (1988). Goals: An approach to motivation and achievement. *Journal of Personality and Social Psychology*, *54*(1), 5–12. doi:10.1037/0022-3514.54.1.5 PMID:3346808

Fadel, C. (2011). Redesigning the Curriculum. Boston, MA: Center for Curriculum Redesign. Retrieved from http://curriculumredesign.org/wp-content/uploads/CCR-Foundational-Whitepaper-Charles-Fadel2.pdf

Foll, D. L., Rascle, O., & Higgins, N. C. (2006). Persistence in a Putting Task During Perceived Failure: Influence of State-attributions and Attributional Style. *Applied Psychology*, *55*(4), 586–605. doi:10.1111/j.1464-0597.2006.00249.x

Goldman, R. D., Hudson, D., & Daharsh, B. J. (1973). Self-estimated task persistence as a nonlinear predictor of college success. *Journal of Educational Psychology*, *65*(2), 216–221. doi:10.1037/h0034989 PMID:4778799

Gollwitzer, P. M., & Bayer, U. (1999). Deliberative versus implemental mindsets in the control of action. *Dual-Process Theories in Social Psychology*, 403–422.

Gunderson, E. A., Gripshover, S. J., Romero, C., Dweck, C. S., Goldin-Meadow, S., & Levine, S. C. (2013). Parent praise to 1-to 3-year-olds predicts children's motivational frameworks 5 years later. *Child Development*, *84*(5), 1526–1541. doi:10.1111/cdev.12064 PMID:23397904

Gusnard, D. A., Ollinger, J. M., Shulman, G. L., Cloninger, C. R., Price, J. L., Van Essen, D. C., & Raichle, M. E. (2003). Persistence and brain circuitry. *Proceedings of the National Academy of Sciences of the United States of America*, *100*(6), 3479–3484. doi:10.1073/pnas.0538050100 PMID:12626765

Hambleton, R. K., Swaminathan, H., & Rogers, H. J. (1991). *Fundamentals of Item Response Theory*. Newbury Park, CA: SAGE Publications, Inc.

Hartshorne, H., May, M. A., & Maller, J. B. (1929). *Studies in the nature of character, II Studies in service and self-control*. Retrieved from http://psycnet.apa.org/psycinfo/2006-22806-000

Hough, L. M. (1992). The 'Big Five' personality variables–construct confusion: Description versus prediction. *Human Performance*, *5*(1-2), 139–155. doi:10.1080/08959285.1992.9667929

Kamins, M. L., & Dweck, C. S. (1999). Person versus process praise and criticism: Implications for contingent self-worth and coping. *Developmental Psychology*, *35*(3), 835–847. doi:10.1037/0012-1649.35.3.835 PMID:10380873

Kennelly, K. J., Dietz, D., & Benson, P. (1985). Reinforcement schedules, effort vs. ability attributions, and persistence. *Psychology in the Schools*, *22*(4), 459–464. doi:10.1002/1520-6807(198510)22:4<459::AID-PITS2310220416>3.0.CO;2-G

Logan, G. D. (1985). Executive control of thought and action. *Acta Psychologica*, *60*(2), 193–210. doi:10.1016/0001-6918(85)90055-1

Lufi, D., & Cohen, A. (1987). A scale for measuring persistence in children. *Journal of Personality Assessment*, *51*(2), 178–185, =185. doi:10.1207/s15327752jpa5102_2 PMID:16372846

MacCann, C., Duckworth, A. L., & Roberts, R. D. (2009). Empirical identification of the major facets of conscientiousness. *Learning and Individual Differences*, *19*(4), 451–458. doi:10.1016/j.lindif.2009.03.007

McClelland, M. M., Acock, A. C., Piccinin, A., Rhea, S. A., & Stallings, M. C. (2013). Relations between preschool attention span-persistence and age 25 educational outcomes. *Early Childhood Research Quarterly, 28*(2), 314–324. doi:10.1016/j.ecresq.2012.07.008 PMID:23543916

McCrae, R. R., & Costa, P. T. (1987). Validation of the five-factor model of personality across instruments and observers. *Journal of Personality and Social Psychology, 52*(1), 81–90. doi:10.1037/0022-3514.52.1.81 PMID:3820081

McCroskey, J. C. (2009). Self-report measurement. In J. Ayres, T. Hopf, J. C. McCroskey, J. Daly, D. M. A. Sonandre, & T. K. Wongprasert (Eds.), *Avoiding communication: Shyness, reticence, and communication apprehension* (3rd ed.; pp. 81–94). New York, NY: Hampton Press.

Messick, S. (1994). The interplay of evidence and consequences in the validation of performance assessments. *Educational Researcher, 23*(2), 13–23. doi:10.3102/0013189X023002013

Meyer, D. E., & Kieras, D. E. (1997). A computational theory of executive cognitive processes and multiple-task performance: Part I. Basic mechanisms. *Psychological Review, 104*(1), 3–65. doi:10.1037/0033-295X.104.1.3 PMID:9009880

Mislevy, R. J., Chudowsky, N., Draney, K., Fried, R., Gaffney, T., & Haertel, G. (2003). *Design patterns for assessing science inquiry.* Menlo Park, CA: SRI International. Retrieved from http://padi.sri.com/downloads/TR1_Design_Patterns.pdf

Mislevy, R. J., Corrigan, S., Oranje, A., DiCerbo, K. E., John, M., Bauer, M. I., … Hao, J. (2014). Psychometrics and Game-Based Assessment. New York, NY: Institute of Play.

Mislevy, R. J., Steinberg, L. S., & Almond, R. G. (2002). Design and analysis in task-based language assessment. *Language Testing, 19*(4), 477–496. doi:10.1191/0265532202lt241oa

Mueller, C. M., & Dweck, C. S. (1998). Praise for intelligence can undermine children's motivation and performance. *Journal of Personality and Social Psychology, 75*(1), 33–52. doi:10.1037/0022-3514.75.1.33 PMID:9686450

Nakamura, J., & Csikszentmihalyi, M. (2002). The concept of flow. In C. R. Snyder & S. J. Lopez (Eds.), *Handbook of positive psychology* (pp. 89–105). New York, NY: Oxford University Press.

O'Rourke, E., Haimovitz, K., Ballweber, C., Dweck, C., & Popović, Z. (2014). Brain points: a growth mindset incentive structure boosts persistence in an educational game. In *Proceedings of the 32nd annual ACM conference on human factors in computing systems* (pp. 3339–3348). New York, NY: ACM. doi:10.1145/2556288.2557157

Ostrow, K. S., Schultz, S. E., & Arroyo, I. (n.d.). *Promoting Growth Mindset Within Intelligent Tutoring Systems.* Retrieved from http://ceur-ws.org/Vol-1183/ncfpal_paper03.pdf

Pearl, J. (1988). *Probabilistic Reasoning in Intelligent Systems: Networks of Plausble Inference.* Burlington, MA: Morgan Kaufmann Pub.

Pellegrino, J., & Hilton, M. (2012). *Education for Life and Work: Developing Transferable Knowledge and Skills in the 21st Century.* Washington, DC: The National Academies Press.

Perry, S. J., Hunter, E. M., Witt, L. A., & Harris, K. J. (2010). P = ƒ (conscientiousness × ability) : Examining the facets of conscientiousness. *Human Performance, 23*(4), 343–360. doi:10.1080/08959285.2010.501045

Presley, R., & Martin, R. P. (1994). Toward a structure of preschool temperament: Factor structure of the Temperament Assessment Battery for Children. *Journal of Personality, 62*(3), 415–448. doi:10.1111/j.1467-6494.1994.tb00304.x PMID:7965566

Ryans, D. G. (1939). The measurement of persistence: An historical review. *Psychological Bulletin, 36*(9), 715–739. doi:10.1037/h0060780

Sabourin, J., Rowe, J. P., Mott, B. W., & Lester, J. C. (2011). When off-task is on-task: The affective role of off-task behavior in narrative-centered learning environments. In *Artificial Intelligence in Education* (pp. 534–536). New York, NY: Springer. doi:10.1007/978-3-642-21869-9_93

Schmeichel, B. J. (2007). Attention control, memory updating, and emotion regulation temporarily reduce the capacity for executive control. *Journal of Experimental Psychology. General, 136*(2), 241–255. doi:10.1037/0096-3445.136.2.241 PMID:17500649

Shernoff, D. J., & Csikszentmihalyi, M. (2009). Cultivating engaged learners and optimal learning environments. In R. Gilman, E. S. Huebner, & M. Furlong (Eds.), *Handbook of positive psychology in schools* (pp. 131–145). New York, NY: Routledge.

Shiffrin, R. M., & Schneider, W. (1977). Controlled and automatic human information processing: II. Perceptual learning, automatic attending and a general theory. *Psychological Review, 84*(2), 127–190. doi:10.1037/0033-295X.84.2.127

Shiner, R. L. (1998). How shall we speak of children's personalities in middle childhood? A preliminary taxonomy. *Psychological Bulletin, 124*(3), 308–332. doi:10.1037/0033-2909.124.3.308 PMID:9849111

Shute, V. J. (2011). Stealth assessment in computer-based games to support learning. In S. Tobias & J. D. Fletcher (Eds.), *Computer games and instruction* (pp. 503–524). Charlotte, NC: Information Age.

Shute, V. J., & Ventura, M. (2013). *Measuring and supporting learning in games: Stealth assessment.* Cambridge, MA: MIT Press.

Sigman, M., Cohen, S. E., Beckwith, L., & Topinka, C. (1987). Task persistence in 2-year-old preterm infants in relation to subsequent attentiveness and intelligence. *Infant Behavior and Development, 10*(3), 295–305. doi:10.1016/0163-6383(87)90018-X

Silva, E., & White, T. (2013). Pathways to improvement: Using psychological strategies to help college students master developmental math. Stanford, CA: Carnegie Foundation for the Advancement of Teaching. Retrieved from http://www.carnegiefoundation.org/sites/default/files/pathways_to_improvement.pdf

Stevenson, H., & Stigler, J. (1994). *Learning Gap: Why Our Schools Are Failing And What We Can Learn From Japanese And Chinese Educ.* New York, NY: Simon and Schuster.

Teng, C.-I. (2011). Who are likely to experience flow? Impact of temperament and character on flow. *Personality and Individual Differences, 50*(6), 863–868. doi:10.1016/j.paid.2011.01.012

Thomas, A., Chess, C., & Birch, H. G. (1968). *Temperament and behavior disorders in children.* Retrieved from http://eric.ed.gov/?id=ED025066

Thomas, A., & Chess, S. (1977). *Temperament and development.* Oxford, UK: Brunner/Mazel.

Tversky, A., & Kahneman, D. (1982). *Judgment under uncertainty: Heuristics and biases.* Cambridge, UK: Cambridge University Press.

Unsworth, N., Redick, T. S., Lakey, C. E., & Young, D. L. (2010). Lapses in sustained attention and their relation to executive control and fluid abilities: An individual differences investigation. *Intelligence, 38*(1), 111–122. doi:10.1016/j.intell.2009.08.002

Van Herk, H., Poortinga, Y. H., & Verhallen, T. M. (2004). Response styles in rating scales evidence of method bias in data from six EU countries. *Journal of Cross-Cultural Psychology, 35*(3), 346–360. doi:10.1177/0022022104264126

Ventura, M., & Shute, V. (2013). The validity of a game-based assessment of persistence. *Computers in Human Behavior, 29*(6), 2568–2572. doi:10.1016/j.chb.2013.06.033

Ventura, M., Shute, V., & Zhao, W. (2013). The relationship between video game use and a performance-based measure of persistence. *Computers & Education, 60*(1), 52–58. doi:10.1016/j.compedu.2012.07.003

Ventura, M., Shute, V. J., & Small, M. (2014). Assessing persistence in educational games. In R. Sottilare, A. Graesser, X. Hu, & B. Goldberg (Eds.), *Design recommendations for adaptive intelligent tutoring systems: Learner modeling* (Vol. 2, pp. 93–101). Orlando, FL: U.S. Army Research Laboratory.

Yeager, D. S., & Dweck, C. S. (2012). Mindsets That Promote Resilience: When Students Believe That Personal Characteristics Can Be Developed. *Educational Psychologist, 47*(4), 302–314. doi:10.1080/00461520.2012.722805

## ADDITIONAL READING

Almond, R. G., DiBello, L. V., Moulder, B., & Zapata-Rivera, J. D. (2007). Modeling diagnostic assessments with Bayesian networks. *Journal of Educational Measurement, 44*(4), 341–359. doi:10.1111/j.1745-3984.2007.00043.x

Almond, R. G., Steinberg, L. S., & Mislevy, R. J. (2002). Enhancing the design and delivery of assessment systems: A four-process architecture. *The Journal of Technology, Learning, and Assessment, 1*(5). http://www.bc.edu/research/intasc/jtla/journal/v1n5.shtml

Ames, C., & Archer, J. (1988). Achievement goals in the classroom: Students' learning strategies and motivation processes. *Journal of Educational Psychology, 80*(3), 260–267. doi:10.1037/0022-0663.80.3.260

Andersson, H., & Bergman, L. R. (2011). The role of task persistence in young adolescence for successful educational and occupational attainment in middle adulthood. *Developmental Psychology, 47*(4), 950–960. doi:10.1037/a0023786 PMID:21639622

Behrens, J. T., & DiCerbo, K. E. (2013). *Technological Implications for Assessment Ecosystems: Opportunities for Digital Technology to Advance Assessment*. Princeton, NJ: The Gordon Commission on the Future of Assessment.

Boe, E. E., May, H., & Boruch, R. F. (2002). *Student Task Persistence in the Third International Mathematics and Science Study: A Major Source of Acheievement Differences at the National, Classroom, and Student Levels*. Retrieved from http://www.eric.ed.gov/ERICWebPortal/content-delivery/servlet/ERICServlet?accno=ED478493

Brandstätter, V., & Frank, E. (2002). Effects of deliberative and implemental mindsets on persistence in goal-directed behavior. *Personality and Social Psychology Bulletin, 28*(10), 1366–1378. doi:10.1177/014616702236868

Carrier, C. A., & Williams, M. D. (1988). A test of one learner-control strategy with students of differing levels of task persistence. *American Educational Research Journal, 25*(2), 285–306. doi:10.3102/00028312025002285

Cloninger, C. R., Svrakic, D. M., & Przybeck, T. R. (1993). A psychobiological model of temperament and character. *Archives of General Psychiatry, 50*(12), 975–990. doi:10.1001/archpsyc.1993.01820240059008 PMID:8250684

Cloninger, C. R., Zohar, A. H., Hirschmann, S., & Dahan, D. (2012). The psychological costs and benefits of being highly persistent: Personality profiles distinguish mood disorders from anxiety disorders. *Journal of Affective Disorders, 136*(3), 758–766. doi:10.1016/j.jad.2011.09.046 PMID:22036800

DiCerbo, K. E. (2014). Game-based assessment of persistence. *Journal of Educational Technology & Society*, *17*(1), 17–28.

DiCerbo, K. E., & Behrens, J. T. (2014). Impacts of the Digital Ocean on Education. London: Pearson; Retrieved from https://research.pearson.com/digitalocean

DiCerbo, K. E., & Kidwai, K. (2013). *Detecting "Serious" Intent in Game Play*. Presented at the Sixth International Conference on Educational Data Mining, Memphis, TN.

Duckworth, A. L., Peterson, C., Matthews, M. D., & Kelly, D. R. (2007). Grit: Perseverance and passion for long-term goals. *Journal of Personality and Social Psychology*, *92*(6), 1087–1101. doi:10.1037/0022-3514.92.6.1087 PMID:17547490

Dudley, N. M., Orvis, K. A., Lebiecki, J. E., & Cortina, J. M. (2006). A meta-analytic investigation of conscientiousness in the prediction of job performance: Examining the intercorrelations and the incremental validity of narrow traits. *The Journal of Applied Psychology*, *91*(1), 40–57. doi:10.1037/0021-9010.91.1.40 PMID:16435937

Dweck, C. (2006). *Mindset: The new psychology of success*. Random House LLC.

El-Nasr, M. S., Drachen, A., & Canossa, A. (2013). *Game analytics: Maximizing the value of player data*. London: Springer. doi:10.1007/978-1-4471-4769-5

Embretson, S. E. (1998). A cognitive design system approach to generating valid tests: Application to abstract reasoning. *Psychological Methods*, *3*(3), 380–396. doi:10.1037/1082-989X.3.3.380

Fadel, C. (2011). Redesigning the Curriculum. Boston, MA: Center for Curriculum Redesign; Retrieved from http://curriculumredesign.org/wp-content/uploads/CCR-Foundational-Whitepaper-Charles-Fadel2.pdf

Gee, J. P. (2007). *What video games have to teach us about learning and literacy* (2nd ed.). New York: Palgrave.

Gee, J. P. (2008). Learning and games. In K. Salen (Ed.), *The ecology of games: Connecting youth, games, and learning* (pp. 21–40). Cambridge, MA: MIT Press.

Goldman, R. D., Hudson, D., & Daharsh, B. J. (1973). Self-estimated task persistence as a nonlinear predictor of college success. *Journal of Educational Psychology*, *65*(2), 216–221. doi:10.1037/h0034989 PMID:4778799

Gunderson, E. A., Gripshover, S. J., Romero, C., Dweck, C. S., Goldin-Meadow, S., & Levine, S. C. (2013). Parent praise to 1-to 3-year-olds predicts children's motivational frameworks 5 years later. *Child Development*, *84*(5), 1526–1541. doi:10.1111/cdev.12064 PMID:23397904

Gusnard, D. A., Ollinger, J. M., Shulman, G. L., Cloninger, C. R., Price, J. L., Van Essen, D. C., & Raichle, M. E. (2003). Persistence and brain circuitry. *Proceedings of the National Academy of Sciences of the United States of America*, *100*(6), 3479–3484. doi:10.1073/pnas.0538050100 PMID:12626765

Hambleton, R. K., Swaminathan, H., & Rogers, H. J. (1991). *Fundamentals of Item Response Theory (1 edition.)*. Newbury Park, CA: SAGE Publications, Inc.

Hough, L. M. (1992). The 'Big Five' personality variables–construct confusion: Description versus prediction. *Human Performance*, *5*(1-2), 139–155. doi:10.1080/08959285.1992.9667929

Ifenthaler, D., Eseryel, D., & Ge, X. (Eds.). (2012). *Assessment in game-based learning: Foundations, innovations, and perspectives*. New York: Springer. doi:10.1007/978-1-4614-3546-4

Kamins, M. L., & Dweck, C. S. (1999). Person versus process praise and criticism: Implications for contingent self-worth and coping. *Developmental Psychology*, *35*(3), 835–847. doi:10.1037/0012-1649.35.3.835 PMID:10380873

Lufi, D., & Cohen, A. (1987). A scale for measuring persistence in children. *Journal of Personality Assessment*, *51*(2), 178–185, =185. doi:10.1207/s15327752jpa5102_2 PMID:16372846

MacCann, C., Duckworth, A. L., & Roberts, R. D. (2009). Empirical identification of the major facets of conscientiousness. *Learning and Individual Differences*, *19*(4), 451–458. doi:10.1016/j.lindif.2009.03.007

McClelland, M. M., Acock, A. C., Piccinin, A., Rhea, S. A., & Stallings, M. C. (2013). Relations between preschool attention span-persistence and age 25 educational outcomes. *Early Childhood Research Quarterly*, *28*(2), 314–324. doi:10.1016/j.ecresq.2012.07.008 PMID:23543916

McCrae, R. R., & Costa, P. T. (1987). Validation of the five-factor model of personality across instruments and observers. *Journal of Personality and Social Psychology*, *52*(1), 81–90. doi:10.1037/0022-3514.52.1.81 PMID:3820081

Messick, S. (1994). The interplay of evidence and consequences in the validation of performance assessments. *Educational Researcher*, *23*(2), 13–23. doi:10.3102/0013189X023002013

Mislevy, R. J., Chudowsky, N., Draney, K., Fried, R., Gaffney, T., & Haertel, G. ... others. (2003). *Design patterns for assessing science inquiry*. Menlo Park, CA: SRI International. Retrieved from http://padi.sri.com/downloads/TR1_Design_Patterns.pdf

Mislevy, R. J., Corrigan, S., Oranje, A., DiCerbo, K. E., John, M., & Bauer, M. I. ... Hao, J. (2014). Psychometrics and Game-Based Assessment. New York, NY: Institute of Play.

Mislevy, R. J., Steinberg, L. S., & Almond, R. G. (2002). Design and analysis in task-based language assessment. *Language Testing*, *19*(4), 477–496. doi:10.1191/0265532202lt241oa

Mueller, C. M., & Dweck, C. S. (1998). Praise for intelligence can undermine children's motivation and performance. *Journal of Personality and Social Psychology*, *75*(1), 33–52. doi:10.1037/0022-3514.75.1.33 PMID:9686450

Nakamura, J., & Csikszentmihalyi, M. (2002). The concept of flow. In C. R. Snyder & S. J. Lopez (Eds.), *Handbook of positive psychology* (pp. 89–105). New York, NY: Oxford University Press.

O'Rourke, E., Haimovitz, K., Ballweber, C., Dweck, C., & Popović, Z. (2014). Brain points: a growth mindset incentive structure boosts persistence in an educational game. In *Proceedings of the 32nd annual ACM conference on human factors in computing systems* (pp. 3339–3348). New York, NY: ACM. doi:10.1145/2556288.2557157

Ostrow, K. S., Schultz, S. E., & Arroyo, I. (n.d.). Promoting Growth Mindset Within Intelligent Tutoring Systems. Retrieved from http://ceur-ws.org/Vol-1183/ncfpal_paper03.pdf

Pearl, J. (1988). *Probabilistic Reasoning in Intelligent Systems: Networks of Plausble Inference*. Burlington, MA: Morgan Kaufmann Pub.

Pellegrino, J., & Hilton, M. (2012). *Education for Life and Work: Developing Transferable Knowledge and Skills in the 21st Century*. Washington, D.C.: The National Academies Press.

Shiner, R. L. (1998). How shall we speak of children's personalities in middle childhood? A preliminary taxonomy. *Psychological Bulletin*, *124*(3), 308–332. doi:10.1037/0033-2909.124.3.308 PMID:9849111

Shute, V. J. (2008). Focus on formative feedback. *Review of Educational Research*, *78*(1), 153–189. doi:10.3102/0034654307313795

Shute, V. J. (2011). Stealth assessment in computer-based games to support learning. In S. Tobias & J. D. Fletcher (Eds.), *Computer games and instruction* (pp. 503–524). Charlotte, NC: Information Age.

Shute, V. J., & Ventura, M. (2013). *Measuring and supporting learning in games: Stealth assessment.* Cambridge, MA: MIT Press.

Sigman, M., Cohen, S. E., Beckwith, L., & Topinka, C. (1987). Task persistence in 2-year-old preterm infants in relation to subsequent attentiveness and intelligence. *Infant Behavior and Development, 10*(3), 295–305. doi:10.1016/0163-6383(87)90018-X

Silva, E., & White, T. (2013). Pathways to improvement: Using psychological strategies to help college students master developmental math. Stanford, CA: Carnegie Foundation for the Advancement of Teaching; Retrieved from http://www.carnegiefoundation.org/sites/default/files/pathways_to_improvement.pdf

Stevenson, H., & Stigler, J. (1994). *Learning Gap: Why Our Schools Are Failing And What We Can Learn From Japanese And Chinese Educ.* New York, NY: Simon and Schuster.

Teng, C.-I. (2011). Who are likely to experience flow? Impact of temperament and character on flow. *Personality and Individual Differences, 50*(6), 863–868. doi:10.1016/j.paid.2011.01.012

Thomas, A., & Chess, S. (1977). *Temperament and development.* Oxford, England: Brunner/Mazel.

Tversky, A., & Kahneman, D. (1982). *Judgment under uncertainty: Heuristics and biases.* Cambridge: Cambridge University Press.

Ventura, M., & Shute, V. (2013). The validity of a game-based assessment of persistence. *Computers in Human Behavior, 29*(6), 2568–2572. doi:10.1016/j.chb.2013.06.033

Ventura, M., Shute, V., & Zhao, W. (2013). The relationship between video game use and a performance-based measure of persistence. *Computers & Education, 60*(1), 52–58. doi:10.1016/j.compedu.2012.07.003

Ventura, M., Shute, V. J., & Small, M. (2014). Assessing persistence in educational games. In R. Sottilare, A. Graesser, X. Hu, & B. Goldberg (Eds.), *Design recommendations for adaptive intelligent tutoring systems: Learner modeling* (Vol. 2, pp. 93–101). Orlando, FL: U.S. Army Research Laboratory.

Wise, S. L., Bhola, D. S., & Yang, S.-T. (2006). Taking the time to improve the validity of low-stakes tests: The effort-monitoring CBT. *Educational Measurement: Issues and Practice, 25*(2), 21–30. doi:10.1111/j.1745-3992.2006.00054.x

Yeager, D. S., & Dweck, C. S. (2012). Mindsets That Promote Resilience: When Students Believe That Personal Characteristics Can Be Developed. *Educational Psychologist, 47*(4), 302–314. doi:10.1080/00461520.2012.722805

## KEY TERMS AND DEFINITIONS

**Characteristic Features:** The elements of an assessment activity that are required in order to assess the construct of interest.

**Evidence Model:** The specification of which elements of a work product will be extracted as evidence of a construct and how they will be combined.

**Evidence-Centered Design:** A framework for explicitly delineating an assessment argument, or the linking of claims to evidence to make a desired inference.

**Invisible Assessment:** The gathering of evidence from learner interactions in digital environments without interrupting their activity. Note that the activity is "invisible" but the learner can certainly be aware that they will be scored on and receive feedback from their activity.

**Student Model:** The definition of the knowledge, skills, or other attributes that are the focus of assessment. This may include defining relationships among skills, subskills, and prerequisite skills.

**Task Model:** The specification of activities that will elicit behaviors and evidence that will provide information about the construct of interest.

**Task Persistence:** Continuation of an activity in the face of difficulty, obstacles, and/or failure.

**Variable Features:** The elements of an assessment task that can be changed to change the way the target construct is expressed in an activity.

# Chapter 31
# Assessing Engagement during the Online Assessment of Real-World Skills

**J. Christine Harmes**
*Assessment Consultant, USA*

**Steven L. Wise**
*Northwest Evaluation Association, USA*

## ABSTRACT

*The assessment of real-world skills will often require complex and innovative types of computer-based test items to provide more authentic assessment. Having information about how students remain engaged with the various innovative elements during an assessment is useful in both assessing the utility of different types of innovative test items and assessing the validity of the inferences made about the test scores of individual students. This chapter introduces the Item Engagement Index (IEI) and the Student Engagement Index (SEI) and demonstrates their use with a variety of innovative items that were pilot tested for a nursing licensure exam. The IEI provided useful information about the amount of student effort each innovative item received, while the SEI was found useful in identifying disengaged test takers.*

## INTRODUCTION

There is a growing interest in skills such as critical thinking, collaborative problem solving, creativity, and global competency in technology-rich environments (often referred to as 21st century skills or real-world skills; e.g., Partnership for 21st Century Learning, 2011). Educators are increasingly expected to help their students develop these real-world skills, and both the formative and summative assessments of such skills should capitalize on the affordances offered by emerging technology (Davies & West, 2014; United States Department of Education, 2014). This *Handbook* represents a compendium of research about computer-based learning and assessment of these types of skills.

When assessing real-world skills, a key challenge can be the match between what is required to perform the target skill in the workplace and the way this skill is assessed. The call for *authentic assessment* has centered on this need. While authentic instruction involves students engaging

DOI: 10.4018/978-1-4666-9441-5.ch031

in activities that involve applying knowledge and skills and have meaning in the world beyond the classroom (King, Newmann, & Carmichael, 2009; Newmann, Marks, & Gamoran, 1996), in the assessment context, preparation for an authentic assessment involves actually practicing the target skill (Wiggins, 1990). With traditional text-based multiple-choice items, the construct match for career, or real-world, skills can be quite low, and thus less authentic. Innovative items offer opportunities to expand an assessment's domain coverage either by assessing particular skills and processes that could not be tested with text-based multiple-choice items, or by improving the ways in which skills and concepts are assessed (Parshall, Harmes, Davey, & Pashley, 2010). Both expanded domain coverage, and improved measurement tools can serve to increase the authenticity of a particular assessment. While innovative items can provide the opportunity for better measurement, it is important to analyze how students are interacting with various types of item innovations, and to devise measurement tools and procedures to gauge the quality and behavior of these new types of items in practice. Similarly, it is critical to gauge the degree to which students are engaged when responding to test items.

This chapter describes a procedure for assessing the degree to which students are engaged with different types of innovative items, and illustrates the use of this procedure with data collected on a set of innovative items designed to target entry-level nursing skills (Wendt & Harmes, 2009). Throughout the chapter, two basic assumptions are made about the typical assessment of real-world skills. First, these types of assessments will be computer-based (i.e., delivered via a desktop or laptop computer or another type of digital device). Second, they will often use innovative items instead of (or at least in conjunction with) traditional text-based multiple-choice items.

## INNOVATIVE ITEMS

One of the most exciting and promising aspects of the use of technology in assessment is the set of expanded possibilities afforded by innovative item formats. In general, innovative items are technology-based test items or tasks that include functionality and features that extend beyond traditional text-based multiple-choice items. These innovative items have also been referred to as "technology-enhanced items" (Zenisky & Sireci, 2013). Helpful discussions of the range of item types and functionalities that can be used in the assessment of real-world skills can be found in Parshall, Harmes, Davey, and Pashley (2010), Scalise (2012), Scalise and Gifford (2006), and Sireci and Zenisky (2006).

The general taxonomy provided by Parshall et al. includes seven dimensions for classifying innovative items: assessment structure, response action, media inclusion, interactivity, complexity, fidelity, and scoring method (2010). Assessment structure describes the continuum from a discrete item, such as an individual selected-response item, to a complete simulated environment. Response action refers to the actions required on the part of the student to record a response. This range could include using a mouse or track pad to select elements, directly interacting with the screen, or operating specialized real-world devices. Media inclusion covers various ways of incorporating multimedia elements such as graphics, audio, or video. Interactivity describes the degree to which the items or tasks respond to input from the student. Complexity refers to the range of components that the student needs to work with in order to complete the item or task. Fidelity is the degree to which an assessment accurately reproduces the context and interactions required for the task in its real-world setting. Scoring method covers how student responses are translated into scores on the item or task and then for the overall test. While each of these dimensions can be considered on its own, one often affects another. For example, increasing the number of elements a student has to interact with to respond to an item (complexity) will often be part of a more complicated assessment structure, and will usually result in a scoring method that is more advanced than a single mark of correct or not correct. Similarly, moving along the assessment structure continuum from discrete items toward situated tasks will tend to increase the interactivity, as well increasing fidelity.

When considering the assessment of real-world skills, the concept of *fidelity* applies most directly (Harmes & Parshall, 2005). A simple example of increased fidelity might be an item in which students watch and listen to a video of a workplace interaction as compared to merely reading a transcript of the interaction. If the real-world skill is being assessed involves looking at a set of literature search results and making decisions about which sources to pursue, fidelity can be enhanced by providing a realistic set of results from a search engine (possibly in an interactive graphical format) and asking the student to interact with this, instead of condensing and describing the results. In both of these examples, media inclusion can serve to increase fidelity. Further increasing fidelity in the second example, students could be asked to generate search queries, selecting from a set of possible words and Boolean operators or by typing in their actual queries, which could then be followed by a realistic set of search results to evaluate. The closer the process followed in the assessment matches that used in the real-world task, the greater the fidelity.

With all of these dimensions of innovation, the focus is on expanding measurement to increase the validity of the inferences made from student assessment scores (Parshall, Harmes, Davey, & Pashley, 2010; Zenisky & Sireci, 2013). These validity enhancements generally result from improving the representation of the construct when skills that could not be measured with traditional methods can now be measured through the use of technology (Huff & Sireci, 2001). In addition to increased domain coverage, other potential direct and indirect benefits to validity from technology-enhanced items include: reducing the ability to correctly guess the correct response, positively affecting instructional practice by measuring higher-order thinking skills, and increasing the efficiency with which higher-order thinking skills can be measured (Huff & Sireci, 2001; Zenisky & Sireci, 2013).

## ENGAGEMENT AND VALIDITY

Whenever we administer a test item to a student, we assume that the student will be engaged and give good effort toward answering the item. Ascertaining the degree of effort that has occurred poses a continual challenge for test givers because, without adequate effort, a student's response to the item is unlikely to reflect what the student knows and can do. Hence, because the goal of the test giver is to obtain valid scores, it is important that non-effortful test-taking behavior be identified whenever possible, and that we have tools to specifically address innovative items.

A claim frequently made about innovative test items is that students find them more interesting and engaging than traditional multiple-choice items (e.g., Strain-Seymour, Way, & Dolan, 2009). However, research has found non-effortful test taking to be associated with items that require greater amounts of reading (Wise, 2006; Wise, Pastor, & Kong, 2009) or are more mentally taxing (Wolf, Smith, & Birnbaum, 1995). Because innovative items tend to be more complex and require more attention and effort from students than traditional multiple-choice items, the nature of their impact on engagement is not inherently clear. This suggests a need for item-analysis methods that can allow test givers to evaluate student engagement, which will help them better identify the types of innovative items that best promote student engagement and valid assessment.

Disengaged, or non-effortful, test taking has been shown to induce a negative bias on test performance, resulting in test scores with diminished validity (Wise & DeMars, 2005; Wise & Kong, 2005; Wolf & Smith, 1995). There are several approaches that one might take to assessing test-taking effort. First, an observer might unobtrusively monitor the test event and rate the level of effort that the student appeared to exhibit during the test. An observation protocol could be devised that would probably yield a reasonably valid effort measure; however, this type of direct observation would usually be prohibitively expensive to use with group-administered tests.

A second method would be to ask students to complete a self-report measure of effort immediately after completing the test. While this is an inexpensive alternative to direct observation, it is difficult to gauge the truthfulness of the students' responses, particularly if they felt that there might be negative consequences associated with their disclosing a lack of effort (Wise & Kong, 2005). Moreover, self-report measures are generally useful for measuring students' overall effort during a test event, and do not provide information about the effort given to specific items.

Recently, a third type of approach to measuring test-taking engagement has emerged that is based on the behavior a student exhibits during a test event. Wise and Kong (2005) developed *response time effort* (*RTE*), which is based on the amount of time a student spends responding to multiple-choice test items. Wise and Kong found evidence that students who had become disengaged from their test would submit rapid, essentially random responses. Such non-effortful responses are characterized by *rapid-guessing behavior*, in contrast to effortful responding (which is termed *solution behavior*). Calculating *RTE* requires classifying each item response as either a rapid guess or a solution behavior, and then aggregating across the items in a student's test event. *RTE* is the

proportion of items on which the student exhibited solution behavior, and is used as an indicator of the student's test-taking effort. Subsequently, Wise (2006) showed that rapid-guessing behavior could also be used to evaluate the effort devoted to specific items. Aggregating item response classifications across students, rather than items (as with *RTE*), yields an indicator of the amount of effort received by an item. This indicator of item effort, termed *response time fidelity (RTF),* is the proportion of students who responded to the item with solution behavior.

Both *RTE* and *RTF* are examples of a general approach to assessing test-taking engagement in which specific test-taking behaviors are identified that would be exhibited by a student who was fully engaged in the test. To the degree to which a particular student does not exhibit those behaviors, an inference may be drawn that the student is not engaged. When considering a student's encounter with a traditional text-based multiple-choice item, the behavioral requirements for an engaged student are straightforward: simply read the item stem and the response options. Although it is challenging to verify directly that the stem and options have been read, one can specify behavior that indicates that the student had not performed the required reading. Specifically, if the student enters an answer to the item rapidly (i.e., so quickly that a very fast reader would not have had time to read the stem and options), it can be inferred that the student responded without reading the item—which would constitute non-effortful behavior. In this fashion, item response time provides useful behavioral information regarding student test-taking effort. In the next section, the same general approach will be applied to assessing engagement on more complex innovative items.

## ENGAGEMENT INDICES FOR INNOVATIVE ITEMS

A common way for innovative items to be evaluated is through the use of traditional item analysis indices, such as p-values and item-total correlations. Such indices are appropriate for evaluating the quality of any multiple-choice items, whether or not they are innovative. However, innovative items often require much more interactivity from a student than do traditional multiple-choice items, which essentially require the student only to read the material included in the item stem and options and to select his or her answer to the item. The only response actions required by traditional items are to click on the radio button next to the chosen response option (action 1) and to click on the button that submits the student's answer (action 2). In contrast, innovative items often expect a more complex set of response actions to be made by the student. For example, if an item uses a video clip, the student should click on a button to begin the video (action 1), watch the video until it has completed (action 2), click on the selected response option (action 3), and submit the answer (action 4). For items that have exhibits for students to read or items for which each response option is a video clip, the number of expected response actions can be much higher.

The more complex set of possible response actions that can be associated with innovative items raises a concern regarding the extent to which students actually complete all of the expected actions as they interact with the item. For instance, if an item provides a button to click that will open a set of three tabbed exhibits, and a student answers the item without looking at the exhibits, then the student did not complete all of the expected actions. This suggests that the degree to which a student is engaged when responding to an item can be inferred from the extent to which he or she completes all of the expected response actions. Similarly, the degree to which students are engaged with an item can provide additional information regarding the quality of the item. For example, if students do not play a video, or play a video multiple times, this may indicate that the item is either difficult, or that the video or instructions are unclear and need to be improved.

Data from student engagement can therefore also be used in item content revision by highlighting items that would benefit from additional types of testing, such as think aloud studies for usability or cognitive processing (see Harmes & Parshall, 2010; Harmes & Wendt, 2009).

The general approach to measuring engagement that was used with *RTE* and *RTF* can be applied to innovative items. With these types of items, however, the behavioral requirements can be much more complex. When presented items of this type, students are often asked to perform multiple actions. For example, consider an item whose stem contains a video-based scenario for which the students are to choose the best response from among four video-based options. In this case there are a total of five response actions the student should complete (initiating the one stem and the four response option videos). To the degree to which these actions were not completed, one can infer that the student was not engaged in the item—which can be interpreted as non-effortful behavior. It is important to note, however, that the actions under consideration should each represent something that an engaged student would need to do to understand the challenge being posed by the item. For each student-item encounter, engagement can be defined as the proportion of the needed actions that were completed. These student-item encounters can then be aggregated across items to provide an engagement score for a student, or aggregated across students to provide an engagement score for an item.

## Engagement Exhibited During a Student-Item Encounter

Let

$c_{ij}$ = the number of response actions completed by student $i$ to item $j$

$a_{ij}$ = the number of actions that should be completed by student $i$ to respond to item $j$

Then, the engagement of student $i$ to item $j$ is given by:

$$e_{ij} = \frac{c_{ij}}{a_{ij}} \tag{1}$$

Thus, $e_{ij}$ is the proportion of expected response actions that were completed by the student when responding to the item. A value of 1.0 indicates that the student was fully engaged, with values less than 1.0 indicating lesser degrees of engagement. For example, if an item had four expected response actions, and the student had completed three, $e_{ij}$ would be .75 for that student-item encounter.

## Overall Engagement of a Student to a Test with $k$ Items

The $e_{ij}$ values can be aggregated across all the items administered during a test event to provide an overall measure of the student's engagement. The Student Engagement Index (*SEI*) for student $i$ is equal to

$$SEI_i = \frac{\sum_{j=1}^{k} e_{ij}}{k}, \tag{2}$$

where $SEI_i$ represents the average item engagement exhibited by the student, taken across $k$ items. The formula for *SEI* is comparable to the *RTE* index developed by Wise and Kong (2005) and has a similar interpretation. *SEI* values of 1.0 indicate full engagement, and values less than 1.0 indicate the average proportion of expected item response actions that were completed.

## Overall Engagement Received by Item $j$ across $n$ Students

Alternatively, the $e_{ij}$ values for a given item can be aggregated across test events to provide a

measure of the amount of engagement the item received. The Item Engagement Index (*IEI*) for item $j$ is given by

$$IEI_j = \frac{\sum_{i=1}^{n} e_{ij}}{n}, \tag{3}$$

where $IEI_j$ represents the average item engagement received by the item, taken across $n$ students. *IEI* is comparable to the *RTF* index (Wise, 2006) and is interpreted in a similar way. *IEI* values of 1.0 indicate full engagement, and values less than 1.0 indicate the average proportion of expected item response actions that were completed. For example, if an item has an *IEI* value of .90, this would indicate that, on average, 90% of the expected response actions had been completed by students who were administered the item.

## EXAMPLE STUDY: INNOVATIVE ITEM DEVELOPMENT AND PILOT TESTING

An initial investigation of the two engagement indices was conducted for a set of innovative items that was designed to measure entry-level nursing skills (Wendt & Harmes, 2009). The purposes of the study were twofold. First, the engagement received by a variety of item types was studied. Second, validity evidence of the *SEI* was investigated. While focused on nursing, these examples should be generalizable to other real-world skills.

A set of 29 innovative items was developed using a template-based approach (Harmes & Wendt, 2009). For each item type, a single screen layout and basic set of student instructions was created, and then used as the framework for individual items of that type. Item types that were used in this study included:

- Video Inclusion

A video is included as the stimulus material for an item, and may also be included as the item's response options.

*Example*: A scenario is presented in which a group of nurses is discussing a conflict. The supervisor comes in and responds to the group. In this example, students must first watch the stem video that portrays the conflict. They then watch a set of videos that offer possible responses that the supervisor could make. The student must select the best response.

- Video Interaction

A video is the primary element in the item. The student interacts with the video by playing the video and then marking the video at one or more points.

*Example:* Students are presented with a scenario in which a nurse is changing the dressing on a patient's wound. The student must watch the video and mark any points at which the nurse makes an error. In this example, the video comprises the entire interaction space and the student clicks directly on the video to record his or her response. Once the student is satisfied that all errors have been marked, a final submit button is pressed.

- Audio Inclusion

An audio clip is included as the stimulus material for an item.

*Example*: A scenario is presented in which a nurse is taking care of several patients who are all calling with requests. The nurse must prioritize the order for attending to the patients. In this example, the student is given several audio clips in which different patients describe their conditions and requests. The student has to listen to these audio clips and choose the patient who should have top priority.

- Animation and Audio Inclusion

An animation with audio is included as stimulus material for an item.

*Example:* The student is presented with an animated graphic depicting lungs. The student must click on the graphic to see the lungs expand and contract, and to hear (through headphones) the breath sounds that correspond with inhaling and exhaling. The student must then select from within a realistic chart the types of breath sounds that were heard in different areas of the lungs.

- Decision Task Item Sets

Each decision task contains three or four items related to a common set of stimulus material. These items are presented in a set sequence, and a student's response to one of the items does not depend on the response to the others. Many of these item sets contain other innovative elements as well (graphics, video, nursing diagnosis lists, client chart information, etc.).

*Example:* Students are presented with a series of related items and patient information. The first item is similar to the above example for animation and audio inclusion. The second item then asks the student to select the most likely diagnosis. The final item requires the students to choose the type of medication that would best suit the patient's condition.

- Graphics Inclusion

A photograph or picture is included as the stimulus material for an item, and may also be included as the item's response options.

*Example:* Students are presented with several images of different syringes and asked to choose the one that should be used to administer a particular injection.

- Graphics Interaction

A photograph or picture is the primary element in the item. The student interacts with the graphic by selecting one or more areas within the graphic.

*Example:* Students are presented with an illustration of a hospital room with an infant in a crib. The graphic comprises the entire interaction area of the screen. Students must evaluate the scene for potential safety concerns, and select these by clicking on various elements in the room.

Two test forms were developed, each of which contained a combination of innovative and text-based multiple-choice items. Once the innovative items had been created, text-based versions of the same items were developed and refined as much as possible to create "parallel" item versions that would allow for comparison of student engagement across item modalities. There were some innovative items for which it was not possible to create a text-based item with any fidelity, so the items appeared in the innovative format on both test forms. Both assessment forms were then constructed to contain a mixture of the innovative and text-based items, for a total of 70 items per form. Items were arranged so that the innovative versions were interspersed throughout, and an item's position in a form was the same regardless of whether or not it was text-based or innovative. Data used in the example study were collected from 89 senior-level nursing students. These students were 97% female, and primarily identified themselves as white, not of Hispanic origin (83%). Other demographic groups included African American (3%), Asian Other (5%), Hispanic (5%), Pacific Islander (1%), and Other (4%). Most participants were native speakers of English (90%). They reported their level of computer experience as experienced or very experienced (86%) and their level of experience with computer-based tests as at least somewhat experienced (97%). Testing was conducted at five institutions, including both Bachelor's and Associate's degree granting nursing programs.

## Procedure for Measuring Student Engagement

The procedure for gathering and analyzing data on student engagement with innovative assessment items can be considered in seven basic steps: capture student behavioral data, construct a single dataset from all student log files, conduct descriptive analysis of behavioral data, relate behavioral data with item performance, define expected response actions, code the item response data, and calculate engagement indexes. These steps are described in general and then illustrated from the example study.

## Capture Student Behavioral Data

One of the advantages of computer-based tests (CBTs) is their capability for collecting detailed information regarding student behavior during tests. This information can be as specific as the individual actions taken by a student. When a mouse click occurs, what action that mouse click performs, and the time that transpires between mouse clicks (e.g., when a video is being played and paused) are all examples of behaviors that can be captured. While this recording can be done in different ways, such as video or screen recording, the simplest to interpret and least intrusive is to have the test delivery software write these actions in the background into a text-based log file. This log file can then be interpreted by the test givers to gain information about how students are interacting with the testing interface and the various item types. Further, this information can aid in understanding how well the actions completed by a student match what the test giver expects.

As part of the pilot testing software used in this example study, each student's actions were tracked by the testing software and written out to a flat text log file. For example, each time a student clicked to play a video, pause a video, view an exhibit, select a response, or deselect a response, that action was tracked, as well as the time signature corresponding to each action.

## Construct a Single Dataset

Whether the recording of student actions is accomplished through log files, video or screen recording, the result is a file (or set of files) that corresponds to each individual student. To perform the necessary analyses, these individual files must first be cleaned and aggregated into a single dataset. In the example study, the text-based log files for each student were read into a statistical software package to first determine the maximum number of actions that had been taken by the entire group for each test item. Once the parameters had been determined for each test item, a program was written to read and combine all student log files into a single dataset for analysis.

## Conduct Descriptive Analyses

Initial descriptive analyses can first be performed on the aggregated dataset. For each test item this might include examining the number of actions taken (minimum, maximum, and average), amount of time spent by students, and the number of item elements that students interacted with and how many times they did so. This dataset was first analyzed from a descriptive perspective, to assess the degree to which students were interacting with the items in the manner in which the item developers expected. In the example study, descriptive analysis questions for each of the items with video included: how many students played the stimulus video file and each of the response video files, how many students played them multiple times (for each file), and how much time was spent playing and replaying the videos before selecting and submitting a response. Similar questions were examined for each item type, and analyses specific to each item type were added as appropriate.

## Relate Behavioral Data with Item Performance

Once the aggregated dataset has been analyzed from a descriptive perspective, the behavioral data can then be combined with student item performance. The purpose of this step is to determine the relationship(s) between the number and types of actions taken by students with each item and whether or not they scored correctly on that item. Once this analysis is completed for each item, it can be viewed across items of a similar type to look for patterns. If the testing software has written the student's score for each item into the log file, no further data processing is required before performing the analysis. If the scored file is separate, it will simply require an additional step to import into the analysis software. In the example study, the above analyses were performed to examine relationships between student actions taken and their performance on the item. When looking at the performance on items with video inclusion, for example, one of the questions posed was whether or not students who played the video file multiple times tended to get those items correct.

## Define Expected Response Action Criteria

To prepare for computing engagement indexes, this step involves examining each item and identifying the actions that students are expected to perform when presented with the item. For example, if an item includes an animation as part of the stimulus material, students would be expected to play the animation and then select their response. With more complex items, this step becomes more detailed. While there may be many actions a student could take when interacting with the item, it is important to identify the set of actions that are required to indicate effortful behavior for each item. In the example study, a set of expected actions was identified for each test item. For items with video inclusion, for example, students were expected to play the entire stem video and all of the response option videos. Thus, if four actions were expected (playing the stem video and all three response option videos), a student's engagement with that item could be 0 (not engaged), 0.25, 0.5, 0.75 (degrees of partial engagement), or 1.0 (fully engaged).

## Calculate Engagement Indexes

The final analysis step is to calculate the engagement indexes. The first of these computations is the engagement exhibited by each student on each item (see Equation 1 above). This is the proportion of expected response actions for each item that were completed by each student. Focusing on the student level, these data can then be used to calculate the overall engagement that a student exhibited across all items on the test (*SEI*; see Equation 2 above). The same data can also be used to focus on each item and calculate the average degree to which students were engaged when interacting with that test item (*IEI*; see Equation 3 above). Once the *SEI* has been calculated for each student, it can be viewed across the set of students to identify patterns. Similarly, once the *IEI* has been computed for each item, the results can be examined for patterns across item type groupings.

## STUDY RESULTS

The first stages of data analysis resulted in a description of the manner in which students from the example study behaved when interacting with the innovative items, along with the relationship between student behavior and item performance. The next stage of the study resulted in a new procedure for assessing student engagement across various item types. This new procedure provided a more comprehensive picture of an item's performance than is currently available through traditional item analysis.

## Student Behavior by Item Type

Items built from the various templates included expectations for student behavior when interacting with the items. Following is a description of these expectations and behaviors by item template type.

## Video Inclusion

There were nine items with video included in the stem and response options. Expected student behavior with items generated from these templates was that students would play the stem video and play each of the response option videos. Results showed that virtually all students did play the stem and response videos, as expected. It was interesting to note that all videos except one (stem video for Q25) were played more than once by at least three students. In some cases, the majority of students played the video more than once.

## Video Interaction

There were three items in which a video clip was the stimulus material as well as the means through which students responded. For items built from this template, it was expected that students would play the entire video clip and place a flag on the video when they identified an error (or multiple errors in one item). Optional actions included re-starting the video, dragging the flag from one place to another, and dragging a slider to rewind or fast-forward the video. In all cases, the video was played by nearly all students, and replayed by more than half of them. All students placed the flag (required for responding), and many placed the flag more than once (i.e., changed their minds and put the flag in a different place). The optional action of dragging the flag to a different position was taken by all students on one item and nearly half of the students on the other two items. In many cases, this was done more than once.

## Audio Inclusion

Two items included audio clips as a portion of the stimulus material. In both items client chart information was also provided. The questions were written with the expectation that students would need to listen to all of the audio files as well as view the chart information for all clients in order to correctly respond to the item. For item Q8, 90% of students played all of the audio files at least once, and 79% opened the exhibits. On item Q38, 96% of students played all of the audio files, and 81% opened the exhibits. The percentage of students who played the audio files more than once for Q8 ranged from 17% (response 3) to 50% (response 1); neither of these was the item key.

## Animation and Audio Inclusion

There were three items that included an animation of a chest expanding and contracting, accompanied by breath sounds. Students were asked to click on each of the four lung quadrants, hear the breath sound that corresponded to that quadrant, and then chart the breath sounds they heard. Across the three items, 95-100% of students played the breath sounds at least once, and 40-98% played sounds more than once. The average percentage of students playing a sound more than once was 87% for Q6, 90% for Q21, and 52% for Q34. It is interesting to note that the most difficult item of the three (Q21; proportion correct [p] =.34) did have slightly more students replay the sounds, but the median response time was virtually the same as for the easiest of these items (Q6; p=.81). Item Q34 was the second item of this type received by students taking Form A. Thus, it is not surprising that fewer students replayed breath sounds, and

that the average response time was considerably lower, as any novelty effect of this different item type would have been diminished.

## Decision Task Item Sets (DTIS)

Only the first item within a DTIS was evaluated for engagement (the results of which are shown below), as the stimulus material did not change with subsequent items within a set. Therefore, although the material was accessible, it was anticipated that many students would not need to replay the videos in order to be able to correctly answer subsequent items. However, it is interesting to see the empirical results. For both those including video and those with client chart information, the number of students accessing the stimulus material decreased as students progressed through the item set.

In the case of the video inclusion item sets, nearly all students played all video files at least once with the first item, and the majority of students played the files more than once. For the second item within a set, the number of students playing the files at least once dropped to an average of 39% for Q13, 38% for Q35, and 21% for Q48. It is interesting to note that in terms of item difficulty on this second item, the one with the highest average number of students playing the video files was the easiest of these items appearing in the second position within a DTIS of this type. The most difficult of these second-position items, Q35, had two files that were played by far more students, which is masked when looking only at the average. In this case, the file with the breath sound for the upper left lobe was played at least once by 64% of the students, and played more than once by 20%. The video for the upper right lobe was played at least once by 43% of the students. These behaviors are indicative that students were having trouble making a decision about the correct response to this second item, and felt the need to access the files again. For the items in the third position within these sets, all of the video files were played at least once by at least one student. However, the percentages of students playing the video files at least once dropped to an average of 14% for Q13, 8% for Q35, and 5% for Q48. It is possible that some students may have played at least one of the files to make sure that nothing had changed (i.e., the breath sounds were still the same as they had been for the prior items in the set).

For the DTIS with client chart information, nearly all students accessed the chart information at least once for the first item in the set (90% for Q3 and 96% for Q47). For Q47, the number of students accessing the chart information declined with each subsequent item. However, with item Q3, one more student accessed the information on the second item in the set. For item Q47, the percentage of students opening the charts declined to 38% on the second item, then to 32% on the third item, and finally to 19% on the fourth item. In both DTIS, there were some students who continued to access this information through the last item in the DTIS.

## Graphics Interaction

Two items that were presented in identical format across the two test forms were image maps that were the means through which students responded to the items. In each photograph, multiple areas could be selected in response to the question (Q9 had eight clickable areas and Q41 had nine). When a student moused over these areas, they turned green, indicating that they could be selected. Once an area was selected, it was then outlined in red. For these items the item stem asked students to identify potential safety hazards, thus the red outline was appropriate. For both of these items, each of the clickable areas was selected at least once by at least one student. Most areas were not clicked on more than once. The area with the most clicks was the IV pump in item Q41, which was selected more than once by five students. Thus, it appears that students did not spend time selecting

and deselecting elements in the pictures. Response times for these items averaged around one minute. Both items were quite difficult, as was expected when applying dichotomous scoring to multiple response items.

## Overall Engagement Received by Items

*IEI* scores for the 29 innovative items, which are shown in Table 1, ranged from .83 to 1.0. There were several items with an average engagement score of 1.0. Four of these items were video inclusion, two were video interaction, and three were graphics inclusion. Items receiving the lowest average engagement included Q3 (.81), Q48 (.83), Q8 (.85), and Q38 (.87). Item Q3 was the first item in a decision task item set in which students were presented with a situation, given client chart information, and instructed to choose a nursing diagnosis from a long list of options. To be engaged, students had to open all of the exhibit tabs. It is interesting to note that no students scored correctly on this item. Item Q48 included a video of a client breathing, with accompanying audio. Students were to click on the video to auscultate the lungs, and heard breath sounds from each quadrant. No students failed to play any of the quadrants; several chose to only play one or two of the possible four, and thus did not receive a full engagement score. The majority of students scored incorrectly on this item. Items Q8 and Q38 were audio inclusion, in which students were presented with four audio clips of clients calling the nursing station, along with client chart information to review. For both items, there was a small group of students who completed some, but not all, of the expected actions (playing all clips and viewing all client chart tabs).

Collectively, if we apply an arbitrary criterion of .90 for acceptably high values of *IEI*, the results in Table 1 show that few of the items received levels of engagement that are cause for concern. The four items with *IEI* less than .90 should be

*Table 1. Item engagement index (IEI) values for the 29 innovative items*

| Item Number | Item Type | IEI | Item Number | Item Type | IEI |
|:---:|:---:|:---:|:---:|:---:|:---:|
| 2 | video inclusion | .91 | 24 | video interaction | 1.00 |
| 3 | DTIS with graphics inclusion | .81 | 25 | video inclusion | .97 |
| 5 | video inclusion | .95 | 28 | video inclusion | 1.00 |
| 6 | animation & audio inclusion | .98 | 29 | video inclusion | .97 |
| 8 | audio inclusion | .85 | 31 | video inclusion | 1.00 |
| 9 | graphics interaction | .97 | 32 | graphics inclusion & interaction | .94 |
| 10 | video interaction | .98 | 34 | animation & audio inclusion | .98 |
| 11 | video inclusion | .97 | 35 | DTIS with video inclusion | .97 |
| 13 | DTIS with video inclusion | .98 | 38 | audio inclusion | .88 |
| 14 | DTIS with graphics inclusion & interaction | .96 | 40 | video interaction | 1.00 |
| 15 | video inclusion | 1.00 | 41 | graphics interaction | 1.00 |
| 16 | video inclusion | 1.00 | 44 | DTIS with graphics inclusion & interaction | 1.00 |
| 19 | graphics inclusion & interaction | .99 | 47 | DTIS with exhibits | .92 |
| 21 | animation & audio inclusion | .95 | 48 | DTIS with video inclusion | .83 |
| 22 | DTIS with graphics inclusion & interaction | 1.00 | | | |

evaluated for possible revision, and they should not be used in operational tests until they have been shown (through future pilot testing) to elicit acceptable levels of student engagement.

## Student Engagement and Test Performance

For each of the students in the pilot study, *SEI* was computed based on their response behaviors to the innovative items. Additionally, *RTE* was computed for each student based on their response times to both the innovative and text-based multiple-choice items. When computing *RTE*, a common five-second threshold was used for differentiating rapid-guessing behavior from solution behavior. For each of the test forms, Table 2 shows descriptive statistics for test performance, *SEI*, and *RTE*. Overall, for each form, the students performed fairly well on the items, with the average scores

around 55% of the maximum attainable score for each form. In terms of student engagement, both *SEI* and *RTE* indicated high average engagement, but the minimum values indicated that there were one or more students who did not give good effort on their test.

Histograms of the *SEI* scores for each test form are shown in Figure 1. In each case, *SEI* exhibited a negatively skewed distribution that resembles the skewed frequency distributions that have been characteristic of *RTE* scores (Wise & Kong, 2005). There were three students (one who received Form A and 2 receiving Form B) whose *SEI* scores were particularly low (< .80). The test scores of these students should be interpreted cautiously, as it is likely that test performance for these students was negatively biased by disengaged test taking.

Descriptively examining the relationships between engagement scores and item scores allowed for exploration of patterns across various item

*Table 2. Descriptive statistics for test performance and student engagement*

| Test Form | Variable | $\overline{X}$ | SD | Minimum | Maximum |
|-----------|----------|-----|-----|---------|---------|
| Form A | Test Score | 40.76 | 6.39 | 22 | 52 |
| (N=42) | Student Engagement Index (*SEI*) | .96 | .05 | .69 | 1.00 |
| | Response Time Effort (*RTE*) | .99 | .03 | .80 | 1.00 |
| Form B | Total Test Score | 38.96 | 5.88 | 18 | 47 |
| (N=47) | Student Engagement Index (*SEI*) | .96 | .11 | .37 | 1.00 |
| | Response Time Effort (*RTE*) | .98 | .08 | .46 | 1.00 |

*Figure 1. Histograms of student engagement index scores for forms A and B*

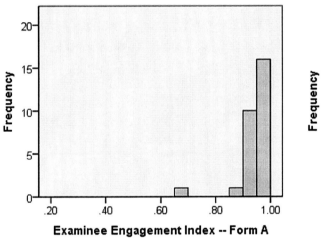
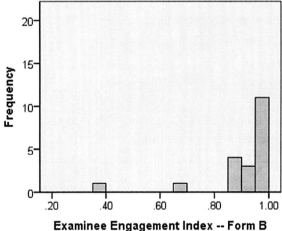

types. For example, of the nine video inclusion items, all students were fully engaged on four of them, while only two to six students were engaged, to a lesser degree, on the remainder. In cases in which students were less than fully engaged, they tended to score incorrectly on the item. On the three video interaction items, all students were fully engaged on two, with only one student not fully engaged (and scoring incorrectly) on the third item.

The two audio inclusion items showed interesting results, with both having several students who fell below the criteria for full engagement with the item. For example, on Q38, 11 students had an engagement score of 0.5. Of this group, nine scored incorrectly and two scored correctly. One student had an engagement score of 0.65 on this item, and scored incorrectly. All other students had an engagement score of one. Out of these 35 students, 20 scored incorrectly, and 15 scored correctly.

## Validating the Student Engagement Index

A primary inference made in this chapter is that the extent to which students complete an item's expected response actions provides a valid indicator of student engagement. Support for this inference can be found by examining the relationship between *SEI* and *RTE*. In each test event, *SEI* was calculated by examining the response actions completed by the student to innovative items. *RTE*, which has well-established evidence as a measure of student engagement (Wise, 2015), is based on the amount of time students take to answer multiple-choice and innovative items. If they are both measures of student engagement, to what extent are the two indices concordant?

Table 3 shows the correlations among test performance, *SEI*, and *RTE* for each of the test forms. The *SEI-RTE* correlations are high, particularly for Form B ($r = .93$). Moreover, in each of the test forms, the two engagement indices showed similar correlations with test performance. Figure

2 shows the scatter plots between *SEI* and *RTE*. These scatterplots suggest that, for the few students appearing disengaged, the two indices provided concordant information.

Additional validation evidence for *SEI* is provided by the accuracy of engaged versus disengaged students. In this analysis, an engaged student is defined as having an *SEI* of 1.0, while disengaged students had *SEI* values less than 1.0. For Form A, responses from engaged students were correct 44% of the time, while responses from disengaged students were correct only 26% of the time. The results were similar for Form B. Engaged students gave correct responses 42% of the time, and disengaged students gave correct responses 23% of the time. These findings indicate that (a) engaged students gave correct answers at a much higher rate than the disengaged students and (b) the accuracy rates of disengaged students resembled the accuracy rates of random responses. Similar findings have been found in numerous studies of RTE (Wise, 2015), which provides additional validity evidence for the SEI.

*Table 3. Correlations among test performance, SEI, and RTE*

| Variable | Form A | | Form B | |
|---|---|---|---|---|
| | RTE | Total Test Score | RTE | Total Test Score |
| SEI | .78 | .28 | .93 | .62 |
| RTE | | .24 | | .58 |

*Figure 2. Scatterplots of SEI by RTE*

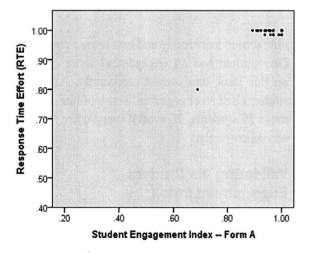

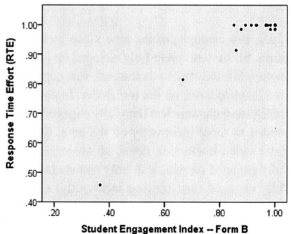

# ASSESSING STUDENT ENGAGEMENT WITH ADDITIONAL INNOVATIVE ITEM TYPES

Both *RTE* and *SEI* can be useful in assessing student engagement with text-based multiple-choice items and the types of innovative items described in this chapter, and such types of items can play a valuable role in the assessment of real-world skills. In addition to these innovative item types, technology offers the opportunity to create many different variations of selected response items, situated tasks, and even more sophisticated simulated environments (Harmes & Parshall, 2005; Parshall, Harmes, Davey, & Pashley, 2010; Zenisky & Sireci, 2013). Leighton (2012) describes these more complex environments as technologically-rich innovative assessments (TRIAs) that use "technology to simulate realistic problem solving environments, where students explore, investigate, test, and select options and courses of action in real time and watch the outcomes of their decisions come alive" (p. 3). Described below are examples of applying *RTE* and *SEI* to a range of additional innovative item types.

As with *RTE* and *SEI* illustrated earlier in the chapter, assessing engagement for items with different response actions (such as dragging and placing elements) or greater complexity requires a similar consideration of the tasks that one would expect to be completed by an engaged student, as well as with the time taken to complete the item. Response time is important in this context because it can help us better understand how to interpret instances in which the student exhibited none of the expected behaviors. For example, for an item that asks students to rearrange into chronological order (by clicking and dragging) a set of key events from the U.S. Civil War, suppose that a student submitted his answer after making zero rearrangements. If he submitted his answer within three seconds, one can probably safely conclude that the student was not engaged and did not make an effort to answer the item. However, if the student submitted his answer after three minutes, then a more plausible interpretation would be that either his knowledge about the Civil War is inadequate or he did not understand how to execute the expected clicking and dragging response actions needed to answer the item. Hence, a short response time to an item may unambiguously indicate a lack of engagement, while a longer response time is more equivocal, though it may indicate that the student did not know how to effectively respond to the item.

Despite the wide (and growing) array of innovative item types that have been proposed, the general idea of defining and looking for expected student behaviors should be useful in assessing engagement with many item types. This will particularly be the case of the types of "intermediate constraint" questions and tasks discussed in Scalise's taxonomy (Scalise, 2012; Scalise & Gifford, 2006). Intermediate constraint items, which lie between fully selected response items (e.g., multiple-choice) and fully constructed response (e.g., demonstrations or projects), often require students to perform some sort of specific response action to indicate their answers such as clicking, dragging, highlighting, selecting information from pop-up menus, or correcting errors. These response actions, which can be captured in log files for later analysis can be evaluated to assess student engagement through calculation of *SEI*, or to conduct item analyses using *IEI*, all using the processes described and shown in this chapter.

To further illustrate this idea, student engagement will be considered for three additional example item types. The first is a substitution/correction item described by Scalise and Gifford (2006) and Zenisky and Sireci (2002). In this item type, the student is asked to edit and correct an onscreen passage or formula by selecting alternative words, phrases, or mathematical expressions from one or more drop-down menus. For this item, an engaged student would be expected to click on each drop-down menu and make at least one correction. The proportion of actions that were exhibited by a particular student in answering the item could be used in calculating the student's *SEI*.

In a second item type, students are asked to select and classify elements from a list (Sireci & Zenisky, 2006). Sireci and Zenisky gave an example of this item in which a list of 10 lakes are shown, and students are asked to drag each lake's name to one of four boxes corresponding to the region of the country to which it belongs. To complete this item, an engaged student would be expected to click on and drag each of the 10 lake names. Thus, there would be 10 expected response actions that could be evaluated in assessing a student's engagement.

The third item type, which was proposed by Dolan, Goodman, Strain-Seymour, Adams, and Sethuraman (2011), and discussed by Leighton (2012), asks students to evaluate the factual accuracy of written information based on external sources of information. In the example item given by Leighton, an item web page is provided about Emperor Penguins, and the student is informed that the web page contains four content errors. The student is directed to research a National Geographic web site to identify the errors in the item web page and then click on four "edit" buttons on the web page to correct the errors. An engaged student would be expected to exhibit at least five actions: click on the National Geographic link and click on each of the four edit buttons. A log file could capture the student's response actions, which could be evaluated to calculate a student's *SEI*.

## CONCLUSION

The integration of technology into assessment has encouraged a re-thinking of what test items can look like and the types of responses that can be expected of students during assessment. This has led to the creation of a new generation of test item types that "can sample as broad a range of

behaviors as needed while preserving a great deal of fidelity to the construct of interest" (Zenisky & Sireci, 2002, p. 337). At the same time, there are implications for student motivation, and technology provides us the capability to peer inside test events and to study test-taking behavior in a more fine-grained fashion than was possible with paper-and-pencil assessments. This is especially important because innovative items tend to ask more effort from students than do traditional multiple-choice items, which can diminish test-taking motivation (Wolf et al., 1995). However, others suggest that innovative items may increase student engagement, and thus increase their test-taking motivation (Zenisky & Sireci, 2013). Hence, there are reasons to be especially attentive to the impact of innovative items on student engagement.

The procedures described and illustrated in this chapter show that by articulating the behaviors we would expect engaged test takers to exhibit, we can identify instances in which students were disengaged during an assessment. In addition, through use of the *IEI*, we can better gauge the amount of effort received by individual test items, which can help inform evaluations of the measurement value of particular item types. For example, knowing how many times a video file was played and replayed can provide an indication of which responses a student was trying to choose between, or which distractors were the most enticing, even if they were not selected. In addition, in cases in which the log files indicated that the expected actions for particular items were not completely understood by students, recommendations can be made for item revision accordingly.

Having more fine-grained information regarding the level of student engagement, as well as the amount of engagement received by particular items, will be helpful in assessing the validity of the inferences that are made from scores on innovative items. As innovative items continue to be developed and evaluated, it is recommended that behavioral components, such as those described in this chapter, continue to be examined. With an increasing emphasis on learning and assessment of real-world skills in K-12 settings (Partnership for 21st Century Skills, 2011) comes a need to advance the tools used by measurement professionals in creating and evaluating these assessments. Innovative items provide a means for addressing the need for greater authenticity in assessing real-world and career skills. As technology advances, the possibilities will continue to expand for innovative items to become more complex and have greater fidelity to the target skills and contexts. This further emphasizes the need for procedures and tools that can be used to evaluate the quality of innovative items and assessments, and insure the validity of the inferences that are made from resulting scores.

# REFERENCES

Davies, R. S., & West, R. E. (2014). Technology integration in schools. In J. M. Spector, M. D. Merrill, J. Elen, & M. J. Bishop (Eds.), *Handbook of research on educational communications and technology* (pp. 841–853). New York, NY: Springer. doi:10.1007/978-1-4614-3185-5_68

Dolan, R. P., Goodman, J., Strain-Seymour, E., Adams, J., & Sethuraman, S. (2011). *Cognitive lab evaluation of innovative items in mathematics and English language arts assessment of elementary, middle, and high school students: Research report.* Pearson.

Harmes, J. C., & Parshall, C. G. (2005). *Situated tasks and simulated environments: A look into the future for innovative computerized assessment.* Paper presented at the annual meeting of the Florida Educational Research Association, Miami, FL.

Harmes, J. C., & Parshall, C. G. (2010, April). *A model for planning, designing, and developing innovative items.* Paper presented at the annual meeting of the National Council on Measurement in Education, Denver, CO.

Harmes, J. C., & Wendt, A. (2009, Winter). Memorability of innovative item types. *CLEAR Exam Review, 20*(1), 16–20.

Huff, K. L., & Sireci, S. G. (2001, Fall). Validity issues in computer-based testing. *Educational Measurement: Issues and Practice, 20*(3), 16–25. doi:10.1111/j.1745-3992.2001.tb00066.x

King, M. B., Newmann, F. M., & Carmichael, D. L. (2009). Authentic intellectual work: Common standards for teaching social studies. *Social Education, 73*(1), 43–49.

Leighton. (2012, April). *Issues of cost, time, and validity: Psychometric perspectives on technologically-rich innovative assessments (TRIAs).* Paper presented at the annual meeting of the American Educational Research Association, Vancouver, Canada.

Newmann, F. M., Marks, H. M., & Gamoran, A. (1996). Authentic pedagogy and student performance. *American Journal of Education, 104*(8), 280–312. doi:10.1086/444136

Parshall, C. G., Harmes, J. C., Davey, T., & Pashley, P. J. (2010). Innovative item types for computerized testing. In W. J. van der Linden & C. A. W. Glas (Eds.), *Elements of adaptive testing* (pp. 215–230). New York: Springer.

Partnership for 21st Century Skills. (2011). *Framework for 21st century learning.* Retrieved from http://www.p21.org/storage/documents/1._p21_framework_2-pager.pdf

Scalise, K. (2012, May). Using technology to assess hard-to-measure constructs in the Common Core State Standards and to expand accessibility. *ETS Invitational Research Symposium on Technology Enhanced Assessments*, Princeton, NJ.

Scalise, K., & Gifford, B. R. (2006). Computer-based assessment in e-learning: A framework for constructing "intermediate constraint" questions and tasks for technology platforms. *Journal of Teaching, Learning, and Assessment, 4*(6), 1–44.

Sireci, S. G., & Zenisky, A. L. (2006). Innovative item formats in computer-based testing: In pursuit of improved construct representation. In S. M. Downing & T. M. Haladyna (Eds.), *Handbook of test development* (pp. 329–347). Mahwah, NJ: Lawrence Erlbaum Associates.

Strain-Seymour, E., Way, W., & Dolan, P. (2009, June). *Strategies and processes for developing innovative items in large-scale assessments.* Retrieved from http://images.pearsonassessments.com/images/tmrs/StrategiesandProcessesforDevelopingInnovativeItems.pdf

United States Department of Education. (2014, June). *Learning technology effectiveness.* Retrieved from http://tech.ed.gov/learning-technology-effectiveness/

Wendt, A., & Harmes, J. C. (2009, May/June). Evaluating innovative items for the NCLEX, Part 2: Item characteristics and cognitive processing. *Nurse Educator, 34*(3), 109–113. doi:10.1097/NNE.0b013e31819fcae8 PMID:19412048

Wiggins, G. (1990). The case for authentic assessment. *Practical Assessment, Research & Evaluation, 2*(2). Retrieved from http://PAREonline.net/getvn.asp?v=2&n=2

Wise, S. L. (2006). An investigation of the differential effort received by items on a low-stakes, computer-based test. *Applied Measurement in Education, 19*(2), 93–112. doi:10.1207/s15324818ame1902_2

Wise, S. L. (2015). Effort analysis: Individual score validation of achievement test data. *Applied Measurement in Education, 28*(3), 237-252.

Wise, S. L., & DeMars, C. E. (2005). Low examinee effort in low-stakes assessment: Problems and potential solutions. *Educational Assessment, 10*(1), 1–17. doi:10.1207/s15326977ea1001_1

Wise, S. L., & Kong, X. (2005). Response time effort: A new measure of student motivation in computer-based tests. *Applied Measurement in Education, 18*(2), 163–183. doi:10.1207/s15324818ame1802_2

Wise, S. L., Pastor, D. A., & Kong, X. J. (2009). Understanding correlates of rapid-guessing behavior in low stakes testing: Implications for test development and measurement practice. *Applied Measurement in Education, 22*(2), 185–205. doi:10.1080/08957340902754650

Wolf, L. F., & Smith, J. K. (1995). The consequence of consequence: Motivation, anxiety, and test performance. *Applied Measurement in Education, 8*(3), 227–242. doi:10.1207/s15324818ame0803_3

Wolf, L. F., Smith, J. K., & Birnbaum, M. E. (1995). Consequence of performance, test motivation, and mentally taxing items. *Applied Measurement in Education, 8*(4), 341–351. doi:10.1207/s15324818ame0804_4

Zenisky, A. L., & Sireci, S. G. (2002). Technological innovations in large-scale assessment. *Applied Measurement in Education, 15*(4), 337–362. doi:10.1207/S15324818AME1504_02

Zenisky, A. L., & Sireci, S. G. (2013, April). *Innovative items to measure higher-order thinking: Development and validity considerations.* Presentation at the annual meeting of the National Council on Measurement in Education, San Francisco, CA.

## KEY TERMS AND DEFINITIONS

**Engagement:** The degree to which a student taking a test directs attention and effort to providing correct answers to a test's items.

**Innovative Items:** Test items delivered on a computer (or some other digital device) that contain functions and features not possible with a traditional, text-based multiple-choice item.

**Item Engagement Index (*IEI*):** A behavior-based index of the amount of effort received by a test item, across a set of test events. *IEI* is based on the proportion of the expected response actions that were completed by students when responding to the item.

**Response Time Effort (*RTE*):** A response time-based index of the amount of effort exhibited by a test taker during a multiple-choice test event. Specifically, *RTE* equals the proportion of a student's responses that were solution behaviors, as opposed to rapid guesses.

**Response Time Fidelity (*RTF*):** A response time-based index of the amount of effort received by a multiple-choice item. Specifically, *RTF* equals, across test events, the proportion of responses to an item that were solution behaviors as opposed to rapid guesses.

**Response Time:** The elapsed time between when a computer-based item is displayed and when a test taker submits an answer.

**Student Engagement Index (*SEI*):** A behavior-based index of the amount of effort exhibited by a student to a set of test items. *SEI* is based on the proportion of expected response actions that were completed by the student when responding to the items.

# Compilation of References

Abel, M. (2005). Find me on Facebook…as long as you are not a faculty member or administrator. *Esource for College Transitions, 3*(3), 1–2.

Achieve. (2014). What is college and career readiness. *The Future Ready Project.* Retrieved from http://www. futurereadyproject.org/sites/frp/files/College_and_Career_Readiness.pdf

ACT. (2005). *Crisis at the core: Preparing all students for college and work.* Iowa City, IA: ACT. Retrieved from: http://www.act.org/research/policymakers/reports/crisis.html

ACT. (2008). ACT-SAT concordance. *Compare ACT & SAT Scores.* Retrieved, from http://www.act.org/aap/concordance/

ACT. (2009). *National overview: Measuring college and career readiness - The class of 2009.* Iowa City, IA: ACT. Retrieved from http://www.act.org/newsroom/data/2009/pdf/output/NationalOverview.pdf

ACT. (2013). *College and career readiness: The importance of early learning.* Retrieved from: http://www.act.org/research/policymakers/pdf/ImportanceofEarlyLearning.pdf

ACT. (2014). *The condition of college and career readiness.* Retrieved from: http://www.act.org/research/policymakers/cccr14/pdf/CCCR14-NationalReadinessRpt.pdf

Adejumo, G., Duimering, R. P., & Zhong, Z. (2008). A balance theory approach to group problem solving. *Social Networks, 30*(1), 83–99. doi:10.1016/j.socnet.2007.09.001

Agresti, A. (1990). *Categorical data analysis.* New York, NY: John Wiley & Sons, Inc.

Ahlgrim-Delzell, L., Browder, D. M., & Wood, L. (2014). Effects of systematic instruction and an augmentative communication device on phonics skills acquisition for students with moderate intellectual disability who are nonverbal. *Education and Training in Autism and Developmental Disabilities, 49,* 517–532.

Ahuja, J., & Webster, J. (2001). Perceived disorientation: An examination of a new measure to assess web design effectiveness. *Interacting with Computers, 14*(1), 15–29. doi:10.1016/S0953-5438(01)00048-0

Ainsworth, S. (2008). The educational value of multiple-representations when learning complex scientific concepts. In J. K. Gilbert, M. Reiner, & M. Nakhleh (Eds.), *Visualization: Theory and practice in science education* (pp. 191–208). Dordrecht: Springer. doi:10.1007/978-1-4020-5267-5_9

Akyol, Z., & Garrison, D. R. (2011). Understanding cognitive presence in an online and blended community of inquiry: Assessing outcomes and processes for deep approaches to learning. *British Journal of Educational Technology, 42*(2), 233–250. doi:10.1111/j.1467-8535.2009.01029.x

Aldunate, R., & Nussbaum, M. (2013). Teacher adoption of technology. *Computers in Human Behavior, 29*(3), 519–524. doi:10.1016/j.chb.2012.10.017

Alexander, P. A., & Jetton, T. L. (2002). Learning from text: A multidimensional and developmental perspective. In M. L. Kamil, P. Mosenthal, P. D. Pearson, & R. Barr (Eds.), *Handbook of reading research* (Vol. 3, pp. 285–310). Mahwah, NJ: Erlbaum.

Algeria, D., Boscardin, C., Poncelet, A., Mayfield, C., & Wamsley, M. (2014). Using tablets to support self-regulated learning in a longitudinal integrated clerkship. *Medical Education Online*, *19*, 1–7. PMID:24646438

All, A. C., Huycke, L. I., & Fisher, M. J. (2003). Instructional tools for nursing education: Concept maps. *Nursing Education Perspectives*, *24*(6), 311–317. PMID:14705401

Allen, E., & Seaman, J. (2010). *Learning on demand: Online education in the United States. Babson Survey Research Group*. Sloan Consortium.

Allen, K. D., Burke, R. V., Howard, M. R., Wallace, D. P., & Bowen, S. L. (2012). Use of audio cuing to expand employment opportunities for adolescents with autism spectrum disorders and intellectual disabilities. *Journal of Autism and Developmental Disorders*, *42*(11), 2410–2419. doi:10.1007/s10803-012-1519-7 PMID:22456818

Allington, R. L. (1977). If they don't read much, how are they ever gonna get good? *Journal of Reading*, *21*, 57–61.

Allington, R. L. (1980). Poor readers don't get much in reading groups. *Language Arts*, *57*(8), 872–877.

Allington, R. L. (1983). The reading instruction provided readers of differing abilities. *The Elementary School Journal*, *83*(5), 548–559. doi:10.1086/461333

Allington, R. L. (1984). Content coverage and contextual reading in reading groups. *Journal of Reading Behavior*, *16*(1), 85–96.

Allington, R. L. (2009). If they don't read much…30 years later. In E. H. Hiebert (Ed.), *Reading more, reading better* (pp. 30–54). New York: Guilford Press.

Allsopp, M. M., Hohlfeld, T., & Kemker, K. (2007). *The Technology Integration Matrix: The development and field-test of an Internet based multi-media assessment tool for the implementation of instructional technology in the classroom*. Paper presented at the annual meeting of the Florida Educational Research Association, Tampa, FL.

Allukian, M. Jr. (2008). The Neglected Epidemic and the Surgeon General's Report: A Call to Action for Better Oral Health. *American Journal of Public Health*, *98*(Suppl 1), S82–S85. doi:10.2105/AJPH.98.Supplement_1.S82 PMID:18687628

Almond, R., Deane, P., Quinlan, T., Wagner, M., & Sydorenko, T. (2012). *A preliminary analysis of keystroke log data from a timed writing task (Research Report, ETS RR-12-23)*. Princeton, NJ: Educational Testing Service.

Al-Smadi, M., & Gütl, C. (2008). *Past, present and future of e-assessment: Towards a flexible e-assessment system*. Paper presented at the International Conference on Interactive Computer Aided Learning, Villach. Retrieved from http://bit.ly/1qDK7JY

Amadieu, F., & Salmerón, L. (2014). Concept maps for comprehension and navigation of hypertexts. In R. Hanewald & D. Ifenthaler (Eds.), *Digital Knowledge Maps in Education* (pp. 41–59). New York: Springer. doi:10.1007/978-1-4614-3178-7_3

Amadieu, F., & Tricot, A. (2006). Utilisation d'un hypermedia et apprentissage: Deux activités concurrentes ou complémentaires?[Hypermedia usage and learning: two competing or complementary activities?]. *Psychologie Française*, *51*(1), 5–23. doi:10.1016/j.psfr.2005.12.001

Ambrose, S., Bridges, M., Lovett, M., DiPetro, M., & Norman, M. (2010). *How learning works: 7 research-based principles for smart teaching*. San Francisco, CA: Jossey-Bass.

American Academy of Arts and Sciences. (2013). *ARISE 2: Unleashing America's research & innovative enterprise*. Cambridge, MA: American Academy of Arts and Sciences.

American Association of Colleges of Nursing. (2008). *The essentials of baccalaureate education for professional nursing practice*. Washington, DC: American Association of Colleges of Nursing.

American Association of Colleges of Nursing. (2010). *The Research-Focused Doctoral Program in Nursing: Pathways to Excellence*. Washington, DC: American Association of Colleges of Nursing.

American Association of Colleges of Nursing. (2011). *The Essentials of Master's Education for Advanced Practice Nursing*. Retrieved August 15, 2015, from http://www.aacn.nche.edu/educationresources/MastersEssentials11.pdf

American Association of Colleges of Nursing. (2012). *New AACN Data Show an Enrollment Surge in Baccalaureate and Graduate Programs amid Calls for More Highly Educated Nurses.* Retrieved August 15, 2015, from http://www.aacn.nche.edu/news/articles/2012/enrollment-data

American Association of State Colleges and Universities. (2006, Spring). Value-added assessment: accountability's new frontier. *Perspectives.* Retrieved from http://www.aascu.org/uploadedFiles/AASCU/Content/Root/PolicyAndAdvocacy/PolicyPublications/06_perspectives%281%29.pdf

American Educational Research Association, American Psychological Association, & National Council on Measurement in Education. (2014). *Standards for educational and psychological testing.* Washington, DC: American Educational Research Association.

American Educational Research Association. American Psychological Association, & National Council for Measurement in Education. (2014). Standards for educational and psychological testing. Washington, DC: American Educational Research Assn.

American Educational Research Association. American Psychological Association, & National Council on Research in Education. (1999). The standards of educational and psychological testing. Washington, DC: American Educational Research Association.

American Library Association (ALA). (1989). *Presidential committee on information literacy: Final report.* Retrieved July 20, 2014, from http://www.ala.org/acrl/publications/whitepapers/presidential

American Library Association (ALA). (2014). *Standards toolkit.* Retrieved July 20, 2014, from http://www.ala.org/acrl/issues/infolit/standards/standardstoolkit

American Library Association. Digital Literacy, Libraries, and Public Policy, Information Technology Policy's Digital Literacy Task Force. (2013). *BC's digital literacy framework* (DRAFT). Retrieved July 20, 2014, from http://www.bced.gov.bc.ca/dist_learning/docs/digital-literacy-framework-v3.pdf

Amershi, S., & Conati, C. (2009). Combining unsupervised and supervised classification to build user models for exploratory learning environments. *Journal of Educational Data Mining, 1*(1), 18–81.

Ames, C., & Archer, J. (1988). Achievement goals in the classroom: Students' learning strategies and motivation processes. *Journal of Educational Psychology, 80*(3), 260–267. doi:10.1037/0022-0663.80.3.260

Amzil, A., & Stine-Morrow, E. (2013). Metacognition: Components and relation to academic achievement in college. *Arab World English Journal, 4*(4), 371–385.

Ananiadou, K., & Claro, M. (2009). 21st century skills and competences for new millennium learners in OECD countries. *OECD Education Working Papers, 41.*

Anastasiades, P., Filippousis, G., Karvunis, L., Siakas, S., Tomazinakis, A., Giza, P., & Mastoraki, H. (2008). Interactive Videoconferencing for collaborative learning at a distance in the school of 21st century: A case study in elementary schools in Greece. *Computers & Education, 54*(2), 321–339. doi:10.1016/j.compedu.2009.08.016

Anctil, T. M., & Adams, N. J. (2002). Computer-based testing in vocational assessment and evaluation: A primer for rehabilitation professionals. *Vocational Evaluation and Work Adjustment Journal, 34,* 5-15. Retrieved from http://bit.ly/1jRKfZ5

Anderman, E. M., & Dawson, H. (2011). Learning and motivation. In R. E. Mayer & P. A. Alexander (Eds.), Handbook of research on learning and instruction (pp. 219-241). New York: Routledge.

Anderman, E. M., & Anderman, L. H. (2010). *Classroom motivation.* Upper Saddle River, NJ: Pearson.

Anderson, E., Gulwani, S., & Popovic, Z. (2013). A trace-based framework for analyzing and synthesizing educational progressions. In *Proceedings of the Special Interest Group on Computer-Human Interaction (SIGCHI) Conference on Human Factors in Computing Systems,* (pp. 773–782). doi:10.1145/2470654.2470764

Anderson-Inman, L. (1992). Electronic studying: Computer-based information organizers as tools for lifelong learning. In N. Estes & M. Thomas (Eds.), *Education "sans frontiers":Proceedings of the ninth annual international conference on technology and education,* (pp. 1104-1106). Austin, TX: The University of Texas at Austin.

Anderson-Inman, L. (1995). Computer-assisted outlining: Information organization made easy. *Journal of Adolescent & Adult Literacy, 39,* 316–320.

Anderson-Inman, L. (1999). Computer-based solutions for secondary students with learning disabilities: Emerging issues. *Reading & Writing Quarterly*, *15*(3), 239–249. doi:10.1080/105735699278215

Anderson-Inman, L. (2009a). Supported etext: Literacy scaffolding for students with disabilities. *Journal of Special Education Technology*, *24*(3), 1–8.

Anderson-Inman, L. (2009b). Thinking between the lines: Literacy and learning in a connected world. *On the Horizon*, *17*(2), 122–141. doi:10.1108/10748120910965502

Anderson-Inman, L., & Ditson, L. (1999). Computer-based concept mapping: A tool for negotiating meaning. *Learning and Leading with Technology*, *26*(8), 6–13.

Anderson-Inman, L., & Horney, M. (2007). Supported etext: Assistive technology through text transformations. *Reading Research Quarterly*, *42*(1), 153–160. doi:10.1598/RRQ.42.1.8

Anderson-Inman, L., Horney, M., Knox-Quinn, C., Ditson, M., & Ditson, L. (1997). *Computer-based study strategies: Empowering students with technology*. Eugene, OR: Center for Electronic Studying, University of Oregon.

Anderson-Inman, L., Knox-Quinn, C., & Horney, M. (1996). Computer-based study strategies for students with learning disabilities: Individual differences associated with adoption level. *Journal of Learning Disabilities*, *29*(5), 461–484. doi:10.1177/002221949602900502 PMID:8870517

Anderson-Inman, L., Knox-Quinn, C., & Szymanski, M. (1999). Computer-supported studying: Stories of successful transition to postsecondary education. *Career Development for Exceptional Individuals*, *22*(2), 185–212. doi:10.1177/088572889902200204

Anderson-Inman, L., & Reinking, D. (1998). Learning from text in a technological society. In C. Hynd, S. Stahl, B. Britton, M. Carr, & S. Glynn (Eds.), *Learning from text across conceptual domains in secondary schools* (pp. 165–191). Mahwah, NJ: Lawrence Erlbaum.

Anderson-Inman, L., Richter, J., Frisbee, M., & Williams, M. (2007). *Computer-based study strategies for handhelds*. Eugene, OR: Center for Advanced Technology in Education, University of Oregon.

Anderson-Inman, L., & Tenny, J. (1989). Electronic studying: Information organizers to help students study better not harder. *The Computing Teacher*, *16*(8), 33–36.

Anderson, J. R., Boyle, C. F., Corbett, A. T., & Lewis, M. W. (1990). Cognitive modeling and intelligent tutoring. *Artificial Intelligence*, *42*(1), 7–49. doi:10.1016/0004-3702(90)90093-F

Anderson, L., & Krathwohl, D. (2001). *A taxonomy for learning, teaching and assessing: A revision of Bloom's taxonomy of educational objectives*. New York: Longman.

Anderson, R. C., Hiebert, E. H., Scott, J. A., & Wilkinson, I. A. G. (1985). *Becoming a nation of readers. U.S. Department of Education, Office of Educational Research and Improvement (ED)*. Washington, DC: U.S. Government Printing Office.

Anderson, R. C., Wilson, P. T., & Fielding, L. C. (1988). Growth in reading and how children spend their time outside of school. *Reading Research Quarterly*, *23*(3), 285–303. doi:10.1598/RRQ.23.3.2

Anderson, T., & Dron, J. (2011). Three Generations of Distance Education Pedagogy. *International Review of Research in Open and Distance Learning*, *12*(3). Retrieved from http://www.irrodl.org/index.php/irrodl/article/view/890/1663

Anderson, W., Krathwohl, R., Airasian, R., Cruikshank, A., Mayer, R., Pintrich, P., & Wittrock, M. (2001). *A taxonomy for learning, teaching, and assessing: A revision of Bloom's Taxonomy of educational objectives (Complete Edition)*. New York: Longman.

Andersson, H., & Bergman, L. R. (2011). The role of task persistence in young adolescence for successful educational and occupational attainment in middle adulthood. *Developmental Psychology*, *47*(4), 950–960. doi:10.1037/a0023786 PMID:21639622

Anohina, A., & Grundspenkis, J. (2007). A concept map based intelligent system for adaptive knowledge assessment. In O. Vasilecas, J. Eder & A. Caplinskas (Eds.), *Databases and information systems IV: selected papers from the Seventh International Baltic Conference DB&IS* (pp. 263-276). Amsterdam: IOS Press.

Apampa, K. M., Wills, G., & Argles, D. (2010). User security issues in summative e-assessment security. *International Journal of Digital Society, 1*(2), 135–147. Retrieved from http://bit.ly/1erjJ6e

Applebee, A. N., & Langer, J. A. (2006). *The state of writing instruction in America's schools: What existing data tell us.* Albany, NY: Center on English Learning and Achievement.

Applebee, A. N., & Langer, J. A. (2009). What is happening in the teaching of writing? *English Journal, 98*(5), 18–28.

Approaches to Information and Communication Literacy. (2007). *Teacher Tap- professional development resources for education & librarians.* Retrieved July 20, 2014, from http://eduscapes.com/tap/topic72.htm

Arendasy, M. E., & Sommer, M. (2010). Evaluating the contribution of different item features to the effect sixe of the gender differences in three-dimensional mental rotation using automatic item generation. *Intelligence, 38*(6), 574–581. doi:10.1016/j.intell.2010.06.004

Arensen, T. (2015). *Internet Access in Secondary Schools and Perseverance in Academic Work: Norway/Sweden Versus Finland.* Paper presented at the 2015 Annual Meeting of the American Educational Research Association, Chicago, IL.

Arthur, W., Day, E. A., McNelly, T. L., & Edens, P. S. (2003). A meta-analysis of the criterion-related validity of assessment center dimensions. *Personnel Psychology, 56*(1), 125–153. doi:10.1111/j.1744-6570.2003.tb00146.x

Arum, R., Roksa, J., & Velez, M. (2008). *Learning to reason and communicate in college: Initial report of findings from the CLA longitudinal study.* Retrieved from Social Science Research Council website: http://www.ssrc.org/workspace/uploads/docs/CLA_Report.pdf

Arum, R., & Roksa, J. (2011). *Academically adrift: Limited learning on college campuses.* Chicago, IL: University of Chicago Press.

Arvaja, M., Hakkinen, P., Rasku-Puttonen, H., & Etelapelto, A. (2002). Social processes and knowledge building during small group interaction in a school science project. *Scandinavian Journal of Educational Research, 46*(2), 161–179. doi:10.1080/00313830220142182

Atkinson, R. (2001). *Standardized tests and access to American universities.* The 2001 Robert H. Atwell Distinguished Lecture. American Council on Education. Retrieved from https://escholarship.org/uc/item/6182126z

Atkinson, R. C., & Geiser, S. (2009). *Reflections on a century of college admissions tests* (CSHE.4.09) Retrieved from Center for Studies in Higher Education website: http://www.cshe.berkeley.edu/sites/default/files/shared/publications/docs/ROPS-AtkinsonGeiser-Tests-04-15-09.pdf

Attali, Y., & Burstein, J. (2006). Automated Essay Scoring with e-rater V.2. *Journal of Technology, Learning, and Assessment, 4*(3). Retrieved from http://www.jtla.org

Attali, Y., & Powers, D. (2008). *Effect of immediate feedback and revision on psychometric properties of open-ended GRE Subject Test items* (ETS Research Report No. RR-08-21, GRE Research Report No. GREB-04-05). Princeton, NJ: Educational Testing Service.

Attali, Y., & Powers, D. (2008). *A developmental writing scale (Report No. ETS RR-08-19).* Princeton, NJ: ETS.

Attali, Y., & Powers, D. (2010). Immediate feedback and opportunity to revise answers to open-ended questions. *Educational and Psychological Measurement, 70*(1), 22–35. doi:10.1177/0013164409332231

Ault, M. J., Wolery, M., Doyle, P. M., & Gast, D. L. (1989). Review of comparative studies in the instruction of students with moderate and severe handicaps. *Exceptional Children, 55*, 346–356. PMID:2521602

Ausubel, D. O., Novak, J. D., & Hanesian, H. (1978). *Educational psychology: A cognitive view* (2nd ed.). Holt, Rinehart and Winston.

Autor, D. H., Levy, F., & Murname, R. J. (2003). The skill content of recent technological change: An empirical exploration. *The Quarterly Journal of Economics, 118*(4), 1279–1333. doi:10.1162/003355303322552801

Avcioglu, H. (2013). Effectiveness of video modeling in training students with intellectual disabilities to greet people when they meet. *Educational Sciences: Theory and Practice, 13*, 466–477.

Avni, E. (2012). *Hitpatkhut mudaut etit shel morim digitaliim* [Development of ethical awareness of digital teachers]. (Unpublished doctoral dissertation). University of Haifa, Israel. (Hebrew)

Avni, E., & Rotem, A. (2009). Pgia mekuvenet. [Cyberbullying]. *Toward Digital Ethics Initiative.* Retrieved July 20, 2014, from http://ianethics.com/wp-content/uploads/2009/10/cyberBullying_IA_oct_09.pdf (Hebrew).

Avni, E., & Rotem, A. (2010). Nohal shimush bemedia khevratit mekuvenet bevatei hasefer [Regulations for usage of online social media in schools]. *Toward Digital Ethics Initiative.* Retrieved July 20, 2014, from http://ianethics.com/wp-content/uploads/2010/12/socail-media-schoo-IA.pdf (Hebrew)

Avni, E., & Rotem, A. (2011). Oryanut etit baidan hadigitali – Mimiyumanut letfisat olam [Ethical literacy in the digital age – From skill to worldview]. *Toward Digital Ethics Initiative.* Retrieved July 20, 2014, from http://ianethics.com/wp-content/uploads/2011/06/Ethical-Literacy-AI.pdf (Hebrew)

Avni, E., & Rotem, A. (2013). Lemida mashmautit 2020 – Tekhnologia meatzevet mashmaut [Meaningful 2020 learning – Technology that forms meaning]. *Toward Digital Ethics Initiative.* Retrieved July 20, 2014, from http://ianethics.com/wp-content/uploads/2013/09/deeper-learning-2020-AI-.pdf (Hebrew)

Avouris, N., Dimitracopoulou, A., & Komis, V. (2003). On analysis of collaborative problem solving: An object-oriented approach. *Computers in Human Behavior, 19*(2), 147–167. doi:10.1016/S0747-5632(02)00056-0

Ayres, K. M., Langone, J., Boon, R. T., & Norman, A. (2006). Computer-based instruction for purchasing skills. *Education and Training in Developmental Disabilities, 41*, 253–263.

Ayres, K., & Cihak, D. (2010). Computer- and video-based instruction of food-preparation skills: Acquisition, generalization, and maintenance. *Intellectual and Developmental Disabilities, 48*(3), 195–208. doi:10.1352/1944-7558-48.3.195 PMID:20597730

Azevedo, R., Moos, D., Johnes, A., & Chauncey, A. D. (2010). Measuring Cognitive and Metacognitive Regulatory Processes During Hypermedia Learning: Issues and Challenges. *Educational Psychologist, 45*(4), 210–223. doi:10.1080/00461520.2010.515934

Babbitt, B. C., & Miller, S. P. (1996). Using hypermedia to improve the mathematics problem-solving skills of students with learning disabilities. *Journal of Learning Disabilities, 29*(4), 391–401. doi:10.1177/002221949602900407 PMID:8763554

Back, S. M. (2009). The bio-entrepreneurship MBA: Options for business schools. *Journal of Commercial Biotechnology, 15*(2), 183–193. doi:10.1057/jcb.2008.57

Bailin, S. (2002). Critical thinking and science education. *Science & Education, 11*(4), 361–375. doi:10.1023/A:1016042608621

Baker, F. B., & Kim, S. H. (2004). *Item response theory: Parameter estimation techniques* (2nd ed.). New York: Marcel Dekker.

Banister, G., Bowen-Brady, H. M., & Winfrey, M. E. (2014). Using Career Nurse Mentors to Support Minority Nursing Students and Facilitate their Transition to Practice. *Journal of Professional Nursing, 30*(4), 317–325. doi:10.1016/j.profnurs.2013.11.001 PMID:25150417

Barab, S. A., Gresalfi, M., & Ingram-Goble, A. (2010). Transformational play using games to position person, content, and context. *Educational Researcher, 39*(7), 525–536. doi:10.3102/0013189X10386593

Baron, J. N., & Kreps, D. M. (1999). *Strategic human resources: Framework for general managers.* Wiley.

Baroody, A. J. (2003). *The development of adaptive expertise and flexibility: the integration of conceptual and procedural knowledge.* Mahwah, NJ: Erlbaum.

Barron, A. E., Kemker, K., Harmes, C., & Kalaydjian, K. (2003, Summer). Large-scale research study on technology in K-12 schools: Technology integration as it relates to the National Technology Standards. *Journal of Research on Technology in Education, 35*(4), 489–507. doi:10.1080/15391523.2003.10782398

Barron, B. (2003). When smart groups fail. *Journal of the Learning Sciences*, *12*(3), 307–359. doi:10.1207/S15327809JLS1203_1

Barron's. (2014). *Barron's profiles of American colleges* (Vol. 31). Hauppauge, NY: Barron's Educational Series.

Barth, C. M., & Funke, J. (2010). Negative affective environnements improve complex solving performance. *Cognition and Emotion*, *24*(7), 1259–1268. doi:10.1080/02699930903223766

Bartle, R. (1996). Hearts, clubs, diamonds, spades: Players who suit MUDs. *Journal of MUD Research*, *1*(1), 19.

Baumeister, R. F., Bratslavsky, E., Muraven, M., & Tice, D. M. (1998). Ego depletion: Is the active self a limited resource? *Journal of Personality and Social Psychology*, *74*(5), 1252–1265. doi:10.1037/0022-3514.74.5.1252 PMID:9599441

Bean, J., & Metzner, B. (1985). A conceptual model of nontraditional undergraduate student attrition. *Review of Educational Research*, *55*(4), 485–650. doi:10.3102/00346543055004485

Beatty, S. J., Kelley, K. A., Metzger, A. H., Bellebaum, K. L., & McAuley, J. W. (2009). Team based learning in therapeutics workshop sessions. *American Journal of Pharmaceutical Education*, *73*(6), 100. doi:10.5688/aj7306100 PMID:19885069

Beaumont, R., & Sofronoff, K. (2008). A multi-component social skills intervention for children with Asperger syndrome: The Junior Detective Training Program. *Journal of Child Psychology and Psychiatry, and Allied Disciplines*, *49*(7), 743–753. doi:10.1111/j.1469-7610.2008.01920.x PMID:18503531

Beck, I. L., McKeown, M. G., & Kucan, L. (2002). *Bringing words to life: Robust vocabulary instruction*. New York, NY: The Guilford Press.

Beck, I. L., Perfetti, C. A., & McKeown, M. G. (1982). Effects of long-term vocabulary instruction on lexical access and reading comprehension. *Journal of Educational Psychology*, *74*(4), 506–521. doi:10.1037/0022-0663.74.4.506

Beetham, H., & Sharpe, R. (Eds.). (2013). Rethinking pedagogy for a digital age (2nd ed.). London: Routledge.

Behrens, J. T., & DiCerbo, K. E. (2013). *Technological Implications for Assessment Ecosystems: Opportunities for Digital Technology to Advance Assessment*. Princeton, NJ: The Gordon Commission on the Future of Assessment.

Beigman-Klebanov, B., Madnani, N., Burstein, J. C., & Sumasundaran, S. (2014). Content importance models for scoring writing from sources. *Proceedings of the 52 Annual Meeting of the Association for Computational Linguistics*. doi:10.3115/v1/P14-2041

Bejar, I. I., Lawless, R., Morley, M. E., Wagner, M. E., Bennett, R. E., & Revuelta, J. (2003). A feasibility study of on-the-fly item generation in adaptive testing. *Journal of Technology, Learning, and Assessment, 2*(3). Available from http://www.jtla.org

Bejar, I. I. (1990). A generative analysis of a three-dimensional spatial task. *Applied Psychological Measurement*, *14*(3), 237–245. doi:10.1177/014662169001400302

Bejar, I. I. (2002). Generative testing: From conception to implementation. In S. H. Irvine & P. C. Kyllonen (Eds.), *Item generation for test development* (pp. 199–217). Hillsdale, NJ: Erlbaum.

Bejar, I. I. (2013). Item generation: Implications for a validity argument. In M. J. Gierl & T. Haladyna (Eds.), *Automatic item generation: Theory and practice* (pp. 40–55). New York: Routledge.

Bejar, I. I., Flor, M., Futagi, Y., & Ramineni, C. (2014). On the vulnerability of automated scoring to construct-irrelevant response strategies (CIRS): An illustration. *Assessing Writing*, *22*, 48–59. doi:10.1016/j.asw.2014.06.001

Bekkerman, R., & Allan, J. (2003). *Using bigrams in text categorization* (Technical Report IR-408). Retrieved April 13, 2012 from the Center for Intelligent Information Retrieval, University of Massachusetts website: http://ciir.cs.umass.edu/pubfiles/ir-408.pdf

Belland, B. R. (2010). Portraits of middle school students constructing evidence-based arguments during problem-based learning: The impact of computer-based scaffolds. *Educational Technology Research and Development*, *58*(3), 285–309. doi:10.1007/s11423-009-9139-4

Bellini, S., & Akullian, J. (2007). A meta-analysis of video modeling and video self-modeling interventions for children and adolescents with autism spectrum disorders. *Exceptional Children, 73*(3), 264–287. doi:10.1177/001440290707300301

Benbunan-Finch, R., & Hiltz, S. (1999). Impacts of Asynchronous Learning Networks on Individual and Group Problem Solving: A Field Experiment. *Group Decision and Negotiation, 8*(5), 409–426. doi:10.1023/A:1008669710763

Benjamin, R., Klein, S., Steedle, J. T., Zahner, D., Elliot, S., & Patterson, J. A. (2012). T*he case for generic skills and performance assessment in the United States and international settings.* CAE – Occasional Paper. Retrieved from: http://www.collegiatelearningassessment.org/files/The_Case_for_Generic_Skills_and_Performance_Assessment_in_the_United_States_and_International_Settings.pdf

Benjamin, R. (2013). The principles and logic of competency testing in higher education. In S. Blomeke, O. Zlatkin-Troitschanskaia, C. Kuhn, & J. Fege (Eds.), *Modeling and measuring competencies in higher education: Tasks and challenges* (pp. 127–136). Rotterdam: Sense Publishers. doi:10.1007/978-94-6091-867-4_9

Benjamin, R. (2014). Two questions about critical thinking tests in higher education. *Change: The Magazine of Higher Learning, 46*(2), 32–39. doi:10.1080/00091383.2014.897179

Bennett, R. E., Persky, H., Weiss, A. R., & Jenkins, F. (2007). *Problem solving in technology-rich environments: A report from the NAEP Technology-Based Assessment Project (NCES 2007-466).* Washington, DC: National Center for Education Statistics, US Department of Education. Retrieved August 25, 2011, from http://nces.ed.gov/pubsearch/pubsinfo.asp?pubid=2007466

Bennett, R. (2001). How the internet will help large-scale assessment reinvent itself. *Education Policy Analysis Archives, 9*(0), 1–23. doi:10.14507/epaa.v9n5.2001

Bennett, R. E., Persky, H., Weiss, A., & Jenkins, F. (2007). *Problem solving in technology rich environments: A report from the NAEP Technology-based Assessment Project, Research and Development Series (NCES 2007-466).* Washington, DC: U.S. Department of Education, National Center for Education Statistics.

Ben-Simon, A., & Bennett, R. E. (2007). Toward More Substantively Meaningful Automated Essay Scoring. *Journal of Technology, Learning, and Assessment, 6*(1). Retrieved from http://files.eric.ed.gov/fulltext/EJ838611.pdf

Bentler, P. M., & Wu, E. J. (2005). *EQS 6.1 for Windows.* Encino, CA: Multivariate Software.

Bereiter, C., & Scardamalia, M. (1987). *The psychology of written composition.* Hillsdale, NJ: Lawrence Erlbaum Associates.

Bereiter, C., & Scardamalia, M. (1998). Beyond Bloom's taxonomy: Rethinking knowledge for the knowledge age. In A. Hargreaves, A. Lieberman, M. Fullan, & D. Hopkins (Eds.), *International handbook of educational change* (pp. 675–692). Boston, MA: Kluwer Academic. doi:10.1007/978-94-011-4944-0_33

Bernard, H. R., & Ryan, G. W. (2010). *Analyzing qualitative data.* Los Angeles: Sage.

Berninger, V. W. (1994). *Reading and writing acquisition: A developmental neuropsychological perspective.* Boulder, CO: Westview Press.

Berninger, V. W., Abbott, R. D., Abbott, S. P., Graham, S., & Richards, T. (2002). Writing and reading: Connections between the language and by hand. *Journal of Learning Disabilities, 35*(1), 39–56. doi:10.1177/002221940203500104 PMID:15490899

Berninger, V. W., Abbott, R. D., Whitaker, D., Sylvester, L., & Nolen, S. B. (1995). Integrating low- and high-level skills in instructional protocols for writing disabilities. *Learning Disability Quarterly, 18*(4), 293–309. doi:10.2307/1511235

Bernstein, B. (2000). *Pedagogy, symbolic control and identity* (Rev. ed.). Lanham, MD: Rowman & Littlefield.

Berthold, K., & Renkl, A. (2009). Instructional aids to support a conceptual understanding of multiple representations. *Journal of Educational Psychology*, *101*(1), 70–87. doi:10.1037/a0013247

Betrancourt, M. (2005). The animation and interactivity principles in multimedia learning. In R. E. Mayer (Ed.), *The Cambridge handbook of multimedia learning* (pp. 287–296). New York, NY: Cambridge University Press. doi:10.1017/CBO9780511816819.019

Bhaerman, R., & Spill, R. (1988). A dialogue on employability skills: How can they be taught? *Journal of Career Development*, *15*(1), 41–52. doi:10.1177/089484538801500105

Biancarosa, C., & Snow, C. E. (2006). *Reading next: A vision for action and research in middle and high school literacy: A report to Carnegie Corporation of New York* (2nd ed.). Washington, DC: Alliance for Excellent Education.

Biddix, J. P., Chung, C. J., & Park, H. W. (2011). Convenience or credibility? A study of college student online research behaviors. *The Internet and Higher Education*, *14*(3), 175–182. doi:10.1016/j.iheduc.2011.01.003

Biesta, G. J. J. (2011). *Experience, meaning and knowledge: A pragmatist view on knowledge and the curriculum.* Paper presented at the ESRC seminar series Curriculum for the 21st Century: Theory, Policy and Practice. Seminar One: Knowledge and the Curriculum, Stirling.

Biesta, G. J. J. (2012) Giving Teaching Back to Education: Responding to the Disappearance of the Teacher. *Phenomenology & Practice, 6* (2), 35-49.

Biesta, G. J. J., Salomon, G., Arnesen, T., & Vavik, L. (2014). *Twenty First Century skills vs. disciplinary studies?* Paper prepared for the Norwegian project "Learning in the 21st Century".

Biesta, G. J. J. (2010). *Good education in an age of measurement: ethics, politics, democracy.* Boulder, CO: Paradigm Publishers.

Biggs, J. (1988). The role of metacognition in enhancing learning. *Australian Journal of Education, 32*(2), 127–138. doi:10.1177/000494418803200201

Bills, D. B. (2003). Credentials, signals, and screens: Explaining the relationship between schooling and job assignment. *Review of Educational Research*, *73*(4), 441–449. doi:10.3102/00346543073004441

Binkley, M., Erstad, O., Herman, J., Raizen, S., Ripley, M., Miller-Ricci, M., & Rumble, M. (2012). Defining twenty first century skills. In P. Griffin, B. McGaw, & E. Care (Eds.), *Assessment and Teaching of 21st Century Skills* (pp. 17–66). Dordrecht: Springer. doi:10.1007/978-94-007-2324-5_2

Birenhak, M. (2010). *Merkhav ishi: hazkhut lepratiut bein mishpat vetekhnologia.* [Personal space: the right to privacy between law and technology]. Nevo Publications. (Hebrew).

Bishop, Y. M. M., Fienberg, S. E., & Holland, P. W. (1975). *Discrete multivariate analysis: Theory and practice.* Cambridge, MA: MIT Press.

Bissbort, D., Järvelä, S., Järvenoja, H., & Nenniger, P. (2011). Advancing conditions for self and shared regulation in collaborative learning settings in higher education. *Proceedings of 36th International Conference 2011- Improving University Teaching.* Bielefeld University.

Biswas, G., Jeong, H., Kinnebrew, J. S., Sulcer, B., & Roscoe, A. R. (2010). Measuring self-regulated learning skills through social interactions in a teachable agent environment. *Research and Practice in Technology-Enhanced Learning*, *5*(2), 123–152. doi:10.1142/S1793206810000839

Biswas, G., Leelawong, K., Schwartz, D., & Vye, N.The Teachable Agents Group at Vande. (2005). Learning by Teaching: A New Agent Paradigm for Educational Software. *Applied Artificial Intelligence*, *19*(3-4), 363–392. doi:10.1080/08839510590910200

Bixler, B. (2008). The effects of scaffolding students' problem-solving process via questions prompts on problem solving and intrinsic motivation in an online learning environment. *Dissertation Abstracts International*, *68*(10), 4261A.

Blachman, B. (1997). *Foundations of reading acquisition and dyslexia: Implications for Early Intervention.* Mahway, NJ: Lawrence Erlbaum Associates.

Black, P., & Wiliam, D. (1998). Assessment and classroom learning. *Assessment in Education: Principles, Policy & Practice, 5*(1), 7–74. doi:10.1080/0969595980050102

Black, P., & Wiliam, D. (2010). Inside the black box: Raising standards through classroom assessment. *Phi Delta Kappan, 92*(1), 81–90. doi:10.1177/003172171009200119

Blattner, G., & Fiori, M. (2009). Facebook in the language classroom: Promises and possibilities. *International Journal of Instructional Technology and Distance Learning, 6*(1), 17–28. Retrieved from http://www.itdl.org/Journal/Jan_09/Jan_09.pdf#page=21

Blischak, D. M., & Schlosser, R. W. (2003). Use of technology to support independent spelling by students with autism. *Topics in Language Disorders, 23*(4), 293–304. doi:10.1097/00011363-200310000-00005

Blömeke, S., Zlatkin-Troitschanskaia, O., Kuhn, C., & Fege, J. (2013). *Modeling and Measuring Competencies in Higher Education.* Springer. doi:10.1007/978-94-6091-867-4

Bloom, B. S., Engelhart, M. D., Furst, E. J., Hill, W. H., & Krathwohl, D. R. (1956). *Taxonomy of educational objectives.* New York: Longmans, Green.

Bloom, B. S., Englehart, M. D., Furst, E. J., Hill, W. H., & Krathwohl, D. R. (Eds.). (1956). *Taxonomy of educational objectives: Handbook I, cognitive domain.* New York: David McKay.

Blum, C. A. (2014). Evaluating Preceptor Perception of Support Using Educational Podcasts. *International Journal of Nursing Education Scholarship, 11*(1), 1–8. doi:10.1515/ijnes-2013-0037 PMID:24615492

Board of Certification for the Athletic Trainer (BOCAT). (2014). *BOC™ sample exam questions* [Sample examination questions]. Retrieved from http://www.bocatc.org/candidates/exam-preparation-tools/sample-exam-questions/

Bock, D. R. (1972). Estimating item parameters and latent ability when responses are scored in two or more nominal categories. *Psychometrika, 37*(1), 29–51. doi:10.1007/BF02291411

Bock, R. D. (1997). A brief history of item theory response. *Educational Measurement: Issues and Practice, 16*(4), 21–33. doi:10.1111/j.1745-3992.1997.tb00605.x

Boe, E. E., May, H., & Boruch, R. F. (2002). *Student Task Persistence in the Third International Mathematics and Science Study: A Major Source of Acheievement Differences at the National, Classroom, and Student Levels.* Retrieved from http://www.eric.ed.gov/ERICWebPortal/contentdelivery/servlet/ERICServlet?accno=ED478493

Bollen, K. A. (1989). A new incremental fit index for general structural equation models. *Sociological Methods & Research, 17*(3), 303–316. doi:10.1177/0049124189017003004

Bonk, C. J., & Smith, G. S. (1998). Alternative instructional strategies for creative and critical thinking in the accounting curriculum. *Journal of Accounting Education, 16*(2), 261–293. doi:10.1016/S0748-5751(98)00012-8

Booth, R., Clayton, B., Hartcher, R., Hungar, S., Hyde, P., & Wilson, P. (2003, May 13). *The development of quality online assessment in vocational education and training.* National Centre for Vocational Education Research. Retrieved from http://bit.ly/1gNYKK5

Bormuth, J. R. (1966). Readability: A new approach. *Reading Research Quarterly, 1*(3), 79–132. doi:10.2307/747021

Bormuth, J. R. (1968a). Cloze test readability: Criterion reference scores. *Journal of Educational Measurement, 5*(3), 189–196. doi:10.1111/j.1745-3984.1968.tb00625.x

Bosch, T. E. (2009). Using online social networking for teaching and learning: Facebook use at the University of Cape Town. *Communicatio: South African Journal for Communication Theory and Research, 35*(2), 185–200. doi:10.1080/02500160903250648

Botafogo, R. A., Rivlin, E., & Shneiderman, B. (1992). Structural analysis of hypertexts: Identifying hierarchies and useful metrics. *ACM Transactions on Information Systems, 10*(2), 142–180. doi:10.1145/146802.146826

Bouchet, F., Harley, J. M., Trevors, G. J., & Azevedo, R. (2013). Clustering and profiling students according to their interactions with an intelligent tutoring system fostering self-regulated learning. *Journal of Educational Data Mining, 5*(1), 104–145.

Boud, D., Keogh, R., & Walker, D. (1985). *Reflection: Turning experience into learning.* New York: Routledge.

Bowser, J., Sivahop, J., & Glicken, A. (2013). Advancing Oral Health in Physician Assistant Education: Evaluation of an Innovative Interprofessional Oral Health Curriculum. *Journal of Physician Assistant Education*, *24*(3), 27–30. doi:10.1097/01367895-201324030-00005 PMID:24261168

Boyle, A., May, T., & Sceeny, P. (2011). *From the festival hall to functional skills: A history of three e-assessment initiatives.* Paper presented at the AEA-Europe conference, Belfast.

Boyle, A., & Hutchinson, D. (2009). Sophisticated tasks in e assessment: What are they and what are their benefits? *Assessment & Evaluation in Higher Education*, *34*(3), 305–319. doi:10.1080/02602930801956034

Boyle, J. R., & Weishaar, M. (1997). The effects of expert-generated versus student-generated cognitive organizers on the reading comprehension of students with learning disabilities. *Learning Disabilities Research & Practice*, *12*(4), 228–235.

Braasch, J. L. G., Rouet, J. F., Vibert, N., & Britt, M. A. (2012). Readers' use of source information in text comprehension. *Memory & Cognition*, *40*(3), 450–465. doi:10.3758/s13421-011-0160-6 PMID:22086649

Bradlow, E. T., Wainer, H., & Wang, X. (1999). A Bayesian random effects model for testlets. *Psychometrika*, *64*(2), 153–168. doi:10.1007/BF02294533

Brady, M., Seli, H., & Rosenthal, J. (2013). "Clickers" and metacognition: A quasi-experimental comparative study about metacognitive self-regulation and use of electronic feedback devices. *Computers & Education*, *65*, 56–63. doi:10.1016/j.compedu.2013.02.001

Braga, J. C. F. (2013). *Fractal groups: Emergent dynamics in on-line learning communities. Revista Brasileira de Linguística Aplicada, 13*(2). doi:10.1590/S1984-63982013000200011

Brand-Gruwel, S., Wopereis, I., & Vermetten, Y. (2005). Information problem solving by experts and novices: Analysis of a complex cognitive skill. *Computers in Human Behavior*, *21*(3), 487–508. doi:10.1016/j.chb.2004.10.005

Brand-Gruwel, S., Wopereis, I., & Walraven, A. (2009). A descriptive model of information problem solving while using internet. *Computers & Education*, *53*(4), 1207–1217. doi:10.1016/j.compedu.2009.06.004

Brandstätter, V., & Frank, E. (2002). Effects of deliberative and implemental mindsets on persistence in goal-directed behavior. *Personality and Social Psychology Bulletin*, *28*(10), 1366–1378. doi:10.1177/014616702236868

Bransford, J. D., Brown, A. L., & Cocking, R. R. (Eds.). (2000). How people learn: Brain, mind, experience, school (Expanded ed.). Washington, DC: National Academy Press.

Bransford, J. D., Brown, A. L., & Cocking, R. R. (2000). *How people learn: Brain, mind, experience, and school.* Washington, DC: National Academy Press.

Brantley-Dias, L., & Ertmer, P. A. (2013). Goldilocks and TPACK: Is the construct "just right?". *Journal of Research on Technology in Education*, *46*(2), 103–128. doi:10.1080/15391523.2013.10782615

Bray, D. W., & Grant, D. L. (1966). The assessment center in the measurement of potential for business development. *Psychological Monographs*, *80*(17), 1–27. doi:10.1037/h0093895 PMID:5970218

Bredo, E. (2006). Conceptual confusion and educational psychology. In P. A. Alexander & P. H. Winne (Eds.), *Handbook of educational psychology* (2nd ed.; pp. 43–57). Mahwah, NJ: Erlbaum.

Brenner, D. G., Timms, M., McLaren, B. M., Brown, D. H., Weihnacht, D., Grillo-Hill, A., … Li, L. (2014). *Exploring the Assistance Dilemma in a Simulated Inquiry Learning Environment for Evolution Theory.* Paper presented at the 2014 Annual Meeting of the American Education Research Association, Philadelphia, PA.

Brindley, J., Blaschke, L., & Walti, C. (2009). Creating Effective Collaborative Learning Groups in an Online Environment. *International Review of Research in Open and Distance Learning*, *10*(3). Retrieved from http://www.irrodl.org/index.php/irrodl/article/view/675/1271

Bromley, K., Irwin-De Vittis, L., & Modlo, M. (1995). *Graphic organizers: Visual strategies for active learning.* New York: Scholastic Professional Books.

Brooks, J. G., & Brooks, M. G. (1993). *In search of understanding: The case for constructivist classrooms.* Alexandria: Association of Supervision and Curriculum Development.

Browder, D., Ahlgrim-Delzell, L., Spooner, F., Mims, P. J., & Baker, J. N. (2009). Using time delay to teach literacy to students with severe developmental disabilities. *Exceptional Children, 75,* 343–364.

Browder, D., Flowers, C., Ahlgrim-Delzell, L., Karvonen, M., Spooner, F., & Algozzine, R. (2004). The alignment of alternate assessment content with academic and functional curricula. *The Journal of Special Education, 37*(4), 211–223. doi:10.1177/00224669040370040101

Bruning, R. H., Schraw, G. J., Norby, M. M., & Ronning, R. R. (2004). *Cognitive psychology and instruction* (4th ed.). Upper Saddle River, NJ: Merrill/Prentice Hall.

Bryant, L. H., & Chittum, J. R. (2013). ePortfolio effectiveness: A(n ill-fated) search for empirical support. *International Journal of ePortfolio, 3*(2), 189-198. Retrieved from: http://www.theijep.com/pdf/IJEP108.pdf

Bryant, D. P., Bryant, B. R., & Hammill, D. D. (2000). Characteristic behaviors of students with LD who have teacher-identified math weaknesses. *Journal of Learning Disabilities, 33*(2), 168–177. doi:10.1177/002221940003300205 PMID:15505946

Buckingham, D. (2007). *Beyond technology: Children's learning in the age of digital culture.* Cambridge, MA: Polity.

Buckley, B. C. (2012). Model-based teaching. In M. Norbert (Ed.), *Encyclopedia of the sciences of learning* (pp. 2312–2315). New York: Springer.

Buckley, B., Gobert, J., Kindfield, A., Horwitz, P., Tinker, R., Gerlits, B., & Willett, J. et al. (2004). Model-based teaching and learning with BioLogica™: What do they learn? How do they learn? How do we know? *Journal of Science Education and Technology, 13*(1), 23–41. doi:10.1023/B:JOST.0000019636.06814.e3

Bui, Y. N., Schumaker, J. B., & Deshler, D. D. (2006). The effects of a strategic writing program for students with and without learning disabilities in inclusive fifth-grade classes. *Learning Disabilities Research & Practice, 21*(4), 244–260. doi:10.1111/j.1540-5826.2006.00221.x

Bullen, K., Moore, K., & Trollope, J. (2002). The influence of pupil generated ground rules on collaborative learning in the classroom: A pilot study. *Evaluation and Research in Education, 16*(4), 202–214. doi:10.1080/09500790208667019

Bull, J., & McKenna, C. (2004). *Blueprint for computer-assisted assessment.* London: Routledge Falmer. doi:10.4324/9780203464687

Burdick, H., Swartz, C. W., Stenner, A. J., Fitzgerald, J., Burdick, D., & Hanlon, S. T. (2013a). Measuring students' writing ability on a computer-analytic developmental scale: An exploratory validity study. *Literacy Research and Instruction, 52*(4), 255–280. doi:10.1080/19388071.2013.812165

Burdick, H., Swartz, C. W., Stenner, A. J., Fitzgerald, J., Burdick, D., & Hanlon, S. T. (2013b). Technological assessment of composing: Response to reviewers. *Literacy Research and Instruction, 52*(4), 184–187.

Burstein, J. (2003). The E-rater(R) Scoring Engine: Automated Essay Scoring with Natural Language Processing. In M. D. Shermis & J. Burstein (Eds.), *Automated Essay Scoring: A Cross-Disciplinary Perspective* (pp. 113–122). Mahwah, NJ: Lawrence Erlbaum Associates.

Burstein, J. (2003). The E-rater® scoring engine: Automated essay scoring with natural language processing. In M. D. Shermis & J. Burstein (Eds.), *Automated essay scoring: A cross-disciplinary perspective* (pp. 113–122). Mahwah, NJ: Lawrence Erlbaum Associates.

Burstein, J., Braden-Harder, L., Chodorow, M., Hua, S., Kaplan, B., Kukich, K., & Wolff, S. (1998). *Computer Analysis of Essay Content for Automated Score Prediction: A Prototype Automated Scoring System for GMAT Analytical Writing Assessment Essays. Research Bulletin RR-98-15.* Princeton, NJ: Educational Testing Service.

Burstein, J., Chodorow, M., & Leacock, C. (2004). Automated essay evaluation: The *Criterion* online writing service. *AI Magazine, 25*(3), 27–36.

Burstein, J., Chodorow, M., & Leacock, C. (2004). Automated essay evaluation: The Criterion Online writing service. *AI Magazine, 25*(3), 27–36.

Butterworth, B. (2006). Mathematical expertise. In K. A. Ericsson, N. Charness, P. Feltovich, & R. R. Hoffman (Eds.), *Cambridge handbook of expertise and expert performance* (pp. 553–568). Cambridge, UK: Cambridge University Press. doi:10.1017/CBO9780511816796.032

Buttler, D. L., & Winne, P. H. (1995). Feedback and self-regulated learning: A theoretical synthesis. *Review of Educational Research, 65*(3), 245–281. doi:10.3102/00346543065003245

Bye, L., Smith, S., & Rallis, H. M. (2009). Reflection using an online discussion forum: Impact on student learning and satisfaction. *Social Work Education, 28*(8), 841–855. doi:10.1080/02615470802641322

Bynum, T. W., & Rogerson, S. (2004). Editors' introduction: Ethics in the information age. In T. W. Bynum & S. Rogerson (Eds.), Computer Ethics and Professional Responsibility (pp. 1-13). Oxford, UK: Blackwell.

Byrne, B. M., & Shavelson, R. J. (1987). Adolescent self-concept: Testing the assumption of equivalent structure across gender. *American Educational Research Journal, 24*(3), 365–385. doi:10.3102/00028312024003365

Byrne, B. M., Shavelson, R. J., & Muthén, B. (1989). Testing for the equivalence of factor covariance and mean structures: The issue of partial measurement invariance. *Psychological Bulletin, 105*(3), 456–466. doi:10.1037/0033-2909.105.3.456

Byrne, B. M., & Watkins, D. (2003). The issue of measurement invariance revisited. *Journal of Cross-Cultural Psychology, 34*(2), 155–175. doi:10.1177/0022022102250225

Caccamise, D. J., Snyder, L., Allen, C., Oliver, W., DeHart, M., & Kintsch, E. (2009). *Teaching comprehension via technology-driven tools: a large scale scale-up of Summary Street.* IES.

Caccamise, D., Franzke, M., Eckhoff, A., Kintsch, E., & Kintsch, W. (2007). Guided practice in technology-based summary writing. In *Reading comprehension strategies: Theories, interventions, and technologies* (pp. 375–396). Mahwah, NJ: Erlbaum.

Cai, L. (2013). flexMIRT version 2: Flexible multilevel multidimensional item analysis and test scoring. Chapel Hill, NC: Vector Psychometric Group.

Cai, S., & Zhao, Y. (2012). A study of technical design-based instrument and multi-dimensional assessment in engineering learning. *Latin American and Caribbean Journal of Engineering Education, 62*, 32-42.

Cai, L., Thissen, D., & du Toit, S. (2011). *IRTPRO for Windows* [Computer software]. Lincolnwood, IL: Scientific Software International.

Cai, Z., Graesser, A. C., Forsyth, C., Burkett, C., Millis, K., Wallace, P., & Butler, H. et al. (2011). Trialog in ARIES: User input assessment in an intelligent tutoring system. In W. Chen, & S. Li (Eds.), *Proceedings of the 3rd IEEE international conference on intelligent computing and intelligent systems* (pp.429-433). Guangzhou, China: IEEE Press.

Cai, Z., Graesser, A. C., Forsyth, C., Burkett, C., Millis, K., Wallace, P., & Butler, H. et al. (2011). Trialog in ARIES: User input assessment in an intelligent tutoring system. In W. Chen, & S. Li (Eds.), *Proceedings of the 3rd IEEE International Conference on Intelligent Computing and Intelligent Systems* (pp.429-433). Guangzhou: IEEE Press.

Calderon, M., August, D., Slavin, R., Duran, D., Madden, N., & Cheng, A. (2010). Bringing words to life in classrooms with English-language learners. In E. H. Hiebert & M. L. Kamil (Eds.), *Teaching and learning vocabulary: Bringing research to practice* (pp. 115–136). New York, NY: Routledge.

Calkins, A., & Vogt, K. (2013). *Next Generation Learning: The Pathway to Possibility*. Washington, DC: EduCause.

Callan, V. J., & Clayton, B. (2010). *Bridging the divide: the challenges and solutions around e-assessment as voiced by practitioners and auditors*. Paper presented at Australian Vocational Education and Training Research Association Conference, Queensland. Retrieved from http://bit.ly/RhC77j

Camara, W. (2013). Defining and measuring college and career readiness: A validation framework. *Educational Measurement: Issues and Practice, 32*(4), 16–27. doi:10.1111/emip.12016

Camilli, G., & Shepard, L. A. (1994). *Methods for identifying biased test items*. Sage Publications.

Campbell, D. T. (1986). Science's social system of validity-enhancing collective belief change and the problems of the social sciences. In Metatheory in social science: Pluralisms and subjectivities (pp. 108-135). Chicago: University of Chicago Press.

Campbell, J., Thompson, E., & Pautz, H. (2011). Apprenticeship training in England: Closing the gap? *Journal of Contemporary European Studies*, *19*(3), 365–378. doi:10.1080/14782804.2011.610606

Cantrell, S. C., Almasi, J. F., Carter, J. C., Rintamaa, M., & Madden, A. (2010). The impact of strategy-based intervention on the comprehension and strategy use of struggling adolescent readers. *Journal of Educational Psychology*, *102*(2), 257–280. doi:10.1037/a0018212

Cárdenas, F., & Velásquez, J. (2011). EFL students speaking their minds to the world through Facebook: Curriculum innovation at a language institute in Bogota, Colombia. *Proceedings of World Conference on E-Learning in Corporate, Government, Healthcare, and Higher Education.*

Carlo, M. S., August, D., McGlaughlin, B., Snow, C. E., Dressler, C., Lippman, D. N., & White, C. E. et al. (2004). Closing the gap: Addressing the vocabulary needs of English-language learners in bilingual and mainstream classes. *Reading Research Quarterly*, *39*, 188–215.

Carlo, M. S., August, D., & Snow, C. E. (2010). Sustained vocabulary-learning strategy instruction for English-language learners. In E. H. Hiebert & M. L. Kamil (Eds.), *Teaching and learning vocabulary: Bringing research to practice* (pp. 137–153). New York, NY: Routledge.

Carmichael, J. (2009). Team based learning enhances performance in introductory biology. *Journal of College Science Teaching*, *38*(4), 54–61.

Carr, P. (2013, September). *NAEP innovations in action: Implications for the next generation science standards*. Presentation at the Invitational Research Symposium on Science Assessment, Washington, DC.

Carrier, C. A., & Williams, M. D. (1988). A test of one learner-control strategy with students of differing levels of task persistence. *American Educational Research Journal*, *25*(2), 285–306. doi:10.3102/00028312025002285

Cascio, W. F., & Phillips, N. F. (1979). Performance testing: A rose among thorns? *Personnel Psychology*, *32*(4), 751–766. doi:10.1111/j.1744-6570.1979.tb02345.x

Case, B. J. (2008). Accommodations to improve instruction and assessment. In R. C. Johnson & R. E. Mitchell (Eds.), *Testing deaf students in an age of accountability*. Washington, DC: Gallaudet Research Institute.

Case, B. J., Brooks, T., Wang, S., & Young, M. (2005). *Administration mode comparability study for Stanford diagnostic Reading and Mathematics tests*. San Antonio, TX: Harcourt Assessment, Inc.

Caspi, A., & Blau, I. (2008). Social presence in online discussion groups: Testing three conceptions and their relations to perceived learning. *Social Psychology of Education*, *11*(3), 323–346. doi:10.1007/s11218-008-9054-2

Casserly, M. (2012, May 11). 10 jobs that didn't exist 10 years ago. *Forbes*. Retrieved from: http://www.forbes.com/sites/meghancasserly/2012/05/11/10-jobs-that-didnt-exist-10-years-ago/

CAST. (2008). *Universal design for learning guidelines version 1.0*. Wakefield, MA: Author.

Cavanaugh, J., & Perlmutter, M. (1982). Metamemory: A critical examination. *Child Development*, *53*(1), 11–28. doi:10.2307/1129635

Chaiprasurt, C., & Esichaikul, V. (2013). Enhancing motivation in online courses with mobile communication tool support: A comparative study. *International Review of Research in Open and Distance Learning*, *14*(3), 377–400.

Chamorro-Premuzic, T., Arteche, A., Bremner, A. J., Greven, C., & Furnham, A. (2010). Soft skills in higher education: Importance and improvement ratings as a function of individual differences in academic performance. *Educational Psychology: An International Journal of Experimental Educational Psychology*, *30*(2), 221–241. doi:10.1080/01443410903560278

Chang, H. H., Mazzeo, J., & Roussos, L. (1996). Detecting DIF for polytomously scored items: An adaptation of the SIBTEST procedure. *Journal of Educational Measurement*, *33*(3), 333–353. doi:10.1111/j.1745-3984.1996.tb00496.x

Chang, K. E., Sung, Y. T., Chang, R. B., & Lin, S. C. (2005). A new assessment for computer-based concept mapping. *Journal of Educational Technology & Society*, *8*(3), 138–148.

Charles, G., & Alexander, C. (2014). An Introduction to Interprofessional Concepts in Social and Health Care Settings. *Relational Child & Youth Care Practice*, *27*(3), 51–55.

Charness, W. G., Krampe, R. T., & Mayer, U. (1996). The role of practice and coaching in entrepreneurial skill domains: An international comparison of life-span chess skill acquisition. In K. A. Ericsson (Ed.), *The road to excellence: The acquisition of expert performance in the arts and sciences, sports, and games* (pp. 51–80). Mahwah, NJ: Erlbaum.

Charness, W. G., Tuffiash, M. I., Krampe, R., Reingold, E., & Vasyukova, E. (2005). The role of deliberate practice in chess expertise. *Applied Cognitive Psychology*, *19*(2), 151–165. doi:10.1002/acp.1106

Chatti, M. A., Agustiawan, M. R., Jarke, M., & Specht, M. (2010). toward a personal Learning Environment Framework. *International Journal of Virtual and Personal Learning Environments*, *1*(4), 66–85. doi:10.4018/jvple.2010100105

Chen, G., Gully, S. M., & Eden, D. (2001). Validation of a new general self-efficacy scale. *Organizational Research Methods*, *4*(1), 62–83. doi:10.1177/109442810141004

Cheng, C., Liou, S., Tsai, H., & Chang, C. (2014). The effects of team-based learning on learning behaviors in the maternal-child nursing course. *Nurse Education Today*, *34*(1), 25–30. doi:10.1016/j.nedt.2013.03.013 PMID:23618848

Cheung, M. W.-L., Leung, K., & Au, K. (2006). Evaluating Multilevel Models in Cross-Cultural Research An Illustration With Social Axioms. *Journal of Cross-Cultural Psychology*, *37*(5), 522–541. doi:10.1177/0022022106290476

Childress, S. (2013, December 19). *Re: Shared attributes of schools implementing personalized learning* [Web blog post]. Retrieved from http://nextgenstacey.com/2013/12/19/shared-attributes-of-schools-implementing-personalized-learning/

Childress, S. (2014, January 1). *Re: Personalized learning will go mainstream* [Web blog post]. Retrieved from https://www.edsurge.com/n/2014-01-01-stacey-childress-personalized-learning-will-go-mainstream

Chi, M. T. H., Glaser, R., & Rees, E. (1982).Expertise in problem solving. In R. Sternberg (Ed.), *Advances in the psychology of human intelligence* (Vol. 1, pp. 7–76). Hillsdale, NJ: Erlbaum.

Chinn, C. A., O'Donnell, A. M., & Jinks, T. S. (2000). The structure of discourse in collaborative learning. *Journal of Experimental Education*, *69*(1), 77–97. doi:10.1080/00220970009600650

Chiu, M. M., & Khoo, L. (2003). Rudeness and status effects during group problem solving: Do they bias evaluations and reduce the likelihood of correct solutions? *Journal of Educational Psychology*, *95*(3), 506–523. doi:10.1037/0022-0663.95.3.506

Cho, M., & Shen, D. (2013). Self-regulation in online learning. *Distance Education*, *34*(3), 290–301. doi:10.1080/01587919.2013.835770

Chow, M., Herold, D. K., Choo, T., & Chan, K. (2012). Extending the technology acceptance model to explore the intention to use Second Life for enhancing healthcare education. *Computers & Education*, *59*(4), 1136–1144. doi:10.1016/j.compedu.2012.05.011

Christensen, R., & Knezek, G. A. (2014). Measuring technology readiness and skills. In J. M. Spector, M. D. Merrill, J. Elen, & M. J. Bishop (Eds.), *Handbook of research on educational communications and technology* (4th ed.; pp. 829–840). New York, NY: Springer. doi:10.1007/978-1-4614-3185-5_67

Chung, E., Rhee, J., Baik, Y., & A, O.-S. (2009). The effect of team-based learning in medical ethics education. *Medical Teacher*, *31*(11), 1013–1017. doi:10.3109/01421590802590553 PMID:19909042

Chung, G. K. W. K., O'Neil, H. F. Jr, & Herl, H. E. (1999). The use of computer-based collaborative knowledge mapping to measure team processes and team outcomes. *Computers in Human Behavior*, *15*(3-4), 463–494. doi:10.1016/S0747-5632(99)00032-1

City and Guilds. (2013). *Managing cases of suspected malpractice in examinations and assessments: guidance notes*. Retrieved from http://bit.ly/1lncKIp

Clare, L., Valdés, R., & Patthey-Chavez, G. G. (2000). *Learning to write in urban elementary and middle schools: An investigation of teachers' written feedback on student compositions* (Center for the Study of Evaluation Technical Report No. 526). Los Angeles: University of California, Center for Research on Evaluation, Standards, and Student Testing (CRESST).

Clark, D., Nelson, B., Sengupta, P., & D'Angelo, C. (2009, October). *Rethinking science learning through digital games and simulations: Genres, examples, and evidence*. Paper presented at Learning science: Computer games, simulations, and education: Workshop conducted from the National Academy of Sciences, Washington, DC.

Clark, M. B., Douglass, A. B., Maier, R., Deutchman, M., Douglass, J. M., Gonsalves, W., ... Bowser, J. (2010). Smiles for Life: A National Oral Health Curriculum. 3rd Edition. *Society of Teachers of Family Medicine*. Retrieved August 15, 2015, from http://www.smilesforlifeoralhealth.com

Clark, R. C., & Mayer, R. E. (2011). *E-learning and the science of instruction: Proven guidelines for consumers and designers of multimedia learning*. Wiley.com.

Clark, D. B., Martinez-Garza, M. M., Biswas, G., Luecht, R. M., & Sengupta, P. (2012). Driving assessment of students' explanations in game dialog using computer-adaptive testing and hidden Markov modeling. In D. Ifenthaler, D. Eseryel, & G. Xun (Eds.), *Assessment in game-based learning: Foundations, innovations, and perspectives* (pp. 173–199). Springer New York. doi:10.1007/978-1-4614-3546-4_10

Clark, D., Tanner-Smith, E., & Killingsworth, S. (2014). *Digital Games, Design and Learning: A Systematic Review and Meta-Analysis (Executive Summary)*. Menlo Park, CA: SRI International.

Clark, H. H. (1996). *Using language*. Cambridge: Cambridge University Press. doi:10.1017/CBO9780511620539

Clauser, B. E., Swanson, D. B., & Clyman, S. G. (2000). A comparison of the generalizability of scores produced by expert raters and automated scoring systems. *Applied Measurement in Education*, *12*(3), 281–299. doi:10.1207/S15324818AME1203_4

Clement, J., & Rea-Ramirez, M. A. (2008). *Model based learning and instruction in science*. Dordrecht: Springer. doi:10.1007/978-1-4020-6494-4

Cloninger, C. R. (2003). Completing the psychobiological architecture of human personality development: Temperament, character, and coherence. In U. M. Staudinger & U. E. R. Lindenberger (Eds.), *Understanding Human Development: Dialogues with Lifespan Psychology* (pp. 159–181). Springer. doi:10.1007/978-1-4615-0357-6_8

Cloninger, C. R., Svrakic, D. M., & Przybeck, T. R. (1993). A psychobiological model of temperament and character. *Archives of General Psychiatry*, *50*(12), 975–990. doi:10.1001/archpsyc.1993.01820240059008 PMID:8250684

Cloninger, C. R., Zohar, A. H., Hirschmann, S., & Dahan, D. (2012). The psychological costs and benefits of being highly persistent: Personality profiles distinguish mood disorders from anxiety disorders. *Journal of Affective Disorders*, *136*(3), 758–766. doi:10.1016/j.jad.2011.09.046 PMID:22036800

Clouder, D. L. (2008). Technology-enhanced learning: Conquering barriers to interprofessional education. *The Clinical Teacher*, *5*(4), 198–202. doi:10.1111/j.1743-498X.2008.00243.x

Cobb, R., & Bowers, J. (1999). Cognitive and situated learning perspectives in theory and practice. *Educational Researcher*, *28*(2), 4–15. doi:10.3102/0013189X028002004

Cohen, A., & Eini, L. (2012). Facebook usage patterns among teenagers and their relation to educational processes. *Proceedings of the 7th Chais Conference for the Study of Innovation and Learning Technologies: Learning In the Technological Era*. Raanana: The Open University of Israel.

Cohn, M. (2004). *User stories applied: For Agile software development*. Boston, MA: Addison-Wesley.

Coiro, J. (2008). *Handbook of research on new literacies*. New York: Lawrence Erlbaum Associates/Taylor & Francis Group.

Cole, J. S., Bergin, D. A., & Whittaker, T. A. (2008). Predicting student achievement for low stakes tests with effort and task value. *Contemporary Educational Psychology, 33*(4), 609–624. doi:10.1016/j.cedpsych.2007.10.002

Coleman-Martin, M. B., Heller, K. W., Cihak, D. F., & Irvine, K. L. (2005). Using computer-assisted instruction and the nonverbal reading approach to teach word identification. *Focus on Autism and Other Developmental Disabilities, 20*(2), 80–90. doi:10.1177/10883576050200020401

Colgoni, A., & Eyles, C. (2010). A new approach to science education for the 21ˢᵗ century. *EDUCAUSE Review, 45*(1), 10–11.

College Board. (2009). *Science: College Boards standards for college success*. Retrieved from http://professionals.collegeboard.com/profdownload/cbscs-science-standards-2009.pdf

College Entrance Examination Board, The National Commission on Writing in America's Schools and Colleges. (2003). *The neglected "R": The need for a writing revolution*. Retrieved from http://www.collegeboard.com

College Entrance Examination Board, The National Commission on Writing in America's Schools and Colleges. (2004). *Writing: A ticket to work . . . Or a ticket out, a survey of business leaders*. Retrieved from http://www.collegeboard.com

College Entrance Examination Board, The National Commission on Writing in America's Schools and Colleges. (2005). *Writing: A powerful message from state government*. Retrieved from http://www.collegeboard.com

Collins, A., Brown, J. S., & Newman, S. E. (1989). Cognitive apprenticeship: Teaching the crafts of reading, writing, and mathematics. In L. B. Resnick (Ed.), *Knowing, learning, and instruction: Essays in honor of Robert Glaser* (pp. 453–494). London: Routledge.

Common Core State Standards Initiative. (2010). *Common core state standards for English language arts & literacy in history/social studies, science, and technical subjects*. Retrieved from http://www.corestandards.org/assets/CCSSI_ELA%20Standards.pdf

Communication Skills. (2014). *Skills You Need*. Retrieved July 20, 2014, from http://education-2020.wikispaces.com/

Conklin, J. (1987). Hypertext: An introduction and Survey. *IEEE Computer, 20*(9), 17–41. doi:10.1109/MC.1987.1663693

Conley, D. T. (2007). Redefining college readiness. Eugene, OR: Educational Policy Improvement Center. Retrieved from http://www.aypf.org/documents/RedefiningCollegeReadiness.pdf

Conley, D. T., & McGaughy, C. L. (2012). College and career readiness: Same or different? *Educational Leadership, 69*(7), 28–34.

Cooke, N. J., Kiekel, P. A., Salas, E., Stout, R., Bowers, C., & Cannon-Bowers, J. (2003). Measuring team knowledge: A window to the cognitive underpinnings of team performance. *Group Dynamics, 7*(3), 179–219. doi:10.1037/1089-2699.7.3.179

Corbett, A. T., & Anderson, J. R. (1995). Knowledge tracing: Modeling the acquisition of procedural knowledge. *User Modeling and User-Adapted Interaction, 4*(4), 253–278. doi:10.1007/BF01099821

Corcoran, T., Mosher, F. A., & Rogat, A. (2009). *Learning progressions in science: An evidence-based approach to reform. CPRE Research Report# RR-63*. Philadelphia: Consortium for Policy Research in Education.

Cornelius-White, J. (2007). Learner-centered teacher-student relationships are effective: A meta-analysis. *Review of Educational Research, 77*(1), 113–143. doi:10.3102/003465430298563

Cory, T. C. (2013). *Aquinas on human self-knowledge*. New York: Cambridge University Press. doi:10.1017/CBO9781107337619

Costanza, R. (1990). Escaping the overspecialization trap. In M. E. Clark & S. A. Wawrytko (Eds.), *Rethinking the curriculum: Toward an integrated interdisciplinary college education* (pp. 95–106). Greenwood.

Costa, S., Cuzzocrea, F., & Nuzacci, A. (2014). Uses of the Internet in Educative Informal Contexts. Implication for Formal Education. *Comunicar*, 22(43), 163–171. doi:10.3916/C43-2014-16

Council of Europe. (2011). *Common European framework of references for languages: Learning, teaching, assessment*. Strasburg: Author.

Council of Europe. Language, Policy Unit. (2001). *Common European framework of reference for languages: Learning, teaching, assessment*. Retrieved from http://www.coe.int/t/dg4/linguistic/Cadre1_en.asp

Coyne, P., Pisha, B., Dalton, B., Zeph, L. A., & Smith, N. C. (2012). Literacy by design: A universal design for learning approach for students with significant intellectual disabilities. *Remedial and Special Education*, 33(3), 162–172. doi:10.1177/0741932510381651

Craven, P. (2009). History and challenges of e-assessment. *Cambridge Assessment*. Retrieved from http://bit.ly/1iU33mY

Creswell, J., & Plano Clark, V. (2007). *Designing and conducting mixed methods research*. London: Sage.

Cronbach, L. J., & Meehl, P. E. (1955). Construct validity in psychological tests. *Psychological Bulletin*, 52(4), 281–302. doi:10.1037/h0040957 PMID:13245896

Cronin, K. (2008). *Transdisciplinary research (TDR) and sustainability*. Environment Science and Research (ESR) Ltd. Retrieved on February 20, 2014 at: http://www.learningforsustainability.org/pubs/Transdisciplinary_Research_and_Sustainability.pdfn

Crow, M. (2010, July/August). Organizing Teaching and Research to Address the Grand Challenges of Sustainable Development. *Bioscience*, 60(7), 488–489. doi:10.1525/bio.2010.60.7.2

Cruz, J. A., & Wishart, D. S. (2007). Applications of machine learning in cancer prediction and prognosis. *Cancer Informatics*, 2, 59–67. PMID:19458758

Cuban, L. (2014). *Larry Cuban on school reform and classroom practice*. Retrieved November 21, 2014, from http://larrycuban.wordpress.com/

Cullen, M. J., Sackett, P. R., & Lievens, F. (2006). Threats to the operational use of situational judgment tests in the college admission process. *International Journal of Selection and Assessment*, 14(2), 142–155. doi:10.1111/j.1468-2389.2006.00340.x

Cunningham, A. E. (2010). Vocabulary growth through independent reading and reading aloud to children. In E. H. Hiebert & M. L. Kamil (Eds.), *Teaching and learning vocabulary: Bringing research to practice* (pp. 45–68). New York, NY: Routledge.

Cunningham, A. E., & Stanovich, K. E. (1998). The impact of print exposure on word recognition. In J. Metsala & L. Ehri (Eds.), *Word recognition in beginning literacy* (pp. 235–262). Mahwah, NJ: Erlbaum.

Currant, N., Haigh, J., Higgison, C., Hughes, P., Rodway, P., & Whitfield, R. (2010). *Designing ePortfolio based learning activities to promote learner autonomy*. Final Report to the Fourth Cohort of the Inter/National Coalition for Research into Electronic Portfolios, University of Bradford. Retrieved from: http://ncepr.org/finalreports/cohort4/University%20of%20Bradford%20Final%20Report.pdf

Currie, L., Devlin, F., Emde, J., & Graves, K. (2010). Undergraduate search strategies and evaluation criteria: Searching for credible sources. *New Library World*, 111(3/4), 113–124. doi:10.1108/03074801011027628

Cutler, L., & Graham, S. (2008). Primary grade writing instruction: A national survey. *Journal of Educational Psychology*, 100(4), 907–919. doi:10.1037/a0012656

D'Mello, S. K., Dowell, N., & Graesser, A. (2011). Does it really matter whether students' contributions are spoken versus typed in an intelligent tutoring system with natural language? *Journal of Experimental Psychology. Applied*, 17(1), 1–17. doi:10.1037/a0022674 PMID:21443377

D'Mello, S. K., & Graesser, A. C. (2012). Dynamics of affective states during complex learning. *Learning and Instruction*, 22(2), 145–157. doi:10.1016/j.learninstruc.2011.10.001

Dabbagh, N., & Kitsantas, A. (2011). Personal Learning Environments, social media, and self-regulated learning: A natural formula for connecting formal and informal learning. *The Internet and Higher Education, 15*(1), 3–8. doi:10.1016/j.iheduc.2011.06.002

Dai, D. Y. (2012). From smart person to smart design: Cultivating intellectual potential and promoting intellectual growth through Design Research. In D. Y. Dai (Ed.), *Design Research on Learning and Thinking in Educational Settings: Enhancing Intellectual Growth and Functioning*. New York, NY: Routledge.

Dale, S. B., & Krueger, A. B. (1999). *Estimating the payoff to attending a more selective college: An application of selection on observable and unobservables.* (NBER Working Paper No. 7322). Cambridge, MA: National Bureau of Economic Research. doi: 10.3386/w7322

Damon, W., & Phelps, E. (1989). Critical distinction among three approaches to peer education. *International Journal of Educational Research, 13*(1), 9–19. doi:10.1016/0883-0355(89)90013-X

Darling-Hammond, L. (2008). The case for university-based teacher education. In M. Cochran-Smith, S., Feiman-Nemser, D. J., McIntyre & K. E. Demers (Eds.), Handbook of research on teacher education (pp. 333-346). New York: Routledge.

Darling-Hammond, L., & Adamson, F. (2010). *Beyond basic skills: The role of performance assessment in achieving 21st century standards of learning.* Stanford, CA: Stanford University, Stanford Center for Opportunity Policy in Education.

Davenport, J. L., Rafferty, A., Timms, M. J., Yaron, D., & Karabinos, M. (2012). ChemVLab+: Evaluating a Virtual Lab Tutor for High School Chemistry. *The Proceedings of the 2012 International Conference of the Learning Sciences*, (pp. 381–385). Academic Press.

Davenport, J. L., Rafferty, A., Yaron, D., Karabinos, M., & Timms, M. (April, 2014). *ChemVLab+: Simulation-based Lab activities to support chemistry learning.* Paper presented at the 2014 Annual Meeting of the American Educational Research Association, Philadelphia, PA.

Davey, T., Ferrara, S., Holland, P., Shavelson, R., Webb, N., & Wise, L. (2015). Psychometric Considerations for the Next Generation Performance Assessment. Washington, DC: Center for K-12 Assessment & Performance Management, Educational Testing Service.

Davidson, R. (2012). Social and emotional aspects of online learning environments. In A. Glassner (Ed.), The arrow head and the warm hand: Narratives concerning ICT and teacher education (pp. 37-72). Tel-Aviv: MOFET Institute. (in Hebrew)

Davidson, R., & Mor, N. (2005, November). Cross-Institutional Team Teaching and Collaborative Learning in an Online Course, In S. Andras, & B. Ingeborg (Eds.), *Lifelong e-learning - bringing e-learning close to lifelong learning and working life: a new period of uptake:proceedings of the EDEN 2005 Annual Conference.* Helsinki: University of Technology, Lifelong Learning Institute TKK Dipoli.

Davies, R. S., & West, R. E. (2014). Technology integration in schools. In J. M. Spector, M. D. Merrill, J. Elen, & M. J. Bishop (Eds.), *Handbook of research on educational communications and technology* (pp. 841–853). New York, NY: Springer. doi:10.1007/978-1-4614-3185-5_68

De Ayala, R. J. (2009). *Theory and practice of item response theory.* Guilford Publications.

De Bruijn, D., de Mul, S., & van Oostendorp, H. (1992). The influence of screen size and text layout on the study of text. *Behaviour & Information Technology, 11*(2), 71–78. doi:10.1080/01449299208924322

de Jong, T., & Pieters, J. (2006). The design of powerful learning environments. In P. A. Alexander & P. H. Winne (Eds.), *Handbook of Educational Psychology* (pp. 739–745). New York: Routledge.

de la Torre, J. (2011). The generalized DINA model framework. *Psychometrika, 76*(2), 179–199. doi:10.1007/s11336-011-9207-7

De Pereyra, G., Britt, M. A., Braasch, J. L. G., & Rouet, J. F. (2014). Reader's memory for information sources in simple news stories: Effects of text and task features. *Journal of Cognitive Psychology, 24*(2), 187–204. doi:10.1080/20445911.2013.879152

Deater-Deckard, K., Petrill, S. A., Thompson, L. A., & DeThorne, L. S. (2005). A cross-sectional behavioral genetic analysis of task persistence in the transition to middle childhood. *Developmental Science, 8*(3), F21–F26. doi:10.1111/j.1467-7687.2005.00407.x PMID:15819750

Dede, C. (2012). *Interweaving assessments into immersive authentic simulations: Design strategies for diagnostic and instructional insights* (Commissioned White Paper for the ETS Invitational Research Symposium on Technology Enhanced Assessments). Princeton, NJ: Educational Testing Service.

Dede, C. (2009). Technologies that facilitate generating knowledge and possibly wisdom. *Educational Researcher, 38*(4), 260–263. doi:10.3102/0013189X09336672

Dede, C. (2014). *The role of technology in deeper learning*. New York, NY: Jobs for the Future.

Deerwester, S., Dumais, S. T., Furnas, G. W., Landauer, T. K., & Harshman, R. (1990). Indexing by Latent Semantic Analysis. *Journal of the American Society for Information Science, 41*(6), 391–407. doi:10.1002/(SICI)1097-4571(199009)41:6<391::AID-ASI1>3.0.CO;2-9

Delano, M. E. (2007). Improving written language performance of adolescents with Asperger syndrome. *Journal of Applied Behavior Analysis, 40*(2), 345–351. doi:10.1901/jaba.2007.50-06 PMID:17624076

Delunas, L. R., & Rouse, S. (2014). Nursing and Medical Student Attitudes about Communication and Collaboration Before and After an Interprofessional Education Experience. *Nursing Education Perspectives, 35*(2), 100–105. doi:10.5480/11-716.1 PMID:24783725

Dennen, V. (2005). From Message Posting to Learning Dialogues: Factors affecting learning participation in asynchronous discussion. *Distance Education, 26*(1), 127–148. doi:10.1080/01587910500081376

Denny, M., Marchand-Martella, N., Martella, R. C., Reilly, J. R., Reilly, J. F., & Cleanthous, C. C. (2000). Using parent-delivered graduated guidance to teach functional living skills to a child with Cri du Chat Syndrome. *Education & Treatment of Children, 23*, 441–454.

Denton, P., Madden, J., Roberts, M., & Rowe, P. (2008). Students' response to traditional and computer-assisted formative feedback: A comparative case study. *British Journal of Educational Technology, 39*(3), 486–500. doi:10.1111/j.1467-8535.2007.00745.x

Department for Business. Innovation and Skills. (2013). *The future of apprenticeships in England: Next steps from the Richard Review*. Retrieved from http://bit.ly/1jK7rYe

Department for Business. Innovation and Skills. (2014). *The future of apprenticeships in England: Guidance for Trailblazers*. Retrieved from http://bit.ly/1fduGlq

Department of Training and Workforce Development. (2012). *Guidelines for assessing competence in VET*. Retrieved from http://bit.ly/SvMnJW

DeStefano, D., & LeFevre, J.-A. (2007). Cognitive load in hypertext reading: A review. *Computers in Human Behavior, 23*(3), 1616–1641. doi:10.1016/j.chb.2005.08.012

Detlor, B., Booker, L., Serenko, A., & Julien, H. (2012). Student perception of information literacy instruction: The importance of active learning. *Education for Information, 29*, 147–161.

Devon, R. (2004). *EDSGN 497 H: Global approaches to engineering design*. Retrieved on July 20. 2014 from http://web.archive.org/web/20050801085903/http://www.cede.psu.edu/~rdevon/EDSGN497H.htm

Dewey, J. (1910). *How we think*. New York: D. C. Heath & Co. doi:10.1037/10903-000

Dewiyanti, S., Brand-Gruwel, S., & Jochem, W. (2005). Applying reflection and moderation in an asynchronous computer-supported collaborative learning environment in campus-based higher education. *British Journal of Educational Technology, 36*(4), 673–676. doi:10.1111/j.1467-8535.2005.00544.x

DiCerbo, K. E., & Behrens, J. T. (2014). Impacts of the Digital Ocean on Education. London: Pearson. Retrieved from https://research.pearson.com/digitalocean

DiCerbo, K. E., & Kidwai, K. (2013). *Detecting "Serious" Intent in Game Play*. Presented at the Sixth International Conference on Educational Data Mining, Memphis, TN.

DiCerbo, K. E. (2014). Game-based assessment of persistence. *Journal of Educational Technology & Society*, *17*(1), 17–28.

DiCerbo, K., & Behrens, J. (2012). Implications of the digital ocean on current and future assessment. In R. Lissitz & H. Jiao (Eds.), *Computers and their impact on state assessment: Recent history and predictions for the future* (pp. 273–306). Charlotte, NC: Information Age.

Digiovanni, L. (2015). Rethinking Instructional Technology in a Graduate Early Childhood Education Class: Moving Away From TPACK. In D. Slykhuis & G. Marks (Eds.), *Proceedings of Society for Information Technology & Teacher Education International Conference 2015* (pp. 2006-2007). Chesapeake, VA: Association for the Advancement of Computing in Education (AACE).

Dikli, S. (2003), Assessment at a distance: Traditional vs. alternative assessments. *The Turkish Online Journal of Educational Technology, 2*(3), 13-19. Retrieved from http://bit.ly/SJBvaD

Dillenbourg, P. (Ed.). (1999). *Collaborative learning: Cognitive and computational approaches*. Amsterdam, NL: Pergamon, Elsevier Science.

Dillenbourg, P., & Traum, D. (2006). Sharing solutions: Persistence and grounding in multi-modal collaborative problem solving. *Journal of the Learning Sciences, 15*(1), 121–151. doi:10.1207/s15327809jls1501_9

Dillon, A. (1994). *Designing Usable Electronic Text: Ergonomics Aspects of Human Information Usage*. London: Taylor and Francis. doi:10.4324/9780203470343

Ditson, L., Kessler, R., Anderson-Inman, L., & Mafit, D. (2001). *Concept-mapping companion* (2nd ed.). Eugene, OR: International Society for Technology in Education.

Dockrell, J. E., Lindsay, G., Connelly, V., & Mackie, C. (2007). Constraints in the production of written text in children with specific language impairments. *Exceptional Children, 73*(2), 147–164. doi:10.1177/001440290707300202

Dolan, R. P., Goodman, J., Strain-Seymour, E., Adams, J., & Sethuraman, S. (2011). *Cognitive lab evaluation of innovative items in mathematics and English language arts assessment of elementary, middle, and high school students: Research report*. Pearson.

Dong, G., & Pei, J. (2007). *Sequence data mining*. New York, NY: Springer.

Donnelly, J. F. (2004). Humanizing science education. *Science Education, 88*(5), 762–784.

Dorans, N. J., & Schmitt, A. P. (1993). Constructed response and differential item functioning: A pragmatic approach. *Construction versus choice in cognitive measurement*, 135-165.

Dorans, N. J., & Kulick, E. (1986). Demonstrating the utility of the standardization approach to assessing unexpected differential item performance on the Scholastic Aptitude Test. *Journal of Educational Measurement, 23*(4), 355–368. doi:10.1111/j.1745-3984.1986.tb00255.x

Dorsey, D., Russell, S., Keil, C., Campbell, G., van Buskirk, W., & Schuck, P. (2009). Measuring teams in action: Automated performance measurement and feedback in simulation-based training. In E. Salas, G. F. Goodwin, & C. S. Burke (Eds.), *Team effectiveness in complex organizations: Cross-disciplinary perspectives and approaches* (pp. 351–381). New York, NY: Routledge.

Dørum, K., & Garland, K. J. (2011). Efficient electronic navigation: A metaphorical question? *Interacting with Computers, 23*(2), 129–136. doi:10.1016/j.intcom.2010.11.003

Douglas, K. H., Ayres, K. M., Langone, J., Bell, V., & Meade, C. (2009). Expanding literacy for learners with intellectual disabilities: The role of supported eText. *Journal of Special Education Technology, 24*, 35–44.

Downes, S. (2012). *Connectivism and connective knowledge: Essays on meaning and learning networks*. National Research Council Canada. Retrieved from: http://www.downes.ca/files/books/Connective_Knowledge-19May2012.pdf

Downing, S. M., & Haladyna, T. M. (2006). *Handbook of test development*. Mahwah, NJ: Erlbaum.

Drasgow, F., Luecht, R. M., & Bennett, R. (2006). Technology and testing. In R. L. Brennan (Ed.), *Educational measurement* (4th ed.; pp. 471–516). Washington, DC: American Council on Education.

Drechsel, J. (1999). Writing into silence: Losing voice with writing assessment technology. *Teaching English in the Two-Year College, 26*(4), 380–387.

Drexler, W. (2010). The networked student model for construction of personal learning environments: Balancing teacher control and student autonomy. *Australasian Journal of Educational Technology, 26*(3), 369–385. Retrieved from http://www.ascilite.org.au/ajet/ajet26/drexler.html

Duckworth, A. L., Peterson, C., Matthews, M. D., & Kelly, D. R. (2007). Grit: Perseverance and passion for long-term goals. *Journal of Personality and Social Psychology, 92*(6), 1087–1101. doi:10.1037/0022-3514.92.6.1087 PMID:17547490

Duckworth, A. L., & Quinn, P. D. (2009). Development and validation of the Short Grit Scale (GRIT–S). *Journal of Personality Assessment, 91*(2), 166–174. doi:10.1080/00223890802634290 PMID:19205937

Dudley, N. M., Orvis, K. A., Lebiecki, J. E., & Cortina, J. M. (2006). A meta-analytic investigation of conscientiousness in the prediction of job performance: Examining the intercorrelations and the incremental validity of narrow traits. *The Journal of Applied Psychology, 91*(1), 40–57. doi:10.1037/0021-9010.91.1.40 PMID:16435937

Duffy, T. M., & Jonassen, D. H. (Eds.). (1992). *Constructivism and the technology of instruction: A conversation.* Hillsdale, NJ: Lawrence Erlbaum Associates.

Duncan, R. G., & Hmelo-Silver, C. E. (2009). Learning progressions: Aligning curriculum, instruction, and assessment. *Journal of Research in Science Teaching, 46*(6), 606–609. doi:10.1002/tea.20316

Dunlosky, J., & Metcalfe, J. (2009). *Metacognition.* Los Angeles: Sage Publishing.

Dunn, L. (2013) Using social media to enhance learning and teaching. In *Social Media 2013: 18th International Conference on Education and Technology.* Retrieved November 4, 2014 from http://eprints.gla.ac.uk/89363/

Duschl, R. A., Schweingruber, H. A., & Shouse, A. W. (2007). *Taking science to school: Learning and teaching science in grades k–8.* Washington, DC: The National Academies Press.

Duschl, R., & Osborne, J. (2002). Supporting and promoting argumentation discourse. *Studies in Science Education, 38*(1), 39–72. doi:10.1080/03057260208560187

Dweck, C. (2000). *Self-theories: Their role in motivation, personality, and development.* New York: Taylor & Francis.

Dweck, C. S. (2007). *Mindset: The new psychology of success.* New York: Random House.

Dymnicki, A., Sambolt, M., & Kidron, Y. (2013). *Improving college and career readiness by incorporating social and emotional learning.* Washington, DC: American Institutes for Research College & Career Readiness and Success Center. Retrieved from http://www.ccrscenter.org/sites/default/files/Improving%20College%20and%20Career%20Readiness%20by%20Incorporating%20Social%20and%20Emotional%20Learning_0.pdf

Ealam, G. (2003). The philosophy and psychology of Vygotzky: From cultural to psychological tools. In A. Kozulin & G. Ealam (Eds.), *Lev Vygotzky: Thought and Culture – An Anthology* (pp. 364–374). Jerusalem: Branco-Weiss Institute. (in Hebrew)

Eckes, T. (2008). Rater types in writing performance assessments: A classification approach to rater variability. *Language Testing, 25*(2), 155–185. doi:10.1177/0265532207086780

Edelen, M. O., Thissen, D., Teresi, J. A., Kleinman, M., & Ocepek-Welikson, K. (2006). Identification of differential item functioning using item response theory and the likelihood-based model comparison approach: Application to the Mini-Mental State Examination. *Medical Care, 44*(11Suppl 3), S134–S142. doi:10.1097/01.mlr.0000245251.83359.8c PMID:17060820

Educational Testing Service (ETS). (2014). *GRE® revised General Test: Quantitative Reasoning question types* [Sample examination questions]. Retrieved from http://www.ets.org/gre/revised_general/about/content/quantitative_reasoning/

Edyburn, D. L. (2007). Technology-enhanced reading performance: Defining a reading agenda. *Reading Research Quarterly, 42*(1), 136–141. doi:10.1598/RRQ.42.1.7

Edyburn, D. L. (2013). Critical issues in advancing the special education technology evidence base. *Exceptional Children, 80*, 7–24.

Efklides, A. (2006). Metacognition and affect: What can metacognitive experiences tell us about the learning process? *Educational Research Review, 1*(1), 3–14. doi:10.1016/j.edurev.2005.11.001

Eisenberg, M. B. (2008). Information Literacy: Essential skills for the information age. *Journal of Library & Information Technology, 28*(2), 39–47. doi:10.14429/djlit.28.2.166

Eisenberg, M., & Berkowitz, R. (1990). *Information problem solving: The big six skills approach to library & information skills instruction.* Norwood, NJ: Ablex.

Eiszler, C. F. (2002). College students' evaluations of teaching and grade inflation. *Research in Higher Education, 43*(4), 483–501. doi:10.1023/A:1015579817194

Eklöf, H. (2006). Development and validation of scores from an instrument measuring student test-taking motivation. *Educational and Psychological Measurement, 66*(4), 643–656. doi:10.1177/0013164405278574

Elbow, P., & Yancey, K. B. (1994). On the nature of holistic scoring: An inquiry composed on Email. *Assessing Writing, 1*(1), 91–107. doi:10.1016/1075-2935(94)90006-X

Elliot, S. (2011). *Computer-assisted scoring for Performance tasks for the CLA and CWRA.* New York, NY: Council for Aid to Education.

Elliott, E. S., & Dweck, C. S. (1988). Goals: An approach to motivation and achievement. *Journal of Personality and Social Psychology, 54*(1), 5–12. doi:10.1037/0022-3514.54.1.5 PMID:3346808

Ellison, N. B., Steinfield, C., & Lampe, C. (2007). The benefits of Facebook "Friends": Social capital and college students' use of online social network sites. *Journal of Computer-Mediated Communication, 12*(4), 1143–1168. doi:10.1111/j.1083-6101.2007.00367.x

Elvevåg, B., Foltz, P. W., Weinberger, D. R., & Goldberg, T. E. (2007). Quantifying incoherence in speech: An automated methodology and novel application to schizophrenia. *Schizophrenia Research, 93*(1-3), 304–316. doi:10.1016/j.schres.2007.03.001 PMID:17433866

Embretson, S. E. (2002). Generating abstract reasoning items with cognitive theory. In S. H. Irvine & P. C. Kyllonen (Eds.), *Item generation for test development* (pp. 219–250). Mahwah, NJ: Erlbaum.

Embretson, S. E., & Reise, S. P. (2000). *Item response theory for psychologists.* Psychology Press.

Engelhard, G. (1994). Examining rater errors in the assessment of written composition with a many-faceted rasch model. *Journal of Educational Measurement, 31*(2), 93–112. doi:10.1111/j.1745-3984.1994.tb00436.x

Ennis, R. H. (1985). A logical basis for measuring critical thinking skills. *Educational Leadership, 43*(2), 44–48.

Ennis, R. H., & Millman, J. (2005). *Cornell Critical Thinking Test, Level 2* (5th ed.). Seaside, CA: The Critical Thinking Co.

Ennis, R. H., & Weir, E. (1985). *The Ennis-Weir Critical Thinking Essay Test.* Pacific Grove, CA: Midwest Publications.

Equal Employment Opportunity Commission. (1978, August25). Uniform Guidelines on Employee Selection Procedures. *Federal Register, 44*, 38290–38315.

Erdogan, Y. (2009). Paper-based and computer-based concept mappings: The effects on computer achievement, computer anxiety and computer attitude. *British Journal of Educational Technology, 40*(5), 821–836. doi:10.1111/j.1467-8535.2008.00856.x

Ericcson, P. F., & Haswell, R. J. (Eds.). (2006). *Machine scoring of student essays: Truth and consequences.* Logan, UT: Utah State University Press.

Ericsson, K. A. (1996a). The acquisition of expert performance: An introduction to some of the issues. In K. A. Ericsson (Ed.), *The road to excellence: The acquisition of expert performance in the arts and sciences, sports, and games* (pp. 1–50). Mahwah, NJ: Erlbaum.

Ericsson, K. A. (2002). Attaining excellence through deliberate practice: Insights from the study of expert performance. In M. Ferrari (Ed.), *The pursuit of excellence in education* (pp. 21–55). Hillsdale, NJ: Erlbaum. doi:10.1002/9780470690048.ch1

Ericsson, K. A. (2004). Deliberate practice and the acquisition and maintenance of expert performance in medicine and related domains. *Academic Medicine, 10*(Supplement), S70–S81. doi:10.1097/00001888-200410001-00022 PMID:15383395

Ericsson, K. A. (2006a). Introduction to Cambridge handbook of expertise and expert performance: Its development, organization, and content. In K. A. Ericsson, N. Charness, P. Feltovich, & R. R. Hoffman (Eds.), *Cambridge handbook of expertise and expert performance* (pp. 3–19). Cambridge, UK: Cambridge University Press. doi:10.1017/CBO9780511816796.001

Ericsson, K. A. (2006b). The influence of experience and deliberate practice on the development of superior expert performance. In K. A. Ericsson, N. Charness, P. Feltovich, & R. R. Hoffman (Eds.), *Cambridge handbook of expertise and expert performance* (pp. 683–703). Cambridge, UK: Cambridge University Press. doi:10.1017/CBO9780511816796.038

Ericsson, K. A. (Ed.). (1996b). *The road to excellence: The acquisition of expert performance in the arts and sciences, sports, and games*. Mahwah, NJ: Erlbaum.

Ericsson, K. A., Krampe, R. T., & Tesch-Romer, C. (1993). The role of deliberate practice in the acquisition of expert performance. *Psychological Review, 100*(3), 363–406. doi:10.1037/0033-295X.100.3.363

Erkens, G., & Janssen, J. (2008). Automatic coding of online collaboration protocols. *International Journal of Computer-Supported Collaborative Learning, 3*(4), 447–470. doi:10.1007/s11412-008-9052-6

Ertas, A. (2010). Understanding of transdiscipline and transdisciplinary process. *Transdisciplinary Journal of Engineering & Science, 1*(1), 55–73.

Ertas, A. (2012). Integrating transdisciplinarity in undergraduate education. *Transdisciplinary Journal of Engineering & Science, 3*, 127–143.

Ertas, A., Frias, K., Tate, D., & Back, S. M. (2015). Shifting engineering education from disciplinary to transdisciplinary practice. *International Journal of Engineering Education, 31*(1), 94–105.

Ertas, A., Kollman, T., & Gumus, E. (2011). Transdisciplinary educational performance evaluation through survey. *International Journal of Engineering Education, 27*(5), 1094–1106.

Ertas, A., Maxwell, T. T., Tanik, M. M., & Rainey, V. (2003). Transformation of higher education: The transdisciplinary approach in engineering. *IEEE Transactions on Education, 46*(1), 289–295. doi:10.1109/TE.2002.808232

Ertmer, P. A., & Ottenbreit-Leftwich, A. (2013). Removing obstacles to the pedagogical changes required by Jonassen's vision of authentic technology-enabled learning. *Computers & Education, 64*, 175–182. doi:10.1016/j.compedu.2012.10.008

Ertmer, P. A., Sadaf, A., & Ertmer, D. J. (2011). Student-content interactions in online courses: The role of question prompts in facilitating higher-level engagement with course content. *Journal of Computing in Higher Education, 23*(2-3), 157–186. doi:10.1007/s12528-011-9047-6

Eshet, Y. (2012).Thinking in the digital era: A revised model for digital literacy. *Issues in Informing Science and Information Technology,* (9), 267-276. Retrieved from: http://iisit.org/Vol9/IISITv9p267-276Eshet021.pdf

Eshet, Y. (2012). Thinking in the Digital Era: A Revised Model for Digital Literacy. *Issues in Informing Science and Information Technology, 9*, 267–276.

European Commission. (2013). *Apprenticeship and traineeship schemes in EU27: Key success factors*. Retrieved from http://bit.ly/1sqazb8

Facione, P. A. (1990). *Critical thinking: A statement of expert consensus for purposes of educational assessment and instruction.* Millbrae, CA: The California Academic Press.

Fadel, C. (2011). Redesigning the Curriculum. Boston, MA: Center for Curriculum Redesign. Retrieved from http://curriculumredesign.org/wp-content/uploads/CCR-Foundational-Whitepaper-Charles-Fadel2.pdf

Fallows, S., & Steven, C. (2000). Building employability skills into the higher education curriculum: A university-wide initiative. *Education + Training, 42*(2), 75–82. doi:10.1108/00400910010331620

Fassbender, E., Richards, D., Bilgin, A., Thompson, W. F., & Heiden, W. (2012). VirSchool: The effect of background music and immersive display systems on memory for facts learned in an educational virtual environment. *Computers & Education, 58*(1), 490–500. doi:10.1016/j.compedu.2011.09.002

Fawcett, L. M., & Garton, A. F. (2005). The effects of peer collaboration on children's problem solving ability. *The British Journal of Educational Psychology, 75*(2), 157–169. doi:10.1348/000709904X23411 PMID:16033660

Fernandez, R. M., & Weinberg, N. (1997). Sifting and sorting: Personal contacts and hiring in a retail bank. *American Sociological Review, 62*(6), 883–902. doi:10.2307/2657345

Ferrara, S., & DeMauro, G. E. (2006). Standardized assessment of individual achievement in K-12. In R. L. Brennan (Ed.), *Educational measurement* (4th ed.; pp. 579–621). Westport, CT: National Council on Measurement in Education and American Council on Education.

Ferrari, A. (2012). Digital competence in practice: An analysis of frameworks. *JRC Technical Reports* [online]. Retrieved July 20, 2014, from http://www.ifap.ru/library/book522.pdf

Ferrari, A. (2013). DIGCOMP: A framework for developing and understanding digital competence in Europe. *European Commission.* Retrieved July 20, 2014, from http://ftp.jrc.es/EURdoc/JRC83167.pdf

Ferrari, A. (2013). *DIGCOMP: A Framework for Developing and Understanding Digital Competence in Europe.* Report EUR 26035 EN. doi: 10.2788/52966

Ferrari, A. (2012). *Digital Competence in Practice: An Analysis of Frameworks. JRC Technical Reports.* Institute for Prospective Technological Studies, European Union.

Ferrell, G., & Gray, L. (2014). *Enhancing student employability through technology-supported assessment and feedback: how the curriculum can help develop the skills and competencies needed in the world of work.* Retrieved from http://bit.ly/1hYHPSA

Fidalgo, A. M., & Madeira, J. M. (2008). Generalized Mantel-Haenszel methods for differential item functioning detection. *Educational and Psychological Measurement, 68*(6), 940–958. doi:10.1177/0013164408315265

*Financial Post.* (2009). Retrieved from http://www.worldhunger.org/articles/08/food_crisis.htm

Finch, D. J., Hamilton, L. K., Baldwin, R., & Zehner, M. (2013). An exploratory study of factors affecting undergraduate employability. *Education + Training, 55*(7), 681–704. doi:10.1108/ET-07-2012-0077

Finch, D. J., Nadeau, J., & O'Reilly, N. (2012). The future of marketing education: A practitioner's perspective. *Journal of Marketing Education, 35*(1), 233–258. doi:10.1177/0273475312465091

Fink, G. A. (2008). *Markov models for pattern recognition.* Berlin, Germany: Springer.

Fiore, S., Rosen, M., Smith-Jentsch, K., Salas, E., Letsky, M., & Warner, N. (2010). Toward an understanding of macrocognition in teams: Predicting process in complex collaborative contexts. *The Journal of the Human Factors and Ergonomics Society, 53*(2), 203–224. doi:10.1177/0018720810369807

Fiore, S., & Schooler, J. W. (2004). Process mapping and shared cognition: Teamwork and the development of shared problem models. In E. Salas & S. M. Fiore (Eds.), *Team cognition: Understanding the factors that drive process and performance* (pp. 133–152). Washington, DC: American Psychological Association. doi:10.1037/10690-007

Fischer, F., Kollar, I., Stegmann, K., & Wecker, C. (2013). Toward a Script Theory of Guidance in Computer-Supported Collaborative Learning. *Educational Psychologist, 48*(1), 56–66. doi:10.1080/00461520.2012.748005 PMID:23378679

Fischer, S. C., Spiker, V. A., & Riedel, S. L. (2009). Critical thinking training for army officers: Vol. 2. *A model of critical thinking. (Technical report).* Arlington, VA: U.S. Army Research Institute for the Behavioral and Social Sciences.

Fishman, B., & Dede, C. (in press). Teaching and technology: New tools for new times. In D. Gitomer & C. Bell (Eds.), *Handbook of research on teaching* (5th ed.). New York, NY: Springer.

Fitzgerald, J., & Shanahan, T. (2000). Reading and writing relations and their development. *Educational Psychologist, 35*(1), 39–50. doi:10.1207/S15326985EP3501_5

Flavell, J. H. (1976). Metacognitive aspects of problem solving. In L. B. Resnick (Ed.), The nature of intelligence (pp. 231-236). Hillsdale, NJ: Erlbaum.

Flavell, J. H. (1976). Metacognitive aspects of problem solving. In L. Resnick (Ed.), *The nature of intelligence* (pp. 231–235). Mahwah, NJ: Lawrence Erlbaum.

Flavell, J. H. (1979). Metacognition and cognitive monitoring: A new area of cognitive–developmental inquiry. *The American Psychologist, 34*(10), 906–911. doi:10.1037/0003-066X.34.10.906

Flavell, J. H. (1987). Speculation about the nature and development of metacognition. In F. E. Weinert & R. H. Kluwe (Eds.), *Metacognition, motivation and understanding* (pp. 21–29). Hillsdale, NJ: Erlbaum.

Fleiss, J. L., Levin, B., & Paik, M. C. (2013). *Statistical methods for rates and proportions.* John Wiley & Sons.

Florida Center for Instructional Technology. (n.d.). *The Technology Integration Matrix.* Retrieved from http://mytechmatrix.org/

Flower, L. S., & Hayes, J. R. (1980). The dynamics of composing: Making plans and juggling constraints. In L. W. Gregg & E. R. Sternberg (Eds.), *Cognitive processes in writing* (pp. 3–29). Hillsdale, NJ: Lawrence Erlbaum Associates.

Fodchuk, A., Schwartz, K., & Hill, T. (2014, June 30). *Say "hello" to TIM! (Technology Integration Matrix).* Presentation at ISTE 2014, Atlanta, GA.

Fogarty, R. (1994). *The mindful school: How to teach for metacognitive reflection.* Glenview, IL: IRI/Skylight Publishing.

Foll, D. L., Rascle, O., & Higgins, N. C. (2006). Persistence in a Putting Task During Perceived Failure: Influence of State-attributions and Attributional Style. *Applied Psychology, 55*(4), 586–605. doi:10.1111/j.1464-0597.2006.00249.x

Foltz, P. W., & Rosenstein, M. (2013). Tracking student learning in a state-wide implementation of automated writing scoring. *Proceedings of the Neural Information Processing Systems (NIPS) Workshop on Data Driven Education.* Retrieved from http://lytics.stanford.edu/datadriveneducation/

Foltz, P. W., Laham, D., & Landauer, T. K. (1999). The Intelligent Essay Assessor: Applications to Educational Technology. *Interactive Multimedia Education Journal of Computer Enhanced Learning, 1*(2).

Foltz, P. W., Lochbaum, K. E., & Rosenstein, M. (2011). *Analysis of student writing for a large scale implementation of formative assessment.* Paper presented at the National Council for Measurement in Education, New Orleans, LA.

Foltz, P. W. (1996). Latent Semantic Analysis for text-based research. *Behavior Research Methods, Instruments, & Computers, 28*(2), 197–202. doi:10.3758/BF03204765

Foltz, P. W., Gilliam, S., & Kendall, S. (2000). Supporting content-based feedback in online writing evaluation with LSA. *Interactive Learning Environments, 8*(2), 111–129. doi:10.1076/1049-4820(200008)8:2;1-B;FT111

Foltz, P. W., Kintsch, W., & Landauer, T. K. (1998). The measurement of textual coherence with Latent Semantic Analysis. *Discourse Processes, 25*(2&3), 285–307. doi:10.1080/01638539809545029

Foltz, P. W., & Martin, M. J. (2008). Automated communication analysis of teams. In E. Salas, G. F. Goodwin, & S. Burke (Eds.), *Team effectiveness in complex organizations and systems: Cross-disciplinary perspectives and approaches* (pp. 411–431). New York: Routledge.

Foltz, P. W., & Martin, M. J. (2008). Automated Communication Analysis of Teams. In E. Salas, G. F. Goodwin, & S. Burke (Eds.), *Team Effectiveness in Complex Organizations and Systems: Cross-disciplinary perspectives and approaches*. New York: Routledge.

Foltz, P. W., Streeter, L. A., Lochbaum, K. E., & Landauer, T. K. (2013). Implementation and applications of the Intelligent Essay Assessor. In M. Shermis & J. Burstein (Eds.), *Handbook of Automated Essay Evaluation* (pp. 68–88). New York: Routledge.

Forbes, T. H. III. (2014). Making the Case for the Nurse as the Leader of Care Coordination. *Nursing Forum*, *49*(3), 167–170. doi:10.1111/nuf.12064 PMID:24393064

Forman, G. (2003). An extensive empirical study of feature selection metrics for text classification. *Journal of Machine Learning Research*, *3*, 1289–1305.

Foss, C. L. (1988). Effective browsing in hypertext systems. In *Proceedings of the Conference on User-Oriented Content-Based Text and Image Handling (RIAO'88)*, (pp. 82–98). Academic Press.

Fox, E., & Riconscente, M. (2008). Metacognition and self-regulation in James, Piaget, and Vygotsky. *Educational Psychology Review*, *20*(4), 373–389. doi:10.1007/s10648-008-9079-2

Fracer, K., & Green, H. (2007). Curriculum 2.0: Educating the digital generation. In S. Perker & S. Perker (Eds.), Unlocking Innovation: Why citizens hold the key to public service reform (pp. 47–58). Retrieved from http://www.demos.co.uk/files/Unlocking%20innovation.pdf

Fraillon, J. (2014). Preparing for Life in a Digital Age. In *The IEA International Computer and Information Literacy Study*. Springer International Publishing. Retrieved Nov 1, 2014, from http://research.acer.edu.au/cgi/viewcontent.cgi?article=1009&context=ict_literacy

Fraillon, J., & Ainley, J. (2013). The IEA international study of computer and information literacy (ICLIS). *Australian Council for Educational Research*. Retrieved July 20, 2014, from http://icils2013.acer.edu.au/wp-content/uploads/examples/ICILS-Detailed-Project-Description.pdf

Franklin, S., & Graesser, A. C. (1996). Is it an agent or just a program? A taxonomy for autonomous agents. *Proceedings of the Agent Theories, Architectures, and Languages Workshop* (pp. 21-35). Berlin: Springer-Verlag.

Frank, M., Reich, N., & Humphreys, K. (2003). Respecting the human needs of students in the development of e-learning. *Computers & Education*, *40*(1), 57–70. doi:10.1016/S0360-1315(02)00095-7

Franzke, M., Kintsch, E., Caccamise, D., Johnson, N., & Dooley, S. (2005). Summary Street ®: Computer support for comprehension and writing. *Journal of Educational Computing Research*, *33*(1), 53–80. doi:10.2190/DH8F-QJWM-J457-FQVB

Frechette, J. (2002). *Developing media literacy in cyberspace: Pedagogy and critical learning for the twenty-first century classroom*. Westport, CT: Praeger Publishers.

French, A. W., & Miller, T. R. (1996). Logistic regression and its use in detecting differential item functioning in polytomous items. *Journal of Educational Measurement*, *33*(3), 315–332. doi:10.1111/j.1745-3984.1996.tb00495.x

Friedman, T. (2005). *The world is flat: A brief history of the 21st Century*. New York, NY: Farrar, Straus, and Giroux.

Fujikura, T., Takeshita, T., Homma, H., Adachi, K., Miyake, K., Kudo, M., & Hirakawa, K. et al. (2013). Team-based learning using an audience response system: A possible new strategy for interactive medical education. *Journal of Nippon Medical School*, *80*(1), 63–69. doi:10.1272/jnms.80.63 PMID:23470808

Funke, J. (2010). Complex problem solving: A case for complex cognition? *Cognitive Processing*, *11*(2), 133–142. doi:10.1007/s10339-009-0345-0 PMID:19902283

Further Education and Training Awards Council. (2007). *Quality assuring assessment: Guidelines for providers*. Retrieved from http://bit.ly/1h7kAoq

Gaines, L., & Kamer, P. M. (1994). The incidence of economic stress in affluent areas: Devising more accurate measures. *American Journal of Economics and Sociology*, *53*(2), 175–185. doi:10.1111/j.1536-7150.1994.tb02584.x

Gallup. (2013). *21st century skills and the workplace: A 2013 Microsoft-Pearson Foundation study on 21st century skills and the workplace*. Washington, DC: Author.

Gambrell, L. B. (1984). How much time do children spend reading during reading instruction? In J. A. Niles, & L. A. Harris (Eds.), *Changing perspectives on research in reading/language processing and instruction* (pp. 127-135). Rochester, NY: National Reading Conference.

Gardner, H. (1999). *Intelligence reframed: Multiple intelligences for the 21st Century*. New York, NY: Basic Books.

Gardner, H. (2006). *Multiple intelligences: New horizons*. New York: Basic Books.

Garrison, D. R., & Cleveland-Innes, M. (2005). Facilitating cognitive presence in online learning: Interaction is not enough. *American Journal of Distance Education*, *19*(3), 133–148. doi:10.1207/s15389286ajde1903_2

Garvin, P. L. (1963). *Natural Language and the Computer*. New York: McGraw-Hill.

Gast, D. L. (2010). *Single subject research methodology in behavioral sciences*. New York, NY: Routledge Publishing Co.

Gaugler, B. B., Rosenthal, D. B., Thornton, G. C. III, & Bentson, C. (1987). Meta-analysis of assessment center validity. *The Journal of Applied Psychology*, *72*(3), 493–511. doi:10.1037/0021-9010.72.3.493

Gee, J. P. (2007). What video games have to teach us about learning and literacy (2nd ed.). Palgrave Macmillan.

Gee, J. P. (2003). *What video games have to teach us about learning and literacy*. New York: Palgrave Macmillan.

Gehlert, S. (2012). Shaping education and training to advance transdisciplinary health research. *Transdisciplinary Journal of Engineering & Science*, *3*, 1–10.

Geiser, S., & Santelices, M. V. (2007). Validity of high-school grades in predicting student success beyond the freshman year: High-school record vs standardized tests as indicators of four-year college outcomes. Berkeley: Center for Studies in Higher Education, University of California. Retrieved from http://files.eric.ed.gov/fulltext/ED502858.pdf

Gersten, R., Compton, D., Connor, C. M., Dimino, J., Santoro, L., Linan-Thompson, S., & Tilly, W. D. (2008). *Assisting students struggling with reading: Response to intervention and multi-tier intervention for reading in the primary grades: A practice guide (NCEE 2009–4045)*. Washington, DC: National Center for Education Evaluation and Regional Assistance, Institute of Education Sciences, U.S. Department of Education.

Gersten, R., Fuchs, L. S., Compton, D., Coyne, M., Greenwood, C., & Innocenti, M. S. (2005). Quality indicators for group experimental and quasi-experimental research in special education. *Exceptional Children*, *71*(2), 149–164. doi:10.1177/001440290507100202

Getzels, J. W. (1979). Problem finding: A theoretical note. *Cognitive Science*, *3*(2), 167–172. doi:10.1207/s15516709cog0302_4

Gibbons, A. M. (2013, March). *Research evidence and AC 2.0: What we know and what we don't*. Presentation at the 33rd Annual Assessment Centre Study Group Conference, Stellenbosch, South Africa.

Gierl, M. J., & Lai, H. (2012). *Using automatic item generation to create items for medical licensure exams*. Paper presented at the annual meeting of the National Council on Measurement in Education, Vancouver, BC.

Gierl, M. J., Latifi, F., Lai, H., Matovinovic, D., & Boughton, K. (April, 2014). *Evaluating the quality of items generated using automatic processes*. Paper presented at the annual meeting of the National Council on Measurement in Education, Philadelphia, PA.

Gierl, M. J., Zhou, J., & Alves, C. (2008). Developing a taxonomy of item model types to promote assessment engineering. *Journal of Technology, Learning, and Assessment, 7*(2). Retrieved from http://www.jtla.org

Gierl, M. J. (1997). Comparing cognitive representations of test developers and students on a mathematics test with Bloom's taxonomy. *The Journal of Educational Research*, *91*(1), 26–32. doi:10.1080/00220679709597517

Gierl, M. J., & Haladyna, T. (2013). *Automatic item generation: Theory and practice*. New York: Routledge.

Gierl, M. J., & Lai, H. (2013). Using automated processes to generate test items. *Educational Measurement: Issues and Practice, 32*, 36–50.

Gierl, M. J., Lai, H., & Turner, S. (2012). Using automatic item generation to create multiple-choice items for assessments in medical education. *Medical Education, 46,* 757–765. doi:10.1111/j.1365-2923.2012.04289.x PMID:22803753

Gilbert, J., & Graham, S. (2010). Teaching writing to elementary students in grades 4-6: A national survey. *The Elementary School Journal, 110*(4), 494–518. doi:10.1086/651193

GlassLab. (2013). *SimCityEDU: Pollution Challenge!* [Computer software]. Retrieved from http://www.simcityedu.org/

Gobert, J. D., & Buckley, B. C. (2000). Introduction to model-based teaching and learning in science education. *International Journal of Science Education, 22*(9), 891–894. doi:10.1080/095006900416839

Gobert, J. D., & Clement, J. J. (1999). Effects of student-generated diagrams versus student-generated summaries on conceptual understanding of causal and dynamic knowledge in plate tectonics. *Journal of Research in Science Teaching, 36*(1), 39–53. doi:10.1002/(SICI)1098-2736(199901)36:1<39::AID-TEA4>3.0.CO;2-I

Gobert, J. D., Sao Pedro, M., Raziuddin, J., & Baker, R. (2013). From log files to assessment metrics: Measuring students' science inquiry skills using educational data mining. *Journal of the Learning Sciences, 22*(4), 521–563. doi:10.1080/10508406.2013.837391

Gobet, F., & Charness, N. (2006). Expertise in chess. In K. A. Ericsson, N. Charness, P. Feltovich, & R. R. Hoffman (Eds.), *Cambridge handbook of expertise and expert performance* (pp. 523–538). Cambridge, UK: Cambridge University Press. doi:10.1017/CBO9780511816796.030

Goh, A. E., & Bambara, L. M. (2013). Video self-modeling: A job skills intervention with individuals with intellectual disability in employment settings. *Education and Training in Autism and Developmental Disabilities, 48,* 103–119.

Goldberg, G. L., & Roswell, B. S. (2000). From perception to practice: The impact of teachers' scoring experience on performance-based instruction and classroom assessment. *Educational Assessment, 6*(4), 257–290. doi:10.1207/S15326977EA0604_3

Goldhammer, F., Naumann, J., & Keßel, Y. (2013). Assessing individual differences in basic computer skills: Psychometric characteristics of an interactive performance measure. *European Journal of Psychological Assessment, 29*(4), 263–275. doi:10.1027/1015-5759/a000153

Goldhammer, F., Naumann, J., Selter, A., Toth, K., Rolke, H., & Klieme, E. (2014). The time on task effect in reading and problem solving is moderated by task difficulty and skill: Insights from a computer-based large-scale assessment. *Journal of Educational Psychology, 106*(4), 608–626. doi:10.1037/a0034716

Goldman, R. D., Hudson, D., & Daharsh, B. J. (1973). Self-estimated task persistence as a nonlinear predictor of college success. *Journal of Educational Psychology, 65*(2), 216–221. doi:10.1037/h0034989 PMID:4778799

Goldstein, I. L., Zedeck, S., & Schneider, B. (1992). An exploration of the job analysis-content validity process. In N. Schmitt & W. C. Borman (Eds.), *Personnel Selection.* San Francisco, CA: Jossey-Bass.

Goldstone, R. L. (2006). The complex systems see-change in education. *Journal of the Learning Sciences, 15*(1), 35–43. doi:10.1207/s15327809jls1501_5

Goldstone, R. L., & Wilensky, U. (2008). Promoting transfer through complex systems principles. *Journal of the Learning Sciences, 17*(4), 465–516. doi:10.1080/10508400802394898

Gollwitzer, P. M., & Bayer, U. (1999). Deliberative versus implemental mindsets in the control of action. *Dual-Process Theories in Social Psychology,* 403–422.

Goodman, S. (2014, May 30) Social media literacy: The five key concepts. The George Lucas Educational Foundation. *Edutopia.* [blog message]. Retrieved July 20, 2014, from http://www.edutopia.org/blog/social-media-five-key-concepts-stacey-goodman

Goodyear, P., Jones, C., & Thompson, K. (2014). Computer-supported collaborative learning: Instructional approaches, group processes and educational designs. In J. M. Spector, M. D. Merrill, J. Elen, & M. J. Bishop (Eds.), *Handbook of research on educational communications and technology* (pp. 439–451). New York, NY: Springer. doi:10.1007/978-1-4614-3185-5_35

Grady, S. E. (2011). Team-Based Learning in Pharmacotherapeutics. *American Journal of Pharmaceutical Education*, 75(7), 136. doi:10.5688/ajpe757136 PMID:21969722

Graesser, A., & Foltz, P. (2013, June). *The PISA 2015 Collaborative Problem Solving Framework*. Paper presented at the 2013 Computer-Supported Collaborative Learning conference, Madison, WI.

Graesser, A. C., Foltz, P., Rosen, Y., Forsyth, C., & Germany, M. (in press). Challenges of assessing collaborative problem solving. In B. Csapo, J. Funke, & A. Schleicher (Eds.), *The nature of problem solving*. OECD Series.

Graesser, A. C., Jeon, M., & Dufty, D. (2008). Agent technologies designed to facilitate interactive knowledge construction. *Discourse Processes*, 45(4), 298–322. doi:10.1080/01638530802145395

Graesser, A. C., Lu, S., Jackson, G. T., Mitchell, H., Ventura, M., Olney, A., & Louwerse, M. M. (2004). AutoTutor: A tutor with dialogue in natural language. *Behavior Research Methods, Instruments, & Computers*, 36(2), 180–193. doi:10.3758/BF03195563 PMID:15354683

Graesser, A. C., & McDaniel, B. (2008). Conversational agents can provide formative assessment, constructive learning, and adaptive instruction. In C. A. Dwyer (Ed.), *The future of assessment: Shaping teaching and learning* (pp. 85–112). New York, NY: Routledge.

Graesser, A., Britt, A., Millis, K., Wallace, P., Halpern, D., Cai, Z., & Forsyth, C. et al. (2010). Critiquing media reports with flawed scientific findings: Operation ARIES! A game with animated agents and natural language trialogues. In V. Aleven, J. Kay, & J. Mostow (Eds.), *Proceedings of the 2nd IEEE international conference on intelligent tutoring systems* (pp. 327-329). Berlin, Germany: Springer. doi:10.1007/978-3-642-13437-1_60

Graham, S., Bollinger, A., Booth Olson, C., D'Aoust, C., MacArthur, C., McCutchen, D., & Olinghouse, N. (2012). Teaching elementary school students to be effective writers: A practice guide (NCEE 2012- 4058). Washington, DC: National Center for Education Evaluation and Regional Assistance, Institute of Education Sciences, U.S. Department of Education. Retrieved from http://ies.ed.gov/ncee/wwc/publications_reviews.aspx#pubsearch

Graham, S., Hebert, M. A., & Harris, K. (under review). *Formative Assessment and Writing: A Meta-analysis with Implications for Common Core*.

Graham, S., Hebert, M., Sandbank, M. P., & Harris, K. (in preparation). *Assessing the writing achievement of young struggling writers: Application of generalizability theory*.

Graham, S., Capizzi, A., Harris, K. R., Hebert, M., & Morphy, P. (2014). Teaching writing to middle school students: A national survey. *Reading and Writing*, 27(6), 1015–1042. doi:10.1007/s11145-013-9495-7

Graham, S., Harris, K. R., Fink-Chorzempa, B., & MacArthur, C. (2003). Primary grade teachers' instructional adaptations for struggling writers: A national survey. *Journal of Educational Psychology*, 95(2), 279–292. doi:10.1037/0022-0663.95.2.279

Graham, S., Harris, K. R., & Hebert, M. (2011). *Informing Writing: The Benefits of Formative Assessment. A Report from Carnegie Corporation of New York*. Carnegie Corporation of New York.

Graham, S., Harris, K. R., & Hebert, M. A. (2011). *Informing writing: The benefits of formative assessment: A Carnegie Corporation Time to Act report*. Washington, DC: Alliance for Excellent Education.

Graham, S., Harris, K., & Hebert, M. (2011). *Informing writing: The benefits of formative assessment. A Carnegie Corporation Time to Act report*. Washington, DC: Alliance for Excellent Education.

Graham, S., & Hebert, M. (2010). *Writing to read: Evidence for how writing can improve reading: A report from Carnegie Corporation of New York*. Carnegie Corporation of New York.

Graham, S., & Hebert, M. (2010). *Writing to read: Evidence for how writing improves reading. — A report to Carnegie Corporation of New York*. Washington, DC: Alliance for Excellent Education.

Graham, S., & Hebert, M. A. (2010). *Writing to read: Evidence for how writing can improve reading. A Carnegie Corporation Time to Act Report*. Washington, DC: Alliance for Excellent Education.

Graham, S., & Perin, D. (2007). A meta-analysis of writing instruction for adolescent students. *Journal of Educational Psychology, 99*(3), 445–476. doi:10.1037/0022-0663.99.3.445

Graham, S., & Perin, D. (2007). *Writing next: Effective strategies to improve writing of adolescents in middle and high schools — A report to Carnegie Corporation of New York*. Washington, DC: Alliance for Excellent Education.

Grasso, D. U., & Martinelli, D. (2007). Holistic engineering. *The Chronicle of Higher Education, 53*(28), B8.

Graves, M. F. (2006). *The vocabulary book*. New York, NY: Teachers College Columbia University.

Greeno, J. G. MSMTAPG. (1998). The situativity of knowing, learning, and research. *The American Psychologist, 53*(1), 5–16. doi:10.1037/0003-066X.53.1.5

Green, S. G., Gavin, M. B., & Aiman-Smith, L. (1995). Assessing a multidimensional measure of radical technology innovation. *IEEE Transactions on Engineering Management, 42*(3), 203–214. doi:10.1109/17.403738

Griffin, M. (2010). How do we fix system engineering. *61st International Astronautical Congress*. Prague, Czech Republic. Paper: IIAC-10.D1.5.4

Griffin, P., & Care, E. (2015). The ATC21S Method. In P. Griffin & E. Care (Eds.), *Assessment and teaching of 21st century skills: Methods and approach* (pp. 3–32). Dordrecht: Springer.

Griffin, P., Care, E., & McGaw, B. (2012). The changing role of education and schools. In P. Griffin, B. McGaw, & E. Care (Eds.), *Assessment and teaching 21st century skills* (pp. 1–15). Heidelberg: Springer. doi:10.1007/978-94-007-2324-5_1

Grimes, D., & Warschauer, M. (2010). Utility in a fallible tool: A multi-site case study of automated writing evaluation. *The Journal of Technology, Learning, and Assessment, 8*(6), 1–44. Retrieved from http://www.jtla.org

Grosseck, G., Bran, R., & Tiru, L. (2011). "Dear teacher, what should I write on my wall?": A case study on academic uses of Facebook. *Procedia: Social and Behavioral Sciences, 15*, 425–1430. doi:10.1016/j.sbspro.2011.03.306

Grotzer, T. A. (2003). Learning to understand the forms of causality implicit in scientifically accepted explanations. *Studies in Science Education, 39*(1), 1–74. doi:10.1080/03057260308560195

Grow, O. (1996). Teaching learners to be self-directed. *Adult Education Quarterly, 41*(3), 125–149. doi:10.1177/0001848191041003001

Gulowsen, J. (1972). A measure of work group autonomy. In L. Davis & J. Taylor (Eds.), *Design of jobs* (pp. 374–390). Harmondsworth, UK: Penguin.

Gunderson, E. A., Gripshover, S. J., Romero, C., Dweck, C. S., Goldin-Meadow, S., & Levine, S. C. (2013). Parent praise to 1-to 3-year-olds predicts children's motivational frameworks 5 years later. *Child Development, 84*(5), 1526–1541. doi:10.1111/cdev.12064 PMID:23397904

Gusnard, D. A., Ollinger, J. M., Shulman, G. L., Cloninger, C. R., Price, J. L., Van Essen, D. C., & Raichle, M. E. (2003). Persistence and brain circuitry. *Proceedings of the National Academy of Sciences of the United States of America, 100*(6), 3479–3484. doi:10.1073/pnas.0538050100 PMID:12626765

Gütl, C., Lankmayr, K., Weinhofer, J., & Höfler, M. (2011). Enhanced Automatic Question Creator – EAQC: Concept, development and evaluation of an automatic test item creation tool to foster modern e-education. *The Electronic Journal of e-Learning, 9*, 23-38.

Gwizdka, J., & Spence, I. (2007). Implicit measures of lostness and success in web navigation. *Interacting with Computers, 19*(3), 357–369. doi:10.1016/j.intcom.2007.01.001

Hadorn, G., Biber-Klemm, S., Grossenbacher-Mansuy, W., Hirsch Hadorn, G., Joye, D., Pohl, C., & Zemp, E. et al. (2008). The emergence of transdisciplinarity as a form of research. In H. Hoffmann-Riem, S. Biber-Klemm, W. Grossenbacher-Mansu, D. Joye, C. Pohl, U. Wiesmann, & E. Zemp (Eds.), *Handbook of Transdisciplinary Research* (pp. 19–39). Springer. doi:10.1007/978-1-4020-6699-3_2

Hadorn, G., Pohl, C., & Bammer, G. (2011). Problem solving through transdisciplinary research integration. *Procedia: Social and Behavioral Sciences, 28*, 636–639.

Haladyna, T. M. (1997). *Writing test items to evaluate higher order thinking*. Boston: Allyn and Bacon.

Haladyna, T. M. (2004). *Developing and validating multiple-choice test items* (3rd ed.). Mahwah, NJ: Lawrence Erlbaum & Associates, Publishers.

Haladyna, T. M. (2006). Roles and importance of validity studies in test development. In S. M. Downing & T. M. Haladyna (Eds.), *Handbook of test development* (pp. 739–758). Mahwah, NJ: Lawrence Erlbaum & Associates, Publishers.

Haladyna, T. M., & Rodriguez, M. C. (2013). *Developing and validating test items*. New York: Routledge.

Hall, G. E. (2010). Technology's Achilles heel: Achieving high-quality implementation. *Journal of Research on Technology in Education*, *42*(3), 231–253. doi:10.1080/15391523.2010.10782550

Hall, G. E., Loucks, S. F., Rutherford, W. L., & Newlove, B. W. (1975, Spring). Levels of use of the innovation: A framework for analyzing innovation adoption. *Journal of Teacher Education*, *26*(1), 52–56. doi:10.1177/002248717502600114

Hall, R., Atkins, L., & Fraser, J. (2014). Defining a self-evaluation digital literacy framework for secondary educators: The DigiLit Leicester project. *Research in Learning Technology*, *22*(0). doi:10.3402/rlt.v22.21440

Halpern, D. F. (1998). Teaching critical thinking for transfer across domains: Dispositions, skills, structure training, and metacognitive monitoring. *The American Psychologist*, *53*(4), 449–455. doi:10.1037/0003-066X.53.4.449 PMID:9572008

Hambleton, R. K. (1996). *Guidelines for Adapting Educational and Psychological Tests*. Academic Press.

Hambleton, R. (2005). Issues, designs, and technical guidelines for adapting tests into multiple languages and cultures. In R. Hambleton, P. Merenda, & C. Spielberger (Eds.), *Adapting educational and psychological tests for cross-cultural assessment* (Vol. 1, pp. 3–38). Lawrence Erlbaum Associates.

Hambleton, R. K., & Murphy, E. (1992). A psychometric perspective on authentic measurement. *Applied Measurement in Education*, *5*(1), 1–16. doi:10.1207/s15324818ame0501_1

Hambleton, R. K., & Patsula, L. (1999). Increasing the validity of adapted tests: Myths to be avoided and guidelines for improving test adaptation practices. *Association of Test Publishers*, *1*(1), 1–13.

Hambleton, R. K., Swaminathan, H., & Rogers, H. J. (1991). *Fundamentals of Item Response Theory*. Newbury Park, CA: SAGE Publications, Inc.

Hamilton, E., & Cherniavsky, J. (2006). Issues in Synchronous versus Asynchronous E-learning Platforms. In H. O'Neil, & R. Perez (Eds.), Web-Based Learning: Theory, Research and Practice (pp. 87-106). Lawrence Erlbaum Associates.

Hammersley, M., & Traianou, A. (2012, May). *Ethics and educational research. British Educational Research Association on-line resource*. Retrieved from http://bit.ly/1x113gJ

Handleman, J. S. (1986). Severe developmental disabilities: Defining the term. *Education & Treatment of Children*, *9*, 153–167.

Hanlon, S. T. (2013). *The relationship between deliberate practice and reading ability* (Doctoral dissertation). Retrieved from ProQuest Dissertations and Theses databases (AAT 3562741).

Hanlon, S. T., Greene, J. A., Swartz, C. W., & Stenner, A. J. (2015). The relationship between deliberate practice and reading ability (manuscript in preparation).

Hanlon, S. T., Neuvirth, K., Tendulkar, J., Houchins, J., Swartz, C. S., & Stenner, A. J. (2015). *EdSphere®*. Retrieved from http://www.EdSphere.com

Hanlon, S. T., Swartz, C. S., Burdick, H., & Stenner, A. J. (2006). *MyWritingWeb®*. Retrieved from http://www.mywritingweb.com

Hanlon, S. T., Swartz, C. S., Burdick, H., & Stenner, A. J. (2007). *MyReadingWeb®*. Retrieved from http://www.myreadingweb.com

Hanlon, S. T., Swartz, C. S., Burdick, H., & Stenner, A. J. (2008). *LearningOasis®*. Retrieved from http://www.alearningoasis.com

Hao, J. (2014). *Statistical models for dependent process data*. Paper presented at the Innovative Assessment of Collaboration Conference, Washington, DC.

Hara, S., Kitaoka, N., & Takeda, K. (2010). Estimation Method of User Satisfaction Using N-gram-based Dialog History Model for Spoken Dialog System. In *Proceedings of International Conference on Language Resources and Evaluation*, (pp. 78–83).

Harlen, W., & Deakin Crick, R. (2003). *A systematic review of the impact on students and teachers of the use of ICT for assessment of creative and critical thinking skills.* London: Evidence for Policy and Practice Co-ordinating Centre Department for Education and Skills.

Harmes, J. C., & Parshall, C. G. (2005). *Situated tasks and simulated environments: A look into the future for innovative computerized assessment.* Paper presented at the annual meeting of the Florida Educational Research Association, Miami, FL.

Harmes, J. C., & Parshall, C. G. (2010, April). *A model for planning, designing, and developing innovative items.* Paper presented at the annual meeting of the National Council on Measurement in Education, Denver, CO.

Harmes, J. C., & Wendt, A. (2009, Winter). Memorability of innovative item types. *CLEAR Exam Review, 20*(1), 16–20.

Hart Research Associates. (2006). *How should colleges prepare students to succeed in today's global economy? - Based on surveys among employers and recent college graduates.* Washington, DC: American Association of Colleges and Universities. Retrieved from https://www.aacu.org/sites/default/files/files/LEAP/2013_EmployerSurvey.pdf

Hart Research Associates. (2006). *How Should Colleges Prepare Students to Succeed in Today's Global Economy? - Based on Surveys Among Employers and Recent College Graduates.* Washington, DC: Hart Research Associates.

Hart Research Associates. (2009). *Learning and assessment: Trends in undergraduate education - A survey among members of the association of American colleges and universities.* Washington, DC: American Association of Colleges and Universities. Retrieved from http://www.aacu.org/sites/default/files/files/LEAP/2009MemberSurvey_Part1.pdf

Hart Research Associates. (2013). *It takes more than a major: Employer priorities for college learning and student success.* Washington, DC: American Association of Colleges and Universities. Retrieved from https://www.aacu.org/sites/default/files/files/LEAP/2013_EmployerSurvey.pdf

Hart, B., & Risley, T. R. (1992). American parenting of language-learning children: Persisting differences in family-child interactions observed in natural home environments. *Developmental Psychology, 28*(6), 1096–1105. doi:10.1037/0012-1649.28.6.1096

Hart, B., & Risley, T. R. (1995). *Meaningful differences in the everyday experiences of young American children.* Baltimore, MD: Paul H. Brookes.

Hartshorne, H., May, M. A., & Maller, J. B. (1929). *Studies in the nature of character, II Studies in service and self-control.* Retrieved from http://psycnet.apa.org/psycinfo/2006-22806-000

Hatano, G., & Inagaki, K. (1991). Sharing cognition through collective comprehension activity. In L. B. Resnick, J. M. Levine, & S. D. Teasley (Eds.), *Perspectives on socially shared cognition* (pp. 331–348). Washington, DC: American Psychological Association. doi:10.1037/10096-014

Hattie, J. A. C. (2009). *Visible learning: A synthesis of 800+ meta-analyses on achievement.* London: Routledge.

Hattie, J., & Timperley, H. (2007). The power of feedback. *Review of Educational Research, 77*(1), 81–112. doi:10.3102/003465430298487

Hayat, M. J., Eckardt, P., Higgins, M., Kim, M., & Schmiege, S. (2013). Teaching Statistics to Nursing Students: An Expert Panel Consensus. *The Journal of Nursing Education, 52*(6), 330–334. doi:10.3928/01484834-20130430-01 PMID:23621121

Hayes, J. R. (1996). A new framework for understanding cognition and affect in writing. In R. B. Ruddell & N. J. Unrau (Eds.), *Theoretical models and processes of reading* (5th ed.; pp. 1399–1430). Newark, DE: International Reading Association.

Hayes, J. R. (2012). Modeling and remodeling writing. *Written Communication*, *29*(3), 369–388. doi:10.1177/0741088312451260

Hearst, M. A. (2000). The debate on automated essay grading. *Intelligent Systems and Their Applications*, *15*(5), 22–37. doi:10.1109/5254.889104

Heatherton, T. F., Kozlowski, L. T., Frecker, R. C., & Fagerstrom, K. (1991). The Fagerstrom Test for Nicotine Dependence: A revision of the Fagerstrom Tolerance Questionnaire. *British Journal of Addiction*, *86*(9), 1119–1127. doi:10.1111/j.1360-0443.1991.tb01879.x PMID:1932883

Hegarty, M. (2004). Dynamic visualizations and learning: Getting to the difficult questions. *Learning and Instruction*, *14*(3), 343–351. doi:10.1016/j.learninstruc.2004.06.007

Helsen, W. F., Starkes, J. L., & Hodges, N. J. (1998). Team sports and the theory of deliberate practice. *Journal of Sport & Exercise Psychology*, *20*, 12–34.

He, Q., Glas, C. A. W., Kosinski, M., Stillwell, D. J., & Veldkamp, B. P. (2014). Predicting self-monitoring skills using textual posts on Facebook. *Computers in Human Behavior*, *33*, 69–78. doi:10.1016/j.chb.2013.12.026

He, Q., Veldkamp, B. P., & de Vries, T. (2012). Screening for posttraumatic stress disorder using verbal features in self-narratives: A text mining approach. *Psychiatry Research*, *198*(3), 441–447. doi:10.1016/j.psychres.2012.01.032 PMID:22464046

Herder, E. (2005). Characterizations of User Web Revisit Behavior. In *Proceedings of Workshop on Adaptivity and User Modelling in Interactive Systems*, (pp. 32-37). Academic Press.

Herman, J., Dai, Y., Htut, A. M., Martinez, M., & Rivera, N. (2011). *Evaluation of the enhanced assessment grants (EAG) SimScientists program: Site visit findings*. Los Angeles: CRESST.

Herrington, A., & Moran, C. (2001). What happens when machines read our students' writing? *College English*, *63*(4), 480–499. doi:10.2307/378891

Hess, H., & Hochleitner, T. (2012). *College rankings inflation: Are you overpaying for prestige?* Retrieved from American Enterprise Institute: http://www.aei.org/publication/college-rankings-inflation-are-you-overpaying-for-prestige

Hesse, F., Care, E., Buder, J., Sassenberg, K., & Griffin, P. (2015). A Framework for Teachable Collaborative Problem Solving Skills. In P. Griffin & E. Care (Eds.), *Assessment and teaching of 21st century skills: Methods and approach* (pp. 37–56). Dordrecht: Springer. doi:10.1007/978-94-017-9395-7_2

Hetzroni, O. E., & Shalem, U. (2005). From logos to orthographic symbols: A multilevel fading computer program for teaching nonverbal children with autism. *Focus on Autism and Other Developmental Disabilities*, *20*(4), 201–212. doi:10.1177/10883576050200040201

Hetzroni, O. E., & Tannous, J. (2004). Effects of a computer-based intervention program on the communicative functions of children with autism. *Journal of Autism and Developmental Disorders*, *34*(2), 95–113. doi:10.1023/B:JADD.0000022602.40506.bf PMID:15162930

Hetzroni, O., Rubin, C., & Konkol, O. (2002). The use of assistive technology for symbol identification by children with Rett syndrome. *Journal of Intellectual & Developmental Disability*, *27*(1), 57–71. doi:10.1080/13668250120119626-1

Hew, K. F. (2011). Students' and teachers' use of Facebook. *Computers in Human Behavior*, *27*(2), 662–676. doi:10.1016/j.chb.2010.11.020

Hibberd, R., Morris, E., & Jones, A. (2004). Use of concept maps to represent students' knowledge of research methods in psychology: A preliminary study. *Journal of Cognitive Education and Psychology*, *3*(3), 276–296. doi:10.1891/194589504787382965

Hibbison, E. P. (1991). The ideal multiple-choice question: A protocol analysis. *Forum for Reading*, *22*(2), 36–41.

Hiebert, E. H. (1983). An examination of ability grouping for reading instruction. *Reading Research Quarterly*, *18*(2), 231–255. doi:10.1598/RRQ.18.2.5

Hiebert, E. H., & Kamil, M. L. (2010). *Teaching and learning vocabulary: Bringing research to practice*. New York, NY: Routledge.

Higgins, D. (2007). *Item Distiller: Text retrieval for computer-assisted test item creation. Educational Testing Service Research Memorandum* (RM-07-05). Princeton, NJ: Educational Testing Service.

Higgins, D., Brew, C., Hellman, M., Ziai, R., Chen, L., Cahill, A., ... Blackmore, J. (2014). *Is getting the right answer just about choosing the right words? The role of syntactically-informed features in short answer scoring.* arXiv: 1404.0801,v2.

Higgins, D., Futagi, Y., & Deane, P. (2005). *Multilingual generalization of the Model Creator software for math item generation. Educational Testing Service Research Report (RR-05-02).* Princeton, NJ: Educational Testing Service.

Higgins, D., & Heilman, M. (2014). Managing what we can measure: Quantifying the susceptibility of automated scoring systems to gaming behavior. *Educational Measurement: Issues and Practice, 33*(3), 36–46. doi:10.1111/emip.12036

Hillage, J., & Pollard, E. (1998). Employability: Developing a framework for policy analysis (ResearchBrief No.85). London: Department for Education and Employment. Retrieved from http://webarchive.nationalarchives.gov.uk/20130401151715/http://www.education.gov.uk/publications/eOrderingDownload/RB85.pdf

Hirschfeld, G., & von Brachel, R. (2014). Multiple-Group confirmatory factor analysis in R–A tutorial in measurement invariance with continuous and ordinal indicators. *Practical Assessment, Research & Evaluation, 19*(7), 2.

Hitchcock, C. H., & Noonan, M. J. (2000). Computer-assisted instruction of early academic skills. *Topics in Early Childhood Special Education, 20*(3), 145–158. doi:10.1177/027112140002000303

Hmelo-Silver, C. E., Chinn, C. A., Chan, C. C., & O'Donnell, A. M. (Eds.). (2013). *The international handbook of collaborative learning.* New York, NY: Routledge.

Hmelo-Silver, C. E., Jordan, R., Liu, L., Gray, S., Demeter, M., Rugaber, S., & Goel, A. et al. (2008). Focusing on Function: Thinking below the Surface of Complex Natural Systems. *Science Scope, 31*(9), 27–35.

Hmelo-Silver, C. E., Nagarajan, A., & Day, R. S. (2000). Effects of high and low prior knowledge on construction of a joint problem space. *Journal of Experimental Education, 69*(1), 36–57. doi:10.1080/00220970009600648

Hoadley, C. M., & Enyedy, N. (1999). Between information and collaboration: Middle spaces in computer media for learning. In C. M. Hoadley & J. Roschelle (Eds.), *CSCL_99 proceedings of computer support for collaborative learning 1999* (pp. 242–251). Mahwah, NJ: Erlbaum. doi:10.3115/1150240.1150270

Hocevar, D., El-Zahhar, N., & Gombos, A. (1989). Cross-cultural equivalence of anxiety measurements in English–Hungarian bilinguals. In Advances in test anxiety research (Vol. 6, pp. 223-231). Netherlands.

Hodges, N. J., & Starkes, J. L. (1996). Wrestling with the nature of expertise: A sport specific test of Ericsson, Krampe, and Tesch-Romer's (1993) "Deliberate Practice". *International Journal of Sport Psychology, 27,* 400–424.

Hoeft, R., Jentsch, F., Harper, M., Evans, A. III, Bowers, C., & Salas, E. (2003). TPL-KATS — concept map: A computerized knowledge assessment tool. *Computers in Human Behavior, 19*(6), 653–657. doi:10.1016/S0747-5632(03)00043-8

Hoffman-Riem, H., Biber-Klemm, S., Grossenbacher-Mansuy, W., Hirsch Hadorn, G., Joye, D., Pohl, C., & Zemp, E. et al. (2008). Idea of the handbook. In H. Hoffmann-Riem, S. Biber-Klemm, W. Grossenbacher-Mansuy, D. Joye, C. Pohl, U. Wiesmann, & E. Zemp (Eds.), *Handbook of transdisciplinary research* (pp. 3–17). Springer. doi:10.1007/978-1-4020-6699-3_1

Hogarty, K., Lang, T., & Kromrey, J. (2003, February). Another look at technology use in classrooms: The development and validation of an instrument to measure teachers' perceptions. *Educational and Psychological Measurement, 63*(1), 139–162. doi:10.1177/0013164402239322

Holland, P. W., & Thayer, D. T. (1988). Differential item performance and the Mantel-Haenszel procedure. *Test validity,* 129-145.

Holland, P. W., & Wainer, H. (1993). *Differential item functioning.* Psychology Press.

Holman, L. (2011). Millennial students' mental models of search: Implications for academic librarians and database developers. *Journal of Academic Librarianship, 37*(1), 19–27. doi:10.1016/j.acalib.2010.10.003

Holmes, V. (2012). Depth of teachers' knowledge: Frameworks for teachers' knowledge of mathematics. *Journal of STEM Education: Innovations and Research, 13*(1), 55–71.

Honey, M. A., & Hilton, M. (Eds.). (2011). *Learning science through computer games and simulations.* Washington, DC: National Academies Press.

Horner, R. H., Carr, E. G., Halle, J., McGee, G., Odom, S., & Wolery, M. (2005). The use of single-subject research to identify evidence-based practice in special education. *Exceptional Children, 71*(2), 165–179. doi:10.1177/001440290507100203

Horn, J. L., & McArdle, J. J. (1992). A practical and theoretical guide to measurement invariance in aging research. *Experimental Aging Research, 18*(3), 117–144. doi:10.1080/03610739208253916 PMID:1459160

Horton, F. W. (2013). *Overview of Information literacy resources worldwide.* Paris: UNESCO. Retrieved July 20, 2014, from http://www.unesco.org/new/fileadmin/MULTIMEDIA/HQ/CI/CI/pdf/news/overview_info_lit_resources.pdf

Houck, C. K., & Billingsley, B. S. (1989). Written expression of students with and without learning disabilities: Differences across grades. *Journal of Learning Disabilities, 22*(9), 561–568. doi:10.1177/002221948902200908 PMID:2809408

Hough, L. M. (1992). The 'Big Five' personality variables–construct confusion: Description versus prediction. *Human Performance, 5*(1-2), 139–155. doi:10.1080/08959285.1992.9667929

Hou, H. (2011). A case study of online instructional collaborative discussion activities for problem-solving using situated scenarios: An examination of content and behavior cluster analysis. *Computers & Education, 56*(3), 712–719. doi:10.1016/j.compedu.2010.10.013

Howard, T. C., & Aleman, G. R. (2008). Teacher capacity for diverse learners. In M. Cochran-Smith, S. Feiman-Nemser, D. J. McIntyre, & K. E. Demers (Eds.), *Handbook of research on teacher education* (pp. 157–174). New York, NY: Routledge.

Hoxby, C. M., & Avery, C. (2012). *The missing "one-offs": The hidden supply of high-achieving, low income students.* Cambridge, MA: National Bureau of Economic Research. doi:10.3386/w18586

Hsieh, I.-L., & O'Neil, H. F. Jr. (2002). Types of feedback in a computer-based collaborative problem solving group task. *Computers in Human Behavior, 18*(6), 699–715. doi:10.1016/S0747-5632(02)00025-0

Hsu, L. L. (2004). Developing concept maps from problem-based learning scenario discussions. *Journal of Advanced Nursing, 48*(5), 510–518. doi:10.1111/j.1365-2648.2004.03233.x PMID:15533089

Hubbard, J. P. (1978). *Measuring medical education: The tests and experience of the national board of medical examiners* (2nd ed.). Philadelphia: Lea & Febiger.

Huffaker, D., & Calvert, S. (2003). The new science of learning: Active learning metacognition, and transfer of knowledge in E-Learning applications. *Journal of Educational Computing Research, 29*(3), 325–334. doi:10.2190/4T89-30W2-DHTM-RTQ2

Huffcutt, A. (2011). An empirical review of the employment interview construct literature. *International Journal of Selection and Assessment, 19*(1), 62–81. doi:10.1111/j.1468-2389.2010.00535.x

Huff, K. L., & Sireci, S. G. (2001). Validity issues in computer-based testing. *Educational Measurement: Issues and Practice, 20*(3), 16–25. doi:10.1111/j.1745-3992.2001.tb00066.x

Hu, L., & Bentler, P. M. (1999). Cutoff criteria for fit indexes in covariance structure analysis: Conventional criteria versus new alternatives. *Structural Equation Modeling, 6*(1), 1–55. doi:10.1080/10705519909540118

Huot, B. (1990). The literature of direct writing assessments: Major concerns and prevailing trends. *Review of Educational Research, 60*(2), 237–263. doi:10.3102/00346543060002237

Hwang, G. J., Chu, H. C., Shih, J. L., Huang, S. H., & Tsai, C. C. (2010). A decision-tree-oriented guidance mechanism for conducting nature science observation activities in a context-aware ubiquitous learning environment. *Journal of Educational Technology & Society, 13*(2), 53–64.

Hyerle, D. (2009). *Visual tools for transformation into knowledge* (2nd ed.). Thousand Oaks, CA: Corwin Press.

IBM. (2013). *IBM Statistics for Windows. Version 22.0.* Armonk, NY: IBM Corp.

Ingeç, S. K. (2009). Analysing concept maps as an assessment tool in teaching physics and comparison with the achievement tests. *International Journal of Science Education, 31*(14), 1897–1915. doi:10.1080/09500690802275820

Inhelder, B., & Piaget, J. (1958). *The growth of logical thinking from childhood to adolescence.* London: Routledge & Kegan Paul. doi:10.1037/10034-000

International Society for Technology in Education. (2007). *ISTE standards for students.* Retrieved from http://www.iste.org/standards/iste-standards/standards-for-students

International Society for Technology in Education. (n.d.). *Student-centered learning.* Retrieved from http://www.iste.org/standards/essential-conditions/student-centered-learning

International Task Force on Assessment Center Guidelines. (2014). *Guidelines and ethical considerations for Assessment Center Operations* (6th ed.). Retrieved from http://www.assessmentcenters.org/Assessmentcenters/media/2014/International-AC-Guidelines-6th-Edition-2014.pdf

Interprofessional Education Collaborative Expert Panel (IPEC). (2011). *Core competencies for interprofessional collaborative practice. Report of an expert panel.* Washington, DC: Interprofessional Education Collaborative.

Ioannidou, A., Repenning, A., Webb, D., Keyser, D., Luhn, L., & Daetwyler, C. (2010). Mr. Vetro: A Collective Simulation for teaching health science. *International Journal of Computer-Supported Collaborative Learning, 5*(2), 141–166. doi:10.1007/s11412-010-9082-8

IOM (Institute of Medicine). (2011). *The Future of Nursing: Leading Change, Advancing Health.* Washington, DC: The National Academies Press.

Irvine, S. H., & Kyllonen, P. C. (2002). *Item generation for test development.* Hillsdale, NJ: Erlbaum.

Irwin, C., Ball, L., Desbrow, B., & Leveritt, M. (2012). Students' perceptions of using Facebook as an interactive learning resource at university. *Australasian Journal of Educational Technology, 28*(7), 1221–1232. Retrieved from http://ascilite.org.au/ajet/ajet28/irwin.html

Israel Ministry of Education. (2011). *Adapting the educational system to the 21st century.* Jerusalem, Israel: Ministry of Education.

Ito, M. (2013). *Connected learning: An agenda for research and design.* Retrieved from http://eprints.lse.ac.uk/48114/

Ito, M., Gutiérrez, K., Livingstone, S., Penuel, B., Rhodes, J., & Salen, K. … Watkins, S. C. (2013). Connected learning: An agenda for research and design. Irvine, CA: Digital Media and Learning Research Hub.

Ito, M., Horst, H. A., Bittanti, M., Boyd, D., Herr-Stephenson, B., Lange, P. G. (2008). *Living and learning with new media: Summary of findings from the digital youth project.* MIT Press. Retrieved July 20, 2014, from http://digitalyouth.ischool.berkeley.edu/report

Ito, M. (2010). *Hanging out, messing around, and geeking out: Kids living and learning with new media.* Cambridge, MA: MIT Press.

Jahnke, J. (2010). Student Perceptions of the Impact of Online Discussion Forum Participation on Learning Outcomes. *Journal of Learning Design, 3*(2), 27–34. doi:10.5204/jld.v3i2.48

Jenkins, H. (2006). *Convergence culture: Where old and new media collide.* New York: New York University Press.

Jensen, J. (2004). It's the information age, so where's the information? Why our students can't find it and what we can do to help. *College Teaching, 52*(3), 107–112.

Jerald, C. D. (2009). Defining a 21st century education. Alexandria, VA: The Center for Public Education. Retrieved from http://www.cfsd16.org/public/_century/pdf/Defininga21stCenturyEducation_Jerald_2009.pdf

Jimenez, B. A., Browder, D. M., & Courtade, G. R. (2008). Teaching an algebraic equation to high school students with moderate developmental disabilities. *Education and Training in Developmental Disabilities, 43*, 266–274.

Joachims, T. (1998). Text categorization with Support Vector Machines: Learning with many relevant features. *Machine Learning: ECML-98. Lecture Notes in Computer Science, 1398*, 137–142. doi:10.1007/BFb0026683

Johnson, V. E. (2003). Grade inflation: A crisis in college education. Ann Arbor, MI: Springer. Retrieved from http://www.springer.com/education+%26+language/book/978-0-387-00125-8

Johnson, D. W., & Johnson, R. T. (2003). Training for cooperative group work. In M. A. West, D. Tjosvold, & K. G. Smith (Eds.), *International handbook for organizational teamwork and cooperative working* (pp. 167–183). Chichester, UK: Wiley.

Johnson-Hofer, P., & Karasic, S. (1988). Learning about Computers. *Nursing Outlook, 36*(6), 293–294. PMID:3186471

Johnson, L. W., & Valente, A. (2008). Tactical language and culture training systems: Using artificial intelligence to teach foreign languages and cultures. In M. Goker, & K. Haigh (Eds.), *Proceedings of the Twentieth Conference on Innovative Applications of Artificial Intelligence* (pp. 1632-1639). Menlo Park, CA: AAAI Press.

Johnstone, C. J., Bottsford-Miller, N. A., & Thompson, S. J. (2006). *Using the Think Aloud Method (Cognitive Labs) to Evaluate Test Design for Students with Disabilities and English Language Learners*. Technical Report 44. National Center on Educational Outcomes, University of Minnesota.

Joint Council for Qualifications. (2013). *General and vocational qualifications suspected malpractice in examinations and assessments: Policies and procedures*. Retrieved from http://bit.ly/1qKJuOE

Joint Information Systems Committee infoNet. (2014). *Learners' perspectives*. Retrieved from http://bit.ly/1EQG1FA

Joint Information Systems Committee. (2007a). *Effective practice with e-Assessment: An overview of technologies, policies and practice in further and higher education*. Retrieved from http://bit.ly/1igM2SK

Joint Information Systems Committee. (2007b). *E-portfolios: an overview of JISC activities*. Retrieved from http://bit.ly/SJKrwI

Joint Information Systems Committee. (2008). *Effective practice with e-portfolios: supporting 21ˢᵗ century learning*. Retrieved from http://bit.ly/1hLnYeG

Joint Information Systems Committee. (2010a). *Effective assessment in a digital age: a guide to technology-enhanced assessment and feedback*. Retrieved from http://bit.ly/1hJwt7V

Joint Information Systems Committee. (2010b). *Making the most of a computer-assisted assessment system, University of Manchester*. Retrieved from http://bit.ly/1HDjK2j

Jonassen, D. H. (1995). Computers as cognitive tools: Learning with technology, not from technology. *Journal of Computing in Higher Education, 6*(2), 40–73. doi:10.1007/BF02941038

Jonassen, D. H. (1996). *Computers in the classroom: Mindtools for critical thinking.* Englewood Cliffs, NJ: Prentice-Hall, Inc.

Jonassen, D. H. (2006). *Modeling with technology: Mindtools for conceptual change*. Columbus, OH: Merrill/Prentice-Hall.

Jonassen, D., Howland, J., Moore, J., & Marra, R. (2003). *Learning to solve problems with technology: A constructivist perspective* (2nd ed.). Upper Saddle River, NJ: Merrill Prentice Hall.

Jones, R., Higgs, R., DeAngelis, C., & Prideaux, D. (2001). Changing face of medical curriculum. *Lancet, 357*(9257), 699–703. doi:10.1016/S0140-6736(00)04134-9 PMID:11247568

Jones, S., & Madden, M. (2002). *The Internet goes to college: How students are living in the future with today's technology*. Washington, DC: Pew Internet & American Life Project.

Jorczak, R., & Dupuis, D. (2014). Differences in Classroom Versus Online Exam Performance Due to Asynchronous Discussion. *Journal of Asynchronous Learning Networks, 18*(2), 67–78.

Jöreskog, K. G., & Sörbom, D. (2014). *LISREL 9.1 for Windows*. Skokie, IL: Scientific Software International.

Julien, H., & Barker, S. (2009). How high-school students find and evaluate scientific information: A basis for information literacy skills development. *Library & Information Science Research*, *31*(1), 12–17. doi:10.1016/j.lisr.2008.10.008

Jurafsky, D., & Martin, J. (2008). *Speech and language processing*. Englewood, NJ: Prentice Hall.

Jurafsky, D., & Martin, J. H. (2009). *Speech and language processing: An introduction to natural language processing, computational linguistics, and speech recognition* (2nd ed.). Upper Saddle River, NJ: Pearson.

Juvina, I., & van Oostendorp, H. (2006). Individual differences and behavioral metrics involved in modeling web navigation. *Universal Access in the Information Society*, *4*(3), 258–269. doi:10.1007/s10209-005-0007-7

Juvina, I., & van Oostendorp, H. (2008). Modeling semantic and structural knowledge in web navigation. *Discourse Processes*, *45*(4-5), 346–364. doi:10.1080/01638530802145205

Kabilan, M. K., Ahmad, N., & Abidin, M. J. Z. (2010). Facebook: An online environment for learning English in institutions of higher education. *The Internet and Higher Education*, *13*(4), 179–187. doi:10.1016/j.iheduc.2010.07.003

Kafai, Y. M., Quintero, M., & Felton, D. (2010). Investigating the 'why' in Whypox: Casual and systematic explorations of a virtual epidemic. *Games and Culture*, *5*(1), 116–135. doi:10.1177/1555412009351265

Kagohara, D. M., van der Meer, L., Ramdoss, S., O'Reilly, M. F., Lancioni, G. E., Davis, T. N., ... Sigafoos, J. (2013). Using iPods and iPads in teaching programs for individuals with developmental disabilities: A systematic review. *Research in Developmental Disabilities: A Multidisciplinary Journal*, *34*, 147-156

Kahneman, D. (2011). *Thinking fast and slow*. New York, NY: Farrar, Strauss and Giroux.

Kalantzis, M., & Cope, B. (2010). The Teacher as Designer: Pedagogy in the new media age. *E-Learning and Digital Media*, *7*(3), 200–222. doi:10.2304/elea.2010.7.3.200

Kamil, M. L., & Hiebert, E. H. (2010). Teaching and learning vocabulary: Perspectives and persistent issues. In E. H. Hiebert & M. L. Kamil (Eds.), *Teaching and learning vocabulary: Bringing research to practice* (pp. 1–23). New York, NY: Routledge.

Kamins, M. L., & Dweck, C. S. (1999). Person versus process praise and criticism: Implications for contingent self-worth and coping. *Developmental Psychology*, *35*(3), 835–847. doi:10.1037/0012-1649.35.3.835 PMID:10380873

Kane, M. T. (2006a). Content-related validity evidence in test development. In S. M. Downing & T. M. Haladyna (Eds.), *Handbook of test development* (pp. 131–154). Mahwah, NJ: Lawrence Erlbaum & Associates, Publishers.

Kane, M. T. (2006b). Validity. In R. L. Brennan (Ed.), *Educational measurement* (pp. 17–64). Westport, CT: Praeger Publishers.

Kane, T. (Ed.). (1998). Racial and ethnic preferences in college admission. Washington, DC: The Brookings Institution. Retrieved from http://www.brookings.edu/research/papers/1996/11/race-kane

Katusic, S. K., Colligan, A. L., & Barbaresi, W. J. (2009). The forgotten learning disability: Epidemiology of written-language disorder in a population-based birth cohort (1976-1982), Rochester, Minnesota. *Pediatrics*, *123*(5), 1306–1313. doi:10.1542/peds.2008-2098 PMID:19403496

Katz, M. (2014). *How the ARE is Scored* [Web log post]. Retrieved from http://blog.ncarb.org/en/2014/April/HowAREScored.aspx

Katzenbach, J., & Smith, D. K. (2003). *The wisdom of teams: Creating the high-performance organization*. New York: Collins Business Essentials.

Keith, T. Z. (2003). Validity and automated essay scoring systems. In M. D. Shermis & J. C. Burstein (Eds.), *Automated essay scoring: A cross-disciplinary perspective* (pp. 147–167). Mahwah, NJ: Lawrence Erlbaum Associates, Inc.

Kelley, K. R., Test, D. W., & Cooke, N. L. (2013). Effects of picture prompts delivered by a video iPod on pedestrian navigation. *Exceptional Children*, *79*, 459–474.

Kellogg, R. T. (1999). *The psychology of writing*. Oxford, UK: Oxford University Press.

Kellogg, R. T. (2006). Professional writing experience. In K. A. Ericsson, N. Charness, P. Feltovich, & R. R. Hoffman (Eds.), *Cambridge handbook of expertise and expert performance* (pp. 389–402). Cambridge, UK: Cambridge University Press. doi:10.1017/CBO9780511816796.022

Kellogg, R. T., & Whiteford, A. P. (2009). Training advanced writing skills: The case for deliberative practice. *Educational Psychologist*, *44*(4), 250–266. doi:10.1080/00461520903213600

Kellogg, R. T., Whiteford, A. P., & Quinlan, T. (2010). Does automated feedback help students learn to write? *Journal of Educational Computing Research*, *42*(2), 173–196. doi:10.2190/EC.42.2.c

Kena, G., Aud, S., Johnson, F., Wang, X., Zhang, J., Rathbun, A., & Kristapovich, P. (2014). The condition of education 2014 (NCES Report 2014-084). Washington, DC: U.S. Department of Education, National Center for Education Statistics. Retrieved from http://nces.ed.gov/pubs2014/2014083.pdf

Kennedy, M. J., & Deshler, D. D. (2010). Literacy instruction, technology, and students with learning disabilities: Research we have, research we need. *Learning Disability Quarterly*, *33*, 289–298.

Kennedy, M., Fisher, M. B., & Ennis, R. H. (1991). Critical thinking: Literature review and needed research. In L. Idol & B. F. Jones (Eds.), *Educational values and cognitive instruction: Implications for reform* (pp. 11–40). Hillsdale, NJ: Lawrence Erlbaum Associates.

Kennelly, K. J., Dietz, D., & Benson, P. (1985). Reinforcement schedules, effort vs. ability attributions, and persistence. *Psychology in the Schools*, *22*(4), 459–464. doi:10.1002/1520-6807(198510)22:4<459::AID-PITS2310220416>3.0.CO;2-G

Kerr, D., & Chung, G. K. W. K. (2012). Identifying key features of student performance in educational video games and simulations through cluster analysis. *Journal of Educational Data Mining*, *4*(1), 144–182.

Kessler, R., Anderson-Inman, L., & Ditson, L. (1997). *Science concept mapping companion*. Eugene, OR: Center for Electronic Studying, University of Oregon.

Ketterlin-Geller, L. R., & Tindal, G. (2007). Embedded technology: Current and future practices for increasing accessibility for all students. *Journal of Special Education Technology*, *22*, 1–15.

Kids Go, P. B. S. (2012). *Lifeboat to Mars* [Computer software]. Retrieved from http://pbskids.org/lifeboat/

Kieran, L., & Anderson, C. (2014). Guiding preservice teacher candidates to implement student-centered applications of technology in the classroom. In M. Searson & M. Ochoa (Eds.), *Proceedings of Society for Information Technology & Teacher Education International Conference 2014* (pp. 2414-2421). Chesapeake, VA: Association for the Advancement of Computing in Education (AACE).

Kim, C. M., Kim, M. K., Lee, C., Spector, J. M., & DeMeester, K. (2013). Teacher beliefs and technology integration. *Teaching and Teacher Education*, *29*, 76–85. doi:10.1016/j.tate.2012.08.005

Kim, H., & Hirtle, S. C. (1995). Spatial metaphors and disorientation in hypertext browsing. *Behaviour & Information Technology*, *4*(4), 239–250. doi:10.1080/01449299508914637

Kim, P., & Olaciregui, C. (2008). The effects of a concept map-based information display in an electronic portfolio system on information processing and retention in a fifth-grade science class covering the Earth's atmosphere. *British Journal of Educational Technology*, *39*(4), 700–714. doi:10.1111/j.1467-8535.2007.00763.x

Kim, S. H., Cohen, A. S., & Park, T. H. (1995). Detection of differential item functioning in multiple groups. *Journal of Educational Measurement*, *32*(3), 261–276. doi:10.1111/j.1745-3984.1995.tb00466.x

Kinchin, I. M. (2000). Concept mapping in biology. *Journal of Biological Education*, *34*(2), 61–68. doi:10.1080/00219266.2000.9655687

King, F. J., Goodson, L., & Rohani, F. (1998). *Higher order thinking skills: definition, teaching strategies and assessment*. Retrieved from http://fla.st/1xek82v

King, M. B., Newmann, F. M., & Carmichael, D. L. (2009, January/February). Authentic intellectual work: Common standards for teaching social studies. *Social Education*, *73*(1), 43–49.

Kingsley, T., & Tancock, S. (2013). Internet inquiry: Fundamental competencies for online comprehension. *The Reading Teacher, 67*(5), 389–399. doi:10.1002/trtr.1223

Kinnebrew, J. S., Loretz, K. M., & Biswas, G. (2013). A contextualized differential sequence mining method to derive students' learning behavior patterns. *Journal of Educational Data Mining, 5*(1), 190–220.

Kinnebrew, J. S., Loretz, K. M., & Biswas, G. (2013). A contextualized, differential sequence mining method to derive students' learning behavior patterns. *Journal of Educational Data Mining, 5*(1), 190–219.

Kinnebrew, J. S., Mack, D. L., & Biswas, G. (2013). Mining temporally-interesting learning behavior patterns.*Proceedings of the 6th International Conference on Educational Data Mining*, (pp. 252–255).

Kintsch, W. (1998). *Comprehension: A paradigm for cognition*. New York: Cambridge University Press.

Kitajima, M., Blackmon, M. H., & Polson, P. G. (2000). A Comprehension-based Model of Web Navigation and Its Application to Web Usability Analysis. *People and Computers, XIV*, 357–373.

Kittur, A., Chi, E. H., & Suh, B. (2008, April). Crowdsourcing user studies with Mechanical Turk. In *Proceedings of the SIGCHI conference on human factors in computing systems* (pp. 453–456). New York, NY: Association for Computing Machinery.

Kiuhara, S. A., Graham, S., & Hawken, L. S. (2009). Teaching writing to high school students: A national survey. *Journal of Educational Psychology, 101*(1), 136–160. doi:10.1037/a0013097

Klein, J. T. (2004, May). *Disciplinary origins and differences*. Paper presented at Fenner Conference on the Environment: Understanding the population-environment debate: Bridging disciplinary divides, Canberra, Australia.

Klein, S., Liu, O. L., Sconing, J., Bolus, R., Bridgeman, B., Kugelmass, H., …Steedle, J. (2009). *Test validity study (TVS) report*. U.S. Department of Education, Fund for the Improvement of Postsecondary Education. Retrieved from http://cae.org/images/uploads/pdf/13_Test_Validity_Study_Report.pdf

Klein, S., Steedle, J., & Kugelmass, H. (2009). CLA Lumina longitudinal study: Summary of procedures and findings. New York, NY: Council for Aid to Education. Retrieved from http://cae.org/images/uploads/pdf/12_CLA_Lumina_Longitudinal_Study_Summary_Findings.pdf

Klein, S., Zahner, D., Benjamin, R., Bolus, R., & Steedle, J. (2013). Observations on AHELO's generic skills strand methodology and findings. New York, NY: Council for Aid to Education. Retrieved from http://www.sheeo.org/sites/default/files/project-files/OBSERVATIONS_FINAL.pdf

Kleinert, J. O., Kearns, J. F., & Kleinert, H. L. (2010). *Students in the AA-AAS and the importance of communicative competence. Alternate assessment for students with significant cognitive disabilities: An educator's guide.* Baltimore, MD: Brookes.

Klein, J. T. (2008a). Education. In H. Hoffmann-Riem, S. Biber-Klemm, W. Grossenbacher-Mansuy, D. Joye, C. Pohl, U. Wiesmann, & E. Zemp (Eds.), *Handbook of Transdisciplinary Research* (pp. 399–410). Springer. doi:10.1007/978-1-4020-6699-3_26

Klein, J. T. (2008b). Evaluation of Interdisciplinary and transdisciplinary research: A literature review. *Journal of Preventive Medicine, 35*(2), S116–S123. doi:10.1016/j.amepre.2008.05.010 PMID:18619391

Klein, S. (2008). Characteristics of hand and machine-assigned scores to college students' answers to open-ended tasks. In D. Nolan & T. Speed (Eds.), *Probability and statistics: Essays in honor of David A. Freedman* (Vol. 2, pp. 76–89). Beachwood, OH: Institute of Mathematical Statistics. doi:10.1214/193940307000000392

Klein, S., Benjamin, R., Shavelson, R., & Bolus, R. (2007). The collegiate learning assessment: Facts and fantasies. *Evaluation Review, 31*(5), 415–439. doi:10.1177/0193841X07303318 PMID:17761805

Klein, S., Freedman, D., Shavelson, R., & Bolus, R. (2008). Assessing school effectiveness. *Evaluation Review, 32*(6), 511–525. doi:10.1177/0193841X08325948 PMID:18981333

Klein, S., Zahner, D., Benjamin, R., Bolus, R., & Steedle, J. (2013). *Observations on AHELO's Generic Skills Strand Methodology and Findings*. Council for Aid to Education.

Klieme, E. (2004). Assessment of cross-curricular problem-solving competencies. In J. H. Moskowitz & M. Stephens (Eds.), *Comparing learning outcomes: International assessments and education policy* (pp. 81–107). London: Routledge.

Klimoski, R., & Brickner, M. (1987). Why do assessment centers work? The puzzle of assessment center validity. *Personnel Psychology*, *40*(2), 243–260. doi:10.1111/j.1744-6570.1987.tb00603.x

Knight, V., McKissick, B. R., & Saunders, A. (2013). A review of technology-based interventions to teach academic skills to students with autism spectrum disorder. *Journal of Autism and Developmental Disorders*, *43*(11), 2628–2648. doi:10.1007/s10803-013-1814-y PMID:23543292

Knight, V., Wood, C., Spooner, F., Browder, D., & O'Brien, C. (2014). An Exploratory Study Using Science eTexts with Students with Autism Spectrum Disorder. *Focus on Autism and Other Developmental Disabilities*. doi:10.1177/1088357614559214

Knowles, M. (1975). *Self-directed learning. A guide for learners and teachers.* Prentice Hall.

Knox, C., & Anderson-Inman, L. (2005). *Project EXCEL: EXcellence through Computer Enhanced Learning.* Final Report to the U.S. Department of Education, Office of Special Education Programs (OSEP).

Kobasigawa, A. (1983). Children's retrieval skills for school learning. *The Alberta Journal of Educational Research*, *29*(4), 259–271.

Kobrin, J. L., Patterson, B. F., Shaw, E. J., Mattern, K. D., & Barbuti, S. M. (2008). Validity of the SAT for predicting first-year college grade point average. New York, NY: The College Board. Retrieved from https://professionals.collegeboard.com/profdownload/Validity_of_the_SAT_for_Predicting_First_Year_College_Grade_Point_Average.pdf

Kodak, T., Fisher, W. W., Clements, A., & Bouxsein, K. J. (2011). Effects of computer-assisted instruction on correct responding and procedural integrity during early intensive behavioral intervention. *Research in Autism Spectrum Disorders*, *5*(1), 640–647. doi:10.1016/j.rasd.2010.07.011

Koehler, M. J., & Mishra, P. (2005). What happens when teachers design educational technology? The development of technological pedagogical content knowledge. *Journal of Educational Computing Research*, *32*(2), 131–152. doi:10.2190/0EW7-01WB-BKHL-QDYV

Koehler, M. J., & Mishra, P. (2009). What is technological pedagogical content knowledge? *Contemporary Issues in Technology & Teacher Education*, *9*(1), 60–70.

Koles, P. G., Stolfi, A., Borges, N. J., Nelson, S., & Parmelee, D. X. (2010). The impact of team based learning on medical students' academic performance. *Academic Medicine*, *85*(11), 1739–1745. doi:10.1097/ACM.0b013e3181f52bed PMID:20881827

Kolowich, S. (2014, April 28). Writing instructor, skeptical of automated grading, pits machine vs. machine. *The Chronicle of Higher Education*. Retrieved from http://chronicle.com/article/Writing-Instructor-Skeptical/146211/

Krajcik, J., Marx, R., Blumenfeld, P., Soloway, E., & Fishman, B. (2000, April). *Inquiry based science supported by technology: Achievement among urban middle school students.* Paper presented at the 2000 Annual Meeting of the American Educational Research Association, New Orleans, LA.

Kranzow, J. (2013). Faculty leadership in online education: Structuring courses to impact student satisfaction and persistence. *MERLOT Journal of Online Learning and Teaching*, *9*(1), 131–139.

Kreijns, K., Kirschner, P. A., & Jochems, W. (2003). Identifying the pitfalls for social interaction in Computer-Supported Collaborative Learning environments: A review of the research. *Computers in Human Behavior*, *19*(3), 335–353. doi:10.1016/S0747-5632(02)00057-2

Kriz, S., & Hegarty, M. (2007). Top-down and bottom-up influences on learning from animations. *International Journal of Human-Computer Studies*, *65*(11), 911–930. doi:10.1016/j.ijhcs.2007.06.005

Kühl, T., Scheiter, K., Gerjets, P., & Edelmann, J. (2011). The influence of text modality on learning with static and dynamic visualizations. *Computers in Human Behavior*, *27*(1), 29–35. doi:10.1016/j.chb.2010.05.008

Ku, K. Y. (2009). Assessing students' critical thinking performance: Urging for measurements using multi-response format. *Thinking Skills and Creativity, 4*(1), 70–76. doi:10.1016/j.tsc.2009.02.001

Kumar, R. (2012). Effective practice with e-assessment: challenges and barriers. *RADIX International Journal of Research in Social Science, 1*(6). Retrieved from http://bit.ly/1qi9N0u

Kuncel, N. R., & Hezlett, S. A. (2010). Fact and fiction in cognitive ability testing for admissions and hiring decisions. *Current Directions in Psychological Science, 19*(6), 339–345. doi:10.1177/0963721410389459

Kurtz, G. (2014). Students' perceptions of using Facebook group and a course website as interactive and active learning spaces. *Proceedings of the 9th Chais Conference for the Study of Innovation and Learning Technologies: Learning In the Technological Era*. Raanana: The Open University of Israel.

LaDuca, A., Staples, W. I., Templeton, B., & Holzman, G. B. (1986). Item modeling procedures for constructing content-equivalent multiple-choice questions. *Medical Education, 20*(1), 53–56. doi:10.1111/j.1365-2923.1986.tb01042.x PMID:3951382

Lai, E. R. (2001). *Critical thinking: A literature review.* Pearson Research Report. Available at http://www.pearsonassessments.com/hai/images/tmrs/CriticalThinkingReviewFINAL.pdf

Lai, E. R., & Viering, M. (2012, April). *Assessing 21st century skills: Integrating research findings.* Paper presented at the Annual Meeting of the National Council on Measurement in Education, Vancouver, Canada.

Lai, H., & Gierl, M. J. (2013). Generating items under the assessment engineering framework. In M. J. Gierl & T. M. Haladyna (Eds.), *Automatic item generation: Theory and practice* (pp. 77–101). New York: Routledge.

Lance, C. E. (2008). Why assessment centers do not work the way they are supposed to. *Industrial and Organizational Psychology: Perspectives on Science and Practice, 1*(1), 84–97. doi:10.1111/j.1754-9434.2007.00017.x

Landauer, T. K., & Dumais, S. T. (1997). A solution to Plato's problem: The Latent Semantic Analysis theory of the acquisition, induction and representation of knowledge. *Psychological Review, 104*(2), 211–240. doi:10.1037/0033-295X.104.2.211

Landauer, T. K., Foltz, P. W., & Laham, D. (1998). Introduction to Latent Semantic Analysis. *Discourse Processes, 25*(2-3), 259–284. doi:10.1080/01638539809545028

Landauer, T. K., Kireyev, K., & Panaccione, C. (2011). Word Maturity: A New Metric for Word Knowledge. *Scientific Studies of Reading, 15*(1), 92–108. doi:10.1080/10888438.2011.536130

Landauer, T. K., Laham, D., & Foltz, P. W. (2001). *Automated essay scoring. IEEE Intelligent Systems.* September/October.

Landauer, T. K., Laham, D., & Foltz, P. W. (2003). Automated essay scoring and annotation of essays with the Intelligent Essay Assessor. In M. D. Shermis & J. C. Burstein (Eds.), *Automated Essay Scoring: A cross disciplinary perspective* (pp. 82–106). Mahwah, NJ: Lawrence Erlbaum Associates.

Landauer, T., Lochbaum, K., & Dooley, S. (2009). A New Formative Assessment Technology for Reading and Writing. *Theory into Practice, 48*(1), 44–52. doi:10.1080/00405840802577593

Landauer, T., McNamara, D. S., Dennis, S., & Kintsch, W. (2007). *Handbook of Latent Semantic Analysis.* Mahwah, NJ: Erlbaum.

Landis, J. R., & Koch, G. G. (1977). The measurement of observer agreement for categorical data. *Biometrics, 33*(1), 159–174. doi:10.2307/2529310 PMID:843571

Lane, S., & Stone, C. A. (2006). Performance Assessment. In R. L. Brennan (Ed.), Educational Measurement (4th ed.). Westport, CT: American Council on Education/Praeger.

Lane, S., & Stone, C. (2006). Performance assessment. In R. L. Brennan (Ed.), *Educational measurement* (4th ed.; pp. 387–431). Westport, CT: Praeger Publishers.

Langer, J. A., & Applebee, A. N. (1987). *How writing shapes thinking: A study of teaching and learning.* NCTE Research Report No.22. Urbana, IL: National Council of Teachers of English.

Langone, J., Clees, T. J., Rieber, L., & Matzko, M. (2003). The future of computer-based interactive technology for teaching individuals with moderate to severe disabilities: Issues relating to research and practice. *Journal of Special Education Technology, 18*, 5–16.

Langone, J., Shade, J., Clees, T. J., & Day, T. (1999). Effects of multimedia instruction on teaching functional discrimination skills to students with moderate/severe intellectual disabilities. *International Journal of Disability Development and Education, 46*(4), 493–513. doi:10.1080/103491299100470

Lankshear, C., & Knobel, M. (Eds.). (2008). *Digital literacies: Concepts, policies and practices.* New York: Peter Lang.

Larmer, J., & Mergendoller, J. R. (2010). Seven essentials for project-based learning. *Educational Leadership, 68*(1), 34–37.

Larson, K., & Czerwinski, M. (1998). Web page design: Implications of memory, structure and scent for information retrieval. In *CHI '98 Proceedings of the SIGCHI conference on Human factors in computing systems* (pp. 25–32). New York, NY: ACM.

Larson, E. L., Cohen, B., Gebbie, K., Clock, S., & Saiman, L. (2011). Interdisciplinary research training in a school of nursing. *Nursing Outlook, 59*(1), 29–36. doi:10.1016/j.outlook.2010.11.002 PMID:21256360

Lasater, M. W., & Brady, M. P. (1995). Effects of video self-modeling and feedback on task fluency: A home-based intervention. *Education & Treatment of Children, 18*, 389–407.

Lattanzio, S. M., Burdick, D. S., & Stenner, A. J. (2012). *The ensemble Rasch model.* Durham, NC: MetaMetrics Paper Series.

Lattuca, L. R., Voigt, L. J., & Fath, K. Q. (2004). Does interdisciplinarity promote learning? Theoretical support and researchable questions. *The Review of Higher Education, 28*(1), 23–48. doi:10.1353/rhe.2004.0028

Laurillard, D. (2009). The pedagogical challenges to collaborative technologies. *International Journal of Computer-Supported Collaborative Learning, 4*(1), 5–20. doi:10.1007/s11412-008-9056-2

LaVoie, N., Streeter, L., Lochbaum, K., Wroblewski, D., Boyce, L. A., Krupnick, C., & Psotka, J. (2010). Automating Expertise in Collaborative Learning Environments. *Journal of Asynchronous Learning Networks, 14*(4), 97–119.

Lawless, K. A., & Kulikowich, J. M. (1996). Understanding hypertext navigation through cluster analysis. *Journal of Educational Computing Research, 14*(4), 385–399. doi:10.2190/DVAP-DE23-3XMV-9MXH

Law, N., Pelgrum, W., & Plomp, T. (2008). *Pedagogy and ICT use in schools around the world: Findings from the IEA SITES 2006 study.* New York: Springer. doi:10.1007/978-1-4020-8928-2

Lawrence, R. J. (2004). Housing and health: From interdisciplinary principles to transdisciplinary. *Futures, 36*(4), 487–502. doi:10.1016/j.futures.2003.10.001

Lazonder, A. W., & Rouet, J.-F. (2008). Information problem solving instruction: Some cognitive and metacognitive issues. *Computers in Human Behavior, 24*(3), 753–765. doi:10.1016/j.chb.2007.01.025

Leacock, T. L., & Nesbit, J. C. (2007). A framework for evaluating the quality of multimedia learning resources. *Journal of Educational Technology & Society, 10*(2), 44–59.

Learn, N. C. (2014). *Performance assessments versus traditional assessments, University of North Carolina.* Retrieved from http://bit.ly/1od3v50

Learning, F. D. (2004). *E-portfolios: their use and benefits.* Retrieved from http://bit.ly/1xCGdHB

Leavy, P. (2011). *Essentials of transdisciplinary research: Using problem-centered methodologies* (Vol. 6). Walnut Creek: Left Coast Press.

Lee, A., Lau, J., Carbo, T., & Gendina, N. (2013). *Conceptual relationship of information literacy and media literacy in knowledge societies*. World Summit on the Information Society – WSIS. UNESCO. Retrieved July 20, 2014 from http://www.unesco.org/new/fileadmin/MULTIMEDIA/HQ/CI/CI/pdf/wsis/WSIS_10_Event/WSIS_-_Series_of_research_papers_-Conceptual_Relationship_between_Information_Literacy_and_Media_Literacy.pdf

Lee, H., Plass, J. L., & Homer, B. D. (2006). Optimizing cognitive load for learning from computer-based science simulations. *Journal of Educational Psychology, 98*(4), 902–913. doi:10.1037/0022-0663.98.4.902

Leelawong, K., & Biswas, G. (2008). Designing Learning by Teaching Systems: The Betty's Brain System. *International Journal of Artificial Intelligence in Education, 18*(3), 181–208.

Lee, Y., & Choi, J. (2011). A review of online course dropout research: Implications for practice and future research. *Educational Research and Technology Development, 59*(5), 593–618. doi:10.1007/s11423-010-9177-y

Lee, Y., Choi, J., & Kim, T. (2013). Discriminating factors between completers of and dropouts from online learning courses. *British Journal of Educational Technology, 44*(2), 328–337. doi:10.1111/j.1467-8535.2012.01306.x

Lehrer, R., Schauble, L., Strom, D., & Pligge, M. (2001). Similarity of form and substance: Modeling material kind. In S. M. Carver & D. Klahr (Eds.), *Cognition and instruction: Twenty-five years of progress* (pp. 39–74). Mahwah, NJ: Lawrence Earlbaum Associates.

Leighton. (2012, April). *Issues of cost, time, and validity: Psychometric perspectives on technologically-rich innovative assessments (TRIAs)*. Paper presented at the annual meeting of the American Educational Research Association, Vancouver, Canada.

Leighton, J. P., & Gierl, M. J. (2011). *The learning sciences in educational assessment: The role of cognitive models*. Cambridge, UK: Cambridge University Press. doi:10.1017/CBO9780511996276

Leighton, J. P., & Gierl, M. K. (2007). Defining and evaluating models of cognition used in educational measurement to make inferences about examinees' thinking processes. *Educational Measurement: Issues and Practice, 26*(2), 3–15. doi:10.1111/j.1745-3992.2007.00090.x

Leong, A. (2012). A comparative study of online self-regulated learning and Its effect on adult learners in the cross-strait regions. *International Journal of Continuing Education and Lifelong Learning, 4*(2), 81–100.

Letassy, N. A., Fugate, S. E., Medina, M. S., Stroup, J. S., & Britton, M. L. (2008). Using team-based learning in an endocrine module taught across two campuses. *American Journal of Pharmaceutical Education, 72*(5), 103. doi:10.5688/aj7205103 PMID:19214257

Leu, D. J., & Reinking, D. (2005). Developing Internet comprehension strategies among adolescent students at risk to become dropouts. Research grant project funded by the U.S. Department of Education, Institute of Education Sciences.

Leu, D. J. Jr. (2000). Developing new literacies: Using the Internet in content area instruction. In M. McLaughlin & M. Vogt (Eds.), *Creativity and innovation in content area teaching* (pp. 183–206). Norwood, MA: Christopher-Gordon.

Leu, D. J. Jr. (2002). The new literacies: Research on reading instruction with the Internet and other digital technologies. In J. Samuels & A. E. Farstrup (Eds.), *What research has to say about reading instruction* (pp. 310–336). Newark, DE: International Reading Association.

Leu, D. J., Kinzer, C. K., Corio, J., & Cammack, D. (2004). Toward a theory of new literacies emerging from the Internet and other information and communication technologies. In R. B. Ruddell & N. J. Unrau (Eds.), *Theoretical models and processes of reading* (5th ed., pp. 1570–1613).Newark, DE: International Reading Association.

Leu, D. J., McVerry, G., O'Byrne, C. K., & Zawilinski, L. (2011). The new literacies of online reading comprehension: Expanding the literacy and learning curriculum. *Journal of Adolescent & Adult Literacy, 55*(1), 5–14.

Leu, D. J., Zawilinski, L., Castek, J., Banerjee, M., Housand, B., Liu, Y., & O'Neil, M. (2007). What is new about the new literacies of online reading comprehension? In L. Rush, J. Eakle, & A. Berger (Eds.), *Secondary school literacy: What research reveals for classroom practices* (pp. 37–68). Urbana, IL: National Council of Teachers of English.

Levin, D., & Arafeh, S. (2002). *The digital disconnect the widening gap between internet-savvy students and their schools.* Washington, DC: Pew Internet & American Life Project.

Liaison Committee on Medical Education. (2011). *Accreditation standards.* Retrieved August 15, 2015, from www.lcme.org/standard.htm

Li, L., An, L., & Li, W. (2010). Nursing students self-directed learning. *Chinese General Nursing, 8*(5), 1205–1206.

Lim, T. (2010). The use of Facebook for online discussions among distance learners. *Turkish Online Journal of Distance Education, 11*(4). Retrieved December 20, 2012 from: http://dergipark.ulakbim.gov.tr/tojde/article/view/5000102541/5000095638

Lim, K. Y., Lee, H. W., & Grabowski, B. (2009). Does concept-mapping strategy work for everyone? The levels of generativity and learners' self-regulated learning skills. *British Journal of Educational Technology, 40*(4), 606–618. doi:10.1111/j.1467-8535.2008.00872.x

Linacre, J. M. (2012). Winsteps® (Version 3.75.0) [Computer software]. Beaverton, OR: Winsteps.com.

Lin, H., & Dwyer, F. (2006). The fingertip effects of computer-based assessment in education. *TechTrends, 50*(6), 27–31. http://bit.ly/1upkbWT doi:10.1007/s11528-006-7615-9

Lin, J., & Wilbur, W. J. (2009). Modeling actions of PubMed users with n-gram language models. *Information Retrieval, 12*(4), 487–503. doi:10.1007/s10791-008-9067-7 PMID:19684883

Linn, M. C., & Eylon, B. S. (2006). Science education: Integrating views of learning and instruction. In P. A. Alexander & P. H. Winne (Eds.), *Handbook of educational psychology* (pp. 511–544). New York, NY: Routledge.

Litman, D. J., Rose, C. P., Forbes-Riley, K., VanLehn, K., Bhembe, D., & Silliman, S. (2006). Spoken versus typed human and computer dialogue tutoring. *International Journal of Artificial Intelligence in Education, 16*, 145–170.

Little, T. D., Card, N. A., Slegers, D. W., & Ledford, E. C. (2007). *Representing contextual effects in multiple-group MACS models.* Academic Press.

Liu, L., & Hmelo-Silver, C. E. (2010). Conceptual representation embodied in hypermedia: An approach to promoting knowledge co-construction. In M. S. Khine & I. M. Saleh (Eds.), *New science of learning: Cognition, computers and collaboration in education* (pp. 341–356). New York, NY: Springer. doi:10.1007/978-1-4419-5716-0_17

Liu, O. L. (2011). Value-added assessment in higher education: A comparison of two methods. *Higher Education, 61*(4), 445–461. doi:10.1007/s10734-010-9340-8

Liu, O. L., Brew, C., Blackmore, J., Gerard, L., Madhok, J., & Linn, M. C. (2014). Automated scoring of constructed-response science items: Prospects and obstacles. *Educational Measurement: Issues and Practice, 33*(2), 19–28. doi:10.1111/emip.12028

Liu, O. L., Bridgeman, B., & Adler, R. M. (2012). Measuring learning outcomes in higher education: Motivation matters. *Educational Researcher, 41*(9), 352–362. doi:10.3102/0013189X12459679

Liu, P. L., Chen, C. J., & Chang, Y. J. (2010). Effects of a computer-assisted concept mapping learning strategy on EFL college students' English reading comprehension. *Computers & Education, 54*(2), 436–445. doi:10.1016/j.compedu.2009.08.027

Livingston Institute of Vocational Training. (2010). *TAE40110 Certificate IV training and assessment: Candidate manual assessment.* Retrieved from http://bit.ly/1qJHx7d

Li, Y., Bolt, D. M., & Fu, J. (2006). A comparison of alternative models for testlets. *Applied Psychological Measurement, 30*(1), 3–21. doi:10.1177/0146621605275414

Lochbaum, K. E., Rosenstein, M., Foltz, P. W., & Derr, M. A. (2013, April). *Detection of gaming in automated scoring of essays with the IEA.* Paper presented at the National Council on Measurement in Education Conference (NCME), San Francisco, CA.

Loehr, L. (1991). Between silence and voice: Communicating in cross-functional project teams. *IEEE Transactions on Professional Communication*, *34*(1), 51–56. doi:10.1109/47.68428

Logan, G. D. (1985). Executive control of thought and action. *Acta Psychologica*, *60*(2), 193–210. doi:10.1016/0001-6918(85)90055-1

Lohman, D. F. (2012, December 3). *An aptitude framework for college admissions testing.* Paper presented at the First International Conference on Assessment and Evaluation sponsored by National Center for Assessment in Higher Education, Riyadh, Saudi Arabia.

London, S. (2005). The Power of Deliberative Dialogue. In R. J. Kingston (Ed.), *Public Thought and Foreign Policy.* Dayton, OH: Kettering Foundation Press.

Long, B. T., & Riley, E. (2007). Financial aid: A broken bridge to college access? *Harvard Educational Review*, *77*(1), 39–63. doi:10.17763/haer.77.1.765h8777686r7357

Loughry, M. L., Ohland, M. W., & Moore, D. D. (2007). Development of a theory-based assessment of team member effectiveness. *Educational and Psychological Measurement*, *67*(3), 505–524. doi:10.1177/0013164406292085

Loveless, A., & Williamson, B. (2013). *Learning identities in a digital age.* London: Routledge.

Love, R. L. (1974). Continuing Education Garnished with Computer Assisted Instruction. *Journal of Allied Health*, *3*, 86–93.

Lowe, R., & Schnotz, W. (Eds.). (2008). *Learning with animation: Research implications for design.* New York, NY: Cambridge University Press.

Luecht, R. M. (2006a, September). *Assessment engineering: An emerging discipline.* Paper presented in the Centre for Research in Applied Measurement and Evaluation, Edmonton, Canada.

Luecht, R. M. (2006b, May). *Engineering the test: From principled item design to automated test assembly.* Paper presented at the annual meeting of the Society for Industrial and Organizational Psychology, Dallas, TX.

Luecht, R. M. (2005). Some useful cost-benefit criteria for evaluating computer-based test delivery models and systems. *Journal of Applied Testing Technology*, *7*(2), 1–31.

Luecht, R. M. (2013). An introduction to assessment engineering. In M. J. Gierl & T. M. Haladyna (Eds.), *Automatic item generation: Theory and practice* (pp. 59–76). New York: Routledge.

Lufi, D., & Cohen, A. (1987). A scale for measuring persistence in children. *Journal of Personality Assessment*, *51*(2), 178–185, =185. doi:10.1207/s15327752jpa5102_2 PMID:16372846

MacArthur, C. A. (2009). Evaluation and revision. In V. W. Berninger (Ed.), *Past, present, and future contributions of cognitive writing research to cognitive psychology* (pp. 461–483). New York, NY: Taylor and Francis.

MacCann, C., Duckworth, A. L., & Roberts, R. D. (2009). Empirical identification of the major facets of conscientiousness. *Learning and Individual Differences*, *19*(4), 451–458. doi:10.1016/j.lindif.2009.03.007

MacDonald, C. J., Archibald, D., Trumpower, D., Cragg, B., Casimiro, L., & Jelley, W. (2010). Quality standards for interprofessional healthcare education: Designing a toolkit of bilingual assessment instruments. *Journal of Research in Interprofessional Practice and Education*, *1*(3), 1–13.

MacLeod, W. B., Butler, D. L., & Syer, K. D. (1996, April). Beyond achievement data: Assessing changes in metacognition and strategic learning. New York: Annual Meeting of the American Educational Research Association. Retrieved from http://ecps.educ.ubc.ca/faculty/Butler/Confer/AERA

McPherson, M. S., & Schapiro, M. O. (Eds.). (2008). College success: What it means and how to make it happen. New York, NY: The College Board. Retrieved from https://net.educause.edu/ir/library/pdf/ff0911s.pdf

Madge, C., Meek, J., Wellens, J., & Hooley, T. (2009). Facebook, social integration and informal learning at University: "It is more of socializing and talking to friends about work than for actually doing work. *Learning, Media and Technology*, *34*(2), 141–155. doi:10.1080/17439880902923606

Madnani, N., Burstein, J., Sabatini, J., & O'Reilly, T. (2013). Automated Scoring of a Summary-Writing Task Designed to Measure Reading Comprehension. In *Proceedings of the North American Association for Computational Linguistics Eighth Workshop Using Innovative NLP for Building Educational Applications*.

Magis, D., Béland, S., Tuerlinckx, F., & De Boeck, P. (2010). A general framework and an R package for the detection of dichotomous differential item functioning. *Behavior Research Methods*, *42*(3), 847–862. doi:10.3758/BRM.42.3.847 PMID:20805607

Magis, D., Raîche, G., Béland, S., & Gérard, P. (2011). A generalized logistic regression procedure to detect differential item functioning among multiple groups. *International Journal of Testing*, *11*(4), 365–386. doi:10.1080/15305058.2011.602810

Mancil, G. R., Haydon, T., & Whitby, P. (2009). Differentiated effects of paper and computer-assisted social stories™ on inappropriate behavior in children with autism. *Focus on Autism and Other Developmental Disabilities*, *24*(4), 205–215. doi:10.1177/1088357609347324

Manning, C. D., & Schütze, H. (1999). *Foundations of statistical natural language processing*. Cambridge, MA: MIT Press.

Manovich, L. (2001). *The language of new media*. MIT Press.

Mansfield, H. C. (2001). Grade inflation: It's time to face the facts. *The Chronicle of Higher Education*, *47*(30). Retrieved from http://chronicle.com/article/Grade-Inflation-It-s-Time-to/9332

Mao, J., & Peck, K. (2013). Assessment strategies, self-regulated learning skills, and perceptions of assessment in online learning. *The Quarterly Review of Distance Education*, *14*(2), 75–95.

Marais, E., Argles, D., & von Solms, B. (2006). *Security issues specific to e-assessments*. Paper presented at the 8th Annual Conference on WWW Applications, Bloemfontein. Retrieved from http://eprints.soton.ac.uk/261433/

Marcovitz, D., & Janiszewski, N. (2015). Technology, models, and 21st-Century learning: How models, standards, and theories make learning powerful. In D. Slykhuis & G. Marks (Eds.), *Proceedings of Society for Information Technology & Teacher Education International Conference 2015* (pp. 1227-1232). Chesapeake, VA: Association for the Advancement of Computing in Education (AACE).

Marriott, P., & Teoh, L. (2012). *Computer-based assessment and feedback: Best practice guidelines. Higher Education Academy*. Retrieved from http://bit.ly/1jkdRZ2

Martinez-Garza, M. M., Clark, D., & Nelson, B. (2013). Advances in Assessment of Students' Intuitive Understanding of Physics through Gameplay Data.[IJGCMS]. *International Journal of Gaming and Computer-Mediated Simulations*, *5*(4), 1–16. doi:10.4018/ijgcms.2013100101

Martinez, R., Yacef, K., Kay, J., Al-Qaraghuli, A., & Kharrufa, A. (2011). Analysing frequent sequential patterns of collaborative learning activity around an interactive tabletop. In *Proceedings of the 4th International Conference on Educational Data Mining*, (pp. 111–120).

Marza, L., & Al-Hafizh, M. (2013). Teaching writing recount text to junior high school students by using Facebook peer-comment. *Journal of English Language Teaching*, *1*(2), 683–692. Retrieved from http://download.portalgaruda.org/article.php?article=100265&val=1486

Marzano, R. J. (2004). *Building background knowledge for academic achievement*. Alexandria, VA: ASCD.

Marzano, R. J. (2007). *The art and science of teaching: A comprehensive framework for effective instruction*. Alexandria, VA: Association for Supervision and Curriculum Development.

Marzano, R. J., & Pickering, D. J. (2005). *Building academic vocabulary: Teacher's manual*. Alexandria, VA: ASCD.

Marzano, R. J., & Sims, J. A. (2013). *Vocabulary for the Common Core*. Bloomington, IN: Marzano Research Laboratory.

Massachusetts Department of Elementary and Secondary Education. (2008). *School reform in the new millennium: Preparing all children for 21ˢᵗ century success.* Recommendations from the Massachusetts Board of Elementary and Secondary Education's Task Force on 21ˢᵗ Century Skills.

Masters, G. N. (1982). A Rasch model for partial credit scoring. *Psychometrika, 47*(2), 149–174. doi:10.1007/BF02296272

Matsumara, L. C., Patthey-Chavez, G. G., Valdés, R., & Garnier, G. (2002). Teacher feedback, writing assignment quality, and third-grade students' revision in lower- and higher-achieving urban schools. *The Elementary School Journal, 103*(1), 3–25. doi:10.1086/499713

Mayer, R. E. (1992). *Thinking, problem solving, cognition* (2nd ed.). New York: Freeman.

Mayer, R. E. (1994). Problem solving, teaching and testing for. In T. Husen & T. N. Postlethwaite (Eds.), *The international encyclopedia of education* (2nd ed.; Vol. 8, pp. 4728–4731). Oxford, UK: Pergamon Press.

Mayer, R. E. (2005). Cognitive theory of multimedia learning. In R. E. Mayer (Ed.), *The Cambridge handbook of multimedia learning* (pp. 31–48). New York, NY: Cambridge University Press. doi:10.1017/CBO9780511816819.004

Mayer, R. E. (2008). *Learning and instruction* (2nd ed.). Upper Saddle River, NJ: Pearson.

Mayer, R. E. (2009). *Multimedia learning* (2nd ed.). New York: Cambridge University Press. doi:10.1017/CBO9780511811678

Mayer, R. E. (2010). *Applying the science of learning.* Upper Saddle River, NJ: Pearson.

Mayer, R. E. (2011). Applying the science of learning to multimedia instruction. In J. Mestre & B. Ross (Eds.), *Cognition in education: Psychology of learning and motivation* (Vol. 55). San Diego, CA: Academic Press. doi:10.1016/B978-0-12-387691-1.00003-X

Mayer, R. E., & Wittrock, M. C. (1996). Problem-solving transfer. In D. C. Berliner & R. C. Calfee (Eds.), *Handbook of educational psychology* (pp. 47–62). New York: Macmillan Library Reference USA, Simon & Schuster Macmillan.

Mayer, R. E., & Wittrock, M. C. (2006). Problem solving. In P. A. Alexander & P. Winne (Eds.), *Handbook of educational psychology* (2nd ed.; pp. 287–304). Mahwah, NJ: Lawrence Erlbaum Associates.

Mazer, J. P., Murphy, R. E., & Simonds, C. J. (2007). I'll see you on "Facebook": The effects of computer-mediated teacher self-disclosure on student motivation, affective learning, and classroom climate. *Communication Education, 56*(1), 1–17. doi:10.1080/03634520601009710

McAllister, C., & Watkins, P. (2012). Increasing academic integrity in online classes by fostering the development of self-regulated learning skills. *The Clearing House: A Journal of Educational Strategies, Issues and Ideas, 85*(3), 96–101. doi:10.1080/00098655.2011.642420

McBeth, R., & Tsacoumis, S. (2014, October). *Going fully automated: A case study.* Presentation at the 38th International Congress on Assessment Center Methods, Alexandria, VA.

McCaffrey, D. F., Lockwood, J. R., Koretz, D. M., & Hamilton, L. S. (2003). *Evaluating value-added models for teacher accountability.* Santa Monica, CA: Rand Corporation. doi:10.1037/e658712010-001

McCallin, R. C. (2006). Test administration. In S. M. Downing & T. M. Haladyna (Eds.), *Handbook of test development* (pp. 625–652). Mahwah, NJ: Lawrence Erlbaum & Associates, Publishers.

McClelland, M. M., Acock, A. C., Piccinin, A., Rhea, S. A., & Stallings, M. C. (2013). Relations between preschool attention span-persistence and age 25 educational outcomes. *Early Childhood Research Quarterly, 28*(2), 314–324. doi:10.1016/j.ecresq.2012.07.008 PMID:23543916

McClure, J., Sonak, B., & Suen, H. (1999). Concept map assessment of classroom learning: Reliability, validity, and logistical practicality. *Journal of Research in Science Teaching, 36*(4), 475–492. doi:10.1002/(SICI)1098-2736(199904)36:4<475::AID-TEA5>3.0.CO;2-O

McCoy, K., & Hermansen, E. (2007). Video modeling for individuals with autism: A review of model types and effects. *Education & Treatment of Children, 30*(4), 183–213. doi:10.1353/etc.2007.0029

McCrae, R. R., & Costa, P. T. (1987). Validation of the five-factor model of personality across instruments and observers. *Journal of Personality and Social Psychology, 52*(1), 81–90. doi:10.1037/0022-3514.52.1.81 PMID:3820081

McCroskey, J. C. (2009). Self-report measurement. In J. Ayres, T. Hopf, J. C. McCroskey, J. Daly, D. M. A. Sonandre, & T. K. Wongprasert (Eds.), *Avoiding communication: Shyness, reticence, and communication apprehension* (3rd ed.; pp. 81–94). New York, NY: Hampton Press.

McDaniel, M. A., Hartman, N. S., Whetzel, D. L., & Grubb, W. L. III. (2007). Situational judgment tests, response instructions and validity: A meta-analysis. *Personnel Psychology, 60*(1), 63–91. doi:10.1111/j.1744-6570.2007.00065.x

McDaniel, M. A., Psotka, J., Legree, P. J., Yost, A. P., & Weekley, J. A. (2011). Toward an understanding of situational judgment item validity and group differences. *The Journal of Applied Psychology, 96*(2), 327–336. doi:10.1037/a0021983 PMID:21261409

McDonald, S., & Stevenson, R. J. (1998). Effects of text structure and prior knowledge of the learner on navigation in hypertext. *Human Factors, 40*(1), 19–27. doi:10.1518/001872098779480541

McEneaney, J. E. (2001). Graphic and numerical methods to assess navigation in hypertext. *International Journal of Human-Computer Studies, 55*(5), 761–786. doi:10.1006/ijhc.2001.0505

McGraw-Hill Education. (2014). *Smarter Balanced Pilot Automated Scoring Research Studies.* Olympia, WA: Smarter Balanced.

McGraw-Hunter, M., Faw, G. D., & Davis, P. K. (2006). The use of video self-modelling and feedback to teach cooking skills to individuals with traumatic brain injury: A pilot study. *Brain Injury: [BI], 20*(10), 1061–1068. doi:10.1080/02699050600912163 PMID:17060139

McKinney, E. H., & Davis, K. (2004). Effects of deliberate practice on crisis decision performance. *Human Factors, 45*(3), 436–444. doi:10.1518/hfes.45.3.436.27251 PMID:14702994

McLeod, S. H. (1992). *Writing Across the Curriculum: An Introduction. Writing Across the Curriculum: A Guide to Developing Program.* Newbury Park, CA: Sage Publications.

McLoughlin, C. (2011). Reinventing the 21st century educator: Social media to engage and support the professional learning of teachers. In G. Williams, P. Statham, N. Brown, & B. Cleland (Eds.), Changing Demands, Changing Directions. Proceedings ascilite Hobart 2011 (pp. 847–851). Retrieved from http://www.ascilite.org.au/conferences/hobart11/procs/McLoughlin-full.pdf

McLoughlin, C., & Lee, M. J. W. (2008). The Three P's of Pedagogy for the Networked Society: Personalization, Participation, and Productivity. *International Journal of Teaching and Learning in Higher Education, 20*(1), 10–27.

McLoughlin, C., & Lee, M. J. W. (2010). Personalised and self regulated learning in the Web 2.0 era: International exemplars of innovative pedagogy using social software. *Australasian Journal of Educational Technology, 26*(1), 28–43.

McLoughlin, C., Lee, M. J., & Chan, A. (2006, October). Fostering reflection and metacognition through student-generated podcasts. In *Proceedings of the Australian Computers in Education Conference (ACEC 2006).*

McNamara, D. S., O'Reilly, T., Rowe, M., Boonthum, C., & Levinstein, I. B. (2007). iSTART: A web-based tutor that teaches self-explanation and metacognitive reading strategies. In D.S. McNamara (Ed.), Reading comprehension strategies: Theories, interventions, and technologies (pp. 397–421). Mahwah, NJ: Erlbaum.

Measuring Digital Skills across the EU: EU wide indicators of Digital Competence. (May, 2014). *DG Connect - European Commission.* Retrieved Nov 1, 2014 http://ec.europa.eu/information_society/newsroom/cf/dae/document.cfm?action=display&doc_id=5406

Mechling, L. C. (2011). Review of twenty-first century portable electronic devices for persons with moderate intellectual disabilities and autism spectrum disorders. *Education and Training in Autism and Developmental Disabilities, 46,* 479–498.

Mechling, L. C., & Bishop, V. A. (2011). Assessment of computer-based preferences of students with profound multiple disabilities. *The Journal of Special Education, 45*(1), 15–27. doi:10.1177/0022466909348661

Mechling, L. C., Gast, D. L., & Fields, E. A. (2008). Evaluation of a portable DVD player and system of least prompts to self-prompt cooking task completion by young adults with moderate intellectual disabilities. *The Journal of Special Education, 42*(3), 179–190. doi:10.1177/0022466907313348

Mechling, L. C., Gast, D. L., & Gustafson, M. R. (2009). Use of video modeling to teach extinguishing of cooking related fires to individuals with moderate intellectual disabilities. *Education and Training in Developmental Disabilities, 44,* 67–79.

Mechling, L. C., Gast, D. L., & Langone, J. (2002). Computer-based video instruction to teach persons with moderate intellectual disabilities to read grocery aisle signs and locate items. *The Journal of Special Education, 35*(4), 224–240. doi:10.1177/002246690203500404

Mechling, L. C., Gast, D. L., & Seid, N. H. (2010). Evaluation of a personal digital assistant as a self-prompting device for increasing multi-step task completion by students with moderate intellectual disabilities. *Education and Training in Autism and Developmental Disabilities, 45,* 422–439.

Mechling, L. C., & Hunnicutt, J. R. (2011). Computer-based video self-modeling to teach receptive understanding of prepositions by students with intellectual disabilities. *Education and Training in Autism and Developmental Disabilities, 46,* 369–385.

Mechling, L. C., & Ortega-Hurndon, F. (2007). Computer-based video instruction to teach young adults with moderate intellectual disabilities to perform multiple step, job tasks in a generalized setting. *Education and Training in Mental Retardation and Developmental Disabilities, 42,* 24–37.

Mechling, L., & O'Brien, E. (2010). Computer-based video instruction to teach students with intellectual disabilities to use public bus transportation. *Education and Training in Autism and Developmental Disabilities, 45,* 230–241.

Media Smarts. (2010). *Digital literacy in Canada: From inclusion to transformation. A submission to the Digital Economy Strategy Consultation.* Retrieved July 20, 2014 from http://mediasmarts.ca/sites/default/files/pdfs/publication-report/full/digitalliteracypaper.pdf

Meishar-Tal, H., Kurtz, G., & Pieterse, E. (2012). Facebook groups as LMS: A case study. *The International Review of Research in Open and Distance Education, 13*(4), 1–16.

MER. (2006). *Program for Digital Kompetanse.* Oslo: Statens Forvaltningsteneste.

Mercer, N. (1995). *The guided construction of knowledge: Talk amongst teachers and learners.* Clevedon: Multilingual Matters.

Merchant, G. (2007). Mind the Gap(s): Discourses and discontinuity in digital literacies. *E-learning, 4*(3), 241–255. doi:10.2304/elea.2007.4.3.241

Meredith, W. (1993). Measurement invariance, factor analysis and factorial invariance. *Psychometrika, 58*(4), 525–543. doi:10.1007/BF02294825

Merrill, D. (1983). Component Display Theory. In C. Reigeluth (Ed.), *Instructional design theories and models* (pp. 279–333). Hillsdale, NJ: Erlbaum Associates.

Messick, S. (1990). Validity of test interpretation and use (ETS RR-90-11). Washington, DC: Educational Testing Service. Available at http://files.eric.ed.gov/fulltext/ED395031.pdf

Messick, S. (1994). The interplay of evidence and consequences in the validation of performance assessments. *Educational Researcher, 23*(2), 13–23. doi:10.3102/0013189X023002013

Meyer, D. E., & Kieras, D. E. (1997). A computational theory of executive cognitive processes and multiple-task performance: Part I. Basic mechanisms. *Psychological Review, 104*(1), 3–65. doi:10.1037/0033-295X.104.1.3 PMID:9009880

Meyers, C., & Jones, T. B. (1993). *Promoting active learning: Strategies for the college classroom.* San Francisco: Jossey-Bass.

Michaelsen, L. K. (1998). Three keys to using learning groups effectively. *Teaching Excellence: Toward the Best in the Academy, 9*(5), 1997-1998.

Michaelsen, L. K. (1983). Team learning in large classes. In C. Bouton & R. Y. Garth (Eds.), *Learning in Groups. New Directions for Teaching and Learning Series* (Vol. 14). San Francisco: Jossey-Bass.

Michaelsen, L. K. (1999). Myths and methods in successful small group work. *National Teaching & Learning Forum, 8*(6), 1–4.

Michaelsen, L. K., Bauman-Knight, A., & Fink, D. (2003). *Team-based learning: A transformative use of small groups in college teaching.* Sterling, VA: Stylus Publishing.

Michaelsen, L. K., & Black, R. H. (1994). Building learning teams: The key to harnessing the power of small groups in higher education. In S. Kadel & J. Keehner (Eds.), *Collaborative learning: A sourcebook for higher education* (Vol. 2). State College, PA: National Center for Teaching, Learning and Assessment.

Michaelsen, L. K., Black, R. H., & Fink, L. D. (1996). What every faculty developer needs to know about learning groups. In L. Richlin (Ed.), *To improve the academy: Resources for faculty, instructional and organizational development* (Vol. 15). Stillwater, Oklahoma: New Forums Press.

Michaelsen, L. K., Fink, L. D., & Knight, A. (1997). Designing effective group activities: Lessons for classroom teaching and faculty development. In D. DeZure (Ed.), *To improve the academy: Resources for faculty, instructional and organizational development* (Vol. 17). Stillwater, OK: New Forums Press.

Michaelsen, L. K., Knight, A. B., & Fink, L. D. (2002). *Team-based learning: A transformative use of small groups.* Westport, CT: Greenwood Publishing Group.

Michaelsen, L. K., Parmalee, D., McMahon, K., & Levine, R. (Eds.). (2008). *Team-based learning for health professions education: A guide to using small groups for improving learning.* Sterling, VA: Stylus Publishing.

Michaelsen, L. K., & Sweet, M. (2008). Teamwork works. *NEA Advocate, 25*(6), 1–8.

Michaelsen, L. K., Sweet, M., & Parmalee, D. (2009). Team-based learning: Small group learning's next big step. *New Directions for Teaching and Learning, 116*, 7–27.

Michaelsen, L. K., Watson, W. E., & Black, R. H. (1989). A realistic test of individual versus group consensus decision making. *The Journal of Applied Psychology, 74*(5), 834–839. doi:10.1037/0021-9010.74.5.834

Milbradt, A. (2008). Quality criteria in open source software for computer-based assessment. In F. Scheuermann & A. Guimarães Pereira (Eds.), Towards a research agenda on computer-based assessment: Challenges and needs for European educational measurement (pp. 53–57). Luxembourg: European Commission. Retrieved from http://bit.ly/1myPtUd

Miller, A. K. (2012, November 28). *Teacher as learning designer.* Huff Post Education [Web log post]. Retrieved from: http://www.huffingtonpost.com/andrew-k-miller/education-reform_b_2169265.html

Miller, G. A., Gallanter, E., & Probam, K. H. (1960). *Plans and the structure of behavior.* New York: Holt, Rinehart, & Winston. doi:10.1037/10039-000

Miller, T. R., & Spray, J. A. (1993). Logistic discriminant function analysis for DIF identification of polytomously scored items. *Journal of Educational Measurement, 30*(2), 107–122. doi:10.1111/j.1745-3984.1993.tb01069.x

Milligan, C., Littlejohn, A., & Margaryan, A. (2013). Patterns of engagement in connectivist MOOCs. *MERLOT Journal of Online Learning and Teaching, 9*(2), 149–159.

Millis, B. J., & Cottell, P. G. Jr. (1998). *Cooperative learning for higher education faculty.* Phoenix, AZ: Oryx Press.

Millis, K., Forsyth, C., Butler, H., Wallace, P., Graesser, A. C., & Halpern, D. (2011). Operation ARIES! A serious game for teaching scientific inquiry. In M. Ma, A. Oikonomou, & J. Lakhmi (Eds.), *Serious games and edutainment applications* (pp. 169–195). London: Springer-Verlag. doi:10.1007/978-1-4471-2161-9_10

Mills, R., Lawless, K., & Pratt, J. (2006). Training groups of end users: Examining group interactions in a computer-based learning environment. *Journal of Computer Information Systems*, 104–109.

Mims, P. J., Hudson, M. E., & Browder, D. M. (2012). Using read-alouds of grade-level biographies and systematic prompting to promote comprehension for students with moderate and severe developmental disabilities. *Focus on Autism and Other Developmental Disabilities, 27*(2), 67–80. doi:10.1177/1088357612446859

Min, S., & He, L. (2014). Applying unidimensional and multidimensional item response theory models in testlet-based reading assessment. *Language Testing, 31*(4), 453–477. doi:10.1177/0265532214527277

Mislevy, R. J., Almond, R. G., & Lukas, J. (2004). A brief introduction to evidence-centered design. CSE Technical Report. Los Angeles: The National Center for Research on Evaluation, Standards, Student Testing (CRESST), Center for Studies in Education, UCLA.

Mislevy, R. J., Almond, R. G., & Lukas, J. F. (2003). *A brief introduction to evidence-centered design* (ETS Research Report RR-03-16). Princeton, NJ: Educational Testing Service.

Mislevy, R. J., Chudowsky, N., Draney, K., Fried, R., Gaffney, T., & Haertel, G. (2003). *Design patterns for assessing science inquiry*. Menlo Park, CA: SRI International. Retrieved from http://padi.sri.com/downloads/TR1_Design_Patterns.pdf

Mislevy, R. J., Corrigan, S., Oranje, A., DiCerbo, K. E., John, M., Bauer, M. I., ... Hao, J. (2014). Psychometrics and Game-Based Assessment. New York, NY: Institute of Play.

Mislevy, R. J., & Haertel, G. D. (2006). Implications of evidence-centered design for educational testing. *Educational Measurement: Issues and Practice, 25*(4), 6–20. doi:10.1111/j.1745-3992.2006.00075.x

Mislevy, R. J., & Riconscente, M. M. (2006). Evidence-centered assessment design. In S. M. Downing & T. M. Haladyna (Eds.), *Handbook of test development* (pp. 131–154). Mahwah, NJ: Lawrence Erlbaum & Associates, Publishers.

Mislevy, R. J., Steinberg, L. S., & Almond, R. G. (2002). Design and analysis in task-based language assessment. *Language Testing, 19*(4), 477–496. doi:10.1191/0265532202lt241oa

Mislevy, R. J., Steinberg, L. S., & Almond, R. G. (2003). On the structure of educational assessments. *Measurement: Interdisciplinary Research and Perspectives, 1*(1), 3–67. doi:10.1207/S15366359MEA0101_02

Mislevy, R. J., Steinberg, L. S., Almond, R. G., & Lukas, J. F. (2006). Concepts, terminology, and basic models of evidence-centered design. In D. M. Williamson, R. J. Mislevy, & I. I. Bejar (Eds.), *Automated scoring of complex tasks in computer-based testing* (pp. 15–47). Hillsdale, NJ: Lawrence Erlbaum Associates.

Mitchell, R., & Nicholas, S. (2006). Knowledge creation in groups: The value of cognitive diversity, transactive memory and open-mindedness norms. *Electronic Journal of Knowledge Management, 4*(1), 64–74.

Mochizuki, N., & Ortega, L. (2008). Balancing communication and grammar in beginning-level foreign language classrooms: A study of guided planning and relativization. *Language Teaching Research, 12*(1), 11–37. doi:10.1177/1362168807084492

Moersch, C. (1995, November). Levels of Technology Implementation (LoTi): A framework for measuring classroom technology use. *Learning and Leading with Technology, 23*(3), 40–42.

Moersch, C. (2010, February). LoTi turns up the H.E.A.T. *Learning and Leading with Technology, 37*(5), 20–23.

Moore, A. (Ed.). (2006). *Schooling, society and the curriculum*. Abingdon: Routledge.

Moore, M., & Calvert, S. (2000). Brief report: Vocabulary acquisition for children with autism: Teacher or computer instruction. *Journal of Autism and Developmental Disorders, 30*(4), 359–362. doi:10.1023/A:1005535602064 PMID:11039862

Moore, P. (1995). Information problem-solving: A wider view of library skills. *Contemporary Educational Psychology, 20*(1), 1–31. doi:10.1006/ceps.1995.1001

Morales, L. S., Flowers, C., Gutierrez, P., Kleinman, M., & Teresi, J. A. (2006). Item and scale differential functioning of the Mini-Mental State Exam assessed using the differential item and test functioning (DFIT) framework. *Medical Care, 44*(11Suppl 3), S143–S151. doi:10.1097/01.mlr.0000245141.70946.29 PMID:17060821

Moreno, R., & Mayer, R. E. (2005). Role of guidance, reflection, and interactivity in an agent-based multimedia game. *Journal of Educational Psychology, 97*(1), 117–128. doi:10.1037/0022-0663.97.1.117

Moreno, R., & Mayer, R. E. (2007). Interactive multimodal learning environments. Special issue on interactive learning environments: Contemporary issues and trends. *Educational Psychology Review, 19*(3), 309–326. doi:10.1007/s10648-007-9047-2

Morgan, J., Shermis, M. D., Van Deventer, L., & Vander Ark, T. (n.d.). *Automated Student Assessment Prize: Phase 1 & Phase 2: A Case Study to Promote Focused Innovation in Student Writing Assessment.* Retrieved 9/1/14 from http://gettingsmart.com/wp-content/uploads/2013/02/ASAP-Case-Study-FINAL.pdf

Morgan, S. A., & Van Dam, A. (2008). Digital visual literacy. *Theory into Practice, 47* (2), 93–101. Retrieved July 20, 2014, from http://stevetrevino.pbworks.com/f/DVL.pdf

Morgan, R. L., & Horrocks, E. L. (2011). Correspondence between video-based preference assessment and subsequent community job performance. *Education and Training in Autism and Developmental Disabilities, 46,* 52–61.

Morocco, C. C. (2001). Teaching for understanding with students with disabilities: New directions for research on access to the general education curriculum. *Learning Disability Quarterly, 24*(1), 5–13. doi:10.2307/1511292

Moses, J. L. (1977). The assessment center method. In J. L. Moses & W. C. Byham (Eds.), *Applying the assessment center method* (pp. 3–11). New York: Pergamon Press. doi:10.1016/B978-0-08-019581-0.50006-2

Mossberger, K., Tolbert, J. C., & McNeal, S. R. (2011). *Digital Citizenship: The internet, society, and participation.* Scribd. Retrieved July 20, 2014, from http://www.scribd.com/doc/13853600/Digital-Citizenship-the-Internetsociety-and-Participation-By-Karen-Mossberger-Caroline-J-Tolbert-and-Ramona-S-McNeal

Moss, P. A., & Koziol, S. M. (1991). Investigating the validity of a locally developed critical thinking test. *Educational Measurement: Issues and Practice, 10*(3), 17–22. doi:10.1111/j.1745-3992.1991.tb00199.x

Mueller, J. (2014a). *Authentic assessment toolbox.* Retrieved from http://bit.ly/1hudUS8

Mueller, J. (2014b). *Portfolios.* Retrieved from http://bit.ly/1oUpEos

Mueller, A., & Fleming, T. (2001). Cooperative learning: Listening to how children work at school. *The Journal of Educational Research, 94*(5), 259–265. doi:10.1080/00220670109598761

Mueller, C. M., & Dweck, C. S. (1998). Praise for intelligence can undermine children's motivation and performance. *Journal of Personality and Social Psychology, 75*(1), 33–52. doi:10.1037/0022-3514.75.1.33 PMID:9686450

Mullenburg, L. Y., & Berge, Z. L. (2007). Student barriers to online learning: A factor analytic study. *Distance Education, 26*(1), 29–48. doi:10.1080/01587910500081269

Muller, J. (2006). Differentiation and progression in the curriculum. In M. Young & J. Gamble (Eds.), *Knowledge Curriculum and Qualifications for South African Further Education.* Cape Town: Human Sciences Research Council.

Muraki, E. (1992). A generalized partial credit model: Application of an EM algorithm. *Applied Psychological Measurement, 16*(2), 159–176. doi:10.1177/014662169201600206

Muraki, E. (1998). *RESGEN:Item response generator* [Program Manual]. Princeton, NJ: Educational Testing Service.

Murnane, R. J., & Willett, J. B. (2011). *Methods matter: Improving causal inference in educational and social science research.* New York, NY: Oxford University Press.

Muthén, B., & Lehman, J. (1985). Multiple group IRT modeling: Applications to item bias analysis. *Journal of Educational and Behavioral Statistics, 10*(2), 133–142. doi:10.3102/10769986010002133

Muthén, B., & Muthén, L. (2010). *Mplus (version 6.00)* [computer software]. Los Angeles, CA: Muthén & Muthén.

Muthén, B., & Muthén, L. (2010). *Mplus Version 6.1* [Software]. Los Angeles, CA: Author.

Nagy, W. (2010). Why vocabulary instruction needs to be long-term and comprehensive. In E. H. Hiebert & M. L. Kamil (Eds.), *Teaching and learning vocabulary: Bringing research to practice* (pp. 27–44). New York, NY: Routledge.

Nakamura, J., & Csikszentmihalyi, M. (2002). The concept of flow. In C. R. Snyder & S. J. Lopez (Eds.), *Handbook of positive psychology* (pp. 89–105). New York, NY: Oxford University Press.

National Academies of Science and Engineering and National Institute of Medicine (NASEIM). (2004). *Facilitating interdisciplinary research.* Washington, DC: National Academies Press. Retrieved on June 12, 2014 from: www.nap.edu/catalog/11153.html

National Academies of Science and Engineering and National Institute of Medicine (NASEIM). (2014). *Convergence: Facilitating transdisciplinary integration of life sciences, physical sciences, engineering and beyond.* Washington, DC: National Academies Press. Retrieved on February 11, 2014 from: http://www.nap.edu/catalog.php?record_id=18722

National Assessment Governing Board. (2013). *Technology and engineering literacy framework for the 2014 National Assessment of Educational Progress.* Washington, DC: National Assessment Governing Board.

National Association of Adult Literacy. (2004). *Average prose, document and quantitative literacy scores of adults: 1992 and 2003.* Retrieved from http://nces.ed.gov/naal/kf_demographics.asp

National Association of Colleges and Employers. (2013). *Job outlook: The candidate skills/qualities employers want.* Retrieved from https://www.naceweb.org/s10022013/job-outlook-skills-quality.aspx

National Center for Education Statistics. (2012). *The Nation's Report Card: Writing 2011 (NCES 2012–470).* Washington, DC: Institute of Education Sciences, U.S. Department of Education.

National Center on Educational Statistics. (2008). *Computer and internet use by children and adolescents in 2008.* Washington, DC: U.S. Department of Education.

National Commission on Writing for America's Families, Schools, and Colleges. (2004). *Writing: A ticket to work… or a ticket out. A survey of business leaders.* Iowa City, IA: The College Board.

National Commission on Writing for America's Families, Schools, and Colleges. (2005). *Writing: A powerful message from state government.* Iowa City, IA: The College Board.

National Education Association. (2008). *Technology in schools: The ongoing challenge of access, adequacy and equity.* Retrieved from http://www.nea.org/assets/docs/PB19_Technology08.pdf

National Education Association. (2014). *Partnership for 21st Century Skills.* Retrieved from: http://www.nea.org/home/34888.htm

National Education Association. (n.d.). *Preparing 21st century students for a global society: An educator's guide to the "Four Cs."* Retrieved from http://www.nea.org/assets/docs/A-Guide-to-Four-Cs.pdf

National Governors Association Center for Best Practices & Council for Chief State School Officers. (2010). *Common Core State Standards for English language arts & literacy in history/social, science, and technical subjects, Appendix A.* Washington, DC: Author. Retrieved from Common Core State Standards Initiative website: http://www.corestandards.org/the-standards

National Governors Association Center for Best Practices & Council of Chief State School Officers. (2010). *Common Core State Standards for English language arts and literacy in history/social studies, science, and technical subjects.* Washington, DC: Authors.

National Governors Association Center for Best Practices & Council of Chief State School Officers. (2010). Common Core State Standards for English language arts and literacy in history/social studies, science, and technical subjects. Washington, DC: National Governors Association Center for Best Practices (NGA Center).

National Governors Association Center for Best Practices and Council for Chief State School Officers. (2010a). *Common core state standards for mathematics.* Washington, DC: Author.

National Governors Association Center for Best Practices and Council for Chief State School Officers. (2010b). *Common core state standards for English language arts and literacy in history/social, science, and technical subjects*. Washington, DC: Author.

National Research Council (NRC). (2009). *A new biology for the 21st century*. Washington, DC: The National Academies Press.

National Research Council (NRC). (2012a). *A framework for k–12 science education: Practices, crosscutting concepts, and core ideas*. Washington, DC: National Academies Press.

National Research Council (NRC). (2012b). *Next generation science standards*. Available at: http://www.nextgenscience.org/next-generation-science-standards

National Research Council. (1999). *Being fluent with information technology*. Washington, DC: The National Academies Press. Retrieved July 20, 2014, from http://www.nap.edu/catalog.php?record_id=6482

National Research Council. (2011). *Assessing 21st Century Skills*. Washington, DC: National Academies Press.

National Research Council. (2012). *Education for life and work: Developing transferable knowledge and skills in the 21st century*. Washington, DC: The National Academies Press. Retrieved from http://www.nap.edu/catalog.php?record_id=13398

National Research Council. (2013). *New directions in assessing performance of individuals and groups: Workshop summary*. Washington, DC: National Academies Press.

National Research Council. (2013). *Next generation science standards: For states, by states*. Washington, DC: The National Academies Press.

National Telecommunications and Information Administration. (2014). *Digital literacy resources and collaboration*. U.S. Department of Commerce. Retrieved July 20, 2014, from http://www.digitalliteracy.gov/

Naumann, J., Richter, T., Christmann, U., & Groeben, N. (2008). Working memory capacity and reading skill moderate the effectiveness of strategy training in learning from hypertext. *Learning and Individual Differences*, *18*(2), 197–213. doi:10.1016/j.lindif.2007.08.007

Naumann, J., Richter, T., Flender, J., Christmann, U., & Groeben, N. (2007). Signaling in expository hypertexts compensates for deficits in reading skill. *Journal of Educational Psychology*, *99*(4), 791–807. doi:10.1037/0022-0663.99.4.791

Nekoueizadeh, M., & Bahrani, T. (2013). Considering challenges in educational system for implementation of e-assessment. *International Journal of Language Learning and Applied Linguistics World*, *4*(2), 89–99. Retrieved from http://www.ijllalw.org/finalversion429.pdf

Nelson, J., Perfetti, Liben, D., & Liben, M. (2011). *Measures of text difficulty: Testing the Predictive Value for Grade Levels and Student Performance*. Retrieved from http://www.ccsso.org/Documents/2012/Measures%20ofText%20Difficulty_final.2012.pdf

Nelson, L. (1999). Collaborative problem-solving. In C. M. Reigeluth (Ed.), *Instruction design theories and models* (pp. 241–267). Mahwah, NJ: Lawrence Erlbaum Associates.

Nersessian, N. J. (2008). *Creating scientific concepts*. Cambridge, MA: MIT Press.

Nesbit, J. C., Li, J., & Leacock, T. L. (2006). Web-based tools for collaborative evaluation of learning resources. *Systemics, Cybernetics, and Informatics*, *3*(5), 102–112.

Nesbit, J., & Adesope, O. (2006). Learning with concept and knowledge maps: A meta-analysis. *Review of Educational Research*, *76*(3), 413–448. doi:10.3102/00346543076003413

Ness, B. M., Sohlberg, M. M., & Albin, R. W. (2011). Evaluation of a second-tier classroom-based assignment completion strategy for middle school students in a resource context. *Remedial and Special Education*, *32*(5), 406–416. doi:10.1177/0741932510362493

Newell, A., Shaw, J. C., & Simon, H. A. (1960). Report on a general problem-solving program for a computer. In *Information processing:* Proceedings of the international conference on information processing (pp. 256–264). Paris: UNESCO House.

Newell, A., & Simon, H. A. (1972). *Human problem solving*. Englewood Cliffs, NJ: Prentice-Hall.

Newell, W. H. (2006). Interdisciplinary integration by undergraduates. *Issues in Integrative Studies, 24,* 89–111.

Newmann, F. M., Marks, H. M., & Gamoran, A. (1996, August). Authentic pedagogy and student performance. *American Journal of Education, 104*(4), 280–312. doi:10.1086/444136

Nickson, D., Warhurst, C., Commander, J., Hurrell, S. A., & Cullen, A. M. (2012). Soft skills and employability: Evidence from UK retail. *Economic and Industrial Democracy, 33*(1), 65–84. doi:10.1177/0143831X11427589

Nicolescu, B. (2010). Methodology of transdisciplinarity – levels of reality, logic of the included middle and complexity. *Transdisciplinary Journal of Engineering & Science, 1*(1), 19–38.

Nielsen, J. (1999). *Designing Web Usability: The practice of simplicity.* Indianapolis: New Riders.

Nilson, L. (2013). *Creating self-regulated learners: Strategies to strengthen students' self-awareness and learning skills.* Sterling, VA: Stylus Publishing.

Noeth, R. J., & Kobrin, J. L. (2007). *Writing changes in the nation's K-12 education system. Research Notes-34.* Iowa City, IA: The College Board.

Norris, D., Oppler, S., Kuang, D., Day, R., & Adams, K. (2006). *The College Board Sat® writing validation study: An assessment of predictive and incremental validity.* New York, NY: The College Board.

Norris, S. P. (1989). Can we test validly for critical thinking? *Educational Researcher, 18*(9), 21–26. doi:10.3102/0013189X018009021

North, B. (2011). Putting the common European framework of reference to good use. *Language Teaching, 47*(2), 228–249. doi:10.1017/S0261444811000206

Northern Advisory Council for Further Education. (2014). *E-portfolio systems.* Retrieved from http://bit.ly/1hLQ75s

NOU 2003: 16. (2003). *I første rekke — Forsterket kvalitet i en grunnopplæring for alle.* Retrieved from https://www.regjeringen.no/nb/dokumenter/nou-2003-16/id147077/?docId=NOU200320030016000DDDEPIS&ch=1&q=NOU%202003:%2016&redir=true&ref=search&term=NOU%202003:%2016

Novak, J. D., & Cañas, A. J. (2008). *The theory underlying concept maps and how to construct them.* (Technical report). IHMC CmapTools, Florida Institute for Human and Machine Cognition. Retrieved from http://cmap.ihmc.us/Publications/ResearchPapers/TheoryUnderlyingConceptMaps.pdf

Novak, J. D. (1998). *Learning, creating, and using knowledge: concept maps as facilitative tools in schools and corporations.* Mahwah, NJ: Lawrence Erlbaum and Associates.

Novak, J. D., & Gowin, D. B. (1984). *Learning how to learn.* Cambridge, NY: Cambridge University Press. doi:10.1017/CBO9781139173469

O'Neil, H. F. Jr, Chen, H. H., Wainess, R., & Shen, C. Y. (2008). Assessing problem solving in simulation games. In E. L. Baker, J. Dickieson, W. Wulfeck, & H. F. O'Neil (Eds.), *Assessment of problem solving using simulations* (pp. 157–176). Mahwah, NJ: Lawrence Erlbaum Associates.

O'Neil, H. F. Jr, & Chuang, S. H. (2008). Measuring collaborative problem solving in low-stakes tests. In E. L. Baker, J. Dickieson, W. Wulfeck, & H. F. O'Neil (Eds.), *Assessment of problem solving using simulations* (pp. 177–199). Mahwah, NJ: Lawrence Erlbaum Associates.

O'Neil, H. F. Jr, Chuang, S. H., & Baker, E. L. (2010). Computer-based feedback for computer-based collaborative problem solving. In D. Ifenthaler, P. Pirnay-Dummer, & N. M. Seel (Eds.), *Computer-based Diagnostics and Systematic Analysis of Knowledge* (pp. 261–279). New York: Springer-Verlag. doi:10.1007/978-1-4419-5662-0_14

O'Neil, H. F. Jr, Chung, G. K. W. K., & Brown, R. (1997). Use of networked simulations as a context to measure team competencies. In H. F. O'Neil Jr., (Ed.), *Workforce readiness: Competencies and assessment* (pp. 411–452). Mahwah, NJ: Lawrence Erlbaum Associates.

O'Rourke, E., Haimovitz, K., Ballweber, C., Dweck, C., & Popović, Z. (2014). Brain points: a growth mindset incentive structure boosts persistence in an educational game. In *Proceedings of the 32nd annual ACM conference on human factors in computing systems* (pp. 3339–3348). New York, NY: ACM. doi:10.1145/2556288.2557157

Oakes, M., Gaizauskas, R., Fowkes, H., Jonsson, W. A. V., & Beaulieu, M. (2001). A method based on chi-square test for document classification. *Proceedings of the 24th Annual International ACM SIGIR Conference on Research and Development in Information Retrieval* (pp. 440–441). New York, NY: ACM. doi:10.1145/383952.384080

Odom, S. L., Collet-Klingenberg, L., Rogers, S. J., & Hatton, D. D. (2010). Evidence-based practices in interventions for children and youth with Autism Spectrum Disorders. *Preventing School Failure, 54*(4), 275–282. doi:10.1080/10459881003785506

OECD - Organization for Economic Co-operation and Development. (2002). *The definition and selection of key competencies.* Retrieved July 20, 2014, from http://www.oecd.org/dataoecd/47/61/35070367.pdf

OECD - Organization for Economic Co-operation and Development. (2005). *Definition and selection of key competencies: Executive summary.* Paris: OECD. Retrieved July 20, 2014, from http://www.oecd.org/dataoecd/47/61/35070367.pdf

OECD - Organization for Economic Co-operation and Development. (2013). *PISA 2015- Draft reading literacy framework.* Paris: OECD. Retrieved July 20, 2014, from http://www.oecd.org/pisa/pisaproducts/Draft%20PISA%202015%20Reading%20Framework%20.pdf

OECD (2011). *PISA 2009 Results: Students on Line: Digital Technologies and Performance (Volume VI).* Paris, France: OECD. 10.1787/9789264112995-en

OECD. (2009). *PIAAC Problem Solving in Technology-Rich Environments: a conceptual framework* (OECD Education Working Paper No. 36.). Paris, France: OECD. 10.1787/220262483674

OECD. (2010). *The Definition and Selection of Key Competencies* (DeSeCo). Retrieved from www.oecd.org/pisa/35070367.pdf

OECD. (2010a). *PISA 2012 Field Trial Problem Solving Framework.* Retrieved from http://www.oecd.org/pisa/pisaproducts/46962005.pdf

OECD. (2010b). *PISA 2015 Draft Reading Literacy Framework.* Retrieved from http://www.oecd.org/pisa/pisaproducts/Draft PISA 2015 Reading Framework.pdf

OECD. (2013). *OECD Skills Outlook 2013. First results from the survey of adult skills.* Retrieved from http://skills.oecd.org/skillsoutlook.html

OECD. (2013). *PISA 2015 Collaborative Problem Solving Framework.* OECD Publishing. Retrieved Dec, 18, 2014, from http://www.oecd.org/pisa/pisaproducts/Draft%20PISA%202015%20Collaborative%20Problem%20Solving%20Framework%20.pdf

OECD. (2013). *PISA 2015 Collaborative Problem Solving framework.* OECD Publishing. Retrieved from: http://www.oecd.org/pisa/pisaproducts/pisa2015draft-frameworks.htm

OECD. (2013a). *OECD skills outlook 2013: First results from the survey of adult skills.* OECD Publishing.

OECD. (2013a). *OECD Skills Outlook 2013: First Results from the Survey of Adult Skills.* Paris, France: OECD Publishing. doi:10.1787/9789264204256-en

OECD. (2013b). *PISA 2015 Collaborative Problem Solving framework.* OECD Publishing.

OECD. (2013b). *Technical Report of the Survey of Adult Skills (PIAAC).* Paris, France: OECD. Retrieved February 17, 2015 from www.oecd.org/site/piaac/_Technical%20Report_17OCT13.pdf

Office of Qualifications and Examinations Regulations. (2010). *E-assessment.* Retrieved from http://bit.ly/1nTsRo9

Olinghouse, N. G., Wilson, J., O'Shea, K., Jagaiah, T., & Troia, G. A. (2014, February). *A framework to evaluate the writing assessment episode.* Paper presented at the meeting of the International Society for the Advancement of Writing Research, Paris, France.

Olinghouse, N. G., Santangelo, T., & Wilson, J. (2012). Examining the validity of single-occasion, single-genre, holistically-scored writing assessments. In E. Van Steendam, M. Tillema, G. Rijlaarsdam, & H. Van den Bergh (Eds.), *Measuring writing. Recent insights into theory, methodology and practices* (pp. 55–82). Leiden, The Netherlands: Brill. doi:10.1163/9789004248489_005

Oliver, R. L. (1993). Cognitive, affective, and attribute bases of the satisfaction response. *The Journal of Consumer Research, 20*(3), 418–430. doi:10.1086/209358

Olson, T. A., Olson, J., Olson, M., Capen, S., Shih, J., Adkins, A., . . . Thomas, A. (2015). Exploring 1:1 tablet technology settings: A case study of the first year of implementation in middle school mathematics classrooms. In D. Slykhuis & G. Marks (Eds.), *Proceedings of Society for Information Technology & Teacher Education International Conference 2015* (pp. 2736-2742). Chesapeake, VA: Association for the Advancement of Computing in Education (AACE).

Organisation for Economic Co-operation and Development. (2009). *PIAAC problem solving in technology-rich environments: A conceptual framework (OECD Education Working Paper No. 36)*. Paris, France: Author.

Organisation for Economic Co-operation and Development. (2010). *PIAAC technical standards and guidelines*. OECD Publishing. Retrieved May 16, 2014, from http://www.oecd.org/site/piaac/PIAAC-NPM(2010_12)PIAAC_Technical_Standards_and_Guidelines.pdf

Organisation for Economic Co-operation and Development. (2012). *Literacy, numeracy and problem solving in technology-rich environments: Framework for the OECD Survey of Adult Skills*. OECD Publishing. 10.1787/9789264128859-en

Organisation for Economic Co-operation and Development. (2013). *Technical Report of the Survey of Adult Skills (PIAAC)*. OECD Publishing. Retrieved August 13, 2014, from http://www.oecd.org/site/piaac/_Technical%20Report_17OCT13.pdf

Organisation of Economic Cooperation and Development. (2013). *Time for the U.S. to Reskill What the Survey of Adult Skills Says, OECD Skills Studies*. Paris, France: OECD Publishing.

Organization for Economic Development (OECD). (2012a). *Better skills, better jobs, better lives: A strategic approach to skills policies*. OECD Publishing.

Organization for Economic Development (OECD). (2012b). *Education at a glance 2012: OECD indicators*. OECD Publishing.

Organization for Economic Development (OECD). (2013). *PISA 2015 collaborative problem solving framework*. OECD Publishing.

Oshima, T., Raju, N. S., & Flowers, C. P. (1997). Development and Demonstration of Multidimensional IRT-Based Internal Measures of Differential Functioning of Items and Tests. *Journal of Educational Measurement, 34*(3), 253–272. doi:10.1111/j.1745-3984.1997.tb00518.x

Ostrow, K. S., Schultz, S. E., & Arroyo, I. (n.d.). *Promoting Growth Mindset Within Intelligent Tutoring Systems*. Retrieved from http://ceur-ws.org/Vol-1183/ncfpal_paper03.pdf

Oswald, F. L., Putka, D. J., & Ock, J. (2014). Weight a minute, what you see in a weighted composite is probably not what you get. In C. E. Lance & R. J. Vandenberg (Eds.), *More statistical and methodological myths and urban legends*. New York: Taylor & Francis.

Otter, M., & Johnson, H. (2000). Lost in hyperspace: Metrics and mental models. *Interacting with Computers, 13*(1), 1–40. doi:10.1016/S0953-5438(00)00030-8

Padovani, S., & Lansdale, M. (2003). Balancing search and retrieval in hypertext: Context-specific trade-offs in navigational tool use. *International Journal of Human-Computer Studies, 58*(1), 125–149. doi:10.1016/S1071-5819(02)00128-3

Paechter, M., Maier, B., & Macher, D. (2010). Students' expectations of, and experiences in e-learning: Their relation to learning achievements and course satisfaction. *Computers & Education, 54*(1), 222–229. doi:10.1016/j.compedu.2009.08.005

Page, E. B., Poggio, J. P., & Keith, T. Z. (1997, March). *Computer analysis of student essays: Finding trait differences in student profile*. Paper presented at the annual meeting of the American Educational Research Association, Chicago, IL.

Page, E. B. (1966). The imminence of grading essays by computer. *Phi Delta Kappan, 48*, 238–243.

Page, E. B. (1966). The imminence of…grading essays by computer. *Phi Delta Kappan, 47*(2), 238–243.

Page, E. B. (1994). Computer grading of student prose, using modern concepts and software. *Journal of Experimental Education, 62*(2), 127–142. doi:10.1080/00220973.1994.9943835

Palincsar, A. S. (1998). Social constructivist perspectives on teaching and learning. In J. T. Spence, J. M. Darley, & D. J. Foss (Eds.), *Annual Review of Psychology, 49* (pp. 345–375). Palo Alto, CA: Annual Reviews. doi:10.1146/annurev.psych.49.1.345

Pallant, J. (2007). *SPSS survival manual: A step by step guide to data analysis using SPSS for Windows* (3rd ed.). Maidenhead, UK: Open University Press.

Pan, B., Hembrooke, H., Joachims, T., Lorigo, L., Gay, G., & Granka, L. (2007). In Google we trust: Users' decisions on rank, position, and relevance. *Journal of Computer-Mediated Communication, 12*, article 3. Retrieved from http://jcmc.indiana.edu/vol12/issue3/pan.html

Pantoya, M., Hughes, P., & Hughes, J. (2013). A case study in active learning: Teaching undergraduate research in an engineering classroom setting. *English Education, 8*(2), 54–64. doi:10.11120/ened.2013.00014

Papaleontiou-Louca, E. (2003). The concept and instruction of metacognition. *Teacher Development, 7*(1), 2–9.

Paris, S., & Paris, A. (2001). Classroom applications of research on self-regulated learning. *Educational Psychologist, 36*(2), 89–101. doi:10.1207/S15326985EP3602_4

Parker, G. M. (2003). *Cross-functional teams.* San Francisco: Jossey-Bass.

Parra, S. (2012). Component display theory design in a foreign language unit. *Journal of Applied Learning Technology, 2*(3), 23–32.

Parshall, C. G., & Harmes, J. C. (2009). Improving the quality of innovative item types: Four tasks for design and development. *Journal of Applied Testing Technology, 10*(1), 1–20.

Parshall, C. G., Harmes, J. C., Davey, T., & Pashley, P. J. (2010). Innovative item types for computerized testing. In W. J. van der Linden & C. A. W. Glas (Eds.), *Elements of adaptive testing* (pp. 215–230). New York: Springer.

Parshall, C. G., Spray, J. A., Kalohn, J. C., & Davey, T. (2002). *Practical considerations in computer-based testing.* New York: Springer-Verlag. doi:10.1007/978-1-4613-0083-0

Parslow, P., Lundqvist, K. Ø., Williams, S., Ashton, R., & Evans, M. (2008). Facebook & BlackBoard: Comparative view of learning environments. In *SSE Systems Engineering Conference 2008.* The University of Reading. Retrieved January 20, 2012 from: http://centaur.reading.ac.uk/1105

Parsons, S., Leonard, A., & Mitchell, P. (2006). Virtual environments for social skills training: Comments from two adolescents with autistic spectrum disorder. *Computers & Education, 47*(2), 186–206. doi:10.1016/j.compedu.2004.10.003

Partnership for 21st Century Skills. (2009). *P21 framework definitions.* Retrieved from http://www.p21.org/storage/documents/P21_Framework_Definitions.pdf

Partnership for 21st Century Skills. (2009). *P21 framework definitions.* Washington, DC: Author.

Partnership for 21st Century Skills. (2011). *Framework for 21st century learning.* Retrieved from http://www.p21.org/storage/documents/1.__p21_framework_2-pager.pdf

Partnership for 21st Century Skills. (2014a). *ICT literacy.* Retrieved July 20, 2014, from http://www.p21.org/about-us/p21-framework/350-ict-literacy

Partnership for 21st Century Skills. (2014a). *Our History.* Retrieved from: http://www.p21.org/about-us/our-history

Partnership for 21st Century Skills. (2014b). *Framework for 21st Century Learning.* Retrieved from: http://www.p21.org/

Partnership for 21st Century Skills. (2014b). *Framework for 21st century learning.* Retrieved July 20, 2014 from http://www.p21.org/our-work/p21-framework

Partnership for 21st Century Skills. (2014c). *Framework for State Action on Global Education.* Retrieved from: http://www.p21.org/

Partnership for 21st Century Skills. (n.d.). *Framework for the 21st century.* Retrieved from http://www.p21.org/storage/documents/p21-stateimp_standards.pdf

Partnership for Assessment of Readiness for College and Career (PARCC). (2014). *Grade 8 Sample Items* [Sample examination questions]. Retrieved from http://parcconline.org/sites/parcc/files/Grade%208%20Sample%20Item%20Set-Revised%204-25-14.pdf

Pascarella, E. T., & Terenzini, P. T. (2005). *How college affects students: A third decade of research*. San Francisco, CA: Jossey-Bass.

Pashler, H., Bain, P. M., Bottge, B. A., Graesser, A., Koedinger, K., McDaniel, M., & Metcalfe, J. (2007). *Organizing instruction and study to improve student learning*. Retrieved from http://ies.ed.gov/ncee/wwc/pdf/practice_guides/20072004.pdf

Paul, R. W. (1992). Critical thinking: What, why, and how? *New Directions for Community Colleges*, *77*(77), 3–24. doi:10.1002/cc.36819927703

Pauschenwein, J., & Sfriri, A. (2010). Adult learners' motivation for the use of micro-blogging during online training courses. *International Journal of Emerging Technologies in Learning*, *5*(1), 22–25.

Pearl, J. (1988). *Probabilistic Reasoning in Intelligent Systems: Networks of Plausble Inference*. Burlington, MA: Morgan Kaufmann Pub.

Pearson, P. D., & Duke, N. K. (2002). Comprehension instruction the primary grades. In C. C. Block & M. Pressley (Eds.), *Comprehension instruction: Research-based best practices* (pp. 247–258). New York, NY: The Guilford Press.

Pellegrino, J. W. (2002, February). Understanding how students learn and inferring what they know: Implications for the design of curriculum, instruction and assessment. In M. J. Smith (Ed.), *NSF k–12 mathematics and science curriculum and implementation centers conference proceedings* (pp. 76–92). Washington, DC: National Science Foundation and American Geological Institute.

Pellegrino, J. W., & Hilton, M. L. (Eds.). (2012). *Education for life and work: Developing Transferable knowledge and skills in the 21ˢᵗ century*. Committee on defining deeper learning and 21ˢᵗ century skills. Board on Testing and Assessment and Board on Science Education, Division of Behavioral and Social Sciences and Education. National Research Council. Washington, DC: The National Academies Press. Retrieved July 20, 2014, from http://www.leg.state.vt.us/WorkGroups/EdOp/Education%20for%20Life%20and%20Work-%20National%20Academy%20of%20Sciences.pdf

Pellegrino, J. W., Chudowsky, N., & Glaser, R. (Eds.). (2001). *Knowing what students know: The science and design of educational assessment*. Washington, DC: National Academy Press.

Pellegrino, J. W., & Hilton, M. L. (Eds.). (2013). *Education for life and work: Developing transferable knowledge and skills in the 21st century*. National Academies Press.

Pellegrino, J., & Hilton, M. (2012). *Education for Life and Work: Developing Transferable Knowledge and Skills in the 21st Century*. Washington, DC: The National Academies Press.

Pempek, T. A., Yermolayeva, Y. A., & Calvert, S. (2009). College students' social networking experiences on Facebook. *Journal of Applied Developmental Psychology*, *30*(3), 227–238. doi:10.1016/j.appdev.2008.12.010

Peña-López, I. (2009). Towards a comprehensive definition of digital skills. *ICTlogy*. Retrieved July 20, 2014, from http://ictlogy.net/20090317-towards-a-comprehensive-definition-of-digital-skills/

Penfield, R. D. (2001). Assessing differential item functioning among multiple groups: A comparison of three Mantel-Haenszel procedures. *Applied Measurement in Education*, *14*(3), 235–259. doi:10.1207/S15324818AME1403_3

Pennington, R. C. (2010). Computer-assisted instruction for teaching academic skills to students with autism spectrum disorders: A review of literature. *Focus on Autism and Other Developmental Disabilities*, *25*(4), 239–248. doi:10.1177/1088357610378291

Pennington, R. C., Stenhoff, D. M., Gibson, J., & Ballou, K. (2012). Using simultaneous prompting to teach computer-based story writing to a student with autism. *Education & Treatment of Children*, *35*(3), 389–406. doi:10.1353/etc.2012.0022

Penuel, W. R., Fishman, B. J., Cheng Hauganm, B., & Sabelli, N. (2011). Organizing research and development at the intersection of learning, implementation, and design. *Educational Researcher*, *40*(7), 331–337. doi:10.3102/0013189X11421826

Perera, D., Kay, J., Koprinska, I., Yacef, K., & Zaiane, O. R. (2009). Clustering and sequential pattern mining of online collaborative learning data. *IEEE Transactions on Knowledge and Data Engineering, 21*(6), 759–772. doi:10.1109/TKDE.2008.138

Perfetti, C. A., Rouet, J.-F., & Britt, M. A. (1999). Towards a theory of documents representation. In H. van Oostendorp & S. R. Goldman (Eds.), *The Construction of Mental Representations During Reading* (pp. 99–122). Mahwah, NJ: Lawrence Erlbaum Associates.

Perkins, D. N., & Grotzer, T. A. (2000). *Models and moves: Focusing on dimensions of causal complexity to achieve deeper scientific understanding.* Retrieved from http://files.eric.ed.gov/fulltext/ED441698.pdf

Perkins, D. (1993). Person plus: A distributed view of thinking and learning. In G. Salomon (Ed.), *Distributed cognitions* (pp. 88–110). New York: Cambridge University Press.

Perkins, D. N. (2014). *Future wise: educating our children for a changing world.* San Francisco, CA: Jossey-Bass.

Perkins, D. N., & Salomon, G. (1989). Are cognitive skills context bound? *Educational Researcher, 18*(1), 16–25. doi:10.3102/0013189X018001016

Perry, S. J., Hunter, E. M., Witt, L. A., & Harris, K. J. (2010). P = ƒ (conscientiousness × ability) : Examining the facets of conscientiousness. *Human Performance, 23*(4), 343–360. doi:10.1080/08959285.2010.501045

Persky, A. M., & Pollack, G. M. (2011). A modified team-based learning physiology course. *American Journal of Pharmaceutical Education, 75*(10), 204. doi:10.5688/ajpe7510204 PMID:22345723

Persky, H. R., Daane, M. C., & Jin, Y. (2002). *The Nation's Report Card: Writing 2002. (NCES 2003-529).* Washington, DC: National Center for Education Statistics, Institute of Education Sciences. U. S. Department for Education.

Pew Research Center. (2009). Teen and young adult Internet use. *Millennials: A portrait of generation next.* Retrieved from www.pewresearch.org/millennials/teen-internet-use-graphic/

Phelps, R. P. (2006). Characteristics of an effective student testing system. *Educational Horizons, 85*(1), 19–29. Retrieved from http://bit.ly/1tK9MCR

Phillips, S. E. (1993). *Legal implications of high-stakes assessment: What states should know.* Retrieved from http://files.eric.ed.gov/fulltext/ED370985.pdf

Phillips, V., & Wong, C. (2010). Tying together the Common Core of standards, instruction, and assessments. *Kappan, 91*(3), 37–42. doi:10.1177/003172171009100511

Phillips, V., & Wong, C. (2012). Teaching to the Common Core by design, not accident. *Kappan, 93*(7), 31–37. doi:10.1177/003172171209300708

Pintrich, P. (1995). Understanding self-regulated learning. In P. Pintrich (Ed.), *Understanding self-regulated learning* (pp. 3–12). San Francisco, CA: Jossey-Bass.

Pintrich, P. R. (2000). The role of goal orientation in self-regulated learning. In M. Boekaerts, P. R. Pintrich, & M. Zeidner (Eds.), *Handbook of self-regulation* (pp. 451–502). San Diego, CA: Academic Press.

Pintrich, P. R. (2002). The role of metacognitive knowledge in learning, teaching, and assessing. *Theory into Practice, 41*(4), 219–225. doi:10.1207/s15430421tip4104_3

Pintrich, P. R., & Schunk, D. H. (2002). *Motivation in education: Theory, research, and applications* (2nd ed.). Upper Saddle River, NJ: Merrill/Prentice Hall.

Pirolli, P., & Card, S. K. (1999). Information Foraging. *Psychological Review, 106*(4), 643–675. doi:10.1037/0033-295X.106.4.643

Pirolli, P., & Fu, W.-T. F. (2003). SNIF-ACT: a model of information foraging on the world wide web. In *Proceedings of the Ninth International Conference on User Modeling.* Berlin: Springer Verlag. doi:10.1007/3-540-44963-9_8

Plant, E. A., Ericsson, K. A., Hill, L., & Asberg, K. (2005). Why study time does not predict grade point average across college students: Implications of deliberate practice for academic performance. *Contemporary Educational Psychology, 30*(1), 96–116. doi:10.1016/j.cedpsych.2004.06.001

Plass, J. L., Homer, B. D., & Hayward, E. O. (2009). Design factors for educationally effective animations and simulations. *Journal of Computing in Higher Education, 21*(1), 31–61. doi:10.1007/s12528-009-9011-x

Pogge, E. (2013). A team-based learning course on nutrition and lifestyle modification. *American Journal of Pharmaceutical Education, 77*(5), 103. doi:10.5688/ajpe775103 PMID:23788814

Pohl, C. (2010). From transdisciplinarity to transdisciplinary research. The ATLAS Transdisciplinary- Trans-national-Transcultural Bi-Annual Meeting. Georgetown, TX: The ATLAS Publications.

Poitras, E., Lajoie, S., & Hong, Y. (2012). The design of technology-rich learning environments as metacognitive tools in history education. *Instructional Science: An International Journal of the Learning Sciences., 40*(6), 1033–1061. doi:10.1007/s11251-011-9194-1

Polly, D., Margerison, A., & Piel, J. (2014). Kindergarten teachers' orientations to teacher-centered and student-centered pedagogies and their influence on their students' understanding of addition. *Journal of Research in Childhood Education, 28*(1), 1–17. doi:10.1080/02568543.2013.822949

Polychronis, S. C., McDonnell, J., Johnson, J. W., Riesen, T., & Jameson, M. (2004). A comparison of two trial distribution schedules in embedded instruction. *Focus on Autism and Other Developmental Disabilities, 19*(3), 140–151. doi:10.1177/10883576040190030201

Pope, L. (2013). *Papers, Please.* [Computer software]. Retrieved from http://papersplea.se/

Porter, A., McMaken, J., Hwang, J., & Yang, R. (2011). Common core standards: The new US intended curriculum. *Educational Researcher, 40*(3), 103–116. doi:10.3102/0013189X11405038

Powers, D. E., Burstein, J. C., Chodorow, M., Fowles, M. E., & Kukich, K. (2002). Stumping *e-rater*: Challenging the validity of automated essay scoring. *Computers in Human Behavior, 18*(2), 103–134. doi:10.1016/S0747-5632(01)00052-8

Prensky, M. (2001). Digital natives, digital immigrants. *On the Horizon, 9* (5). Retrieved July 20, 2014, from http://www.marcprensky.com/writing/Prensky%20-%20Digital%20Natives,%20Digital%20Immigrants%20-%20Part1.pdf

Prensky, M. (2001, October). Digital natives, digital immigrants. *On the Horizon, 9*(5), 1–6. doi:10.1108/10748120110424816

Presley, R., & Martin, R. P. (1994). Toward a structure of preschool temperament: Factor structure of the Temperament Assessment Battery for Children. *Journal of Personality, 62*(3), 415–448. doi:10.1111/j.1467-6494.1994.tb00304.x PMID:7965566

Pressley, M., Allington, R. L., Wharton-McDonald, R., Collins Block, C., & Mandel Morrow, L. (2001). Learning to read: Lessons from exemplary first-grade classrooms. New York, NY: The Guilford Press.

Pressley, M., Forrest-Pressley, D., Elliott-Faust, D. L., & Miller, G. E. (1985). Children's use of cognitive strategies, how to teach strategies, and what to do if they can't be taught. In M. Pressley & C. J. Brainerd (Eds.), *Cognitive learning and memory in children* (pp. 1–47). New York: Springer-Verlag. doi:10.1007/978-1-4613-9544-7_1

Pressley, M., & Ghatala, E. S. (1990). Self-regulated learning: Monitoring learning from text. *Educational Psychologist, 25*(1), 19–33. doi:10.1207/s15326985ep2501_3

Prineas, M., & Cini, M. (2011). *Assessing learning in online education: The role of technology in improving student outcomes.* National Institute for Learning Outcomes Assessment. Retrieved from http://bit.ly/1vsSyOF

Pringle, R. M., Dawson, K., & Ritzhaupt, A. D. (2015). Integrating science and technology: Using technological pedagogical content knowledge as a framework to study the practices of science teachers. *Journal of Science Education and Technology, 24*(5), 648–662. doi:10.1007/s10956-015-9553-9

Professional Development Program, Rockefeller College, University at Albany, State University of New York. (n.d.). *Tobacco Recovery Resource Exchange.* Retrieved August 15, 2015, from http://www.tobaccorecovery.org/

Programs, U. S., & the Bill and Melinda Gates Foundation. (2012). *Innovations in education.* Retrieved from http://www.gatesfoundation.org/

Promnitz-Hayashi, L. (2011). A learning success story using Facebook. *Studies in Self-Access Learning Journal, 2*(4), 309-316. Retrieved October 20, 2013 from: http://sisaljournal.org/archives/dec11/promnitz-hayashi

Prose, F. (2006). *Reading like a writer*. New York, NY: Harper Collins.

Protopsaltis, A. (2008). Reading strategies in hypertexts and factors influencing hyperlink selection. *Journal of Educational Multimedia and Hypermedia, 17*, 191–213.

Puentedura, R. R. (2006). *Transformation, technology, and education*. Retrieved from http://hippasus.com/resources/tte/

Punie, Y. (2007). Learning Spaces: An ICT-enabled model of future learning in the knowledge-based society. *European Journal of Education, 42*(2), 185–199. doi:10.1111/j.1465-3435.2007.00302.x

Purdue University. (2015). *The evolution of technology in the classroom*. Retrieved from http://online.purdue.edu/ldt/learning-design-technology/resources/evolution-technology-classroom

Putka, D. J. (2014, March). *Transitioning from traditional ACs to automated simulations: Insights for practice and science*. Invited keynote presentation at the 34th Annual Assessment Centre Study Group (ACSG) Conference, Stellenbosch, South Africa.

Putka, D. J., Le, H., McCloy, R. A., & Diaz, T. (2008). Ill-structured measurement designs in organizational research: Implications for estimating interrater reliability. *The Journal of Applied Psychology, 93*(5), 959–981. doi:10.1037/0021-9010.93.5.959 PMID:18808219

Puzziferro, M. (2008). Online technologies self-efficacy and self-regulated learning as predictors of final grade and satisfaction in college level online courses. *American Journal of Distance Education, 22*(2), 72–89. doi:10.1080/08923640802039024

Qualifications and Curriculum Authority. (2007). *Regulatory principles for e-assessment*. Retrieved from http://bit.ly/1dGAkNy

Quality Assurance Agency. (2005). *Reflections on assessment: Volume II*. Retrieved from http://bit.ly/1AZPTMP

Quellmalz & Silberglitt (2011, February) *Integrating simulation-based science assessments into balanced state science assessment systems: Findings and implications*. Workshop from the 2011 Meeting of the Technical Issues in Large-Scale Assessment, State Collaboratives on Assessment and Student Standards, Atlanta, GA.

Quellmalz, E. S., & Moody, M. (2004). *Models for multilevel state science assessment systems*. Paper commissioned by the National Research Council Committee on Test Design for K-12 Science Achievement.

Quellmalz, E., Timms, M., & Buckley, B. (2005). *Using science simulations to support powerful formative assessments of complex science learning*. Paper from the annual meeting of the American Educational Research Association, San Diego, CA.

Quellmalz, S., & Timms, B. (2012). Multilevel assessments of science systems: Final report. Redwood City, CA: WestEd.

Quellmalz, Timms, Buckley, Loveland, & Silberglitt. (2012). *Calipers II: Using simulations to assess complex science learning: Final report*. Redwood City, CA: WestEd.

Quellmalz, E. S., Davenport, J. L., Timms, M. J., DeBoer, G., Jordan, K., Huang, K., & Buckley, B. (2013). Next-generation environments for assessing and promoting complex science learning. *Journal of Educational Psychology, 105*(4), 1100–1114. doi:10.1037/a0032220

Quellmalz, E. S., & Haertel, G. D. (2008). Assessing new literacies in science and mathematics. In J. Coiro, M. Knobel, C. Lankshear, & D. J. Leu (Eds.), *Handbook of research on new literacies* (pp. 941–972). Mahwah, NJ: Lawrence Erlbaum Associates.

Quellmalz, E. S., & Pellegrino, J. W. (2009). Technology and testing. *Science, 323*(5910), 75–79. doi:10.1126/science.1168046 PMID:19119222

Quellmalz, E. S., Timms, M. J., Buckley, B. C., Davenport, J., Loveland, M., & Silberglitt, M. D. (2012). 21st century dynamic assessment. In M. Mayrath, J. Clarke-Midura, & D. H. Robinson (Eds.), *Technology-based assessments for 21st century skills: Theoretical and practical implications from modern research*. Charlotte, NC: Information Age.

Quellmalz, E. S., Timms, M. J., & Schneider, S. A. (2009). *Assessment of student learning in science simulations and games*. Washington, DC: National Research Council.

Quellmalz, E. S., Timms, M. J., Silberglitt, M. D., & Buckley, B. C. (2012). Science assessments for all: Integrating science simulations into balanced state science assessment systems. *Journal of Research in Science Teaching, 49*(3), 363–393. doi:10.1002/tea.21005

Quellmalz, E., & Kozma, R. (2003). Designing assessments of learning with technology. *Assessment in Education: Principles, Policy & Practice, 10*(3), 389–407. doi:10.1080/0969594032000148208

Quintana, C., Zhang, M., & Krajcik, J. (2005). A framework for supporting metacognitive aspects of online inquiry through software-based scaffolding. *Educational Psychologist, 40*(4), 235–244. doi:10.1207/s15326985ep4004_5

R. (2014). *R: A Language and Environment for Statistical Computing*. Vienna, Austria: R Foundation for Statistical Computing. Retrieved from http://www.R-project.org

Rabiner, L. (1989). A tutorial on hidden Markov models and selected applications in speech recognition. *Proceedings of the IEEE, 77*(2), 257–286. doi:10.1109/5.18626

Raju, N. S. (1988). The area between two item characteristic curves. *Psychometrika, 53*(4), 495–502. doi:10.1007/BF02294403

Raju, N. S. (1990). Determining the significance of estimated signed and unsigned areas between two item response functions. *Applied Psychological Measurement, 14*(2), 197–207. doi:10.1177/014662169001400208

Raju, N. S., Laffitte, L. J., & Byrne, B. M. (2002). Measurement equivalence: A comparison of methods based on confirmatory factor analysis and item response theory. *The Journal of Applied Psychology, 87*(3), 517–529. doi:10.1037/0021-9010.87.3.517 PMID:12090609

Ramdoss, S., Lang, R., Mulloy, A., Franco, J., O'Reilly, M., Didden, R., & Lancioni, G. (2011). Use of computer-based interventions to teach communication skills to children with autism spectrum disorders: A systematic review. *Journal of Behavioral Education, 20*(1), 55–76. doi:10.1007/s10864-010-9112-7

Rap, S., & Blonder, R. (2014). Learning science in social networks: Chemical interactions on Facebook. *Proceedings of the 9th Chais Conference for the Study of Innovation and Learning Technologies: Learning In the Technological Era*. Raanana: The Open University of Israel.

Rasch, G. (1960). *Probabilistic models for some intelligence and attainment tests*. Copenhagen: Danish Institute for Educational Research.

Raudenbush, S. W., & Bryk, A. S. (2002). *Hierarchical linear models: Applications and data analysis methods* (2nd ed.). Thousand Oaks, CA: Sage.

Raudenbush, S. W., Bryk, A. S., & Congdon, R. T. (1988). *HLM: Hierarchical linear modeling*. Chicago: Scientific Software International, Inc.

Ray, L. C. (1963). Programming for natural language. In P. L. Garvin (Ed.), *Natural Language and the Computer*. New York: McGraw-Hill.

Raymond, M., & Neustel, S. (2006). Determining the content of credentialing examinations. In S. M. Downing & T. M. Haladyna (Eds.), *Handbook of test development* (pp. 181–224). Mahwah, NJ: Lawrence Erlbaum & Associates, Publishers.

Reckase, M. D. (2009). *Multidimensional item response theory*. Springer. doi:10.1007/978-0-387-89976-3

Reese, G. M., & Snell, M. E. (1991). Putting on and removing coats and jackets: The acquisition and maintenance of skills by children with severe multiple disabilities. *Education and Training in Mental Retardation, 26*, 398–410.

Rehder, B., Schreiner, M., Laham, D., Wolfe, M., Landauer, T., & Kintsch, W. (1998). Using latent semantic analysis to assess knowledge: Some technical considerations. *Discourse Processes, 25*(2-3), 337–354. doi:10.1080/01638539809545031

Reid, J. (2011). "We don't Twitter, we Facebook": An alternative pedagogical space that enables critical practices in relation to writing. *English Teaching, 10*(1), 58–80. Retrieved from http://education.waikato.ac.nz/research/files/etpc/files/2011v10n1art4.pdf

Reid, J. R., & Anderson, P. R. (2012). Critical thinking in the business classroom. *Journal of Education for Business, 87*(1), 52–59. doi:10.1080/08832323.2011.557103

Reiss, M. J., & White, J. (2013). *An aims-based curriculum: The significance of human flourishing for schools.* London: IOE Press.

Ren, Y. (2014). Information and communication technologies in education. In J. M. Spector, M. D. Merrill, J. Elen, & M. J. Bishop (Eds.), *Handbook of research on educational communications and technology* (pp. vii–xi). New York, NY: Springer.

Resnick, M. (2009, May 27). Kindergarten is the model for lifelong learning: Let's keep teaching creativity throughout school and adulthood. *Edutopia.* Retrieved from http://www.edutopia.org/kindergarten-creativity-collaboration-lifelong-learning

Ribble, M. (2014). Nine themes of digital citizenship. In: *Digital Citizenship: Using Technology Appropriately.* Retrieved July 20, 2014, from http://www.digitalcitizenship.net/Nine_Elements.html

Richard, D. (2012, November). *The Richard review of apprenticeships.* School for Startups. Retrieved from http://bit.ly/QFz6gX

Richter, S., & Test, D. (2011). Effects of multimedia social stories on knowledge of adult outcomes and opportunities among transition-aged youth with significant cognitive disabilities. *Education and Training In Autism and Developmental Disabilities, 46,* 410–424.

Rideout, V. J., Foehr, U. G., & Roberts, D. F. (2010). Generation M2: Media in the lives of 8-18 year-olds. Menlo Park, CA: Kaiser Family Foundation.

Ridgway, J., McCusker, S., & Pead, D. (2004). Literature review of e-assessment (Futurelab Series Report 10). Bristol: Futurelab. Available at www.futurelab.org.uk/research/lit_reviews.htm

Rieber, L. P., Tzeng, S. C., & Tribble, K. (2004). Discovery learning, representation, and explanation within a computer-based simulation: Finding the right mix. *Learning and Instruction, 14*(3), 307–323. doi:10.1016/j.learninstruc.2004.06.008

Rijmen, F. (2010). Formal relations and an empirical comparison among the bi-factor, the testlet, and a second-order multidimensional IRT model. *Journal of Educational Measurement, 47*(3), 361–372. doi:10.1111/j.1745-3984.2010.00118.x

Rimor, R., & Arie, P. (2013). An English play is hosted by Facebook: Students' achievements and attitudes towards studying an English play using the Facebook environment. In L. Gómez Chova, A. López Martinez & I. Cadel Torres (Eds). *Proceedings of ICERI2013 Conference. 6th International Conference of Education, Research and Innovation.* International Association of Technology, Education and Development (IATED).

Rimor, R., & Kozminsky, E. (2004). An Analysis of the Reflections of Students in Online Courses. *EARLI-SIG on Metacognition.* Amsterdam, the Netherlands.

Rimor, R., Reingold, R., & Kalay, A. (2006). *The relationship between students' metacognition and instructor's scaffolding in online academic courses.* Paper presented at SIG16 Metacognition: 2nd Biennial Conference, Cambridge, UK.

Rimor, R., Reingold, R., & Heiman, T. (2008). Instructor's scaffolding in support of students' metacognition through an online course: Why to promote and how to investigate. In J. Zumbach, N. Schwartz, T. Seufert, & L. Kester (Eds.), *Beyond knowledge: The legacy of competence- meaningful computer-based learning environments* (pp. 43–53). Springer. doi:10.1007/978-1-4020-8827-8_6

Rimor, R., & Rosen, Y. (2010). Collaborative knowledge construction in online Learning Environment: Why to promote and how to investigate. In S. Mukerji & P. Tripathi (Eds.), *Cases on Technological Adaptability and Transnational Learning: Issues and Challenges.* IGI-Global. doi:10.4018/978-1-61520-749-7.ch010

Rimor, R., Rosen, Y., & Naser, K. (2010). Are two better than one? A study of social interaction patterns in an online collaborative database environment. IJELLO special series of Chais Conference 2010 best papers. *Interdisciplinary Journal of E-Learning and Learning Objects, 6,* 355–365.

Rimor, R., Rosen, Y., & Naser, K. (2010). Complexity of social interactions in collaborative learning: The case of online database environment. *Interdisciplinary Journal of E-Learning and Learning Objects, 6,* 355–365.

Ritchhart, R., Church, M., & Morrison, K. (2011). *Making thinking visible: How to promote engagement, understanding, and independence for all learners.* San Francisco, CA: Jossey-Bass.

Ritchhart, R., Turner, T., & Hadar, L. (2009). Uncovering students' thinking about thinking using concept maps. *Metacognition and Learning, 4*(2), 145–159. doi:10.1007/s11409-009-9040-x

Rittel, H. W. J., & Weber, M. M. (1973). Dilemmas in a general theory of planning. *Policy Sciences, 4*(2), 155–169. doi:10.1007/BF01405730

Rivera, L. A. (2011). Ivies, extracurriculars, and exclusion: Elite employers' use of educational credentials. *Research in Social Stratification and Mobility, 29*(1), 71–90. doi:10.1016/j.rssm.2010.12.001

Rivera, L. A. (2012). Hiring as cultural matching: The case of elite professional service firms. *American Sociological Review, 77*(6), 999–1022. doi:10.1177/0003122412463213

Rizzo, A. A., Buckwalter, J. G., Bowerly, T., Van Der Zaag, C., Humphrey, L., Neumann, U., & Sisemore, D. et al. (2000). The virtual classroom: A virtual reality environment for the assessment and rehabilitation of attention deficits. *Cyberpsychology & Behavior, 3*(3), 483–499. doi:10.1089/10949310050078940

Roberts, J. B., Crittenden, L. A., & Crittenden, J. C. (2011). Students with disabilities and online learning: A cross-institutional study of perceived satisfaction with accessibility compliance and services. *The Internet and Higher Education, 14*(4), 242–250. doi:10.1016/j.iheduc.2011.05.004

Rogers, E. M. (1962). *Diffusion of innovations.* New York: Free Press of Glencoe.

Rogoff, B. (2003). *The cultural nature of human development.* Oxford University Press.

Rogoff, B. (1990). *Apprenticeship in thinking: Cognitive development in social context.* New York, NY: Oxford University Press.

Rokach, L. (2010). Ensemble-based classifiers. *Artificial Intelligence Review, 33*(1–2), 1–39. doi:10.1007/s10462-009-9124-7

Romero, C., & Ventura, S. (2010). Educational data mining: A review of the state of the art. Systems, Man, and Cybernetics, Part C: Applications and Reviews. *IEEE Transactions on Systems, Man, and Cybernetics, 40*(6), 601–618. doi:10.1109/TSMCC.2010.2053532

Romrell, D., Kidder, L. C., & Wood, E. (2014). The SAMR model as a framework for evaluating mLearning. *Journal of Asynchronous Learning Networks, 18*(2).

Root-Bernstein, R., & Root-Bernstein, M. (2011, March 16). *Turning STEM into STREAM: writing as an essential component of science education.* Retrieved on July 12, 2014 from: http://www.nwp.org/cs/public/print/resource/3522

Roschelle, J. (1992). Learning by collaborating: Convergent conceptual change. *Journal of the Learning Sciences, 2*(3), 235–276. doi:10.1207/s15327809jls0203_1

Roschelle, J. (1996). Learning by collaborating: Convergent conceptual change. In K. Tobin (Ed.), *The practice of constructivism in science education* (pp. 91–119). Hillsdale, NJ: Erlbaum.

Roschelle, J. M., Pea, R. D., Hoadley, C. M., Gordin, D. N., & Means, B. M. (2000). Changing how and what children learn in school with computer-based technologies. *The Future of Children: Children and Computer Technology, 10*(2), 76–101. doi:10.2307/1602690 PMID:11255710

Roschelle, J., & Teasley, S. D. (1995). The construction of shared knowledge in collaborative problem-solving. In C. E. O'Malley (Ed.), *Computer-supported collaborative learning* (pp. 69–97). Berlin: Springer-Verlag. doi:10.1007/978-3-642-85098-1_5

Roscoe, R. D., & McNamara, D. (2013). Writing Pal: Feasibility of an intelligent writing strategy tutor in the high school classroom. *Journal of Educational Psychology, 105*(4), 1010–1025. doi:10.1037/a0032340

Rose, D. H., & Gravel, J. W. (2010). Universal design for learning. In E. Baker, P. Peterson, & B. McGaw (Eds.), *International Encyclopedia of Education* (3rd ed.). Oxford, UK: Elsevier. doi:10.1016/B978-0-08-044894-7.00719-3

Rose, D., & Meyer, A. (2000). Universal Design for Learning. *Journal of Special Education Technology, 15*(1), 67–70.

Rosen, Y. (2014a). Assessing collaborative problem solving through computer agent technologies. In M. Khosrow-Pour (Ed.), Encyclopedia of information science and technology (3rd ed.; pp. 94-102). Hershey, PA: Information Science Reference, IGI Global.

Rosen, Y., & Rimor, R. (2009). Using a collaborative database to enhance students' knowledge construction. *Interdisciplinary Journal of E-Learning and Learning Objects, 5,* 187-195.

Rosen, Y., & Rimor, R. (2013). Teaching and assessing problem solving in online collaborative environment. In R. Hartshorne, T. Heafner, & T. Petty (Eds.), Teacher education programs and online learning tools: Innovations in teacher preparation (pp. 82-97). Hershey, PA: Information Science Reference, IGI Global. doi:10.4018/978-1-4666-1906-7.ch005

Rosen, Y., & Tager, M. (2013). *Computer-based assessment of collaborative problem solving skills: Human-to-agent versus human-to-human approach.* Retrieved March, 18, 2014, from http://researchnetwork.pearson.com/wp-content/uploads/CollaborativeProblemSolvingResearchReport.pdf

Rosen, Y., & Tager, M. (2013). *Computer-based performance assessment of creativity skills: A pilot study.* Pearson. Retrieved from http://bit.ly/1yMHkU2

Rosen, Y., & Tager, M. (2013). *Evidence-centered concept map as a thinking tool in critical thinking computer-based assessment.* Pearson Research Report. Available at: http://researchnetwork.pearson.com/wp-content/uploads/CriticalThinkingAssessmentResearchReport.pdf [Accessed 9 June 2014]

Rosen, Y., & Wolf, I. (2014). *Learning and Assessing Collaborative Problem Solving Skills.* Paper presented at the International Society for Technology in Education (ISTE) conference, Atlanta, GA.

Rosenfield, P. L. (1992). The potential of transdisciplinary research for sustaining linkages between the health and social sciences. *Social Science & Medicine, 35*(11), 1343–1357. doi:10.1016/0277-9536(92)90038-R PMID:1462174

Rosen, Y. (2009). Effects of animation learning environment on knowledge transfer and learning motivation. *Journal of Educational Computing Research, 40*(4), 439–455. doi:10.2190/EC.40.4.d

Rosen, Y. (2014). Thinking tools in computer-based assessment: Technology enhancements in assessing for learning. *Educational Technology, 54*(1), 30–34.

Rosen, Y. (2014b). Comparability of conflict opportunities in human-to-human and human-to-agent online collaborative problem solving. *Technology Knowledge and Learning, 19*(1-2), 147–174. doi:10.1007/s10758-014-9229-1

Rosen, Y., & Beck-Hill, D. (2012). Intertwining digital content and one-to-one laptop learning environment. *Journal of Research on Technology in Education, 44*(3), 223–239. doi:10.1080/15391523.2012.10782588

Rosen, Y., & Foltz, P. (2014). Assessing collaborative problem solving through automated technologies. *Research and Practice in Technology Enhanced Learning, 9*(3), 389–410.

Rosen, Y., & Rimor, R. (2009). Using collaborative database to enhance students' knowledge construction. *Interdisciplinary Journal of E-Learning and Learning Objects, 5,* 187–195.

Rosen, Y., & Tager, M. (2013). *Computer-based assessment of collaborative problem-solving skills: Human-to-agent versus human-to-human approach.* Boston, MA: Pearson Education.

Rosen, Y., & Tager, M. (2014). Making student thinking visible through a concept map in computer-based assessment of critical thinking. *Journal of Educational Computing Research, 50*(2), 249–270. doi:10.2190/EC.50.2.f

Roseth, C. J., Fang, F., Johnson, D. W., & Johnson, R. T. (2006, April). Effects of cooperative learning on middle school students: A meta-analysis. Paper presented at the Annual Meeting of the American Educational Research Association, San Francisco, CA.

Rosseel, Y. (2012). Lavaan: An R package for Structural Equation Modeling. *Journal of Statistical Software, 48*(2), 1–36.

Rotem, A., & Avni, E. (2008). Reshet khevratit khinuchit [Social education network]. *Toward Digital Ethics Initiative.* Retrieved July 20, 2014, from http://ianethics.com/?page_id=2577 (Hebrew)

Rotem, A., & Avni, E. (2010). Hamoreh bemalkodet haresbet hakhevratit – Moreh or khaver? [The teacher in a social network trap: Teacher or friend?] *Toward Digital Ethics Initiative.* Retrieved July 20, 2014, from http://ianethics.com/wp-content/uploads/2010/11/teacher-student-facebook.pdf (Hebrew)

Rotem, A., & Avni, E. (2011). Yisum horaa-limida bemedia khevratit mekuvenet [Teaching-learning implementation in the online social media]. *Machon Mofet Journal, 46*, 42-46. Retrieved July 20, 2014, from http://www.mofet.macam.ac.il/ktiva/bitaon/Documents/bitaon46.pdf (Hebrew)

Rotem, A., & Avni, E. (2012). Muganut hamoreh haretzuya bemisgeret medinuyut hitnahalut bakita [Desired teacher protection in the framework of policy of conduct in the digital classroom]. *Toward Digital Ethics Initiative.* Retrieved July 20, 2014, from http://ianethics.com/wp-content/uploads/2012/04/muganutIA4-2012.pdf (Hebrew)

Rotem, A., & Avni, I. (2012). *Facebook in education: Tools and educational applications.* Retrieved April 22, 2013 from http://ianethics.com/wp-content/uploads/2012/01/facebook-in-education-toolsAI.pdf (in Hebrew)

Rotem, A., & Peled, Y. (2008). Digital text. In A. Rotem & Y. Peled (Eds.), Likrat beit sefer mekuvan [School turns on line] (pp. 79–90). Tel Aviv: Klil Pub. (Hebrew)

Rothstein, J. (2004). College performance predictions and the SAT. *Journal of Econometrics, 121*(1-2), 297–317. doi:10.1016/j.jeconom.2003.10.003

Rouet, J.-F. (1990). Interactive text processing by inexperienced (hyper-) readers. In A. Rizk, N. Streitz, & J. André (Eds.), *Hypertexts: Concepts, systems, and applications* (pp. 250–260). Cambridge, UK: Cambridge University Press.

Rouet, J.-F. (2006). *The skills of document use: From text comprehension to Web based learning.* Mahwah, NJ: Lawrence Erlbaum.

Rouet, J.-F., & Britt, M. A. (2011). Relevance processes in multiple document comprehension. In M. T. McCrudden, J. P. Magliano, & G. Schraw (Eds.), *Text Relevance and Learning from Text* (pp. 19–52). Greenwich, CT: Information Age Publishing.

Rouet, J.-F., Favart, M., Britt, M. A., & Perfetti, C. A. (1997). Studying and using multiple documents in history: Effects of discipline expertise. *Cognition and Instruction, 15*(1), 85–106. doi:10.1207/s1532690xci1501_3

Rouet, J.-F., & Passerault, J.-M. (1999). Analyzing Learner-hypermedia interaction: An overview of online methods. *Instructional Science, 27*(3/4), 201–219. doi:10.1023/A:1003162715462

Rovai, A. (2002). Building a Sense of Community at a Distance. *The International Review of Research in Open and Distance Learning, 3*(1), 1-16.

Rovai, A. P. (2002). Building sense of community at distance. *International Review of Research in Open and Distance Learning, 3*(1). Retrieved from http://www.irrodl.org/index.php/irrodl/article/view/79/152

Rowe, F., & Rafferty, J. (2013). Instructional design interventions for supporting self-regulated learning: Enhancing academic outcomes in postsecondary E-learning environments. *MERLOT Journal of Online Learning and Teaching, 9*(4), 590–601.

Rudner, L. (2010). Implementing the Graduate Management Admission Test Computerized Adaptive Test. In W. van der Linden & C. A. W. Glas (Eds.), *Elements of adaptive testing* (pp. 151–165). New York, NY: Springer.

Rudner, L. M. (2001). Informed test component weighting. *Educational Measurement: Issues and Practice, 20*(1), 16–19. doi:10.1111/j.1745-3992.2001.tb00054.x

Rudner, L., & Liang, T. (2002). Automated essay scoring using Bayes' theorem. *The Journal of Technology, Learning, and Assessment, 1*(2), 1–21.

Ruiz-Primo, M. A. (2004). *Examining concept maps as an assessment tool. Concept Maps: Theory, Methodology, Technology.* Proceeding of the First International Conference on Concept Mapping.

Ruiz-Primo, M. A., Schultz, S. E., Li, M., & Shavelson, R. J. (2001). Comparison of the reliability and validity of scores from two concept-mapping techniques. *Journal of Research in Science Teaching, 38*(2), 260–278. doi:10.1002/1098-2736(200102)38:2<260::AID-TEA1005>3.0.CO;2-F

Ruiz-Primo, M. A., & Shavelson, R. J. (1996). Problems and issues in the use of concept maps in science assessment. *Journal of Research in Science Teaching, 33*(6), 569–600. doi:10.1002/(SICI)1098-2736(199608)33:6<569::AID-TEA1>3.0.CO;2-M

Ruiz-Primo, M. A., Shavelson, R. J., Li, M., & Schultz, S. E. (2001). On the validity of cognitive interpretations of scores from alternative concept-mapping techniques. *Educational Assessment*, 7(2), 99–141. doi:10.1207/S15326977EA0702_2

Rummel, N., & Spada, H. (2005). Learning to collaborate: An instructional approach to promoting problem-solving in computer-mediated settings. *Journal of the Learning Sciences*, 14(2), 201–241. doi:10.1207/s15327809jls1402_2

Rupp, A., Templin, J., & Henson, R. (2010). *Diagnostic measurement: Theory, methods, and applications.* New York: Guilford.

Rutkowski, L., Gonzalez, E., von Davier, M., & Zhou, Y. (2014). Assessment design for international large-scale assessments. In L. Rutkowski, M. von Davier, & D. Rutkowski (Eds.), *Handbook of international large-scale assessment* (pp. 75–95). Boca Raton, FL: Taylor & Francis.

Ryan, R. M., & Deci, E. L. (2002). An overview of self-determination theory. In E. L. Deci & R. M. Ryan (Eds.), *Handbook of self-determination research* (pp. 3–33). Rochester, NY: University of Rochester Press.

Ryans, D. G. (1939). The measurement of persistence: An historical review. *Psychological Bulletin*, 36(9), 715–739. doi:10.1037/h0060780

Rynes, S. L., & Connerley, M. L. (1993). Applicant reactions to alternative selection procedures. *Journal of Business and Psychology*, 7(3), 251–277. doi:10.1007/BF01015754

Saavedra, A. R., & Opfer, V. D. (2012, October). Learning 21st-century skills requires 21st-century teaching. *Phi Delta Kappan*, 94(2), 8–13. doi:10.1177/003172171209400203

Sabatini, J., O'Reilly, T., Halderman, L., & Bruce, K. (2014). Broadening the scope of reading comprehension using scenario-based assessments: Preliminary findings and challenges. *International Journal of Topics in Cognitive Psychology*, 114, 693–723.

Sabot, R., & Wakeman-Linn, J. (1991). Grade inflation and course choice. *The Journal of Economic Perspectives*, 5(1), 159–170. doi:10.1257/jep.5.1.159

Sabourin, J., Rowe, J. P., Mott, B. W., & Lester, J. C. (2011). When off-task is on-task: The affective role of off-task behavior in narrative-centered learning environments. In *Artificial Intelligence in Education* (pp. 534–536). New York, NY: Springer. doi:10.1007/978-3-642-21869-9_93

Sadler, R. D. (1989). Formative assessment and the design of instructional systems. *Instructional Science*, 18(2), 119–144. doi:10.1007/BF00117714

Salen, K., & Zimmerman, E. (2003, November). This is not a game: Play in cultural environments. In *DiGRA '03 – Proceedings of the 2003 DiGRA International Conference: Level Up*. Retrieved from http://www.digra.org/digital-library/forums/2-level-up

Salmerón, L., Cañas, J. J., Kintsch, W., & Fajardo, I. (2005). Reading strategies and hypertext comprehension. *Discourse Processes*, 40(3), 171–191. doi:10.1207/s15326950dp4003_1

Salmerón, L., Kammerer, Y., & García-Carrión, P. (2013). Searching the Web for conflicting topics: Page and user factors. *Computers in Human Behavior*, 29(6), 2161–2171. doi:10.1016/j.chb.2013.04.034

Salmerón, L., Kintsch, W., & Cañas, J. J. (2006). Reading strategies and prior knowledge in learning from hypertext. *Memory & Cognition*, 34(5), 1157–1171. doi:10.3758/BF03193262 PMID:17128614

Salmerón, L., Kintsch, W., & Kintsch, E. (2010). Self-regulation and link selection strategies in hypertext. *Discourse Processes*, 47(3), 175–211. doi:10.1080/01638530902728280

Salomon, G., & Globerson, T. (1989). When teams do not function the way they ought to. *International Journal of Educational Research*, 13(1), 89–99. doi:10.1016/0883-0355(89)90018-9

Salomon, G., & Perkins, D. N. (1998). Individual and social aspects of learning. *Review of Research in Education*, 23, 1–24.

Samejima, F. (1997). Graded response model. Handbook of modern item response theory, 85-100.

Samejima, F. (1969). *Estimation of latent ability using a response pattern of graded scores (Psychometric Monograph No. 17)*. Richmond, VA: Psychometric Society.

Sandholtz, J. H., Ringstaff, C., & Dwyer, D. C. (1997). *Teaching with technology: Creating student-centered classrooms*. New York: Teachers College Press.

Sanger, L. (2010). Individual knowledge in the Internet age. *EDUCAUSE Review*, (45), 14–24. Retrieved from http://www.educause.edu/ero/article/individual-knowledge-internet-age

SAS. (2011). *The SAS system for Windows. Release 9.2*. Carey, NC: SAS Institute Inc.

Scalise, K. (2012, May). Using technology to assess hard-to-measure constructs in the Common Core State Standards and to expand accessibility. *ETS Invitational Research Symposium on Technology Enhanced Assessments*, Princeton, NJ.

Scalise, K., & Gifford, B. R. (2006). Computer-based assessment in e-learning: A framework for constructing "intermediate constraint" questions and tasks for technology platforms. *Journal of Teaching, Learning, and Assessment*, 4(6), 1–44.

Scardamalia, M., & Bereiter, C. (2003). Knowledge building environments: Extending the limits of the possible in education and knowledge work. In A. Distefano, K. E. Rudestam, & R. Silverman (Eds.), Encyclopedia of distributed learning. Thousand Oaks, CA: Sage. Retrieved from http://ikit.org/fulltext/2003_KBE.pdf

Scardamalia, M. (2002). Collective cognitive responsibility for the advancement of knowledge. In B. Smith (Ed.), *Liberal education in a knowledge society* (pp. 67–98). Chicago: Open Court.

Scardamalia, M. (Ed.). (2002). *Collective cognitive responsibility for the advancement of knowledge*. Chicago, IL: Open Court.

Schaal, S., Bogner, F. X., & Girwidz, R. (2010). Concept mapping assessment of media assisted learning in interdisciplinary science education. *Research in Science Education*, 40(3), 339–352. doi:10.1007/s11165-009-9123-3

Schalock, R. L., Borthwick-Duffy, S. A., Bradley, V. J., Buntinx, W. E., Coulter, D. L., Craig, E. M., & Yeager, M. H. et al. (2010). *Intellectual disability: definition, classification, and systems of supports* (11th ed.). Washington, DC: American Association On Intellectual And Developmental Disabilities.

Schatztnann, J., Stuttle, M. N., Weilhammer, K., & Young, S. (2005). Effects of the user model on simulation-based learning of dialogue strategies. In *Proceedings of IEEE Workshop on Automatic Speech Recognition and Understanding*, (pp. 220–225). doi:10.1109/ASRU.2005.1566539

Scheuermann, F., & Guimarães Pereira, A. (Eds.). (2008). Towards a research agenda on computer-based assessment: Challenges and needs for European educational measurement. Luxembourg: European Commission. Retrieved from http://bit.ly/1myPtUd

Schleicher, A. (Ed.). (2012). Preparing Teachers and Developing School Leaders for the 21st Century: Lessons from Around the World. OECD Publishing. doi:10.1787/9789264xxxxxx-en

Schleicher, A. (2008). PIAAC: A new strategy for assessing adult competencies. *International Review of Education*, 54(5-6), 627–650. doi:10.1007/s11159-008-9105-0

Schmeichel, B. J. (2007). Attention control, memory updating, and emotion regulation temporarily reduce the capacity for executive control. *Journal of Experimental Psychology. General*, 136(2), 241–255. doi:10.1037/0096-3445.136.2.241 PMID:17500649

Schmeiser, C. B., & Welch, C. J. (2006). Test development. In R. L. Brennan (Ed.), *Educational measurement* (4th ed.; pp. 307–353). Westport, CT: National Council on Measurement in Education and American Council on Education.

Schmidt, F. L., Greenthal, A. L., Hunter, J. E., Berner, J. G., & Seaton, F. W. (1977). Job sample versus paper-and-pencil trades and technical tests: Adverse impact and examinee attitudes. *Personnel Psychology*, 30(2), 187–197. doi:10.1111/j.1744-6570.1977.tb02088.x

Schmidt, F. L., & Hunter, J. E. (1998). The validity and utility of selection methods in personnel psychology: Practical and theoretical implications of 85 years of research findings. *Psychological Bulletin, 124*(2), 262–274. doi:10.1037/0033-2909.124.2.262

Schmitt, N., & Ostroff, C. (1986). Operationalizing the "behavioral consistency" approach: Selection test development based on a content-oriented approach. *Personnel Psychology, 39*(1), 91–108. doi:10.1111/j.1744-6570.1986. tb00576.x

Schon, D. (1983). *The reflective practitioner: How professionals think in action.* New York: Basic Books.

Schumaker, J. B., & Deshler, D. D. (2006). Teaching adolescents to be strategic learners. In D. D. Deshler & J. B. Schumaker (Eds.), *Teaching adolescents with disabilities: Accessing the general education curriculum* (pp. 121–156). Thousand Oaks, CA: Corwin Press.

Schunk, D. (2012). *Learning Theories: An Educational Perspective* (6th ed.). Boston: Pearson.

Schunk, D. H. (2012). *Learning theories: An educational perspective.* Boston, MA: Pearson.

Schunk, D. H., & Rice, J. M. (1991). Learning goals and progress feedback during reading comprehension instruction. *Journal of Reading Behavior, 23,* 351–364.

Schunk, D. H., & Swartz, C. W. (1993a). Goals and progress feedback: Effects on self-efficacy and writing achievement. *Contemporary Educational Psychology, 18*(3), 337–354. doi:10.1006/ceps.1993.1024

Schunk, D. H., & Swartz, C. W. (1993b). Writing strategy instruction with gifted students: Effects of goals and feedback on self-efficacy and skills. *Roeper Review, 15*(4), 225–230. doi:10.1080/02783199309553512

Schwartz, D. L., & Heiser, J. (2006). Spatial representations and imagery in learning. In R. K. Sawyer (Ed.), *The Cambridge handbook of the learning sciences.* New York, NY: Cambridge University Press.

Scientific Software International, Inc. (2003). *PARSCALE, version 4.1.2328.4* [Computer software]. Skokie, IL: Publisher.

Scottish Qualifications Authority. (2014a). *E-portfolios.* Retrieved from http://www.sqa.org.uk/sqa/42718.html

Scottish Qualifications Authority. (2014b). *CPD toolkit for assessors and internal verifiers of SVQ.* Retrieved from http://bit.ly/1qGbq8f

Scott, J. A. (2010). Creating new opportunities to acquire new word meanings from text. In E. H. Hiebert & M. L. Kamil (Eds.), *Teaching and learning vocabulary: Bringing research to practice* (pp. 69–91). New York, NY: Routledge.

Scott, P. A., Matthews, A., & Kirwan, M. (2014). What is nursing in the 21st century and what does the 21st century health system require of nursing? *Nursing Philosophy, 15*(1), 23–34. doi:10.1111/nup.12032 PMID:24320979

Scott, R., Collins, B., Knight, V., & Kleinert, H. (2013). Teaching adults with moderate intellectual disability ATM use via the iPod. *Education and Training in Autism and Developmental Disabilities, 48,* 190–199.

Scoular, C., & Awwal, N. (2014). Module 3: ATC21S Collaborative Problem Solving Assessments [ATC21S professional development modules]. In E. Care & P. Griffin (Eds.), Assessment and Teaching of 21st Century Skills. Springer.

Sefton-Green, J., Nixon, H., & Erstad, O. (2009). Reviewing approaches and perspectives on "Digital Literacy". *Pedagogies, 4*(2), 107–125. doi:10.1080/15544800902741556

Selander, S. (2008). Designs for learning and ludic engagement. *Digital Creativity, 19*(3), 145–152. doi:10.1080/14626260802312673

Selig, J. P., Card, N. A., & Little, T. D. (2008). *Latent variable structural equation modeling in cross-cultural research: Multigroup and multilevel approaches.* Academic Press.

Seo, Y. J., & Bryant, D. P. (2009). Analysis of studies of the effects of computer-assisted instruction on the mathematics performance of students with learning disabilities. *Computers & Education, 53*(3), 913–928. doi:10.1016/j. compedu.2009.05.002

Shanahan, T. (1998). The reading-writing relationship: Seven instructional principles. *The Reading Teacher*, *41*(6-9), 636–647.

Shane, H. C., & Albert, P. D. (2008). Electronic screen media for persons with autism spectrum disorders: Results of a survey. *Journal of Autism and Developmental Disorders*, *38*(8), 1499–1508. doi:10.1007/s10803-007-0527-5 PMID:18293074

Shapiro, A., & Niederhauser, D. (2004). Learning from hypertext: Research issues and findings. In D. H. Jonassen (Ed.), *Handbook of research on educational communications and technology* (pp. 605–620). Mahwah, NJ: Lawrence Erlbaum Associates.

Sharples, M., McAndrew, P., Weller, M., Ferguson, R., FitzGerald, E., Hirst, T., . . . Whitelock, D. (2012). *Innovating Pedagogy 2012: Exploring new forms of teaching, learning and assessment to guide educators and policy makers*. Open University Innovation Report 1. Retrieved from http://bit.ly/1uwYH78

Sharp, P. A., & Langer, R. (2011). Promoting convergence in biomedical science. *Science*, *333*. PMID:21798916

Shavelson, R. J. (2012). Assessing business-planning competence using the Collegiate Learning Assessment as a prototype. *Empirical Research in Vocational Education and Training*, *4*(1), 77–90.

Shaw, E. J., & Mattern, K. D. (2009). Examining the accuracy of self-reported high school grade point average. New York, NY: The College Board. Retrieved from https://research.collegeboard.org/sites/default/files/publications/2012/7/researchreport-2009-5-examining-accuracy-self-reported-high-school-grade-point-average.pdf

Shealy, R., & Stout, W. (1993). A model-based standardization approach that separates true bias/DIF from group ability differences and detects test bias/DTF as well as item bias/DIF. *Psychometrika*, *58*(2), 159–194. doi:10.1007/BF02294572

Sherman, D., & Cornick, S. (2015). Assessment of PreK-12 educators' skill and practice in technology & digital media integration. In D. Slykhuis & G. Marks (Eds.), *Proceedings of Society for Information Technology & Teacher Education International Conference 2015* (pp. 1286-1291). Chesapeake, VA: Association for the Advancement of Computing in Education (AACE).

Shermis, M. D., & Hammer, B. (2012). *Contrasting state-of-the-art automated scoring of essays: Analysis*. Retrieved from ASAP: http://www.scoreright.org/NCME_2012_Paper3_29_12.pdf

Shermis, M. D., & Hamner, B. (2012). *Contrasting state-of-the-art automated scoring of essays: Analysis*. Retrieved from http://www.scoreright.org/NCME_2012_Paper3_29_12.pdf

Shermis, M. D., Burstein, J. C., & Bliss, L. (2004, April). *The impact of automated essay scoring on high stakes writing assessments*. Paper presented at the annual meeting of the National Council on Measurement in Education, San Diego, CA.

Shermis, M. D., Wilson Garvan, C., & Diao, Y. (2008, March). *The impact of automated essay scoring on writing outcomes*. Paper presented at the annual meeting of the National Council on Measurement in Education, New York, NY.

Shermis, M., & Hamner, B. (2012). *Contrasting state-of-the-art automated scoring of essays: Analysis*. Paper presented at Annual Meeting of the National Council on Measurement in Education, Vancouver, Canada.

Shermis, M. D. (2014). State-of-the-art automated essay scoring: Competition, results, and future directions from a United States demonstration. *Assessing Writing*, *20*, 53–76. doi:10.1016/j.asw.2013.04.001

Shermis, M. D., & Burstein, J. (2013). *Handbook of Automated Essay Evaluation: Current Applications and Future Directions*. New York: Routledge.

Shermis, M. D., & Burstein, J. (Eds.). (2003). *Automated essay scoring: A cross-disciplinary perspective*. Mahwah, NJ: Lawrence Erlbaum Associates.

Shermis, M. D., & Burstein, J. (Eds.). (2003). *Automated Essay Scoring: A Cross-Disciplinary Perspective*. Mahwah, NJ: Lawrence Erlbaum Associates.

Shermis, M. D., Burstein, J., & Leacock, C. (2006). Applications of computers in assessment and analysis of writing. In C. A. MacArthur, S. Graham, & J. Fitzgerald (Eds.), *Handbook of Writing Research* (pp. 403–416). New York, NY: Guilford.

Shernoff, D. J., & Csikszentmihalyi, M. (2009). Cultivating engaged learners and optimal learning environments. In R. Gilman, E. S. Huebner, & M. Furlong (Eds.), *Handbook of positive psychology in schools* (pp. 131–145). New York, NY: Routledge.

Shiffrin, R. M., & Schneider, W. (1977). Controlled and automatic human information processing: II. Perceptual learning, automatic attending and a general theory. *Psychological Review*, *84*(2), 127–190. doi:10.1037/0033-295X.84.2.127

Shih, P.-C., Mate, R., Sanchez, F., & Munoz, D. (2004). *Quantifying user navigation patterns: a methodology proposal.* Paper presented at the 28th International Congress of Psychology. Retrieved August 15, 2011, from http://www.uam.es/personal_pdi/psicologia/pei/download/Shih2004quantifying_ICP.pdf

Shih, R. (2011). Can Web 2.0 technology assist college students in learning English writing? Integrating Facebook and peer assessment with blended learning. *Australasian Journal of Educational Technology*, *27* (Special issue, 5), 829-845.

Shiner, R. L. (1998). How shall we speak of children's personalities in middle childhood? A preliminary taxonomy. *Psychological Bulletin*, *124*(3), 308–332. doi:10.1037/0033-2909.124.3.308 PMID:9849111

Shin, J., Deno, S. L., Robinson, S. L., & Marston, D. (2000). Predicting classroom achievement from active responding on a computer-based groupware system. *Remedial and Special Education*, *21*(1), 53–60. doi:10.1177/074193250002100107

Shiotsu, T., & Weir, C. J. (2007). The relative significance of syntactic knowledge and vocabulary breadth in the prediction of reading comprehension test performance. *Language Testing*, *24*(1), 99–128. doi:10.1177/0265532207071513

Shukla-Mehta, S., Miller, T., & Callahan, K. J. (2010). Evaluating the effectiveness of video instruction on social and communication skills training for children with autism spectrum disorders: A review of the literature. *Focus on Autism and Other Developmental Disabilities*, *25*(1), 23–36. doi:10.1177/1088357609352901

Shuster, D. M. (2008, August). The arts and engineering. *IEEE Control Systems Magazine*, *28*(4), 96–98. doi:10.1109/MCS.2008.924881

Shute, V. J. (2008). Focus on formative feedback. *Review of Educational Research*, *78*(1), 153–189. doi:10.3102/0034654307313795

Shute, V. J. (2011). Stealth assessment in computer-based games to support learning. In S. Tobias & J. D. Fletcher (Eds.), *Computer games and instruction* (pp. 503–524). Charlotte, NC: Information Age.

Shute, V. J., Rieber, L., & Van Eck, R. (2011). Games... and... learning. In R. Reiser & J. Dempsey (Eds.), *Trends and issues in instructional design and technology* (3rd ed.; pp. 321–332). Upper Saddle River, NJ: Pearson Education.

Shute, V. J., & Ventura, M. (2013). *Measuring and supporting learning in games: Stealth assessment.* Cambridge, MA: MIT Press.

Siegel, M., & Lee, J. (2001). *"But electricity isn't static": Science discussion, identification of learning issues, and use of resources in a problem-based learning education course.* Paper presented at the annual meeting of the National Association for Research in Science Teaching, St. Louis, MO.

Siemens, G. (2005). Connectivism: A learning theory for the digital age. *International Journal of Instructional Technology and Distance Learning*, *2*(1). Retrieved from http://www.itdl.org/Journal/Jan_05/article01.htm

Sigman, M., Cohen, S. E., Beckwith, L., & Topinka, C. (1987). Task persistence in 2-year-old preterm infants in relation to subsequent attentiveness and intelligence. *Infant Behavior and Development*, *10*(3), 295–305. doi:10.1016/0163-6383(87)90018-X

Silva, E., & White, T. (2013). Pathways to improvement: Using psychological strategies to help college students master developmental math. Stanford, CA: Carnegie Foundation for the Advancement of Teaching. Retrieved from http://www.carnegiefoundation.org/sites/default/files/pathways_to_improvement.pdf

Silva, E. (2008). *Measuring skills for the 21st century.* Washington, DC: Education Sector at American Institutes for Research. doi:10.1177/003172170909000905

Silver, N. (2013). Reflective pedagogies and the metacognitive turn in college teaching. In M. Kaplan, N. Silver, D. LaVaque-Manty, & D. Meizlish (Eds.), *Using reflection and metacognition to improve student learning* (pp. 1–17). Sterling, VA: Stylus Publishing.

Simon, S., Erduran, S., & Osborne, J. (2002). Enhancing the quality of argumentation in school science. Paper presented at the annual meeting of the *National Association for Research in Science Teaching.* New Orleans, LA.

Singer, J. D., & Willett, J. B. (2003). Applied longitudinal data analysis: Modeling change and event occurrence. New York, NY: Oxford. doi:10.1093/acprof:oso/9780195152968.001.0001

Singley, M. K., & Bennett, R. E. (2002). Item generation and beyond: Applications of schema theory to mathematics assessment. In S. H. Irvine & P. C. Kyllonen (Eds.), *Item generation for test development* (pp. 361–384). Mahwah, NJ: Erlbaum.

Sireci, S. G., & Zenisky, A. L. (2006). Innovative item formats in computer-based testing: In pursuit of improved construct representation. In S. M. Downing & T. M. Haladyna (Eds.), *Handbook of test development* (pp. 329–347). Mahwah, NJ: Lawrence Erlbaum Associates.

Skinner, B. F. (1954). The science of learning and the art of teaching. *Harvard Educational Review, 24,* 86–97.

Skov, O., Le Bigot, L., Vibert, N., de Pereyra, G., & Rouet, J.-F. (2014). *The Role of Popularity Cues in Students' Selection of Scholarly Literature Online.* Paper presented at the EARLI SIG2 Conference, Rotterdam, The Netherlands.

Slotta, J. D., & Chi, M. T. H. (2006). The impact of ontology training on conceptual change: Helping students understand the challenging topics in science. *Cognition and Instruction, 24*(2), 261–289. doi:10.1207/s1532690xci2402_3

Smarter Balanced Assessment Consortium. (2010). *Race to the Top Assessment Program Application for New Grants: Comprehensive Assessment Systems CFDA Number 84.395B. Proposal submitted by Washington State on Behalf of the Smarter Balanced Assessment Consortium.* Olympia, WA: Author.

Smedshammar, H., Frenckner, K., Nordquist, C., & Romberger, S. (1989). *Why is the difference in reading speed when reading from VDUs and from paper bigger for fast readers than for slow readers?* Paper presented at WWDU 1989, Second International Scientific Conference, Montreal, Canada.

Smith, M., Turner, J., & Lattanzio, S. (2014). *The NC CAP "Road map of Need" supports the need for the Read to Achieve Act.* Retrieved from http://cdn.lexile.com/m/cms_page_media/135/NC%20CAP%20II_4.pdf

Smith, B. R., Spooner, F., & Wood, C. L. (2013). Using embedded computer-assisted explicit instruction to teach science to students with autism spectrum disorder. *Research in Autism Spectrum Disorders, 7*(3), 433–443. doi:10.1016/j.rasd.2012.10.010

Smith, G. F. (2002). Thinking skills: The question of generality. *Journal of Curriculum Studies, 34*(6), 659–678. doi:10.1080/00220270110119905

Smith, J. III, diSessa, A., & Roschelle, J. (1993). Misconceptions reconceived: A constructive analysis of knowledge in transition. *Journal of the Learning Sciences, 3*(2), 115–163. doi:10.1207/s15327809jls0302_1

Smith, P. A. (1996). Towards a practical measure of hypertext usability. *Interacting with Computers, 4*(4), 365–38. doi:10.1016/S0953-5438(97)83779-4

Snow, R. E., & Lohman, D. F. (1989). Implications of cognitive psychology for educational measurement. In R. L. Linn (Ed.), *Educational measurement* (3rd ed.; pp. 263–332). New York: American Council on Education and Macmillan.

Society for Human Resource Management & Achieve. (2012). *The future of the U.S. workforce.* Washington, DC: Achieve. Retrieved from http://www.achieve.org/future-us-workforce

Society for Industrial and Organizational Psychology. (2003). *Principles for the validation and use of personnel selection procedures.* Bowling Green, OH: Author.

Soland, J., Hamilton, L. S., & Stecher, B. M. (2013, November). *Measuring 21st century competencies: Guidance for educators.* Santa Monica, CA: RAND Corporation.

Solano-Flores, G., & Li, M. (2009). Generalizability of cognitive interview-based measures across cultural groups. *Educational Measurement: Issues and Practice, 28*(2), 9–18. doi:10.1111/j.1745-3992.2009.00143.x

Soller, A., & Stevens, R. (2008). Applications of stochastic analyses for collaborative learning and cognitive assessment. In G. R. Hancock & K. M. Samuelson (Eds.), *Advances in latent variable mixture models* (pp. 109–111). Charlotte, NC: Information Age Publishing.

Sonamthiang, S., Cercone, N., & Naruedomkul, K. (2007). Discovering Hierarchical Patterns of Students' Learning Behavior in Intelligent Tutoring Systems. In *Proceedings of IEEE International Conference on Granular Computing*, (pp. 485–489).

Songer, N. B., Kelcey, B., & Gotwals, A. W. (2009). How and when does complex reasoning occur? Empirically driven development of a learning progression focused on complex reasoning about biodiversity. *Journal of Research in Science Teaching, 46*(6), 610–631. doi:10.1002/tea.20313

Spärck Jones, K. (1972). A statistical interpretation of term specificity and its application in retrieval. *The Journal of Documentation, 28*(1), 11–21. doi:10.1108/eb026526

Spencer, M., Quinn, J. M., & Wagner, R. K. (2014). Specific reading comprehension disability: Major problem, myth, or misnomer? *Learning Disabilities Research & Practice, 29*(1), 3–9. doi:10.1111/ldrp.12024 PMID:25143666

Spetz, J. (2014). How Will Health Reform Affect Demand for RNs? *Nursing Economics, 32*(1), 42–44. PMID:24689158

Spooner, F., Knight, V. F., Browder, D. M., & Smith, B. R. (2012). Evidence-based practices for teaching academics to students with severe developmental disabilities. *Remedial and Special Education, 33*(6), 374–387. doi:10.1177/0741932511421634

Sprayberry, L. D. (2014). Transformation of America's Health Care System: Implications for Professional Direct-Care Nurses. *Medsurg Nursing, 23*(1), 61–66. PMID:24707672

Squire, K. (2006). From content to context: Videogames as designed experience. *Educational Researcher, 35*(8), 19–29. doi:10.3102/0013189X035008019

Squire, K. D., & Jan, M. (2007). Mad City Mystery: Developing scientific argumentation skills with a place-based augmented reality game on handheld computers. *Journal of Science Education and Technology, 16*(1), 5–29. doi:10.1007/s10956-006-9037-z

St.meld. nr. 16 (2006-2007). *- og ingen sto igjen…: Tidlig innsats for livslang læring.* Retrieved from https://www.regjeringen.no/nb/dokumenter/stmeld-nr-16-2006-2007-/id441395/

Stadtler, M., & Bromme, R. (2013). Multiple document comprehension: An approach to public understanding of science. *Cognition and Instruction, 31*(2), 122–129. doi:10.1080/07370008.2013.771106

Stahl, G. (2006). *Group cognition: Computer support for building collaborative knowledge.* Cambridge, MA: MIT Press.

Stahl, S. A. (2010). Four problems with teaching word meanings (and what to do to make vocabulary an integral part of instruction). In E. H. Hiebert & M. L. Kamil (Eds.), *Teaching and learning vocabulary: Bringing research to practice* (pp. 95–114). New York, NY: Routledge.

Staker, H., & Horn, M. B. (2012). *Classifying K-12 blended learning.* Mountain View, CA: Innosight Institute.

Standen, P. J., & Brown, D. J. (2005). Virtual reality in the rehabilitation of people with intellectual disabilities[Review]. *Cyberpsychology & Behavior*, *8*(3), 272–282. doi:10.1089/cpb.2005.8.272 PMID:15971976

Stanovich, K. E. (2000). *Progress in understanding reading: Scientific foundations and new frontiers*. New York: Guilford Press.

Stanovich, K. E., West, R. F., Cunningham, A. E., Cipielewski, J., & Siddiqui, S. (1996). The role of inadequate print exposure as a determinant of reading comprehension problems. In C. Cornoldi & J. Oakhill (Eds.), *Reading comprehension difficulties: Processes and intervention* (pp. 15–32). Mahwah, NJ: Erlbaum.

Starkes, J. L., Deakins, J., Allard, F., Hodges, N. J., & Hayes, A. (1996). Deliberate practice in sports: What is it anyway? In K. A. Ericsson (Ed.), *The road to excellence: The acquisition of expert performance in the arts and sciences, sports, and games* (pp. 81–106). Mahwah, NJ: Erlbaum.

Stark, S., Chernyshenko, O. S., & Drasgow, F. (2006). Detecting differential item functioning with confirmatory factor analysis and item response theory: Toward a unified strategy. *The Journal of Applied Psychology*, *91*(6), 1292–1306. doi:10.1037/0021-9010.91.6.1292 PMID:17100485

Starr, S. S. (2010). Associate degree nursing: Entry into practice -- link to the future. *Teaching and Learning in Nursing*, *5*(3), 129–134. doi:10.1016/j.teln.2009.03.002

Steedle, J. T. (2009). Advancing institutional value-added score estimation. New York, NY: Council for Aid to Education. Retrieved from http://cae.org/images/uploads/pdf/04_Improving_the_Reliability_and_Interpretability_of_Value-Added_Scores_for_Post-Secondary_Institutional_Assessment_Programs.pdf

Steedle, J. T. (2012). Selecting value-added models for postsecondary institutional assessment. *Assessment & Evaluation in Higher Education*, *37*(6), 637–652. doi:10.1080/02602938.2011.560720

Steeves, V. (2014). Young Canadians in a Wired World, Phase III: Life Online. Ottawa: MediaSmarts.

Steinkuehler, C., & Duncan, S. (2008). Scientific habits of mind in virtual worlds. *Journal of Science Education and Technology*, *17*(6), 530–543. doi:10.1007/s10956-008-9120-8

Stendal, K., Balandin, S., & Molka-Danielsen, J. (2011). Virtual worlds: A new opportunity for people with lifelong disability? *Journal of Intellectual & Developmental Disability*, *36*(1), 80–83. doi:10.3109/13668250.2011.526597 PMID:21070118

Stenner, A. J., Burdick, H., Sanford, E. F., & Burdick, D. S. (2006). How accurate are Lexile text measures? *Journal of Applied Measurement*, *7*(3), 307–322. PMID:16807496

Stenner, A. J., Fisher, W. P., Stone, M. H., & Burdick, D. S. (2013). Causal Rasch models. *Frontiers in Psychology*, *4*, 1–14. doi:10.3389/fpsyg.2013.00536 PMID:23986726

Stephenson, J., & Limbrick, L. (2013). A review of the use of touch-screen mobile devices by people with developmental disabilities. *Journal of Autism and Developmental Disorders*, 1–15. PMID:23888356

Sternberg, R. J. (1986). Critical thinking: Its nature, measurement, and improvement. Washington, DC: National Institute of Education. Available at http://www.eric.ed.gov/PDFS/ED272882.pdf

Sternberg, R. J. (1987). Most vocabulary is learned from context. In M. G. McKeowon & M. E. Curtis (Eds.), *The nature of vocabulary acquisition* (pp. 89–105). Hillsdale, NJ: Erlbaum.

Stevens, K. R., & Ovretveit, J. (2013). Improvement research priorities: USA survey and expert consensus. *Nursing Research and Practice*, *2013*, 1–8. doi:10.1155/2013/695729 PMID:24024029

Stevenson, H., & Stigler, J. (1994). *Learning Gap: Why Our Schools Are Failing And What We Can Learn From Japanese And Chinese Educ*. New York, NY: Simon and Schuster.

Stewart, C. O., Setlock, L. D., & Fussell, S. R. (2007). Conversational argumentation in decision-making: Chinese and U.S. participants in face-to-face and instant-messaging interactions. *Discourse Processes*, *44*(2), 113–139. doi:10.1080/01638530701498994

Stewart, J., Cartier, J. L., & Passmore, C. M. (2005). Developing understanding through model-based inquiry. In M. S. Donovan & J. D. Bransford (Eds.), *How students learn* (pp. 515–565). Washington, DC: National Research Council.

Stewart, V. (2012). *A world-class education: Learning from international models of excellence and innovation.* Arlington, VA: ASCD.

Stieff, M., & Wilensky, U. (2003). Connected chemistry—incorporating interactive simulations into the chemistry classroom. *Journal of Science Education and Technology, 12*(3), 285–302. doi:10.1023/A:1025085023936

Stiggins, R. J. (2005). From formative assessment to assessment FOR learning: A path to success in standards-based schools. *Phi Delta Kappan, 87*(4), 324–328. doi:10.1177/003172170508700414

Stiwne, E. E., & Jungert, T. (2010). Engineering students' experiences of transition from study to work. *Journal of Education and Work, 23*(5), 417–437. doi:10.1080/13639080.2010.515967

Stock, S. E., Davies, D. K., & Wehmeyer, M. L. (2004). Internet-based multimedia tests and surveys for individuals with intellectual disabilities. *Journal of Special Education Technology, 19*, 43–48.

Stock, S. E., Davies, D. K., Wehmeyer, M. L., & Palmer, S. B. (2008). Evaluation of cognitively accessible software to increase independent access to cellphone technology for people with intellectual disability. *Journal of Intellectual Disability Research, 52*(12), 1155–1164. doi:10.1111/j.1365-2788.2008.01099.x PMID:18647214

Stokols, D., Harvey, R. G., Fuqua, J., & Phillips, K. (2004). In vivo studies of transdisciplinary scientific collaboration, lessons learned and implications for active living research. *American Journal of Preventive Medicine, 28*(2), 202–213. doi:10.1016/j.amepre.2004.10.016 PMID:15694529

Strain-Seymour, E., Way, W., & Dolan, P. (2009, June). *Strategies and processes for developing innovative items in large-scale assessments.* Retrieved from http://images.pearsonassessments.com/images/tmrs/StrategiesandProcessesforDevelopingInnovativeItems.pdf

Strain-Seymour, E., Way, W., & Dolan, R. P. (2009). *Strategies and processes for developing innovative items in large-scale assessments.* Pearson Education, Inc. Available at: http://images.pearsonassessments.com/images/tmrs/StrategiesandProcessesforDevelopingInnovativeItems.pdf

Strautmane, M. (2012). Concept map-based knowledge assessment tasks and their scoring criteria: An overview. In A. J. Cañas, J. D. Novak, & J. Vabhear (Eds.), *Proceedings of the Fifth International Conference on Concept Mapping.* Valletta, Malta.

Street, B. V. (1984). *Literacy in theory and practice.* Cambridge University Press.

Streeter, L., Lochbaum, K., LaVoie, N., & Psotka, J. (2007). Automated tools for collaborative learning environments. In T. Landauer, D. McNamara, S. Dennis, & W. Kintsch (Eds.), *Latent Semantic Analysis: A Road to Meaning.* Mahwah, NJ: Lawrence Erlbaum.

Sukkarieh, J. Z., von Davier, M., & Yamamoto, K. (2012). *From biology to education: Scoring and clustering multilingual text sequences and other sequential tasks.* (ETS Research Report No. RR-12-25). Princeton, NJ: Educational Testing Service.

Sutton, R. I., & Hargadon, A. (1996). Brainstorming groups in context: Effectiveness in a product design firm. *Administrative Science Quarterly, 41*(4), 685–718. doi:10.2307/2393872

Su, Z., Yang, Q., Lu, Y., & Zhang, H. (2000). WhatNext: A prediction system for Web requests using n-gram sequence models. In *Proceedings of the First International Conference on Web Information Systems Engineering,* (vol. 1, pp. 214–221).

Svetina, D., & Rutkowski, L. (2014). Detecting differential item functioning using generalized logistic regression in the context of large-scale assessments. *Large-scale Assessments in Education, 2*(1), 1–17.

Swaminathan, H., & Rogers, H. J. (1990). Detecting differential item functioning using logistic regression procedures. *Journal of Educational Measurement, 27*(4), 361–370. doi:10.1111/j.1745-3984.1990.tb00754.x

Swartz, C. W., & Sanford-Moore, E. (2008). *Implications of The Lexile Framework® for Writing for North Carolina's General Model of Writing Assessment.* A MetaMetrics Research Report submitted to the North Carolina Department of Public Instruction.

Swartz, C. W., & Williamson, G. L. (2014). *Bending the curve of reader ability estimates from third grade back to pre-kindergarten: Results from an exploratory study of early literacy.* Unpublished technical report.

Swartz, C. W., Emerson, C., Kennedy, A. J., & Hanlon, S. T. (2015). Impact of deliberate practice on reader ability for students Taiwanese students learning to read English as a foreign language. (Manuscript in preparation).

Swartz, C. W., Hanlon, S. T., Stenner, A. J. (2011-2013, Grant No. OPP1020128). *Literacy by Technology: Technology Solutions Designed to Help Educators Create Literacy Rich Content Area Classrooms.* Funds provided by The Bill and Melinda Gates Foundation.

Swartz, C. W., Hanlon, S. T., Tendulkar, J., & Williamson, G. W. (2015). Impact of different amounts of reading on early adolescents' growth in reading ability. (Manuscript in preparation).

Swartz, C. W., Burdick, D. S., Hanlon, S. T., Stenner, A. J., Kyngdon, A., Burdick, H., & Smith, M. (2014). Toward a theory relating text complexity, reader ability, and reading comprehension. *Journal of Applied Measurement, 16*(1), 359–371. PMID:25232670

Swartz, C. W., Hanlon, S. T., Stenner, A. J., Burdick, H., Burdick, D. S., & Emerson, C. (2011). *EdSphere®: Using technology to enhance literacy through deliberate practice. (MetaMetrics Research Brief).* Durham, NC: MetaMetrics.

Swartz, C. W., Stenner, A. J., Hanlon, S. T., Burdick, H., Burdick, D. S., & Kuehne, K. W. (2012). *From novice to expert: Applying research principles to promote literacy in the classroom. (MetaMetrics Research Brief).* Durham, NC: MetaMetrics.

Sweet, M. S., & Michaelsen, L. K. (2012). *Team-based learning in the social sciences and humanities: Group work that works to generate critical thinking and engagement.* Sterling, VA: Stylus Publishing.

Sweller, J. (1998). Cognitive load during problem solving: Effects on learning. *Cognitive Science, 12*(2), 257–285. doi:10.1207/s15516709cog1202_4

Taber, T. A., Alberto, P. A., Seltzer, A., & Hughes, M. (2003). Obtaining assistance when lost in the community using cell phones. *Research and Practice for Persons with Severe Disabilities, 28*(3), 105–116. doi:10.2511/rpsd.28.3.105

Tan, C. M., Wang, Y. F., & Lee, C. D. (2002). The use of bigrams to enhance text categorization. *Information Processing & Management, 38*(4), 529–546. doi:10.1016/S0306-4573(01)00045-0

Tan, N. C., Kandiah, N., Chan, Y. H., Umapathi, T., Lee, S. H., & Tan, K. (2011). A controlled study of team-based learning for undergraduate clinical neurology education. *BMC Medical Education, 11*(1), 91. doi:10.1186/1472-6920-11-91 PMID:22035246

Tashakkori, A., & Teddlie, C. (1998). *Mixed methodology: Combining qualitative and quantitative approaches.* London: Sage.

Taylor, M. C. (2011). Crash course; U.S. universities unprepared to meet the challenges of the 21st century. *The Buffalo News.* Retrieved from http://www.buffalonews.com/article/20110220/OPINION02/302209877

Technology in Schools Task Force. (2002). *Technology in schools: Suggestions, tools, and guidelines for assessing technology in elementary and secondary education.* Washington, DC: U.S. Department of Education, National Center for Education Statistics.

Teng, C.-I. (2011). Who are likely to experience flow? Impact of temperament and character on flow. *Personality and Individual Differences, 50*(6), 863–868. doi:10.1016/j.paid.2011.01.012

Terman, L. M. (1916). *The measurement of intelligence.* Boston, MA: Houghton Mifflin. doi:10.1037/10014-000

Thaiss, C., & Porter, T. (2010). The State of WAC/WID in 2010: Methods and Results of the U.S. Survey of the International WAC/WID Mapping Project. *College Composition and Communication, 61*(3), 524–570.

The European Commission. (2001). *European report on the quality of school education: Sixteen quality indicators.* Luxembourg: Office for Official Publications of the European Communities. Retrieved July 20, 2014, from http://europa.eu/legislation_summaries/education_training_youth/lifelong_learning/c11063_en.htm

The European Commission. (2014). Enhancing digital literacy, skills and inclusion (Pillar VI). *Digital Agenda for Europe.* Retrieved July 20, 2014, from http://ec.europa.eu/digital-agenda/en/our-goals/pillar-vi-enhancing-digital-literacy-skills-and-inclusion

The European Parliament and the Council of the EU. (2006). Recommendation of the European Parliament and the Council of 18 December 2006 on key competences for lifelong learning. *Official Journal of the European Union, L, 394*(310). Retrieved from http://eur-lex.europa.eu/LexUriServ/LexUriServ.do?uri=OJ:L:2006:394:0010:0018:en:PDF

TheATLAS. (2014). *LENSOO: Active learning & group collaboration platform.* Retrieved on July 5, 2014 at: http://www.theatlas.org/index.php?option=com_content&view=article&id=244

Therrien, W. J., Taylor, J. C., Hosp, J. L., Kaldenberg, E. R., & Gorsh, J. (2011). Science instruction for students with learning disabilities: A meta-analysis. *Learning Disabilities Research & Practice, 26*(4), 188–203. doi:10.1111/j.1540-5826.2011.00340.x

Thissen, D., Steinberg, L., & Wainer, H. (1988). *Use of item response theory in the study of group differences in trace lines.* Academic Press.

Thissen, D., Steinberg, L., & Wainer, H. (1993). *Detection of differential item functioning using the parameters of item response models.* Academic Press.

Thissen, D. (1991). *MULTILOG user's guide.* Chicago: Scientific Software.

Thissen, D., Nelson, L., Rosa, K., & McLeod, L. D. (2001). Item response theory for items scored in more than two categories. In D. Thissen & H. Wainer (Eds.), *Test scoring* (pp. 141–186). Mahwah, NJ: Lawrence Erlbaum Associates.

Thissen, D., & Steinberg, L. (1988). Data analysis using item response theory. *Psychological Bulletin, 104*(3), 385–395. doi:10.1037/0033-2909.104.3.385

Thissen, D., Steinberg, L., & Gerrard, M. (1986). Beyond group-mean differences: The concept of item bias. *Psychological Bulletin, 99*(1), 118–128. doi:10.1037/0033-2909.99.1.118

Thomas, A., Chess, C., & Birch, H. G. (1968). *Temperament and behavior disorders in children.* Retrieved from http://eric.ed.gov/?id=ED025066

Thomas, A., & Chess, S. (1977). *Temperament and development.* Oxford, UK: Brunner/Mazel.

Thomas, P. A., & Bowen, C. W. (2011). A controlled trial of team-based learning in an ambulatory medicine clerkship for medical students. *Teaching and Learning in Medicine, 23*(1), 31–36. doi:10.1080/10401334.2011.536888 PMID:21240780

Thomas, S. L. (2003). Longer-term economic effects of college selectivity and control. *Research in Higher Education, 44*(3), 263–299. doi:10.1023/A:1023058330965

Thompson, D. R., & Darbyshire, P. (2013). Reply... Thompson D.R. & Darbyshire P. (2013) Is academic nursing being sabotaged by its own killer elite? Journal of Advanced Nursing 69(1), 1–3. *Journal of Advanced Nursing, 69*(5), 1216–1219. doi:10.1111/jan.12123 PMID:23521594

Thornton, G. C., & Byham, W. C. (1982). *Assessment centers and managerial performance.* New York: Academic Press.

Thornton, G. C. III. (1992). *Assessment centers in human resource management.* Reading, MA: Addison Wesley.

Thornton, G. C. III, & Mueller-Hanson, R. A. (2004). *Developing organizational simulations: A guide for practitioners and students.* Mahwah, NJ: Lawrence Erlbaum Associates.

Thurlow, M., Hermann, A., & Foltz, P. W. (2010). *Preparing MSA Science Items for Artificial Intelligence (AI) Scoring.* Paper presented at the Maryland Assessment Group Conference, Ocean City, MD.

Thurlow, M., Lazarus, S., Albus, D., & Hodgson, J. (2010, September). *Computer-based testing: Practices and considerations.* Retrieved from http://bit.ly/1q3azPj

Tierney, R. J., & Shanahan, T. (1992). Research on the reading-writing relationship: Interactions, transactions, and outcomes. In R. Barr, M. I. Kamil, P. B. Mosenthal, & P. D. Pearson (Eds.), *Handbook of Reading Research* (Vol. 2, pp. 246–280). Mahway, NJ: Lawrence Erlbaum Associates.

Tinto, V. (1975). Dropout from higher education: A theoretical synthesis of recent research. *Review of Educational Research, 45*(1), 89–125. doi:10.3102/00346543045001089

Tosun, N., & Baris, M. (2011). E-portfolio applications in education. *The Online Journal of New Horizons in Education, 1*(4), 42-52. Retrieved from http://bit.ly/SuGFqE

Tovey, A. (2014, July 17). Degree losing attraction for smaller employers. *The Telegraph.* Retrieved from http://bit.ly/1jAxm5m

Towles-Reeves, E., Kearns, J., Kleinert, H., & Kleinert, J. (2009). An analysis of the learning characteristics of students taking alternate assessments based on alternate achievement standards. *The Journal of Special Education, 42*(4), 241–254. doi:10.1177/0022466907313451

Tracey, D. H., & Mandel Morrow, L. (2002). Preparing young learners for successful reading comprehension: Laying the foundation. In C. C. Block & M. Pressley (Eds.), *Comprehension instruction: Research-based best practices* (pp. 219–233). New York, NY: The Guilford Press.

Trading Standards Institute. (2014). *Internal verifier.* Retrieved from http://bit.ly/1lotOBT

*Transdisciplinary Skills.* (2012). Retrieved on July 6, 2014 at: http://www.amersol.edu.pe/es/pyp/PYPskills.asp

Tremblay, K., Lalancette, D., & Roseveare, D. (2012). *Assessment of Higher Education Learning Outcomes feasibility study report: volume 1-design and implementation.* Academic Press.

Trier, U. P. (2003). Twelve countries contributing to DeSeCo: A summary report. In D. S. Rychen, L. H. Salganik, & M. E. McLaughlin (Eds.), *Contributions to the Second DeSeCo Symposium: Definition and selection of key competencies.* Retrieved from http://www.deseco.admin.ch/bfs/deseco/en/index/02.parsys.26255.downloadList.54824.DownloadFile.tmp/2003.symposiumvolume.pdf

Trötschel, R., Hüffmeier, J., Loschelder, D. D., Schwartz, K., & Gollwitzer, P. M. (2011). Perspective taking as a means to overcome motivational barriers in negotiations: When putting oneself into the opponent's shoes helps to walk toward agreements. *Journal of Personality and Social Psychology, 101*(4), 771–790. doi:10.1037/a0023801 PMID:21728447

Trundle, K. C., & Bell, R. L. (2010). The use of a computer simulation to promote conceptual change: A quasi-experimental study. *Computers & Education, 54*(4), 1078–1088. doi:10.1016/j.compedu.2009.10.012

Tsacoumis, S. (2014, October) *Do role plays need the human touch?* Presentation at the 38th International Congress on Assessment Center Methods, Alexandria, VA.

Tsacoumis, S. (2007). Assessment centers. In D. L. Whetzel & G. R. Wheaton (Eds.), *Applied measurement: Industrial psychology in human resources management* (pp. 259–292). Mahwah, NJ: Lawrence Erlbaum.

Tufano, P. (2014, February 24). Business schools are stuck in a self-reinforcing bubble. *Business Week.*

Tversky, A., & Kahneman, D. (1982). *Judgment under uncertainty: Heuristics and biases.* Cambridge, UK: Cambridge University Press.

Tversky, B., Heiser, J., Mackenzie, R., Lozano, S., & Morrison, J. (2008). Enriching animations. In R. K. Lowe & W. Schnotz (Eds.), *Learning with animation: Research implications for design* (pp. 263–285). New York, NY: Cambridge University Press.

Tyson, R. B. (2001). Applying the Design Structure Matrix to system decomposition and integration problems: A review and new directions. *IEEE Transactions on Engineering Management, 48*(3), 292–306. doi:10.1109/17.946528

Tziner, A., Ronen, S., & Hacohen, D. (1993). A four-year validation study of an assessment center in a financial corporation. *Journal of Organizational Behavior, 14*(3), 225–237. doi:10.1002/job.4030140303

U. S. Census Bureau. (2011). *Profile of selected social characteristics: Suffolk County, N.Y. Author.*

U. S. Department of Education, Office of the Deputy Secretary, Implementation and Support Unit. (2012a). *Race to the Top assessment: Partnership for Assessment of Readiness for College and Careers year one report.* Washington, DC: Author. Downloaded from: http://www2.ed.gov/programs/racetothetop-assessment/performance.html

U. S. Department of Education, Office of the Deputy Secretary, Implementation and Support Unit. (2012b). *Race to the Top assessment: Smarter Balanced Assessment Consortium year one report.* Washington, DC: Author. Downloaded from: http://www2.ed.gov/programs/racetothetop-assessment/performance.html

U.S. Department of Education, Office of Educational Technology. (2010). *Transforming American education: Learning powered by technology.* Washington, DC: Author.

U.S. Department of Education, Office of Educational Technology. (2012). *Enhancing teaching and learning through educational data mining and learning analytics: An issue brief.* Washington, DC: Author.

U.S. Department of Education, Office of Educational Technology. (2013). *Expanding evidence approaches for learning in a digital world.* Washington, DC: Author.

U.S. Department of Education. (2003, December 9). *Improving the academic achievement of the disadvantaged: Final rule,* 68 Fed. Reg. 236.

U.S. Department of Education. (2010). *Transforming American education – Learning powered by technology: National Education Technology Plan 2010.* Washington, DC: Office of Educational Technology, U.S. Department of Education.

U.S. Department of Education. (2010). *Transforming American education: Learning powered by technology (National Educational Technology Plan 2010).* Washington, DC: Office of Educational Technology, U.S. Department of Education.

U.S. Department of Health and Human Services, Health Resources and Services Administration, National Center for Health Workforce Analysis. (2014). The Future of the Nursing Workforce: National- and State-Level Projections, 2012-2025. Rockville, MD: Author.

U.S. Department of Health and Human Services, National Institutes of Health, National Institute of Child Health and Human Development. (2000). *Teaching children to read: An evidence-based assessment of the scientific literature on reading and its implications for reading instruction.* Retrieved from http://www.nichd.nih.gov/publications/pubs/ nrp/documents/report.pdf

U.S. Merit Systems Protection Board. (2009). *Job simulations: Trying out for a federal job.* Washington, DC: Author.

Ulbrich, F., Jahnke, I., & Mårtensson, P. (2011). Special issue on knowledge development and the net generation. *International Journal of Sociotechnology and Knowledge Development.*

Uline, C., Tschannen-Moran, M., & Perez, L. (2003). Constructive conflict: How controversy can contribute to school improvement. *Teachers College Record, 105*(5), 782–816. doi:10.1111/1467-9620.00268

UNESCO – The United Nations Educational, Scientific and Cultural Organization. (2005). Beacons of the Information Society. *The Alexandria proclamation on information literacy and lifelong learning.* Retrieved July 20, 2014, from http://www.codyassociates.com/alexandria-proclamation.html

UNESCO – The United Nations Educational, Scientific and Cultural Organization. (2013). *Global media and information literacy assessment framework: Country readiness and competencies.* Paris: UNESCO. Retrieved July 20, 2014, from http://unesdoc.unesco.org/images/0022/002246/224655e.pdf

United Nations. (2014). *We can end poverty: Millennium development goals and beyond 2015.* Author.

United States Department of Education. (2004). *Paying for college: Changes between 1990 and 2000 for full-time dependent undergraduates* (NCES Publiacton 2004-075). Washington, DC: United States Department of Education. Retrieved from http://nces.ed.gov/pubs2004/2004075.pdf

United States Department of Education. (2006). *A test of leadership: Charting the future of US higher education.* Washington, DC: United States Department of Education. Retrieved from https://www2.ed.gov/about/bdscomm/list/hiedfuture/reports/pre-pub-report.pdf

United States Department of Education. (2013). *Total tuition, room and board rates charged for full-time students in degree-granting institutions.* Retrieved from http://nces.ed.gov/fastfacts/display.asp?id=76

United States Department of Education. (2014, June). *Learning technology effectiveness.* Retrieved from http://tech.ed.gov/learning-technology-effectiveness/

Unsworth, N., Redick, T. S., Lakey, C. E., & Young, D. L. (2010). Lapses in sustained attention and their relation to executive control and fluid abilities: An individual differences investigation. *Intelligence, 38*(1), 111–122. doi:10.1016/j.intell.2009.08.002

Vale, C. D. (2006). Computerized item banking. In S. M. Downing & T. M. Haladyna (Eds.), *Handbook of test development* (pp. 261–285). Mahwah, NJ: Lawrence Erlbaum Associates, Publishers.

Valenti, S., Neri, F., & Cucchiarelli, A. (2003). An overview of current research on automated essay grading. *Journal of Information Technology Education, 2,* 319–330.

Van de Vijver, F. J. (1998). Towards a theory of bias and equivalence. *Zuma Nachrichten, 3,* 41–65.

Van de Vijver, F. J., & Leung, K. (1997). *Methods and data analysis for cross-cultural research* (Vol. 1). Sage.

Van de Vijver, F. J., & Poortinga, Y. H. (1997). Towards an integrated analysis of bias in cross-cultural assessment. *European Journal of Psychological Assessment, 13*(1), 29–37. doi:10.1027/1015-5759.13.1.29

Van de Vijver, F. J., & Poortinga, Y. H. (2002). Structural equivalence in multilevel research. *Journal of Cross-Cultural Psychology, 33*(2), 141–156. doi:10.1177/0022022102033002002

Van de Vijver, F., & Hambleton, R. K. (1996). Translating tests: Some practical guidelines. *European Psychologist, 1*(2), 89–99. doi:10.1027/1016-9040.1.2.89

Van de Vijver, F., & Leung, K. (1997). *Methods and data analysis of comparative research.* Allyn & Bacon.

Van de Vijver, F., & Tanzer, N. K. (2004). Bias and equivalence in cross-cultural assessment: An overview. *Revue Européenne de Psychologie Appliquée. European Review of Applied Psychology, 54*(2), 119–135. doi:10.1016/j.erap.2003.12.004

van der Linden, W. J. (2005). *Linear models for optimal test design.* New York, NY: Springer. doi:10.1007/0-387-29054-0

van der Linden, W. J., & Glas, C. A. W. (2000). *Computerized adaptive testing: Theory and practice.* Boston, MA: Kluwer Academic Publishers. doi:10.1007/0-306-47531-6

Van Doorn, G., & Eklund, A. A. (2013). Face to Facebook: Social media and the learning and teaching potential of symmetrical, synchronous communication. *Journal of University Teaching & Learning Practice, 10*(1), article 6. Retrieved September 20, 2014 from: http://ro.uow.edu.au/cgi/viewcontent.cgi?article=1268&context=jutlp

Van Herk, H., Poortinga, Y. H., & Verhallen, T. M. (2004). Response styles in rating scales evidence of method bias in data from six EU countries. *Journal of Cross-Cultural Psychology, 35*(3), 346–360. doi:10.1177/0022022104264126

Van Laarhoven, T., Johnson, J. W., Van Laarhoven-Myers, T., Grider, K. L., & Grider, K. M. (2009). The effectiveness of using a video iPod as a prompting device in employment settings. *Journal of Behavioral Education, 18*(2), 119–141. doi:10.1007/s10864-009-9077-6 van Merriënboer, J. J. G., & Paas, F. (2003). Powerful learning and the many faces of instructional design: Towards a framework for the design of powerful learning environments. In E. de Corte, L. Verschaffel, N. Entwistle, & J. J. G. van Merriënboer (Eds.), *Powerful learning environments: Unravelling basic components and dimensions* (pp. 3–21). Oxford, UK: Elsevier Science.

Van Merrienboer, J. J., & Kester, L. (2005). The four-component instructional design model: Multimedia principles in environments for complex learning. In R. E. Mayer (Ed.), *The Cambridge handbook of multimedia learning* (pp. 71–93). New York, NY: Cambridge University Press. doi:10.1017/CBO9780511816819.006

Vandenberg, R. J., & Lance, C. E. (2000). A review and synthesis of the measurement invariance literature: Suggestions, practices, and recommendations for organizational research. *Organizational Research Methods*, *3*(1), 4–70. doi:10.1177/109442810031002

VanLehn, K., Graesser, A. C., Jackson, G. T., Jordan, P., Olney, A., & Rose, C. P. (2007). When are tutorial dialogues more effective than reading? *Cognitive Science*, *31*(1), 3–62. doi:10.1080/03640210709336984 PMID:21635287

Vaughan, M., & Dillon, A. (2006). Why structure and genre matter to users of digital information: A longitudinal study with readers of a web-based newspaper. *International Journal of Human-Computer Studies*, *64*(6), 502–526. doi:10.1016/j.ijhcs.2005.11.002

Veenman, M. V. J., Van Hout-Wolters, B. H. A. M., & Afflerbach, P. (2006). Metacognition and learning: Conceptual and methodological considerations. *Metacognition and Learning*, *1*(1), 3–14. doi:10.1007/s11409-006-6893-0

Veenman, M. V. J., Wilheim, P., & Beishuizen, J. J. (2004). The relation between intellectual and metacognitive skills from a developmental perspective. *Learning and Instruction*, *14*(1), 89–109. doi:10.1016/j.learninstruc.2003.10.004

Vellas, B., Villars, H., Abellan, G., Soto, M. E., Rolland, Y., Guigoz, Y., & Garry, P. et al. (2006). Overview of the mini nutritional assessment: Its history and challenges. *The Journal of Nutrition, Health & Aging*, *10*(6), 456–465. PMID:17183418

Ventura, M., & Shute, V. (2013). The validity of a game-based assessment of persistence. *Computers in Human Behavior*, *29*(6), 2568–2572. doi:10.1016/j.chb.2013.06.033

Ventura, M., Shute, V. J., & Small, M. (2014). Assessing persistence in educational games. In R. Sottilare, A. Graesser, X. Hu, & B. Goldberg (Eds.), *Design recommendations for adaptive intelligent tutoring systems: Learner modeling* (Vol. 2, pp. 93–101). Orlando, FL: U.S. Army Research Laboratory.

Ventura, M., Shute, V., & Zhao, W. (2013). The relationship between video game use and a performance-based measure of persistence. *Computers & Education*, *60*(1), 52–58. doi:10.1016/j.compedu.2012.07.003

Vescio, V., Ross, D., & Adams, A. (2008). A review of research on the impact of professional learning communities on teaching practice and student learning. *Teaching and Teacher Education*, *24*(1), 80–91. doi:10.1016/j.tate.2007.01.004

Vogt, J., Fisser, P., Roblin, N., Tondeur, J., & van Braak, J. (2013, April). Technological pedagogical content knowledge – A review of the literature. *Journal of Computer Assisted Learning*, *29*(2), 109–121. doi:10.1111/j.1365-2729.2012.00487.x

Von Bertalanffy, L. (1969). *General system theory*. George Braziller.

Von Davier, A. A., & Halpin, P. F. (2013). *Collaborative problem solving and the assessment of cognitive skills: Psychometric considerations* (Research Report 13-41). Princeton, NJ: Educational Testing Service.

Von Davier, A. A., & Halpin, P. F. (2013, December). *Collaborative problem solving and the assessment of cognitive skills: Psychometric considerations*. Research Report ETS RR-13-41. Educational Testing Service.

von Davier, M., Sinharay, S., Oranje, A., & Beaton, A. (2006). Statistical procedures used in the National Assessment of Educational Progress (NAEP): Recent developments and future directions. In C. R. Rao & S. Sinharay (Eds.), Handbook of statistics (Vol. 26): Psychometrics. Amsterdam, Netherlands: Elsevier.

von Davier, M., & Sinharay, S. (2014). Analytics in international large-scale assessments: Item response theory and population models. In L. Rutkowski, M. von Davier, & D. Rutkowski (Eds.), *Handbook of international large-scale assessment* (pp. 155–174). Boca Raton, FL: Taylor & Francis.

Vonderwell, S., Liang, X., & Alderman, K. (2007). Asynchronous discussions and assessment in online learning. *Journal of Research on Technology in Education, 39*(3), 309–328. doi:10.1080/15391523.2007.10782485

Vörös, Z., Rouet, J.-F., & Pléh, C. (2011). Effect of high-level content organizers on hypertext learning. *Computers in Human Behavior, 27*(5), 2047–2055. doi:10.1016/j.chb.2011.04.005

Vygotsky, L. S. (1978). *Mind in society: The development of higher psychological processes.* Cambridge, MA: Harvard University Press.

Wade-Stein, D., & Kintsch, E. (2004). Summary Street: Interactive computer support for writing. *Cognition and Instruction, 22*(3), 333–362. doi:10.1207/s1532690xci2203_3

Wadmany, R., Rimor, R. & Rozner, E. (2011). The relationship between attitude, thinking and activity of students in an e-learning course. *REM – Research on Education and Media, 3*(1), 103- 121

Wagner, T. (2008). *The global achievement gap: Why even our best schools don't teach the new survival skills our children need--and what we can do about it.* New York, NY: Basic Books.

Wagner, T. (2012). *Creating innovators: The making of young people who will change the world.* New York, NY: Scribner.

Wainer, H. (1976). Estimating coefficients in linear models: It don't make no nevermind. *Psychological Bulletin, 83*(2), 213–217. doi:10.1037/0033-2909.83.2.213

Wainer, H., Bradlow, E. T., & Du, Z. (2000). Testlet response theory. An analog for the 3-PL useful in testlet-based adaptive testing. In W. J. van der Linden & C. A. W. Glas (Eds.), *Computerized adaptive testing: Theory and practice* (pp. 245–270). Boston, MA: Kluwer Academic Publishers. doi:10.1007/0-306-47531-6_13

Wainer, H., Bradlow, E. T., & Wang, X. (2007). *Testlet response theory and its applications.* New York, NY: Cambridge University Press. doi:10.1017/CBO9780511618765

Wainer, H., Dorans, N. J., Flaugher, R., Green, B. F., Mislevy, R. J., Steinberg, L., & Thissen, D. (1990). *Computerized adaptive testing: A primer.* Hillsdale, NJ: Lawrence Erlbaum Associates.

Wainer, H., & Kiely, G. L. (1987). Item clusters and computerized adaptive testing: A case for testlets. *Journal of Educational Measurement, 24*(3), 185–201. doi:10.1111/j.1745-3984.1987.tb00274.x

Walton, K. M., & Ingersoll, B. R. (2013). Improving social skills in adolescents and adults with autism and severe to profound intellectual disability: A review of the literature. *Journal of Autism and Developmental Disorders, 43*(3), 594–615. doi:10.1007/s10803-012-1601-1 PMID:22790427

Wang, C., Shannon, D., & Ross, M. (2013). Students' characteristics, self-regulated learning, technology self-efficacy, and course outcomes in online learning. *Distance Education, 34*(3), 302–323. doi:10.1080/01587919.2013.835779

Wang, M. W., & Stanley, J. C. (1970). Differential weighting: A review of methods and empirical studies. *Review of Educational Research, 40*(5), 663–705. doi:10.3102/00346543040005663

Wang, Q., Woo, H. L., Quek, C. L., Yang, Y., & Liu, M. (2012). Using Facebook group as learning management system: An exploratory study. *British Journal of Educational Technology, 43*(3), 428–438. doi:10.1111/j.1467-8535.2011.01195.x

Wang, S. (2005). *Online or paper: Does delivery affect results? Administration mode comparability study for Stanford diagnostic Reading and Mathematics tests.* San Antonio, TX: Harcourt Assessment.

Wan, Z., Compeau, D., & Haggerty, N. (2012). The effects of self-regulated learning processes on E-learning outcomes in organizational settings. *Journal of Management Information Systems, 29*(1), 307–339. doi:10.2753/MIS0742-1222290109

Ware, C. (2004). *Information visualization: Perception for design*. San Francisco: Morgan Kaufmann.

Warfield, J. N. (1982). *Interpretive structural modeling. In Group Planning and problem-solving methods in engineering* (pp. 155–201). New York: Wiley.

Warfield, J. N., & Cardenas, A. R. (2002). *A handbook of interactive management. Palm Harbor*, FL: Ajar Publishing Company.

Warschauer, M., & Grimes, D. (2008). Automated writing assessment in the classroom. *Pedagogies*, *3*(1), 22–36. doi:10.1080/15544800701771580

Watson, G., & Glaser, E. M. (2008). *Watson-Glaser Critical Thinking Appraisal*. Pearson Education, Inc.

Webb, N. M. (1995). Group collaboration in assessment: Multiple objectives, processes, and outcomes. *Educational Evaluation and Policy Analysis*, *17*(2), 239–261. doi:10.3102/01623737017002239

Webb, N. M., Nemer, K. M., Chizhik, A. W., & Sugrue, B. (1998). Equity issues in collaborative group assessment: Group composition and performance. *American Educational Research Journal*, *35*(4), 607–651. doi:10.3102/00028312035004607

Wehmeyer, M. L. (2014). Framing for the future: Self-determination. *Remedial and Special Education*. doi:10.1177/0741932514551281

Wehmeyer, M. L., Smith, S. J., Palmer, S. B., & Davies, D. K. (2004). Technology use by students with intellectual disabilities: An overview. *Journal of Special Education Technology*, *19*, 7–21.

Weinberger, A., & Fischer, F. (2006). A framework to analyze argumentative knowledge construction in computer-supported collaborative learning. *Computers & Education*, *46*(1), 71–95. doi:10.1016/j.compedu.2005.04.003

Weinerth, K., Koenig, V., Brunner, M., & Martin, R. (2014). Concept maps: A useful and usable tool for computer-based knowledge assessment? A literature review with a focus on usability. *Computers & Education*, *78*, 201–209. doi:10.1016/j.compedu.2014.06.002

Wellman, N. (2010). The employability attributes required of new marketing graduates. *Marketing Intelligence & Planning*, *28*(7), 908–930. doi:10.1108/02634501011086490

Welsh, J., Harmes, J. C., & Winkelman, R. (2011). Florida's Technology Integration Matrix. *Principal Leadership*, *12*(2), 69–71.

Wendt, A., & Harmes, J. C. (2009, May/June). Evaluating innovative items for the NCLEX, Part 2: Item characteristics and cognitive processing. *Nurse Educator*, *34*(3), 109–113. doi:10.1097/NNE.0b013e31819fcae8 PMID:19412048

Wenglinsky, H. (1999). *Does it compute? The relationship between educational technology and student achievement in mathematics*. Educational Testing Service Policy Information Center.

Wenglinsky, H. (2002). The link between teacher classroom practices and student academic performance. *Education Policy Analysis Archives*, *10*(12).

Werner, O., & Campbell, D. T. (1970). Translating, working through interpreters, and the problem of decentering. In A handbook of method in cultural anthropology (pp. 398-419). New York: American Museum of Natural History.

Wernimont, P. F., & Campbell, J. P. (1968). Signs, samples, and criteria. *The Journal of Applied Psychology*, *52*(5), 372–376. doi:10.1037/h0026244 PMID:5681116

Wertsch, J. V. (1991). A sociocultural approach to socially shared cognition. In L. B. Rensick, J. M. Levine, & S. D. Teasley (Eds.), *Perspectives on Socially Shared Cognition* (pp. 85–100). Washington, DC: APA. doi:10.1037/10096-004

Whalen, C., Liden, L., Ingersoll, B., Dallaire, E., & Liden, S. (2006). Behavioral improvements associated with computer-assisted instruction for children with developmental disabilities. *The Journal of Speech and Language Pathology-Applied Behavior Analysis*, *1*(1), 11–26. doi:10.1037/h0100182

What Works Clearinghouse. (2014). *Procedures and standards handbook. Version 3.0*. Retrieved December 4, 2014. http://ies.ed.gov/ncee/wwc/pdf/reference_resources/wwc_procedures_v3_0_standards_handbook.pdf

Wheelahan, L. (2010). *Why knowledge matters in curriculum*. New York, NY: Routledge.

Wheeler, S. (2012). Digital literacies for engagement in emerging online cultures. *eLC Research Paper Series*, *5*, 14-25.

White, B. Y., & Frederiksen, J. R. (1990). Causal model progressions as a foundation for intelligent learning environments. *Artificial Intelligence, 42*(1), 99–157. doi:10.1016/0004-3702(90)90095-H

White, B. Y., & Frederiksen, J. R. (1998). Inquiry, modeling, and metacognition: Making science accessible to all students. *Cognition and Instruction, 16*(1), 3–118. doi:10.1207/s1532690xci1601_2

White, B., & Frederisken, J. (2005). A theoretical framework and approach for fostering metacognitive development. *Educational Psychology, 40*(4), 211–223. doi:10.1207/s15326985ep4004_3

Wiener, H., Plass, H., & Marz, R. (2009). Team-based learning in intensive course format for first-year medical students. *Croatian Medical Journal, 50*(1), 69–76. doi:10.3325/cmj.2009.50.69 PMID:19260147

Wiesmann, U., Biber-Klemm, S., Grossenbacher-Mansuy, W., Hirsch Hadorn, G., Hoffmann-Riem, H., Joye, D., & Zemp, E. et al. (2008). Enhancing transdisciplinary research: a synthesis in fifteen propositions. In H. Hoffmann-Riem, S. Biber-Klemm, W. Grossenbacher-Mansuy, D. Joye, C. Pohl, U. Wiesmann, & E. Zemp (Eds.), *Handbook of transdisciplinary research* (pp. 433–441). Springer. doi:10.1007/978-1-4020-6699-3_29

Wiggins, G. (1990). The case for authentic assessment. *Practical Assessment, Research & Evaluation, 2*(2). Retrieved from http://PAREonline.net/getvn.asp?v=2&n=2

Wiggins, G., & McTighe, J. (1998). *Understanding by design*. AlexandrIa, VA: ASCD.

Wildman, J. L., Shuffler, M. L., Lazzara, E. H., Fiore, S. M., Burke, C. S., Salas, E., & Garven, S. (2012). Trust development in swift starting action teams: A multilevel framework. *Group & Organization Management, 37*(2), 138–170. doi:10.1177/1059601111434202

Wiliam, D. (2011). *Embedded formative assessment*. Bloomington, IN: Solution Tree Press.

Williamson, D. M., Bennett, R., Lazer, S., Bernstein, J., Foltz, P. W., … Sweeney, K. (2010, June). *Automated Scoring for the Assessment of Common Core Standards*. Retrieved July 1 2014 from http://www.ets.org/s/commonassessments/pdf/AutomatedScoringAssessCommonCoreStandards.pdf

Williamson, D., Xi, X., & Breyer, J. (2012). A framework for evaluation and use of automated scoring. *Educational Measurement: Issues and Practice, 31*(1), 2–13. doi:10.1111/j.1745-3992.2011.00223.x

Williamson, G. L. (2008). A Text Readability Continuum for Postsecondary Readiness. *Journal of Advanced Academics, 19*(4), 602–632.

Williamson, G. L., Fitzgerald, J., & Stenner, A. J. (2013). The Common Core State Standards quantitative text complexity trajectory: Figuring out how much complexity is enough. *Educational Researcher, 42*(2), 59–69. doi:10.3102/0013189X12466695

Williamson, G. L., Tendulkar, J., Hanlon, S. T., & Swartz, C. W. (2012). *Growth in reading ability as a response to using EdSphere®. (MetaMetrics Research Brief)*. Durham, NC: MetaMetrics.

Willis, J. (2007). *Research-based strategies to ignite student learning: Insights from a neurologist and classroom teacher*. Alexandria, VA: Association for Supervision & Curriculum Development.

Wilson, J., & Andrada, G. N. (2013, April). *Examining patterns of writing performance of struggling writers on a statewide classroom benchmark writing assessment*. Paper presented at the presented at that annual meeting of the American Educational Research Association, Classroom Assessment SIG, San Francisco, CA.

Wilson, J., & Wing Jan, L. (2008). Smart thinking: Developing reflection and metacognition. Newtown, Australia: Primary English Teaching Association.

Wilson, S., Liber, O., Johnson M.W., Beauvoir, P., Sharples, P. & Milligan, C. (2007). Personal Learning Environments: challenging the dominant design of educational systems. *Journal of e-Learning and Knowledge Society, 3* (2), 27-38.

Wilson, J., Olinghouse, N. G., & Andrada, G. N. (2014). Does automated feedback improve writing quality? *Learning Disabilities (Weston, Mass.), 12*, 93–118.

Wilson, M. (2005). *Constructing measures*. Mahwah, NJ: Lawrence Erlbaum Associates.

Windschitl, M. (1998). The WWW and classroom research: What path should we take? *Educational Researcher, 27*(1), 28–33.

Windschitl, M. (2000). Supporting the development of science inquiry skills with special classes of software. *Educational Technology Research and Development, 48*(2), 81–97. doi:10.1007/BF02313402

Winerip, M. (2012, April 22). Facing a Robo-Grader? Just Keep Obfuscating Mellifluously. *New York Times.* Retrieved from http://www.nytimes.com/2012/04/23/education/robo-readers-used-to-grade-test-essays.html?_r=0

Winkley, J. (2010). *E-assessment and innovation.* AlphaPlus. Retrieved from http://bit.ly/1HD3IFD

Winne, P. H. (1982). Minimizing the black box problem to enhance the validity of theories about instructional effects. *Instructional Science, 11*(1), 13–28. doi:10.1007/BF00120978

Wiseman, C. S. (2012). Rater effects: Ego engagement in rater decision-making. *Assessing Writing, 17*(3), 150–173. doi:10.1016/j.asw.2011.12.001

Wise, S. L. (2006). An investigation of the differential effort received by items on a low-stakes, computer-based test. *Applied Measurement in Education, 19*(2), 93–112. doi:10.1207/s15324818ame1902_2

Wise, S. L. (2015). Effort analysis: Individual score validation of achievement test data. *Applied Measurement in Education, 28*(3), 237-252.

Wise, S. L., & DeMars, C. E. (2005). Low examinee effort in low-stakes assessment: Problems and potential solutions. *Educational Assessment, 10*(1), 1–17. doi:10.1207/s15326977ea1001_1

Wise, S. L., & Kong, X. (2005). Response time effort: A new measure of student motivation in computer-based tests. *Applied Measurement in Education, 18*(2), 163–183. doi:10.1207/s15324818ame1802_2

Wise, S. L., Pastor, D. A., & Kong, X. J. (2009). Understanding correlates of rapid-guessing behavior in low stakes testing: Implications for test development and measurement practice. *Applied Measurement in Education, 22*(2), 185–205. doi:10.1080/08957340902754650

Wolf, M. A. (2010, November). *Innovate to educate: System [re]design for personalized learning.* Washington, DC: Software and Information Industry Association.

Wolf, R., Zahner, D., Kostoris, F., & Benjamin, R. (2014). *A Case Study of an International Performance-Based Assessment of Critical Thinking Skills.* Paper presented at the American Educational Research Association, Philadelphia, PA.

Wolfe, E. W. (1997). The relationship between essay reading style and scoring proficiency in a psychometric scoring system. *Assessing Writing, 4*(1), 83–106. doi:10.1016/S1075-2935(97)80006-2

Wolfe, E. W. (2005). Uncovering rater's cognitive processing and focus using think-aloud protocols. *Journal of Writing Assessment, 2,* 37–56.

Wolf, L. F., & Smith, J. K. (1995). The consequence of consequence: Motivation, anxiety, and test performance. *Applied Measurement in Education, 8*(3), 227–242. doi:10.1207/s15324818ame0803_3

Wolf, L. F., Smith, J. K., & Birnbaum, M. E. (1995). Consequence of performance, test motivation, and mentally taxing items. *Applied Measurement in Education, 8*(4), 341–351. doi:10.1207/s15324818ame0804_4

Wolf, R. M. (1998). Validity issues in international assessments. *International Journal of Educational Research, 29*(6), 491–501. doi:10.1016/S0883-0355(98)00044-5

Wong, C., Odom, S. L., Hume, K., Cox, A. W., Fettig, A., Kucharczyk, S., ... Schultz, T. R. (2014). Evidence-based practices for children, youth, and young adults with Autism Spectrum Disorder. Chapel Hill, NC: The University of North Carolina, Frank Porter Graham Child Development Institute, Autism Evidence-Based Practice Review Group.

Workman, J., & Stenard, A. (1996). Student support services for distance learners. *DEOSNEWS, 6*(3). Retrieved June 18, 2014, from the Distance Education Online Symposium Website: http://learningdesign.psu.edu/deos/deosnews6_3.pdf

World, O. R. T. (2014). *Mission Statement*. Retrieved from: http://www.ort.org/

Wu, P. H., Hwang, G. J., Milrad, M., Ke, H. R., & Huang, Y. M. (2012). An innovative concept map approach for improving students' learning performance with an instant feedback mechanism. *British Journal of Educational Technology*, *43*(2), 217–232. doi:10.1111/j.1467-8535.2010.01167.x

Yang, S. H. (2009). Using blogs to enhance critical reflection and community of practice. *Journal of Educational Technology & Society*, *12*(2), 11–21.

Yeager, D. S., & Dweck, C. S. (2012). Mindsets That Promote Resilience: When Students Believe That Personal Characteristics Can Be Developed. *Educational Psychologist*, *47*(4), 302–314. doi:10.1080/00461520.2012.722805

Yen, W. M. (1993). Scaling performance assessments: Strategies for managing local item dependence. *Journal of Educational Measurement*, *30*(3), 187–214. doi:10.1111/j.1745-3984.1993.tb00423.x

Yin, Y., Vanides, J., Ruiz-Primo, M. A., Ayala, C. C., & Shavelson, R. J. (2005). Comparison of two concept-mapping techniques: Implications for scoring, interpretation, and use. *Journal of Research in Science Teaching*, *42*(2), 166–184. doi:10.1002/tea.20049

Young, M., & Lambert, D. (2014). *Knowledge and the future school: Curriculum and social justice*. London: Bloomsbury Academic.

Young, M., & Muller, J. (2010). Three educational scenarios for the future: Lessons from the sociology of knowledge. *European Journal of Education*, *45*(1), 11–27. doi:10.1111/j.1465-3435.2009.01413.x

Zahner, D. (2013). Reliability and validity of the CLA. New York, NY: CAE. Retrieved from http://cae.org/images/uploads/pdf/Reliability_and_Validity_of_CLA_Plus.pdf

Zahner, D., & Steedle, J. (2014). *Evaluating Performance Task Scoring Comparability in an International Testing Program*. Paper presented at the American Educational Research Association, Philadelphia, PA.

Zapata-Rivera, D., Jackson, T., Liu, L., Bertling, M., Vezzu, M., & Katz, I. R. (2014) Science Inquiry Skills using Trialogues. In S. Trausan-Matu, K. E. Boyer, M. Crosby, & K. Panourgia (Eds.), *Proceedings for 12th International conference on Intelligence Tutoring Systems* (pp. 625-626). Springer.

Zenisky, A. L., & Sireci, S. G. (2013, April). *Innovative items to measure higher-order thinking: Development and validity considerations*. Presentation at the annual meeting of the National Council on Measurement in Education, San Francisco, CA.

Zenisky, A. L., & Sireci, S. G. (2002). Technological innovations in large-scale assessment. *Applied Measurement in Education*, *15*(4), 337–362. doi:10.1207/S15324818AME1504_02

Zgheib, N. K., Simaan, J. A., & Sabra, R. (2010). Using team-based learning to teach pharmacology to second year medical students improves student performance. *Medical Teacher*, *32*(2), 130–135. doi:10.3109/01421590903548521 PMID:20163228

Zhang, J. (1998). A distributed representation approach to group problem solving. *Journal of the American Society for Information Science*, *49*(9), 801–809. doi:10.1002/(SICI)1097-4571(199807)49:9<801::AID-ASI5>3.0.CO;2-Q

Zhao, Y. (2012). *World class learners: Educating creative and entrepreneurial students*. Thousand Oaks, CA: NAESP, Corwin.

Zhou, M., Xu, Y., Nesbit, J. C., & Winne, P. H. (2010). Sequential pattern analysis of learning logs: Methodology and applications. Handbook of educational data mining, 107–121.

Zickuhr, K., & Smith, A. (2012). *Digital differences*. Pew Internet & American Life Project. Retrieved from www.pewinternet.org/files/oldmedia/Files/Reports/2012/PIP_Digital_differences_041312.pdf

Zimmerman, B. J. (2002). Becoming a Self-Regulated Learner: An overview. *Theory into Practice*, *41*(2), 64–70. doi:10.1207/s15430421tip4102_2

Zimmerman, B. J. (2008). Investigating self-regulation and motivation: Historical background, methodological developments, and future prospects. *American Educational Research Journal*, 45(1), 166–183. doi:10.3102/0002831207312909

Zimmerman, E. (2009). Gaming literacy: Game design as a model for literacy in the twenty-first century. In B. Perron & M. J. P. Wolf (Eds.), *The video game theory reader, 2* (pp. 23–31). New York: Routledge.

Zingone, M. M., Franks, A. S., Guirguis, A. B., George, C. M., Howard-Thompson, A., & Heidel, R. E. (2010). Comparing team based and mixed active learning methods in an ambulatory care elective course. *American Journal of Pharmaceutical Education*, 74(9), 160. doi:10.5688/aj7409160 PMID:21301594

Zisimopoulos, D., Sigafoos, J., & Koutromanos, G. (2011). Using video prompting and constant time delay to teach an internet search basic skill to students with intellectual disabilities. *Education and Training in Autism and Developmental Disabilities*, 46, 238–250.

Zoanetti, N. (2010). Interactive computer based assessment tasks: How problem-solving process data can inform instruction. *Australasian Journal of Educational Technology*, 26, 585–606.

Zucker, S., Sassman, C., & Case, B. J. (2004). Cognitive labs. *San Antonio, TX: Harcourt Assessment. Retrieved*, 10(11), 2006.

Zula, K., Yarrish, K., & Christensen, S. D. (2010). Initial assessment and validation of an instrument to measure student perceptions of leadership skills. *The Journal of Leadership Studies*, 4(2), 48–55. doi:10.1002/jls.20168

Zumbach, J., & Mohraz, M. (2008). Cognitive load in hypermedia reading. *Computers in Human Behavior*, 24(3), 875–887. doi:10.1016/j.chb.2007.02.015

Zumbo, B., & Thomas, D. (1997). *A measure of effect size for a model-based approach for studying DIF*. Working Paper. Edgeworth Laboratory for Quantitative Behavioral Science.

Zumbo, B. D. (1999). *A handbook on the theory and methods of differential item functioning (DIF)*. Ottawa: National Defense Headquarters.

Zumbo, B. D. (2003). Does item-level DIF manifest itself in scale-level analyses? Implications for translating language tests. *Language Testing*, 20(2), 136–147. doi:10.1191/0265532203lt248oa

Zurkowski, P. G. (1974). *The information service environment: Relationships and priorities*. Washington, DC: National Commission on Libraries and Information.

Zwick, R., Donoghue, J. R., & Grima, A. (1993). Assessment of differential item functioning for performance tasks. *Journal of Educational Measurement*, 30(3), 233–251. doi:10.1111/j.1745-3984.1993.tb00425.x

Zwick, R., & Himelfarb, I. (2011). The effect of high school socioeconomic status on the predictive validity of SAT scores and high school grade-point average. *Journal of Educational Measurement*, 48(2), 101–121. doi:10.1111/j.1745-3984.2011.00136.x

Zwick, R., & Sklar, J. (2005). Predicting college grades and degree completion using high school grades and SAT scores: The role of student ethnicity and first language. *American Educational Research Journal*, 42(3), 439–464. doi:10.3102/00028312042003439

# About the Contributors

**Yigal Rosen** is a Senior Research Scientist in The Vice Provost for Advances in Learning (VPAL) at Harvard University. He leads the Harvard VPAL Research Team that enables faculty to create and implement research-enabled online learning experiences for residential and online use, such as HarvardX Massively Open Online Courses. Prior to joining Harvard he was a Senior Research Scientist at Pearson, leading research and development of innovative learning and assessment technologies for real-life skill development. Yigal was a Head of Assessment & Evaluation at Time To Know. He was a member of OECD's PISA 2015 Assessment Framework Expert Group and consulted to Microsoft, Intel, ETS, Ministry of Education in Israel and the National Authority for Measurement & Evaluation. Yigal previously held academic appointments at the University of Haifa, the Open University of Israel and Ben-Gurion University. In 2009 he received the University of Haifa Faculty of Education's Outstanding Lecturer Award. He obtained his Ph.D. degree from the University of Haifa. Yigal was a post-doctoral fellow at Harvard University Graduate School of Education and at Tel Aviv University School of Education. He began his career as a computer science, math and science teacher in grades 5 through 12. Yigal co-edited the book during his work as a Senior Research Scientist at Pearson.

**Steve Ferrara** is Vice President, Performance Assessment, and leads the Center for Next Generation Learning and Assessment in Pearson's Research and Innovation Network. The center designs, develops, validates, and conducts research on performance assessment for summative and formative uses to support learning. Prior to joining Pearson, Steve was a Principal Research Scientist at CTB/McGraw-Hill, Managing Research Director in the assessment program at American Institutes for Research, and State Assessment Director in Maryland, and a Head Start and high school special education teacher. Steve conducts psychometric research and designs large scale and formative assessments for K-12 educational achievement. He serves on technical advisory panels for assessment programs and research projects. He was Editor of Educational Measurement: Issues and Practice and serves on journal editorial advisory boards. Steve was co-recipient, AERA Cognition and Assessment Special Interest Group 2014 award for Outstanding Contribution to Practice in Cognition and Assessment; and co-recipient, AERA Division D 2006 award for Significant Contributions to Educational Measurement and Research Methodology.

**Maryam Mosharraf** has been working at Pearson since 2009. She has managed a number of national and global assessment product lines. In her most recent role she works as a Research to Practice Manager. In this role she brings innovation, research and new technology into educational solutions for teachers and students. Maryam has conducted research on developing innovative 21st century skills assessment tasks which have been administered in Turkey, South Africa, Singapore, UK, US and other countries. Some of her previous experience includes working at Procter and Gamble. Prior to moving to the States to attend business school, Mosharraf lived in Iran and worked at the British Embassy in Tehran as an interpreter. She holds a master's degree in Business Administration from the University of Texas in Austin and a bachelor's degree in Translation from Azad University.

* * *

**Lynne Anderson-Inman** is a professor of education at the University of Oregon and past Director of the university's Center for Advanced Technology in Education. Dr. Anderson-Inman is a nationally and internationally recognized expert on the use of technology to improve reading, writing, and studying, with special emphasis on strategies for using technology to enhance the academic success of struggling learners. She pioneered the concept of "computer-supported studying," conducting research on strategy-based instruction to promote effective reading and learning online. Recent work has focused on investigating "supported etext" as a means to improve content-area reading and studying. Dr. Anderson-Inman is a widely published author on effective uses of technology and a frequent speaker at national and international conferences.

**Gilbert Andrada**, PhD., State Education Consultant, has been with the Connecticut State Department of Education for 21 years. In addition to having been the program manager for the Connecticut Benchmark Assessment System (CBAS), his duties involve psychometric and statistical analyses, applied research projects, program evaluations, and large-scale student assessment. He holds a Connecticut school administrator's license (092). Gil is an active researcher with colleagues from the Neag School of Education at the University of Connecticut. He is a frequent adjunct faculty member teaching courses in statistics, measurement and research methods. Gil holds a BA in psychology from California State University, Stanislaus; an MS in Psychology from the School of Psychological Sciences at Purdue University; and a PhD in Educational Psychology from the Measurement, Evaluation and Assessment program at the University of Connecticut, Neag School of Education.

**Perla Arie**, M.Ed. Honors Degree in Educational Technology from Kibbutzim College of Education, Technology and the Arts. EFL and English-Hebrew Translation teacher at Kugel High School (Holon, Israel). Main fields of interest: Language teaching (English, French and Spanish), Innovative teaching methods, Computer Assisted Learning, Web 2.0 tools and Facebook use for educational purposes.

**Edith Avni**, Ph.D. in Education, Haifa University, Israel. Charge of ICT in Education, Ministry of Education, Haifa District, Israel. Lecturer in professional development courses for educational leadership and teachers. Establishing with Dr A. Rotem "Toward Digital Ethics Initiative", Israel, contains original articles related to technology, pedagogical and ethical aspects in learning and teaching.

**Susan Malone Back**, PhD, MBA, is a Research Scientist in the Institute for Measurement, Methodology, Analysis and Policy of the College of Education at Texas Tech University and Director of the university Small Business Innovation Research/ Small Business Technology Transfer (SBIR/STTR) Resource Center. She has extensive experience managing federal and private foundation grants and working with public/private partnerships. Her areas of research are community engagement, STEM education, and new frontiers in business education. Dr. Back received her M.Ed. and PhD in Educational Psychology from Temple University and her MBA from the University of Denver.

**Sara Bakken**'s education career began in 2001 as a high school science teacher. After leaving the classroom, she worked as an instructional designer and advocate for online learning in both the K-12 and higher education environments. She has worked extensively with the Texas Virtual School Network (TxVSN), and served as committee co-chair for the 2011 publication of the International Association for K-12 Online Learning (iNACOL) National Standards for Quality Online Teaching. She has presented on the effective incorporation of 21st century skills into the virtual classroom at several national conferences including the Texas Distance Learning Association (TxDLA) and iNACOL's Virtual School Symposium. She now develops new and innovative online assessments at Pearson, where she won the Pearson Innovative Assessment Idea competition in 2012. She holds a Master of Science degree in instructional design from the University of Houston-Clear Lake.

**Kirk A. Becker** is a senior research scientist with Pearson and consulting editor for the Journal of Computer Adaptive Testing. He has over fifteen years' experience conducting research and performing operational work in measurement and psychometrics. Dr. Becker's current research focuses on efficient methods for evaluating and coding large item pools using natural language processing, especially within the context of adaptive testing, LOFT, and automated test assembly. This research on natural language processing is currently being extended to automated item generation, item modeling, and the evaluation of item quality. Additionally Kirk has continued to research methods for developing, evaluating, and scoring innovative test items and performance tasks, with current research looking at the application of polytomous scoring models on information functions and adaptive administration. Dr. Becker has presented research on applications of natural language processing at the annual conferences of the American Educational Research Association, the Association of Test Publishers, and the National Council on Measurement in Education. Kirk received his Ph.D. in Educational Psychology from the University of Illinois at Chicago.

**Valerie Beltran**, Ed.D., is an Associate Professor of Education at the University of La Verne. In the K-12 field, she has been a teacher, a resource specialist, and a principal. At the university level, she teaches courses in both the teacher credential and Master's programs. She chairs the Master's of Education Special Emphasis program. Her research interests include writing instruction, bilingual education, online teaching, and student engagement.

**Roger Benjamin** has been President of CAE (Council for Aid to Education) since 2005. He was a research scientist at RAND from 1990 to 2005 (director of RAND Education, 1994-1999). Previous to his appointment to RAND, he was professor of political science at the University of Minnesota, 1966 to 1983 and associate dean and executive officer, College of Liberal Arts, University of Minnesota, 1980 to 1983, vice chancellor for academic affairs and provost at the University of Pittsburgh, 1983 to 1986, and vice president for academic affairs and provost, University of Minnesota, 1986 to 1988, and professor of political science, 1988 to 1990. He is the author or co-author of numerous books, monographs and articles in political economy and public policy, including governance, strategic planning, and educational assessment. His latest book is The New Limits of Education Policy: Avoiding A Tragedy of the Commons. London: Edward Elgar, 2012. He directs CAE, an educational assessment testing organization, implementing performance assessments and related 21st century assessments throughout the K-16 education system in the United States and beyond.

**John Bielinski** has worked in educational assessment as a developer and researcher since 1995. He earned a PhD in quantitative methods through the Educational Psychology department at the University of Minnesota. His research includes gender differences in math achievement, test accommodation validation, DIF, and growth modeling. Since joining Pearson in 2002, John has directed the development of several clinical and educational assessment including the KeyMath-3 Diagnostic Assessment and the Bruininks-Oseretsky Test of Motor Proficiency, 2nd Edition, and aimsweb. He is currently leading development on next generation curriculum-based measurement and formative assessment. In addition to his research and development work, John volunteers as a middle school math coach.

**Keith A. Boughton** is a Senior Research Scientist at CTB/McGraw-Hill Education. His areas of specialization include automatic item generation, adaptive testing, mixture/latent class models, hierarchical IRT models, and multidimensional IRT models.

**Daniel G. Brenner,** a Senior Research Associate at WestEd's Science, Technology, Engineering, and Mathematics (STEM) program, is Co-Principal Investigator on multiple projects developing simulation-based assessments in various science content areas: the NSF-funded Human Body System and SimScientists Assessment System: Physical Science Links projects as well as the IES-Funded SimScientists Assessment System: Life Sciences and SimScientists Model Progressions (Genetics and Evolution) providing scientific content expertise, managing the assessment programming, and overseeing the SimScientists learning management system that serves over 10,000 students annually. Dr. Brenner is also Principal Investigator on the Institute of Education Sciences-funded Voyage to Galapagos project to develop a differentiated assistance model that is based on knowledge about what kinds of assistance are most effective for students of differing abilities as they work in an inquiry-driven learning environment for evolution science content. Brenner's research interests focus on online education and assessment, and on the application of new technologies to these areas, and on application of the arts to STEM research. He has done extensive research and project management in academic and industrial research in the areas of bioorganic chemistry and biopharmaceuticals. Prior to joining WestEd, Brenner worked as an instructional designer heading the production of over 500 in-depth online media rich courses for the Academy of Art University. Dr. Brenner received an AB in Chemistry and Visual & Environmental Studies from Harvard College, and a PhD in Chemistry from Harvard University.

**Diane Browder** is the Lake and Edward P. Snyder Distinguished Professor of Special Education at the University of North Carolina at Charlotte. Dr. Browder has over two decades of research and writing on assessment and instruction for students with severe developmental disabilities. Dr. Browder's research has been recognized through multiple awards. She received the 2009 Distinguished Researcher Award in Special Education from the American Education Research Association and was the 2009 First Citizens Bank Scholar at the University of North Carolina at Charlotte. In 2011 Dr. Browder was recognized by the state of North Carolina with the O. Max Gardner Award for research that has made a contribution to humanity.

**Barbara Buckley,** a Senior Research Associate at WestEd's Science, Technology, Engineering, & Mathematics (STEM) program is Principle Investigator of the SimScientists Human Body Systems (HBS) project funded by NSF (DR K12), and co-PI of two current SimScientists projects in the life sciences funded by IES. As a proponent of model-based learning, Dr. Buckley guides the evidence-centered design process used by the SimScientists team to create simulation-based instructional and assessment suites that incorporate model-based learning, complex systems thinking, and Next Generation Science Standards. Prior to joining WestEd, Dr. Buckley was a researcher at the Concord Consortium, playing a central role in the Modeling Across the Curriculum Project (IERI #0115699). At TERC, she contributed to the GLOBE and Global Lab projects.

**Michael B. Bunch** is Senior Vice-President of Measurement Incorporated, a test development and scoring company serving the large-scale assessment and professional licensure/certification fields. He oversees a research and development unit of over 80 assessment professionals and serves as a company director. Dr. Bunch earned a doctorate in psychology with a specialty in measurement and human differences from the University of Georgia in 1976. Prior to joining MI in 1982, he served as research psychologist at the American College Testing Program (ACT) and senior professional at NTS Research Corporation. Since joining MI, he has been active not only in the profession but in the Durham community as well, serving on and chairing boards of local education and human service organizations. He is past chairman of the Graduate Education Advancement Board of the University of Georgia.

**Dolores Cannella** earned her PhD in Social and Health Psychology. She is the Director of Behavioral Sciences and the Acting Chair in the Department of General Dentistry at Stony Brook University, School of Dental Medicine. Her teaching and research interests focus on the development of patient-centered interprofessional healthcare teams to improve health outcomes.

**E. Lee Childress** has been superintendent of the Corinth School District for 13 years. A native of Clarksdale, Mississippi, Childress is a graduate of Delta State University. He served as a social studies teacher in the Clarksdale Public Schools before becoming Program Manager for the School Executive Management Institute for the Mississippi Department of Education, which provided training for over 2,000 Mississippi school administrators. Childress was also Director of School Improvement for the DeSoto County School District before serving for nine years as Assistant Superintendent for the Corinth School District. Dr. Childress has been active in several educational organizations and is currently serving as a Trustee for Mississippi Public Employees Retirement System representing public school and community college educators; serves as Chairman of the Mississippi Commission on School Accreditation, President, of the Program for Research and Evaluation in Public Schools; and serves on the Advisory Board for the Mississippi School for Math and Science.

**Rafi Davidson** received his PH.D in Biochemistry from the Weizmann Institute in Rechovot, Israel. He is a senior lecturer in the department of science & technology in Kaye College of education, where, for 20 years, he teaches courses for B.Ed. and M.ED. in the subjects of "ICT in education", "information literacy and critical thinking" and "teaching and learning in an information age". In 1999 he founded the Center for Educational Technology Initiatives which supports, advises and provides pedagogical-technological assistance to lecturers and student at Kaye College. For the last 4 years he is responsible for the development and implementation of programs for professional development of lecturers and pedagogical supervisors in the colleges for education in Israel. These programs are part of the national program for the adaptation of the Israeli education system to the 21st century. His areas of research and development include integration of ICT in teaching and learning, social and emotional aspects of online learning and the factors that influence the digital divide.

**Jessica Decker** is an Assistant Professor of Education at the University of La Verne. Previously, she has worked as an elementary school teacher. Her areas of research include improving writing skills, technology, and mentoring.

**Kristen DiCerbo** is a Principal Research Scientist in the Center for Digital Data, Analytics, and Adaptive Learning at Pearson. Her research program centers on how to use evidence from learner activity in games and simulations to understand what learners know and can do. Dr. DiCerbo has also engaged with teachers to understand how to best communicate information about student performance to inform instructional decisions. Prior to joining Pearson, Kristen provided research support to the Networking Academies at Cisco and worked as a certified school psychologist. Kristen received her Master's Degree and Ph.D. in Educational Psychology at Arizona State University. She received a B.A. in Psychology and Sociology at Hamilton College.

**Patricia Eckardt** is an educator with a PhD in Quantitative Methods for Research, Educational Psychology. She has taught research and statistics to nurses and health professionals across undergraduate and graduate studies. She has been a registered professional nurse for over thirty years.

**Sammy Elzarka** is the Director of the Center for the Advancement of Faculty Excellence at the University of La Verne in La Verne, California. He has worked in education for nearly 20 years including roles as teacher, curriculum developer, assessment analyst, and accreditation liaison. His current focus is on the effective use of new technologies for teaching and learning.

**David P. Erlanger** is an educator and research director. His interests include how to apply educational theory to ensure students learn best in both traditional and non-traditional settings. He has a focus on identifying methods needed to make distance learning effective, especially for research students.

**Peter Foltz** is a Vice President for research and development and works to bring innovative technologies to learning and assessment. He is one of the original developers of automated scoring technologies and holds a patent on methods for scoring of writing. Dr. Foltz's research has focused on language comprehension, 21st Century skills learning and assessment, and uses of machine learning and natural language processing in educational technology. The methods he has pioneered improve student achievement, expand student access, and make learning materials more affordable. He has led the framework development for a new assessment of collaborative problem solving for the Organisation of Economic Cooperation and Development's Programme for International Student Assessment (PISA) test. A former professor of psychology at New Mexico State University, he has authored more than 100 journal articles, book chapters, conference papers, and other publications. He previously worked at Bell Communications Research and the Learning Research and Development Center at the University of Pittsburgh. Dr. Foltz holds doctorate and master's degrees in Cognitive Psychology from the University of Colorado, Boulder, and a bachelor's degree from Lehigh University.

**Kellilynn M. Frias** is an Assistant Professor in the Marketing Department at Texas Tech University. Her research agenda focuses on understanding the technology, firm, and environmental factors that impact a firm's decision of "where to participate in the value chain" or "what to sell". This research has implications for product development and innovation, design of inter-firm ties, and intellectual property enforcement.

**Mark Gierl** is Professor of Educational Psychology and the Director of the Centre for Research in Applied Measurement and Evaluation (CRAME) at the University of Alberta. His specialization is educational and psychological testing, with an emphasis on the application of cognitive principles to assessment practices. Professor Gierl's current research is focused on automatic item generation and automated essay scoring. His research is funded by the Medical Council of Canada, Elsevier, ACT Inc., and the Social Sciences and Humanities Research Council of Canada. Dr. Gierl holds the Tier I Canada Research Chair in Educational Measurement.

**Amnon Glassner** was trained as a math teacher and then completed his M.A. and PhD in the center of cognition, instruction and computers at the Hebrew University in Jerusalem. He participated in some researches about learning and argumentation in the frame of Kishurim Group in the leadership of Prof. Baruch Schwarz. His current educational interest is to lead some new progressive programs of teacher training, such as those who use PBL (project or product based learning) as main direction for learning and instruction. He serves as the head of Education Department, the head of Informal Studies and a pedagogical guide in Kaye Academic College of Education in Beer-Sheva. His current researches directions include infusion of creative and critical thinking during learning of any content, learning with PBL, learning by successes, and moderation of dialogical learning discussion.

**Heather Greenhalgh-Spencer** is an Assistant Professor of Curriculum and Instruction at Texas Tech University. Her research focuses on diversity and equity issues in online education. This research has implications for the ways we teach in online spaces, and implications for creating greater access and engagement in education for underrepresented students.

**Sean T. Hanlon** creates student- and teacher-centered educational technology applications that blend assessment and instruction. He received his undergraduate degree in computer science from The George Washington University (GW), his master's degree in computer science and his Ph.D. in educational psychology from the University of North Carolina at Chapel Hill. During his senior year at GW, Sean received the Gary Bard Entrepreneur award for Blaise, an online essay-writing system with gesture-based scoring. This application was deployed in the GW Writing Center and used in the compulsory freshmen composition course. Since joining MetaMetrics, Sean has led the design, development, deployment, and enhancement of multiple educational technologies including MyWritingWeb, MyReadingWeb, MyMathWeb, Learning Oasis, EdSphere, Module Creator, and Guided Literacy. Sean supplements his technological expertise with the instructional and assessment principles necessary to create research-based technologies that impact the everyday lives of students and teachers.

**Jiangang Hao** is a Research Scientist in the Center for Advanced Psychometrics at ETS. Prior to joining in ETS, he has been working on modeling and mining Terabyte-scale data in physics at Fermi National Accelerator Laboratory after getting his PhD in physics and MA in Statistics both from the University of Michigan. He has been working extensively on data mining & machine learning, statistical modeling & inference, data standardization and data model schema design for big data. He published over 40 papers in peer-reviewed journals with over 2400 total citations and his work has been reported by *Wired, MIT Technology Review* and etc. Jiangang's current research centers on collaborative problem solving, game and simulation based assessment, educational data mining, log file structuring and analysis. He is also applying natural language processing techniques to analyze the conversations in collaboration to develop intelligent (adaptive) facilitation mechanism.

**J. Christine Harmes** is a consultant in the areas of assessment, measurement, and technology integration. She holds a Ph.D. with dual concentrations in Educational Measurement and Research and Instructional Technology. Dr. Harmes' research in computer-based testing has most recently focused on the design, cognitive processing, memorability, and usability of innovative items. Her recent projects regarding technology integration in K-12 settings have included developing tools for teacher professional development with and use of technology, and developing technology-related assessments, observation tools, and surveys. She has taught courses in mixed methods research, scholarly communication, performance assessment, computer-based testing, measurement for teachers, and instructional design.

**Qiwei He** is an Associate Research Scientist in ETS's Research & Development Division, Global Assessment Center. Her background and expertise is in psychometrics, data mining, text mining and natural language processing with a focus on building applications for educational and psychological technology. She currently focuses on exploration research of process data in large scale assessments. Previously, Dr. He has conducted research in the areas of text-based online assessment for psychiatric and psychological assessment in the University of Twente, the Netherlands. She also won the Best Dissertation Prize of Abbas Fund in the field of psychological assessments in the Netherlands.

**Bridget Hildreth**, M.F.A., is a Research Assistant at the Center for Advanced Technology in Education at the University of Oregon. She was a secondary teacher and ELA Intervention Specialist for over ten years, and she taught writing, remedial ELA, and eLiteracy at the community college level. Her research with federally funded projects (SSOAR, SAIL, SOAR, and MeTRC) primarily involves improving education outcomes for middle school students with learning disabilities through the use of technology.

**Cheryl Johnson** has worked in professional, clinical, and education assessment development since 1998. She has written content and managed teams to successfully execute multi-year assessment research projects that include the Kaufman Assessment Battery for Children, 2nd Edition, the Kaufman Test of Educational Achievement, 2nd and 3rd Editions, Sensory Profile, 2nd Edition, and aimsweb. She currently leads research on early literacy, and effective progress monitoring toward achievement goals for school-aged children, as Research Director at Pearson. In addition to her research work, she is an advocate for Montessori education, approaches to help maximize cognitive and physical performance in adults, and new technology and experiences that foster a person's natural curiosity.

**Carolyn Knox** has a Ph.D. in Digital Learning with an emphasis on students with special needs and English Learners. She is Assistant Director of CATE at the University of Oregon. Dr. Knox is PI of the Stepping up to SOAR: Strategies for Online Academic Reading project, developing both the project's strategies and its video-based instructional website. She was a seminal part of the development of CATE's original "computer-based study strategies" for using technology to enhance the academic success of struggling learners. She is a nationally recognized expert on the use of digital note-taking systems in the classroom for students with disabilities. For the last 25 years, Dr. Knox has been conducting research and development projects that create and promote innovative uses of technology for learning, innovative instructional materials, and evidence-based strategies designed to help struggling learners use technology for effective learning and academic success.

**Zach Kornhauser** is an Associate Measurement Scientist at the Council for Aid to Education. Prior to joining CAE Zach worked as a Senior Research Assistant for the Community College Research Center. His research interests include examining quality of educational programming in colleges and universities, understanding factors that affect student motivation on low-stakes assessments, studying students' use of technology in college classrooms, and investigating factors that explain student performance in college over and above student ability. Zach received a Master's in Applied Developmental Psychology from Fordham University in 2011, and is currently finishing his doctorate at Fordham.

**Patrick Kyllonen** is Senior Research Director of the Center for Academic and Workforce Readiness and Success at Educational Testing Service (ETS) in Princeton, N.J. Center scientists conduct innovative research on (a) higher education assessment, (b) workforce readiness; (c) international large scale assessment (e.g., Program for International Student Assessment; PISA); and (d) 21st century skills assessment, such as creativity, collaborative problem solving, and situational interviews. Dr. Kyllonen received his B.A. from St. John's University and Ph.D. from Stanford University and is author of Generating Items for Cognitive Tests (with S. Irvine, 2001); Learning and Individual Differences (with P. L. Ackerman & R.D. Roberts, 1999); Extending Intelligence: Enhancement and New Constructs (with R. Roberts and L. Stankov, 2008), and Innovative Assessment of Collaboration (with A. von Davier and M. Zhu, forthcoming). He is a fellow of the American Psychological Association and the American Educational Research Association, recipient of The Technical Cooperation Program Achievement Award for the "design, development, and evaluation of the Trait-Self Description (TSD) Personality Inventory," and was a coauthor of the National Academy of Sciences 2012 report, Education for Life and Work: Developing Transferable Knowledge and Skills in the 21st Century.

**Hollis Lai** is Assistant Professor of Dentistry and the Director of Assessment for Undergraduate Medical Education program at the University of Alberta. His specialization is educational and psychological testing, with an emphasis on assessment designs in medical education, curriculum mapping, educational data mining, and item generation.

**Syed F. Latifi** is a doctoral candidate in Educational Psychology at the University of Alberta and a graduate researcher in the Center for Research in Applied Measurement and Evaluation (CRAME) at the same university. He holds a M.S. in Computer Science from LUMS, and an M.Ed. in Measurement, Evaluation and Cognition from University of Alberta. He has published numerous papers and articles in reputed peer-reviewed conferences and journals. His current research interests include automatic item generation, automated essay scoring, evolutionary programming and application of swarm intelligence in assessment systems.

**Lei Liu** is a research scientist from the Cognitive and Learning Sciences Center at Educational Testing Service. She is leading multiple projects focusing on the design of innovative and technology-rich science assessments that are competency-based and NGSS aligned. Her research has drawn heavily on cognitive and socioconstructivist learning theories. Her research interest is on the role of technology in learning and assessing. She has developed simulation-based learning environment and assessments, learning progression based assessments, conversation-based assessments, and collaborative problem solving assessments. She has published numerous journal articles and book chapters in the field of learning about complex systems, computer-supported collaborative learning, and learning sciences. She earned her PhD from Rutgers University and her dissertation won the best Doctoral Research Award by the National Association of Research in Science Teaching.

**William Lorié**, Ph.D., is Director of Education Research at Questar Assessment, Inc. A graduate of Notre Dame (B.A, Philosophy, B.S. Physics) and Stanford (M.S. Statistics, Ph.D. Education), Dr. Lorié has worked at CTB/McGraw-Hill, ETS, the World Bank, and Metrica, an assessment company he co-founded. Dr. Lorié has lead R&D for large-scale testing programs and has advised on assessment-related capacity building for states and ministries of education. His focus at Questar is on R&D innovation.

**Mark Loveland**, a Senior Research Associate at WestEd's Science, Technology, Engineering, & Mathematics (STEM) program is Co-Principal Investigator of the IES funded SimScientists Assessment System and SimScientists Model Progressions projects, and the NSF funded SimScientists Assessments: Physical Science Links project. Dr. Loveland has over 20 years of experience working in scientific research and STEM education. Prior to joining WestEd, Dr. Loveland coordinated research efforts to transform middle school mathematics and science teaching and learning in San Francisco public schools. He has conducted cancer research and taught biology, chemistry, and environmental science in formal and informal environments.

**Marie Ann Marino** is the Associate Dean for Academic Affairs and Strategic Partnerships at the Stony Brook University School of Nursing. Dr. Marino received a Bachelor of Science from Molloy College, a Master of Science in Nursing from Stony Brook University and a Doctor of Education at Teachers College, Columbia University. She completed a Post-Doctoral Fellowship in Family Violence Research at The Children's Hospital/Harvard University School of Medicine. Dr. Marino has maintained a clinical practice as a pediatric nurse practitioner/forensic medical examiner conducting medical evaluations of child victims of abuse and violence. Dr. Marino is an active member of several professional organizations, including the International Association of Forensic Nurses. She is a key driver on several academic-practice partnerships aimed at innovating care management and improving transitional care, as well as development of competence in interprofessional collaborative practice.

**Donna Matovinovic** is Vice President of Test Development at ACT. Donna has over 25 years of experience providing leadership and strategic direction for the design and development of assessment products and services across the K through career continuum. Her focus it to ensure tight alignment between content development and psychometric principles as well as with product, program, and customer requirements.

**Mark Matzaganian** is Associate Professor of Education at the University of La Verne. He teaches in the areas of Assessment and Research. His scholarly interests include the role of technology in education, online learning, and student motivation.

**Shayne Miel** is currently the Vice President of Software Development at LightSide Labs, an ed-tech startup focused on providing automated writing support to K-12 students around the world through the use of their automated scoring and feedback technology. His role at LightSide is primarily research and development of the automated assessment and feedback software. Prior to his experience at LightSide Labs, Shayne was the Sr. Director of AI Technology at Measurement Incorporated, where he led a group of researchers and developers in the creation and development of modern day PEG.

**Edys Quellmalz** is Director of Technology-Enhanced Assessment and Learning Systems in WestEd's Math, Science and Technology program. She leads SimScientists projects funded by NSF and the U.S. Department of Education related to simulation-based science curricula and assessments for formative and summative uses that can serve as components of balanced state science assessment systems. Projects include Calipers II: Using Simulations to Assess Complex Science Learning (NSF); Foundations of 21st Century Science Assessment (NSF); Model Progressions (IES); SimScientists Assessments: Physical Science Links (NSF); SimScientists Crosscutting Concepts: Progressions in Earth Systems (NSF); SimScientists Assessment System (IES); SimScientists: Interactive Simulation-based Learning Environments (IES); Mutilevel Assessments of Science Standards (IES); Transformative Assessments for Science (Carnegie Corporation); and Integrating Science Simulations into Balanced State Science Assessment System (OESE). She co-directed the development of the framework and specifications for the 2014 Technological Literacy (TEL) National Assessment of Educational Progress and served on the Steering Committee for the 2011 NAEP Writing Framework. She has consulted for numerous state, national, international assessment programs. She was Associate Director of the Center for Technology and Learning at SRI International and the Director of Assessment Research and Design. She served on the faculty at the Stanford School of Education and as research faculty in the UCLA Graduate School of Education.

**Rikki Rimor**, Ph.D., Senior Lecturer, Technology in Education Graduate Program, Department of Education at Kibbutzim College of Education, Technology and the Arts, Israel. Past experience: developer and instructor of online graduate course "From Search for Information to Construction of Knowledge in Technology-Based Environments" at the Open University of Israel. This course won Excellence Prize in the Open University Online Courses Contest. She was the Head of the Center for Pedagogy & Innovative Technologies (PITEC) at the Teachers College of Technology, Tel-Aviv. She was also Head of the Unit for Research and Evaluation at the Department of Education in the Municipality of Jerusalem. Most of her publications deal with why and how to promote collaborative knowledge construction in online learning environments, teaching and assessing problem solving in an online collaborative environment, complexity of social interactions in collaborative online learning environment as well as analysis of cognitive and metacognitive aspects of learning on Facebook.

**Jenny Root**, M.Ed. is the Snyder Fellow at UNC Charlotte where she is a doctoral student in Special Education. She is a graduate research assistant for The Solutions Project, an IES grant, developing a mathematics problem-solving curriculum for students with severe disabilities. Jenny has over seven years of experience working with children and adolescents with disabilities in school settings. Jenny's research focuses on giving students with autism and intellectual disability access to the general curriculum through technology, systematic instruction, and positive behavior supports. Future directions for her research include systematic instruction to increase independence within academic tasks for students with developmental disabilities and using technology to overcome barriers to critical thinking and problem solving skills.

**Abraham Rotem**, Ph.D in Physics and Electrical Engineering, KSU USA and Ben-Gurion University, Israel (1983); Founder SENTOP Ltd (1990); Establishing Teachers Development center with Branco Weiss Institute, Israel (1994). Establishment of the first social educational network in Israel, to schools and student (1998). Wrote the Book "School turns on line" with Dr Y. Peled (2008). Lecturer in professional development courses for school administrators and teachers. Establishing with Dr E. Avni "Toward Digital Ethics Initiative", Israel, contains original articles related to technology, pedagogical and ethical aspects in learning and teaching; Academic advisor ICT program in Israel (Ministry of Education) for the last decade.

**Jean-François Rouet** is a Senior research scientist with the French Centre National de la Recherche Scientifique (National Center for Scientific Research). He was trained as a developmental and language psychologist and he has published extensively on the cognitive underpinnings of reading literacy and skilled uses of information technology (e.g., "Reading: From words to multiple documents", coedited with Britt and Goldman, Routledge, 2013). Jean-François Rouet has been involved since 2006 as an expert in the OECD's PISA and PIAAC surveys of teenage and adult literacy, respectively. He has served as the director of the Center for Research on Cognition and Learning at the University of Poitiers, France, from 2004 to 2011. After his PhD (1991), Jean-François Rouet spent several years as a post-doctoral fellow at the Learning Research and Development Center (University of Pittsburgh, USA). He has developed numerous collaborations with scholars from various countries including Argentina, Germany, Japan, Norway, Spain and the USA. He is on the board of several major academic journals and a former associate editor of Learning and Instruction.

**Gavriel Salomon** (PhD at Stanford, 1968) is professor of educational psychology at the Haifa University in Israel where he served as dean of the Faculty of Education. As editor of Educational Psychologist, he has published four books and about a 150 research, theory, and methodology journal articles. He is the recipient of the Israel Award for scientific achievements and holds an honorary doctorate from the Leuven University in Belgium. His fields are the use and abuse of computers in education and research on peace education in regions of conflict.

**Alicia Saunders**, Ph.D., is the Project Coordinator and Research Associate for the Solutions Project, an IES grant, developing a mathematical word problem solving curriculum for students with severe disabilities at the University of North Carolina at Charlotte. She has conducted research in the areas of general curriculum access, specifically in science, mathematics, and English language arts, as well as in technology, including video modeling and computer-assisted instruction. Additionally, she has published multiple peer reviewed journal articles and book chapters, developed and conducted professional development webinars on aligning instruction to alternate achievement standards and the Common Core State Standards, and is a co-author of Early Numeracy, a mathematics curriculum for students with severe disabilities. Dr. Saunders received her bachelor's degree in psychology from the University of North Carolina at Chapel Hill, and both her master's and doctoral degrees in special education from the University of North Carolina at Charlotte. She taught students with severe disabilities and autism in North Carolina prior to obtaining her doctorate. She also worked as a research associate on an IES funded grant investigating mathematics and science instruction for students with severe disabilities, and as a research associate for one of the two national consortia called to develop an alternate assessment and curricular materials based on alternate achievement standards aligned to the Common Core State Standards for students with significant cognitive disabilities.

**Matt Silberglitt**, a Senior Research Associate at WestEd's Science, Technology, Engineering, & Mathematics (STEM) program is Co-Principal Investigator of the SimScientists Assessments: Physical Science Links and SimScientists Crosscutting Concepts: Progressions in Earth Science projects funded by NSF and the SimScientists Assessment Systems project funded by IES. As a former science teacher and experienced assessment developer, Mr. Silberglitt provides content expertise in physical science and expertise in standards for educational assessments. Prior to his current position, Mr. Silberglitt managed development of science assessments for WestEd in several states. Prior to joining WestEd, Mr. Silberglitt oversaw development of science assessments at the Minnesota Department of Education and developed assessments at Data Recognition Corporation. Mr. Silberglitt started his career as a high school science teacher.

**Jeffrey T. Steedle** is a Research Scientist at Pearson, where he provides psychometric support for state testing programs and conducts research with the Center for Next Generation Learning and Assessment. His research interests include student motivation, comparative judgment, item difficulty modeling, and science assessment. He earned a Ph.D. in Educational Psychology and a M.S. in Statistics from Stanford University in 2008.

**A. Jackson Stenner** is a co-founder of MetaMetrics and is its Chief Executive Officer and Chairman of the Board. With colleagues, he developed The Lexile Framework for Reading, The Quantile Framework for Mathematics, and the Lexile Framework for Writing. Dr. Stenner has published more than 60 papers, monographs and books, primarily on statistical and measurement methodology. Currently, he is a Research Professor in the Department of Applied Developmental and Special Education Program in the School of Education at the University of North Carolina-Chapel Hill. Dr. Stenner received his Ph.D. in educational psychology, with an emphasis in measurement, research design and evaluation methodology, from Duke University, and dual undergraduate degrees in psychology and education from the University of Missouri–Saint Louis. He has taught graduate seminars at Duke University and the University of North Carolina at Chapel Hill and guest lectured at several dozen universities.

**Carl W. Swartz** conducts research on models and technologies for blending learning and assessment and use of technology as a component of educational programs to enhance personalized learning for students with learning, attention, and language differences. He is currently a Research Professor in the Department of Applied Developmental and Special Education in the School of Education at the University of North Carolina-Chapel Hill where he was a Research Scientist in the School of Medicine and Clinical Assistant Professor in the School of Education at The University of North Carolina at Chapel Hill. Currently, He received his undergraduate degree in education from Indiana University and his master's and doctorate degrees in education from The University of North Carolina at Chapel Hill. Dr. Swartz taught early adolescents with severe emotional disturbances and behavior disorders at a middle school in Greenville, South Carolina (1983-1986).

**Noel Tagoe** is the Executive Director of Education at CIMA, where he was previously Head of Research and Development. Prior to joining CIMA Noel had held accounting, strategy and financial consulting positions with BP and KMPG in Ghana. He has also taught at various universities in the UK including Manchester University and Oxford University. Noel's current interests are in designing professional accounting curricula that address business needs and ensuring that they are assessed rigorously and robustly using technology where possible.

**Fatima E. Terrazas-Arellanes** is PI of Project ESCOLAR, an OSEP-funded project to create online modules for teaching science to middle school students with learning disabilities. Dr. Terrazas-Arellanes was a teacher from Mexico, coordinating research projects in areas of Spanish literacy instruction, second language acquisition, and eText supports. Dr. Terrazas-Arellanes' areas of expertise include designing and conducting research to learn how technology addresses the educational needs of children and youths, particularly students with learning disabilities and English Language Learners. Dr. Terrazas-Arellanes received her Bachelor of Arts in Psychology from the Universidad Autonoma de Sinaloa in 2000, a Master's of Science in Special Education from the University of Oregon in 2008, as well as a Doctor of Philosophy from the University of Oregon's School of Psychology in 2009.

**Suzanne Tsacoumis** has built her professional career conducting and managing projects associated with the research, development, and implementation of personnel assessments and human capital systems, often in litigious environments. Her expertise revolves around job analysis, selection, promotion, leadership assessment, and performance evaluation. Currently, she is spearheading innovative work in the development of valid, online simulations, such as virtual role plays and interactive in-baskets, for use in both promotion systems and self-assessment processes. She often consults on a range of policy and implementation issues. In addition to her technical work, Suzanne is a corporate officer and HumRRO's vice president of business development. In this role, she is responsible for providing leadership and direction to the business development and marketing team. Suzanne has been an active volunteer for the Society of Industrial-Organizational Psychology (SIOP) and she is a fellow of SIOP and the American Psychological Association (APA). Suzanne has served as an adjunct professor at both The George Washington University and George Mason University. She earned her Ph.D. from the University of Georgia, specializing in Industrial-Organizational Psychology and her B.A. from Bucknell University.

**David Vaughn** is a software engineer with over ten years of experience in the field of artificial intelligence (AI) and machine learning. As a Senior Software Developer he designs, develops, and enhances automated scoring technologies. Mr. Vaughn was the primary architect of MI's winning submissions to the Automated Student Assessment Prize (ASAP) contest, an automated scoring competition sponsored by the Hewlett Foundation. He subsequently enhanced the AI scoring system used in the ASAP competition to improve its accuracy, speed, efficiency, and scalability for use on the Smarter Balanced Pilot Test automated scoring project. Previously, Mr. Vaughn developed and implemented machine learning algorithms in a variety of contexts including email classification, genome research, and human/computer voice dialogue systems. He received his B.S. in Computer Science from Harvard University.

**Lars Vavik** is a professor in interactive educational technology at Stord/Haugesund University College. He has been working with design of digital media since 1980 and has been given European Academic Software Award for developing of modeling and simulation tools. His work the last 15 years has been dedicated to developing a master program in ICT and learning and the leadership of several research program as "Education on Curriculum and Technology" (2008-2012) and "Learning in the 21st century" (2012-2016) supported by The Research Council of Norway.

**Alina von Davier** is a Senior Research Director and leader of the Center for Advanced Psychometrics at ETS. She also is an Adjunct Professor at Fordham University. At ETS, von Davier is responsible for developing a team of experts and a psychometric research agenda in support of next generation of assessments. Computational psychometrics, which include machine learning and data mining techniques, Bayesian inference methods, stochastic processes and psychometric models are the main set of tools employed in her current work. She also works with psychometric models applied to educational testing: test score equating methods, item response theory models, adaptive testing. She published several books, authored or edited; she also published numerous papers in peer reviewed journals.

**Matthias von Davier** is a Senior Research Director in ETS's Research & Development Division, managing the international large-scale assessment methodology group in the ETS center for global assessment. At ETS, Dr. von Davier manages a group of researchers concerned with methodological questions arising in large-scale international comparative studies in education. He is currently editor-in-chief of the British Journal of Mathematical and Statistical Psychology and co-editor of the journal "Large Scale Assessments in Education", which is jointly published with the International Association for the Evaluation of Educational Achievement (IEA) and ETS through the IEA -ETS Research Institute (IERI). His current work at ETS involves the psychometric methodologies used in analyzing cognitive skills data and background data from large-scale educational surveys, such as the Organization for Economic Co-operation and Development's upcoming PIAAC and the ongoing PISA, as well as IEA's TIMSS and PIRLS. His work at ETS also involves the development of software for multidimensional models for item response data, and the improvement of models and estimation methods for the analysis of data from large scale educational survey assessments. Prior to joining ETS, Dr. von Davier led a research group on computer assisted science learning, was co-director of the "Computer as a tool for learning" section at the Institute for Science Education (IPN) in Kiel, Germany, and was an associate member of the Psychometrics & Methodology Department of IPN.

**Zsofia Voros** is currently research associate in the Center for Research on Cognition and Learning, CNRS and University of Poitiers, France. Her research investigates cognitive dimensions that may underlie electronic reading, learning and problem solving. Previously, she worked as a research consultant for the Educational Testing Service. She explored Programme for the International Assessment of Adult Competencies (PIAAC) processing data to identify cognitive/metacognitive skills and solution strategies linked to success in various electronic problem solving tasks. She earned her Ph.D in psychology from the University of Poitiers, France (2009).

**Emily Walden**, M.A., is a Research Assistant at the Center for Advanced Technology in Education at the University of Oregon in Eugene, Oregon. She completed a bachelor's degree in English and psychology at the University of Oregon in 2010 and a master's degree in developmental psychology at the

University of Oregon in 2011. Her research with federally funded projects (ESTRELLAS, COPELLS, SSOAR, and ESCOLAR) primarily involves improving education outcomes, especially in science, for middle school students with learning disabilities and English learners through the use of technology.

**Nancy T. Walker** is currently a Professor of Education at the University of Laverne. For the past fifteen years, she has overseen the teacher education literacy faculty and worked with adjunct faculty in online learning. Her research has focused on content area literacy, disciplinary literacy, visual literacy, and online learning in higher education. Previously, she taught Language Arts at the middle school level for eight years and mentored new teachers in effective literacy instruction. Dr. Walker is a published author on the use of multiple texts in the classroom and is a frequent speaker at national and international conferences.

**James Welsh** is the Director of the Florida Center for Instructional Technology and holds a Ph.D. in Literacy Studies from the University of South Florida College of Education. A former elementary school teacher, James is the program coordinator for technology integration support in the USF College of Education and the project leader for the Technology Integration Matrix K-12 evaluation tools. James conducts research with the Contemporary Literacies Collaborative at USF. His research interests include evaluation of educational technology, critical media literacy, student creation of multimedia texts, and the role of genre in student composition.

**Joshua Wilson** is an Assistant Professor in the School of Education at the University of Delaware. He earned his Ph.D. in Special Education from the University of Connecticut in 2014. His research focuses on methods of assessing and instructing struggling writers, and on the application of automated essay evaluation (AEE) technology in Response to Intervention (RtI) contexts. He currently teaches courses on elementary special education methods. Prior to earning his Ph.D., Dr. Wilson was a special education teacher for six years.

**Roy Winkelman** has spent two decades in K-12 education and two decades in higher education. Formerly director of the Florida Center for Instructional Technology, he now works on special projects for the Center and creates digital resources for K-12 students and teachers.

**Steven Wise** is a Senior Research Fellow at Northwest Evaluation Association. Dr. Wise has published extensively during the past three decades in applied measurement, with particular emphases in computer-based testing and the psychology of test taking. In addition, he sits on the editorial board of several academic journals and provides psychometric consultation to a variety of organizations. In recent years, Dr. Wise's research has focused primarily on methods for effectively dealing with the measurement problems posed by low examinee effort on achievement tests.

**Raffaela Wolf** completed her PhD in Research Methodology from the University of Pittsburgh in December 2013. Dr. Raffaela Wolf joined CAE in January 2014 as a Measurement Scientist. In this role, Dr. Raffaela Wolf is involved in research projects that pertain to validity and reliability studies of the Collegiate Learning Assessment-Plus. Other responsibilities include running psychometric analyses for national and international clients. Research interests include equating, scaling, and linking; item response theory; structural equation modeling; and, cross-national assessments in higher education.

**Doris Zahner** joined CAE in March 2011 as the Director of Test Development and a Measurement Scientist. Her responsibilities include overseeing all item development for CAE as well as conducting research studies pertaining to the CLA+ and other CAE assessment instruments. Prior to her position with the CAE, she was a Program Director with a professional licensure and certification firm and managed a variety of clients, including a medical certification board, an information systems auditing certification program, various nursing specialties, and plastics engineers. She has experience managing large-scale item development projects and is knowledgeable about all aspects of assessment development including task analyses, test specifications, item writing, exam construction, score reporting and equating, and standard setting. She holds a Ph.D. in Cognitive Psychology and a M.S. in Applied Statistics from Teachers College, Columbia University. Her post-doctoral work at the Stevens Institute of Technology was on the use of diagrams in information systems design and her own research interests pertain to the use of diagrams in probability and mathematics problem solving. In addition to her responsibilities at CAE, Dr. Zahner is an adjunct assistant professor at Barnard College where she teaches a course on statistics to undergraduate students in the social sciences.

**Diego Zapata-Rivera**, PhD, is a senior research scientist in the Cognitive Science Research Group at Educational Testing Service. His research focuses on innovations in score reporting and technology-enhanced assessment, including work on assessment-based learning environments and game-based assessments. His research interests also include Evidence-Centered Design, Bayesian student modeling, open student models, conversation-based assessments, virtual communities, authoring tools and program evaluation. He has been a committee member and organizer of international conferences and workshops in his research areas. He is a member of the Board of Special Reviewers of the User Modeling and User-Adapted Interaction journal and an Associate Editor of the IEEE Transactions on Learning Technologies Journal. Most recently, Dr. Zapata-Rivera has been invited to contribute his expertise to projects sponsored by the National Research Council, the National Science Foundation and NASA.

# Index

# I

ICT Skills 10, 421, 437, 581, 717

Individual Cognitive Skills 348, 356, 359

Information Literacy 13, 16, 25-26, 33, 40

Innovative Items 385-386, 392-397, 400-401, 403, 406, 410-411, 414, 804-809, 811, 813, 815-816, 818-821, 823

Innovative Item Types 394-395, 397, 400-401, 406, 819

Innovative Pedagogy 15, 320

Institutional Selectivity 232, 246, 257

Instruction 68-72, 84-86, 91, 95-98, 105, 107, 110-111, 115, 137-140, 142, 144-147, 150-151, 158-159, 162, 165-168, 170-171, 174, 177, 182-183, 191-194, 197, 201, 203, 206, 211, 214-215, 217, 286, 289, 294, 296-297, 299-300, 302, 304, 306, 310, 325, 364, 370, 372, 376, 394, 445-446, 448-454, 456, 458-459, 461-462, 464, 471-472, 503, 564-565, 578, 591, 621, 625, 659, 665, 671, 679, 681, 683, 686, 693-697, 703, 726, 744-746, 804

instructional design 110-111, 168, 450

Intellectual Disability 445-447, 449, 451-457, 460-462

interactive 16, 18, 24, 29-31, 40, 47, 52, 54-55, 59, 85, 113-114, 138, 149, 156, 167, 169, 182, 192, 194-196, 198, 209, 228-229, 261-262, 266, 268, 271, 277-280, 350, 352, 393, 449, 451, 457, 463-464, 491, 503, 505, 508, 517, 527, 564, 624, 668-669, 728, 750, 775, 806

Interdisciplinarity 43-44, 46, 67, 180

Internal Verification 421, 444

Internet 2, 6-7, 13-14, 16-17, 20-21, 25, 31-32, 40, 68-69, 71-74, 80, 82-87, 89, 91-94, 96-98, 103, 114, 147, 149, 153, 165, 418, 420, 433, 439, 458-461, 508-509, 511, 516, 543, 547, 559-560, 562, 564-566, 576-577, 581, 591-592, 661, 679, 705, 707, 709, 717

interprofessional education 172, 180-181

Invisible Assessment 785, 793-794, 802

Isomorphs 594, 596, 601, 604-605, 610

Item Engagement Index (IEI) 804, 809, 823

Item Model 593-594, 596-597, 601, 604-607, 610

Item Response Theory (IRT) 292, 475, 499, 628, 631, 647, 654, 656, 789, 793

Item Responsibilities 404, 414

# L

Learning Disabilities 68, 70-74, 83-85, 91-94, 96-98, 679

Learning Management System (LMS) 206

Life Competencies 558-560, 562, 565-566, 576, 587

Lifelong Learning 4, 24, 108-109, 113, 129, 562, 577, 587

LMS (Learning Management Systems) 587

Locus of Control 110, 122, 135, 145

Log Files 213, 323, 709, 717, 731, 750, 754, 767-768, 775, 786, 811-812, 819-820

Low-Stakes Assessment 444

Lynne Anderson-Inman 70, 72

# M

machine learning 617, 624-625, 627-629, 727, 731, 733, 735

Malpractice 421, 444

Mapping Task 634, 656

measurement 135, 162, 209, 249, 261-263, 265-266, 272-274, 276-279, 288, 296, 303, 323-324, 331, 333-335, 344-345, 390, 393-396, 411, 414, 473-480, 483-485, 487, 490-492, 499, 504, 518, 520, 613-614, 642, 647, 679, 724-725, 727-728, 732, 740-741, 745-747, 777, 785, 788-791, 794, 805-806, 820-821

Measurement Equivalence 477-480, 483, 490-492, 499

Measurement Incorporated 613-614, 679

Medium-Stakes Assessment 444

Metacognition 105-110, 113-118, 120, 122, 125-127, 129, 135, 144-145, 196, 528-529, 538-539, 549, 554

Mindset 82, 104, 437, 777, 780-781, 783-784, 793-794

mixed methods 169, 181

Model-Based Learning 195-196, 198, 219, 228

Moderate and Severe Developmental Disabilities 445-447, 449-450, 453, 459, 461-465, 471

Motivation 28, 31, 109, 112-113, 135, 173, 195, 222, 229, 241, 323, 325, 370, 449-450, 458, 474, 490, 516, 530-532, 537, 539, 543, 545, 547, 571, 577, 623, 697, 777, 779-780, 820

Multicomponent Task 628-631, 633-634, 636-638, 643-644, 654-657

Multidisciplinarity 43-44, 67

# Become an IRMA Member

Members of the **Information Resources Management Association (IRMA)** understand the importance of community within their field of study. The Information Resources Management Association is an ideal venue through which professionals, students, and academicians can convene and share the latest industry innovations and scholarly research that is changing the field of information science and technology. Become a member today and enjoy the benefits of membership as well as the opportunity to collaborate and network with fellow experts in the field.

## IRMA Membership Benefits:

- **One FREE Journal Subscription**

- **30% Off Additional Journal Subscriptions**

- **20% Off Book Purchases**

- Updates on the latest events and research on Information Resources Management through the IRMA-L listserv.

- Updates on new open access and downloadable content added to Research IRM.

- A copy of the Information Technology Management Newsletter twice a year.

- A certificate of membership.

## IRMA Membership $<u>195</u>

Scan code to visit irma-international.org and begin by selecting your free journal subscription.

Membership is good for one full year.

CPSIA information can be obtained at www.ICGtesting.com
Printed in the USA
BVOW04*0721161215

428404BV00026B/59/P